前言

20 世纪 80 年代初期，中国内地居民赴港澳地区探亲兴起，成为中国出境旅游的雏形；20 世纪 90 年代前后，东南亚旅游目的地相继开放，标志着中国"出境游"的正式启动。到今天，中国经济持续发展，社会保障水平不断提升，老百姓可支配收入增加，这一切均使得中国出境旅游快速增长，出境旅游正被越来越多的中国人接受。迄今为止，中国已成为世界上最大的出境旅游客源国，成为日本、泰国、俄罗斯、韩国等主要旅游目的地国家的第一大游客来源地，成为全球国际旅游增长的重要支撑。据中国旅游研究院（文化和旅游部数据中心）统计，2019 年，中国出境旅游人数为 1.55 亿人次，同比增长 3.3%。从出境旅游目的地数量来看，截至 2020 年 3 月，中国公民出境旅游目的地国家和地区达到 150 多个，中国游客的出境旅游目的地更加广泛，中国出境旅游者遍布世界各地。

出境旅游大规模兴起的直接原因是文化差异以及对异质文化的好奇和了解欲望，然而，与中国出境旅游高速增长相伴的则是中国公民在境外旅游时与当地的文化碰撞，有时甚至会因文化差异引起冲突。当今世界的竞争已不仅仅是经济实力的竞争，更是文明环境的竞争、文化软实力的竞争。为适应新形势下旅游发展的需要，有必要扩大旅游类专业学生的知识面，使学生对中国主要出境旅游目的地国家和地区的概况、民俗风情、旅游资源等有一个较为全面、准确的认识和了解。本书以党的二十大精神为引领，全面贯彻党的教育方针，落实立德树人根本任务，推进习近平新时代中国特色社会主义思想进教材、进课堂、进头脑，力求成为培根铸魂、启智增慧、适应时代要求的精品教材。本书针对高职院校旅游类专业人才培养的目标，着力培养学生汉、英双语的表达能力和综合职业素养，力求充分挖掘学生的主动性和创造性。

本书根据中国出境旅游市场的发展和需求，对近年来中国公民主要出境旅游目的地国家和地区进行了论述；采用校企合作的独特编写模式，使用汉、英双语，培养国际化旅游专业人才；注重实用性和可操作性，要求学生对各旅游目的地的经典旅游线路和案例进行分析，将理论知识与实际应用紧密结合。

本书的主要对象为高职院校旅游类专业的学生，也可作为旅行社、旅游景区、酒店以及相关旅游企业员工的培训教材。

本书的所有作者、译者在过去几年分别有在亚洲、欧洲、美洲、大洋洲等大洲的

30多个国家和地区学习、考察和访问的经历，其在海外的切身感受，以及在国内长期从事旅游职业教育的经历夯实了本书的内容；同时，旅游企业的参与编写为本书增添了亮点。本书由饶华清担任主编，负责全书大纲的设计与制定，并负责全书的统稿、定稿和修改完善；李德煜担任副主编，负责全书的修订；袁青担任主审。具体编写分工如下：导论、第二章、第三章、第四章由饶华清（浙江旅游职业学院）编写，第一章由徐辉（浙江旅游职业学院）编写，第五章、第六章由张智雄（浙江光大国际旅游有限公司）编写。其中，第一章由徐辉翻译，第三章的英国、法国、德国和意大利由饶华清翻译，第三章的瑞士、西班牙和俄罗斯由厉玲玲（浙江旅游职业学院）翻译，第二章、第四章由杨志超（浙江旅游职业学院）翻译，第五章由向玲玲（浙江旅游职业学院）翻译，第六章由程迎春（浙江越秀外国语学院）翻译。本书涉及的部分案例和旅游线路由朱小军（浙江省中青国际旅游有限公司）收集与整理。

在本书的编写过程中，编者吸收和借鉴了有关出境旅游研究的同类教材、学术著作、文章和报道，参阅了大量的统计资料（除去本书已注明的参考书目，恕不一一列出）。在此，谨向所有这些论著、资料的作者表示真诚的谢意。同时，感谢宋丽珍对本书的友情帮助。

由于编者水平有限，书中的不足之处望广大读者批评指正。

编者

目录

导论
中国出境旅游市场概述

导航

随着改革开放的深入、综合国力的增强，人民生活逐步富裕，居民可自由支配收入的明显增多，中国居民的旅游需求日益高涨，国内旅游和出境旅游都得到了迅猛发展。出境旅游涵盖的内容可以细分到各目的地，中国出境旅游目的地由两部分组成：一部分是其他国家和地区，另一部分是中国香港、澳门和台湾地区。近年来，虽然国际金融市场急剧动荡、国际旅游消费需求走低、全球旅游市场竞争加剧，但是中国旅游业仍保持了平稳较快增长。2019 年，中国出境旅游人数为 1.55 亿人次，同比增长 3.3%。从绝对数量来看，中国已经成为世界第一大出境旅游客源国。本导论主要介绍了中国出境旅游市场的发展历程、特点和发展趋势，使读者能了解中国出境旅游市场的现状和基本特点，了解中国出境旅游目的地市场的概况。

第一节　中国出境旅游的发展现状

出境旅游作为旅游市场的重要组成部分，已成为一国旅游业国际化的重要体现。国外学者把出境旅游定义为一国公民跨越国界到其他国家或地区开展的旅游消费活动，包括公务旅行、商务旅行和观光旅游等。由于国情的特殊性，国内学者一般把出境旅游定义为不包括港澳台地区居民在内的中国公民到其他国家或地区（目前包括港澳台地区）连续停留不超过 12 个月，并不以通过所从事的活动获取报酬为主要目的开展的旅游活动。

为了赢得庞大的中国出境旅游客源市场，许多国家通过外交努力，希望成为中国公民出境旅游的目的地。因此，出境旅游的快速发展有利于我国政府大力构建独立自主的多边外交关系。旅游活动是一种文化交往和审美体验行为，不同国家具有不同的语言文字、风俗习惯、价值观念以及道德标准等独具特色的文化。因此，出境旅游的快速发展还有利于不同文化背景下的人们相互接触和了解，促进不同国家之间的民族文化交流。伴随着世界经济一体化和区域化的飞速发展，国际经济交往与区域经济合作继续深化，出境旅游的快速发展更有利于加强国际经济交往以及区域旅游合作。作为一种高档次的消费活动，出境旅游既是一个国家或地区经济发达、居民生活水平提高的重要标志，又是一个国家或地区综合实力增强、改革开放程度加深的有力象征。同时，出境旅游对于扩大我国在全球范围的影响、增强国际社会地位等，具有极其重要的政治意义。

一、中国出境旅游发展历程

中国出境旅游产生于 20 世纪 80 年代。1983 年 11 月，为适应国家改革开放政策的基本要求，广东省作为试点首先开放本省居民赴港澳地区旅游，主要目的是方便内地居民到香港和澳门探亲，这成为出境旅游的先河。1984 年，国务院批准开放内地居民赴港澳地区探亲旅游，从此拉开中国公民出境旅游的序幕。而中国出境旅游市场的真正开放是从东南亚各国开始的。1988 年，为了满足归侨、侨眷及相关人员的探亲需要，经国务院批准，规定由海外亲友付费、担保，允许公民赴泰国探亲旅游，这是我国出境旅游的起点，泰国成为我国出境旅游的第一个目的地国家。自 1990 年起，政府又陆续将新加坡、马来西亚、菲律宾确定为公民出境旅游目的地国家，批准我国公民到新加坡、马来西亚、菲律宾探亲旅游。第一阶段的出境旅游有以下特征：以探亲为主要旅游动机；目的地仅限于新加坡、马来西亚、泰国、菲律宾四国；出境旅游费用一律自理，并要求海外亲友付费。此外，边境旅游作为出境旅游的一种形式，也开始在一些沿边省份出现，并且得到了较快的发展。1987 年，国家首先开放辽宁丹东—朝鲜新义州一日游。经过 20 多年的努力，我国的边境旅游得到了迅速发展，先后开放了中朝、中蒙、中哈、中越、中缅等边境口岸和边境旅游线路。1997年7月，国家旅游局①、公安部发布《中国公民自费出国旅游管理暂行办法》②，标志着我国出境旅游市场的形成。更重要的是，它标志着中国旅游业初步形成了入境旅游、国内旅游、出境旅游三足鼎立的市场格局。1983—2003年，中国政府根据各方条件的变化，从最初批准港澳探亲游，到开放新加坡、马来西亚、泰国出境游，再到逐步开放澳大利亚、新西兰等西方国家为中国公民出境旅游目的地，我国政府对出境旅游的限制性政策逐步放开。

二、中国出境旅游人数

进入21世纪，随着经济发展水平的不断提高和改革开放的继续深化，中国公民出境旅游目的地不断增加，出境旅游人数也越来越多（见表1）。从出境旅游的人次规模来看，2000年首次突破1 000万人次；2003年达到2 022.19万人次，比2002年增长21.8%，并且在人数方面超过日本，成为亚洲出境旅游人数最多的国家；2005年，我国公民出境旅游人数持续上升，突破3 102.63万人次，比2004年增长7.53%；2010年，我国出境市场规模继续保持旺盛增长的态势，出境旅游人数达到5 739万人次，同比增长20.44%，其中，因私出境的主体格局进一步强化，因公出境人数占比首度降至10%以下，仅为9.92%；2011年，我国经济虽受欧美债务危机、国内通货膨胀、合理调控产业发展等因素影响，但是受人民币汇率稳步提升、境外目的地国家签证政策进一步放宽等利好因素刺激，出境总人数达7 025万人次，比2010年同期增长22.42%，其中，因私出境人数为6 412万人次，占出境总人数的91.3%，同比增长24.5%；2012年，中国出境旅游人数为8 318.27万人次，同比增长18.41%；2013年，中国出境市场仍保持快速发展态势，出境旅游人数为9 730万人次，同比增长17%；2014年，中国公民出境旅游人数首次破亿，达到1.07亿人次；2019年，中国公民出境旅游人数突破1.5亿，达到1.55亿人次。

表1　1992—2019年中国出境旅游人数一览表

年　份	出境旅游人数（万人次）	比上年增长（%）
1992	298.87	—
1993	374.00	25.13
1994	373.36	－0.17
1995	452.05	21.07
1996	506.07	11.95
1997	532.39	5.2
1998	842.56	58.25
1999	923.24	9.57

① 2018年3月，原文化部、国家旅游局职责整合，现为文化和旅游部。

②《中国公民出国旅游管理办法》自2002年7月1日起施行，原《中国公民自费出国旅游管理暂行办法》同时废止。

续前表

年　份	出境旅游人数（万人次）	比上年增长（%）
2000	1 047.26	13.4
2001	1 213.31	15.85
2002	1 660.23	36.8
2003	2 022.19	21.8
2004	2 885.29	42.68
2005	3 102.63	7.53
2006	3 452	11.26
2007	4 095	18.63
2008	4 600	12.33
2009	4 765	3.6
2010	5 739	20.44
2011	7 025	22.42
2012	8 318.27	18.41
2013	9 730	17
2014	10 700	19.5
2015	11 700	9.0
2016	12 200	4.3
2017	13 100	7
2018	14 972	14.7
2019	15 500	3.3

资料来源：中国旅游研究院《中国旅游业统计公报》；中华人民共和国文化和旅游部《中国文化和旅游发展统计公报》。

三、已开放的出境旅游目的地

20世纪90年代，我国旅游界出现了一个新词——Approved Destination Status（ADS），这就是通常所说的“中国公民出境旅游目的地”。依照规定，任何国家想在中国开拓旅游客源市场，必须事先与中国政府有关部门协商，经批准同意后，才能被确定为“中国公民出境旅游目的地”。我国公民出境旅游发展非常迅速，出境旅游市场十分活跃。从出境旅游目的地数量来看，截至2020年3月，中国公民出境旅游目的地国家和地区达到150多个；从客流分布来看，尽管中国已正式开展组团业务的出境旅游目的地国家和地区达131个，但出境游客大多集中于港澳台地区、韩国及东南亚等周边目的地；从统计数据来看，2019年，前往大洋洲、欧洲、北美、非洲等中长线目的地的游客显著增加，尤其是在“一带一路”倡议的指引下，欧洲及中亚市场表现强劲，旅游目的地品种持续增长，中长线旅游作为中国出境旅游的高端市场表现出非常大的增长潜力。

四、出境旅游客源市场

由于国民收入水平的提高、人民币升值以及提高生活质量的需求等因素，出境旅游正被越来越多的中国人接受。迄今为止，中国已成为世界最大的出境旅游客源国，是日本、泰国、俄罗斯、韩国等主要旅游目的地国家的第一大游客来源地。从出境旅游客源市场分布来看，目前出境旅游者主要集中在经济发达的东部地区和沿海地区。出境旅游客源在空间分布上表现出较强的地域性，其主要特征相对稳定，根据近几年来的数据，广东一直是出境旅游的客源大省，占出境旅游总人数的30%左右，其他依次为北京、上海、福建和浙江；在边境旅游方面，以云南、黑龙江、广西、内蒙古、辽宁等为主。此外，中国公民出境旅游目的地也相对集中。从目的地来看，亚洲国家仍然保持着市场优势，泰国、日本、越南等周边国家成为中国出境游客热门选择；俄罗斯、塞尔维亚、克罗地亚等国在“中欧旅游年”、2018年俄罗斯世界杯、东欧多国签证优化的推动下，成为中国出境游客想要探寻的新晋热门目的地；墨西哥、阿根廷、格鲁吉亚等国成为新生代年轻出境游客的个性化、小众目的地。对于在互联网大环境浸染下的中国出境游客而言，目的地距离渐渐不再是考量的首因，具有新奇感、话题度、个性化、花样玩法的目的地更能吸引其眼球。从游客的流向来看，目前，中国出境游客前往的目的地有89%在亚洲，3.83%在欧洲，2.44%在北美地区，1.26%在大洋洲，0.4%在非洲，另有3.04%流向南北极及邮轮等。中国出境游旅客有3种，分别为团队、自由行游客和会展旅游（MICE）。其中，以团队方式出境游客的特点为：年龄在35岁以上、文化程度为高中以上、拥有与技术相关的职务、消费能力在1 200美元左右、60%为女性、每两年出游一次、多数来自中国二线城市。自由行游客的特点为：年龄在38岁以下、60%为男性、拥有稳定的工作、消费能力在3 400美元、每年出游2～3趟、多数来自中国一线城市。以MICE方式出境游客的特点为：大多来自全球性企业、每晚消费在145美元以上、停留时间为5～7天、消费能力达12 000美元。中国公民出游的主要动机是游览地标性的景观、购物、体验、冒险和感受文化差异。其中，在购物方面，一般集中在名牌衣服、手表、化妆品和珠宝。

第二节　中国出境旅游的特点

一、出境旅游人数大幅增加

近年来，中国公民出境旅游人数大幅增加，成为世界第一大客源输出国和全球出境旅游市场增幅最快、潜力最大、影响力最广泛的国家之一。自1990年中国公民自费赴新加坡、马来西亚和菲律宾三国旅游率先开启，1997年发布《中国公民自费出国旅游管理暂行办法》，中国公民出境旅游市场开始逐步形成。进入21世纪以来，中国出境旅游市场一直保持着20%左右的高速增长态势。从出境规模来看，中国的出境游客数量已经多年位列全球第一，且在出境旅游的总消费上也是第一。虽然拥有巨大的市场基数，但是中国的出境旅游仍然处于发展的初级阶段。仅就国民旅游数量而言，目前还处于大众化旅游时代发展初期，这其中存在多次出境的游客和大量新增的初次出境的游客，成为整个市场规模增长的主要动力。

从区域分布来看，出境旅游主要集中在东部地区，西部地区的家庭与个人出境旅游人数在总人口中占比较低，中西部地区的农村居民出境旅游的就更少了。从区域发展状况来看，由于我国东、中、西部经济发展差异，大多数小城镇居民和农民依然没有能力外出旅游，东部地区一直是中国出境旅游市场占比最大的区域，但是随着中西部地区的经济实力和开放程度的进一步提升，中西部地区出境旅游市场增长潜力正在得到不断释放。在出境旅游的初级阶段，由于多数出境旅游者的旅游经验尚不成熟，对旅行社的依赖程度较高，因此，在未来一段时期内，中国公民出境旅游的出境方式仍以旅行社组团、观光游览为主，旅游目的地还是以周边国家和地区为主，消费形式则主要体现在购物消费。

二、出境旅游者旅游方式单一，消费观念尚不成熟

由于中国出境旅游的发展尚处于起步阶段，大多数旅游者是第一次出国，缺乏出境旅游经验，他们往往会选择团队包价的单一的旅游方式。在现有条件下，价格依然是影响旅游者选择旅游目的地的重要参数，但出境旅游开始由高收入人群的高消费活动向中等收入人群和中等消费转变，中国公民出境旅游的动机有所改变，团队包价旅游依然是中国出境旅游者主要的旅游方式。品牌是旅游者选择旅行社的重要参考标准。

随着公民生活水平的提高和消费观念的转变，因私出境旅游成为旅游市场的热点。从2000年起，我国因私出境人数超过因公出境人数，成为出境旅游市场的绝对主体。购物是中国旅游者的一项重要的消费支出。根据调查，约1/3的游客认为购物是花费最高的项目。随着境外支付的日趋便利，经济全球化，旅游业成为一些国家振兴经济的希望，各国纷纷出台措施为中国游客提供便利，因此消费规模大幅增长。在总量上，中国出境旅游市场与消费持续增长；在客源产出上，经济增长是中国出境旅游的主要推动因素，中西部地区与二、三、四线城市的市场活跃度进一步上升。世界旅游组织表示，过去10年间，中国国际旅游市场的发展一直是全球最快的，至今依然如此，这要归功于中国城镇化的发展、居民可支配收入的增长以及对国际旅游限制的放松。2018年，中国公民在海外旅游消费额达1 300亿美元，增速超过13%。中国已经多年保持世界第一大国际旅游消费国地位。购物成为推动消费规模增长的重要因素，但出境旅游者的消费观念不够成熟。受短期内难以再次出境旅游等因素的影响，中国公民在境外的消费行为突出表现为密集性购物，缺乏理性的消费观念。

三、出境旅游的目的地更加广泛，亚洲仍然是出境旅游首选目的地，欧美等中长线逐渐升温

作为亚洲最大的出境旅游客源国，中国出境旅游自1997年开放以来一直以超过20%的年增长率高速发展。截至2019年初，全国有出境旅游资质的旅行社已增至4 442家；出境人数也有明显增长，出境旅游目的地则由东南亚各国及中国港澳地区扩展到150多个国家和地区。由于价格、人缘、地域、语言等方面的优势，中国出境旅游目的地仍主要集中在中国港澳台地区、东南亚、东亚和边境国家，其中中国港澳台地区的旅游者占了出境人数的60%左右，东亚的日本、韩国，东南亚较早对中国开放的新加坡、马来西亚、泰国等地，边境国家越南等都成为中国公民首次出境旅游的首选地。随着开放目的地数量的稳中有升，境外旅游目的地不断加大对中国游客的促销力度，签证、免税、支付、中文接待环境等便利措施的出台，欧元、英镑的贬值以及后奥运旅游等因素，进一步拉动了中国公民的出境旅游需求。在“一带一路”倡议下，中国公民在签证办理方面更趋便利。2018年，中国游客到“一带一路”沿线国家旅游人次突破3 000万人次，超过日本、美国，“一带一路”沿线国家成为中国游客第一大海外旅游目的地区域。开放旅游签证是促进国际旅游快速发展的重要因素。截至2019年4月1日，已经有51个共建“一带一路”国家面向中国游客开放便利签证政策。其中，单方面允许中国公民免签入境的国家有7个，包括印度尼西亚、韩国（济州岛等地区）、突尼斯、摩洛哥等；与中国互免普通护照签证的国家有11个，包括阿联酋、巴巴多斯、斐济、格林纳达、塞舌尔等；对中国游客实施落地签证政策的国家有33个，包括泰国、印度尼西亚、越南、老挝、柬埔寨、马尔代夫等。

四、问题与发展伴生，出境旅游亟待规范

由于当前我国有关出境旅游的法律法规还不健全，行业管理部门对出境旅游的管理也不够完善，导致我国出境旅游的发展伴生着各种问题。主要表现为：

（一）价格竞争

影响中国出境旅游市场有序健康发展的重要因素之一是价格竞争。近年来，中国出境旅游呈现高速增长的态势，但在某些出境旅游路线或者目的地，仍存在低价、低质的旅游产品、“零团费”及强制购物等问题。价格竞争带来低成本经营、低层次的服务；产品雷同也使中国出境旅游市场在高速发展的同时，出境旅游服务质量一再下降，严重地影响了出境旅游市场的健康发展，不仅危害了旅游者的消费利益，而且损害了我国旅游企业的国际形象。很多经营出境旅游业务的旅行社都会自愿或者不自愿地被卷进价格竞争的怪圈。另外，新开发的目的地市场也会很快被卷入价格竞争中。导致价格竞争的原因主要有两方面：一是经营旅游业务的企业自身的因素；二是中国游客在旅游方面的受教育程度不够高，游客只论价格的消费行为推动了价格竞争，从某种程度上使价格竞争愈演愈烈。这也是中国出境旅游市场发展多年来难有质的飞跃的原因。

（二）中国出境旅游如何讲好中国故事

近两年来，中国每年有大约1.5亿人次的游客出境，几乎在世界各旅游目的地都能见到中国游客的身影，中国游客正成为世界旅游业的中坚力量，中国游客巨大的出游数字、惊人的消费能力，给世人留下了深刻的印象。在文化和旅游融合的大背景下，如何借助出境旅游推广中国文明、加入文化元素、讲好中国故事也是出境旅游高速发展的过程中要思考的问题。

（三）旅游安全开始备受关注

出境旅游的游客已经从精英群体变成了大众群体，出境游客越多，安全问题就越明显，因此旅游安全备受关注，旅游保险亟待规范。近年来，由于国际旅行常识储备不足、自身安全防范意识不足、缺乏自我保护能力，中国公民在海外各类旅游活动安全事故时有发生，使得出境旅游安全日益为人们所关注和重视。

中国旅游市场不正当竞争问题愈加突显，但在2013年以前，中国尚没有一部专门的旅游法，这与中国作为世界旅游大国的地位不相匹配。第八届全国人民代表大会之后，社会上要求制定旅游法的呼声进一步提高。2013年10月1日起，《中华人民共和国旅游法》施行，有利于行业整体规范、有序、健康发展，使消费者的旅行体验和旅游质量得到保障。从国家层面来立法，以保障旅游者和旅游经营者的合法权益为宗旨，明确各方权利、责任，旅游者和经营者的维权、政府部门的监管执法都将有明确的法律依据。中国旅游业从此进入依法治理、依法维权的新时代。

第三节　中国出境旅游的发展趋势

一、后疫情时代对出境旅游市场的挑战

近年来，中国出境旅游市场维持稳步上升态势。2019年虽然受宏观经济下行的影响，整体增速有所放缓，但仍较2018年实现了4.5%的增长。出境旅游人数继续增长，二、三线客源地区是新的增长点，市场也更趋成熟。2020年，由于全球疫情形势严峻，各国针对新冠肺炎的防控措施严格，出境游行业整体停摆。由于疫情的不可控，因此预计出境旅游将需要更长的恢复周期。待疫情结束，出境游势必将迎来又一次井喷式增长。未来的出境旅游将会向与中国地缘政治较好的国家，如日本、韩国，以及“一带一路”沿线国家导流。后疫情时代，由于疫情导致收入紧缩，游客会更偏向市场性价比较高的出境游产品、小团旅游和自由行，科技和出境游的结合会成为增长亮点，游客也会对目的地的安全环境、服务质量及旅游产品的优质体验提出更高要求。

二、团队游产品竞争更加激烈，产品创新和升级将成趋势

由于中国出境旅游还处于初级发展阶段，以观光为主导的产品结构还会长期存在，因

此价格主导市场的情况也将会在一段时期内长期存在。大多数游客还是会选择团队出游，但团队游产品竞争更加激烈，产品创新和升级将成趋势。旅游业界纷纷利用市场增长的机会对旅游产品不断细化，随着市场的细分，享受型、休闲型、探索型等深度体验游在未来会比较受欢迎，针对不同人群细分旅游产品，提升团队游消费主体的稳定性和忠诚度，将是主流团队游市场的必然趋势。同时，区域出游的增长潜力正在释放。东部地区长期以来占据着中国出境旅游的主力位置，但随着中西部地区经济实力和开放程度的进一步提升，中西部地区出境旅游市场的增长潜力正在得到不断释放。中西部地区所占比重在不断提高，由 2010 年的 30% 提高到 2017 年的 62.4%，这也跟一些 OTA（在线旅游）平台不断扩张，布局三、四线城市有关。

三、自助旅游愈发受到青睐，在线预订将持续增长

中国出境旅游最大的特点是从原来的大众观光旅游开始进入体验旅游，未来的深度游有更大的发展潜力。从出行的方式来看，团队旅游仍占主要地位，但个性化的自由行会有更大的增长。目前，自由行、在线预订人数持续增长。2012 年的市场已出现散客化、自助化、网络化三大趋势。由于境内外旅游电子商务的普及，各方面技术更为完善，再加上在线支付便捷与特价的重要优势，因此出境游客会更依赖互联网预订，通过网络在线预订机票、酒店的比重显著增加。自主性较强的“80 后”和“90 后”成为市场的主要推动力量。2018 年，通过携程平台报名境外私家团的游客同比增长 240%。2019 年上半年较 2018 年同期增长翻倍，新一线城市涨幅明显。此外，由于自助游和半自助游的比重攀高，成熟的自助游、深度游产品将占据越来越多的市场份额。例如：东南亚、南亚自助海岛游；法国葡萄酒产区深度游线路，包括“酒窖游”；苏格兰的高端旅游，邀请中国游客前往“高尔夫球和威士忌的故乡”；丹麦哥本哈根自行车游，体验当地健康的生活方式和现代绿色环保理念。对于自助游游客来说，旅游的质量越来越重要，跟团游走马观花似的形式已不能满足他们的需要。而自驾游因国外特殊的地理、人文环境开始受到推崇，欧美国家普遍高速公路网发达，而且少有收费公路，大大降低了出行成本，使得自驾游顺理成章地成为主要的出行方式。除了方式的变化，亲子游、家庭游、研学旅游等新业态也成为旅游产品供应商们争相开拓的市场。

四、出境游客消费动机更趋多元化，消费行为更趋理性

经过多年的发展，中国游客的旅游消费观念已经发生明显转变，市场需求结构在不断变化，随着中国出境游市场继续稳定增长的态势，中国出境游客的境外花销仍保持全球领先，但增势已出现回落，这说明中国出境游客仍具有很强的消费能力，但消费行为更趋理性。以前的观光、购物导向型出境游方式已经逐渐被追求个性化的目的地体验取代，游玩体验已经成为出境游客决策的关键因素，出境游客的消费重心也从原来的境外购物转向体

验差异化、个性化的旅游服务。同时，随着出境旅游市场的不断成熟，中国公民在出境旅游时开始追求更加经济的旅行方式。统计数据表明，越来越多的中国游客，尤其是自由行游客，开始选择体验感强的民宿，“80后”和“90后”正在逐步成为出境旅游市场的重要消费群体。

五、小众目的地更受欢迎，深度游需求增强

中国游客出境自由行呈现出更高频、更深度的特征：在旅游广度上，目的地选择更加多样化，出行频次大幅提升；在旅游深度上，个性化、定制化、品质化的旅游产品和服务正在成为主流，日益多元化的需求正在促进中国旅游休闲消费的新升级。

“一带一路”倡议的提出，推动了中国与相关国家和地区的旅游合作，让中国游客更加关注和了解这些国家的风土人情和旅游资源，并在出行时优先选择“一带一路”沿线相关旅游目的地。如在中俄建交70周年之际，俄罗斯旅游热度环比上涨29%。

出境旅游目的地选择多样化，中国游客的足迹已经遍布全球各大洲、超过60 000个目的地。在目的地选择上，中国的年轻游客越来越热衷于去往“小众”地方。无论是塞舌尔、格鲁吉亚这样小众目的地国家，还是泰国、马来西亚等热门国家的小众城市，都受到了中国游客，尤其是年轻中国游客的青睐。

旅游方式个性化，深度游需求增强。随着越来越多的中国游客走出国门，国人的旅游方式也正在发生变化。休闲度假和深度体验正在取代以购物为主的观光游，中国游客对于“文化旅游”的关注度也显著提升。大数据显示，2019年上半年，“博物馆”的搜索量上涨了41%，“购物”的搜索量则下降了11%。个性化和定制化成为中国游客热衷的出行方式，以一站式服务、个性化体验为核心的定制游快速增长。

六、出境旅游目的地市场发展趋势

（一）亚洲游市场与产品特点

由于价格相对便宜、距离近、时间短，且文化差异小，因此亚洲仍为中国出境旅游的基础市场，东南亚等国的海岛游仍为热点，关岛等新兴目的地充满市场机遇。随着各大旅行社在越南、柬埔寨等线路开通包机旅游，包机旅游市场的潜力巨大。而马尔代夫等地蜜月旅游、马来西亚等地医疗旅游、泰国康体旅游等特殊或私人定制的旅游产品也有很大的市场潜力。除了传统的日本、韩国、东南亚国家，印度、尼泊尔、斯里兰卡、阿联酋等南亚、西亚目的地正在迅速发展。

（二）大洋洲游市场与产品特点

大洋洲的澳大利亚和新西兰较早对中国开放，因其独特的动物资源、成熟的生态旅游、相反的季节等使旅行社能提供丰富的、差异性的产品，可以满足不同游客的需求。此外，澳大利亚和新西兰的旅游产品开发还包含更多旅游目的地和旅游体验，更为深入、多

元化而且能提供更好的质量保证。除了传统的澳大利亚和新西兰市场，斐济和塔希提岛等新兴目的地的探索将使大洋洲旅游产品进一步多样化。

（三）欧洲游市场与产品特点

由于欧洲市场的成熟和其深厚的历史文化底蕴，以及申根签证的优越性，欧洲旅游正逐渐深入化、个性化，深度游和主题游将变成新的市场关注焦点。目前，前往欧洲的游客大部分是中等以上收入的知识分子和商界人士，他们具有丰富的出境旅游经验。极具个性、高质量的欧洲旅游产品将越来越受中国游客的欢迎，尤其是散客旅游市场份额将上升。赴欧洲旅游的中国游客数量将稳步增加，但不会有急剧的增长。

（四）北美游市场与产品特点

随着 2012 年初，美国、加拿大两国对华签证政策的进一步放宽，大大降低了旅游门槛，整个美洲市场正成为目前我国公民出境旅游增速最快的市场之一。美国签证申请时间明显缩短，随着签证政策的改善，美国旅游市场在未来有很大的发展潜力。随着美国旅游的深入化，主题旅游和私人定制产品数量将会增加。赴美国、加拿大旅游的中国游客将逐渐从东、西海岸转向深入游览。美国和加拿大的独立深度旅游将越来越具吸引力，赴美国、加拿大的年轻人将越来越多。其中，30 ～ 40 岁的游客比率将显著增加。这一年龄层的游客主要消费中、短线及与休闲、购物、观光和主题活动相关的产品，此外，暑假赴美国、加拿大的游学旅游也会占据一定的市场份额。随着高端线路的问世，中、南美洲的旅游产品将更加多元化。市场增长速度将取决于促销策略、航班和价格等因素。

（五）非洲游市场与产品特点

截至 2019 年底，在非洲 54 个国家中，共有 28 个国家成为中国（不含港澳台）公民组团出境旅游目的地。到非洲的中国人主要分为三类：商务以及公务考察群体、国内旅行社组织的团队旅游和小众的个人自助游，其中以团队旅游为主，旅游目的国则以埃及、南非、肯尼亚三国为主。此外，这几年也有不少中国游客选择前往毛里求斯、津巴布韦、塞舌尔、坦桑尼亚、突尼斯等新兴的旅游目的地。《2018 中国公民非洲旅游报告》显示，中国赴非游客人数增长速度持续保持高位，年均增幅超过 40%；中国游客出境游十大首选目的地非洲国家占比达 30%。尤其在突尼斯和摩洛哥免签之后，前往突尼斯的中国游客人数同比增长 240%，前往摩洛哥的中国游客人数同比增长 378%。非洲地区逐渐成为关注深度游、品质游、个性游、猎奇游的中国游客首选目的地，非洲游将朝更深入和多元化的方向发展。

第一章
亚洲

本章导航

亚洲（Asia）是亚细亚洲的简称。亚洲东面是太平洋，北面是北冰洋，南面濒临印度洋，西面以乌拉尔山脉、乌拉尔河、里海、大高加索山脉、黑海、土耳其海峡（博斯普鲁斯海峡和达达尼尔海峡）与欧洲分界，西南面隔亚丁湾、曼德海峡、红海、苏伊士运河与非洲相邻，东北面隔白令海峡与北美洲相望。亚洲是世界七大洲中面积最大、人口最多的一个洲，其绝大部分土地位于东半球和北半球。亚洲共有48个国家和地区，在地理上习惯分为东亚、东南亚、南亚、西亚、中亚和北亚。亚洲人口总数约为47亿，约占世界总人口的60%。中国是亚洲最大的出境旅游客源国，中国公民出境旅游目的地主要集中在亚洲。本章主要从国家概况、民俗风情、主要旅游城市及景点、旅游资讯等几个方面增加学习者对日本、韩国、新加坡、马来西亚、泰国、印度尼西亚、菲律宾等主要目的地国家的认识和了解。

第一节 日本

一、国家概况

（一）地理环境

日本是东亚的一个岛国，坐落在太平洋，东临日本海、中国、朝鲜、韩国和俄罗斯，从鄂霍次克海到中国东海一直向南延伸到中国台湾地区。日本由 6 800 多个岛屿组成。四个最大的岛屿是本州、北海道、九州和四国，其国土面积约 377 900 平方千米。

> Japan is an island nation in East Asia. Located in the Pacific Ocean, it lies to the east of the Sea of Japan, China, the Democratic People's Republic of Korea (DPRK), Republic of Korea (ROK) and Russia, stretching from the Sea of Okhotsk in the north to the East China Sea and Taiwan, China in the south. Japan is an archipelago of more than 6,800 islands. The four largest islands are Honshū, Hokkaidō, Kyūshū and Shikoku, and its land area covers around 377,900 square kilometers.

日本属于温带海洋性季风气候，有四个不同的季节。樱花是日本的国花，到了春天到处可见此花。日本群岛位于环太平洋火山地震带，全球有 1/10 的火山位于日本，1/5 的地震发生在日本。破坏性地震往往造成海啸，在每个世纪都会发生多次。最近的大地震是 2011 年本州岛东北部地震，达到了里氏 9.0 级，于 2011 年 3 月 11 日爆发，引发了大海啸。

> The climate of Japan is predominantly temperate maritime monsoon climate with four distinct seasons. Sakura (cherry blossom) is Japan's national flower prevailing all over the natural landscape in spring. The islands of Japan are located in Circum-Pacific Volcanic Belt. One tenth of the world's volcanoes are located in Japan, and one fifth of the earthquakes occurred in Japan. Destructive earthquakes, often resulting in tsunami, occur several times in each century. The latest major earthquake is the 2011 Tōhoku earthquake, the 9.0-magnitude earthquake which hit Japan on March 11, 2011 and triggered a massive tsunami.

（二）人文概况

1. 历史

日本第一次出现在历史记载中是在中国的《汉书》。根据三国历史的记载，在 3 世纪出现的最强大的王国被称为邪马台国。8 世纪的奈良时代（公元 710—794 年）标志着日本的强大，集中体现在奈良王朝。日本封建时代的特征是作为统治阶级的武士的出现。1185 年，平氏家族衰败后，平家武士源赖朝被任命为将军并在镰仓建立了基地。他死后，北条家族上台，成为摄政的幕府将军。美国海军准将马休·佩里策划的“黑船”事件直接导致日本于 1854 年 3 月 31 日签署了《神奈川条约》，迫使日本向外部世界开放。

> Japan first appears in the Chinese *Book of Han* in historical records. According to the accounts of Three Kingdoms, the most powerful kingdom on the archipelago during the 3rd century was called Yamataikoku. The Nara period (710–794) of the 8th century marked the emergence of a strong Japanese state, centered on an imperial court in Heijō-kyō (modern Nara). Japan's feudal era was characterized by

the emergence and dominance of a ruling class of warriors, the samurai. Following the defeat of the Taira Clan in 1185, Minamoto no Yoritomo, a samurai, was appointed shogun and established a base of power in Kamakura. After his death, the Hojo Clan came to power as regents for the shoguns. On March 31,1854, USS “Black Ships” led by Commodore Matthew C.Perry forced the opening of Japan to the outside world with the *Convention of Kanagawa*.

1868 年，革新派实行明治维新，废除封建割据的幕藩体制，建立统一的中央集权国家，恢复天皇至高无上的统治。明治维新后，日本资本主义发展迅速，对外逐步走上侵略扩张的道路。1894 年，日本发动甲午战争；1904 年，日本挑起日俄战争；1910 年，日本侵吞朝鲜半岛。日本在第二次世界大战中战败，1945 年 8 月 15 日宣布无条件投降。战后初期，美军对日本实行单独占领。1947 年 5 月实施新宪法，日本由绝对天皇制国家变为以天皇为国家象征的议会内阁制国家。

In 1868, the reformists practiced Meiji Restoration, abolishing the feudal separatism Bakuhan system, and established a unified and centralized country, restoring the emperor’s supreme reign. After the Meiji Restoration, Japan’s capitalism experienced rapid development, and was gradually on road toward invasion and expansion. In 1894, Japan provoked the Sino-Japanese War and then the Russo-Japanese War in 1904. In 1910, Japan annexed Korean Peninsula. Japan was defeated in the Second World War as it announced the unconditional surrender on August 15, 1945. During the initial post-war period, Japan was under the exclusive occupation by the US Army. With the implementation of the new constitution in May 1947, the absolute emperor system was transformed into the parliamentary cabinet system with the emperor as the national symbol.

2. 经济

尽管地域有限、资源贫乏，但日本从 20 世纪 60 年代到 80 年代，战后整体经济增长创造了奇迹：在 60 年代和 70 年代平均增长率为 7.5%，80 年代和 90 年代初为 3.2%。20 世纪 90 年代增长明显放缓，当时在日本被称为“失落的十年”，主要是因为日本资产价格泡沫的副作用和国内政策旨在抵消过度投机的股票和房地产市场。2000 年，日本政府努力恢复经济增长的举措收效甚微，进一步加剧了全球经济增长放缓。2005 年后，日本经济表现出强劲复苏的迹象，当年的国内生产总值增长率为 2.8%，超过了同一时期的美国和欧盟。2008 年以来，先后受到国际金融危机和 2011 年本州岛东北部地震的冲击，日本经济复苏势头受挫。现任首相安倍晋三上台后推出“安倍经济学”，实施了一系列刺激经济政策，一定程度上提振了日本经济。2011 年，日本在名义国内生产总值方面是美国和中国之后的世界第三大经济体。

Despite limited area and poor resources, the overall real economic growth in the era from the 1960s to the 1980s has been called the Japanese post-war economic miracle: its growth rates averaged 7.5 percent in the 1960s and 1970s, and 3.2 percent in the 1980s and early 1990s. Growth slowed markedly in the 1990s during what the Japanese call the Lost Decade, largely because of the after-effects of the Japanese property price bubble and domestic policies intended to wring speculative excesses from the stock and real estate markets. Government efforts to revive economic growth met with little success and thus further accelerated the global slowdown in 2000. The economy showed strong signs of recovery after 2005 with GDP growth for that year reaching 2.8 percent, surpassing the growth rates of the US and European Union during the same period. Since 2008, it has been hit by the international financial crisis and the 2011 Tōhoku earthquake, and the momentum of economic recovery of Japan has been frustrated. After the current Prime Minister Shinzo Abe took office, he launched "abenomics" and implemented a series of economic stimulus policies, which to some extent boosted the Japanese economy. In 2011, Japan is the third largest economy in the world in terms of nominal GDP, after the United States and China.

3. 社会文化

日本民族的主体是大和民族，占人口的 99.3% 以上。少数民族只有阿伊努族，旧称"虾夷"族，生活在北海道地区。日本人口约 1.25 亿，男性平均寿命为 81.25 岁，女性平均寿命为 87.32 岁，是世界上人均寿命最长的国家。日本的官方语言为日本语。日本是个多宗教的国家，主要有神道教、佛教、基督教三大宗教。大多数日本人既信奉神道教，又信奉佛教。

The main body of the Japanese nationality is Yamato, accounting for more than 99.3% of the population. The only ethnic minority group is Ainu, formerly known as the "Ainu" family, who live in the Hokkaidō area. Japan's population is about 125 million, with the male's average life expectancy 81.25 years old and female 87.32 years old. Japanese is the country of the longest average life expectancy in the world. The official language of Japan is Japanese. Japan is a country of multiple-religions, mainly Shinto, Buddhism and Christianity. Most Japanese believe in both Shinto and Buddhism.

日本在 100 多年的现代化社会发展过程中，人口大为膨胀。以人口数量计算，日本已位居世界前十位。日本国土的 76% 是山地，大部分日本人居住在高度发达的东海岸和南部地区，占 45% 的人口居住在东京、大阪、名古屋及其周边地区。第二次世界大战之前，丈夫是一家之主，具有绝对权威，妻子作为主妇，双方在家庭中处于不平等的地位。1947 年，日本颁布了《民法修正案》，赋予女性与男性同等的法律地位，从而打破了家庭中的家长制。

Over its past 100 year's social development, Japan has experienced dramatic population expansion. In terms of demography, Japan has already ranked among the world's top ten. 76% of Japan's land is mountain. Most Japanese live in highly-developed east coast and southern regions, and 45% of the population live in Tokyo, Osaka, Nagoya and their surrounding areas. Before the Second World War, the husband was the master of the family with absolute authority, and the wife was just a housewife with an unequal status. In 1947, Japan enacted the *Civil Law Amendment*, giving women equal legal status, thus breaking the family paternalism.

日本文化至今发展迅猛。当代文化结合了来自亚洲、欧洲和北美各派的影响。日本传统艺术包括茶道、花道、武术、书法、折纸、温泉、艺伎和游戏。日本有一项保护并促进有形和无形文化财产以及国宝完善的制度。日本共有 23 处遗产已被联合国教科文组织列入世界遗产名录。

Japanese culture has evolved greatly from its origins. Contemporary culture combines influences from Asia, Europe and North America. Traditional Japanese arts include practices such as the tea ceremony, ikebana, martial arts, calligraphy, origami, onsen, geisha and games. Japan has a well-established system for the protection and promotion of both tangible and intangible Cultural Properties and National Treasures. Twenty-three sites in total have been inscribed on the UNESCO World Heritage List.

茶仪式，也被称为茶道，是日本传统的文化活动，涉及礼仪准备和抹茶粉（即绿茶叶沫）的介绍。在日本，它被称为茶之汤或茶道。这种展示方式或表演艺术，被称为“otemae”。禅宗佛教对茶道的发展具有主要影响。

Tea ceremony, also called the Way of Tea, is a Japanese traditional cultural activity involving the ceremonial preparation and presentation of matcha, a powdered green tea. In Japan, it is called Chanoyu or Chado. The manner in which it is performed or the art of its performance, is called otemae. Zen Buddhism is believed to exert primary influence on the development of the tea ceremony.

日本花道，这一插花艺术的主要理念，是在茶室里提高装饰瓶的吸引力并用花来寄托感情。茶道和插花历来是日本的传统艺术，两者都旨在表现纯洁和朴实，而非创造优雅之美。花道旨在创造线性结构、韵律和颜色的和谐，花瓶、茎、叶、枝条与花共同构成这一艺术形式。不同于西方人对花草的欣赏强调数量和颜色，日本插花是基于三条主线，分别象征着天堂、地球和人类。碎叶和枯萎的芽以及盛开的鲜花都被视为提升插花之美的元素。

Ikebana, the main idea behind art of flower arranging, is to arrange the flowers to heighten the appeal of a vase in a tea room and use flowers to represent emotions. The tea ceremony and flower arrangement has always been the traditional Japanese arts, with the objective of both expressing purity and simplicity rather than creating something of elegant beauty. Flower arrangement seeks to create a harmony of linear construction, rhythm and color in which the vase, stems, leaves and branches are part of the art form as well as the flowers. Unlike Western appreciation of flowers, which emphasizes quantity and color, Japanese flower arrangement is based on three main lines that symbolize heaven, earth and humankind. Broken leaves and blighted buds as well as blooming flowers are all seen as objects that enhance the beauty of the arrangement.

相扑是日本式摔跤和日本的国家运动。它起源于古代招待道教神的演出，至今仍然遵循该仪式与宗教背景。相扑的基本规则很简单：在比赛时，相扑手除了脚掌之外的任何部位触及地面，或谁最先出圈则失败。该比赛在被称为“dohyo”的高台上进行，该高台由黏土堆起来，上面蒙了一层沙子。战斗通常只持续几秒钟，或在极少数情况下约一分钟。横纲站（冠军）是相扑手的最高级别。一旦一个相扑手达到横纲等级，他就不会再失去这一地位，但是当他的成绩开始退步时，人们便期望他引退。许多前相扑手作为日本相扑协会的成员仍然活跃在相扑界。

Sumo is a Japanese style of wrestling and Japan's national sport. It originated in ancient times as a performance to entertain the Shinto gods. Many rituals with religious background are still followed today. The basic rules of sumo are very simple: the wrestler who first touches the ground with anything besides the soles of his feet, or who leaves the ring before his opponent, loses out. The game takes place on an elevated ring, called "dohyo", which is made of clay and covered in a layer of sand. The fights usually last only a few seconds, or in rare cases, about one minute. On the top of the sumo wrestlers' hierarchy stand the Yokozuna (grand champion). Once a wrestler reaches the rank of Yokozuna, he won't lose this status but he will be expected to retire when his results begin to worsen. Many former wrestlers remain active in the sumo world as members of the Japan Sumo Association.

知识拓展

艺伎

艺伎（Geisha）在原则上是艺术表演者，与日本的茶道、书道一样同属于日本传统文化的一部分。最初的艺伎全部是男性，在娱乐场所以演奏传统鼓乐、说唱逗乐为生。18世纪中叶，艺伎渐渐成为女性职业，这一传统也一直沿袭至今。艺伎从事的是表演艺术，不是卖弄色相，更不卖身。艺伎行业规定，艺伎在从业期内不得结婚，否则必须先引退，以保持艺伎“纯洁”的形象。在日本，担任艺伎的条件非常苛刻，不仅学艺费用高昂，并非一般家庭可以承担，而且学艺历程艰辛，不是所有人都能坚持的。“自我修养”和“自我重塑”的能力是日本人恒久追求的一种品质，而艺伎正体现了这种品质。艺伎的“自我重塑”是由表及里的，她们一丝不苟、不遗余力地把自己打造成才貌双全的极品女子。艺伎通过多年的勤学苦练，最终成为通晓琴棋书画，能歌善舞，精通插花、茶道等传统技艺的才女，因此被称为“日本古典文化的活化石”。

二、民俗风情

（一）礼仪禁忌

日本人见面多以鞠躬为礼，一般行30度和45度的鞠躬礼。鞠躬弯腰的深浅表示的含义不同，弯腰最低、最有礼貌的鞠躬被称为“最敬礼”。鞠躬时，两手自然下垂放在衣裤两侧；对对方表示恭敬时，多以左手搭在右手上，放在身前行鞠躬礼。交换名片时，地位低或者年轻的一方先给对方，这种做法被认为是一种礼节。递交名片时，要将名片正对着对方。名片在日语中写为“名刺”，大多数女性名片的规格比男性名片要小一些。

Bowing is very common to show etiquette in Japan. Generally, bowing is achieved by 30 degrees and 45 degrees, and different degrees of bowing show different meanings. The lowest and the politest bow is called "the salute". In bowing, hands are naturally put down on both sides of the dress. To show respect, the left hand should rest on the right hand, bowing down with both hands in the front. In business card exchange, the one with lower status or younger age should give the card first, which is considered to be a kind of etiquette. The card should directly face the other when it is handed over. Written as "meishi" in Japanese, most business cards for women are smaller than those for men.

在社交活动中，日本人爱用自谦语，如“请多关照”“粗茶淡饭”“照顾不周”等。在与日本人交谈时，不要边说边指手画脚，别人讲话时切忌插话打断。在交谈中，不要打听日本人的年龄、婚姻状况、工资收入等私事。对年事高的人不要用“年迈”“老人”等字样。

In social activities, the Japanese prefer to use humble languages, such as “thank you for your kind consideration”, “hope you like the simple tea and meal”, “please forgive me if there’s anything wrong with hospitality”, etc. In Japanese conversations, don’t talk while making gestures and don’t interrupt when others are speaking. Also don’t ask privacy such as age, marital status and salary. Don’t refer to senior people as “old”.

日本人大多数信奉神道教和佛教。他们不喜欢紫色，认为紫色是悲伤的色调，最忌讳绿色。日本人忌讳 3 人一起“合影”，他们认为中间的人被左右两人夹着，是不祥的预兆。日本人忌讳荷花，认为荷花会带来坏运气。在探望病人时，忌用山茶花及淡黄色、白色的花。日本人不愿接受菊花或有菊花图案的物品，因为它是皇室的标志。日本人喜欢的图案是松、竹、梅、鸭子、乌龟等。通信时，信的折叠、邮票的贴法都要合乎规范，如寄慰问信忌用双层信封，双层被认为是祸不单行；寄给恋人的信件的邮票不能倒贴，否则意味着分手。日本人在饮食方面的忌讳也很多。一般而言，日本人不吃肥肉和猪内脏，也有人不吃羊肉和鸭子；招待客人忌讳将饭盛得过满、过多，也不可一勺就盛好一碗；忌讳客人吃饭一碗就够，只吃一碗象征无缘；忌讳用餐过程中整理自己的衣服或用手抚摸、整理头发，因为这是不卫生和不礼貌的举止；日本人使用筷子时，忌把筷子放在碗、碟上面。

Most Japanese believe in Shinto and Buddhism. They don’t like purple, which is considered having a sad tone, the top taboo in color is green. Three people together cannot take pictures, because they think the one being sandwiched by the other two in the middle is an omen of misfortune. The Japanese avoid lotus, which means bad luck. When visiting patients, the Japanese don’t send camellias or pale yellow, white flowers. They would not accept chrysanthemum or things with chrysanthemum pattern, because it is the symbol of the royal family. What the Japanese like using as patterns are pine, bamboo, plum, duck and turtle. There are rules for letter folding, stamps sticking in correspondence, such as not to use a double envelope to send a letter of condolence, because double is considered as “disasters don’t happen alone”. When sending a letter to one’s lover, the stamp cannot be upside down, otherwise it means a Dear John Letter. There are also many taboos in Japanese diet. Generally, they don’t eat fat and pig intestines, and some people don’t eat the mutton and the duck. It is inappropriate to serve too much rice in a bowl for guests, nor a spoonful to fill a bowl. It is a taboo for guests to just eat a bowl of rice, which means no further development of relationship. It is also a taboo to neat the clothes or touch hair when dining, because it is considered as an unhealthy and rude behavior. Japanese also avoid putting chopsticks on a bowl or dish.

日本人有不少语言忌讳，如“苦”和“死”。因为“4”的发音与“死”相同，“42”的发音是“死”的动词形式，所以医院一般没有号码为 4 和 42 的房间和病床。用户的电话也忌讳用 42，监狱一般也没有 4 号囚室。13 也是日本人忌讳的数字，许多宾馆没有 13 楼和 13 号房间，羽田机场也没有 13 号停机坪。

There are many taboos in Japanese language, such as “bitter” and “death”. The word “4” has the same pronunciation as “death”, and “42” sounds like the verb of the word “die”, so there is no room or bed with number 4 or 42 in a hospital. 42 is also avoided in telephone numbers and there is no number 4 in a prison either. 13 is another taboo number, so there are no floors or rooms of 13 in many hotels, there is also no apron 13 in Haneda Airport.

日本人送礼时，通常送成双成对的礼物，如一对笔、两瓶酒很受欢迎。但送新婚夫妇红包时，忌讳送 2 万日元或 2 的倍数，日本民间认为"2"这个数字容易导致夫妻感情破裂，一般送 3 万日元、5 万日元或 7 万日元。礼品包装纸的颜色也有讲究，黑白色代表丧事，绿色为不祥，也不宜用红色包装纸，最好用花色纸包装礼品。

When Japanese give gifts, the gifts will usually be in pair, for example, two pens or two bottles of liquor. When giving money to newly wedded couples, never give 20,000 Japanese yen or the amount as multiples of 2, because the Japanese believe 2 will break up the couple's relationship. So generally 30,000 Japanese yen, 50,000 Japanese yen or 70,000 Japanese yen will be acceptable. The color of packaging materials for gift is another thing which need attention. Black and white stand for something about funeral and green means something unlucky, while red is also not appropriate. Colorful papers are preferred for packaging.

日本人对坐姿很有讲究。在公司里，日本人都坐椅子，但在家里，日本人保持着坐"榻榻米"的传统习惯。坐榻榻米的正确坐法叫"正座"，即把双膝并拢跪地，臀部压在脚跟上。轻松的坐法有"盘腿坐"和"横坐"。"盘腿坐"是把脚交叉在前面，臀部着地，这是男性的坐法；"横坐"是双腿稍许横向一侧，身体不压住双脚，这通常是女性的坐法。现在，不坐"榻榻米"的年轻一代在逐渐增多。

The Japanese are careful about sitting. In the company the Japanese usually sit on chairs, but at home they sit on "tatami" as a tradition. The correct way to sit on tatami is to kneel down with hips pressed on the heel. An easy way to sit is "cross-legged" and "cross sitting". "Cross-legged" means crossing in front of the feet with hips forward, which is male's sitting; and "cross sitting" is to put legs slightly to lateral side, while the body does not suppress the feet, which is often a way for women to sit. Nowadays, there are more and more young people who don't sit on "tatami".

（二）节庆风情

1. 玩偶节（Doll's Festival）

玩偶节是在 3 月 3 日庆祝，也称女儿节，这是一年一度为年轻女孩子乞求幸福和健康成长的日子。在这一天，家家户户摆放着穿着传统宫廷装束的玩具娃娃和桃花，还供奉一种钻石形状的米饼和干米团。玩偶节来源于古代关于仪式涤罪的信念。人们相信，人类的罪行和污秽可以通过在河边的净化仪式冲洗干净。后来，人们在这些仪式上使用纸做的玩偶。江户时期（1603—1868 年）之后，这些玩偶被设计成现在的玩具的样子。

Doll's Festival is celebrated on March 3rd, also called Girls' Day, which is a day once a year for young girls to pursue happiness and healthy growth. On this day, each and every family display dolls in traditional court costume with peach blossom, and offer diamond-shaped rice cakes and dried rice balls. Doll's Festival comes from the faith of ancient ritual of purgatory. People believed that the crimes and filth of humanity could be cleaned in the purification ritual by the river. People have since made paper dolls in the ceremony. Ever since the Edo Period (1603–1868), these dolls have been designed as what look like current toys.

2. 樱花节（Cherry Blossom Festival）

3 月末 4 月初，在日本的大多数地方，象征着日本的樱花盛开了。日本人在樱花树下举行野餐，尽情游乐。自江户时期以来，在樱花树下野餐的传统习俗一直在日本普通百姓中十分流行。

From the end of March to early April, cherry flowers blossom in most of the places in Japan as the national symbol. The Japanese people enjoy picnic under cherry trees. Since the Edo Period, it has been very popular for Japanese people to have picnic under cherry trees as traditional customs.

三、主要旅游城市及景点

（一）东京（Tokyo）

东京是日本首都，是全国政治、经济、文化、交通中心，也是世界特大城市之一。东京位于本州岛东南部，临东京湾。东京全称东京都，为一级行政区，辖 23 个特别区、26 个市、5 个町（镇）和 8 个村（包括海上的伊豆诸岛和小笠原群岛），面积 2 194 平方千米，人口 1 385 万。其中，23 个区相当于市区，面积为 621.97 平方千米。夏季高温多雨，冬季寒冷干燥。年降水量约为 1 400 毫米。

Tokyo, as Japan's capital and the political, economic, cultural and transportation center, is one of the largest metropolitan cities in the world. Located in the southeast part of Honshū, the city faces Tokyo Bay. With the full name Tokyo Prefecture, the city as the first level administrative region administers 23 special districts, 26 cities, 5 towns and 8 villages (including Izu Islands and Ogasawara Islands on the ocean). It covers an area of 2,194 square kilometers with a population of 13.85 million. 23 districts belong to downtown with an area of 621.97 square kilometers. It is featured by high temperature and frequent rainfalls in summer, but cold and dry climate in winter, with annual precipitation about 1,400 millimeters.

◆ 浅草寺（Sensoji Temple）

浅草寺创建于公元 628 年，是东京都内最古老的寺庙。浅草寺本堂被称作观音堂，以其主梁的构型优美而闻名，内部分为外阵和内阵。观音堂内阵中央有放置着本尊的宫殿，三面开门，是日本第一大宫殿，也是日本现存的具有“江户风格”的民众游乐之地。

Sensoji Temple, the oldest of its kind in Tokyo, was founded in the year 628. Sensoji Temple Hondo is referred to as the Goddess of Mercy Hall, which is famous for its beautiful architecture of the main beam and is divided into the outer and inner array for its interior. In the central of the inner side of the Goddess of Mercy Hall, there is a statue enshrined in the palace, which is open on three sides and is Japan's largest palace. Now it is a popular "Edo style" amusement land in Japan.

◆ 皇居（Imperial Palace）

皇居是指日本天皇居住的宫殿。由于古代日本没有“定都”的想法，因此皇居的位置经常变更，几乎都是以该天皇的即位地为国都，并以该天皇原本居住之宫室为皇居。

Imperial Palace refers to the Japanese emperor's palace. Due to the fact that in ancient Japan there was no capital, so Imperial Palace's location had to change often. The capital was almost always in where the emperor took the throne. Therefore the emperor's original residence became Imperial Palace.

◆ 东京塔（Tokyo Tower）

东京塔又名日本东京电视塔，位于东京都港区芝公园西侧，即东经 139° 44′ 55″，北纬 35° 39′ 20″。1958年12月建成，于1968年7月对游客开放。塔高333米，占地2 118平方米。这座日本最高的独立铁塔上部装有东京 7 个电视台、21 个电视中转台和广播台等的无线电发射天线。东京塔使用的建筑材料是埃菲尔铁塔的一半，造塔费时一年半，不到埃菲尔铁塔施工时间的 1/3。日本用这样少的材料和这样短的时间，平地竖起这座防台风、抗地震的庞然大物，震惊了全世界。

Tokyo Tower—also known as Japan Tokyo TV Tower, located to the west of the Shiba Park, Minato, at longitude 139° 44' 55″, latitude 35° 39' 20″. It was finished in December 1958 and opened to visitors in July 1968. The tower is 333 meters high, covering 2,118 square metres. This independent tower, highest of its kind in Japan, is equipped with transmitting antennas for 7 TV stations, 21 TV relay stations and radio broadcasting stations in Tokyo. Tokyo Tower used half the construction materials of the Eiffel Tower. It takes 1.5 years to construct the whole tower, less than one-third of that for the Eiffel Tower. In such a short time with so few materials, the whole world was stunned by the erection of this against typhoon, earthquake-resistant behemoth tower.

◆ 东京晴空塔（Tokyo Sky Tree）

东京晴空塔是位于日本东京都墨田区的电波塔。东京晴空塔于2008年7月14日动工，2012年2月29日竣工，同年5月22日正式对外开放。东京晴空塔的高度为634米，于2011年11月17日获得吉尼斯世界纪录认证为“世界第一高塔”，成为全世界最高的自立式电波塔，也是目前世界第二高的建筑物，仅次于迪拜的哈利法塔。

Tokyo Sky Tree is a radio tower located in the Sumida District of Tokyo, Japan. The construction started on July 14, 2008, completed on February 29, 2012, and officially opened to the public on May 22, 2012. The height of the Tokyo Sky Tree is 634 meters. It was certified as the "World's Tallest Tower" by the Guinness World Record on November 17, 2011, becoming the world's highest self-supporting radio tower. Nowadays, it is also the second tallest building in the world, only next to Burj Khalifa Tower in Dubai.

（二）大阪（Osaka）

大阪是日本第二大都市，日本三大都市圈之一的大阪都市圈的中心城市。广义上的“大阪”指日本关西地区，或以大阪市作为府厅所在地的大阪府，也指以大阪市为中心的大阪都市圈。大阪也是关西地区经济、文化的中心，拥有古都、副都的历史。

Osaka, the second largest city in Japan, is the center of Osaka metropolitan area, one of the three metropolitan areas in Japan. In a broad sense, "Osaka" can refer to Kansai Prefecture of Japan, or Osaka Prefecture with Osaka City as the seat of government office, or Osaka metropolitan area with Osaka City as the center. Osaka is also the economic and cultural center of Kansai area, with the history of ancient capital and vice capital.

◆ 大阪城（Osaka Castle）

大阪城是大阪的著名地标。公元1583年，丰臣秀吉花费了两年七个月的时间和四万民夫建造而成。大阪城分为三部分，四周有护城河。公元1615年，原大阪城与丰臣一族毁于战火，后德川家光增建后才有今天的面貌。现在的大阪城已规划成为公园，作为市民休闲的场所。大阪城为日本三大名城之一。

Osaka Castle is Osaka's famous landmark. In 1583, Toyotomi Hideyoshi spent two years and seven months building this castle with 40,000 laborers. The moat-surrounded Osaka Castle is divided into three parts. It was destroyed in war fire in 1615, followed by Tokugawa Iemitsu's reconstruction to achieve the present shape today. Now Osaka Castle has been renovated into a park for public leisure. Osaka Castle itself is one of the three Japanese famous cities.

（三）京都（Kyoto）

京都位于东京西南500千米，大阪以东41千米。从东京乘新干线特快车，只需3小时。日本或外国组织的旅游团体，把京都作为必游之地，群山围绕的京都，历史古迹与神奇传说众多。从794年至1868年，它是日本的古都，故有“千年古都”之称。市内多名胜古迹，现尚存1 877个寺庙和神社，被定为国宝的文物有211件，占日本全国总数的15%。京都的宫殿、园林与建筑皆完好无损，是日本保存得最完好的城市，其中包括京都最著名的寺庙——清水寺，它是由山坡上的支柱支撑着的一座宏伟的寺庙。古城平安京（京都古称）的设计和建筑风格模仿唐代的洛阳城和长安城，故京都简称“洛”。

Kyoto is located 500 kilometers southwest to Tokyo, 41 kilometers east on Osaka. From Tokyo by Shinkansen, it takes only 3 hours. It is a must for both Japanese tourist groups and foreign visitors, which has surrounding mountains, historical relics and mysterious legends. From 794 to 1868, it had been Japan's ancient capital, so it is called the "ancient capital of the millennium". The whole city now has 1,877 temples and shrines, and 211 cultural relics have been designated as national treasure, which is a share of 15% for the nation's total. Palaces, gardens and architecture also remain intact, it is one of the best preserved cities in Japan. Among the temples is the most famous in Kyoto—Kiyomizu-dera, a magnificent wooden temple supported by pillars on a mountain slope. The design and construction of the city are in imitation of that of Luoyang and Chang'an in the Tang Dynasty, so Kyoto is referred to as "Los" for short.

到京都旅游的最佳时间是春秋两季。每当樱花盛开和秋季来临时，岚山游人如织。在岚山山麓的龟山公园内有为纪念周恩来同志而建的“雨中岚山”诗碑。

Spring and autumn are the best time to visit Kyoto. Whenever cherry blossoms and autumn comes, Arashiyama is thronged with visitors. Kameyama Park has a stone monument "Arashiyama in the Rain" built in memory of Chinese ex-premier Zhou Enlai.

◆ 清水寺（Kiyomizu-dera）

清水寺是一座位于日本京都府京都市东山区的寺院，建于 778 年。清水寺的山号为音羽山，主要供奉千手观音，原本属于法相宗这一宗派，但目前已独立，成为北法相宗的大本山。自平安时代以来，清水寺就经常出现于日本文学作品中。1994 年，清水寺作为古都京都历史遗迹的一部分，被列入世界文化遗产名录。

Kiyomizu-dera, founded in 778, is a temple located in Higashiyama-ku, Kyoto Prefecture. Kiyomizu-dera is also called Otowa-san. Kiyomizu-dera, which is mainly dedicated to the Thousand-hand Bodhisattva. Originally, Kiyomizu-dera belonged to the Dharma sect. But now, it becomes independent as the center of North Dharma. Since the Heian Period, Kiyomizu-dera has been often seen in Japanese literary works. In 1994, the Kiyomizu-dera, as part of the Historic monuments of Ancient Kyoto, was listed into World Cultural Heritage Site.

◆ 金阁寺（Kinkaku-ji）

金阁寺是日本最美丽的建筑之一，与富士山、艺伎并列为外国人对于日本的三大典型印象。该寺于 1397 年以足利义满将军之名所建，专为举办佛教纪念活动所设。金阁寺最高的两层楼被金叶全部包裹，一只金色凤凰矗立屋顶，十分夺目，金阁寺也因此得名。1950 年，金阁寺被一个日本疯和尚付之一炬，后于 1955 年重建。阁亭和周围的花园、池塘是日本最美丽的取景地之一。1994 年被列入世界文化遗产名录。

Kinkaku-ji is one of the most beautiful buildings in Japan. The Temple, Mount Fuji and Geisha are the three typical impression of Japan in the eyes of foreigners. It was constructed in 1397 for General Ashikaga Yoshimitsu and designed for holding the Buddhist observance. The top two floors are all wrapped in gold leaves and a golden phoenix perches on the rooftop, which is an eye-catching scene and hence the name. In 1950, the temple was torched by a crazy Japanese monk and was rebuilt in 1955. The pavilions and gardens around the pond are one of the best sites for photograph in Japan. In 1994, it was listed into the World Cultural Heritage Site.

（四）其他著名旅游景点

◆ 富士山（Mount Fuji）

富士山在日语中的意思是"火山"，海拔 3 776 米，是日本的最高峰，屹立于本州中南部，跨静冈、山梨两县，距东京 80 千米，富士山占地面积约 1 200 平方千米。这座被日本人奉为"圣岳"的圆锥形火山，自公元 781 年有文字记载以后，共喷发了 18 次，最后一次喷发是在 1707 年，以后休眠至今。冬季半山腰以上均为大雪覆盖，有"玉扇倒悬东海天"和"富士白雪映朝阳"的赞誉。山北麓有独具特色的富士五湖，湖光山色十分宜人。每年7月、8月是登山的好季节。2013年6月，作为信仰的对象与艺术的源泉，富士山被列入世界文化遗产名录。

Mount Fuji, which means "volcano" in Japanese, is at 3,776 meters above sea level and the highest mountain in Japan. It stands in the mid south of Honshū Island, straddling the prefectures of Shizuoka and Yamanashi. Coving an area of about 1,200 square kilometers, it is 80 kilometers from Tokyo. As a "Holy Mountain", this conical volcano, has erupted a total of 18 times since the year 781. The last eruption took place in 1707, and it has been dormant since then. Half way up the mountain is covered with snow during the winter. Northern foot of the mountain is featured by picturesque Fuji Five Lakes. July and August every year are good time to climb the mountain. In June 2013, Mount Fuji, scared place and source of artistic inspiration, was listed as the World Cultural Heritage site by UNESCO.

◆ 箱根町（Hakone）

箱根町以山景而闻名，温泉古迹颇多，主要的名胜包括芦之湖，以湖水倒映着富士山和箱根神社而著名。

Well-known for its hot springs and mountain views, Hakone's main sights include Lake Ashi, renowned for reflecting the famous Mount Fuji and Hakone Gongen.

◆ 北海道（Hokkaidō）

北海道位于日本最北端，约占日本国土面积的22%。森林覆盖面积占总面积的70%以上，人口密度极低。全年气候寒冷、冬季漫长。北海道是日本屈指可数的游览胜地，其中札幌是北海道的空中门户。札幌最著名的是一年一度的冰雪节，人们纷纷前来观赏作为札幌象征的钟塔大楼。札幌是冬季运动的主要场所，如在札幌做短程旅行，定山溪是理想之选，可以看到深谷和沟壑。

Located in the northernmost Japan, Hokkaidō accounts for about 22% land area of Japan. Forest covers 70% of its land and population density is extremely low. The climate is cold during long winter. As a main Japanese tourist attraction, Hokkaidō has an air gateway at Sapporo, which is famous for its annual snow festival when people come to admire its symbol, the Sapporo Clock Tower. Sapporo is the main place for winter sports. A getaway from Sapporo may provide you with a glimpse at Jōzankei Dam, an ideal spot to view the deep canyons and ravines.

四、旅游资讯

（一）美食

由于日本是一个岛国，因此人们常食用海鲜，由于佛教的限制，直到近年日本除生鱼片以外的肉食仍比较少见。但是严格的素食食品还是罕见的，因为菜肴的风味得由无处不在的出汁调料制作，该调料通常由鲣节（干鲣鱼片）做成。当然佛教僧侣们的一些斋菜（精致料理）是例外。面条是日本料理中不可缺少的一部分，通常将面条作为以稻米为基础的膳食的一种替代。荞麦面（荞麦粉制成的灰褐色面条）和乌冬面（小麦粉制成的粗面条）是主要的传统面条，并可由出汁调味料做成热的或冷的食物。中式面条可以放在肉汤中，称为拉面，在过去的一个世纪中非常受欢迎。由于普通食品成本上升，日本家庭的蔬菜消费量减少，而加工食品的购买量增多。日本料理的一个特色是生食，任何食物如鲔鱼、鲑鱼、章鱼、牛肉、鸡蛋都可以生食入菜。日本饮食中比较有特色的是寿司、刺身（生鱼片）、清酒、便当（盒饭）、天妇罗、章鱼烧、荞麦面等。

As Japan is an island nation, its people eat a lot of seafood. Meat-eating has been rare until recently due to restrictions of Buddhism. However, strictly vegetarian food is rare since even vegetable dishes are flavored with the ubiquitous dashi stock, usually made with katsuobushi (dried skipjack tuna flakes). An exception is shōjin ryōri, vegetarian dishes developed by Buddhist monks. Noodles are an essential part of Japanese cuisine usually as an alternative to a rice-based meal. Soba (thin, grayish-brown noodles containing buckwheat flour) and udon (thick wheat noodles) are the main traditional noodles, and can be served hot or cold with soy-dashi flavorings. Chinese-style wheat noodles served in a meat stock broth, which is known as ramen, have become extremely popular over the last century. Vegetable consumption has dwindled while processed foods have been on the rise in Japanese households due to the rising costs of general foodstuffs. Raw food is one of the features of the Japanese cuisine. Any food such as tuna, salmon, octopus, beef, eggs can be eaten raw. Special Japanese diet includes sushi, sashimi, sake, bento, tempura, Takoyaki, soba noodles, etc.

（二）购物及退税

日本清酒：清酒是日本酒文化的代表，是借鉴中国黄酒的酿造方法而发展起来的日本国酒。其味甘醇温和，与我国白酒相比，酒精度数较低。清酒是日本的国粹之一。

Japanese sake: Sake is a representative of the Japanese alcohol culture and its national wine developed by drawing lessons from China's brewing method of glutinous rice wine. With a mild taste, sake's alcoholic content is lower compared with China's liquor. It is one of Japan's national essences.

玩偶玩具：日本的玩偶玩具小巧精美，有些品牌大家耳熟能详，如和服人偶娃娃、Hello Kitty 系列等。它们可爱的样子和精致的做工，让游客忍不住会动心。

Toy dolls: Japanese toy dolls are small and exquisite. Some of such brands are highly popular, such as the Kimono Doll, Hello Kitty, etc. Customers may show keen interest in those dolls for their cute shape and elaborate craftsmanship.

电子产品：日本有许多著名的电子品牌，如东芝、日立、索尼、尼康等。这些品牌的最新款 DV、相机、电脑等产品，有些只能在日本本地才能买到。因为免税，价格相对便宜。

Electronic products: Japan has many well-known electronic brands like Toshiba, Hitachi, Sony, Nikon, etc. Some of the latest models for DV, camera, PC of those brands are only available in Japan. Duty-free policy means price is also relatively lower.

护肤品：日本的护肤品价格便宜，质量上乘，卫生和原料控制严格有保证，是亚洲女性的最爱。特别是近年来人气很旺的药妆，一定不能错过。著名的品牌有资生堂、高丝等。

Skin care products: Japan's skin care products are inexpensive and of high quality with guarantee of health and material control, and thus favourite with Asian ladies. Especially not to be missed are the popular cosmeceuticals in recent years. Famous brands of such products are SHISEIDO, KOSE, etc.

在日本购物，要加收消费总额 10% 的消费税。因此在商场或土特产店，购买标价为 100 日元的物品时，实际支付额为 110 日元。但在日本刷卡退税较为方便，规模较大的商场都有专门的退税点。游客当天购买 5 000 日元以上、50 万日元以下的商品，离开前可凭发票和护照到退税点办理退税。

When shopping in Japan, you have to pay 10% of the total amount as consumption tax. Therefore, in the mall or specialty shops, you need to actually pay 110 yen for an item priced 100 yen. However, it is very convenient to get the tax refund by swiping the cards. Large shopping malls have specialized refund counters. The purchase of 5,000 yen to 500,000 yen enables you to get tax refund with invoice and passport before leaving.

（三）时差

日本首都东京的时间比北京时间早 1 个小时。

Tokyo time is an hour earlier than Beijing time.

思考练习

1. 经典旅游线路分析

日本风情 6 日游

第 1 天：上海——大阪

早上在上海浦东国际机场集合，由领队带领办理出境手续后，搭乘国际航班飞往日本第一大工业城市——大阪，降落于全世界耗资最昂贵的人造岛屿空港——关西国际空港。导游接机后，前往入住大阪市内酒店。之后游客可自行前往大阪最热闹的中心地带——心斋桥商业街，游客在此处可尽情享受在日本的快乐时光。

第 2 天：大阪——京都——高山

酒店享用早餐后，参观日本著名的大阪城公园（不上天守阁，约 40 分钟）。历史悠久的大阪城是由丰臣秀吉于 1583 年建造，由雄伟的石墙砌造而成，占地广阔。之后乘专车前往千年古都——京都，参观以清水舞台及求姻缘著名的清水寺（约 60 分钟）。现存清水寺于 1633 年重修。寺院建筑气势宏伟，结构巧妙，依悬崖峭壁而建，未用一颗钉子。后前往为纪念京都建都 1 100 年而建的平安神宫外苑。外苑是平安时代大内皇宫的复原之作，正门的朱红神殿和大鸟居将当年皇宫盛貌展现在游客眼前，加上茂密的红枝垂樱在旁衬托，更是丰色无边。正殿里的神苑是日本池泉回游式庭园的代表杰作，是京都必游景点之一。晚餐后前往有"小京都"称号的高原城市——高山市入住酒店。

第 3 天：高山——松本——白川乡

酒店享用早餐后，首先在德川幕府时期建造的旧式官府高山阵屋迹（不入内）前摄影留念（停留约 10 分钟），追忆当年番主生活的情景。高山也因这些建筑物而被列为日本的国家重要遗产。然后前往日本四大国宝城之一的松本城游览，松本城建于永正元年（1504 年），位于日本长野县松本市，是日本的 12 座现存天守之一，与姬路城、犬山城、彦根城同为被日本政府指定为国宝的四座古城。最后前往 1995 年被指定为联合国教科文组织世界文化遗产的白川乡，参观"合掌造"（茅草的人字形木屋顶）式民宅（停留约 30 分钟）。白川乡是四面环山、水田纵横、河川流经的安静山村。那里有 110 多栋连成一片"合掌造"式的民宅。晚上入住温泉酒店，品尝日式美食并体验日式温泉的乐趣，消除旅途疲劳。

第 4 天：平和公园——富士山——新宿都厅大厦

酒店享用早餐后，前往箱根，游览平和公园（停留约 30 分钟），远眺日本最高峰——富士山（天气晴朗、云淡风轻时可以拍到背依富士山的美丽风景）。之后游览有"地狱"之称的大涌谷：白烟弥漫、硫黄刺鼻、地热喷涌，堪称世界一大奇迹。此外可自费品尝火山熏陶的长寿蛋——黑玉子蛋。团友可选择自费前往富士山五合目，零距离接触富士山或富士山五合目 + 忍野八海（视天气而定）。然后乘车前往东京，在导游带领下登新宿都厅大厦俯瞰东京全景（停留约 3C 分钟）。

第 5 天：银座——台场海滨公园

酒店享用早餐后，前往银座大街自由购物（停留约 60 分钟），浏览台场海滨公园（维纳斯名店坊和丰田汽车会馆），结束后可选择自费项目——前往东京迪士尼乐园游玩。迪士尼乐园是大人与小孩的梦幻天堂，游客可与米奇、米妮、唐老鸭、维尼熊一同遨游探险乐园、明日世界、梦幻世界、动物天地等，这里有灰姑娘的城堡、丛林巡航、巨雷山、鬼屋、小小世界、太空山、巴斯光年的星际历险等老少咸宜的娱乐设施；午后时分，华丽的花车以及耳熟能详的卡通人物会在街头游行表演，必让游客置身其中，重拾童年的欢乐，并带给游客甜美的回忆。

第 6 天：东京——上海

酒店享用早餐后，继续在东京观光皇居二重桥。最后由专人协助办理搭机手续后，搭乘国际航班飞往上海，在互道珍重的再见声中结束这次日本欢乐之旅。

分析：这条经典旅游线路约主要旅游景点与行程特色，以及适合旅游的人群。

2. 案例分析

[案例 1] 某旅游团在日本旅游，游客在欣赏樱花时兴致很高，其中两人要求与当地导游一起合影，但被导游婉言拒绝了。这是为什么？

[案例 2] 某游客去日本一位朋友家做客，吃饭时主人给客人盛饭。该游客肚子比较饿，但看见主人没有给自己碗里盛满饭，心里稍微有点不高兴。请问是主人太小气而不让客人吃饱吗？

3. 练一练

（1）列举四个日本主要的旅游城市。

（2）简述日本茶道和中国茶道的异同点。

第二节　韩国

一、国家概况

（一）地理环境

大韩民国（韩国）位于东亚朝鲜半岛的南半部，西部与中国隔海相望，东部与日本隔海相望，北接朝鲜，南面是中国台湾。韩国由于东、南、西三面环海，因此属温带季风气候。韩国面积为 100 329 平方千米，约 5 200 万人口。首都和最大的城市是首尔，人口超过 1 000 万。行政首都是世宗市。

Republic of Korea (South Korea) is a country in East Asia, located on the southern portion of the Korean Peninsula. South Korea and China face each other across the sea to the west, Japan to the east, DPRK to the north and Taiwan to the south. As east, south and west surrounded on three sides by the sea, South Korea has a temperate monsoon climate. Its territory covers a total area of 100,329 square kilometers and has a population of almost 52 million. The capital and largest city is Seoul, with a population of more than 10 million. Sejong City is the administrative capital.

（二）人文概况

1. 历史

根据神话记载，神王檀君在公元前 2333 年建立了高丽王国。韩国历史上经历了高句丽、百济和新罗三国鼎立的时代。韩国在历史上多次被较大的邻国入侵。尽管国内意见不一致，韩国还是击退了众多外国侵略者，部分是由于在朝鲜王朝（1392—1897 年）期间，其政治模式使其当时在以中国为中心的区域中处于受保护的地位。19 世纪末，中国势力的影响减弱，韩国在日本和西方势力的胁迫下逐渐开放。1910 年，日本吞并韩国并开始了在韩国长达 35 年的殖民统治。日本一直努力取代韩国语言及韩国文化，众多韩国人，尤其是年龄较大的韩国人，至今仍对日本吞并韩国有深深的敌意和怨恨。

According to the mythology, Korea Kingdom was founded by the god-king Tangun in 2333 BC. An important historical period is the so-called Three Kingdoms including Goguryeo, Baekje and Silla. Korea has suffered many invasions by its larger neighbors in its recorded history. The country repelled numerous foreign invasions despite domestic strife, in part due to its political model of protected status in the Sino-centric region during the Kingdom of Joseon (1392–1897). With the declining Chinese power at the end of the 19th century, Korea was coerced to open by the Japanese and Western encroachment. In 1910, Japan annexed Korea and began a 35-year period of colonial rule over there. As a result of Japan's efforts to supplant the Korean language and its culture, memories of Japanese annexation still recall fierce animosity and resentment, especially among elderly Koreans.

1945 年日本向盟军投降，标志着第二次世界大战的结束，却进一步加剧了外国势力在朝鲜半岛的纷争。北纬三八分界线标志着苏联和美国分别占领朝鲜半岛北部和南部。1948 年 8 月 15 日，大韩民国成立，李承晚为第一任总统。

Japan's surrender to the Allied Forces in 1945, signaling the end of the Second World War but further intensifying foreign rivalries in the Korean Peninsula. Division at the 38th parallel north latitude marked the respective occupation of the North and South by Soviet Union and the United States. On August 15, 1948, Republic of Korea was established, with Syngman Rhee as the first president.

2. 经济

在过去的几十年，韩国经济高速增长，达到非常高的水平，韩国也因此从朝鲜战争的废墟中崛起。1996 年，韩国加入了经济合作与发展组织（简称经合组织）。韩国由 16 个行政区域组成，属于发达国家，人民生活水平很高。它是亚洲第 4 大经济实体，在世界经济排行榜中位列第 12。韩国的国民经济属于出口导向型，生产集中在电子、汽车、船舶、钢铁、纺织等行业。韩国是联合国会员国，也是经合组织和世界贸易组织成员方、G20 主要国家之一。同时，韩国也是亚太经济合作组织、东亚峰会的创始成员国。

Over the past several decades, Republic of Korea has achieved a remarkably high level of economic growth, witnessing the country's rise from the rubble of the Korean War. In 1996, South Korea joined in the the Organization for Economic Co-operation and Development (OECD). South Korea, consisting of sixteen administrative divisions, is a developed country with a very high standard of living. It is Asia's fourth largest economy and the world's twelfth (nominal) largest economy. The economy is export-oriented, with industries focusing on electronics, automobiles, ships, steel and textile, etc. South Korea is a member of the United Nations, WTO, OECD and G20. It is also a founding member of Asia-Pacific Economic Cooperation (APEC) and East Asia Summit.

3. 社会文化

韩国人使用单一语言朝鲜语，但英语也可在旅游区及商业区通用。宗教为佛教、基督教新教、天主教。

The Koreans speak Korean only, but English is also widely used in tourist and commercial areas. Its religions are Buddhism, Protestantism and Catholicism.

韩国人是单一民族，只讲一种语言。他们有一定的独特性，使其区分于其他亚洲人，包括中国人和日本人，并且自身带有很强的文化特性。事实上，韩国人使用同一种语言讲话和书写，是他们具有强烈的民族认同感的一个关键因素。现代韩国有几种不同的方言，包括标准的首尔方言和中部地区方言，但它们很接近，不同地区的人相互很容易理解。

The Koreans are one ethnic family speaking one language. They share certain distinct physical characteristics which differentiate them from other Asian people including the Chinese and the Japanese, and have a strong cultural identity by themselves. The fact that all Koreans speak and write in the same language has been a crucial factor in their strong national identity. Modern South Korea has several different dialects including the standard one used in Seoul and central areas, but they are similar enough that speakers/listeners do not have trouble understanding each other.

家庭是韩国人生活中最重要的一部分。在儒家传统中，父亲是一家之主，他的任务是提供食物、衣服和住所，并批准家庭成员的婚姻。长子在家庭中应承担的职责有一定的排序：首先是对父母，然后是对他的兄弟，再次是对他的儿子，接着是对他的妻子，最后是对他的女儿。家庭福利比个人的需要更重要。家族中的成员相互联系在一起，是因为一个家庭成员的行动反映了其他家庭成员的情况。在许多情况下，家庭登记可以通过男性祖先追溯超过 500 年的家族历史。儒家理论描述了个体在韩国社会的地位。它是一套行为和道德系统，强调人们彼此之间的关系。基本的原则是基于五种不同的关系：君臣、夫妇、父子、长幼、朋友。儒家思想强调责任、忠诚、荣誉、孝顺、尊老、真诚。祖先是基于男性家族的。大人会教育孩子们，他们永远无法偿还父母的养育之恩，因此祭祖非常普遍。韩国人祭拜前三代祖先（即父母、祖父母和曾祖父母），一年举行数次，中秋节和新年尤为重要。在中秋节那天，人们烹饪食品来祭拜他们的祖先。

The family is the most important part of Korean life. In Confucian tradition, the father is the head of the family. His responsibility is to provide food, clothing and shelter, and to approve the marriages of family members. The eldest son has special duties: first to his parents, then to all his younger siblings, next to his sons and his wife, and finally to his daughters. Family welfare is much more important than the needs of the individual. Members of the family are tied to each other because the actions of one family member reflect on the rest of the family. In many cases, the family register can trace a family's history through male ancestors for over 500 years. Confucianism describes the position of the individual in Korean society. It is a system of behaviour and ethics that stress the obligations of people towards one another based upon their relationship. The basic tenets are based upon five different relationships: ruler and subject, husband and wife, parents and children, brothers and sisters and between friends. Confucianism stresses duty, loyalty, honor, filial piety, respect for the aged and seniority, and sincerity. Ancestors are based on the male family line. Children are raised to believe they can never repay their indebtedness to their parents, hence the popularity of ancestor worship. They hold ancestral ceremonies for the previous three generations (parents, grandparents and great grandparents) several times a year, particularly on Chuseok and New Year's Day. On Chuseok, people cook and set out food to celebrate their ancestors.

二、民俗风情

（一）礼仪禁忌

在会议中，相互间问候遵循严格的规则。许多韩国人先鞠躬，再和外籍人士握手，这样结合了两种文化风格。地位较低的人通常向地位较高的人鞠躬，但应由最年长的人提出握手。首先鞠躬的人会说“man-na-seo ban-gap-sum-mi-da”，意思是“见到你很高兴”。在实际见面前，双方的信息会被提前介绍。在社交聚会中，应等待别人介绍自己。当离开一个社交聚会时，应向每个人单独说再见。

During a meeting, greetings follow strict rules of protocol. Many South Koreans shake hands with foreigners after the bow, thereby blending both cultural styles. The person of lower status bows to the person of higher status, yet it is the most senior person who initiates the handshake. The person who initiates the bow says, “man-na-seo ban-gap-sum-mi-da”, which means “pleased to meet you”. Information about the other person will be given to the person he or she will be introduced to in advance of their encounter. You need to wait to be introduced at a social gathering. When you leave a social gathering, say goodbye and bow to each person individually.

在赠送礼物的礼节方面，礼品很大程度上表现了双方的关系。如果你知道对方无法承受相应的回报，还是不要送昂贵的礼物。如果应邀到韩国的家庭做客，一般可以带水果或质量上乘的巧克力或鲜花。在韩国，数字 4 是不吉利的，所以礼物数量不应是 4 的倍数。数字 7 被认为是幸运数字。礼物应精心包装。礼物应包裹在红色或黄色的纸中，因为这两种颜色是皇家的颜色，象征着幸福。不要用绿色、白色或黑色的纸包裹礼物。不要用红色墨水在卡片上签字。应使用双手赠送礼物。收到礼物时，别马上打开。

As for gift giving etiquette, gifts express a great deal about a relationship. It is inconsiderate to give someone an expensive gift if you know that they cannot afford to reciprocate accordingly. Bring fruit or good quality chocolates or flowers if you are invited to a Korean’s house. The number 4 is considered unlucky in South Korea, so gifts should not be given in multiples of 4, but the number 7 is considered lucky. Gifts should be wrapped nicely. Wrap gifts in red or yellow paper, since they are royal colors and they denote happiness. Do not wrap gifts in green, white and black paper. Do not sign a card in red ink. Use both hands when offering a gift. Gifts should not be opened at the moment you receive.

如果你被邀请到韩国人家里用餐，通常客人会在一个常规的地点会合，然后一起出发前往。一般客人可以晚到 30 分钟。客人在进屋前须脱鞋。主人会在门口单独迎接每一位客人，并为客人奉上饮料。主人通常会亲自送客人到门口或车上，因为他们认为在屋内和客人告别是对客人的不尊重。在被邀请吃饭后的第二天，应回送一张感谢的卡片。

If you are invited to a South Korean’s house for dining, it is common for guests to meet at a common spot and then go together. You may arrive up to 30 minutes late without offending your host. Remove your shoes before entering the house. The host greets each guest individually and pours drinks for the guests in their presence. The hosts usually accompany guests to the gate or to their car because they believe that it is insulting to wish the guests farewell indoors. Send a thank-you note the following day after being invited to dinner.

餐桌礼仪是很重要的。客人应该等着主人安排入座。韩国有比较严格的吃饭礼仪。年龄最长的应该第一个分到食物。年龄最大或级别最高的人应该第一个进食。在餐桌上，不要用筷子指东西，更不要用筷子戳食物。当你吃了几口饭，准备喝东西或者停下来说话时，应把筷子放在筷架上，但不能交叉放置。不要用手拿食物。吃水果时，应使用牙签。骨头和外壳应放在桌上或额外的盘子里。客人应品尝每一道菜，对于不知道的菜，可以向主人请教。客人应吃完盘里的食物。当客人已经吃完时，可以把筷子放在筷子架上或桌子上。不要把筷子和碗平行放在一起。

Table manners are very important. You should wait to be told where to sit. There is often a strict protocol to be followed. The eldest are served first. The most senior or highest-ranking person is the one who starts the eating process. Never point with your chopsticks. Do not pierce the food with chopsticks. Chopsticks should be returned to the chopstick rest after every few bites and when you drink or stop to speak. Do not cross your chopsticks while putting them on the chopstick rest. Do not pick up food with your hands. Fruits should be speared with a toothpick. Bones and shells should be put on the table or an extra plate. Try a little bit of every dish. It is acceptable to ask the host of an unknown dish. Finish everything on your plate. Indicate you are finished eating by placing your chopsticks on the chopstick rest or on the table. Never place them parallel to your rice bowl.

（二）节庆风情

1. 辣椒节（The Pepper Festival）

韩国人对泡菜的热爱直接决定了他们对红辣椒，特别是干红辣椒和辣椒面的热爱，也决定了他们对辣椒质量的高标准、严要求。虽然早已告别了缺衣少食的年代，但韩国人在年末储藏大白菜和制作泡菜的习俗保留了下来。泡菜的味道首先取决于大白菜，然后就是干辣椒的优劣。6 月 16 日，在首尔市中心，人们用各种颜色的辣椒拼出硕大的辣椒造型，迎接即将到来的辣椒节。

Koreans love of kimchi determines their love of red pepper and chilly powder as well as their high standards on the quality of hot pepper. Although the age with lack of food and clothing is long gone, the Koreans preserve the tradition of storage of cabbages and making kimchi during winter. The taste of kimchi depends primarily on the cabbage, then the quality of dried pepper. On June 16, in the downtown of Seoul, people use peppers of a variety of colors to piece together huge pepper modelings to mark the upcoming Pepper Festival.

2. 开天节（Gaecheonjeol）

每年的 10 月 3 日是韩国的公假日——开天节，亦称“建国日”。开天节是纪念传说中的韩民族始祖檀君于公元前 2333 年建立古朝鲜的节日，原本定在农历十月初三，但于 1949 年改成公历的 10 月 3 日。在开天节这一天，政府和民间宗教团体都会举行各种隆重的庆典，首尔的祭奠主要是在社稷坛举行。

October 3 is South Korea's public holiday—Gaecheonjeol, also known as "National Foundation Day". Gaecheonjeol is to commemorate the legendary ancestor of the Korean nationality Dan Gun who founded Gojoseon in the year 2333 BC. Originally set on the third day of the tenth lunar month, it was changed to October 3 in the Gregorian Calendar in 1949. On that day, both the government and the civil religious groups will hold grand celebration, and in Seoul the ceremony is held on Sajikdan.

三、主要旅游城市及景点

（一）首尔（Seoul）

首尔的历史超过 2 000 年，在公元前 18 年由三国时代之一的百济王国建立。当时的百济王国建都于现在的首尔市东南。在朝鲜王朝与大韩帝国时期，首尔一直作为韩国的首都。首尔都市圈有 5 处联合国教科文组织世界遗产：昌德宫、水原华城、宗庙神殿、朝鲜王朝的皇家陵墓和南汉山城。

Seoul's history stretches back over 2,000 years, when it was founded in 18 BC by Baekje, one of the Three Kingdoms of Korea, and established its capital in what is now southeastern Seoul. It continued as the capital of Korea under the Joseon Dynasty and the Korean Empire. The Seoul Metropolitan Area contains five UNESCO World Heritage Sites: Changdeok Palace, Hwaseong Fortress, Jongmyo Shrine, the Royal Tombs of the Joseon Dynasty and Namhansanseong.

如今，首尔被认为是全球领先的城市，位居 2019 年全球城市指数排名前 10 位。它是世界十强之一的金融和商业中心，有多家跨国集团公司，如三星、LG 和现代。

Today, Seoul is considered to be a leading global city, ranking among the top ten global cities in the 2019 Global Cities Index. It is one of the world's top ten financial and commercial centers, home to major multinational conglomerates such as Samsung, LG and Hyundai.

◆ 景福宫（Gyeongbokgung）

景福宫是首尔规模最大、最古老的宫殿之一，是韩国封建社会后期的政治中心。1592 年“壬辰倭乱”时，宫苑的大部分建筑物被破坏，只有 10 处宫殿保持完整。直到高宗同治七年（1868 年）才在高宗的父亲兴宣大院君的主持下重建。景福宫的正殿勤政殿是韩国古代最大的木结构建筑物，是举行正式仪式以及接受百官朝贺的大殿。

The Gyeongbokgung is one of the largest and most ancient palaces in Seoul, and served as the political center of the late feudal society. During the Japanese Invasion of 1592, most structures in the palace were destroyed with only 10 houses remaining intact. Until 1868, the palace underwent reconstruction under the leadership of Prince Regent Heungseon Daewongun. Geunjeongjeon, the main hall in Gyeongbokgung, is the largest wooden building in ancient time, designed for holding official ceremonies and receiving congratulations from the court officials.

◆ 崇礼门（Sungnyemun）

崇礼门位于韩国首都首尔市中区，一般叫作南大门。南大门在诸多城门中规模最大，它邻近平民化的南大门市场，是首尔乃至韩国的一个主要地标，曾经是首尔留存历史最悠久的木制建筑。不幸的是，2008 年 2 月，崇礼门木造二重楼阁遭到纵火，仅存石基，木结构城楼被焚毁，2013 年 5 月，崇礼门历时五年复建正式竣工。

The Sungnyemun is located in the central district of Seoul, generally called the South Gate. It is the largest one among the gates of Seoul, adjacent to the commoners' Namdaemun market. It is one of the main landmarks and also the oldest original wooden structure retained in Seoul. Unfortunately, in February 2008, Sungnyemun's wooden two storied pavilion was set on fire, only stone base left, the wooden structure were burned. In May 2013, Sungnyemun took five years to complete the reconstruction.

（二）釜山（Busan）

釜山位于韩国首尔东南端 450 千米，是韩国的第二大城市和第一大港口城市，泛太平洋物流中心。釜山的设施和吞吐能力位居世界前列。釜山东南濒临朝鲜海峡，与日本对马岛相望，西临洛东江，西北山地耸峙，南有群岛屏障。釜山的温泉星罗棋布，群山环抱，是一座风景秀丽的海滨城市，已经发展为多种文化共存的国际性现代都市。釜山电影节从 1996 年创办至今，已成为汇聚亚洲乃至全球电影商和明星、媒体的电影盛会。

Busan, located 450 kilometers southeast to Seoul, is South Korea's second largest city and the largest port city, and also the logistics center of the Pan-Pacific Ocean. Its facilities and capacity rank in the forefront of the world. It is adjacent to the southeastern coast of Korea Strait and faces the Japan Tsushima Island. The Nakdong River lies on its west side. Northwest stands the mountains and south provides island barriers. The city is dotted with hot springs and surrounded by mountains. It is also a beautiful seaside city and has developed into an international and modern metropolis with cultural pluralism. The Busan International Film Festival was created in 1996 and has become a popular film festival venue for Asian and even global film industry as well as for media and stars.

◆ 龙头山公园（Yongdusan Park）

釜山塔所在的龙头山公园内约有 700 多种生长繁茂的植物，是深受釜山市民喜爱的休憩场所。龙头山公园位于龙头山上，面积约 6.9 平方千米。釜山塔高 120 米，可一览釜山市内及釜山港口的全景。此外，公园内还竖立着朝鲜时代名将李舜臣将军的铜像和 4 · 19 纪念碑。

There are more than 700 species of plants in the Yongdusan Park, where many local citizens prefer to enjoy themselves. The park is located in the Yongdusan Mountain, covering an area of about 6.9 square kilometers. Busan Tower is 120-meter-high with a bird's-eye view of the downtown and port. In addition, the park also erects General Yi Sunshin's statue and the commemorative monument for the April 19th anti-government student protests.

（三）庆州（Gyeongju）

历史上，庆州曾是韩国的一个商业中心，1995 年与附近的庆州县合并，形成乡镇一体化，与韩国其他 53 个中小型城市类似，人口约 30 万。除了丰富的历史遗产，今天的庆州受到了塑造现代韩国文化的经济、人口和社会趋势的影响。旅游业是庆州主要的经济来源，但其工业生产水平已经发展到接近主要工业中心蔚山和浦项的水平。庆州有很多文化遗产，曾是新罗王朝的首都，1979 年被联合国教科文组织指定为世界十大历史遗迹地，它还有“无围墙博物馆”之称。

As a commercial center of Korea in history, Gyeongju was merged with the nearby rural Gyeongju County in 1995 and is now an urban-rural complex. It is similar to 53 other small-and-medium-sized cities in South Korea with a population around 300,000. In addition to its rich historical heritage, Gyeongju today is affected by the economic, demographic and social trends that are shaping modern South Korean culture. Tourism remains the major economic resources, but its industrial production has developed up to the major industrial centers such as Ulsan and Pohang. Rich in cultural heritage and as the capital of the Silla Dynasty, Gyeongju was inscribed in 1979 by the UNESCO one of the ten World Heritage Sites, and it is also nicknamed as the “Museum without Walls”.

◆ 佛国寺（Bulguksa Temple）

佛国寺坐落在庆州东南 13 千米的吐含山山腰处，被称为韩国五岳之东岳，海拔 745 米。释迦塔、多宝塔等佛塔体现了新罗时期登峰造极的艺术。寺内诸多的国宝与文化遗产令游客目不转睛，乃至不觉时间之流逝。

Bulguksa Temple is located on the slopes of Tohamsan, 13 kilometers southeast of the city of Gyeongju, which is known as the east one of the five Korean mountains with elevation of 745 meters. Some Buhhdist towers and statues reveal the peak of the cultural development of the Silla period. Many national treasures and the cultural heritage inside enable the visitors to feel that time flies quickly.

（四）济州岛（Jeju Island）

济州岛，也被称为“神之岛”，是深受亚洲人喜爱的度假胜地。古代时建有名为“耽罗国”的独立国家，因此岛上保留着独特的风俗习惯。济州岛上有很多火山岩，经常下雨，气候温和，有风多、石头多和女人多的特点，这使其非常类似于美国的夏威夷群岛。济州岛为游客提供了多种多样的活动：徒步爬汉拿山、在海边看日出日落、看瀑布、骑马，或者只是躺在海边的沙滩上。济州岛也是很多韩国电视剧的拍摄基地，如《大长今》等。

Jeju Island, also known as the “Island of the Gods”, is a popular vacationland for Asians. Once built an independent kingdom called the Tamna in ancient time, it has preserved distinguished customs. The island’s mixture of volcanic rocks, frequent rains, temperate climate and its featured windy weather, numerous stones and many women, make it very similar to the Hawaiian Islands in the United States. The island offers visitors a wide range of activities: hiking on Hallasan, catching sunrises and sunsets on the beach, viewing majestic waterfalls, riding horses, or just lying comfortably on the sandy beaches. It is also a popular scene to shoot Korean TV series such as *Dae Jang Geum*.

◆ 城山日出峰（Seongsan Ilchulbong）

城山日出峰凝灰岩火山锥高 182 米，是 5 000 年前海底火山爆发而形成的，城山日出峰是一块高耸的巨岩，其顶部有巨大的火山口。99 块尖石围绕在火山口周围，如同一顶巨大的皇冠。2007 年，城山日出峰被列入联合国教科文组织世界自然遗产名录。

The Seongsan Ilchulbong tuff cone is 182 meters high, was formed 5,000 years ago from the eruption of an undersea volcano. Seongsan Ilchulbong is now a towering rock with a huge volcano mouth on its top. 99 sharp stones around the volcano mouth look like a huge crown. In 2007, Seongsan Ilchulbong was inscribed on UNESCO's World Natural Heritage Site.

◆ 汉拿山国家公园（Hallasan National Park）

汉拿山高度为 1 950 米，是韩国第一高峰。该山峰为海底延伸，坡度缓和。济州岛亦是汉拿山火山喷发后形成的。汉拿山上生长着亚热带、寒带的 1 800 余种植物与野生昆虫。前来此地的游客可以欣赏春天的杜鹃花、夏天的高山植物、秋天的红叶与冬天的雪景。登山的最佳季节是气候适宜的 5 月和 10 月。

Hallasan with a height of 1,950 meters is the highest peak in South Korea. The mountain extends from submarine mountain range with relatively flat slope. Jeju Island was also formed in the period of Hallasan volcanic eruption. There are more than 1,800 subtropical and frigid species of plants and wild insects. Visitors may come here to enjoy the spring rhododendrons, summer alpine plant, autumn maple leaves and winter snow. The best seasons with moderate climate for hiking are May and October.

四、旅游资讯

（一）美食

韩国气候适合发展农业。早在新石器时代，随着水稻种植的普及，谷物开始大范围种植。此后，谷物成为韩国饮食文化的中心，并在三国时代后期形成了由主食、副食构成的韩国固有的饮食结构。主食有米饭、粥、面条、饺子、年糕汤，副食有酱汤、烤肉、酱肉、炒肉、野菜、蔬菜、酱鱼、干鱼、酱菜、炖食、火锅、泡菜等很多种类。除了这些日常饮食之外，韩国饮食还包括多种多样的糕饼、点心、茶、酒等，以及各种发酵食品。比较有名的菜肴有泡菜、冷面、煎饼、烤五花肉、石锅拌饭和参鸡汤等。

South Korea's climate is suitable for the development of agriculture. As early as the New Stone Age, grain planting began with the popularity of the rice planting. Thereafter, the grains became the center of Korean food culture, and in the period of the Three Kingdoms the dietary system was formed with staple food and non-staple food as Korean inherent home-cooked meals. Staple food include rice, porridge, noodles, dumplings and rice cake soup, while non-staple food include miso soup, barbecue, braised pork with soy sauce, sauted meat, wild vegetables, vegetables, dried fish, pickles, boiled food, stew pot, kimchi, etc. In addition to the daily diet, the Korean diet also includes a wide variety of pastry, snacks, tea, wine, and all kinds of fermented foods. Some famous dishes are kimchi, cold noodles, pancakes, streaky bacon, bibimbap and Samgyetang.

（二）购物及退税

高丽参：在韩国，高丽参被公认为是能使元气旺盛的神秘名药，其保健效果居世界之冠。人参分水参、干参、红参三种，其价格相差悬殊。除了可直接食用根以外，为方便顾客，商家还为顾客提供参精、粉制品等多种产品。

Ginseng: In South Korea, ginseng is widely recognized as a precious drug widely believed to make the mysterious strength for humans and to have the top medicinal effects in the world. It can be classified as water ginseng, dried ginseng and red ginseng, and their prices vary greatly. Apart from the direct use of root, ginseng essence or powder products are also available for the convenience of customers.

韩式器皿：韩式器皿有青瓷、白瓷、粉青砂器等，式样、颜色、质地多种多样。除家庭日用品外，可用于装饰的艺术器皿也有很多。一般家用的器皿种类繁多，漆器、木器、玻璃器皿等均价廉物美。

The Korean-style household utensils: Korean-style household utensils include blue, white and pink green porcelains with different styles, colors and texture. In addition to the household daily necessities, there are many artistic vessels available as well. There are various vessels for family use. Products like lacquer, woodwork and glassware are all of high quality and low price.

济州土产蜂蜜：济州土产蜂蜜的优良品质是其他地方无法比拟的。蜜柑蜜和油菜蜜是从济州产的蜜柑和油菜的花中提取出来的，具有独特的芳香和味道。以此精制的蜂王浆对养生、肠胃疾病相当有效，虽然价格较高，但仍有许多人购买。近来，在土产蜂蜜中加入仙人掌而制成的产品广受游客的喜爱。

The Jeju native honey: the quality of the Jeju native honey is really unique which others cannot compare with. Mandarin orange honey and rape honey are extracted from the Jeju mandarin and rape flowers with unique aroma and taste. The refined royal jelly is helpful to health and gastrointestinal disease. Many people are interested in this product despite its high price. Recently, this product laced with cactus becomes very popular among visitors.

在相关税务机关指定的商店中，购物 30 000 韩元以上，3 个月内携带所购商品出境的外国游客可以享有 10% 的退税。顾客需在标有“全球退税”或“韩国退税”标志的指定商店中购物后，取得退税发票。出境时，游客向海关出示所购商品，发票经确认后加盖“物品出境”图章。在出境处的退税窗口，现场领取所返还的税金，或者在未设退税窗口的机场、港口或退税窗口关闭时，准确填写所规定样式的表格后，投入指定的邮筒。这样 1 ～ 2 个月内，就可通过信用卡转账或现金邮寄的形式收到应退税款。

10% of VAT is applied in South Korea. VAT is returned to foreign customers when the goods are taken outside South Korea in three months after purchasing goods at “Global Blue Tax Free” or “Tax Free KOREA” participating stores and receiving a tax refund slip. Tax refund slip is only available for purchasing over KRW 30,000. Receive a customs “All Goods Exported” stamp by showing passport and the purchased goods at the Customs Desk before departure. At the tax refund office of the Customs Desk, tourists may have their tax refund cashed. They also need to fill in an application form as requested before putting it in the designated mail box at the airport or harbor without a tax refund office, or when the tax refund office is closed. Then they will receive the tax refund through credit card fund transfer or cash in mail within one or two months.

（三）时差

韩国首都首尔的时间比北京时间早1个小时。

Seoul time is an hour earlier than Beijing time.

思考练习

1. 经典旅游线路分析

韩国炫动5日游

第1天：上海——首尔

游客在上海浦东国际机场指定时间、地点集合，在专业领队的带领下搭乘国际航班飞往韩国仁川国际机场。导游接机后，前往市区具有韩国特色的汗蒸房（约2个小时），晚餐后入住酒店休息。

第2天：金浦——济州

早餐后乘车前往京畿道的滑雪场（滑雪道具和衣服自费），后自费前往龙仁爱宝乐园或加勒比水上乐园（门票自费），然后前往金浦机场搭乘飞机到济州岛。

第3天：济州岛

早餐后前往游览仿佛神话传说中的一条巨龙，屹立于波涛澎湃的海岸，由汉拿山火山口喷出的熔岩在海上凝结而成，犹如龙头的龙头岩（约30分钟）；攀登东海岸被列为联合国教科文组织世界自然遗产名录的城山日出峰（约1小时）；欣赏韩剧《洛城生死恋》的拍摄地涉地岬（约20分钟），随后前往城邑民俗村（约60分钟）。午餐后前往济州岛最大的瀑布——天地渊瀑布（约30分钟），潭水中栖息着被指定为济州天然纪念物的巨鳗。之后赴济州岛的“神奇之路”（约30分钟），逛乐天免税店（约1个小时），观看搞笑功夫秀，晚餐后入住酒店。

第4天：济州岛——首尔

早餐后搭乘韩国国内航班前往首尔，到达首尔后前往建于1395年、有600余年历史的朝鲜时代第一正宫——景福宫，参观文武大臣朝见典礼之勤政殿、摆设国宴之庆会楼、国王之寝室康宁殿、王后之寝室交泰殿，去民俗博物馆了解韩国的民俗发展史，远看现在的总统府——青瓦台外景等。然后去做美容体验，再去化妆品免税店。随后在护肝宝店购买精美的礼品，去人参公卖局购买人参。最后到韩国唯一豪华赌场——华克山庄，游客可自由活动或选择欣赏精彩的韩国民族歌舞表演及类似美国拉斯维加斯的歌舞表演——华克秀（自费）。结束后入住酒店休息。

第 5 天：首尔——上海

早餐后可以选择参观统一展望台 + 临津阁 + 自由之桥 + 第三隧道（自费），之后逛韩国土特产商店（约 1 小时），然后赴仁川国际机场搭乘国际航班飞往上海。游客抵达上海浦东国际机场，结束愉快的旅程。

分析：这条经典旅游线路的主要旅游景点与行程特色，以及适合旅游的人群。

2. 案例分析

[案例 1] 某旅游团在韩国旅游，游客在结束行程后，觉得当地女导游的服务很好，为了表示感谢，团长拿出一瓶中国的茅台酒要送给该导游，但是该导游并未表现出很高兴的样子。领队见状，立即走上前去和该导游说了一句话。该导游听后才对茅台酒欣然接受。请问领队说了一句什么话？

[案例 2] 某游客在首尔一家税务机关指定的商店消费了 40 万韩元后，即将离开，但导游提醒了该游客。该游客后来非常感激导游的提醒。请问导游提醒了那位游客什么？

3. 练一练

（1）韩国的新年风俗有哪些和中国的风俗相似？

（2）首尔有哪几个著名的购物点？

第三节　新加坡

一、国家概况

（一）地理环境

新加坡，全称新加坡共和国，坐落在马来半岛南端，赤道以北 137 千米。新加坡是一个岛国，由新加坡岛及附近的 63 个岛屿组成，北隔柔佛海峡与马来西亚相邻，南隔新加坡海峡与印度尼西亚的廖内群岛相望。新加坡高度城市化，但几乎一半的国土覆盖着绿色植被，更多的土地正在通过复垦来开发。新加坡主要的岛屿被称为新加坡岛或蒲罗中（马来语）。有 2 条人造通道连接马来西亚柔佛：北面的柔佛—新加坡通道和西面的大士二环线。裕廊岛、德光岛、乌敏岛和圣淘沙是新加坡最大的四座小岛。新加坡的最高点是武吉知马，海拔 163.63 米。

Singapore, officially the Republic of Singapore, is located in the southern tip of the Malay Peninsula, 137 kilometers to the north of the equator. An island country made up of one mainland and 63 islands nearby, it is separated from Malaysia by the Straits of Johor to its north and from Indonesia's Riau Islands by Singapore Strait to its south. Singapore is highly urbanized but almost half of the country is covered by greenery. More lands are created for development through land reclamation. Singapore's main island is widely known as Singapore Island or Pulau Ujong (Malay). There are two man-made connections to Johor, Malaysia: the Johor-Singapore Causeway in the north and the Tuas Second Link in the west. Jurong Island, Tekong Island, Ubin Island and Sentosa are the largest four Singapore's outlying islands. The highest natural point is Bukit Timah at an altitude of 163.63 metres.

（二）人文概况

1. 历史

新加坡最早有人定居是在 2 世纪。当时的苏门答腊室利佛逝王国将其命名为淡马锡（海镇）。从 16 世纪到 19 世纪初，它是柔佛王国的一部分。1613 年，葡萄牙入侵者烧毁了该居住区和岛屿，在随后的两个世纪中，新加坡陷入黑暗时期。1819 年，托马斯·斯坦福德·莱佛士来到此地，代表不列颠东印度公司和苏丹侯赛因·沙赫签约，发展新加坡南部作为英国贸易站。

The earliest known settlement on Singapore was in the 2nd century AD. It was an outpost of the Sumatran Sri Vijaya Empire, named Temasek ("sea town"). Between the 16th and early 19th centuries, it was part of the Johor Sultanate. In 1613, Portuguese raiders burnt down the settlement and the island sank into obscurity for the next two centuries. In 1819, Thomas Stamford Raffles arrived and signed a treaty with Sultan Hussein Shah on behalf of the British East India Company to develop the southern part of Singapore as a British trading post.

支持独立的工党领袖戴维·马歇尔赢得了 1955 年新加坡的第一次大选。在 1959 年 5 月的选举中，人民行动党赢得压倒性的胜利。自此，新加坡在英联邦中实现了国家自治，成立了自治政府，李光耀出任第一任总理。总督威廉·阿尔蒙德·科德林顿担任第一任国家元首，1965 年由尤索夫·宾·伊萨克接任成为新加坡首任总统。1965 年 8 月 9 日，新加坡脱离马来西亚，宣布独立。

Singapore's first general election in 1955 was won by the pro-independence David Marshall, leader of the Labour Front. In elections in May 1959, the People's Action Party won a landslide victory. Singapore had become an internally self-governing state within the Commonwealth, with Lee Kuan Yew as the first prime minister. Governor Sir William Allmond Codrington Goode served as the first head of state, and was succeeded by Yusof Bin Ishak who became the first president of Singapore in 1965. Singapore seceded from Malaysia and declared independence on August 9, 1965.

2. 经济

新加坡是一个经济高度发达的、国有经济占主导的国家，国家通过淡马锡控股等主权财富基金占有整个新加坡国内生产总值 60% 以上的份额。新加坡的商业环境较为开放，相对廉洁和透明，物价稳定，相比其他发达国家税率较低，位居世界人均国内生产总值最高的国家之列。新加坡的创新机制和稳定模式，综合了计划经济与自由市场的优点，由此成为独特的“新加坡模式”。出口，特别是在电子、化学、服务行业的出口，是新加坡经济收入的主要来源。

Singapore has a highly-developed state capitalist mixed economy; the state owns stakes in firms that comprise over 60% of the GDP through entities such as the sovereign wealth fund Temasek. It has an open business environment, relatively corruption-free and transparent, stable prices, low tax rates compared to other developed economies, and one of the highest per-capita GDP in the world. Its innovative yet steadfast form of economy that combines economic planning with free-market has given it the nickname "the Singapore Model". Exports, particularly in electronics, chemicals and services provide the main source of revenue for the economy.

3. 社会文化

新加坡人口约 564 万，包括华人、马来人、印度人和其他种族，其中华人占 74.2%。官方语言为英语、汉语、马来语和泰米尔语。马来语为国语，英语为行政用语。新加坡是一个多元宗教国家，主要宗教有佛教、伊斯兰教、基督教、印度教。

With a population of about 5.64 million, Singapore has Chinese, Malay, Indian and other nationalities, of which ethnic Chinese accounts for 74.2%. The official languages are English, Chinese, Malay and Tamil. The national language is Malay and administrative language is English. Singapore is a multi-religious country with major religions including Buddhism, Islam, Christianity and Hindu.

新加坡是一个多元化的年轻国家，多种语言、文化和宗教并存。由于语言和文化的差异很大，公众行为呈现多元化。

Singapore is a very diverse and young country. It has many languages, cultures and religions for a country of its size. Due to the many different languages and cultures in the country, there is no single set of culturally acceptable behaviours.

1963 年，新加坡脱离英联邦独立，大多数的新加坡公民是来自中国、马来西亚和印度的未受过教育的劳工。他们中的许多人是短期打工者，只是希望赚一些钱，并不打算永久居住在新加坡。此外，新加坡还有相当数量的中产阶级以及土生土长的当地居民。除了当地人会发誓效忠新加坡，大多数劳工只忠诚于他们各自的国家，如中国、马来西亚和印度。获得独立后，新加坡开始打造独立的身份和文化。虽然英语是新加坡的第一语言，但根据政府 2010 年的人口调查，20% 的新加坡人不会讲英语。

When Singapore became independent from the United Kingdom in 1963, most of the newly minted Singaporean citizens were uneducated laborers from China, Malaysia and India. Many of them were transient laborers who were seeking to make some money in Singapore and they had no intentions of staying for good. A sizable number of middle-class and local-born people, known as the Peranakans also existed. With the exception of the Peranakans who pledged their loyalties to Singapore, most of the laborers' loyalties lie with their respective homelands of China, Malaysia and India. After independence, the process of crafting a Singaporean identity and culture began. Even though English is the first language of the nation, according to the government's 2010 census, 20% of Singaporeans, or one in five, are illiterate in English.

知识拓展

新加坡是一个罚款的地方

到过新加坡的许多人都知道这样一句话，“Singapore is a fine place”。这是一句双关语，一是指“新加坡是一个美好的地方”，二则指“新加坡是一个罚款的地方”。“fine”有“美好的”和“罚款”两层意思。

新加坡政府的罚款措施颇具特色。有人说新加坡的法治社会实质上是“罚治社会”，新加坡的社会文明是罚出来的。在新加坡，罚款无处不在，而且罚款名目繁多，几乎涉及所有公共领域；罚款程序明确具体，可操作性强；罚款数额较大，足以使受罚者心疼。在新加坡街头，罚款告示牌随处可见。在公园里，竖立着“不准钓鱼”“不准乱丢垃圾”“不准骑自行车”等告示牌；在地铁站外，竖立着“不准坐矮墙”的告示牌；在影剧院内，挂有“不准吸烟”的告示牌。此外，随地吐痰、骑摩托车不戴安全帽、电梯内吸烟、损坏树木等不良行为，均要受到处罚。就连在地铁里吃东西、上厕所后不冲水也要被罚款。如果你留意的话，几步就可能见到一个告示牌，而旁边则标着罚款的“价格”。众多的告示牌时刻提醒着新加坡人应处处小心谨慎。有时，在商店还能看见印满各种罚款标志和罚款金额的T恤衫。

二、民俗风情

（一）礼仪禁忌

在新加坡旅游，游客必须注意如下事项：不要嚼口香糖，这在新加坡是禁止的，否则可能会被逮捕。不能乱扔垃圾，对此法律有严格规定。不能在公共场所吸烟，在封闭的公共场所（包括餐厅）吸烟是违法的，在街道上丢弃烟头或吸烟会立即被罚款。不能参与任何毒品交易，拥有或使用毒品会被判死刑。不讨论宗教和政治，不开上述话题的玩笑。不要触摸他人的头部，因为头部被认为是神圣的。不暴露脚底，别用脚指指点点，因为脚被认为是肮脏的。不在地铁车厢内吃东西，违者将被处以高达200新元的罚款。不用食指指人，因为这是非常粗鲁的。不坐出租车，在新加坡坐出租车是非常昂贵的，新加坡的公共交通系统非常完善。与穆斯林在一起时，不要用左手吃东西或递食物，更不要用左手与穆斯林握手。小费不是必需的，给小费在新加坡并非约定俗成的习惯，政府对此并不提倡。不要在送礼人面前立即打开礼物。忌用白色纸张包裹礼物，因为白色代表丧葬。别向华人赠送钟表、手帕或花，因为它们代表死亡和葬礼。不要立即接受礼物，通常应拒绝2～3次以表明你不贪心。不能赠送酒类或猪皮制品给马来人，因为马来人大多是穆斯林。在离开的时候给予礼物，而并非到达的时候，使用右手或双手给予或接受礼物。不能赠送酒类或皮革制品给印度人。

There are many things a visitor has to pay attention to as follows: Do not chew gums, which is banned in Singapore and may get you arrested. Do not litter in Singapore, while laws are strictly enforced relating to littering. Do not smoke in public. Smoking is illegal in enclosed public places (including restaurants) and dropping a cigarette end in the street or smoking illegally can lead to an immediate fine. Do not get involved in any drugs, because Singapore carries a mandatory death penalty for drug-trafficking and harsh penalties for possession and use within the country. Do not discuss religion or politics or make jokes either. Do not touch someone's head which is considered sacred. Do not show the bottoms of your feet or use your feet to point which are considered dirty. Do not bring in food into MRT (Mass Rapid Transport), offenders will be fined up to SGD 200. Do not point at someone with your index finger, which is considered very rude. Do not take cabs which are very expensive in Singapore, and Singapore transportation system is exceptionally well planned. Do not eat or offer anything with your left hand when with Muslims and do not use your left hand when shaking hands with a Muslim. Do not tip, because tipping is not customary in Singapore and it is even frowned down upon by the government. Do not open a gift immediately in front of the giver. Do not wrap gifts in white, which is a mourning color. Do not, for a Chinese descent, give clocks, handkerchiefs or flowers as they are associated with death and funerals. Do not accept a gift immediately, refuse a gift two to three times before accepting to show that you're not greedy. Do not, for a Malay descent, give alcohol or anything made of pigskin, as Malays are Muslims. Give the gift upon departing not arriving, and use your right hand or both hands to give or receive presents. Do not, for an Indian descent, give alcohol or something made of leather.

（二）节庆风情

1. 屠妖节（Deepavali Festival）

屠妖节期间，新加坡的小印度的大街小巷、大小庙宇都会升起幡带、点亮灯火，欢迎神仙与凡人。届时维达帕提雅卡拉曼兴都庙、维拉巴蒂拉卡拉曼兴都庙、斯里尼瓦沙柏鲁马兴都庙都会举行壮观的灯火展出。实龙岗路也将灯火通明，迎接屠妖节的到来。甘贝尔巷将化身欢乐的市集，张灯结彩的店铺纷纷出售丰富多彩的印度特色物品：精巧的珠宝首饰、传统服饰、手工艺品等。

During the Deepavali Festival, there will be lights and belts all over Little India's temples, streets and lanes in order to welcome gods and mortals. There will be show of lights in Sri Veeramakaliamman Temple, Sri Vadapathira Kaliamman Temple, Sri Srinivasa Perumal Temple. Serangoon Road will also be brightly lit to mark the Deepavali Festival. And Campbell Lane will be the embodiment of the joy of the bazaar, where decorated shops offer varieties of goods with Indian characteristics such as exquisite jewelry, traditional clothing and handicrafts.

2. 卫塞节（Vesak Day）

卫塞节是庆祝释迦牟尼佛祖诞生、成道、涅槃的节日。东南亚及南亚国家如斯里兰卡、泰国、缅甸、新加坡、马来西亚、印度尼西亚、尼泊尔等国的佛教徒，均在这一年一度的重要节日中举行盛大的庆典活动。每年卫塞节的日期根据历法而定，通常是在5月的月圆之日。

It is the day of birth, enlightenment and nirvana of Shakyamuni. Buddhists from South East Asian and South Asian countries such as Sri Lanka, Thailand, Myanmar, Singapore, Malaysia, Indonesia, Nepal and others will celebrate this festival once a year. According to the official calendar, the annual Vesak Day is usually the day of full moon in May.

三、主要旅游城市及景点

（一）牛车水（Chinatown）

新加坡的牛车水是一个具有明显的中国文化特征的华人聚集地，历史上集中居住着华裔人口，坐落于广阔的欧南区。虽然华人是新加坡最大的族群，但现在的牛车水比过去小多了。然而，该地区仍保留着重要的历史文化意义。很多商店和餐馆逐渐取代了以往的香烛店。牛车水现在已是游客最佳购物地之一。

Singapore's Chinatown is an ethnic neighborhood featuring distinctly Chinese cultural elements and a historically concentrated ethnic Chinese population. Chinatown is located within the large district of Outram. As the largest ethnic group in Singapore is Chinese, Chinatown is considerably less of an enclave than it once was. However, the district does retain significant historical and cultural significance. Many shops and restaurants are gradually overtaking the venerable incense-selling professions. It is one of the best places for visitors to go shopping.

（二）小印度（Little India）

小印度是新加坡印度族群的聚集地，犹如印度的缩影。每逢周六和周日傍晚，小印度会格外热闹，新加坡的印度籍劳工都喜欢到这里与朋友吃饭或购物。在屠妖节，小印度被装点成金碧辉煌的神话世界。

The Little India is a popular place for Indians to gather, like the epitome of India. Every Saturday and Sunday evening, the Little India is in hustle and bustle. Indian workers living in Singapore all like to eat here or do shopping with friends. On the Deepavali Festival, Little India is decorated as a mythical world like a wonderland.

（三）鱼尾狮公园（Merlion Park）

鱼尾狮公园里有一座神秘的动物雕塑，鱼身狮头，它是新加坡的吉祥物。它的名字结合了“海”和“狮子”。“鱼身”代表新加坡最初是一个渔村，当时被称为淡马锡，爪哇语意为“海镇”。“狮头”是新加坡原有的名字，意思是“狮城”。

The Merlion Park is a mythical creature with the head of a lion and the body of a fish, used as a mascot of Singapore. Its name combines “mer” meaning the sea and “lion”. The fish body represents Singapore's origin as a fishing village when it was called Temasek, which means “sea town” in Javanese. The lion head represents Singapore's original name — Singapura — meaning “lion city”.

（四）圣淘沙（Sentosa）

“圣淘沙”在马来语里的意思是“和平安宁”。可能因为这个小岛曾经是英军的军事基地的缘故，新加坡政府才在收回此地并决定将其建成度假地时，赋予其这么一个美丽的名字。圣淘沙距离新加坡本岛南部仅 0.5 千米，由一座堤道跨海大桥与本岛连接起来。这个占地面积为 390 公顷的度假小岛名不虚传，几乎每一寸土地都带着休闲的味道。圣淘沙延续了新加坡“花园城市”的路线，放眼望去，一片青翠，郁郁葱葱。阳光、沙滩等自然景观自不必多说，更有精致的人文景观耐人寻味。游客可以在沙滩上赤足行走，沐浴海风；可以到世界昆虫博物馆观赏；可以到高尔夫球乐园里挥杆；可以到梦幻岛里体验。无论是白天还是黑夜，圣淘沙都会时时刻刻传递美丽与快乐，来到这里的每一个人都无一例外地陶醉在岛上的时光里。

Sentosa in Malay means “peace”. Probably because the island was once a British military base, the Singapore government gave it such a name when recovering it and deciding to make it a resort. Sentosa is only half a kilometer away to the south of the island of Singapore, connected by a Causeway Bridge across the sea. The island covered an area of 390 hectares is a renowned island resort. Almost every inch of land is characterized by a sense of leisure. The island further represents Singapore as a “garden city” with verdant trees all over the sight. The sun on the beach and other natural landscape are needless to say, and there are more exquisite natural scenes for tourists to explore. You can walk barefoot on the beach, enjoy the sea breeze, and visit the World Insect Museum; you may also swing your brassie in the golf field and experience the fantasy on the island. Whether it is day or night, Sentosa will emit all its beauty and happiness all the time, and everyone coming here will be carried away with no exception.

四、旅游资讯

（一）美食

新加坡的特色菜是由马来西亚裔、新加坡的华侨，融合中国菜与马来菜所发展出来的家常菜，称为“娘惹”。具有代表性的新加坡食物有海南鸡饭、肉骨茶、炒粿条、酿豆腐、云吞面等。早期的中国移民沿袭了福建和广东的饮食习惯和风味，再加上当地的风格，逐渐形成了新加坡的特色食物。

Singapore’s own specialties are cuisine developed by the Malaysian, Singapore overseas Chinese with mixture of Chinese and Malay food, known as Nyonya. Representatives of the Singaporean food include Hainanese Chicken Rice, Bak Kut Teh, Char Kway Teow, Yong Tau Foo, Wonton Noodle, etc. These foods were brought by early Chinese immigrants, incorporated with Fujian and Guangdong style and flavor with local own style, and gradually formed the local own characteristics of food in Singapore.

新加坡附近水域的海产丰富，品质鲜美，如龙虾、螃蟹、对虾、贻贝、鱿鱼及各种海产品。一些餐厅专卖各种海鲜。一般而言，东海岸一带的海鲜餐厅的价位较市区的许多餐馆低。菜色中最受欢迎的是黑胡椒蟹，是将肥美的螃蟹连肉带壳加上番茄汁及黑胡椒一起拌炒，令人回味无穷。

Singapore enjoys abundant seafood of good quality, such as lobster, crab, prawn, mussel, squid and all kinds of other seafood. Some restaurants only specialize in a wide variety of seafood. Generally speaking, seafood restaurants along the east coast charge less than those of the urban areas. The most popular dish, for example, is the black pepper crab, which is made of plump crab flesh and shell with tomato sauce and black pepper together for frying. Its taste is just unforgettable for visitors.

（二）购物及退税

香水：香水是送人的最佳礼品。尤其是那些限量版的香水，除极具收藏价值外，漂亮的瓶子本身也让人爱不释手。

Perfume: It is the best gift for friends. Especially those of limited editions, in addition to collection value, the perfume's bottles are also perfect to attract customers.

饰品：饰品往往传达出时尚女性对细节和品位的把握，与众不同的审美也许就在那个靓丽的点缀中。

Ornaments: Ornaments often convey lady's grasp of the details and taste for fashion. Maybe the aesthetic value just lies in that piece of beautiful decoration.

鱼尾狮纪念品：鱼尾狮在新加坡是相当有名的。自然，这里会有许多与鱼尾狮相关的饰品。既然不能把鱼尾狮带回去，游客可以买一些鱼尾狮的小饰品，如钥匙扣、项链等。

Merlion souvenirs: Merlion is quite famous in Singapore. Naturally, there are many ornaments associated with the Merlion. As you cannot take back the Merlion, why don't you buy some Merlion souvenirs such as key ring, necklace and so on?

在新加坡购物，游客可获得 5% ～ 7% 的商品及服务税（GST）退税。游客可寻找贴有“退税”标识的商家或者在同一店铺消费满 100 新元以上即可享受退税。对于带往新加坡境外的商品，可在特定商家、樟宜国际机场或特定机场进行退税。退税款项中可能会扣除退税服务的手续费。需要注意的是，退税仅适用于乘飞机离境。

As a tourist in Singapore, you can claim a refund of 5% to 7% for goods and services tax (GST) paid on your purchases made at participating retail shops. You may look for stores with labels "Tourist Refund" or spend a minimum of SGD 100 in the same shop for tax refund. You may have your tax refund cashed for goods to be taken out of Singapore at specified shops, Changi International Airport or specified airports. A handling fee for the refund service may be deducted from the total amount. Mind you that the tax refund is only available for departure by air.

（三）时差

新加坡时间与北京时间一样。

There is no time difference between Singapore and Beijing.

思考练习

1. 经典旅游线路分析

新加坡自由6日游

第1天：宁波——新加坡

游客在16:00点之前自行到达宁波栎社国际机场，办理登机手续后搭乘国际航班直飞新加坡。抵达后自行前往V Hotel酒店休息。

第2天：新加坡自由活动

建议游客上午前往市中心一带的市政厅、高等法院、旧国会大厦看看，还可前往鱼尾狮公园，与新加坡的象征——鱼尾狮来个亲密接触。与鱼尾狮遥遥相对的滨海艺术中心是新加坡最新的地标，宛若两颗大榴莲，独具匠心的设计让人印象深刻。游客可以品尝一下地道的新加坡美食，如海南鸡饭、黑胡椒蟹、叻沙等。华灯初上之时，游客可前往新加坡河畔的克拉码头，这里有超过30家餐厅和酒吧，游客可以在享受美食的同时欣赏河岸风光，十分惬意。

第3天：新加坡自由活动

建议游客前往"市"外桃源——圣淘沙，可从港湾城第二大厦或花柏山搭乘缆车入岛（每天8:30—21:00），也可以在港湾中心巴士转换站搭乘圣淘沙巴士前往（每天7:00—23:00）。岛上的活动丰富精彩，旅游设施一应俱全。游客可搭乘岛上免费巴士，抵达任何景区、游乐场所和沙滩等休闲场地。英比奥山顶景区汇集了多个刺激好玩的景点：惊险刺激的斜坡滑车、万象新加坡、鱼尾狮塔，还有360度旋转的摩天塔、4D魔幻剧院、蝴蝶园与世界昆虫博物馆等，这些都是不错的选择。游客还可前往新加坡海底世界观赏各种罕见的海底精灵，到海豚乐园观看海豚的精彩表演。每晚的音乐激光喷泉都会上演激动人心的节目。更可以去名胜世界购物，或去环球影城体验最新电影科技。

第4天：新加坡自由活动

游客可以自由选择休息或逛街，可以逛逛新加坡的民族文化区——牛车水、小印度、阿拉伯街，体会新加坡的多元文化。新加坡有着"购物天堂"的美誉，游客也可选择去乌节路"血拼"。

第5天：新加坡自由活动

前往新加坡最大的一站式购物、美食、休闲中心"怡丰城"（Vivo City），可品尝新加坡美食海南鸡饭、黑胡椒蟹等。

第 6 天：新加坡——宁波

游客自行前往樟宜国际机场 1 号航站楼（提早 2 小时到达），搭乘国际航班飞回宁波，返回温馨家园。

分析：该条旅游线路的主要旅游景点与行程特色，以及适合旅游的人群。

2. 案例分析

[案例 1] 某旅游团于 2016 年 12 月 6 日出发前往新加坡旅游，该旅游团计划在第二天与当地一家有业务往来的私营企业签署一份合作协议，并举行一个小型仪式。但是该企业负责人却建议客人第二天先去游玩，第三天再来拜访并签署协议。该企业 12 月 7 日并没有其他事情冲突，为何要做如此安排？

[案例 2] 某游客前往新加坡时，忘记从家里带上安眠药，便想在国内机场候机时购买。但领队建议不要购买，请问为什么？

3. 练一练

（1）列举四种能携带进新加坡境内且无须支付关税的物品。

（2）请说出新加坡有哪几个种族。

第四节　马来西亚

一、国家概况

（一）地理环境

马来西亚是君主立宪联邦制国家，分为 13 个州和 3 个联邦直辖区，面积为 330 257 平方千米。全境被南海分成西马来西亚（马来西亚半岛）和东马来西亚（沙巴、沙捞越）两部分。马来西亚陆地与泰国、印度尼西亚和文莱接壤，海洋濒接新加坡、越南和菲律宾。马来西亚首都为吉隆坡，是联邦政府所在地。

Malaysia is a federal constitutional monarchy country. It consists of thirteen states and three federal territories and has a total land of 330,257 square kilometers. It is separated by the South China Sea into two regions: Peninsular Malaysia and Malaysian Borneo. Land borders are shared with Thailand, Indonesia and Brunei, and maritime borders are close to Singapore, Vietnam and the Philippines. The capital city is Kuala Lumpur, the seat of the federal government.

（二）人文概况

1. 历史

15 世纪初，以马六甲为中心的满剌加王国统一了马来半岛的大部分，并发展成当时东南亚的主要国际贸易中心。16 世纪开始先后遭到葡萄牙、荷兰和英国的侵略。1911 年，沦为英国殖民地。沙捞越、沙巴历史上属文莱，1888 年两地沦为英国殖民地。第二次世界大战期间，马来亚、沙捞越、沙巴被日本占领。1957 年 8 月 31 日，联邦主席端姑·阿卜杜勒·拉赫曼宣布马来亚联邦独立。1963 年，马来亚联邦同新加坡、沙巴及沙捞越组成了马来西亚联邦。1965 年，马来西亚国会以 126 票赞成、0 票反对，迫使新加坡退出马来西亚联邦。2018 年 5 月 9 日，反对党阵营希望联盟赢得大选，终结了执政联盟国民阵线长达 60 年的统治。

At the beginning of the fifteenth century, the Malacca Kingdom reigned most of the Malay Peninsula, and developed into the main international trade center in Southeast Asia. In the sixteenth century it was invaded by Portugal, Holland and Britain. In 1911, the British colonized the country. Sarawak and Sabah historically belonged to Brunei, but both of them became a British protectorate in 1888. During the Second World War, Malaya, Sarawak and Sabah were occupied by Japan. On August 31, 1957, chairman of the alliance — Tunku Abdul Rahman declared the independence of Malaya. In 1963, Malaya together with Singapore, Sabah and Sarawak formed the Federation of Malaysia. In 1965, the Congress of Malaysia, with 126 votes to 0, forced Singapore to withdraw from the Federation of Malaysia. On May 9, 2018, the opposition Pakatan Harapan win the general election, ending 60 years of governance of the National Front.

2. 经济

马来西亚拥有相对开放的国家导向与新兴工业化市场经济。通过宏观经济计划指引经济活动，国家虽然在经济方面发挥了重要作用，但其重要性正在逐渐下降。马来西亚拥有亚洲最佳的经济纪录，国内生产总值从 1957 年至 2005 年平均每年增长 6.5%。2018 年，马来西亚国内生产总值为 3 543.5 亿美元，是东盟第四大经济体。但经济不平等存在于不同的族群之间，华人占有马来西亚 70% 的市场资本，即使他们的人口只占全国的 1/3。

Malaysia is a relatively open state-oriented and newly industrialized market economy. The state plays a significant but declining role in guiding economic activity through macroeconomic plans. Malaysia has had one of the best economic records in Asia, with GDP growing an average 6.5 percent annually from 1957 to 2005. In 2018, the GDP was 3,543.5 billion dollars, the 4th largest economy in ASEAN. However, economic inequality exists in different ethnic groups. The Chinese own 70% of Malaysia's market capital, even though their population only takes up one third of the whole country.

紧邻马六甲海峡航线所产生的国际贸易以及制造业是马来西亚经济的关键部门。马来西亚是自然资源和农业资源的出口国，最值钱的出口物资是石油。有一段时间，它是世界上锡、橡胶和棕榈油的最大生产国。虽然马来西亚的经济结构已逐渐远离制造业，但制造业仍对国家经济有很大的影响。马来西亚是世界上最大的棕榈油生产国之一。

International trade, facilitated by the adjacent Strait of Malacca shipping route, and manufacturing are key sectors of the country's economy. Malaysia is an exporter of natural and agricultural resources, the most valuable exported resource being petroleum. At one time, it was the largest producer of tin, rubber and palm oil in the world. Manufacturing has a large influence in the country's economy, although Malaysia's economic structure has been moving away from it. Malaysia remains one of the world's largest producers of palm oil.

3. 社会文化

马来西亚人口约 3 238 万。马来人、华人、印度人是马来西亚的三大种族。马来语为马来西亚的国语，英语为通用语。马来西亚把伊斯兰教定为国教，其他宗教有佛教、印度教、道教。此外，还有居民信奉基督教和锡克教。

Malaysia has a population about 32.38 million. The Malay, Chinese and Indian are three main nationalities here. Malay is the official language and English is also widely used. Islam is the national religion. Other religions include Buddhism, Hindu and Taoism and there are also people believing in Christianity and Sikhism.

马来西亚是个多元族群、多元文化和多种语言的社会。其文化源自当地的土著部落，随后马来人搬到这里。中国文化和印度文化所具有的实质影响力，可追溯到外国贸易开始活跃于这个区域之时。对于马来西亚产生重要影响的文化还包括波斯、阿拉伯与英国文化。由于政府的政治体制，再加上社会契约理论，因此马来西亚的少数族群产生了一定程度的文化同化。

Malaysia has a multi-ethnic, multi-cultural, and multi-lingual society. The original culture of the area stemmed from indigenous tribes, along with the Malays who later moved here. Substantial influence exists from Chinese and Indian culture, dating back to when foreign trade began. Other cultural influences include the Persian, Arabic and British cultures. Due to the structure of the government, coupled with the social contract theory, there has been minimal cultural assimilation of ethnic minorities.

1971 年，政府创立了一套“国家文化政策”。这套政策明确界定了马来西亚的文化，指出马来西亚文化必须建立在马来西亚土著（马来人）的文化基础之上，它可能包括来自其他文化的适当元素，而且强调伊斯兰教必须在马来西亚文化中扮演重要角色。这套政策也提升了马来语的地位。

In 1971, the government created a set of “National Cultural Policy”, defining what Malaysian culture is. It stated that Malaysian culture must be based on the culture of the indigenous people of Malaysia, that it may incorporate suitable elements from other cultures, and that Islam must play a significant part in it. It also promoted the Malay language above others.

二、民俗风情

（一）礼仪禁忌

一般而言，男女可互相握手问候，然而，一些穆斯林女性可能只会以点头和微笑来代替握手，向新认识的男性表示友好，故男性应等女性伸出手来，才可与她握手。在马来西亚，传统的“Salam”问候方式更为普遍。拜访别人之前，礼貌上要先致电对方。到马来西亚人家中做客之前，需先脱鞋。主人通常会奉上饮品，客人接受饮品是礼貌的表现。吃饭或接受礼物时应使用右手。在指示地点、物品或他人时，通常不可使用右手的食指，正确的指示方法是用右手的拇指且另外四指紧握。进入祈祷和参拜的场所，如清真寺和庙宇时，均须脱掉鞋子，一些清真寺还会为女性参观者提供长袍。在这些场所通常是可以拍照的，但应事先请求批准及同意。马来西亚人不喝含有酒精的饮品。

Generally, males and females may greet each other by shaking hands. However, some Muslim women can only smile or nod to other men instead of shaking hands, so men should not be the first to reach out hands for shaking. The traditional way of Salam is more popular in greeting to others. One must make a call before visiting others. Shoes should be taken off before entering local people's houses. The host will normally offer drinks to guests, and it is polite for the guests to accept the drinks. Right hand is usually used to take meals or receive gifts. The right index finger is normally not used when pointing at locations, objects or other people. On the contrary, the correct way is to use the right thumb with the other four fingers in a grip. Shoes should also be taken off when entering the Muslim place or shrine. Robes could be offered to female visitors. Photos are allowed with prior approval. Alcoholic drinks are not consumed for the Malays.

（二）节庆风情

1. 独立日（Hari Merdeka）

在端姑·阿卜杜勒·拉赫曼及其团队的争取下，马来亚联邦终于在 1957 年 8 月 31 日宣布独立，结束了长达 446 年的殖民时期。在 1957 年 8 月 31 日午夜 12 点，英国国旗正式降下，马来亚国旗正式升起。同一天，端姑·阿卜杜勒·拉赫曼和人民在独立广场高喊 7 声“默迪卡”（merdeka：马来语，意为独立）。从此以后，8 月 31 日被定为马来西亚的国庆日。

With the efforts by the Tunku Abdul Rahman and his team, Malaya finally declared independence on August 31, 1957, ending 446 years of the colonial period. On midnight of August 31, 1957, British national flag officially fell, Malay national flag officially rose. On the same day, Tunku Abdul Rahman and the people in Merdeka Square shouted " Merdeka " for 7 times (merdeka means independence in Malay). Since then, August 31 has been designated as the National Day in Malaysia.

2. 花卉节（Flower Festival）

马来西亚充足的雨水和常年阳光普照的气候环境为植物提供了极佳的生长环境，也带来了缤纷绚丽的花卉。每年的 7 月，为了庆祝鲜花的盛开，各式各样的花卉盛会如期举办。在为期一周的庆典中，有壮丽的花车游行，花车把整个街道装点得绿意盎然。伴随着花车的还有乐队、马队和舞蹈团，为观众献上精彩的表演。各个公园、酒店也会借机推出形形色色的活动，如寻花赛、花展等。整个活动期间，举国欢庆，热闹非凡，每年都会吸引大批游客前来参观。

Malaysia's ample rain and year-round sunny climate environment provide an excellent environment for the growth of plants, and also create rich and colorful flowers. In July each year , flower contests of various kinds are held to celebrate the blooming flowers. The week-long celebration witnesses a magnificent parade that decorates the whole street in green. With the bands, the train of horses and dancing groups, an excellent show is performed. Parks and hotels also offer all kinds of activities such as flower finding competition and flower show. During this period, the whole country is soaked in a happy atmosphere, attracting lots of visitors to come.

三、主要旅游城市及景点

（一）吉隆坡（Kuala Lumpur）

吉隆坡，简称为“K.L.”，是马来西亚的焦点。这座城市的过去仍然可以在令人回味的独立广场的英国殖民地建筑和茨厂街午夜露天夜市中找到，并与其现在和未来相融合。吉隆坡繁华的街道、光辉、现代化办公大楼以及大都市的氛围体现了城市的不断发展，象征着马来西亚正快速地跃入未来。作为一个商业中心，吉隆坡汇聚着世界各地的商人和游客。在国家博物馆，令人炫目的多样性的马来西亚文化历史向来是参观重点。作为大多数游客和会议参加者的往来门户，吉隆坡是一个迷人的目的地。石油双塔是世界上最高的建筑物之一，矗立于吉隆坡天际。毫无疑问，它们已经成为马来西亚过去20年惊人发展的标志。

Kuala Lumpur, or commonly known as “K.L.”, is the focal point of Malaysia. While the city’s past is still present in the evocative British colonial buildings of the Merdeka square and the midnight lamps of the Petaling Street night market, that past is everywhere met with insistent reminders of K.L.’s present and future. The city’s bustling streets, its shining, modern office towers, and its cosmopolitan air project an unbounded spirit of progress and symbolize Malaysia’s unhesitating leap into the future. K.L.’s commercial center is a grand meeting place for merchants and travelers from all over the world. And in the National Museum, the dizzying multiplicity of Malaysia’s cultural history comes into focus. As the entry point for most visitors and the meeting point of the country’s many attractions, Kuala Lumpur is a grand gateway to a fascinating destination. Petronas Twin Towers, one of the world’s tallest buildings, rise above the skyline of Kuala Lumpur. Inevitably, they have become the symbols for the astounding growth that has taken place in Malaysia over the last two decades.

◆ 独立广场（Merdeka Square）

独立广场坐落在苏丹阿都沙末大厦的前方，是吉隆坡的标志性建筑，也是每年举办国庆日庆祝活动的地点。独立广场面积约为8公顷，绿草如茵。1957年8月31日，马来亚国旗在这里第一次升起，标志着该国脱离英国统治而独立。广场南端矗立着全世界最高的旗杆，高达100米。广场上还有喷水池、廊柱和花坛组成的休息处。广场下的Plaza Putra是一条地下美食娱乐街。宽阔广场的一边是欧式风格的草坪和荷兰式的建筑，而另一边是古老的穆斯林风格的苏丹阿都沙末大厦。

Merdeka Square, located in front of the Sultan Abdul Samad Building, is the landmark building of K.L., and also a place for the annual National Day celebration. The square covers an area of about 8 hectares full of green grass. On August 31, 1957, Malay flag rose right here for the first time, marking the country’s independence from Britain. South of the square stands the world’s highest flagpole up to 100 meters. There is also a complex of fountain, columns and a flower bed. Under the square is the Plaza Putra: an underground food entertainment street. One side of the spacious square is a European style lawn with Holland style structures, and the other side is the old Sultan Abdul Samad Building with entirely Muslim style.

◆ 石油双塔（Petronas Twin Towers）

马来西亚国家石油公司的双塔大楼别名为“双子星大厦”，建成于 1997 年，是当今世界最高的双塔楼，也是吉隆坡的新象征。石油双塔位于吉隆坡市中心商务区，共有 88 层，高 452 米。两座一模一样的大厦并肩耸立，中间有栈桥相连，设计灵感来自伊斯兰教教义。

Built in 1997, the Petroliam Nasional Berhad Twin Towers, with the alias “the Twin Towers”, are the world’s highest twin towers and also the new symbol of K.L. The 88-storied building, located in CBD of K.L., is 452 meters high. They are a pair of towers standing side by side connected by a bridge, the design of which was inspired by the teachings of Islam.

◆ 黑风洞（Batu Cave）

黑风洞所在的石灰岩溶洞群位于吉隆坡北郊 11 千米处，石灰岩面积为 255 公顷，洞穴不下 20 处，以暗洞和光洞最为有名。它是马来西亚的印度教圣地，每年 1 月底 2 月初的大宝森节期间，虔诚的印度教教徒来到这里，唱着宗教圣歌游行步入石洞参拜，朝圣者可达 30 万人。

Batu Cave, located 11 kilometers north suburb of Kuala Lumpur, is a limestone cave, with an area of 255 hectares and at least 20 caves. Among them, the Dark Cave and Light Cave are most famous. It is Malaysia’s Hindu holy place. During the Thaipusam Festival from late January to early February every year, pilgrims of Hindu come to visit here, singing religious chanting and parading into the cave shrine. The number of pilgrims may reach as many as 300,000.

◆ 云顶高原（Genting Highlands）

云顶高原位于吉隆坡东北约 50 千米处，海拔 1 772 米，是东南亚最大的高原避暑地。云顶高原的赌场是马来西亚唯一合法的赌场，有“东南亚的蒙特卡洛”之称。在赌场门口贴着“穆斯林不准入内”的告示，即使进入赌场，他们也不能够下注。游客进入赌场须出示护照，年龄未满 21 岁不得入内。

Genting Highlands, located approximately 50 kilometers northeast of Kuala Lumpur at an elevation of 1,772 meters, is Southeast Asia’s largest plateau summer resort. Genting Highlands owns Malaysia’s only legal casino, commonly known as “the Southeast Asia’s Monte Carlo”. In the casino entrance hangs a warning sign that reads “No entry for the Muslim”, and even if they enter the casino, they are not allowed to bet. Visitors entering the casino must show their passports, and they must be above 21 years old.

（二）槟城（Penang）

在 15 世纪，槟城岛被称为槟榔屿，中国明代郑和下西洋时在航海图上用到过该名称。15 世纪的葡萄牙水手前往香料群岛（东印度群岛）时往往会在该岛停留，他们称之为 Pulo Pinaom 岛。早期马来人称它为 Pulau Ka-Satu 或“第一（或独立）岛”，因为它是林伽和吉打州贸易航道间最大的岛。暹罗族——之后的吉打苏丹王国霸主，称之为 Koh

Maak。“槟城”的名字来自现代马来语槟榔屿，即种有槟榔的岛屿。槟城这个名字可能是指槟城岛（槟榔屿）或槟城州。在马来语中，槟城首府乔治镇被称为丹本那加，并标记在古地图上，这是以海岸上众多滚珠螺帽树（也被称为亚历山大桂冠）命名的，但现在一般简称“丹戎”（海角）。

In the 15th century, Penang Island was referred to as *Bīnláng Yǔ* in the navigational drawings used by Admiral Zheng He of China's Ming-dynasty in his fleet's expeditions overseas. Fifteenth-century Portuguese sailors heading for the Spice Islands (East Indies) often made stopovers on the island which they called Pulo Pinaom. Early Malays called it Pulau Ka-Satu or "First (or Single) Island" because it was the largest island encountered on the trading sea-route between Lingga and Kedah. The Siamese, then the overlord of the Kedah Sultanate, referred to the island as Koh Maak. The name "Penang" comes from the modern Malay name Pulau Pinang, which means island of the areca nut palm. The name Penang may refer either to the island of Penang (Pulau Pinang) or the state of Penang. In Malay, Penang's capital George Town was called and labeled in old maps as Tanjung Penaga (Cape Penaigre), named after the many ballnut trees (also known as Alexandrian laurels) on the coast, but now usually shortened as Tanjung (the Cape).

◆ 极乐寺（Kek Lok Si Temple）

极乐寺是由福州鼓山涌泉寺方丈妙莲禅师于1889年开山兴建的，历时20多年才完成。1903年，康有为曾为极乐寺题匾，书“勿忘救国”四字。现在，游客在极乐寺还可见到慈禧太后题的“海天佛地”和光绪皇帝题的“大雄宝殿”等匾额，足见当年清廷对极乐寺的重视。该寺结合了中国、泰国和缅甸三种不同的建筑风格。寺内五彩缤纷的建筑鳞次栉比，无论是当地华人还是游客都乐于前往。

Kek Lok Si Temple was constructed in 1889 by Abbot Miao Lian from Fuzhou's Yongquan Temple and took 20 years to finish. In 1903, Chinese scholar Kang Youwei also once wrote on the temple's plaques: Don't forget to save the nation. Now visitors can still see, on those plaques, Empress Dowager Ci Xi's words "the Buddhist World" and Emperor Guang Xu's words "the Grand Hall", both from China's Qing Dynasty. Such inscriptions reflected the Qing imperial court's special attention to the temple. The temple combines architectural styles of China, Thailand and Burma. The temple owns a variety of building techniques, attracting both local Chinese residents and tourists.

（三）马六甲（Malacca）

马六甲位于马来半岛的东南海滨，距吉隆坡约160千米，是马来西亚最古老的一座城市。在过去的一个世纪，有很多人征服过马六甲：中国人、葡萄牙人、荷兰人和英国人。在过去，马六甲扼守马六甲海峡的咽喉，战略地位十分重要。在当时，马六甲是香料贸易的主要港口，整天飘扬着来自世界各地的香料贸易船的风帆和桅杆。在马六甲交易的商品还包括：来自中国的丝绸和瓷器，来自印度古吉拉特和科罗曼德的纺织品，来自婆罗洲的樟脑，来自东帝汶的檀香，来自摩鹿加群岛的肉豆蔻、肉豆蔻衣、丁香，来自苏门答腊岛的黄金和辣椒，以及马来西亚西部的锡。

Malacca, located on the southeast coastal line of the country about 160 kilometers away from Kuala Lumpur, is the oldest city in Malaysia. Malacca had a lot of conquerors in the past century: Chinese, Portuguese, Dutch and Britons. In the past, the city was a strategic place at the border of the Strait of Malacca. It was a major port along the spice-route, and its harbor bristled with the sails and masts of spice-loaded vessels from all over world. What others were traded here include: silk and porcelain from China; textiles from Gujarat and Coromandel in India; camphor from Borneo; sandalwood from Timor; nutmeg, mace and cloves from the Moluccas, gold and pepper from Sumatra; and tin from western Malaysia.

◆ 马六甲行政中心（The Administrative Center of Malacca）

马六甲行政中心是位于圣保罗丘陵广场的行政官邸，系荷兰式建筑，建于 1660 年。在行政中心的左边，有一道高墙，上面装饰着古代战船。行政中心附近有马六甲志愿团纪念碑，纪念在第二次世界大战中阵亡的将士。

Located in the St. Paul Hills Plaza, it is an executive mansion in Holland style built in 1660. On its left side, there is a high wall decorated with ancient warship. Near the administrative center is the Malacca Volunteer Regiment Monument commemorating the soldiers who sacrified their lives in the Second World War.

◆ 三宝山（Bukit China）

三宝山意为“中国山”，它是位于马来西亚马六甲州首府马六甲的市郊小丘，为纪念三宝太监郑和而得名。山下青云亭附近有汉丽宝井，又称三宝井，传说为郑和所凿。山脚耸立着纪念碑，以纪念在第二次世界大战中抗日殉难的志士。在三宝山下有宝山庙，为纪念郑和访问马六甲而建。该庙采用了中国传统建筑形式，红墙配琉璃瓦，房顶飞檐描有彩龙戏珠的图案，庙内供有郑和坐像。

Bukit China means Chinese hill. It is located on the outskirt of the capital of the Malacca state and commemorates the eunuch admiral Zheng He. There is Hang Li Poh's Well near the Cheng Hoon Teng, which is said to have been dug by Zheng He. At the foot of the hill stands the monument, in recognition of the Second World War's anti-Japanese martyrs. There is Poh San Teng Temple at the hill foot, dedicated to the memory of Zheng He's visit to Malacca. The construction of the temple preserves the traditional Chinese style, such as red wall with glazed tile roof, depicting the dragon pearl motifs. Inside the temple is the sitting Zheng He's statue.

四、旅游资讯

（一）美食

作为一个多元社会，马来西亚的饮食也体现着多元化。这里汇集了中国、印度、西方、马来西亚土著民族的食物，使得各种风味的美食琳琅满目，可供任意选择。

As a pluralistic society, Malaysia is also evident in food for that feature. It is a collection of Chinese, Indian, Western and Malaysian local indigenous food, making all kinds of flavor available to choose.

马来西亚人的主食是米饭，但面食也相当普遍。从街边小摊贩到酒店，中餐无处不在。马来西亚的小吃包括酿豆腐、虾面、炒粿条、咖喱面、薄饼、海南鸡饭、瓦煲鸡饭、云吞面、香港点心、肉骨茶、槟城叻沙等，种类繁多。

Malaysia's staple food is rice, but noodle is also quite common. You may find Chinese food from local food vendors to restaurants. Snacks include Yong Tau Foo, shrimp noodles, Char Kway Teow, curry mee, pan cake, Hananese Chicken Rice, Claypot Chicken Rice, Wonton Noodles, HongKong snacks, Bak Kut Teh, Penang Laksa and other varieties.

马来西亚人的食物以辣为主，其中较出名的有椰浆饭、香喷喷的沙嗲（鸡肉、牛肉及羊肉串）、马来糕点、竹筒饭、黄姜饭等。与东南亚其他国家的美食相比，马来西亚美食的口味更加浓重一些，喜欢放咖喱和辣椒。因为当地气候炎热、潮湿，吃一些辛辣的食物有助于排汗，这样人们会感到清爽些。由于信奉伊斯兰教，因此马来人不吸烟，不吃猪肉、死了的动物或动物血液。马来人习惯用右手抓饭，进餐前必须把手洗干净，用餐时十分讲究卫生和礼节。

Malay food is mainly hot. Well-known foods include coconut rice, delicious satay (chicken, beef and mutton kebab), Malay cakes, bamboo rice, yellow rice, etc. Compared with other countries in Southeast Asia, the Malay food taste somewhat stronger, and they like curry and spices. Because the local climate is hot and humid, eating some spicy food makes the body feel refreshed with sweat let off. As they believe in Muslim, the Malay do not smoke, and do not eat pork, the dead animal or animal blood. The Malays use right hands to pick up rice, before the meal they must wash hands and think highly of polite and dining etiquette.

知识拓展

马来西亚代表菜

1. 娘惹菜系（Nyonya）

娘惹菜系是由中国菜系和马来菜系合并而成的马六甲菜肴，传统的中国菜烹饪方法与马来香料完美结合，融会了甜酸、辛香、微辣等多种风味，口味浓重，所用的酱料都由起码10种香料调配而成。叻沙（Laksa）是娘惹美食中最具盛名的一种。许多马来西亚土著人认为：娘惹美食见证了马来人与华人的联姻，代表了浪漫、丰富的美食特色。除了马六甲地区，娘惹菜还流传到了槟榔屿、新加坡、印度尼西亚和泰国。

2. 肉骨茶（Bak Kut Teh）

肉骨茶是马来西亚的美食之一，是以猪肉和猪骨配合中药煲成的汤底，其独特的风味享誉全马，甚至名扬四海，深受各地游客的喜爱。其中，以巴生肉骨茶最为闻名。肉骨茶分为新加坡的海南派及马来西亚的福建派，海南肉骨茶有较重的胡椒味，而福建肉骨茶有较重的药材味。

3. 沙嗲（Satay）

沙嗲是传统马来西亚美食。将腌好的牛肉、羊肉、鸡肉块串成串，以适度的火候炭烤后，最重要的是要蘸一层厚厚的沙嗲酱一起入口。沙嗲酱由花生酱、椰浆、幼虾等调制而成，香醇无比，令人眷恋不已。享用一串串沙嗲的同时，配以椰叶或班兰叶包裹的传统马来米饭、小黄瓜及洋葱等，入口的沙嗲味道会更加分明。

4. 罗惹（Rojak）

罗惹来自马来语，是“混合物”的意思，是一种在马来半岛非常受欢迎的餐前开胃菜和配菜。马来西亚各族群之间普遍采用一种被称为“罗惹”的说话方式交谈，即混杂了当地几种语言的说话方式。因为“罗惹”实际上是大杂烩的色拉，所以当地人便借用“罗惹”来称呼这种美食。它的用料是东南亚的各式新鲜水果和蔬菜，如菠萝、青瓜、苹果、豆芽、芒果等，当然，少不了用来吊味的酸橘子皮和山姜花。把上述食材切成细块，与油豆腐、油条、虾片、墨鱼片、海蜇皮、碎花生屑等混合，最后拌入虾膏酱、罗望子汁、糖、辣椒、柠檬汁、酸橙汁等搅拌均匀后即可。而在沙巴地区，罗惹指的是一道浇上花生酱，加入牛肉块和白水煮蛋的面食，是沙巴人最爱的印度尼西亚爪哇风味美食。

（二）购物及退税

蝴蝶：种类多达几千种，吸引着大批游客前来观赏。本地人将绚烂多彩的蝴蝶制成栩栩如生的标本和装饰物出售，成为马来西亚一大特产。

> Butterfly: There are thousands of species of butterfly attracting a large number of tourists. Local people produce colorful and lifelike butterfly specimens and ornaments for sales.

香水：马来西亚盛产兰花，出产高质量的香水。当地产的“兰”系列香水，品质甚佳，不亚于法国香水，但价格比法国香水便宜得多。

> Perfume: Malaysia abounds in orchid and produces quality perfume. A premium local brand named the “orchid” series is as perfect as French perfume, but the price is much lower than French perfume.

蜡染：马来西亚的蜡染产品以花和蝴蝶的图案居多，色彩艳丽，价格适中，为馈赠佳品。

> Batik: Malaysian batik products exhibit patterns of flower and butterfly, with gorgeous color and reasonable price.

马来西亚是低税收的国家，除了烟、酒以外，其他的物品税收都不高，所以马来西亚目前没有针对外国游客的退税政策。

> Malaysia is a low tax country. Except alcohol and tobacco, all the other articles are not subject to high tax, so there is no tax refund policy currently available to foreign visitors.

（三）时差

马来西亚首都吉隆坡与北京没有时差。

There is no time difference between Kuala Lumpur and Beijing.

思考练习

1. 经典旅游线路分析

马来西亚风情6日游

第1天：北京——吉隆坡——亚庇

游客搭乘马来西亚航空公司航班经吉隆坡转机前往沙巴州首府亚庇。抵达后入住酒店休息。

第2天：亚庇

游客乘船前往沙比岛。全程约5小时，游客可以看到五光十色的热带鱼遨游蔚蓝大海，也可以躺在沙滩上，戴上太阳眼镜，品尝椰子或者沙巴最美味的榴莲雪糕（自费），还可以免费租用岛上浮潜用具下海，或者自费参加水上活动：海底漫步、水肺潜水、双人拖曳伞、摩托艇、香蕉船等。午餐于岛上享用海鲜烧烤。约14:00，返回酒店休息。17:00，在导游的安排下，前往第一沙滩（视天气状况），欣赏令人叹为观止的落日美景，留下美妙的回忆。

第3天：亚庇

全天自由活动。游客可自由享受泳池、沙滩、高尔夫休闲时光，亦可自费前往凯尔斯长鼻猴生态萤河之旅保护区。

第4天：亚庇

全天自由活动。游客可自由享受泳池、沙滩、高尔夫休闲时光，亦可自费前往民族文化村或激流等。

第5天：亚庇——吉隆坡

游客于中午12:00前办理退房手续，而后享用午餐。之后，前往敦马士达化大厦（31层楼高的基金局大厦），该大厦是由96根钢条呈辐射状支撑的圆体型建筑。然后游览亚庇市区最大的伊斯兰教建筑，因其建造在人造湖上，所以又被称为“水上清真寺”。最后参观沙巴普陀寺，该寺由华人捐献建造，承袭了中式寺院一贯的建筑风格，寺院每日开放2次给信徒诵经。寺外有个巨大的观音雕像，仿佛好像在欢迎游客的到来。前往机场前，品尝具有当地特色的拉茶、抛饼等招待各位游客。行程结束后，游客前往机场办理离境手续，搭乘马来西亚航空公司航班经吉隆坡转机返回北京。

第6天：吉隆坡——北京

游客乘国际航班抵达首都北京。

分析：这条经典旅游线路的主要旅游景点与行程特色，以及适合旅游的人群。

2. 案例分析

[案例 1] 某旅游团在马来西亚旅游，客人在某商场购完物后，感觉很满意。其中一位男士为表示感谢，伸出手来要求与戴着头巾的女经理握手，但女经理显得比较尴尬。这是为什么？

[案例 2] 某旅游团搭乘亚洲航空公司的航班从杭州前往吉隆坡，一位乘客在飞机上口渴了，却怎么也等不到空姐提供水或饮料。请问这是为什么？

3. 练一练

（1）简述“槟城”这一名称的来历。

（2）简述马来西亚有哪些特产。

第五节　泰国

一、国家概况

（一）地理环境

泰国全称为泰王国，原名为暹罗，坐落在中南半岛和东南亚的中心。它北邻缅甸和老挝，东临老挝和柬埔寨，南到泰国湾和马来西亚，西接安达曼海和缅甸南端。泰国的 513 120 平方千米的国土处于东南亚中部。其中轴线位置影响了泰国社会和文化的许多方面，并控制了唯一通向马来西亚和新加坡的陆路。

Thailand, officially the Kingdom of Thailand, formerly known as Siam, is a country located at the center of the Indo-China Peninsula and Southeast Asia. It is bordered to the north by Burma and Laos, to the east by Laos and Cambodia, to the south by the Gulf of Thailand and Malaysia, and to the west by the Andaman Sea and the southern extremity of Burma. Thailand's 513,120 square kilometers lie in the middle of mainland Southeast Asia. The nation's axial position influenced many aspects of Thailand's society and culture. It controls the only land route to Malaysia and Singapore.

（二）人文概况

1. 历史

最早的泰国人据说是在公元 10 年左右从中国南部迁移到东南亚的。13 世纪，泰国从高棉帝国获得主权，坤邦克朗刀成立了一个独立的王国。这是一个经济繁荣和民众生活安逸的时期，直到国王兰坎亨于 1317 年去世。同时，另外一个泰王朝在北方地区兰纳建立了。以拉玛铁菩提一世为泰王的素可泰王国沦陷后，大城府王国开始兴盛，它持续了 5 代 33 位国王，一直到 1767 年缅甸军队攻击首都。在很短的时间内，泰国由他信将军统治，直到却克里王朝却克里将军建立了新首都曼谷。1932 年，民党发动政变，君主立宪制正式成为泰国的国体。现任国王玛哈·哇集拉隆功（拉玛十世）是国家元首、武装部队最高统帅，2016 年 12 月 1 日继位。第二次世界大战后，泰国军人集团长期把持政权，局势动荡。20 世纪 90 年代军人淡出政坛后，泰国政坛党派林立，纷争不断，政府更迭频仍。

It is believed that the earliest Thais migrated into the region of Southeast Asia all the way from southern China at some point in 10 AD. When Thailand gained sovereignty from the Khmer Empire during the 13th century, Pho Khun Si Indrathit founded an independent empire. It was a glorious and joyful period for the Thais until King Ramkhamhaeng died in 1317. At the same time, another Thai state also existed in the northern region of Lanna. The Kingdom of Ayutthaya began its grandeur after the fall of the Kingdom of Sukhothai with its first monarch, Ramathibodi Ⅰ. It had a total of 5 dynasties with 33 kings and lasted until 1767 when Burmese army attacked the capital. For a short period of time, Thailand was under the rule of General Taksin until the first king of the Chakri Dynasty, General Chakri as Rami, succeeded and established Bangkok as the new capital. In 1932, constitutional monarchy became the official state system of Thailand through the Siamese Revolution. King Maha Vajiralongkorn served as the highest ranking officer in military troops, and he took over the throne on December 1, 2016. After the Second World War, the military groups ruled the country for a long time with unstable political situation. The quit of these military groups in 1990s led to a number of political parties stepping upon the stage for complicated struggle.

2. 经济

泰国是一个新兴经济体和新兴工业化国家。1985 年至 1996 年，泰国拥有世界上最高的经济增长率——平均每年以 12.4% 的速度增长。1997 年，泰国货币——泰铢面临很大的压力，导致该年泰国经济萎缩了 1.9%，引发了经济危机，暴露了金融部门的弱点。

Thailand is an emerging economy and considered as a newly industrialized country. After enjoying the world's highest growth rate from 1985 to 1996 — averaging 12.4% annually, increased pressure on Thailand's currency, the baht, in 1997, the year in which the economy contracted by 1.9% led to a crisis that uncovered financial sector weaknesses.

泰国每年出口的产品和服务价值超过 1 050 亿美元，主要出口产品包括大米、纺织品和鞋类、渔业产品、橡胶制品、珠宝、汽车、电脑及电器。泰国是世界第一的大米出口国，每年出口超过 650 万吨精米。水稻是泰国最重要的农作物。泰国在湄公河流域国家中拥有最高比重的耕地，达到 27.25%。约 55% 的可耕种土地面积用于水稻生产。

Thailand exports over 105 billion dollars worth of goods and services annually. Major exports include rice, textiles and footwear, fishery products, rubber, jewellery, cars, computers and electrical appliances. Thailand is the world's No.1 exporter of rice, exporting more than 6.5 million tons of milled rice annually. Rice is the most important crop in the country. Thailand has the highest percentage of arable land, 27.25%, of any nation in the Greater Mekong Subregion. About 55% of the arable land area is used for rice production.

3. 社会文化

泰国人口约 6 903 万，包含泰族、华族、老挝族、高棉族等民族。官方语言是泰语。泰国以佛教为国教，90% 以上的民众信奉佛教。

Thailand's population is about 69.03 million, including Thai, Chinese, Lao, Khmer, etc. The official language is Thai. Buddhism is the state religion and more than 90% residents believe in Buddhism.

泰国文化受到许多国家的影响，包括印度、老挝、缅甸、柬埔寨和中国。其传统融合了大量来自印度、中国、柬埔寨和东南亚其他地方的元素。泰国国教上座部佛教对现代泰国人具有重要影响。随着时间的演变，泰国佛教吸纳了源自印度教、万物有灵论以及祭祖的地方信仰等的诸多内容。泰国的官方日历是基于东方版本的佛教日历，比西方的公历早 543 年。例如：公元 2020 年在泰国是 2563 年。

Thai culture has been shaped by many influences, including India, Laos, Burma, Cambodia and China. Its traditions incorporate a great deal of influence from India, China, Cambodia and the rest of Southeast Asia. Thailand's national religion — Theravada Buddhism is important to modern Thai identity. Thai Buddhism has evolved over time to include many regional beliefs originating from Hinduism, Animism as well as ancestor worship. The official calendar in Thailand is based on the eastern version of the Buddhist Era, which is 543 years ahead of the Gregorian calendar from the West. For example, the year 2020 AD is 2563 BE in Thailand.

"Wai" 是泰国传统的问候方式，一般是先由年纪较轻的一方提出。行礼时，要微微鞠躬，手掌合十如祈祷状，男性通常会说 "Sawasdee khrap"，女性通常会说 "Sawasdee ka"，年长者则以相同的方式回复。社会地位（如政府职位）也会影响谁先开始问候礼。例如：虽然某人可能比省长年纪要大，但见面时通常是来访者首先问候。当孩子离开家去学校时，他们应先向父母致意以示尊敬。回家时也一样。这种问候表示尊重和崇敬，类似于印度和尼泊尔的"合十礼"问候方式。

The traditional form of Thai greeting, the wai, is generally offered first by the younger of the two people meeting. The wai consists of a slight bow, with the palms pressed together in a prayer-like fashion, usually coinciding with the spoken word "Sawasdee khrap" for male speakers and "Sawasdee ka" for females. The elder then is to respond afterwards in the same way. Social status and position, such as in government, will also have an influence on who performs the wai first. For example, although one may be considerably older than a provincial governor, it is usually the visitor who pays respect first when meeting. When children leave to go to school, they are taught to wai to their parents to represent their respect for them. They do the same when they come back. The wai is a sign of respect and reverence for another, similar to the namaste greeting of India and Nepal.

正如其他亚洲文化，尊重祖先是泰国文化的一个重要组成部分。泰国人比较好客和慷慨，但也有强烈的社会等级观念。资历在泰国文化中是一个重要的概念。根据传统，年长者掌管家族事务。年长者应对年纪小的兄弟姐妹负起责任。

Like most Asian cultures, respect towards ancestors is an essential part of Thai spiritual practice. Thais have a strong sense of hospitality and generosity, but also have a strong sense of social hierarchy. Seniority is an important concept in Thai culture. Elders by tradition rule in family decisions or ceremonies. Elder siblings have duties to younger ones.

二、民俗风情

（一）礼仪禁忌

佛教形成了泰国文化的根本，这一国教把所有泰国人联系在了一起。当进入房屋或寺庙时，应将鞋放在门口。泰国人对无知的访客稍微违反禁忌是相对宽容的，通常会面带微笑地忽略。一个微笑能帮助解决很多难题或化解尴尬的状况，泰国人常说“mai pen rai”（没关系）。游客应该尽可能遵守泰国人的礼节，这包括以下几个方面：

The Thai culture is shaped by Buddhism, which as the national religion presents a connecting element of all Thais. When entering a house or even a temple, one will put the shoes on the threshold. Thais are relatively tolerant against small violations of taboo by the unknowing visitor, and will ignore it with a smile. A smile helps to survive any problematic or awkward situation, as well as the frequently used formula “mai pen rai” (it does not matter). One should strive nevertheless as much as possible to observe the politeness forms observed for Thais. These comprise the following things:

作为一项基本原则，人们应尊重其他宗教的人。在泰国，对所有佛像都应表示尊重，对于皇室也应一样虔诚。参观寺庙时必须循规蹈矩，不能穿短裤或透明的衣服去寺庙。人们可以安全地进入任何寺庙并拍照，但玉佛寺除外。泰国人不会为其他事情中断他们的参拜和祈祷，至少不会对佛像显示出任何形式的不敬，没有人会爬上雕像拍照留念。游客应该非常谨慎，不能拍陌生人的照片，因为许多泰国人相信照片上的人将被剥夺一小块灵魂。参观寺庙时，要面对大佛跪在地上，但要保证人脚远离佛像。

As a basic principle, one should respect the religion of other people, and in Thailand respect must be paid to all Buddha images and to the royal family who in Thailand enjoys almost religious devotion. One must behave decently when visiting a temple and should not go to the temple in shorts or transparent blouses. One can safely go into any temple and take photographs of everything, with the exception of the Temple of the Emerald Buddha (Wat Phra Kaew). The Thais will not be disrupted in their worship and their prayers, at least one does not show any sort of disrespect to a Buddha statue, no one should ever climb on a statue to get a photo as a souvenir. One should be very cautious not to take photographs of strange people because many Thais believe that with every photo the rightful owner will be deprived of a small piece of his soul. If visiting a temple, one has to crouch on the ground facing the Buddha statue, but always leave one’s feet away from Buddha.

和尚绝对不能与女性有任何身体接触。女性在任何情况下都不能触摸和尚，否则会给他带来很大麻烦。普通人触摸异性也被认为是不妥当的，即使仅仅是一个友好的动作（如触摸手臂）。在公共场所，任何亲昵的举动都是不道德的，即使是配偶间的亲吻。你会经常看到两个女孩或两个男孩手牵手走在街上，但在公共场所，异性之间的牵手却被认为是不体面的。

A monk should never have physical contact with women. Under no circumstances can a woman touch him, as that would bring him serious trouble. It is also considered unbecoming for laymen to touch a strange person of the opposite gender, even if it is only a friendly gesture as touching the arm. It is also unethical to have intimate behavior in public, even if it is just a kiss between spouses. You can often see two young girls or two boys walking hand in hand on the street, but for people of different genders, it is considered unseemly to be hand in hand in public.

头部是人类灵魂所在。即使是小孩子的头，也不能随便触摸，甚至要避免在别人头部的上方传递东西，否则在某些情况下可能会惹恼对方。人们通常用右手拿东西，而用左手触摸并支持该动作。当走近坐着的人时，应该将头向下低些，让人感觉到并不比别人高。当向他人表示尊重时，甚至会微微弯曲膝盖或上半身。

In the head resides the soul of humans. It should therefore not be touched, even if it is the head of a small child. This rule goes so far as to avoid the head of people while passing things over—this might be very aggravating in some situations. One gives and takes something with the right hand, while touching with the left hand to facilitate the movement. When walking close to sitting people, one should bend the head to indicate that one feels no higher than the others. When showing respect to others, one will even bent the knees a little bit, or bow the upperpart of the body.

脚应谨慎使用。它们是身体最低的一部分，用脚对着他人是不礼貌的。在公共场所应避免用脚移动东西。

The feet should be used with caution. They are the lowest part of the body, and it is impolite to point with your foot towards someone. In public one should even avoid to move things with the feet.

即使是无知的游客也应知道，在进入庙寺前需要脱鞋。但同样重要的是，进入他人房间前也要脱鞋。这不仅是为了不弄脏地板，更是因为穿鞋进入他人家里是对主人的侮辱。泰国人家里通常没有椅子，大家坐在地板上，甚至食物通常也是放在地板上享用。

Even the ignorant tourists know that before entering into a temple one should take off their shoes. But it is also important to take off the shoes each time before going into a house. This is not only in order not to soil the floor, but also because it is an insult to the residents to enter a house with shoes. Thais usually have no chairs, everybody sits on the floor, and even the food is usually served on the floor.

（二）节庆风情

1. 泰国父亲节（The King's Birthday）

12 月 5 日是前任国王拉玛九世的生日，这一天也被称为“泰国父亲节”。这一天，所有泰国的建筑都会装饰上象征君主和国王的标志。

December 5 is Rama Ⅸ, the former King's Birthday. This public holiday is also known as the Thailand Father's Day. In this day, all the buildings of Thailand are covered up with symbols of the monarchy and the king.

2. 水灯节（Loy Krathong）

水灯节是一个宗教节日，在每年泰历12月（11月的第一个月圆之日）。所有泰国人会购买或自己做一个“水灯”。它是由香蕉叶包围的泡沫塑料制成的，花和蜡烛放在中间。当夜晚来临时，泰国人会去河流或池塘放下“水灯”任其漂流。

Loy Krathong (Festival of Lights) is a religious event which falls every year on the full moon of the 12th month in the traditional Thailand Calendar (first full moon day of November). All Thai people buy or make a “krathong”. It is made of styrofoam surrounded by banana leaves, with flowers and a candle in the middle. During the evening, Thai people go to places where there is a river or a pound to launch their “krathong”.

3. 宋干节（Songkran Festival）

宋干节（“宋干”是梵语的音译）也叫“泼水节”，是在每年公历的4月13日到15日。在宋干节期间，人们抬着或用车载着巨大的佛像出游，佛像后面跟着一辆辆花车，车上站着化了妆的“宋干女神”。在游行队伍经过的道路两旁，善男信女夹道而行，将银钵里用贝叶浸泡过的、渗有香料的水，泼洒到佛像和“宋干女神”身上，祈求新年如意，风调雨顺，然后人们相互洒水，祝愿长辈健康长寿，祝愿亲朋新年幸运。未婚的青年男女则用泼水来表示彼此间的爱慕之情。新年第一天，泰国人会在窗台、门口放一盆清水，家家户户都要到郊外江河中去进行新年沐浴。为庆贺新年，泰国人会举行规模盛大的“赛象大会”，活动包括：人象拔河、跳象拾物、象跨人身、大象足球赛、古代象阵表演等。

Songkran (“Songkran” is the Sanskrit transliteration), also called the “Water-Splashing Festival”, falls from April 13 to 15 of the Gregorian Calendar. In the festival, people carry or use vehicles to carry huge statues of Buddha for travel, followed by floats on which “Goddess Songkran” wearing makeup stands. As the procession proceeds, on both sides of the road walk the devout men and women who splash with a silver bowl filled with leaf soaked, flavor-laced water, to Buddha, and pray for a happy new year, good weather, then people splash water, wishing elderly health and longevity, and relatives and friends good fortune in the New Year. Unmarried youth use water to express their love to each other. In the first day of the new year, Thai people usually put a basin of water at the window and the door, each and every family will go to the river in the countryside for a new year bath. To celebrate the new year, large-scale elephant race is held in Thailand with the following events: people-elephant tug-of-war, jumping elephant to pick up objects, elephant stepping across person, elephant soccer and ancient elephant array performances.

三、主要旅游城市及景点

（一）曼谷（Bangkok）

曼谷原意为“天使之城”，有“佛庙之都”的美誉，是泰国首都，是泰国政治、经济、文化和交通中心。曼谷位于湄南河畔，距泰国湾 4 千米，离入海口 15 千米，全市面积为 1 568 平方千米，人口 1 370 万。市内河道纵横，货运频繁，有“东方威尼斯”之称。曼谷港是泰国乃至世界著名的大米输出港。

Bangkok originally means “the City of Angels”, has a reputation of Buddhist city, and is Thailand’s political, economic, cultural and transportation center. Located along the Chao Phraya River, Bangkok is 4 kilometers away from the Gulf of Thailand, and 15 kilometers away from the estuary. It covers an area of 1,568 square kilometers with a population of 13.7 million. With vertical and horizontal river network, shipping is easy and frequent and the city is also known as “Venice of the East”. Bangkok port is famous for rice shipment in Thailand even the world.

曼谷是国际活动中心之一，每年有多达两三百场的国际会议在此举行。曼谷是联合国亚太经社委员会总部所在地，以及世界银行、世界卫生组织、国际劳工组织以及其他 20 多个国际机构的区域办事处所在地。曼谷还是世界佛教徒联谊会（有 32 个成员国）总部及亚洲理工学院所在地。

Bangkok is one of the centers for international events. Each year, there are up to two to three hundred international conferences held here. The city has the headquarters of United Nations Economic and Social Commission for Asia and the Pacific, and regional offices of the World Bank, the World Health Organization, International Labor Organization and over 20 other international agencies. The World Buddhist Association (with 32 member states) headquarters and the Asian Institute of Technology are also located in Bangkok.

◆ 大皇宫（Grand Palace）

大皇宫位于曼谷市中心，是泰国建筑艺术的巨作。这座宫殿自 1782 年以来一直是暹罗（后来的泰国）的国王官邸。1925 年之前，国王、宫廷及皇家政府都在这里。目前的君主，国王玛哈·哇集拉隆功（拉玛十世）居住在吉拉达宫，但大皇宫仍然是官方活动举办地。每年都有数项皇家和国家活动在大皇宫举行。

The Grand Palace is a complex of buildings at the heart of Bangkok. The palace has been the official residence of the Kings of Siam (later Thailand) since 1782. The king, his court and his royal government were based on the grounds of the palace until 1925. The present monarch, King Maha Vajiralongkorn (Rama X), currently resides at Chitralada Palace, but the Grand Palace is still used in official events. Several royal and national functions are held here every year.

◆ 玉佛寺（Temple of the Emerald Buddha）

玉佛寺始建于 1782 年，与卧佛寺、金佛寺一并被列为“泰国三大国宝”。它位于首都曼谷大皇宫东北角，是大皇宫的组成部分，也是泰国所有寺庙中最崇高的代表。该寺占地

2.1 万平方米，面积为整个大皇宫的 1/4，是泰国最著名的佛寺，也是泰国唯一没有和尚居住的佛寺。

Temple of the Emerald Buddha, also known as Wat Phra Kaew, was founded in 1782 and is well-known, together with Temple of the Sleeping Buddha and Temple of the Golden Buddha in Thailand, as the three national treasures. Located in the northeast of the Grand Palace, it is part of the Grand Palace, and is also the lofty representative of all the monasteries. The temple covers an area of 21,000 square meters, one fourth of the Grand Palace. It is the most famous temple in Thailand and also the only Thai temple without Buddist monk residence.

（二）芭堤雅（Pattaya）

芭堤雅曾经是个渔村，最初在越南战争期间成为一个度假地，并逐渐发展为家庭游海景度假胜地。每年来此旅游的外国游客超过 1 200 万人次。

Once as a fishing village, Pattaya first boomed as a resort destination during the Vietnam War and has developed into a family-orientated seaside destination. The number of foreign tourists every year amounted over 12 million.

游客在芭堤雅的游乐活动包括打高尔夫（高尔夫球场 21 个，距芭堤雅 1 小时车程），卡丁车赛车，参观不同的主题公园和动物园，如大象村等，那里每天都会展示训练方法和古代礼仪。其他景点包括百万年石林、芭堤雅鳄鱼公园、芭堤雅公园海滩度假村、水上乐园、斯里波恩兰花农场、银湖酒厂、泰国文化芭堤雅剧院（文化表演）、瓶艺术博物馆、信不信由你博物馆和海底世界水族馆。海底世界水族馆是一个世界级的水族馆，它集中了泰国湾的多个海洋物种，包括鲨鱼和黄貂鱼。该市也以歌舞表演而闻名，特别是华丽的人妖表演。

Activities in Pattaya include playing golf (21 golf courses within 1 hour drive to Pattaya), kart racing, and visiting different theme parks and zoos such as the Elephant Village, where demonstrations of training methods and ancient ceremonial re-enactments are performed daily. Other attractions in Pattaya include The Million Years Stone Park, Pattaya Crocodile Farm, Pattaya Park Beach Resort, Water Park, Siriporn Orchid Farm, Silverlake Winery, the Thai Alangkarn Theater Pattaya (cultural show), Bottle Art Museum, Ripley's Believe It or Not Museum and Underwater World Pattaya (world-class aquarium), an aquarium where there is a collection of marine species in the Gulf of Thailand including sharks and stingrays. The city is also famous for singing and dancing, especially flamboyant kathoey cabaret shows.

知识拓展

泰国人妖

泰国人妖（Thai Ladyboy）的产生是由于泰国的色情旅游业猖獗，一些男性为谋生，想方设法把自己变成“女人”。于是，“人妖”这个特殊群体就逐渐产生了。到了 20 世纪

90年代，泰国人妖已达2万人，年龄均在14～50岁，主要集中在芭堤雅的人妖歌舞团及酒吧和夜总会。凡到泰国旅游的游客都会看人妖，但“她们”到底是男人还是女人，“她们”是怎样变成人妖的，怪异为身体造成了“她们”怎样的畸形内心世界，这一切却鲜为人知。人妖们所表演的歌舞具有相当高的艺术水准，表演内容通常涵盖各国的歌舞等，每晚都有很多游客前往观看。

（三）清迈（Chiang Mai）

清迈是泰国北部最大和文化上最重要的城市。它是清迈省首府，在1296年到1768年间是兰纳王国的首都，也是自1774年到1939年清迈王国的附庸国。近年来，清迈已经成为一个日益现代化的城市，每年吸引超过500万的游客，其中外国游客达到140万～200万。清迈在政治领域中也有突出贡献。2006年5月，清迈举办了“东盟+3”（东盟10国和中、日、韩3国）首脑会议，会议发表了“清迈协议”。

Chiang Mai is the largest and most culturally significant city in northern Thailand and the capital of Chiang Mai province. It was a former capital of the Kingdom of Lanna from 1296 to 1768 and the tributary Kingdom of Chiang Mai from 1774 to 1939. In recent years, Chiang Mai has become an increasingly modern city and has been attracting over 5 million visitors each year, of which between 1.4 million and 2 million are foreign tourists. Chiang Mai gained prominence in the political sphere in May 2006, when the *Chiang Mai Initiative* was announced here at the summit meeting of ASEAN plus Three (10 ASEAN member states plus China, Japan and South Korea).

◆ 素贴山和素贴寺（Doi Suthep and Wat Phra That Doi Suthep）

素贴山位于清迈市西7 000米，海拔约1 053米，是最著名的避暑胜地，这里建有泰国国王的避暑行宫——普屏宫。素贴山是清迈市的标志。当地华人称此山为“遇仙山”或“会仙山”，因山上有著名的素贴寺而闻名。山坡上开满五色玫瑰，山顶白云缭绕，风光秀丽。

Doi Suthep is located 7 kilometers west of Chiang Mai, and is about 1,053 meters above sea level. It is the most famous summer resort, which was built there as Summer Palace for the king of Thailand — Phu Phing Palace. It is the landmark of the city of Chiang Mai. The local Chinese call it Meeting God Mountain because of the famous temple, Wat Phra That Doi Suthep. The hillside is full of colored rose and provides a view of clouds and other beautiful scenery.

（四）普吉岛（Phuket）

普吉岛是泰国最大的岛屿，面积和新加坡差不多，位于印度洋安达曼海东北部，离泰国首都曼谷南部867千米。普吉岛具有得天独厚的宏伟海湾、种满棕榈树的白色沙滩、环绕周围的各式岛屿、好客的主人、美味的海鲜和令人赏心悦目的跨世纪中葡建筑；这儿会给人们许多运动和休闲的机会，同时游客会欣赏到郁郁葱葱的热带景观——所有这些都创造了一个愉快的氛围和真正难忘的假期。这儿有最著名的海滩，如巴东、卡塔、卡隆、卡玛拉和奈汉海滩。普吉岛及周边岛屿是出海、潜水和浮潜的理想地，也有游客期望的高尔夫球场及各种体育和娱乐项目。游客可以乘坐潜艇探索丰富多彩的海底生活。岛上住宿有众多选择，从普通标准间到五星级酒店的海景房应有尽有。

Phuket is Thailand's largest island, approximately the size of Singapore. Phuket nestles in Andaman Sea of Indian Ocean, located 867 kilometers south of Bangkok. Phuket is blessed with magnificent coves and bays, powdery and palm-fringed white beaches, smaller surrounding islands, hospitable people and seafood, delightful trans-century Sino-Portuguese architecture, numerous sporting and leisure opportunities, as well as a lush tropical landscape — all of which combine to create a delightful ambiance for truly memorable holidays. The most famous beaches are Patong Beach, Kata Beach, Karon Beach, Kamala Beach and Nai Harn Beach. Phuket and its islands are ideal for sailing, diving, snorkeling, golfing and all kinds of sports and entertainment you can wish for. You can also take a trip with a submarine to discover the colorful marine lives under the sea. There is plenty of accommodations available ranging from standard rooms to sea-view rooms 5 star hotels.

四、旅游资讯

（一）美食

泰国菜混合了五种基本味道：甜、酸、苦、辣、咸。泰国菜中一些常见的食材有大蒜、辣椒、柠檬汁、柠檬草和鱼露。在泰国，大米是主食，特别是名为茉莉香米的水稻品种几乎每餐都有。泰国是世界最大的大米出口国。泰国饮食和柬埔寨、老挝、越南、印度尼西亚等东南亚国家基本相同。泰国菜是以鱼为原料的酸辣菜。因泰国三面环海，海鲜产品丰富，海鲜成为泰国菜的一大特色。泰国大米晶莹剔透，蒸熟后有一种特殊的香味，是世界稻米中的珍品。传统料理是除去黏性的米饭淋上掺满香辣作料的调味品。调味品的做法十分考究，一般是根据家传秘方烹调，堪称一门艺术。泰国人最喜欢的民族风味食品是咖喱饭，它是用大米调以辣椒、椰浆、肉片或鱼片，再配蔬菜和竹笋烹制的椰浆辣汤做成的。在泰国餐桌上，无论饭菜是否丰富，餐汤都是不能缺少的。泰国的餐汤主要分三大类：第一类是一种清淡的肉和菜汤；第二类是稀米汤；第三类是冬阴功汤，被称为"王者之汤"。汤的材料包括甘草、胡椒、柠檬、冬葱、鱼露等，再配上各种海鲜，由一个金鼎炭炉奉上，令人回味无穷。比较受欢迎的泰国菜有冬阴功汤、绿咖喱鸡肉、泰式炒面等。

Thai cuisine blends five fundamental tastes: sour, sweet, bitter, spicy and salty. Some common ingredients used in Thai cuisine include garlic, chili, lemon juice, lemon grass and fish sauce. The staple food in Thailand is rice, particularly jasmine rice which is included in almost every meal. Thailand is the world's largest exporter of rice. Thai cuisine is similar to that of Cambodia, Laos, Vietnam, Indonesia and other Southeast Asian countries. The main course is a hot and sour dish using fish as raw materials. Because the country is surrounded on three sides by the sea, there are rich seafood products, which is a major feature of Thai diet. The Thai steamed rice is crystal clear with a special flavor, and is the top species in the world. Its traditional food is stickiness-free rice garnished with hot seasoning spices. Condiment approach is very sophisticated, generally based on ancestral secret recipe, and can be regarded as an art. People in Thailand most like curry rice with national flavor, it is the rice garnished with chili, coconut milk, meat or fish, along with vegetables and bamboo shoots cooked in spicy soup of coconut milk. On the table, regardless of whether there are abundant foods, soup is always necessary. Thai soup is mainly divided into three categories: the first is a light meat and vegetable soup, the second is the dilute rice soup, and the third is Tom Yum Goong Soup, which can be considered the king of the soup. The materials of Tom Yum Goong Soup include liquorice, pepper, lemon, shallots and fish sauce, complemented with a variety of seafood, served in a golden charcoal oven. Popular dishes include Tom Yum Goong Soup (spicy shrimp soup), Kaeng Khiao Wan Kai (green chicken curry), Phat Thai (fried noodles of Thai style), etc.

（二）购物及退税

泰丝：近几十年来，因为独到的手工制作工艺、独特的外表质地，泰丝已成为别具一格的产品，在世界各地广受欢迎。泰丝被用来制作高贵的服饰、手帕、领带、围巾等。

Thai silk: Because of the unique handmade craftsmanship, appearance and texture, Thai silk has in recent years become distinctive in style and popular around the world. Thai silk is used to make sumptuous costumes, handkerchief, necktie and scarf, etc.

宝石：曼谷是世界上的有色宝石之都。红宝石和蓝宝石是本地产的宝石，但是事实上所有的有色宝石以及钻石都可以在这里买到。购物者要小心，应只在声誉好的经销商那里购买。

Gem: Bangkok is the capital of world colored gems. Ruby and sapphire are the local jewels, but in fact all colored gemstones and diamonds can be bought here. Customers are advised to be cautious and only shop from the established dealers.

漆器：漆器是清迈及泰国北部的特产。这种工艺包括在劈开的竹子和木头上涂漆，然后加上精致的手绘设计，典型的是黑底金线或棕红底黄绿线。游客可以购买漆器碗、盒子、盘子以及其他装饰品或纪念品。

Lacquer: That is the specialty of Chiang Mai and Northern regions. This process includes painting in a split bamboo and wood and then carefully designing the hand-painting. Typical types are black bottom with gold lines or brown red bottom with yellow and green lines. You can see lacquer bowls, boxes, trays and other decorations or souvenirs.

游客在泰国购买商品，离境时可以要求退还 7% 的增值税。如果购买了有“VAT Refund for Tourists”标志的商品，单一店购买超过 2 000 泰铢以上并且累积消费超过 5 000 泰铢，可在购物当天凭护照填写一张“旅客退税申请表”，然后打印一张“原始税费凭证”（这些表格可在服务中心或退税专用柜台索取，要求店员填写两份退税表格，将发票贴在表格上并盖章），在离境当天就可到机场退税。

Tourists who make purchases in Thailand are entitled 7% value added tax refund when returning home. Products with label "VAT Refund for Tourists", purchase above 2,000 baht in a single shop and a total expense above 5,000 baht in different shops can be accompanied with a VAT Refund Application for Tourist Form and an Original Tax Invoice for tourists' tax refund (these papers can be collected at the service center or tax refund counter, and will be made in two copies with the invoice sticking to the form of a seal). The tax refund can be made at the airport on the departure day.

（三）时差

泰国首都曼谷时间比北京时间晚一个小时。

Bangkok time is an hour later than that of Beijing.

思考练习

1. 经典旅游线路分析

新马泰完美10日游

第1天：杭州——曼谷

游客在指定时间、地点集合，在专业领队的带领下搭乘国际航班飞往曼谷素万那普国际机场。导游接机后入住酒店休息。

第2天：曼谷

早餐后，前往参观大皇宫。大皇宫汇集了泰国建筑、绘画、雕刻和装潢艺术的精粹，玉佛寺在大皇宫东北角，是全泰国唯一没有僧侣住持的佛寺，但供奉着一座价值连城的国宝——玉佛，该玉佛是由整块翡翠雕成的。之后参观马车博物馆。午餐后前往桂河大桥，带您前往观看拥有奇异神功的尼姑浮水表演。搭乘桂河地区特有的竹筏漂流屋，展开浪漫唯美的桂河之旅，在薄雾夜色中、晚风伴随下，乘坐竹筏顺流而下，边享用晚餐边起舞欢唱，后返回酒店。

第3天：曼谷——芭堤雅

早餐后，前往珠宝中心，欣赏闻名世界的泰国出产的红、蓝宝石，参观皮革展示中心。随后前往有"东方夏威夷"之称的度假胜地——芭堤雅，途中前往观赏独具特色的龙虎园，园内可欣赏到鳄鱼、老虎的表演及小猪赛跑等。

随后，充分体验放松身心的茉莉嘉泰式SPA养生之旅，享受专业按摩师亲切、细心的服务。从皇家药草烤箱、蒸汽浴、舒体百草芳香疗（全身精油按摩）到滋润护肤等泰式健康养生疗程，可令全身舒缓，并有美白兼去除暗沉之效果。最后再来上一杯独特的调制芳香养生茶及泰式小点心，保证让人身心更具活力，神采飞扬。亦可选择泰国国粹之一的泰式古法指压按摩（2小时），疏解连日来的疲劳。（二者任选其一）

第4天：芭堤雅

早餐后，乘快艇出海，蓝蓝的天、碧绿的海，让人陶醉于大自然的怀抱中。金沙岛有

“泰国仙境”之称，美丽的海湾、清澈的海水，徜徉在宁静的暹罗湾中，令人赞叹不已。

前往泰国最具特色的东芭乐园，此为景色秀丽的乡间度假胜地，园内有一个大型的表演场，可观看泰国传统民俗歌舞表演、独特的泰拳表演及精彩有趣的大象表演（跳舞、作画、踢足球）。

之后前往芭堤雅乡村俱乐部，体验趣味丛林骑大象，试试最原始的交通工具，并体验古代泰国人利用大象作为交通工具的情形。休息片刻后搭乘竹筏＋卡拉OK在湖中享受大自然的宁静，竹筏内准备了多首歌曲，不妨高歌一曲；还可以用专人准备的钓竿、鱼饵，体会一下垂钓的乐趣。上岸后前往观赏恐龙造型雕像，体验侏罗纪探险之旅。前往著名的猴子学校参观，观看训练猕猴的情形，并欣赏到猕猴在受训后所表演的各种逗趣画面。最后安排有趣的射飞镖比赛，比比看谁的奖品最丰富。之后特别安排品尝热带水果。

第5天：芭堤雅——曼谷

早餐后，前往七珍佛山上仿佛一斧劈开半山、镶上金粉金箔的大壁佛，九世皇庙是当今国王最爱的庙宇，庙中供奉着高僧的舍利子。休息一下再前往栩栩如生的蜡像馆参观，蜡像由泰国著名的师傅精心雕刻而成，犹如真人。

前往金三角少数民族文化村，此地模仿泰北“金三角”美斯乐而建，观赏毒王坤沙纪录片及博物馆内展览的海洛因、枪支、水烟管等物品，而后返回曼谷。

随后逛皇权（King Power）免税店，晚餐安排于湄南河上昭拍耶公主号游船，欣赏湄南河沿岸大皇宫、饭店、郑王庙等知名建筑交织的湄南河迷人景色，并品尝精致晚宴。随后欣赏独一无二的东方人妖秀（VIP座位），大型的舞台、华丽的服饰、亮丽的布景，表演完后可自由和这些“佳丽们”拍照。

温馨提示：

七珍佛山的大壁佛是为了庆祝泰王拉玛九世登基50周年，特别用激光雕刻的一座释迦牟尼佛像，此为芭堤雅最大的释迦牟尼佛像，用总计18吨重的24K黄金雕塑而成，七珍佛山中也曾挖掘出许多古佛像。

第6天：曼谷——新加坡

乘机前往新加坡，抵达后游览鱼尾狮公园（约30分钟），鱼尾狮演绎了新加坡如何从一个渔港“淡马锡”成为狮城的传奇故事，在这里还可以看到新加坡最新的文化艺术殿堂——滨海艺术中心，感受国际大都会的内涵，观赏英殖民地时代的建筑——国会大厦（约20分钟）。而后前往新加坡的“世外桃源”——圣陶沙岛音乐喷泉（约60分钟）。

第7天：新加坡——吉隆坡

早餐后，前往新加坡南部最高山——花芭山（约30分钟），观赏新加坡市区、南部岛屿及世界上数一数二的海港美景，参观珠宝店（约90分钟）、百货店（约45分钟）、免税店（约45分钟）。随后乘车前往马来西亚首都吉隆坡，沿途观赏棕榈园及橡胶林。

第8天：吉隆坡——云顶高原

早餐后，游览吉隆坡市区的国家清真寺（约20分钟）、独立广场（约20分钟）及皇宫（约20分钟），可与门前衣着华丽的侍卫拍照留念。而后参观珠宝加工厂（约90分钟）、巧克力店（约45分钟）。参观石油双塔（外观）（约20分钟）、首相官邸或首相府马哈迪故居（外观）（约15分钟）、水上清真寺（外观）＋太子广场＋首相署（外观）（约45分钟）、马来民居（约40分钟）后前往云顶高原，参观云顶赌场。

第9天：云顶高原——马六甲——新山

早餐后，前往马来西亚古城马六甲，参观葡萄牙殖民地时期遗留的建筑物，前往郑和下西洋时代遗留的古迹三宝山、三宝庙、三宝井（约20分钟），荷兰红屋（约20分钟），圣保罗教堂（约20分钟）等名胜。接着前往马来西亚的手工艺品锡器雕刻工厂（约45分钟）及土产店（约90分钟）参观选购，可带些小礼物回去馈赠亲友。

第10天：新山——新加坡——杭州

早餐后返回新加坡，前往机场办理登机手续，搭乘航班返回杭州，结束愉快的旅程。

分析：这条经典旅游线路的主要旅游景点与行程特色，以及适合旅游的人群。

2. 案例分析

[案例1] 某旅游团在泰国旅游，客人在导游的带领下参观了很多寺庙，回来后大家的袜子都有些脏了，这是为什么？

[案例2] 某游客看到一名泰国小孩很可爱，希望上前与之合影，便想要去抱那个小孩。导游见状，上前和客人说了一句话，但并未阻拦，请问导游说了什么？

3. 练一练

（1）请列举出五种具有泰国特色的旅游纪念品。

（2）请简述泰国特有的节日（至少两个）。

第六节　印度尼西亚

一、国家概况

（一）地理环境

印度尼西亚位于亚洲东南部，地跨赤道，是由太平洋和印度洋之间的约17 508个岛屿所组成的国家，陆地面积约为190万平方千米。这些岛屿均散布于赤道两旁，约6 000个岛屿有人居住，其中最大的岛屿为爪哇岛、苏门答腊岛、加里曼丹岛（与文莱、马来西亚共有）、新几内亚岛（与巴布亚新几内亚共有）和苏拉威西岛。印度尼西亚海岸线长54 716千米。印度尼西亚属于热带雨林气候，平均温度为25℃～27℃，是有名的"跨越赤道翠绿带"，高山地区气温要低一些。印度尼西亚分为旱、雨两季，旱季从5月到

10月，雨季从11月到次年的4月。

Located in southeast Asia, Indonesia goes through the Equator. Consisting of about 17,508 islands between the Indian Ocean and the Pacific Ocean, the country covers an area of 1.9 million square kilometers. These islands are scattered over both sides of the Equator, around 6,000 of which islands have local inhabitants. The largest are Java, Sumatra, Kalimantan (shared with Brunei and Malaysia), New Guinea (shared with Papua New Guinea) and Sulawesi. Its coastal line covers 54,716 kilometers. Indonesia has tropical rain forest climate with average temperature from 25℃ to 27℃, commonly known as "a green ribbon spanning over the Equator", while it is relatively cool in mountainous areas. It is divided into the dry season from May to October, and the rain season from November to the next April.

（二）人文概况

1. 历史

印度尼西亚在公元3—7世纪建立了一些分散的王朝。13世纪末14世纪初，东爪哇出现了强大的信奉印度教的麻诺巴歇封建帝国，对印度尼西亚产生了重要影响。15世纪，印度尼西亚先后遭葡萄牙、西班牙和英国入侵。1602年，荷兰在印度尼西亚建立了具有政府职能的荷兰东印度公司，开始了长达300多年的殖民统治。1942年日本入侵印度尼西亚，1945年日本投降后爆发了"八月革命"。1945年8月17日，印度尼西亚宣告独立，成立印度尼西亚共和国，苏加诺为首任总统，雅加达为首都。

There were some scattered dynasties established from the 3rd century to 7th century AD in Indonesia. The Hindu Majapahit Kingdom was founded in eastern Java in the late 13th century and early 14th century, and its influence stretched over much of Indonesia. In 15th century, the country was invaded by the Portuguese, the Spaniards and the Britons. In 1602, the Dutch established the Dutch East India Company (VOC) and became the dominant European power, which lasted more than 300 years. Japan invaded Indonesia in 1942 and the Revolution of August broke out in 1945 after the surrender of Japan. On August 17, 1945, Indonesia declared independence and founded Republic of Indonesia, Bung Sukarno became its first president and Jakarta has been the capital.

2. 经济

印度尼西亚的经济呈现多样化，私营部门和政府共同发挥着重要作用。该国是东南亚最大的经济体，也是20国集团的主要成员。2018年，印度尼西亚国内生产总值为1.042万亿美元。工业是该国经济最大的领域，占国内生产总值的46.04%（2013年），其次是服务业（37.1%）和农业（15.04%）。然而，从2010年开始，服务业雇用人员数量高于其他产业，占劳动力总数的48.9%，其次是农业（38.3%）和工业（12.8%）。但是农业一直集中了几个世纪来全国最多的劳动力数量。

Indonesia has a mixed economy in which both the private sector and the government play significant roles. The country is the largest economy in Southeast Asia and a key member of the G20. In 2018, Indonesia's gross domestic product was USD 1,042 billion. The industry sector is the economy's largest and accounts for 46.04% of GDP (2013), this is followed by services (37.1%) and agriculture (15.04%).

However, since 2010, service sector has employed more people than other sectors, accounting 48.9% of the total labor force, this has been followed by agriculture (38.3%) and industry (12.8%). Agriculture, however, had been the country's largest employer for centuries.

3. 社会文化

印度尼西亚人口约2.62亿，共有100多个民族，主要民族有爪哇族、巽他族、马都拉族。印度尼西亚的官方语言为印度尼西亚语，大多数民族拥有自己的语言。印度尼西亚的主要宗教有伊斯兰教、基督教新教、天主教、印度教、佛教和原始拜物教，全国约87.2%的人口信奉伊斯兰教，是世界上穆斯林人口最多的国家。

Indonesia has a population of about 262 million with a total of more than 100 nationalities. Its main ethnic groups are Java, Sunda and Madura. Indonesian is the official language of Indonesia. Most people have their own language. The main religions are Islam, Protestantism, Catholicism, Hinduism, Buddhism and primitive Fetishism. Across Indonesia, about 87.2% of the people believe in Islam, and it is the most populous Muslim country in the world.

近年来，印度尼西亚经济迅速发展，积累了大量社会财富，虽然人民生活水平有了较大的提高，但贫富悬殊的现象仍然是一大挑战。作为发展中的新兴经济体，印度尼西亚的产业结构调整正处在起步阶段，需要解决的问题还有很多。例如：农业发展滞后、科学技术落后，这是阻碍印度尼西亚经济结构调整甚至影响国民经济可持续发展的两大瓶颈。

Recently, Indonesia has witnessed rapid economic development and the social wealth has been accumulated immensely, but the gap between the rich and the poor still remains unchanged despite improvement in people's living standard. As a new emerging economy, the adjustment of the industrial structure is in the initial stage with many problems waiting to be resolved. For example, agricultural development lags behind, and also science and technology develop slowly, which are the two bottlenecks that hinder the Indonesian economic structural adjustment and even affect the sustainable development of nation's economy.

印度尼西亚国内有超过100多个种族，每个种族都有其不同文化，并已经发展了好几个世纪。这些种族的文化受到印度、阿拉伯国家、中国及欧洲的影响。例如：传统的爪哇和巴厘舞蹈蕴含印度教文化和神话元素，还有皮影戏演出。不同地区的纺织品呈现印度尼西亚跨度较大的艺术风格，如蜡染布、锦缎等。印度尼西亚建筑最主要的影响来自印度，但中国、阿拉伯国家及欧洲建筑的影响也是相当重要的。

Indonesia has about 100 ethnic groups, each with cultural identities developed over centuries, and influenced by Indian, Arabic, Chinese and European sources. Traditional Javanese and Balinese dances, for example, contain aspects of Hindu culture and mythology, as do wayang kulit (shadow puppets) performances. Textiles such as batik and brocade are created across Indonesia in styles that vary by region. The most dominant influences on Indonesian architecture have traditionally been Indian; however, Chinese, Arabic and European architectural influences are also significant.

二、民俗风情

（一）礼仪禁忌

在印度尼西亚，不要做如下行为：用左手给予、接受东西或吃东西。这是不被接受的，被认为是不礼貌的。左手是肮脏之手，通常在上完厕所后使用。这也正是人们认为左手肮脏的原因。

In Indonesia, don't do the following: to give, receive and eat with the left hand. To give, receive and eat with the left hand is unacceptable and considered impolite. The left hand is toilet hand. People usually use their left hand to clean up after relieving oneself. That is why they consider the left hand dirty.

不要触摸或拍别人的头部。头部是神圣的，应该得到尊重。成年人是不会拍别人的头的，小孩子的头也不能拍。

Don't touch or pat on other's head. The head is sacred and should be respected. Patting on other's head should not be done among adults and even should be avoided among children.

不要在别人面前吐痰。当印度尼西亚人很厌恶或看到恶心的东西时，他们通常会吐痰。如果你吐痰的话，别人会认为你在侮辱对方或你讨厌看到他们。唾沫也被认为是令人恶心的。

Don't spit in the presence of the others. When Indonesians are disgusted or see something disgusting, they usually spit. They would presume that you insult them or that you are disgusted at seeing them. Spittle is also considered nauseating.

另外，熟人、朋友相遇，用右手按住胸口互相问好，与人谈话应摘下太阳镜，将手放在臀部是不礼貌的。印度尼西亚人一般不会要求客人带礼物，但应邀赴宴时，客人送鲜花是合乎礼貌的。主人若有馈赠，推却不受是不礼貌的。印度尼西亚人敬蛇如神，但忌讳老鼠和乌龟。当地人不喜欢外国人当众接吻，裸体太阳浴是非法的。爪哇岛流行斗牛，在西班牙，斗牛是人牛相斗，而在这里是两牛相斗。

Besides, when acquaintances or friends meet, they greet each other by the right hand putting on the chest, and talk with others after taking off sunglasses. It is impolite to put one's hand on the hip. Indonesia people generally do not ask the guests invited to dinner to bring the gift, but it is polite to send flowers. If the host has a gift, it is impolite to decline it. They also respect the snake as god, but they regard mice or turtle as a taboo. Local people don't like foreigners kissing in public, and nude sunbathing is illegal. It is popular to organize bull fighting in Java Island. Unlike Spanish bullfighting, which is a man versus a bull in fighting, here it is a fight between two bulls.

（二）节庆风情

1. 建国五基诞生日（Pancasila Day）

印度尼西亚立国的基础是建国五项原则（又称“建国五基”），即潘查希拉，是建立该国基本制度的依据。印度尼西亚的国徽是神话中的鹰，鹰的胸前挂着一个盾牌，盾牌分为五个部分，分别代表五项原则，每项原则以一个物件为标志：五角星象征信仰安拉，榕树象征民族主义，野牛象征民主，铁链象征人道主义，棉花和谷穗象征社会公平。这一法定假日定为每年的6月1日。

The foundation of Indonesia's nation-founding is the five founding principles, namely, the Pancasila, and acts as rationale for its basic system. Indonesia's national emblem is a mythological eagle, with a shield on its chest. The shield is divided into five parts, each representing one of the five principles, each of which is embodied by an object as a symbol: the star symbolizes faith in Allāh, the banyan symbolizes nationalism, the bison symbolizes democracy, the chains symbolize humanitarianism, the cotton and cereal symbolize social fairness. This holiday is on June 1 every year.

2. 开斋节（Eid al-Fitr）

这是印度尼西亚最重要的节日。每年伊斯兰教历9月，全国的伊斯兰教信徒都要白天斋戒禁食，斋月后第一天便是开斋节。开斋节前夕，伊斯兰教信徒要进行慈善捐赠活动。开斋节法定只放假1天，但实际上一般都要放假3天以上，有的单位甚至放假1周以上。外出工作的人都要赶在开斋节前返回老家与亲人团聚。开斋节前夕是个不眠之夜，各个清真寺整夜念长经，诵经声通过高音喇叭传到四面八方。开斋节当天，家家户户打扫得干干净净，门前挂着用嫩椰叶制作的装饰物。人们都身着盛装，相互拜访。有些组织还会聚会，气氛热烈，一片喜庆景象。

This is the most important festival in Indonesia. During annual September of the Islamic calendar, the Islamists observe the fast of Ramadan, the first day after which is the Eid al-Fitr. On the eve of Eid al-Fitr, the Islamists must conduct charity activities. The legal festival is only one day off, but generally there are three days or more, some organizations or businesses even have more than one week. People working outside have to hurry to return home for family reunion before the festival. Eid al-Fitr's eve is a sleepless night, with reading all night in every mosque, chants spreading all around through loudspeakers. On the Eid al-Fitr day, every family clean houses with ornaments made of tender coconut leaves hanging on doors. Dressed in costumes, people visit each other. Some organizations even arrange the gathering in such a warm atmosphere and a festive scene.

三、主要旅游城市及景点

（一）雅加达（Jakarta）

印度尼西亚首都雅加达是东南亚第一大城市，世界著名的海港。它位于爪哇岛西北部沿海，人口1 027.7万。雅加达的历史悠久，早在14世纪就已成为初具规模的港口城市，当时叫巽他加拉巴，意思是“椰子”，当地华人称其为“椰城”。

Jakarta is Southeast Asia's top city and a world famous port. Located on the northwest coast of Java Island, it has a population of 10.277 million. Jakarta has a long history, and became a port city with certain scale as early as in the fourteenth century. At that time, it was called the Sunda Kalapa, which means coconut, and the local overseas Chinese called it city of coconut.

雅加达的旅游名胜众多。在东郊距市中心 26 千米处，有世界著名的印尼缩影公园，也称“迷你公园”，也有人称其为“缩影国”。公园占地 120 公顷，1984 年正式开放。全市有清真寺 200 余座，基督教新教及天主教教堂 100 余所，佛教与道教寺院数十座。班芝兰是华人集中地，附近的小南门是华人商业中心区。雅加达以东 10 千米的丹戎不碌是世界著名的海港。这里的寻梦园，也称“幻想公园”，是东南亚最大的游乐园之一。

Jakarta has many tourist attractions. In the eastern suburbs 26 kilometers from the city center, there is a world famous Miniature Park, also known as Mini Park, and some call it the epitome of the country. The park covers an area of 120 hectares, and has officially opened since 1984. The city has more than 200 mosques, over 100 Protestant and Catholic churches, as well as dozens of Buddhist and Taoist temples. Pancoran is the place for overseas Chinese, and nearby the South Gate is the Chinese central business district of Jakarta. Tanjung Priok, 10 kilometers east of Jarkata, is a world famous port. The Dream Garden here, also known as Fantasy Park, is one of the largest amusement parks in Southeast Asia.

（二）巴厘岛（Bali Island）

巴厘岛是印度尼西亚著名的旅游区，距印度尼西亚首都雅加达 1 000 多千米，与雅加达所在的爪哇岛隔海相望。巴厘岛面积约 5 620 平方千米，人口约 315 万。巴厘岛处于热带地区，气候炎热且潮湿。

Bali Island is a famous tourist district of Indonesia, 1,000 kilometers from the capital Jakarta, and faces across the sea to the Java Island where Jakarta is situated. Bali Island has an area of about 5,620 square kilometers, a population of about 3.15 million. Bali Island belongs to tropical area, so the climate is hot and humid.

巴厘岛上大部分为山地，全岛山脉纵横，地势东高西低。岛上还有四五座完整的锥形火山峰，其中阿贡火山海拔 3 142 米，是岛上的最高点。沙努尔、努沙杜瓦和库塔等处的海滩，是岛上景色最美的海滨浴场，这里沙质细腻、海水湛蓝且清澈。每年来此游览的各国游客络绎不绝。

Bali Island is mostly a mountainous island with mountain range going down from east to west. There are four to five complete conical volcano peaks on the island, including the Mount Agung with an elevation of 3,142 meters, which is the highest point on the island. Beaches on Sanur, Nusa Dua and Kuta are the island's most beautiful scenery, featured by fine sand beach and clear blue water. This scenery attracts millions of visitors every year.

巴厘岛的居民主要是巴厘人。因为历史上受印度宗教文化的影响，他们大都信奉印度教。全岛有庙宇 12 500 多座，因此，巴厘岛又有“千寺之岛”的美称。巴厘人的古典舞蹈典雅多姿，在世界舞蹈艺术中具有独特的地位。其中，狮子舞与剑舞最具代表性。

Residents of Bali Island are mainly local Bali people. Due to historical influence from Indian religion, the island mainly believes in Hinduism. Bali Island has more than 12,500 temples, so Bali Island is also known as "Island of Thousand Temples". Bali's elegant classical dance is another pretty scene. The art of dance takes up a unique position in the world cultures. Among them, the lions and the sword dances are the most typical ones.

巴厘岛的雕刻（木雕、石雕）、绘画和手工艺品也以其精湛的技艺、独特的风格闻名遐迩。在岛上处处可见木、石的精美雕像和浮雕，因此，该岛又有“艺术之岛”之誉。巴厘岛的绘画别具一格，大都是用胶和矿物颜料画在粗麻布或白帆布上，主题取材于田园风光和人们的生活习俗，具有浓郁的地方色彩。因此，巴厘岛素有“诗之岛”和“东方的希腊”的美称。

Bali Island's carving (wood carving, stone carving), painting and handicrafts are also well-known for its superb artistry and unique style. Everywhere on the island, you may be able to see exquisite statues and reliefs in wood or stone carvings, therefore, the island is also called “the Island of Art”. Bali's paintings have a style of their own, mostly glue and mineral pigments painted on the coarse linen or white canvas, and their themes are drawn from the pastoral scenery and people's living habits with strong local taste. Therefore, Bali Island is also known as “Poetry Island” or “Oriental Greece”.

巴厘岛风景如画，完美无瑕。岛上有许多休眠火山、火山湖、河流、热带雨林和白沙海滩。巴图火山锥和一个湖填补了一半的周边火山口，形成了巴厘岛最壮观的一处风景。

Bali Island's scenery is extraordinarily picturesque and immaculate. The island boasts numerous dormant volcanoes, crater lakes, rivers, tropical rain forests and white sand beaches. The volcanic cone of Mount Batur and a lake that fills half of the surrounding caldera, forming one of Bali Island's most spectacular landscapes.

（三）其他旅游城市及景点

◆ 婆罗浮屠（Borobudur）

婆罗浮屠位于印度尼西亚日惹，大约于公元 750 年至 850 年间，由当时统治爪哇岛的夏连特拉王朝的统治者兴建。“婆罗浮屠”这个名字的意思很可能来自梵语“Vihara Buddha Ur”，意思是“山顶的佛寺”。后来因为火山爆发，使得佛塔群下沉并在茂密的热带丛林中隐藏了近千年，直到 19 世纪初才被清理出来。婆罗浮屠与中国的长城、印度的泰姬陵、柬埔寨的吴哥窟并称为“古代东方四大奇迹”。联合国教科文组织将婆罗浮屠列入世界文化遗产名录。

Located in Yogyakarta of Indonesia, Borobudur was built by the ruler of Sailendra Dynasty between 750 and 850 AD. The name “ Borobudur” probably comes from the Sanskrit “Vihara Buddha Ur”, meaning “mountain temple”. Because of the later volcanic eruption, this complex of statues sank and were covered in dense tropical jungles for nearly a millennium, until the beginning of the nineteenth century. Along with the Great Wall of China, the Taj Mahal in India, the Angkor Wat in Cambodia, it has been known as one of the ancient oriental four wonders. UNESCO has put Borobudur in the list of World Cultural Heritage Site.

◆ 民丹岛（Bintan Island）

民丹岛是印度尼西亚廖内群岛中最大的岛屿。早在15世纪，郑和下西洋的记载中就已提及民丹岛。由于离新加坡很近，从新加坡搭乘渡轮到民丹岛只需45分钟，因此新加坡人把它当作后花园，这里也吸引了世界各地的游客。

Bintan Island is the largest island in Indonesia Riau Islands and is mentioned by Zheng He in his ship's log as early as the fifteenth century. Close to Singapore, it takes only 45 minutes in a ferry to reach there. The Singaporeans regard it as a backyard garden, and it also attracts a lot of tourists from all over the world.

民丹岛的面积是新加坡的3倍，人口却只有新加坡的1/10。踏上民丹岛，浓绿斑斓的热带植物、银色的绵长沙滩、碧蓝的海洋、各种国际级度假酒店以及一系列热带休闲活动令度假者心旷神怡。

Bintan Island is as big as three Singapore nations in size, but its population is one tenth as many as that of Singapore's. A tour on the island provides you with a view of green beautiful tropical plants, a long silver beach, blue sea, a number of world-class resort hotels as well as a series of leisure tropical holiday activities, making visitors feel refreshed.

四、旅游资讯

（一）美食

印度尼西亚地处热带，当地居民的主食一般为米饭。与东南亚其他国家相似，印度尼西亚菜肴总体偏辣，喜欢放各种香料调味，并且大量使用咖喱。各个地区的食材和调味料都不同：苏门答腊岛人喜欢把辣椒加入浓浓的椰子酱中调味，常吃牛肉和牛内脏；西爪哇岛人的酸辣汤是一大特色；中爪哇岛人习惯以虾酱佐餐，而北苏拉威西省人则喜欢将各式鱼类做成烩饭。由于天气炎热，因此当地还有用各种水果制作的冷饮和甜品。

Indonesia is located in intertropical area, and the staple food for local residents is rice. Like other countries in Southeast Asia, Indonesia food is overall hot with all kinds of spices and additional use of curry. In each region, the ingredients and seasonings are different. For example, Sumatra people like to add chili to thick coconut sauce seasoning and enjoy beef and beef offals. The hot and sour soup in West Java is one of the local delicacies. People in Middle Java are accustomed to shrimp paste for meal, and people in North Sulawesi like using fish to make risotto. Due to the hot weather, they also use a variety of local fruits to make cold drinks and dessert.

（二）购物及退税

银制品：分两大类，一类是我们熟悉的纯银或银合金制作的装饰品，另一类则是用一条纤细的银缕按图案设计焊接而成的装饰品。这些银制品做工精湛，玲珑剔透，十分美观。银制工艺品有很多的造型，有一些小巧玲珑的花形银胸针、银耳环，既美观又便于携带，常成为游客的首选之物。

Silver products: It can be divided into two categories. One is sterling silver or silver alloy, the other silver products are made of a thin silver thread welded according to the pattern design. The works are characterized with perfect workmanship, exquisite carving and beautiful appearance. Silver handicrafts have a variety of shapes, including little and dainty flower-shaped silver brooch, silver earrings, which are both beautiful and portable, and often become the first choice of the tourists.

木雕：印度尼西亚的木雕，尤其是巴厘木雕，享誉国内外，到印度尼西亚旅游的外国游客几乎无人不买一两件巴厘木雕留作纪念。巴厘木雕是一种传统工艺品，它最初与巴厘人的宗教信仰息息相关。人们把自己崇拜的印度教诸神用石头或木头雕刻出来，供奉在庙宇、庭院、堂室内。后来代代相传，便产生了无数能雕善刻的巧匠。巴厘木雕大都是用质地坚硬、花纹细密的乌木、柚木等木料雕刻而成，其造型千姿百态，有栩栩如生的神鹰、神牛、雄狮等动物及各种禽鸟，有惟妙惟肖的巴厘渔夫、少女，有民间故事中脍炙人口的传奇人物，也有当代各种抽象艺术形象。

Woodcarving: Indonesian woodcarving, especially Bali woodcarving, is renowned at home and abroad. When traveling to Indonesia, virtually foreign guests will buy one or two pieces of wood carving of Bali as a souvenir. Bali woodcarving is a kind of traditional handicraft, which is closely related to people's religious beliefs. People worship their Hindu gods carved with stone or wood, and enshrined in the temple, courtyard or indoors hall. With such a practice handed down from generation to generation, it has produced many good carving craftsmen. Most of Bali carvings are crafted from hard wood like ebony and teak with a wide range of shapes. These include condor, bull, lion and various birds really true to life, and lifelike Bali fishermen, girls and well-known legends in folklore as well as the images of contemporary abstract art.

巴迪布：巴迪布是一种蜡染印花布，其特点是布上印有多姿多彩的彩色图案，包括几何图形、花鸟图案、对称图案及不对称图案。其色彩一般以黑、红、黄为主，鲜艳明快，也有以蓝、褐、白为主的，看上去凝重、深沉。这种布不仅深受当地民众的喜爱，而且早已世界闻名。用它制作的长袖男衬衣和布裙已被指定为印度尼西亚的国服，适用于各种正式和非正式场合。游客在选购巴迪布时，原则上要注意其制造工艺，用传统手工绘制印染的巴迪布做工精细，具有较高的艺术价值，但因耗时费力，一般价格较贵。而机制的巴迪布，由于产量高，价格相对便宜，更经济实惠，但艺术价值逊于手工制品。

Batiks: It is a kind of batik printed cloth, which is characterized by the colorful patterns, including various geometric figures and flower motifs, symmetrical patterns and asymmetric patterns. Its color is generally bright such as black, red and yellow, and also featured dark colors like blue, brown and white. This cloth is not only deeply loved by the people of Indonesia, but also has long been world-renowned. The long sleeve shirt and Sarong produced from this fabric has been set as the Indonesian national dress, suitable for a variety of formal and informal occasions. While purchasing batiks, tourists should pay attention to the manufacturing process. The traditional handicraft dyeing batiks boast fine workmanship and thus the artistic value, but are relatively pricey out of the time-consuming effort. While the machine-made batiks, due to the high yield and lower price, seem more cost-effective but are less than the handmade products in artistic value.

游客同一天在同一个商店购买金额超过 50 万印尼卢比即可开具退税单，并在机场获得 10% 的退税。

If the purchase amount of tourists in the same shop exceeds 500,000 rupiah on the same day, a tax refund form can be issued. And the tourist can get a 10% refund at the airport.

（三）时差

印度尼西亚首都雅加达的时间比北京时间晚一个小时。

Jakarta time is an hour later than that of Beijing.

思考练习

1. 经典旅游线路分析

印度尼西亚新奇 5 日游

第 1 天：南宁——雅加达——巴厘岛

游客于指定时间在南宁吴圩国际机场集合，乘坐直航航班赴印度尼西亚首都雅加达，抵达后转内陆航班前往有“世外桃源”和“永远的度假天堂”之称的巴厘岛，到达后身穿传统服装的当地美女会为贵宾献上鲜花，由专业华语导游接机送往酒店休息。

第 2 天：巴厘岛

早餐后参观巴厘岛艺术重地马斯木雕、蜡染艺术村，接着参观闻名的乌布传统市场，选购巴厘岛当地民俗工艺品。午餐后前往巴厘岛的地标、海上明珠——海神庙，并将在金巴兰最浪漫的海滩享用晚餐。在这里，可以一边享用巴厘岛特色的海鲜烧烤，一边可以欣赏黄昏时美丽的海景。

第 3 天：巴厘岛

早餐后，前往海滨戏水胜地南湾海滩。午餐后，前往有着神话色彩的乌鲁瓦度望夫崖，观赏悬崖断壁的大自然奇景，远眺望夫崖，欣赏海天一色的美景，气势磅礴宛如一幅画，沿途亦可参观栖息于此的顽皮猴群。而后前往神鹰文化村，继而前往巴厘岛最著名的库塔海滩，享受惬意的阳光与椰树沙滩，这里是冲浪、滑水等水上活动的乐园。夜游巴厘岛最热闹的洋人街，此处有繁华的商业景象，可尽情地享受购物乐趣，餐后返回酒店休息。

第 4 天：巴厘岛

自由活动。

第 5 天：巴厘岛——雅加达——南宁

早餐后整理行李，由专人送往机场，乘机前往雅加达后，搭乘航班回南宁。游客抵达南宁机场后散团，返回温暖的家，结束浪漫的印度尼西亚之旅。

分析：这条经典旅游线路的主要旅游景点与行程特色，以及适合旅游的人群。

2. 案例分析

[案例1] 某旅游团在印度尼西亚旅游，在旅游大巴上，当地导游正在用手机打电话。其中一位游客想看一下那面很别致的导游旗，就要求导游拿给他看一下。由于导游正在用右手拿着手机接电话，他就用左手给客人把旗子递了过去，但同时说了声“对不起”，这是为什么？

[案例2] 某旅游团在印度尼西亚爪哇岛旅游，当地导游询问游客是否要前往观看斗牛比赛。因为该团有不少人曾去过西班牙旅游并亲眼看过西班牙斗牛，所以对爪哇岛的斗牛兴趣不大。但导游却说爪哇岛的斗牛与西班牙斗牛是不同的，请问有何区别？

3. 练一练

（1）印度尼西亚有哪些特色工艺品？

（2）印度尼西亚的景点特色与马来西亚有哪些相同和不同之处？

第七节 菲律宾

一、国家概况

（一）地理环境

菲律宾共和国位于亚洲东南部，西濒南海，东临太平洋，是一个群岛国家，共有大小岛屿7 000多个，其中2 400个岛有名称，1 000多个岛有居民。吕宋岛、棉兰老岛、萨马岛等为主要岛屿，被称为“西太平洋明珠”。全国划分为吕宋、维萨亚和棉兰老三大部分。

The Republic of the Philippines, located in Southeast Asia, is surrounded by the South China Sea in the west, Pacific Ocean in the east. As a country of islands, it has more than 7,000 islands, of which 2,400 have the names and 1,000 are inhabited by residents. Known as the “Pearl of the West Pacific Ocean”, its main islands are Luzon, Mindanao and Samar. Therefore, the country is divided into three parts: Luzon, Visayas and Mindanao.

菲律宾大部分由山地、高原和丘陵构成。多活火山，地震频繁。棉兰老岛的阿波火山是菲律宾最高的山峰。吕宋岛的马荣火山是菲律宾最大的活火山，也是世界最小的活火山。菲律宾的主要河流有棉兰老河、卡加延河，贝湖是菲律宾的最大湖泊。

The Philippines is geographically composed of mountainous areas, high lands and hilly regions. It is characterized by many live volcanoes and frequent earthquakes. Mount Apo on Mindanao is the highest mountain in the Philippines. Mayon Volcano on Luzon is the largest one and meanwhile the smallest one in the world. Mindanao River and Cagayan River are the main rivers in the country and the Laguna de Bay is the largest lake in the Philippines.

菲律宾北部属海洋性热带季风气候，南部属热带雨林气候，年平均气温为27℃，年降水量为2 000毫米～3 000毫米。夏秋季多雨、多台风。菲律宾海岸线长18 533千米，多天然良港，森林面积在40%以上，矿藏有金、银、铬、铜、锰、铁等。

The northern part of the country belongs to ocean tropical climate while the southern part belongs to tropical rain forest climate with annual average temperature of 27 ℃ and annual precipitation of 2,000 to 3,000 millimeters. The summer and autumn seasons witness frequent rainfalls and typhoons. Its 18,533 kilometers coastline offers many natural harbors. The forests cover 40% of the land with rich mines of gold, silver, chromium, copper, manganese, iron, etc.

（二）人文概况

1. 历史

在西班牙殖民主义者入侵之前，菲律宾沿海不少地区进入了早期封建社会。16世纪，葡萄牙著名航海家麦哲伦发现了这个东方群岛。1565年，菲律宾沦为西班牙的殖民地，西班牙用王储菲利普斯的名字命名该群岛为“菲律宾”，从此统治菲律宾长达300多年。直到19世纪末，菲律宾诗人何塞·黎刹领导独立运动。菲律宾于1898年6月12日宣布独立，可是在同年又沦为美国的殖民地。1942年太平洋战争中被日军占领。1945年美军反攻，光复了菲律宾。1946年7月4日宣告独立，成立菲律宾共和国，首都为马尼拉。美国对菲律宾的影响：英语占有主导地位以及对西方文化的认同。

Before invasion of the Spanish colonists, some coastal areas in the Philippines entered into the early feudal society. In the 16th century, the famous Portuguese navigator Magallanes discovered this oriental island complex. In 1565, the Philippines became a colony of Spain, and these islands were named after one Spanish royal member Duke Phillips, marking the 300-year colony over the Philippines until the end of the 19th century when the revolutionary poet Jose Rizal launched the independence campaign. The country announced independent on June 12, 1898. In the same year, however, it was placed under the United States colony again. It was occupied by Japanese troops in 1942. The US army counterattacked the Japanese in 1945 and recovered the Philippines. It gained independence on July 4, 1946 and the Republic of the Philippines was founded with Manila as the capital. The United States made English the dominant language in the Philippines and its identification of western cultures.

2. 经济

菲律宾是发展中国家、新兴工业国家及世界的新兴市场之一，但贫富差距很大。独立至今，菲律宾曾经历数次经济的快速成长。然而，政局时常动荡以及社会的不安定已成为阻碍其继续发展的一大因素。菲律宾的经济结构是以农业及工业为主，尤其着重于食品加工、纺织以及电子、汽车组件等轻工业。大部分的工业企业集中于马尼拉的市郊。此外，宿务近来成为外国投资集中地。菲律宾的矿产业有很大的发展潜力。除了地热及煤炭资源，近来发现的天然气也是菲律宾能源储备的一部分。

The Philippines is a developing country, emerging industrialized country and one of the emerging markets in the world, but the gap between rich and poor is large. Since independence, the Philippines has experienced rapid economic growth. However, frequent political turbulence and social unrest have become the obstacle to social development. Agriculture and industry are the mainstay of its national economy, particularly on food processing, textile, electronics and auto parts. Most industrial businesses are located around the suburb of Manila. Besides, Cebu is another focus for foreign investment. There is a great potential in the Philippines mine industry. Rich natural gas reserve has been found recently in addition to its geothermal and coal mines.

3. 社会文化

菲律宾的人口约1.2亿，主要民族是马来族，少数民族有华人、印度尼西亚人、阿拉伯人、印度人、西班牙人、美国人以及土著伊洛戈人。菲律宾的国语是他加禄语，电台、电视台主要使用英语。在菲律宾居民中，约85%信奉天主教，其他宗教还有基督教新教、佛教、伊斯兰教等。

The Philippines has a population of about 100.2 million. Main nationality is Malay. Ethnic minorities include Chinese, Indonesian, Arabic, Indian, Spanish, Americans and native Igorot. The Philippine's national language is Tagalog, but what is spoken in radio and television is mainly English.The Philippine's residents include about 85% Catholic and and those of other religions like Protestant, Buddhism, Islam, etc.

在菲律宾，等级保护制度存在于社会的各个角落。行政管理系统成了一个盘根错节的关系网络。这种与现代法理格格不入的机制与传统上人们对家庭、族群等的忠诚结合起来，便形成了一种公开的特权机制。国家权力被家族化、种族化、集团化，国家原则成了家族关系的放大。每一个官员的任命和升迁，都是政客和官员们在亲友中和家族中分配权力而发财致富的机会。因此，社会和组织运转都是以个人、家庭、密友关系为基础，保护与被保护关系是各个组织在民众中寻找追随者的基础。

In the Philippines, hierarchy protection system is filled in every corner of the society. Administrative management system has become complicated and difficult to deal with the relationship network. This modern jurisprudence mechanism is mixed with loyalty of traditional people on family, village groups, and thus forms a public privilege mechanism. The national power is based on the family, race and clique with amplification of national principles embodied from family relationship. Most official appointments and promotions are all manipulated by politicians and officials in their friends and family circles for distribution of power and wealth. Therefore, social and organizational operation are based on personal, family, close friends relationship. The protectors and protected relations served as the foundation for social organizations to look for the followers.

菲律宾文化结合了东西方文化。菲律宾文化中含有其他亚洲国家的元素，如马来西亚文化遗产，但也展现出大量西班牙和美国文化的影响。常见的传统庆祝节日主要是为了纪念节日的守护神，其中的莫里奥内斯节和仙奴诺节是最著名的。这些庆祝活动主要是聚餐、享受音乐和跳舞。然而由于现代化的发展，一些传统正在被改变或被逐渐遗忘。百雅尼汉菲律宾民族民间舞蹈公司因致力于维护菲律宾的传统民间舞蹈而闻名。该公司著名的标志性演出为菲律宾舞蹈如竹竿舞和辛基尔扇舞（singkil），其特点是使用碰撞的竹竿。

The Philippine culture is a combination of Eastern and Western cultures. The Philippines exhibits aspects found in other Asian countries with a Malay heritage, yet its culture also displays a significant amount of Spanish and American influences. Traditional festivities to commemorate the feast days of patron saints are common. The Moriones Festival and Sinulog Festival are a couple of the most well-known. These community celebrations are times for feasting, music and dancing. Some traditions, however, are changing or gradually being forgotten due to modernization. The Bayanihan Philippine National Folk Dance Company has been lauded for preserving many of the various traditional folk dances found throughout the Philippines. They are famed for their iconic performances of Philippine dances such as the tinikling and singkil that both feature the use of clashing bamboo poles.

知识拓展

菲律宾的海外劳工

鉴于国内经济不景气和政治上反对势力滋生等原因，菲律宾第10任总统——“强人”总统马科斯（1965年12月30日至1986年2月25日在任）开启国门，准许和鼓励本国人民赴海外打工，希望在改善国内民生的同时，缓解政治压力。自那时起，海外菲劳（OFW）渐渐成了菲律宾社会生活中不可或缺的重要角色。其中，菲律宾女佣更是成为国际劳务市场中的一大亮点。

菲律宾政府非常重视海外劳工，每年圣诞节海外劳工集中归国探亲时，政府就会在首都国际机场铺设红地毯，设立特殊快速通道。总统及海外劳工福利署等部门的官员还会专门举行接机欢迎仪式。

除了女佣，菲律宾的海外劳工还包括男性技工、海员和建筑工人等。这些海外劳工的汇款是菲律宾政府重要而稳定的收入，海外劳工也因此成为国家的“新英雄”。有统计表明，2016年，菲律宾收到海外劳工通过合法途径的汇款269亿美元，占GDP的7.3%以上。

二、民俗风情

（一）礼仪禁忌

菲律宾人对个人尊严很敏感，坦率和直言被视为鲁莽。菲律宾人喜欢送礼，也喜欢收取礼物，但接受礼物后不会当面打开。在社交活动中，遵守时间被视为过分热衷，菲律宾人一般会迟到15～30分钟。招呼别人时要伸直手臂，手掌向下，摆动手指，手掌向上被认为是一种侮辱。不能把手掌放在臀部或长时间用眼光直视别人，这往往是挑衅的象征。菲律宾人尽量回避13这个数字，集会聚餐不宜13个人，旅馆也没有13号房间。如果某月13日又逢星期五，则认为是大不吉利。如果被邀请到某人家里做客，被邀请者不可拒绝，否则会被认为是对邀请者的轻视。日常话题以婚姻、家庭、职业、烹饪等为主，避免谈论菲律宾内政、天主教会及政治人物。菲律宾人喜欢外国人赞扬他们的国家、家庭，适当得体的称赞会使双方成为朋友。

The Filipinos are sensitive to personal respect. Being frank or straightforward may be regarded as rudeness. They enjoy giving gifts as well as receiving gifts. They do not open the gift in front of the others. Punctuality for social activity is seen as over-enthusiasm, so normally they are 15 to 30 minutes later than the agreed time. In greeting, the arm should be stretched with the hand pointing downward and shaking hands. Hand pointing upward is considered disrespectful. One cannot put his hands upon his hip or stare at the others for a while, which would be seen as a provocation. The Filipinos avoid the number 13. They don't have parties with 13 people and there is no room 13 in hotels. If one day is the 13th and Friday, it is considered very unfortunate. One should not turn down others' invitation to their homes. Daily topics deal chiefly with marriage, family, profession and cuisine, etc. The internal politics, Catholic Church and political figures should be avoided. They enjoy being flattered for their country or family. Appropriate compliments may lead to good friendship.

（二）节庆风情

1. 国父逝世纪念日（Rizal Day）

何塞·黎刹祖籍中国福建，是一名医生，精通包括粤语在内的22种语言，并在文理各方面多才多艺。早在西班牙统治时期，年轻的黎刹就进行了改革运动，他是菲律宾反抗西班牙殖民统治、争取独立自由的民族英雄，于1896年12月30日被西班牙殖民者杀害。于是每年的12月30日被定为国父逝世纪念日，标志着菲律宾人民继承和发扬国父留下的宝贵财富，做一名对国家和社会有贡献的公民。

Jose Rizal, with ancestors from China's Fujian province, was a doctor and proficient in 22 languages including Cantonese, as well as in the arts and science. Since a young man, he has begun the reform under the Spanish domination, and became a national hero leading the Philippines against Spanish colonial rule. He was executed by the Spanish colonists on December 30, 1896. This memorial day is held on December 30th each year, marking the Filipinos inherit and carry forward these valuable treasures and become a citizen with contributions to the country and the society.

2. 五月花节（The May Flower Festival）

五月花节在5月的最后一个星期天举行。节日那天，小女孩们手捧花束献给圣母玛利亚。这天会举行圣母像大游行，未婚的少女们身穿缀满鲜花的白色长袍，跟随在圣母像后游行。

Held on the last Sunday in May, this festival witnesses the little girls holding bouquets of flowers in worship to the Blessed Virgin Mary. In a grand parade, unmarried girls in white and flowery robes follow the statue of the Notre Dame.

三、主要旅游城市及景点

（一）马尼拉（Manila）

马尼拉是菲律宾的首都。马尼拉之名源于一种生长着白艳花朵的湿地树，许多观赏过的人都以“那些白色的花开着，像一双双亮晶晶的眼睛”来形容它。马尼拉是一座具有悠久历史的城市。它在印度文明、中国文明及中亚古文明的基础上，融合西班牙、美国等国的西方文明，形成东西合璧的文化。

Manila is the capital of the Philippines. The name derives from the growth of white bright flowers wetland tree. Many who have watched the white flowers describe them as pairs of bright eyes. Manila is a city with a long history. Based on the Indian civilization, Chinese civilization and ancient civilization of Central Asia, it has fused with civilizations of Spain, the United States and the West, thus achieving the combination.

1571 年，西班牙殖民者米格尔·洛佩斯·德·莱加斯皮从马尼拉登陆，入侵、占领了菲律宾，并在现在的马尼拉市中心巴石河南岸建立了城堡和炮台。自那时起，这里便成了西班牙殖民统治当局的首府。如今的马尼拉已发展为一个世界级城市，以美丽的岛国风光和独特的文化背景吸引了来自世界各地的游客。由于受西班牙统治达 300 多年，因此马尼拉颇具西欧情调。马尼拉大都会区面积为 638.55 平方千米，人口 1 288 万，是全国最大的城市和经济、文化、交通中心，是亚洲最具欧洲特色的城市，有“亚洲的纽约”之称。

In 1571, the Spanish colonists Miguel López de Legazpi landed in Manila, followed by invasion and occupation of the Philippines. Then in what is now downtown Manila, castles and forts were built. Since then, it became the capital of the Spanish colonial authorities. Now Manila has developed into a world-class city, with beautiful island scenery and unique cultural background, attracting the visitors from all over the world. As a result of the Spanish rule for over 300 years, it has the Western European style. Metro Manila covers an area of 638.55 square kilometers with a population of 12.88 million. As the country's largest city and economic, cultural and transportation center, it is the most European style city in Asia and is also called “the New York of Asia”.

◆ 马拉卡南宫（Malacañang Palace）

马拉卡南宫原来是西班牙总督避暑的地方，西班牙语意为“有一个贵族”，具有 150 年历史，属于 18 世纪的新殖民主义风格，类似于美国的白宫。如果想追寻菲律宾历任领导人物的历史，这个地方可能是一个好的开始。

Originally as the summer house of the Spanish governor general, the Malacañang Palace (Spanish for “there's a nobleman”) is a 150-year-old, 18th century complex built in neocolonial style, resembling the White House of the United States. If you want to trace the history of the leadership that shaped the Filipinos, this place could be a good start.

◆ 西班牙古城（Intramuros）

西班牙古城是西班牙人在占领马尼拉时期所建的，对于游客来说，是非常值得一看的地方。它位于帕西格河南岸，是 16 世纪由西班牙人在马尼拉最古老的城区修建的。“Intramuros”取自拉丁文，字面意思为“墙内”，即城市或城堡内的墙壁，也描述了其结构及其周围有很厚很高的城墙及护城河。

Intramuros, the multifaceted city built by the Spaniards upon their occupation of Manila, is a marvelous place to spend the day in Manila. It is located along the southern bank of the Pasig River and was built by the Spaniards in the 16th century in the oldest district of the city of Manila. The name is taken from the Latin, literally meaning "within the walls", namely within the wall enclosure of the city or the fortress, and also describing its structure which is surrounded by thick, high walls and moats.

◆ 黎刹公园（Rizal Park）

黎刹公园，又名伦礼沓公园，俗称伦礼沓，是坐落在马尼拉市中心的一座历史性公园，毗邻马尼拉老城区。自西班牙殖民时期以来，该公园已成为市民喜爱的放松、社交、假日家庭野餐的选择地。它是马尼拉的一个主要旅游景点。

Rizal Park, also known as Luneta Park or colloquially Luneta, is a historical urban park located in the heart of the city of Manila, adjacent to the old city of Manila. Since the Spanish colonial era, the park has been a favorite spot for unwinding, socializing and an urban oasis for family picnics on holidays. It is one of the major tourist attractions of Manila.

（二）宿务（Cebu）

宿务是菲律宾最早开发的城市，被誉为"南方皇后市"。1521 年，葡萄牙航海家麦哲伦由西班牙出发进行环球航行，途中惊喜地发现了这个美丽、静谧的小岛。宿务位于维萨亚斯群岛的中心位置，全市人口 180 万，由 167 个岛屿构成，是菲律宾与国际衔接的第二大通道。宿务四周被群岛环绕，其间散布着棕榈环绕的渔村。

Cebu is the earliest developed city in the Philippines, known as the Queen City of the South. In 1521, the Portuguese navigator Magellanes sailed from Spain for around-the-globe voyage and surprisingly found this beautiful quiet island. Cebu is located in the center of Visayas Islands with a total population of 1.8 million, and is composed of 167 islands. It provides the Philippines with the second international access. Cebu is surrounded by the islands and scattered with fishing villages of palm trees.

◆ 圣奥古斯丁教堂（San Agustin Church）

圣奥古斯丁教堂建于 1565 年。自建造以来即被当作基督教传教的据点。这座教堂中最值得参观的是相传由麦哲伦运来的耶稣圣婴像，这座高约 40 厘米的圣像是麦哲伦在 1521 年送给女皇胡安，象征友谊的礼物。它受到了市民的热烈欢迎。

San Agustin Church was built in 1565. Since the construction, it has served as a Christian missionary base. The most worthwhile part for visitors is the statue of St. Baby Jesus, about 40 cm in height, believed to be transported from Magellanes according to the legend. It was a gift of friendship by Magellanes in 1521 to the Empress. It has been very popular among the citizens.

（三）长滩岛（Boracay）

长滩岛是位于菲律宾中部阿克兰省的苏禄海中的一个小岛，长 7 000 米、宽 4 000 米。

早在 1994 年，一家国际知名的英国旅游杂志就将其沙滩评选为世界最美沙滩之一，也是世界排名前十位的沙滩。

Located in Sulu Sea in the middle of the Philippines, Boracay of the Province of Aklan is a small island 7 kilometers long and 4 kilometers wide. It was awarded in 1994 by a famous tourism magazine of UK as one of the best beaches in the world, and also ranks top ten in the world.

长滩岛的魅力无穷，有热闹的集市、绚丽的夜晚、神秘的 SPA、各色酒吧等。游客在长滩岛可以进行多种活动，如乘着螃蟹船出海、海上垂钓、珊瑚花园浮潜、海底漫步以及品尝海鲜烧烤。

The Boracay is a charming place, where there are bustling markets, colorful night, mysterious SPA and various kinds of bars. Tourists have a variety of activities to do on the sea, such as taking crab boat, fishing, diving among coral reefs, walking at the sea bottom as well as enjoying seafood barbecue.

四、旅游资讯

（一）美食

多元化是菲律宾饮食的特点。由于有较多的中国移民，因此菲律宾的饮食也深受中餐的影响，米饭、粥、面条、饺子等中国食品在菲律宾随处可见，已成为菲律宾饮食文化的一部分。另外，由于曾受西班牙和美国的统治，菲律宾人也非常容易接受西班牙菜、美国菜、法国菜、意大利菜等西方菜系。在菲律宾，早餐多为西式，但中午和晚上则多为中餐，但中餐具有菲律宾的本土特色。

The Philippines' diet is characterized by plurality. With many Chinese immigrants, the Philippines' diet is also influenced by Chinese cuisine such as rice, porridge, noodle, dumpling and other Chinese food everywhere in the Philippines as part of the Philippines' diet culture. Having been colonized by Spain and the United States, the Filipinos are very ready to accept the Western cuisine like Spanish, American, French, Italian and so on. In the Philippines, most breakfasts are Western-style, but lunch and supper are mostly of Chinese style with the local characteristics of the Philippines.

当然，最受菲律宾人欢迎的当数本土菜肴。菲律宾菜肴的特点是大量使用醋、大蒜等辛辣调味料。菲律宾人最喜欢吃的是椰子汁煮木薯、椰子汁煮饭，然后用香蕉叶包饭。玉米作为食物，先是晒干，磨成粉，再做成各种食品。风味浓郁的海鲜则是菲律宾菜肴中最令人称道的。菲律宾也有众多颇具特色的小吃，包括烤乳猪“勒琼”、菲律宾春卷“鲁必亚”、椰子甜粽“苏曼”以及烤猪腿等，让游客一路走来嘴巴不停。菲律宾任何一家饭店的主餐厅中都会供应地道的菲律宾菜肴，以风味浓郁的海鲜最为有名。餐厅中常常有乐队演奏和民族舞蹈表演。游客若想品尝菲律宾风味，建议去菲律宾人开的小饭馆，既便宜，又地道。

Of course, the most popular cuisine in the Philippines is the local food. The Philippine cuisine is characterized by extensive use of vinegar, garlic and other pungent seasonings. The Filipinos like eating coconut juice boiled cassava, rice stewed by coconut juice with banana leaf. Corn can be dried first and then grounded into powder for various foods. Strong-flavored seafood is the most acclaimed item of the Philippine cuisine. The Philippines also has many distinguished snacks, including roasted suckling pig (Lechon), the Philippine spring rolls (Lumpia), rice cake (Suman) and roasted pork leg, allowing the visitors to keep eating on their way. The main hall of any of the Philippines' restaurants supplies authentic Philippine cuisine, with the rich flavor of seafood as the most famous. The restaurants often have the band and folk dance performance. The visitors are suggested to dine in small restaurants run by the Filipinos for their low cost and authentic taste.

知识拓展

烤乳猪

烤乳猪是菲律宾宴席上的主菜。菲律宾的烤乳猪是将一整只猪的内脏掏干净后，填入香蕉叶和其他香料，然后在炭火上慢烤，烤的时候在猪皮上刷上油，油里面加入了一种叫作 atsuwete 的调料，这样猪皮就会呈现出暗红色。在菲律宾，你可以买一整只烤乳猪或按斤称。马尼拉的 La Loma（一条美食街）有很多烤乳猪的连锁店。烤乳猪的食材最好的是年纪比较小的猪，这种猪的皮比较嫩、油脂少。

（二）购物及退税

菲律宾以丰富的手工艺品而闻名。有各种各样的手工艺品可供选择，如马尼拉麻帽、杯垫、贝壳风铃、竹托盘和陶瓷花盆等。这些工艺品可以作为馈赠亲友的上佳礼品。推荐可购买的纪念品是篮筐、垫、鞋和包，以及刺绣、木雕、珠宝、古董和铜器等。

The Philippines enjoys high reputation on rich handicrafts. There are many choices for customers such as Manila linen hats, cup mats, shell wind bells, bamboo tray and ceramic vases, etc. These products are great gifts for friends or relatives. The recommended souvenirs are basketries, mats, shoes, bags as well as embroidery, woodcarving, jewelries, antiques and bronze wares.

吕宋雪茄：菲律宾是上等雪茄的原产地之一。如果有喜欢或者需要的朋友，可以购买一些自用或送人。

Luzon cigars: The Philippines is one of the original places for the finest cigars. Cigar lovers may buy local products here for themselves or friends.

水果干：水果干是很好的礼品，如芒果干。与新鲜的芒果风味不同，芒果干有一种特别的味道。此外，还有香蕉干等其他水果干。

Dried fruit: Dried fruit is a good gift such as dried mango. Unlike fresh mango flavor, it offers a kind of special taste. There are also other varieties like dried bananas.

菲律宾木雕：菲律宾的木雕工艺品比较有名，大多具有欧洲风格。建议游客到当地的木雕作坊去挑选或定做。

The Philippine wood carving: the Philippine wooden crafts are relatively well-known and most have European style. The tourists are advised to visit the local wood workshop to pick a product or get it tailor-made.

（三）时差

菲律宾首都马尼拉与北京之间没有时差。

There is no time difference between Manila and Beijing.

思考练习

1. 经典旅游线路分析

菲律宾奇幻5日游

第1天：上海——马尼拉——长滩岛

游客在上海浦东国际机场集合，办理好登机手续后搭乘航班前往菲律宾首都马尼拉，后转国内航班飞往卡利博国际机场，抵达后转车到码头，继而乘快船直达目前菲律宾宣传力度最为强劲的观光地之一——长滩岛。

第2天：长滩岛

清晨享用早餐后，搭乘菲律宾特有的螃蟹船出海。首先来趟海上垂钓之旅，接着前往珊瑚花园浮潜、游泳，欣赏铺满珊瑚的海底。近午，前往景致优美的海湾，在大自然的美景下，享用独具菲式风味的海鲜烧烤，餐毕后返回度假酒店。

第3天：长滩岛

自由活动。

第4天：长滩岛——马尼拉

早餐后，乘船转车搭乘飞机返回马尼拉，抵达后驱车前往参观菲律宾著名的旅游胜地黎刹公园、象征民族独立的历史纪念碑、马尼拉大教堂，后途经日落大道游览建筑新颖的菲律宾文化中心及气派宏伟的国际会议中心。结束后可以前往大型商场自由购物。后返回酒店休息。

第5天：马尼拉——上海

早餐完办理退房手续后全天自由活动。游客也可选择自费参加各种境外配套活动项目或到岛上的水上活动中心体验一系列刺激而有趣的海上活动项目。后返回马尼拉机场搭机返回上海。

分析：这条经典旅游线路的主要旅游景点与行程特色，以及适合旅游的人群。

2. 案例分析

[案例1] 某旅游团在菲律宾旅游，游客入住酒店后，团友甲要求与团友乙和丙住隔壁。已知甲住1012房间，乙住1011房，那么丙应该住几号房间?

[案例2] 某旅游团在菲律宾旅游，全体团员将要出席一场晚宴。晚宴准时开始，但当地的客人还没到。请问这是一种不礼貌的行为吗?

3. 练一练

（1）请简述黎刹公园的历史。

（2）请讨论菲律宾人社会生活中最重要的两个方面。

第二章
大洋洲

本章导航

大洋洲（Oceania）的名字源于西班牙语，意思是“大洋中的陆地”，主体部分是澳大利亚大陆，因此，直到今天还有人把大洋洲称为澳洲。大洋洲位于太平洋西南部和赤道南北广大海域中，在亚洲和南极洲之间，西邻印度洋，东临太平洋，并与南、北美洲遥遥相对。大洋洲一般包括澳大利亚大陆、塔斯马尼亚岛、新西兰南北二岛、新几内亚岛，以及波利尼西亚、密克罗尼西亚、美拉尼西亚三大群岛，共有10 000多个岛屿。大洋洲共有16个独立国家，还有美、英、法等国的属地，如美国的塞班岛、法国的塔希提岛。目前，中国出境游客前往大洋洲的主要旅游目的地为澳大利亚、新西兰、塞班岛和塔希提岛。

第一节　澳大利亚

一、国家概况

（一）地理环境

澳大利亚，全称澳大利亚联邦，又称澳洲，位于南半球的大洋洲，属于东半球。澳大利亚面积为 769.2 万平方千米，国土面积位列全球第 6，是大洋洲最大的国家，东南邻新西兰，西北邻近印度尼西亚，北边邻巴布亚新几内亚及东帝汶。

Australia, officially the Commonwealth of Australia, or known as the Continent of Australia, is part of Oceania in south and in the east hemisphere. Covering an area of 7.692 million square kilometers, it is by area the 6th largest country in the world and the largest in Oceania. Across the sea, Australia is neighbored by New Zealand to the southeast, Indonesia to the northwest, Papua New Guinea and East Timor to the north.

澳大利亚四面环海，占有大洋洲的大部分土地。澳大利亚所处的位置又称为澳大利亚大陆，是地球上最小的大陆板块。澳大利亚境内多沙漠和半沙漠（约占 44%），平均海拔为 300 米。澳大利亚东部和东南部地势较高，西部为高原，中部为平原。东北部的大堡礁是世界上最大的珊瑚礁群。

Australia is surrounded by sea and occupies most of the land in Oceania. The location of Australia is known as Australian continent. It is the smallest continental plate on the earth. Most of the Australia land is covered by desert or semi-desert (44%) with an average altitude of 300 meters above the sea level. The eastern and southeastern part of the terrain is higher. The west is highland and the central is plain. The Great Barrier Reef in the northeast is the largest coral reefs in the world.

澳大利亚是全球最干燥的地区之一，西部和内陆沙漠为热带沙漠气候，北部属热带稀树草原气候，少数地区为亚热带气候。年平均气温北部为 27℃，南部为 14℃。

Australia is one of the driest area in the world. The west and the desert of inland is in the tropical desert climate zone, the north part is in the tropical savanna climate zone with few areas in the subtropical zone. The annual average temperature is 27℃ in the north and 14℃ in the south.

（二）人文概况

1. 历史

在英国人来澳大利亚大陆以前，这块大陆生活着土著人。1657 年，荷兰人最早来到这块大陆，但他们认为该地无资源，因此选择放弃。1770 年，英国航海家詹姆斯・库克发现这块大陆并将其命名为“新南威尔士”，宣布其为英国领土。美国独立战争后，英国需要一块地方安置犯人，1788 年 1 月 26 日，阿瑟・菲利普船长带着第一批犯人登陆澳大利亚，并建立了第一个英国殖民区。1 月 26 日也被定为澳大利亚的国庆日。此后很长一段时间，澳大利亚成为英国的犯人流放地。由于需要技术人员来生产粮食、建造房屋，英国又陆续迁移了许多民众，悉尼成为第一座城市。1797 年，英国军官约翰·麦克阿瑟由好望角引进一批西班牙美丽诺羊，澳大利亚畜牧业迅速发展起来。19 世纪 50 年代，在新南威尔士和维多利亚两州发现金矿，大批来自欧洲、美洲的淘金者蜂拥而至，澳大利亚人口迅速增长。1901 年 1 月 1 日，6 个殖民区组成联邦，建立澳大利亚联邦，成为大英帝国的自治领，实际是个独立国家。1931 年，取得内政和外交权。第二次世界大战以后，澳大利亚政府启动移民计划，该计划已为澳大利亚带来 600 多万移民。1986 年，英国女王签署《与澳大利亚关系法》，英国法律在澳大利亚失效，澳大利亚正式脱离英国成为真正意义上的独立国家。

Before the arrival of the Britons, the Continent of Australia had long been inhabited by indigenous Australians. In 1657 the first group of Dutch explorers visited here but failed to settle down simply because it was lack of resources. It was not until 1770 when Captain James Cook, the great navigator, found this continent and named it New South Wales before claiming it a British territory. After the American Revolutionary War, Britain needed a location for the prisoners. On January 26, 1788 Captain Arthur Philip and the first British fleet arrived here, and later the first British colony was established. The date January 26 was later designated as the National Day of Australia. Australia had since served as the penal colony for a long time. Meanwhile, due to the need of labors for farming and house building, many British free men emigrated to Australia and Sydney was established as the first city. In 1797, John MacArthur, a British army officer, purchased a portion of a small flock of Spanish merinos imported from the Cape Colony, contributing them to the fast development of animal husbandry in Australia. In 1850s, gold mines were discovered in New South Wales and Victoria, attracting a great many gold diggers from Europe and America, which accelerated the growth of population in Australia. On January 1, 1901, the six crown colonies federated, forming the Commonwealth of Australia, as a dominion of the British Empire, but actually it was already an independent country. In 1931, it obtained the right to deal with its domestic and foreign affairs. After the Second World War, Australian government launched a migration program, as a result of which more than 6 million people have come to Australia as new settlers. In 1986, the British Queen signed *the Australia Act* that ended all power of the UK Parliament for effective legislation in Australia, and Australia has since become a truly independent country.

2. 经济

澳大利亚国民的生活水平很高，是全球经济最发达、生活水平最高的国家之一。2013 年，澳大利亚在世界人均国内生产总值排名中位列第 5，在 2 000 万人口以上国家中排在第 1 位。农业、采矿业、制造业和服务业是澳大利亚的支柱产业。澳大利亚农业、畜牧业发达，自然资源丰富，享有“骑在羊背上的国家”“坐在矿车上的国家”“手持麦穗的国家”“南半球的聚宝盆”“野生动物的世外桃源”“珍奇植物的王国”等美称。澳大利亚凭借其得天独厚的自然条件和地理优势大力发展服务业，特别是旅游业和教育业。教育业是澳大利亚继旅游业之后的一项新兴产业，在世界范围内占有重要地位。每年全球有不少学生来澳大利亚深造，为该国带来丰厚的外汇收入。

Australians enjoy a high quality life and it is one of the most developed countries with the highest standard of living. In 2013, Australia ranked the 5th in GDP per capita worldwide and the first among the countries with the population of more than 20 million. Agriculture, mining, manufacturing and service are the pillar industries in Australia. Rich in natural resources and developed in agriculture and animal husbandry, it is reputed as "the country riding on sheep's back", "the country on a mine car", "the country holding wheat ears", "the cornucopia of the south hemisphere", "the paradise for wild animals" and "the kingdom of rare plants". The natural blessings and geographical advantages combined greatly promoted the development of service sector, especially tourism and education. Education is another booming industry after tourism and it takes the leading position in the world. Every year a large number of students come to Australia to further their studies, bringing with abundant foreign exchange earnings for the country.

3. 社会文化

自英国移民踏上这片土地，已经先后有 120 个国家、140 个民族的移民来到澳大利亚谋生与发展。这是一个典型的移民国家，被社会学家们称为“民族的大拼盘”，多民族形成的多元文化是澳大利亚社会的一个显著特征。澳大利亚总人口约 2 544 万，其中英国及爱尔兰后裔占 74%，亚裔占 5%，土著人占 2.7%，其他民族占 18.3%。大多数居民信奉基督教。据统计，澳大利亚的亚裔人口正在迅速增长，他们来自中国大陆和中国台湾、印度以及越南等。澳大利亚的通用语言是英语，其次是意大利语、汉语（粤语、普通话）、希腊语、阿拉伯语和越南语。

Ever since British immigrants disembarked on this land, immigrants from 120 countries and 140 nationalities have come to Australia to seek a livelihood. It is a typical immigrant country and is compared to the melting pot of nations by the sociologists. Multi-cultures created by different nations are a prominent characteristic of Australian society. The total population of Australia is about 25.44 million, among which 74% are British and Irish descendants, 5% Asian descendants, 2.7% indigenous Australians and 18.3% the rest. Most of them believe in Christianity. According to a survey, the population of Asian Australians is growing rapidly, such as those from the mainland of China, Taiwan, India and Vietnam, etc. English is the most commonly-used language in Australia, followed by other languages like Italian, Chinese (Cantonese and Mandarin), Greek, Arabic and Vietnamese.

澳大利亚是一个移民国家，澳大利亚的发展史从 1788 年第一批英国人登陆澳大利亚东海岸算起来才 200 余年，独立建国史从 1901 年澳大利亚联邦成立算起才 100 余年，而且它至今还是个英联邦国家，与英国有着密切的联系，英国文化一直是主流。但 20 世纪 60 年代后，随着美国文化的输入和新生代移民的成长，以及音乐、艺术、电影、文学等方面和当地土著文化的交融，新的澳大利亚文化形成了。一方面，它体现在土著人的绘画、文学和音乐中；另一方面，也体现在西方传统的艺术、文学、现代舞蹈、电影、歌剧和戏剧中。亚太地区文化也是影响澳大利亚文化的一个重要因素。

Australia is an immigrant country with short history. It has only over 200 years of history since 1788 when the first group of British settlers arrived at the east coast of the continent, and a little more than 100 years of history since 1901 when the Commonwealth of Australia was established. Even till now it has still been a country of Commonwealth of Nations and has close touch with the UK. The British culture has always been the main stream. Since 1960s, with the import of American culture and the grown-up of the new generation of immigrants, as well as the blending with the aboriginal culture in the form of music, art, film and literature, a new Australian culture has come into being. It is reflected in both aboriginal paintings, literature and music on the one hand, and traditional western arts, literatures, modern dance, films, operas and plays on the other hand. The Asian-Pacific culture is also an important element in forming Australian culture.

澳大利亚土著文化的历史可以追溯到20 000年前。土著人有丰富的口头传说以及与祭祀有关的原始舞蹈，但最突出的还是绘画。绘画是土著人记录历史、延续文化的一种重要手段。土著人绘画的内容以梦幻为永恒的主题，描绘了各种神话传说及土著人的风俗习惯和生活情景。土著人绘画的形式主要有岩画、树皮画和沙石画，这些都笼罩着一层神秘的色彩。

The history of Australian aboriginal culture can be traced back to 20,000 years ago. Indigenous Australians have abundant oral lores and primitive sacrificial dances, but the most prominent one is painting, which is an important means to record history and carry on the culture. Indigenous painting features the theme of dreamtime story, depicting variety of myths and legends, as well as the indigenous customs and scenes of life. It includes works in a wide range of media, such as painting on rocks, barks and sandpainting, which are all wreathed in mystery.

澳大利亚出现了一批著名的作家，其中帕特里克·怀特和托马斯·基尼利无疑是澳大利亚文学巨匠。1973年，帕特里克·怀特以《风暴眼》获得诺贝尔文学奖，是澳大利亚第一位获得诺贝尔文学奖的作家。托马斯·基尼利的许多作品都被拍成电影，如《辛德勒名单》等。

A large number of famous authors appeared, among whom Patrick White and Thomas Kenealy were undoubtedly the great masters. For his novel *The Eye of the Storm,* Patrick White was awarded the Nobel Prize in literature in 1973, and thus became the first Nobel laureate in literature in Australia. Many works of Thomas Kenealy have been made into films such as *Schindler's List*.

澳大利亚的绘画和建筑丰富多彩，独具特色，风格也不同于其他地区。澳大利亚在文化遗产保护方面颇有成效，而且政府也非常关注能源节约和环境保护。

Rich, colorful and distinctive, the Australian styles of painting and architecture are different from the other areas. Architectural heritages are well preserved and attentions have also been paid to energy conservation and environmental protection.

二、民俗风情

（一）礼仪禁忌

从主流文化的角度而言，澳大利亚属于西方文化，民众的生活方式与西欧和北美相似。澳大利亚的生活轻松、舒适且充满各种可能。来自世界各地的移民大都喜欢这里的生活。澳大利亚人既有西方人的爽朗，又有东方人的矜持。澳大利亚人的风俗礼仪在许多方面同英国人十分相似。澳大利亚人在公共场合不会喧哗，讲究礼貌，待人谦恭有礼。人们相见总是热情打招呼，握手致意，彼此称呼对方的名字，男女老幼均是如此。在社交场合，澳大利亚人显得非常随和，喜爱同陌生人交往，对待客人也是如此。如同英国社会，澳大利亚社会同样遵循“女士优先”的原则。在社交场合打哈欠、伸懒腰也是不礼貌的。

The main stream of Australian culture essentially belongs to the western culture. The lifestyle is similar to that of Western Europe and North America. The life here is slow-paced, comfortable and full of possibilities. Those immigrants from all corners of the world enjoy living here. Australians have both the candidness of the western people and the reservedness of the oriental people. The Australian customs are quite similar to the British in many aspects. Australians usually do not talk aloud in public, and are polite and courteous.They greet each other warmly with handshakes. They tend to call each other's names, regardless of gender and age. On social occasions, Australians are very easygoing and like to make contact with strangers, so is it with guests. Like Britain, Australia advocates the practice of “lady first”. It is considered rude to yawn or stretch oneself in social situations.

澳大利亚人的时间观念很强，约会要提前联系并准时赴约。如果被邀请到澳大利亚人家中做客，最合适的礼物是给女主人带上一束鲜花，澳大利亚人喜欢喝酒，也可以给男主人送一瓶葡萄酒。告别时，客人最好对主人的款待表示感谢。澳大利亚人好流动，频频变换居住之地，很少固定在一个地方终其一生。澳大利亚人也爱旅游，并乐在其中。他们兴趣广泛，喜欢体育运动，如冲浪、帆板、赛马、钓鱼、澳式橄榄球及游泳等。

Australians have a strong sense of time. Appointment should be made in advance if you want to meet someone and be punctual. If you are invited to an Australian family, a proper gift could be a bunch of flowers for the hostess or a bottle of wine for the host, as they love drinking. When you leave, you had better express your gratitude for their hospitality. Australians are fond of being mobile and changing their residences frequently. Few of them would stay at one place for his or her whole life. They enjoy traveling and have wide interests, especially sports, such as surfing, sailing, horse racing, fishing, Australian rugby and swimming, etc.

澳大利亚是一个非常重视生态环境保护和建设的国家。在有序、高效的管理体制下，整个澳大利亚就像是一个生态乐园。澳大利亚是世界上最早出台环境保护法的国家之一。政府和国民的生态环境意识都很强，政府在生态环境保护和建设中发挥了非常重要的作用。在澳大利亚，不论是个人、企业，还是政府机构，只要违反了环保法律、法规，都会受到严惩。在著名的大堡礁绿岛公园，游客不允许带走任何自然物体（包括贝壳），违者将处以高额罚款。在昆士兰州北部地区，有人曾因砍伐20多棵树而被判刑10年。在维多利亚州，环保局每年都要向法院起诉40～50起损害环境的案件。例如：澳大利亚曾遭遇百年不遇的大旱，一些地方终年滴雨未下，许多城市都出台了严厉的节水措施，严格限制洗车、浇草坪等的用水时间。任何人违反，都要受到处罚。

Australia lays great emphasis on ecological and environmental protection and construction. Due to the effective administration system, the whole country is essentially a large ecological park. Australia is one of the first countries that implemented the law of environmental protection. Both the government and citizens have a strong ecological and environmental consciousness. The government plays a very important role in ecological and environmental protection and construction. In Australia, any one, any company or even government agencies will face investigation and punishment in case it should violate the laws and regulations of environmental protection. In the well-known Green Island of Great Barrier Reef, the visitors are forbidden to take any natural object (including shells) from it, and violators have to pay large amount of fines. In the north of Queensland, a man was jailed for 10 years for having cutting down more than 20 trees. In Victoria, Environmental Protection Agency files 40–50 lawsuits every year over environmental destruction. A devastating drought once occurred in Australia, and in certain area you never see even a drop of falling rain, thus, very strict water conservation measures were implemented to limit the time spent on some water consumption such as car washing and watering lawn. Any violator will be punished.

居住在澳大利亚的土著人仍然保留着自己的风俗习惯。他们以狩猎为生，"飞去来器"是他们独特的狩猎武器。很多土著人仍居住在用树枝和泥土搭成的窝棚里，围一块布或用袋鼠皮蔽体。他们喜欢文身并在身上涂抹各种颜色，一些土著人会佩戴臂环、项圈、前额箍和骨制鼻针。随着时代的变迁，一些土著人渐渐离开部落，搬迁到城市居住。在旅游区，土著人的艺术品和手工艺品深受游客的喜爱，这也是土著人的主要收入来源。

Australian aborigines or indigenous people still hold onto their traditional customs and habits. They make a living by hunting with their characteristic hunting weapon Boomerang. Many of them live in shacks made by tree branches and mud, their bodies covered by a piece of cloth or kangaroo fur. They like tattoos and painting all kinds of colors on their bodies. Some wear arms band, collar, forehead hoop and nose piercing bone needles. With the passage of time, some aborigines have left their tribes and settled down in city. In tourist areas, the aboriginal works of art and handicrafts are favored by tourists, and it becomes the main source of income for the aborigines.

（二）节庆风情

1. 澳大利亚日（Australia Day）

1788年1月26日，阿瑟·菲利普船长和他的第一舰队携带1 350人（其中多数是囚犯）抵达悉尼港，英国殖民者开始在澳大利亚定居。后来，这一天被定为澳大利亚国庆日，即澳大利亚日。每年1月26日这天，澳大利亚各大城市都会举行各种大型的庆祝活动，其中之一是入籍仪式。近年来，澳大利亚日的活动非常强调"多元文化构成澳大利亚"的重要特质，即各族居民分享传统习惯、文化、语言和宗教信仰。

On January 26, 1788, Captain Arthur Phillip and his First Fleet arrived at Sydney harbour with more than 1,350 people, among whom most were prisoners, and it marked the day when British colonists started settling in Australia. Later this special day was designated the National Day of Australia or known as Australia Day. On this day, all kinds of celebrations will be launched in the big cities all over the country, and naturalization ceremony is one of them. Over the recent years, the National Day celebrations have stressed on an important characteristic that Australia is made by multi-cultures. People of different races learn about different traditional customs, cultures, languages and religious beliefs.

2. 墨尔本赛马节（Melbourne Cup）

虽然澳大利亚仅有200多年的历史，但始于1861年的“国民运动”——墨尔本赛马节已经有近150年的传统。墨尔本赛马节是澳大利亚最重要的赛马盛事，是澳大利亚人众所周知的“让整个国度屏住呼吸的赛事”。每年11月的第一个星期二为全国公假日，家家户户都穿着节日盛装，兴致勃勃地参加这一盛典。全球的澳大利亚人无论身处世界何处，都会驻足观看这场赛事并为他们喜爱的赛马冲线而兴奋喝彩。墨尔本赛马节深深地嵌入澳大利亚的文化，并成为这个国家的一个象征。

Australia has only a short history of more than 200 years, but Melbourne Cup considered as the national sport, which originated in 1861, boasts a tradition of nearly 150 years. Marked as “the race that stops the nation”, Melbourne Cup is the most important horse race event in Australia. The event falls on the first Tuesday of November, also a public holiday. Every family will be dressed up and take part in this event with great enthusiasm. Wherever Australians are around the world, they would stop to cheer in excitement for their favorite horse dashing the line. Melbourne Cup is deeply rooted in Australian culture and, therefore, has become a symbol of the country.

三、主要旅游城市及景点

（一）悉尼（Sydney）

悉尼位于澳大利亚东南部，是新南威尔士州的首府，是澳大利亚最早开发的城市，它是以当时英国内务大臣悉尼子爵的名字命名的。悉尼是澳大利亚的经济中心与文化中心，澳大利亚第一大城市，也是著名的旅游城市。同时，悉尼是澳大利亚最繁华的现代化、国际化城市，有“南半球纽约”之称。

Located in the southeast of Australia, Sydney is the capital of New South Wales. It is the earliest developed city and was named after the British Home Secretary, Viscount Sydney. As the largest city of the country, Sydney is the economic and cultural center and a well-known tourist city as well. The city is reputed as the New York in south hemisphere for its modern and metropolitan splendors.

悉尼拥有众多的名胜古迹，其中以悉尼歌剧院、海港大桥、悉尼塔、情人港、中国城、岩石区、维多利亚女王大厦、邦迪海滩等最为著名。

Sydney boasts a large number of places of interests, among which Sydney Opera House, Harbor Bridge, Sydney Tower, Darling Harbor, China Town, The Rocks, Queen Victoria Building, Bondi Beach are the most famous ones.

◆ 悉尼歌剧院（Sydney Opera House）

悉尼歌剧院是20世纪最具特色的建筑之一，是世界著名的艺术表演中心之一。在现代建筑史上，它被认为是巨型雕塑式的典型作品，是悉尼的标志性建筑。悉尼歌剧院于1959年开始修建，1973年建成，外形犹如即将乘风出海的白色风帆，与周围景色相映成趣，其特有的风帆造型每年吸引着无数的游客。悉尼歌剧院不仅是悉尼艺术文化的殿堂，更是悉尼的灵魂，是公认的20世纪世界十大奇迹之一，该剧院的设计者为丹麦设计师约恩·乌松。2007年6月28日，悉尼歌剧院被联合国教科文组织评为世界文化遗产。

Sydney Opera House is one of the 20th century's most distinctive buildings and one of the most famous performing arts centers in the world. It is recognized as a typical work of giant statue style in modern architecture history and the landmark of Sydney. Sydney Opera House was commenced in 1959 and finished in 1973, designed in the shape of a white swollen sail, forming a nice ballance with its neighbors. Every year, millions of tourists are attracted by its unique design. Sydney Opera House is more than just a hall for arts and culture, but the soul of Sydney. Built by a Danish architect Jørn Utzon, it is reputed as one of ten wonders of the 20th century. On June 28, 2007, it was elected by UNESCO as one of the World Cultural Heritage.

◆ 海港大桥（Harbor Bridge）

1932年建成的悉尼海港大桥长达1 149米，最高处高出海平面134米，是南半球第一大拱桥，是早期悉尼的代表建筑，与举世闻名的悉尼歌剧院隔海相望。澳大利亚人形容悉尼海港大桥的造型像一个“老式的大衣架”，并把它誉为悉尼的象征。

Sydney Harbor Bridge was built in 1932, with a span of 1,149 meters and 134 meters from top to water level. It is the biggest arch bridge in south hemisphere and the representative of Sydney's early architecture, matching the world famous Sydney Opera House across the sea. Nicknamed "the coat-hanger" by Australians, it is an iconic symbol of Sydney.

◆ 悉尼塔（Sydney Tower）

悉尼塔是悉尼的又一标志，它与悉尼歌剧院、海港大桥并列为悉尼三大标志性建筑。悉尼塔金黄色的外观闪耀夺目，塔高305米，为南半球第二高的建筑物。游客登上圆锥形塔楼，纵目四望，悉尼市容一览无余。

Sydney Tower is another landmark of Sydney. Together with Sydney Opera House and Harbor Bridge, they are known as three landmarks of Sydney. It has a dazzling golden exterior, with a height of 305 meters, making it the second tallest observation tower in the Southern Hemisphere. On the top of its cone-shaped tower, you may have a panoramic view of the whole Sydney city.

◆ 岩石区（The Rocks）

岩石区的名称源于1788年殖民地刚形成的时候，最早的建筑大多是用当地的砂岩建成的。岩石区是每个来到悉尼的观光客的必游之地，这里是悉尼最早开发的地区，有着许多代表悉尼开拓史的古老房屋和街道。现在，岩石区已成为展示澳大利亚最初20年的艰辛开发历程的“活的博物馆”。

The name of the Rocks stemmed from when the colony was just established in 1788, as the original buildings were mostly made of local sandstones. It is a must-see scenic spot for every tourist to Sydney. It is the earliest developed area in Sydney, with many old houses and streets as the testimony of the development of the city. Now the Rocks is a living museum to show the hard time of the first 20 years of development of the country.

◆ 蓝山（Blue Mountains）

蓝山国家公园坐落在新南威尔士州境内，该州共有 7 座澳大利亚国家公园。蓝山曾被英国女王伊丽莎白二世誉为“世界上最美丽的地方”，在 2000 年被列入世界自然遗产名录。蓝山的得名源于满山的桉树（当地称由加利树）。由于桉叶时时散发出浓郁的芬芳，在阳光的折射下，这种芬芳的挥发性蒸汽使蓝山笼罩在蓝色的氤氲中。蓝山的标志是著名的三姐妹峰。

Blue Mountains National Park is situated in New South Wales in which there are altogether 7 national parks. Described as the most beautiful place in the world by Queen Elizabeth Ⅱ, it was later inscribed on the list of World Natural Heritage in 2000. Blue Mountains derive its name from eucalyptus all over the mountains. It is based on the fact that the constant fragrance emitted by the eucalyptus forest becomes evaporated and dispersed under the refraction of the sunlight, thus making the mountain shrouded in the blue veil of mist. The Three Sisters sandstone rock formation are a famous symbol of the Blue Mountains.

（二）墨尔本（Melbourne）

墨尔本是澳大利亚第二大城市，是有“花园之州”之称的维多利亚州的首府，知名的国际大都市。1901 年至 1927 年，墨尔本曾是澳大利亚的首都。墨尔本也是澳大利亚的文化重镇和体育之都，具有深厚的文化底蕴，被称为“澳大利亚的文化首都”，曾主办 1956 年夏季奥运会，也是一年一度的澳大利亚网球公开赛、一级方程式赛车澳大利亚大奖赛比赛的常年主办城市。全球都很有影响力的墨尔本赛马节每年都会在墨尔本举行。墨尔本是在 19 世纪中期淘金热潮中迅速发展起来的城市，目前仍保留着许多 19 世纪华丽的维多利亚式建筑，是澳大利亚最具有欧洲韵味的城市，被称为“澳大利亚的伦敦”。墨尔本成功地融合人文与自然，城市的绿化面积高达 40%，连续多年被评为世界上最适合人类居住的城市之一 。

Melbourne, a famous metropolis and the second largest city in Australia, is the capital city of the state of Victoria renowned as “the state of gardens”. From 1901 to 1927, it served as the capital of the country. Often referred to as “the cultural capital of Australia”, the city is the hub of culture and sports, boasting profound cultural implications. It was the host city of the Olympic Games in 1956 and is the perennial host city for annual Australian Open and Formula 1 Australian Grand Prix. The Melbourne Cup, a world famous horse racing event, is held in Melbourne every year. Melbourne is the city bred by the gold rush in mid 19th century. At present, it still retains many splendid Victorian style buildings dating from the 19th century, making it a distinctive city with strong European flavor and thus gaining itself a nickname “London in

Australia". Melbourne is a perfect blend of culture and nature, with the green area taking up 40% of the city proper. It has been ranked as one of the world's most livable cities for many years.

◆ 大洋路（The Great Ocean Road）

大洋路位于墨尔本西南，是一条全长近 300 千米的海滨公路。20 世纪 80 年代初，大洋路被确定为国家自然公园，对游客开放，是世界著名的观光景点之一。大洋路是为纪念参加第一次世界大战的士兵修建的，参与建设的人包括许多参战老兵，共有 3 000 余名工人为此付出了艰辛的汗水。这条路于 1919 年开始动工，1932 年全线贯通。大洋路沿着维多利亚州西海岸蜿蜒伸展，带给游客壮丽的海洋风光，游客可体验各种海滩活动。

Located in the southwest of Melbourne, the Great Ocean Road is a 300 kilometers stretch of road along the coast. In the early 1980s, the Great Ocean Road was open to public as a national nature park. It is a world famous tourist attraction. Dedicated to the veterans of the First World War, the road was built by over 3,000 laborers, including many retired veterans from the First World War. The construction started in 1919 and finished in 1932. The road winds alongside the west coast of Victoria, providing tourists with splendid ocean view and beach amusements.

◆ 菲利普岛（Phillip Island）

菲利普岛位于墨尔本东南 124 千米的海上。由于这里可以观赏到世界上最小的蓝企鹅，因此也被称为"企鹅岛"，并成为澳大利亚最知名的观光胜地之一。菲利普岛自然公园的"企鹅列队"每年吸引着上百万的国内外游客来此目睹企鹅登陆的生态奇景。

Phillip Island is located on the sea about 124 kilometers southeast from Melbourne. It is the area where little penguins can be seen, hence the name Penguin Island. As the habitat of little penguins, Phillip Island is a renowned tourist destination visited by millions of people annually. The Penguin Parade at Phillip Island Nature Park, in which little penguins come ashore in groups, attracts visitors from all over the world.

（三）堪培拉（Canberra）

堪培拉是澳大利亚的首都，纯粹的政治中心。堪培拉是个年轻的花园城市，1901 年，澳大利亚联邦政府成立以后，为定都问题，悉尼和墨尔本两大城市争执不下，直到 1911 年，联邦政府通过决议，选择位于这两大城市之间的堪培拉作为新首都，由美国著名设计师沃尔特·伯利·格里芬设计。1913 年按规划始建，1927 年联邦政府从墨尔本迁至此，使用了当地居民的传统名称——堪培拉，意思是"汇合之地"。

Canberra is the capital of Australia, purely a political center. It is a young garden city. After the founding of the Commonwealth of Australia in 1901, Sydney and Melbourne were competing for the location of the national capital. The site of Canberra was selected for the location of the nation's capital in 1911 as a compromise between rivals Sydney and Melbourne, when a resolution was made by the Federal Government to settle the dispute. Following a blueprint by the American architects Walter Burley Griffin, the construction commenced in 1913. In 1927, the Federal Government moved from Melbourne, the temporary seat of government, to Canberra, which means "meeting place", a traditional name borrowed from the local residents.

◆ 国会大厦（Parliament House）

澳大利亚国会大厦是世界最著名的建筑之一。它建于国会山顶上，其位置就如同其权力一样高。国会大厦以大量使用砖石和优质木材，以及收藏包括世界上最大的挂毯在内的艺术精品为特色。堪培拉是世界上向公众开放国会大厦的少数首都之一，每隔30分钟会提供免费导游，使游客更进一步了解其奥秘。

Parliament House is one of the most famous buildings in the world. Crowning the Parliament Hill, its location is as high as its power. Its uniqueness lies in the fact that a large number of stones and fine timbers were used in the building and a fantastic collection of works of art is housed in it, including one of the biggest tapestry in the world. Canberra is one of the few capitals where the Parliament House is open to the public, providing free guide services at the interval of 30 minutes to explain to the tourists the mystery of the House.

◆ 格里芬湖（Lake Burley Griffin）

如果不去格里芬湖，不看喷射式喷泉，就不能说到过堪培拉。格里芬湖是以昔日首都建设总监沃尔特·伯利·格里芬命名的长达11千米的人工湖，湖岸周长为35千米，湖中有为纪念库克船长而建造的喷泉。

A visit to Canberra without seeing the jet fountain in Lake Burley Griffin is not complete. This artificial lake, named after Walter Burley Griffin, the federal capital director of design and construction, is 11 kilometers long. It has a shoreline of 35 kilometers. A fountain was built in the lake to commemorate Captain Cook.

（四）布里斯班（Brisbane）

布里斯班是有“阳光之州”美誉的昆士兰州的首府，布里斯班因此被称为“阳光之城”，是澳大利亚第三大城市，有“考拉之都”的美誉。整个城市由布里斯班河环绕，拥有美丽的自然风景和四季如春的气候，有女王花园、维多利亚公园、考拉动物园等观光游览胜地。布里斯班是澳大利亚东部前往热带地区的中转站，搭乘火车可以直达凯恩斯、黄金海岸、阳光海岸等旅游胜地。

Brisbane, the third largest city in Australia, is the capital of the sunshine state Queensland. Thus it is proclaimed as “sunshine city” and also as “koala capital”. The whole city is encircled by the Brisbane River, boasting beautiful natural scenery and pleasantly mild climate. It has the attractions such as Queen’s Garden, Victoria Park, Koala Zoo, etc. Brisbane is the junction to the tropical area on the east coast of Australia, linking directly to tourist resorts such as Cairns, Gold Coast and Sunshine Coast by railway.

（五）黄金海岸（Gold Coast）

黄金海岸位于澳大利亚东部海岸中段、布里斯班以南，它由一段长约42千米、10多个连续排列的优质沙滩组成，因沙滩为金色而得名。这里气候宜人、日照充足、海浪险急，适合冲浪和滑水，尤其是在著名的“冲浪者天堂”。这里拥有完备的旅游和娱乐设施，包括酒店、风景名胜、30多个富有吸引力的主题游览区，如华纳兄弟电影世界、梦幻世界和海洋世界，因此享有“主题公园之都”的美誉。

Located at central of east coast of the country and south of Brisbane, Gold Coast is a popular resort in the country. It consists of more than 10 best gold beaches about 42 kilometers long in total, hence the name. With cozy climate, ample sunshine and surging waves in particular, Gold Coast is a major destination for surfing and water skiing, especially in the renowned Surfer Paradise. Reputed as the “capital of theme parks”, it has a complete facilities of tourism and amusement, including hotels, tourist attractions, and more than 30 theme parks, among which Warner Bros. Movie World, Dream World and Sea World enjoy the worldwide fame.

（六）凯恩斯（Cairns）

凯恩斯是地处热带的昆士兰州北部的旅游城市，它位于澳大利亚大陆东海岸最北端，是最接近世界七大自然景观之一——大堡礁的观光城市。靠近赤道的凯恩斯，被称为“热带之都”，保有大片原始热带雨林。凯恩斯是前往大堡礁和热带雨林的必经大门。

As a tourist city of tropical North Queensland, Cairns is at the north tip of east coast of Australia, closest to the Great Barrier Reef, one of the Seven Natural Wonders of the world. As it is close to the Equator and home to vast pristine tropical rain forest, Cairns is often referred to the “tropical capital”. It serves as a gateway for people to visit the Great Barrier Reef and tropical rain forest.

◆ 大堡礁（The Great Barrier Reef）

大堡礁是世界上最长、最大的珊瑚礁群，是澳大利亚人最引以为豪的天然景观，被称为“透明清澈的海中野生王国”。它纵贯蜿蜒于澳大利亚的东海岸，全长 2 011 千米，最宽处 161 千米，南端离海岸 241 千米，北端离海岸仅 16 千米。在落潮时，部分的珊瑚礁露出水面形成珊瑚岛。大堡礁上生存着 400 余种不同类型的珊瑚礁，其中有世界上最大的珊瑚礁。1981 年，大堡礁被联合国教科文组织列入世界自然遗产名录。

The Great Barrier Reef, referred to as “the clear and transparent wild marine world”, has the world’s longest and largest coral reef system. It winds along the Australia’s east coast, with overall length of 2,011 kilometers and maximum width as large as 161 kilometers. Furthermost in the south is 241 kilometers off the coast, whereas in the north is just 16 kilometers off the coast. When the tides fall, part of coral reefs above the water surface form coral island. There are over 400 types of coral reefs in the Great Barrier Reef, including the biggest one of its kind in the world. It was listed as a World Natural Heritage Site by UNESCO in 1981.

（七）其他著名旅游景点

◆ 艾尔斯岩石（Uluru/Ayers Rock）

北方领土地区是古代土著文化的发源地，以自然景观和文化特色著称，特别是著名的“红土中心”及世界上最大的独立巨石“艾尔斯岩石”。艾尔斯岩石底面呈椭圆形，形状有些像两端略圆的长面包，长约 3 600 米，宽约 2 000 米，高约 335 米，周长约 9 400 米。该岩石主要成分为砾石，含铁量高，其表面因被氧化而发红，整体呈红色，因此又被称作“红石”。艾尔斯岩石俗称为“人类地球上的肚脐”，号称“世界七大奇景”之一 。如今这里成为国家公园，每年有数百万人从世界各地纷纷慕名前来观赏巨石风采。这块独体岩随着太阳高度的不同而变色，因此被土著人膜拜为圣石。1987 年，艾尔斯岩石及其所处的国家公园被列入世界自然遗产名录。

Northern Territory is the origin place of ancient aboriginal culture, renowned for its natural landscape and cultural features, especially the famous Red Center and Uluru (Ayers Rock), the biggest free standing monolith in the world. Ayers Rock is oval at the bottom, resembling a long loaf of bread with two round ends. It is about 3.6 kilometers long, about 2 kilometers wide, and about 335 meters high with a total circumference of 9.4 kilometers. The rock is mainly composed of gravel containing high level of iron. Weathering of iron-bearing minerals by the process of oxidation gives the surface layer of rock a red-brown rusty color, thus, it is also called Red Rock. Nicknamed the "Belly Button of the Earth", it is one of the "Seven Natural Wonders of the World". It is now a national park, receiving millions of visitors from different parts of the world. It was worshiped by the aboriginal as the sacred rock as its color changes with the height of sun. In 1987, Ayers Rock and the surrounding National Park were inscribed as a World Natural Heritage Site.

四、旅游资讯

（一）美食

到澳大利亚旅游，游客一定要品尝这里的美酒佳肴。澳大利亚是个移民国家，在这里不仅可以找到世界各地的正宗美食，而且有澳大利亚独有的特色风味。澳大利亚传统的饮食文化以英格兰、爱尔兰风味为主。澳大利亚饮食文化的多元化是从 20 世纪 50 年代开始的，随着世界各地移民的大量涌入和定居，他们也带来了各自家乡的风味，其中影响最大的是地中海和亚洲的烹饪风格。

Australian wine and food is something you should not miss while visiting the country. As it is an immigrant country, you can find both authentic cuisine from all parts of the world and unique food native to Australia. The traditional Australian food can find its root in English and Irish traditions. Diversification of Australian food began in 1950s when immigrants from around the world flocked into and settled down here, bringing with them their ethnic flavors, among which the most influential ones are Mediterranean and Asian cooking styles.

鱼和海鲜是澳大利亚美食的特色，澳大利亚的海鲜肉嫩味美，如帝王蟹、牡蛎、鲍鱼、龙虾、鲑鱼等，源于澳大利亚适宜的气候和无污染的环境。传统快餐是英式炸鱼片和炸薯条。澳大利亚的畜牧业发达，因此可以品尝到美味的牛肉、羊肉和袋鼠肉。亚洲美食则以中国、泰国、日本、韩国和越南的为主。除此以外，澳大利亚还是水果之乡、著名的葡萄酒产地，四大产区分别是南澳大利亚、新南威尔士、维多利亚（包括塔斯马尼亚岛）、西澳大利亚。四大产区的葡萄酒各有特色，质量均堪称世界水平。

Fish and seafood are very distinctive in Australian food. The delicacy of Australian seafood, such as king crabs, oysters, abalones, lobsters and salmons, can be well explained by its favorable climate and pollution-free environment. Traditional fast food is the English style fish and chips. Australia is developed in livestock husbandry, so beef, mutton and kangaroo meat are fresh and tasty. In Asian food, Chinese, Thai, Japanese, Korean, Vietnamese food are the most popular ones. Besides, Australia is home of fruits and wines, with South Australia, New South Wales, Victoria (including Tasmania) and West Australia as its four major world class wine producing regions.

（二）购物及退税

澳大利亚物产丰富，独具特色。澳大利亚特产包括欧泊（一种珍贵的彩色宝石）、羊皮、牛皮、绵羊油、葡萄酒、土著文化手工艺品和艺术品等。

Australia is abundant in resources with unique features. For shopping you may have variety of choices including Opal (a precious colored gem), sheep skin, cow leather, sheep oil, wines, aboriginal handicrafts and artworks.

澳大利亚羊毛：澳大利亚出产的羊毛质量远近驰名。其中美丽诺羊毛的纤维是世界最长的，澳大利亚设计师巧用这种优质的羊毛制成各种精美的服装。除了服装之外，还有羊毛被褥等羊毛制品。由于高超的处理工艺和优良品质，羊毛制品冬暖夏凉，柔软，不易生蛀虫。

Australian wool: The wool produced in Australia enjoys great reputation for its superior quality. Merino Wool has the longest fiber in the world, with which Australian designers make fine featured clothes. Apart from the clothing, there are other woolen products such as woolen blanket. Due to its super workmanship and quality, woolen products are cool in summer and warm in winter, soft and resistent to moths.

健康保健品：澳大利亚具有优越的自然环境，是世界上空气污染最少的地区之一。由于澳大利亚还有着近乎苛刻的药检标准及保健品管理制度，因此这里出产的健康食品早已享誉全球，如鱼油、蜂胶等。

Health care products: Australia has superior natural environment, suffering the least pollution in the world. Besides that, the harsh drug test standard and health care products supervision system ensure the renowned quality products such as fish oil and propolis, etc.

土著文化艺术品：澳大利亚的土著文化是世界上一种十分独特的古老文化，土著人设计的艺术品最具澳大利亚风情，拥有独特的神话传说和图腾造型。这些工艺品包括“飞去来器”、树皮画、布画、木雕、木制乐器等，极具纪念意义。

Aboriginal artworks: Aboriginal culture is a characteristic ancient culture in the world. Aboriginal artworks are the most Australian featured souvenirs with the design of legendary and totem images, such as boomerang, bark painting, cloth painting, wood carving, wooden musical instruments which are all quite memorable.

澳大利亚的购物退税制对游客来说极为方便。游客于 30 天内在 GST（goods and services tax）注册商店购买 300 澳元或以上的含有货物服务税（GST 10%）或酒类平价税（WET 14.5%）的物品，在离境前可以提出退税申请。游客必须于离境前随身携带需退税的物品。购物退税柜台设于各国际机场的出境区。游客在海关查验护照后，即可至退税柜台办理。游客须出示购买的物品、商店开立的税单、护照及国际航班的登机证。若退税金额低于 200 澳元，游客可选择领取现金。

The Tax Refund System (TRS) in Australia is very convenient for the tourists. Those who purchase goods more than AUD 300 with GST (goods and services tax) 10% or WET (wine equalization tax) 14.5% in the GST registered shops, can apply for the tax refund before they depart within 30 days after the purchase. When they apply for tax refund, they should carry the goods with them before departing. All the tax refund counters are located in the departing area of the international airports. After the passports control, the tourists can go to the counter to apply for it with the goods, tax invoice, passport and international boarding pass. Tourists can choose to have the refund in cash if the amount is less than AUD 200.

（三）时差

澳大利亚有三个时区：东部标准时间比北京时间快 2 个小时，包括昆士兰州、新南威尔士州、维多利亚州、塔斯马尼亚州和澳大利亚首都地区。中部标准时间比北京时间快 1.5 小时，包括南澳大利亚州、新南威尔士州西部的布罗肯山镇以及北领地。西部标准时间同北京时间一样，覆盖西澳大利亚州。

Australia is divided into three separate time zones: Australian Eastern Standard Time (AEST) covers the eastern states of Queensland, New South Wales, Victoria, Tasmania and the Australian Capital Territory. AEST is 2 hours earlier than Beijing time. Australian Central Standard Time (ACST) covers the state of South Australia, the town of Broken Hill in western New South Wales and Northern Territory. ACST is 1.5 hours earlier than Beijing time. Australian Western Standard Time (AWST) covers Western Australia. It is the same as Beijing time.

澳大利亚部分地区夏季实行夏令时（DST），夏令时从 10 月的第 1 个星期日凌晨 2:00（澳大利亚东部标准时间）开始，到次年 4 月的第 1 个星期日的凌晨 3:00（澳大利亚东部夏令时）结束。新南威尔士、维多利亚、塔斯马尼亚和澳大利亚首都地区将时钟调快 1 小时。南澳大利亚和新南威尔士的布罗肯山镇从澳大利亚中部标准时间调到澳大利亚中部夏令时，调快 1 小时。昆士兰州、北领地和西澳大利亚州均不采用夏令时。

Daylight Saving Time (DST) is observed in summer in some areas of Australia, which begins at 2:00 am (AEST) on the first Sunday of October and ends at 3:00 am (AEDT) on the first Sunday of next April. New South Wales, Victoria, Tasmania and the Australian Capital Territory turn their clocks one hour forward to DST. South Australia and the town of Broken Hill in New South Wales move from ACST to Australian Central Daylight Time (ACDT). DST is not observed in Queensland, Northern Territory and Western Australia.

知识拓展

澳大利亚的动植物检疫

澳大利亚迷人的自然风光吸引了世界各地的游客。澳大利亚有许多植物和动物种类是地球上独一无二的。澳大利亚是一个人为污染程度较低的国家，农牧及园艺业对澳大利亚而言相当重要。为了保护本国的动植物、公众健康、农业和环境，尽可能维护与保持生态原始风貌，澳大利亚严格禁止各种可能危害其自然或人文景观的物品入境。澳大利亚海关和检疫部门对入境旅客的检查非常严格，禁止或限制游客携带动植物及其制品。任何形式的食品，包括新鲜食品、熟食、腌制食品等，特别是肉类，其他如动物或植物的任何部分、传统的药材或草药等都是明令禁止的。若真的需要携带食品入境，游客最好提前声明并接受检验。澳大利亚检验检疫局承担了此项任务。在航班抵达澳大利亚之前，乘客会收到一张入境旅客卡。如果携带任何食品、植物或动物产品，必须在“是”(YES) 一栏打钩，并进行申报。如果不想申报，也可将禁止携带的入境物品弃置于机场的检疫箱内。所有申报物品必须交检疫局官员检查，违禁物品将被扣留并销毁。如果经检查发现乘客携带违禁物品或做出虚假申报，乘客可能会被当场罚款 220 澳元，情节严重者可被罚款 6 万澳元以上甚至处以 10 年监禁。

澳大利亚之所以在动植物检疫方面如此小心谨慎，是因为这块大陆实在是与众不同。澳大利亚大陆远古时就已同世界其他大陆分开，形成其今天为人们所熟知的、特有的动植物种群。澳大利亚的生物链很短，任何外来的动植物病害或人为的疏忽，都可能给本地区动植物群落带来灾难性的后果。早年的英国移民为了维持狩猎的爱好带来几只狐狸和野兔，不想这里草肥水美又无天敌遏制，野兔大量繁殖，泛滥成灾，危害植被，破坏环境，造成土地裸露沙化，给这个“骑在羊背上的国家”带来了大麻烦。而狐狸因为没有天敌，迅速繁衍，很快就消灭了 20 种本地的动物，并威胁到另外 40 多种动物的生存。鲤鱼在中国是喜庆的象征，但在澳大利亚，它们被视为一害。自 100 多年前从欧洲引进后，鲤鱼大量繁殖，吃光了水草，把本地鱼种推到了灭绝的边缘。澳大利亚人把它们称作“水兔”，与坏了名声的兔子相提并论。这就是澳大利亚为了防止外来物种入侵而严格进行动植物检疫的原因。

澳大利亚独特的动物

澳大利亚被称为“世界活化石博物馆”。澳大利亚的特有生物是在地球演化过程中保留下来的古老生物种类。它们虽然显得有些原始，却是人类研究地球演化历史的活化石。据统计，澳大利亚有植物 12 000 种，其中 9 000 种是其他国家没有的；有鸟类 650 种，其中 450 种是澳大利亚特有的。全球的有袋类动物，除南美洲外，大部分都分布在澳大利亚。

考拉（Koala）：考拉只生活在澳大利亚，既是澳大利亚的国宝，又是澳大利亚奇特的珍贵原始树栖动物，属哺乳类中的有袋目树袋熊科。考拉又叫树袋熊、无尾熊、可拉熊，以桉树叶和嫩枝为食，一般很少饮水，所以当地人称它“克瓦勒”，意思就是“不喝水”。它们性情温顺，体态憨厚，深受人们喜爱。

鸸鹋（Emu）：鸸鹋是出现在澳大利亚国徽上的动物之一，是一种飞翔功能已经退化的大鸟。它是澳大利亚最大的鸟，也是世界上最大的陆地鸟之一，是世界上最古老的鸟类之一。

袋鼠（Kangaroo）：袋鼠是澳大利亚著名的哺乳动物，在澳大利亚占有很重要的生态地位，被澳大利亚人视为国家的象征。在澳大利亚的国徽上，就有袋鼠的形象。袋鼠通常作为澳大利亚的国家标志出现，如绿色三角形袋鼠用来代表澳大利亚制造。袋鼠图案还经常出现在澳大利亚公路上，表示附近常有袋鼠出现。

鸭嘴兽（Platypus）：鸭嘴兽是单孔类哺乳动物，澳大利亚的20分硬币上印有鸭嘴兽图案。它们分布于澳大利亚东部约克角至南澳大利亚之间，是最古老而又十分原始的哺乳动物，早在2 500万年前就出现了。

思考练习

1. 经典旅游线路分析

澳大利亚经典8日游

第1天：上海——悉尼

游客在上海浦东国际机场2号航站楼集合并出发，乘机飞往澳大利亚第一大城市——悉尼。

第2天：悉尼

抵达后前往市区，途中游览澳大利亚最著名的邦迪海滩，体验澳大利亚风情。参观富人区玫瑰湾、双湾。中午前往悉尼最大的海鲜批发市场，尽情挑选当天的生猛海鲜，享用海鲜大餐。下午前往游览皇家植物园，于最佳角度欣赏悉尼歌剧院、海港大桥的雄伟外观，参观澳大利亚最大的圣玛丽大教堂，感受哥特式建筑的宏伟。游览位于市中心的海德公园，感受悉尼都市的繁华。前往参观澳大利亚标志性建筑——悉尼歌剧院（外观），近距离接触这座伟大建筑。傍晚前往情人港码头，乘坐游船畅游著名的情人港，夕阳西下，远眺悉尼歌剧院、海港大桥的雄伟外观，并在船上享用正宗三道式西式晚餐。结束后入住酒店休息。

第3天：悉尼——蓝山——悉尼

早餐后乘车前往位于悉尼以西100千米，被列为世界自然遗产的蓝山国家公园；游览回音谷，在此远眺蓝山全景及享誉世界的三姐妹峰。午餐后前往蓝山美景世界。乘坐近乎垂直的小矿车下到蓝山峡谷，漫行于热带雨林中。后乘坐缆车横越原始山谷，饱览峡谷风貌。结束后乘车返回悉尼市区，晚餐后入住酒店休息。

第4天：悉尼——布里斯班——黄金海岸

早餐后乘机飞往昆士兰州首府布里斯班。抵达后在布里斯班市区观光：参观南岸公园（1988年世界博览会的举办地），参观公园内精美绝伦的雕塑精品尼泊尔神庙，沿着布里斯班河岸感受公园内的休闲气氛，参观公园内的人造海滩。后前往游览袋鼠角，俯瞰市区全景。下午乘车抵达度假胜地黄金海岸。傍晚漫步于著名的滑浪者天堂海滩，体验澳大利亚人的悠闲生活。晚餐后入住酒店休息。

第 5 天：黄金海岸

早餐后前往天堂牧场参观，在此可与澳大利亚特有的袋鼠、考拉、鸸鹋等特色动物来一次亲密接触。观看精彩的剪羊毛表演，并可自愿参与其中，同时还能观看澳大利亚牛仔及牧羊犬的精彩表演。随后前往耗资千万、南半球唯一一座电影主题公园——华纳兄弟电影世界。

第 6 天：黄金海岸——布里斯班——墨尔本

早餐后，乘机飞往澳大利亚第二大城市——墨尔本，抵达后享用午餐。参观澳大利亚最大的天主教堂之一的圣派翠克大教堂。游览费瑞滋花园，参观“澳大利亚之父”库克船长小屋。晚餐后入住酒店休息。

第 7 天：墨尔本

早餐后在市区观光，游览皇家植物园，植物园内有着世界各地 6 000 多种的植物，以及栖息在此的黑天鹅等澳大利亚特色动物，参观战争纪念馆，漫步亚拉河畔，体验澳大利亚花园城市的独特魅力。午餐后游览位于市中心的标志性建筑——维多利亚广场，感受都市繁华。

第 8 天：墨尔本——上海

早餐后前往墨尔本国际机场，乘机飞往上海浦东国际机场，结束本次行程。

分析：这条经典旅游线路的主要旅游景点与行程特色，以及适合旅游的人群。

2. 案例分析

[案例 1] 蛋黄派、方便面、自制食品……不少游客出国，担心吃不惯，喜欢在行李中装一些自备食物。某旅游团到澳大利亚旅游，一位游客在行李中放了一盒方便面，在澳大利亚过海关时，检查人员打开了方便面，取出里面的肉酱包后再归还；另一位游客携带的蛋黄派，因为里面含有蛋黄，也被查扣；还有一位游客，因为随身携带的包里有一个苹果和五个橘子，通关时忘记申报被查出，结果水果被没收销毁，并处罚款折合人民币 5 000 元。请分析原因以及到澳大利亚旅游时，游客和领队需要注意的相关事项。

[案例 2] 2019 年春节期间，某旅游团到澳大利亚凯恩斯酒店入住后，半夜里一个游客突然跑到领队房间大喊要求换房间，原来他入住后发现房间里有蜥蜴和蚂蚁。由于春节期间客房爆满，无法调换，凯恩斯酒店的工作人员说在澳大利亚，人与动物共同分享大自然，一般靠近森林的宾馆时常会有小动物来光顾，但这些动物不会伤害人，为此酒店在每个房间的告示牌上解释了原因并告知客人不要在房间里留下食物残渣并随时关好门。而该游客依然不予理解，回国后投诉旅行社和领队。请问：前往澳大利亚的旅游团，领队该如

何做行前说明，才能避免以上尴尬和投诉？

3. 练一练

了解澳大利亚的主要信息、文化历史和自然地貌，分析澳大利亚的旅游宣传口号“澳大利亚，尽是不同”体现在哪些方面。

第二节　新西兰

一、国家概况

（一）地理环境

新西兰，毛利语音译“奥特亚罗瓦”（Aotearoa，意为“长白云之乡”），新西兰人自称Kiwi。新西兰是个岛屿国家，位于太平洋西南部，介于赤道和南极洲之间。新西兰西隔塔斯曼海与澳大利亚相望，相距 1 600 千米；北邻新喀里多尼亚、斐济、汤加。作为一个海洋孕育的国家，新西兰的陆地面积约 27 万平方千米，在世界各国中仅居第 75 位，海域面积超过 400 万平方千米，有 120 万平方千米的专属经济区，居世界第 7 位。新西兰是世界最南端的陆地之一，其南海岸距南极洲只有 2 400 多千米，因此，美国海军选择它作为南极探险基地，新西兰也被誉为“世界边缘的国家”。

New Zealand has widely accepted Māori name Aotearoa, meaning “the land of long white cloud”. New Zealanders colloquially call their country as Kiwi. New Zealand is an island country located between the Equator and the Antarctica, in the southwest of Pacific Ocean, with Australia 1,600 kilometers to its west across the Tasman Sea, New Caledonia, Fiji and Tonga to its north. As a nation born and bred in ocean, it occupies a land area of 270,000 square kilometers, ranking the 75th in the world, and a sea area of over 4,000,000 square kilometers, an exclusive economic zone of 1,200,000 square kilometers, ranking the 7th around the world. New Zealand is one of the lands in the farthest south, with its south coast only 2,400 kilometers away from the Antarctica. Therefore, the US navy selects it as its base for Antarctic expedition, and New Zealand is known as “the country on the verge of the world”.

新西兰由南岛、北岛及附近的一些小岛组成。境内多山，75% 以上的面积为山地和丘陵，森林覆盖面积超过 31%，天然牧场或农场占国土面积的一半。北岛多火山和温泉，南岛多冰河和湖泊。

New Zealand consists of South Island, North Island and a number of smaller islands. Its territory is predominantly mountainous, of which above 75% are mountains and hills. 31% of the land is covered by forest and half of its land are natural pastures or farms. There are lots of volcanoes and thermal springs on the North Island, glaciers and lakes on the South Island.

新西兰属于温带海洋性气候，四季温差不大。12 月至次年 2 月为夏季，6 月至 8 月为冬季。夏季平均气温在 20℃左右，冬季 10℃左右。

New Zealand has a mild and equable temperate maritime climate. Summer begins from December to next February and winter from June to August, with the summer average temperature of 20℃ and winter 10℃.

（二）人文概况

1. 历史

新西兰的历史比较短，是世上最年轻的移民国家之一。最早的土著人是14世纪从波利尼西亚移民来此的毛利人。荷兰人埃布尔·杨森·塔斯曼所带领的船队，在1642年抵达这里并将其命名为“Nieuw Zealand”。1769年至1777年，英国的库克船长先后5次来到这里，并绘制地图。随后，英国向新西兰大批移民并宣布占领新西兰，把名字改为“新西兰”。1840年，英国迫使毛利人族长签署《怀唐伊条约》，新西兰纳入英帝国版图。1907年，新西兰独立，但仍为英国自治领。1947年，新西兰成为主权国家，同时为英联邦成员。

As one of the youngest immigrant countries in the world, New Zealand has a very short history. The earliest settlers were a group of Māori who migrated from Polynesia in 14th century and settled in New Zealand. A Dutch man named Abel Janszoon Tasman arrived here with his fleet in 1642 and named the place “Nieuw Zealand”. During the year of 1769 to 1777, Captain Cook had come here for five times and mapped the coastlines. Whereafter, the migrants from UK came, occupied this land and named the land New Zealand. New Zealand was annexed as part of the British Empire after the *Treaty of Waitangi* signed with Māori cacique in 1840. It declared independence in 1907 but still remained a dominion of the United Kingdom. In 1947, New Zealand became a completely independent country and joined the Commonwealth of Nations.

2. 经济

新西兰经济发达，是一个发达国家。畜牧业是新西兰的经济基础，羊肉、奶制品出口量居世界第一，羊毛出口量居世界第二位。新西兰是全球最大的鹿茸生产国和出口国，出口量约占全球的30%。新西兰森林资源丰富，工业以农林牧产品加工、造纸和木材加工为主。新西兰渔产丰富，拥有世界第四大专属经济区，200海里专属经济区内捕鱼潜力每年约50万吨。新西兰气候宜人、环境清新、风景优美，旅游胜地遍布全境、地表景观富于变化，旅游业发达，旅游业收入约占新西兰国内生产总值的10%，是仅次于乳制品业的第二大创汇产业。

New Zealand has an advanced economy and is one of the developed countries. Animal husbandry is the foundation of New Zealand’s economy. The value of exporting mutton, dairy products ranks the first in the world and raw wool ranks the second in the world. New Zealand is the largest country of producing and exporting pilose antler, making up 30% of the total global exporting amount. It has rich forest resources. Its main industries are farming, forestry and animal products processing, paper making and timber processing industry. New Zealand boasts the world’s fourth largest exclusive economic zone on its abundant aquatic products. In this 200 miles long exclusive economic zone, 500,000 tons of fishes are captured every year. Blessed with pleasant climate, tranquil environment, beautiful landscapes, varied landforms and resources, tourism in New Zealand is highly developed. The total revenue from tourism industry takes up 10% of GDP, making tourism the second largest industry to earn foreign exchange, next to the dairy industry.

3. 社会文化

新西兰人口约 492 万，奥克兰的人口占全国总人口的 30.7%，首都惠灵顿的人口约占全国总人口的 11%。奥克兰、惠灵顿和克赖斯特彻奇是人口最多的三个城市。其中，欧洲移民后裔占 74%，毛利人占 15%，亚裔占 12%，太平洋岛国裔占 7%。毛利族是人口最多的少数民族。新西兰 48.9% 的居民信奉基督教新教和天主教，是世界上人口城市化程度最高的国家之一。英语、毛利语是官方语言。

New Zealand has a population of 4.92 million, with Auckland (30.7% of the total population), Wellington (11% of the total population) and Christchurch the three most populous cities. The whole population is composed of 74% the descendants of the European immigrants, 15% Māori, 12% Asian descendants and 7% Pacific Islands descendants. The Māori is the ethnic minority group with the biggest population. 48.9% of New Zealand citizens believe in Protestantism and Catholicism. It is one of the countries which enjoy the highest degree of population urbanization. The official languages are English and Māori.

新西兰毛利人的历史可追溯到乘着瓦卡（一种独木舟）横渡辽阔的太平洋的祖先。毛利人有着丰富、充满活力的文化，体现在他们对传统艺术和当代艺术的追求中保留着精神与自然世界的结合。毛利人的传统艺术包括世代相传的雕刻、编织和刺青术等。组舞艺术中融合了合唱、节奏舞步和气势凶猛的传统舞蹈哈卡舞。哈卡舞来源于毛利人开战前用以鼓舞士气的舞蹈。如今，新西兰国家橄榄球队在开赛前总要表演哈卡舞来鼓舞士气，是游客必看的节目。许多新西兰作家把毛利人的文化及传说写入作品中，创造了别具特色的新西兰文化。

The history of Māori people in New Zealand can be traced back to the ancestors who crossed the vast Pacific Ocean on wakas, a type of canoe. Māori people have rich and dynamic culture, reflected in the bond with the spiritual and natural world when pursuing the traditional and contemporary art. Traditional art includes carving, weaving and Ta Moko (a kind of the permanent body and face tatoo), passed down from generation to generation. A kapa haka performance involves choral singing, movements and the vigorous traditional haka dance which originated from the dance to raise the morale of Māori soldiers before the combat. Nowadays, the National Rugby Team of New Zealand will always perform the haka dance to keep up the morale of the players and it has developed into a popular tourist program. Many New Zealand writers created distinctive New Zealand culture by adapting Māori culture and legends into their works.

好莱坞有史以来的最大制作之一《指环王》是由彼得·杰克逊在新西兰拍摄完成的，新西兰的地方电影工业正是随着这部大片的成功而不断发展的。得益于许多影片的取景地位于新西兰的国家公园与保护区内，新西兰更多地能为世界所了解。出生于新西兰的安德鲁·亚当森以动画片《怪物史莱克》而闻名，他导演的《纳尼亚传奇：狮子、女巫和魔衣柜》也在新西兰很多著名的地点选景。

The Lord of the Rings, one of the biggest blockbusters from Hollywood, was shot in New Zealand by Peter Jackson. Fueled by the success of this movie, the movie industry in New Zealand has been growing continuously. Nowadays, New Zealand is better known to the outside world, thanks to the movies with many scenes set in national parks and reserves throughout the country. Andrew Adamson, born in New Zealand and known for his animation *Shrek*, also chose many famous scenic sites in the country as the locations for his movie *The Chronicles of Narnia: The Lion, the Witch and the Wardrobe*.

二、民俗风情

（一）礼仪禁忌

新西兰的大部分国民是欧洲移民的后裔，特别是英国移民的后裔，故一直保持着早期白人殖民者所带来的纯英国式的生活方式，即享受生活。社会上流行的礼仪也主要是英国式的。握手是新西兰人见面和告别时的常用礼仪，标准的握手方式是紧紧握住对方的手，目光平视对方。初次见面时，一般要在称呼上冠上“先生”“小姐”等，熟悉后会直呼名字。新西兰人的时间观念很强，约会要提前联系并准时赴约。拜访时，客人最好带上一束鲜花、一瓶威士忌酒或一盒巧克力等。新西兰人的生活悠闲，节奏较慢，除了正餐以外，新西兰人每天要喝 6 次茶，而且他们很喜欢喝酒，几乎每家都有自己的酒窖。新西兰人的生活一般很朴素，他们的住房和花园却很漂亮。新西兰人热爱运动，有近一半的人参加至少一种运动或一家健身俱乐部。新西兰最主要的运动是橄榄球，其具有非正式“国民运动”的地位。其他流行的运动有板球、足球、赛车、高尔夫球、游泳和网球等。新西兰的极限运动和探险旅行全球知名，如登山运动在该国颇为流行。著名的登山家埃德蒙·珀西瓦尔·希拉里爵士，是全球第一位成功登上珠穆朗玛峰峰顶的人。

Most citizens of New Zealand are of European origins, especially the British. Therefore, like those white settlers in the early days, they have held onto pure British life style, enjoying life. The prevailing social etiquette is also British style. A handshake is commonly used when people meet and bid farewell. A normal handshake involves grasping the hands of the other person and looking into his eyes. You should address the person with “Mr.” or “Ms.” when meeting for the first time, but first name is preferred when you are familiar with each other. New Zealand people have strong time concept. You should make an appointment in advance for your visit and arrive on time. It is customary to bring a bunch of flowers to the hostess or a bottle of whiskey or a box of chocolate with you. The life of New Zealand people is slow-paced and easy. Besides the regular meals, they drink tea for 6 times one day. They enjoy drinking so much that almost every family has their own cellar. Most of them live a simple life but their houses and gardens are usually very elegant. Known for being sporty, half of people join at least one sport or fitness club. The major sport in New Zealand is rugby, and it’s almost an unofficial national sport. Other popular sports include cricket, football, car racing, golf, swimming and tennis, etc. The country enjoys world reputation for its extreme sports and adventure travels, such as the popular mountaineering. Sir Edmund Percival Hillary, a renowned mountaineer, is the first climber in the world to have reached the summit of Mount Everest.

毛利人是新西兰最早的定居者，仍保留着自己的传统礼仪和文化，散发着独特的魅力。毛利文化是新西兰独具特色的民族文化，突出反映在刺青、歌舞及民间艺术上。毛利人刺青是一种身份的象征。毛利人擅长雕刻和编织，这两者被视为毛利艺术的精髓。尽管现在的毛利人身居都市，但他们依然继承了传统文化。他们尊重长者，对族人聚首的时刻，如葬礼，尤为重视，分散各地的家人都会珍惜难得的见面时刻，赶回家乡。毛利人对传家宝物极为重视，如权杖、翡翠项链等，深信它们蕴藏着祖先的灵气，他们会将这些传家之宝传给子孙们。毛利人相信灵魂不灭，拍照会把灵魂摄走，因此他们非常厌恶游客对着自己拍照、摄像。毛利人是波利尼西亚人的一支，有着自己独特的礼仪。欣赏毛利人礼仪的最佳场所是毛利会堂。新西兰的很多旅行社都会组织游客到毛利会堂一睹风采。碰鼻礼是毛利人特有的迎接客人的礼仪。在客人抵达部落时，欢迎仪式以挑战打开序幕，毛利人身着色彩艳丽的民族服装，载歌载舞，做出各种各样的鬼脸，挥舞手中的剑或长矛表示欢迎，然后会依次用鼻尖碰对方三次。根据毛利人的传统，双方碰鼻的时间越长，表示客人越尊贵。在许多毛利会堂里，毛利长者会教授本部落的知识、礼仪和宗谱，通过讲述古老的故事和神话传说，口述历史这一传统一直持续至今。

Māori people were the earliest settlers of New Zealand. They still preserve their own traditional etiquette and culture, representing its unique charm. Māori culture is a distinctive ethnic culture, reflected in the form of Māori tattoo (or Ta Moko), dance and folk art. Māori tattoo is a symbol of identity. They are skilled in carving and weaving which is recognized as the essence of Māori culture. Though modern Māori people are living in cities, they still inherit the traditional Māori culture. They have a reverence for the elderly. They treasure the time of clan members reunion, especially the funeral, a moment when all the members hurry home to meet each other for this important occasion. Māori people cherish their family treasures such as scepter, emerald necklace, etc., with a firm belief that they bear the spirits of the ancestors and those treasures will be passed down to their descendants. They believe that souls never die and a snapshot can take away one's soul, so they hate to be photographed or recorded in a video by tourists. Māori is a branch of Polynesians and has its characteristic etiquette. The best place to watch the Māori etiquette is the marae. Many travel agencies in New Zealand will arrange a visit to marae for tourists. Hongi is the unique way to greet guests by pressing one's nose and forehead (at the same time) to another person. When the guests arrive at the tribe, the welcome ceremony begins with a challenge. They are dressed in colorful ethnic costumes, singing, dancing, making all kinds of faces, swinging their swords or spears, as a way of welcome, before touching the nose of the other for three times with his own tip of nose. According to their tradition, the longer the touching lasts, the deeper respect they have for the guests. At many maraes, senior Māori will teach tribal knowledge, etiquette and genealogy. By telling ancient stories and myths, the tradition of oral history has been preserved till now.

（二）节庆风情

1. *怀唐伊日*（Waitangi Day）

2月6日是新西兰一个非常重要的节日——怀唐伊日。1974年，这一天被定为新西兰的国庆日，举国上下共同欢庆新西兰的立国条约——《怀唐伊条约》的签订，它于1840年由毛利人族长和英国王室的代表签署，条约签署地点在岛屿湾的怀唐伊。如今，怀唐伊已成新西兰最重要的、具有历史意义的地点之一。每年的2月6日，《怀唐伊条约》签订的地方成为全新西兰关注的焦点，举国上下共同参与为期四天的庆典活动，包括一场正式的典礼、新西兰皇家海军和地方文化团体带来的阅兵式及表演，以及各式各样的体育活动和文化活动。

February 6 is a very important holiday, Waitangi Day, designated as the national day of New Zealand in 1974. On this day, people throughout the country celebrate the signing of *Treaty of Waitangi* in 1840 by caciques of Māori tribes and the representatives of the British monarch on Waitangi at Bay of Islands. Nowadays, Waitangi has become one of the most important historic places. The place where the treaty was signed became the focus of attentions around the country. People all over the country join in the four-day long celebration, including a formal ceremony, a military parade and performances by New Zealand Royal Navy and art troupes as well as variety of sports and cultural activities.

2. 澳新军团日（ANZAC Day）

澳新军团日，又称澳纽军团日，是纪念1915年的4月25日在加里波利之战牺牲的澳大利亚和新西兰军团（简称澳新军团）将士的日子。澳新军团日在澳大利亚和新西兰现均被定为公众假日，以缅怀将士们为国牺牲的勇敢精神。澳新军团日是两国最重要的节日之一。

ANZAC Day is to commemorate the day of April 25, 1915 when Australian and New Zealand troops suffered heavy casualties and endured great hardships in the Battle of Gallipoli. Declared as a public holiday in memory of the sacrifices those soldiers made for the country, ANZAC Day is one of the most important holidays in both countries.

三、主要旅游城市及景点

（一）奥克兰（Auckland）

奥克兰位于新西兰北岛的中北部，依海而建，景色优美，是新西兰第一大城市，是新西兰的工业、商业和经济、贸易中心，也是新西兰人口最多的城市。奥克兰在1841年至1865年为新西兰第二任首都（原首都为拉塞尔，后迁都至现在的首都惠灵顿）。奥克兰的气候温和多雨，四季分明，全年气温在6℃～28℃。奥克兰港风大浪小，非常适合帆船运动。这里每年都会吸引世界各国的帆船爱好者，奥克兰是全世界拥有私人船只比例最高的城市，有“千帆之都”的美誉（每年1月的帆船竞赛场面十分壮观）。从奥克兰启程，可以当天往返奥斯卡获奖影片《钢琴课》的拍摄地黑沙滩、诗人顾城曾经居住的怀赫科岛以及火山熔岩形成的朗伊托托岛等必游之地。作为世界上最适宜居住的城市之一，奥克兰拥有完善的旅游设施、海港、岛屿、波利尼西亚文化和世界一流的餐饮、夜生活、购物环境，是展开新西兰之旅的最佳起点。

Located in the north center of the North Island, Auckland is the largest and most populous city and the industrial, commercial and trade center of the country. It borders the sea and have a beautiful harbour view. Auckland used to be the second capital of the country from 1841 to 1865 (the first was Russell and the current is Wellington). Auckland is warm and rainy with four distinct seasons and the temperatures of the year vary from 6℃ to 28℃. The strong wind and calm waves make Auckland harbour a wonderful place for sailing, so sailing enthusiasts flock to the harbour every year. Auckland has the biggest number of private yachts worldwide, thus popularly known as the "city of sails". Every January, large scale sailing competition will be held here. Starting from Auckland, the journey includes other popular tourist places such as Bethells Beach where *The Piano*—an Oscar winning movie was set, Waiheke Island on which the famous Chinese poet Gu Cheng once lived, and Rangitoto Island created by volcanic lava. As one of the most livable cities in the world, Auckland boasts complete facilities for tourism, harbour, islands, Polynesian culture, first-class dining, night life and shopping. It is an ideal place to start the tour of New Zealand.

（二）罗托鲁阿（Rotorua）

罗托鲁阿，又译罗托鲁瓦，是新西兰北岛中北部著名的地热观光城市，因坐落在火山多发区，被喻为“火山上的城市”。罗托鲁阿距奥克兰市221千米，市内多天然温泉，热泉及泥浆池数不胜数。空气中硫黄弥漫，温泉在灰黄泥浆中翻滚、吐泡，泡地热温泉对旅客来说是必不可少的节目。罗托鲁阿位于罗托鲁阿湖南畔，毛利语中意为“双湖”。作为一个旅游城市，吸引游客的除了令人惊讶的火山口、高山和湖泊景观外，罗托鲁阿还有美丽的英国哥特式建筑和园林。

Rotorua, a geothermal sightseeing city in central north part of North Island of New Zealand, is popularly known as the "city on the volcano", as it is located in a volcanic area. 221 kilometers away from Auckland, the city is known for its natural hot springs, particularly geysers and mud pools. The smell of sulfur permeates in the air, and hot springs and yellow muds are bubbling. A geothermal spring bath here is a must for most travelers. Rotorua, whose name means "double lakes" in Māori, sits on the south bank of Rotorua Lake. As a tourist city, Rotorua has so much to offer, from the crater, high mountains and lakes, to British style gothic architecture and gardens.

罗托鲁阿是毛利人聚居区，毛利族历史文化的荟萃之地，素有“毛利之乡”的美誉。毛利人的历史源远流长，手工艺品引人入胜。毛利人擅长用地热烧煮食物，游客在罗托鲁阿可以品尝到地道的石头火锅。石头火锅是把经地热烘烫的石块放进地洞内，再把食物烩熟，风味独特。在新西兰流传着这样一句名言：“没到过罗托鲁阿，就不算到过新西兰。”

Rotorua, a Māori enclave, is the flourishing land of culture and history, gaining the reputation as the "home of Māori". Māori enjoys a time-honored history and impressive folk crafts. Māori people are adept at cooking with geothermal heat. Tourists can feast their tongues with authentic stone chafing dish, a kind of hotpot stewed with pieces of stones which are heated by geothermal heat. A saying in New Zealand goes like this "No trip to New Zealand is complete without visiting Rotorua".

（三）惠灵顿（Wellington）

惠灵顿是新西兰首都，位于北岛的最南端，是往来南、北二岛的交通枢纽，也是世界最佳深水港之一。惠灵顿是处于世界最南端的首都，三面环山，一面朝海。惠灵顿由于濒临海湾，城市依山而建，而且地势较高，时常受到海风的侵袭，一年之中大部分日子都会刮风，因而有“风城”之称。

Located at the south tip of the North Island, the capital city Wellington is the pivot of transportation between South Island and North Island, and one of the best deepwater ports in the world as well. Wellington is a capital in the world's furthest south, surrounded by mountains on three sides with one side facing the sea. Bordered by the harbour, the city is built against hillside. Because of its position and high terrain, it often suffers from the high winds of sea. As most of days in a year are windy, it is called "windy city".

惠灵顿是新西兰地理、文化和政治中心，城市紧凑，文化气息浓厚并充满了个性，它与悉尼和墨尔本一起成为大洋洲的文化中心。许多艺术家在此定居或活动，这里还有众多艺术咖啡馆和生动的夜生活。惠灵顿也是新西兰的电影业中心，彼得·杰克逊《指环王》的拍摄地就位于惠灵顿。惠灵顿还有许多文化节日，包括每两年举办一次的新西兰国际艺术节、每年举办的国际爵士节等。惠灵顿也是著名的旅游胜地。建于 1876 年的旧政府大厦是南太平洋最宏伟的木结构建筑之一。

Wellington is the geological, cultural and political center of New Zealand. This compact city has rich cultural atmosphere and unique personality. In addition to Sydney and Melbourne, Wellington is another cultural center of Oceania. Many artists are settled down here or have a short stay, partly for its artistic cafes and dynamic night life. Wellington is the national movie center. Peter Jackson's movie *the Lord of the Rings* was set in Wellington region. In Wellington, there are many festivals such as biennial New Zealand Festival and annual International Jazz Festival, etc. Wellington is also a famous tourist city. Its old Government Buildings built in 1876 is one of the most magnificent wooden structure architecture in South Pacific Ocean.

（四）克莱斯特彻奇（Christchurch）

克莱斯特彻奇，又称基督城，西临南阿尔卑斯山，东临太平洋海岸，是南岛第一大城市，新西兰第三大城市，也是仅次于奥克兰通往世界各地的第二大门户。它还是进入南极的门户，其国际机场是新西兰、意大利及美国南极计划的主要基地。国际南极中心涵盖基地设施、博物馆和游客中心。基督城的艺术文化气息浓厚，处处洋溢着英国气息，是除英国本土以外最具英国特色的城市。基督城是世界级的花园城市，每年 2 月、3 月举办的鲜花节享有盛誉。基督城变化多样的地形地貌特征为冒险和探索运动创造了充分的条件，这里游客有机会欣赏到各种各样的野生动物与大自然的奇妙景观。但近年来，基督城附近地区已接连发生多次地震。

Bordered by Southern Alps to its west and Pacific Ocean to its east, Christchurch is the largest city of South Island, the third largest city of New Zealand, and the second gateway to the world next to Auckland. Serving as the gateway to the Antarctica, Christchurch International Airport is the main base for the Antarctic expeditions of New Zealand, Italy and the United States. International Antarctic Centre includes base facilities, museum and tourist center. Christchurch is a very artistic and cultural city. Featured in British ambiance, it is the most British style city outside UK. It is also a world-class garden city, where the famed flowers festival is held here in February or March. The varied landforms of Christchurch make it an ideal place for exploration and adventure travels. Here travelers are able to see different kinds of wild animals and spectacular natural landscapes. However, the area around Christchurch has been stricken by earthquakes several times over the past years.

（五）皇后镇（Queenstown）

新西兰南岛皇后镇位于瓦卡蒂普湖的北岸，被南阿尔卑斯山包围。依山傍水的环境，使得皇后镇成为新西兰最受欢迎的旅游目的地之一。据说因为此地美得适合维多利亚女王居住，因此被命名为“皇后镇”。新西兰的极限运动和探险旅行全球知名，皇后镇拥有各种各样超乎想象的户外探险运动，四周自然景观更是令人叹为观止。早在1988年，皇后镇便已建立全球首座商业化的高空弹跳场，这里的卡瓦劳悬索大桥是世界蹦极跳的发源地。在皇后镇，游客可以坐四驱车越野，欣赏《指环王》拍摄地的奇妙风光；乘上喷射快艇，在激流中快速穿梭于高山峡谷间；或是骑马、徒步旅行、漂流、骑山地自行车、登山等。

Nestled by South Alps Mountain and bordered by Lake Wakatipu in its south, Queenstown is one of the most popular tourist destinations in New Zealand for the proximity to the mountain and lake. This place is so beautiful that it was said to be the perfect living place for the Queen, hence the name Queenstown. The extreme sports and adventure travels in New Zealand enjoy the worldwide fame. Queenstown is where you can experience unimaginable outdoor adventure sports in breathtaking natural surroundings. As early as 1988, the world first commercial bungee jump site was established on Kawarau Gorge Suspension Bridge in Queenstown, which is known as the birthplace of bungee jump now. In Queenstown, you will be amazed by the choices you have here, crossing the country in four-wheel-drive vehicles to see the picturesque scenery of the shooting location of *the Lord of the Rings,* piercing through the currents of canyons on a jet, or horse riding, trekking, drifting, mountain biking and mountaineering.

四、旅游资讯

（一）美食

新西兰经济以农牧业和渔业为主。新西兰的物产丰富，素有“美食天堂”之誉，盛产瓜果蔬菜、海产和禽肉。新西兰“环太平洋”式的烹饪风格，汲取了欧洲以及泰国、马来西亚、印度尼西亚、日本、越南的烹调艺术的精华。典型的新西兰式的食物有羊肉、猪肉、鹿肉、鲑鱼、龙虾、布拉夫牡蛎、鲍鱼、贻贝、扇贝、红薯、猕猴桃和树茄果。蛋白蛋糕是新西兰的国民甜点。石头火锅是毛利人的传统做法。把石头烤热放入洞中，再把包好的食物放在石头上煮熟，这种做法保留了食材原有的风味。

New Zealand mainly relies on agriculture, livestock husbandry and marine economy. Known as the food paradise, the country abounds with fruits, vegetables, seafood and poultry meat. The pan-pacific cooking style of New Zealand is the fusion of European, Thai, Malaysian, Indonesian, Japanese and Vietnamese culinary art. Typical New Zealand ingredients include mouton, pork, venison, salmon, lobster, bluff oyster, paua, mussel, scallop, kumara, kiwi fruit and tamarillo. Pavlova is the national dessert of New Zealand. Stone chafing dish is the traditional cooking method of Māori people. The stones are heated and placed in the cave together with wrapped food. After a while the food will be cooked, but it still retains its original taste and flavor.

新西兰人的饮食习惯大体上与英国人相同，以西餐为主。但是当地人非常热爱烧烤，各种鱼类、扇贝都是烧烤的食材。新西兰人喜欢饮酒，特别是啤酒和葡萄酒。新西兰的白葡萄酒，特别是霞多丽和长相思赢得了国际声誉。饮茶也是新西兰人的爱好。

Generally speaking, the diet habit of New Zealanders is similar with the Britons, mostly dining on Western food. But local people are also enthusiastic about grilled food. All kinds of fishes and scallops are all the good ingredients for grilling. New Zealanders enjoy drinking, especially beer and wine. New Zealand white wines, particularly Chardonnay and Sauvignon Blancs, have won global reputation. New Zealanders are also obsessed with tea drinking.

（二）购物及退税

游客到新西兰喜欢购买的商品有保健品、蜂产品、绵羊油和毛利人特色纪念品。传统的新西兰纪念品包括用木头、骨头和翡翠制成的精制的毛利雕刻品、用五彩斑斓的鲍鱼壳做成的首饰和装饰品。几个世纪以来，毛利人一直把它们视为珍宝。新西兰的陶瓷艺术世界闻名。新西兰的羊毛工业十分发达，游客可以买到美丽的手工编织的羊毛衫、漂亮的壁挂、家纺的毛线与上乘的羊皮。由于有着纯天然的环境，新西兰的蜂蜜和蜂胶质量上乘，享誉世界。

The New Zealand goods that the tourists favor are healthcare products, honey products, lanolin oil and characteristic Māori souvenir. Those traditional souvenirs include exquisite Māori carvings made of wood, bone or emerald, jewelry and adornments made of colorful abalone shells. For centuries, they have been cherished as treasures for Māori people. The ceramic art of New Zealand enjoys world reputation. The wool industry is highly-developed in New Zealand where you can buy fine hand-knitted woolen sweaters, pretty wall hangings, woolen knitting yarn and superb sheepskins. The honey and propolis in New Zealand are known around the world for its natural environment.

新西兰无针对游客的购物退税政策，但凭机票到免税店购买商品可以享受免税。

There is no special policy of the tax refund for the visitors in New Zealand, but visitors can purchase the duty free goods in the duty free shops by air tickets.

（三）时差

新西兰是地球上最早开始新的一天的国家之一，比世界标准时间早 12 小时。新西兰实行夏令制，夏季时钟向前拨 1 小时，比世界标准时间早 13 小时。新西兰位于东十二区，新西兰时间比北京时间快 4 个小时。但是每当新西兰实施夏令时时，新西兰时间会比北京时间快 5 个小时。新西兰的夏令时是从每年 10 月的第 1 个星期天到次年 3 月的第 3 个星期天。

New Zealand is one of the first countries to begin a new day, 12 hours in advance of Coordinated Universal Time (UTC). Daylight Saving Time (DST) is observed and clocks are set one hour earlier. New Zealand Daylight Time (NZDT) is thus 13 hours ahead of UTC. The time zone of New Zealand is UTC+12

(4 hours ahead of Beijing time). When the DST is observed in New Zealand, the time is 5 hours ahead of Beijing time. The DST begins from the first Sunday of October to the third Sunday of March next year.

知识拓展

奇异鸟

奇异鸟（Kiwi，又译几维鸟）分布于新西兰，因为它们的鸣叫声非常尖锐，听起来特别像“kiwi”，所以被当地土著的毛利人叫作奇异鸟。奇异鸟由于翅膀退化，因此无法飞行。奇异鸟是新西兰的特产，也是新西兰的国鸟及象征。在新西兰人的生活中，有的银行名字叫奇异鸟，新西兰的20分与1元的硬币上一面印的是英国女王伊丽莎白二世的头像，另一面便是奇异鸟。新西兰人更是坦然地以奇异鸟自称，新西兰人常常自豪地说“我是一只奇异鸟”，意思是“我是一个新西兰人”。

思考练习

1. 经典旅游线路分析

新西兰经典8日游

第1天：上海——奥克兰

游客搭乘飞机前往新西兰第一大城市——奥克兰，班机于隔日上午抵达。

第2天：奥克兰——基督城

抵达奥克兰后，由领队协助通关，随即转往南岛第一大城——素有“花园城市”之称的基督城。基督城保持了南岛优雅而传统的文化气质，建有古色古香的哥特式教堂以及19世纪的石砌建筑。最早的英国移民有计划地把该城建设为家乡的模样，因此又被称为“英国以外最像英国的城市”，深具浓厚的古典英国风味，宛如花园城堡、缤纷多彩。抵达后，参观基督城这座新西兰最具有英国风味的传统都市，欣赏杨柳垂岸的回忆之桥（艾芬河上）、植物园、大教堂广场。参观艺术中心，这里富有维多利亚式的建筑和美轮美奂的花园景致。

第3天：基督城——梯卡坡——皇后镇

早餐后，专车前往新西兰美丽的度假城市——皇后镇，沿途欣赏位于南阿尔卑斯山的库克山国家公园以及途经有“世外桃源”之称的美丽的梯卡坡小镇。午餐后可欣赏美丽的湖边景色，尽情地享受大自然的美景。抵达皇后镇，晚餐后入住酒店休息，全天游览结束。

第4天：皇后镇

早餐后，前往新西兰最大的米尔福德峡湾国家公园（Milford Sound National Park）。

毛利语称米尔福德峡湾为Piopiotahi，占地面积达125万公顷，于1986年被列入世界自然遗产名录。此外，前往米佛峡湾的道路被人称为“全世界风景最好的高地公路之一”。沿途行车欣赏峡湾国家公园内的壮丽景致。中午抵达米尔福德峡湾，搭乘游艇游览由冰河及海水切割而成的峡湾景观，其中教冠峰（Mitre Peak）由海平面向上直拔1 692米，是直接从海上拔起的世界上最高的独立岩石，在峡湾巡弋航程中有机会观赏到新西兰特有的寒带动物，如软毛海豹、凸吻海豚等或峡湾鸡冠企鹅或蓝企鹅等野生动物。之后返回皇后镇入住酒店休息。

第5天：皇后镇——奥克兰

早餐后，在市区观光，包括在瓦卡蒂普湖边漫步、摄影等。皇后镇迷人的湖光山色令人流连忘返。后搭乘飞机前往新西兰“千帆之都”——奥克兰，抵达后享用晚餐，入住酒店休息，全天游览结束。

第6天：奥克兰——怀托摩——罗托鲁阿

早餐后专车前往怀托摩，参观怀托摩萤火虫洞，星光点点的萤火虫洞犹如漫天繁星，蔚为壮观。午餐后专车前往新西兰地热中心——罗托鲁阿，它是南半球最有名的泥火山和温泉区，也是当地毛利人聚集的首府。随后参观毛利文化地热中心——著名的旅游景点Te Puia（意为喷泉），它以部落里的几个地热喷泉而闻名。独有的毛利文化一直为来自世界各地的游客所喜爱，其中波呼图间歇喷泉向空中射出高达30米的热水柱，世界闻名。此外，硅石台地、沸腾的泥浆及独特的植被，都不容错过，园区内还有新西兰国宝奇异鸟。晚上搭乘天空缆车至山顶一览罗托鲁阿的全景。

第7天：罗托鲁阿——奥克兰——上海

早上前往搭乘“皇后号”游轮畅游罗托鲁阿湖，并在船上享用自助早餐的同时游湖观景。专车前往爱歌顿皇家牧场，它是罗托鲁阿的五星级景点，罗托鲁阿地区是新西兰农产品出口的重镇之一。在爱歌顿牧场参与一系列活动，馆内有全世界19种各类训练有素的羊只，在此观赏精彩的剪羊毛秀及乖巧的牧羊犬赶羊表演。然后参观政府花园和红森林公园等。之后返回奥克兰，市区观光包括途经海湾大桥、皇后街、美国帆船杯比赛村、战争湾以及伊甸山观看死火山口遗留下来的痕迹，并在此可一览奥克兰市的全景。

第8天：上海

清晨，抵达上海，结束精彩愉快的新西兰之旅。

分析：这条经典旅游线路的主要旅游景点与行程特色，以及适合旅游的人群。

2. 案例分析

[案例] 某旅行团到新西兰旅游，在参观毛利民俗村时，游客看到毛利人的欢迎仪式大不一样，情不自禁地拿起相机对着欢迎的队伍猛拍。突然，一位毛利人冲过来，对着旅行团大喊大叫，游客们都被吓坏了。请问：毛利人想要表达什么不满？作为游客与领队，

如何消除两国之间的文化差异？

3. 练一练

（1）随着导演彼得·杰克逊执导的电影《指环王》三部曲在银屏上大获成功，新西兰丰富多样的地貌特征和纯净美丽的自然风光便吸引了大批来自世界各地的影迷。在荣获奥斯卡大奖的《指环王》影片中，150多个壮美的场景遍布新西兰全境。影片中的大部分场景均在重要的地标和旅游中心附近取景，如影片中的霍比屯（Hobbiton）位于北岛的马塔马塔镇（Matamata）郊外，在这里可以欣赏到惊人的建筑细节之美；在汤加里罗步道（Tongariro Alpine Crossing）远足行走可以感受魔多（Mordor）摄人心魄的美景；在皇后镇附近的格林诺奇（Glenorchy）可以欣赏到宏伟矗立的艾辛格（Isengard）堡垒；新西兰的首都惠灵顿是该部影片的制作大本营，这里可以享受到新西兰的美食和文化大餐。请观看电影《指环王》，随电影踏上出游探险的征程，分析“指环王观光之旅”的主要旅游景点的分布城市及其特色。

（2）了解新西兰的主要信息、文化历史和旅游景点。如何理解新西兰的旅游宣传口号“百分之百纯净保证（100% Pure New Zealand）”？

第三章
欧洲

本章导航

欧洲（Europe）是西方文化的起源地，全称为欧罗巴洲。“欧罗巴”一词相传来源于希腊神话中的腓尼基公主欧罗巴的名字。欧洲面积为 1 016 万平方千米，是世界第六大洲，但人口居于世界第三位，达到 7.4 亿，仅次于亚洲和非洲。欧洲东以乌拉尔山脉、乌拉尔河，东南以里海、大高加索山脉和黑海与亚洲为界，西边、西北隔大西洋、格陵兰海、丹麦海峡与北美洲相望，北接北冰洋，南隔地中海与非洲相望。通常，根据政治、经济、文化或实际考虑，欧洲的边界线并不总是一样的。这就使得人们产生了几个不同“欧洲”的观念。欧洲共有 50 个独立国家，按照地理上习惯分为北欧、东欧、中欧、西欧及南欧。欧洲的文化是西方社会文化的源头，几乎渗透到世界的每个角落，欧洲人始终为此深感骄傲。同时，深厚的文化底蕴让他们表现出的谦虚与彬彬有礼，使整个欧洲都展现出一种含蓄与浪漫。本章主要从国家概况、民俗风情、主要旅游城市及景点等方面增加学习者对英国、法国、德国、意大利、瑞士、西班牙和俄罗斯七国的认识和了解。

第一节　英国

一、国家概况

（一）地理环境

大不列颠及北爱尔兰联合王国是位于欧洲西部的岛国，简称“联合王国”，由大不列颠岛（包括英格兰、苏格兰、威尔士）、爱尔兰岛东北部和一些小岛组成，首都为伦敦。英国坐落于欧洲大陆西北部，被大西洋包围。英国东临北海，西临大西洋，南面是英吉利海峡和多佛尔海峡，与欧洲大陆隔海相望，陆界与爱尔兰接壤。面积为24.41万平方千米。由于英格兰是全国的重心，经济最发达，政治占优势，人口占绝大多数，因此人们非正式地以“英格兰”来代表整个“联合王国”。

The United Kingdom of Great Britain and Northern Ireland commonly referred to as the UK or Britain, consists of the Great Britain Island (including England, Scotland and Wales), Northeastern Ireland and some small isles. The capital is London. It is located off the northwest of Continental Europe and is surrounded by the Atlantic Ocean. To its east is the North Sea, the west is the Atlantic Ocean and its south is English Channel and Strait of Dover which separate Britain from the continent of Europe and it borders Ireland. The UK covers an area of 244,100 square kilometers. Sometimes, people unofficially use England instead of the United Kingdom as England is the most important part of the country for its developed economy, influential political forces and its large number of population.

从地形上看，英国地势由西北向东南逐渐倾斜，北部的苏格兰为山地，到处牛羊成群；南部英格兰原野风光令人陶醉；西部的威尔士以崎岖的山岭和碧绿的河谷而闻名。英国河流、湖泊众多，主要河流有大不列颠岛上的第一长河——塞文河和流经牛津、伦敦的泰晤士河。

Geographically, the Great Britain descends gradually from the northwest to the southeast. The northern part in Scotland is highland where flocks of sheep and cows can be seen everywhere. The southern part is England which is plain with the beautiful natural scenic view. And the west part is Wales which is famous for its rugged mountains and green valleys. The UK is full of lakes and rivers. The main rivers are River Severn which is the longest in Great Britain and the River Thames which passes through Oxford and London.

英国属海洋性温带阔叶林气候，终年温和湿润。冬暖夏凉，夏天最高温度不超过32℃，冬天平均温度为4℃～6℃。英国雨量充沛，四季晴雨常常不定。多雨雾是英国气候的显著特点，故雨伞成了英国人外出必备之物。

The climate of the UK belongs to oceanic temperate broad-leaved forest. It is mild and moist all year round. Warm in winter and cool in summer, the highest temperature in summer is not higher than 32℃, and the average temperature in winter is 4℃ to 6℃. Rainfall is plentiful here but the rain is often unpredictable in four seasons. The signature of the UK weather is frequent fogs and rains so that an umbrella is an outdoor must for the Britons.

知识拓展

欧洲联盟

欧洲联盟（European Union，EU），简称欧盟，是根据1991年签署的《欧洲联盟条约》(又称《马斯特里赫特条约》)所建立的国际组织，总部设在比利时首都布鲁塞尔。欧盟是世界上最有影响力的国际组织之一，在贸易、农业、金融等方面趋近于一个统一的联邦国家，而在内政、国防、外交等其他方面则类似于一个由独立国家所组成的同盟。欧盟的政治体制与世界其他大规模的国际组织不同，应把它视作邦联。欧盟的宗旨是促进和平，追求公民富裕生活，实现社会、经济可持续发展，确保基本价值观，加强国际合作。“在多元中团结”是欧盟的官方口号。它清楚地再现了欧洲人是如何走到一起共同追求和平与富裕，又能容纳不同的种族、语言和文化的。欧盟的主要机构有欧洲理事会、欧盟理事会、欧盟委员会、欧洲议会、欧盟对外行动署等。欧元是欧盟的官方货币，目前已经被19个成员国采纳为流通货币；《申根协定》取消了部分成员国之间的边境管制，目前已有22个欧盟成员国和4个非成员国实施。到目前为止，欧盟共有27个成员国，分别是：奥地利、比利时、保加利亚、塞浦路斯、捷克、克罗地亚、丹麦、爱沙尼亚、芬兰、法国、德国、希腊、匈牙利、爱尔兰、意大利、拉脱维亚、立陶宛、卢森堡、马耳他、荷兰、波兰、葡萄牙、罗马尼亚、斯洛伐克、斯洛文尼亚、西班牙、瑞典。英国于2020年1月31日正式脱离欧洲联盟。

（二）人文概况

1. 历史

英国与欧洲大陆拥有同一祖先。大不列颠岛原本是和欧洲大陆连在一起的，在后冰川时期，冰山融化导致海平面上升，大不列颠岛于是与欧洲大陆分离。公元前500年，凯尔特人大批涌入大不列颠岛，并在此定居。随着时间流逝，凯尔特系英国人成为英国最早的居民。

The ancestors of the UK should be the same as those in the Continental Europe with which the British Isles used to be connected. In the last Ice Age, the melting of last glaciers caused the sea level to rise and the British Isles were thus separated from the Continent. In the year of 500 BC, the Celts poured into Britain and settled down. They lived together with the original residents, and years passed, the Britons with Celtic origin became the first inhabitants in the UK.

公元55年到450年，罗马帝国两次入侵并统治英格兰约350年。在这期间，拉丁文化被带入上层阶级，基督教文化开始传播至整个英格兰。公元450年到1066年，英格兰进入了盎格鲁-撒克逊时代，在这段时期，北欧海盗不断入侵并移居到英格兰，进而形成了盎格鲁-撒克逊人。他们迫使一部分凯尔特人逃到威尔士，形成了今天的威尔士人。在与北欧海盗的抗争过程中，于公元829年，威塞克斯国王埃格伯特统一了英格兰。

The Roman Empire had invaded the land twice and dominated the England for almost 350 years from 55 AD to 450 AD. In the meantime, Latin culture was brought into the upper class. During this period, the Christian practices spread throughout the country. The Anglo-Saxons period had remained from 450 AD to 1066 AD. During this period, the Vikings invaded the island and gradually settled down. They either mixed with existing population or pushed the Celts to westward. Some of them mixed with the residents and became the Wales. In 829 AD, England was united under the King Egbert of Wessex during the war against the Vikings.

而英格兰真正实行君主制的社会制度是在 1066 年，来自法国的诺曼底公爵威廉率兵打败盎格鲁–撒克逊人，成为英格兰的国王，创建诺曼底王朝后才开始的。此后，英格兰经历了十个王朝，再无其他大陆外族的大规模入侵和占领，并相继完成和威尔士、苏格兰的合并，其后逐步完成由封建制度向资本主义制度的转变，成为最强大的国家。1689 年，英国通过了《权利法案》，1701 年通过了《王位继承法》，这两部法律大大加强了议会的权力，确立了英国资产阶级和新贵族专政的君主立宪制。19 世纪英国第一个完成工业革命，成为当时最发达的国家。至 1914 年，英国占有的殖民地比本土大 111 倍，成为第一殖民大国，特别是把澳大利亚和新西兰纳入其殖民体系后，英国成了真正的“日不落帝国”。第二次世界大战后，英国经济实力大为削弱，政治地位下降。随着 1947 年印度和巴基斯坦相继宣布独立，到 20 世纪 60 年代，英殖民体系逐渐瓦解。

England became a monarchy when the French Norman invader led by William, the Conqueror, invaded in 1066 and defeated the Anglo-Saxons. After King William's Norman Dynasty, there were 10 successive dynasties in total and England has never been under invasion by any continental countries since then. England gradually united with Wales and Scotland. It turned into the most powerful country after it ended the feudal social system and adopted the capitalism system. The enactment of *The Bill of Rights* in 1689 and *The Act of Settlement* in 1701 strengthened the power of the Parliament and established the United Kingdom dictatorship of the bourgeoisie and the new nobility under a constitutional monarchy. It was UK that had completed the first industrial revolution in the 19th century. UK has become the most developed country in the world since then. By the year of 1914, UK had colonized an area 111 times more than its own land and became the largest ever colonial power. It became "the empire on which the sun never sets" after it colonized Australia and New Zealand. After the Second World War, its economic power weakened and political position decreased. In 1947, India and Pakistan declared independence. The colonial system of the British Empire collapsed in the 1960s.

2. 经济

英国是世界上第一个实行市场经济的国家，是 19 世纪至 20 世纪世界上最发达的国家，但经过两次世界大战和 20 世纪下半叶大英帝国的瓦解，已失去昔日荣光。不过，英国仍是一个在世界范围内拥有巨大影响力的强国。英国的石油、天然气、煤矿和水资源丰富，能源工业在西欧国家中位列第一。在金融、保险、通信、咨询业及某些高科技领域，英国仍具有相当的优势和领先地位。英国的农业以乳畜业为主，高度机械化。目前，英国是世界上第六大经济体，首都伦敦更是世界上数一数二的金融、航运和服务中心，与纽约并列为全球两大国际金融中心。英国的教育、学术和科学研究亦处于世界领先地位，拥有众多如剑桥大学、牛津大学和伦敦政治经济学院等国际知名学府。英国是除美国外的全球最重要的教育中心。旅游业是英国最重要的经济部门之一，年产值700多亿英镑，旅游收入占世界旅游收入的5%左右。与以自然风光为主的国家不同，英国的王室文化和博物馆是旅游业的最大看点。英国经济被广泛形容为盎格鲁-撒克逊经济。

The United Kingdom was the first country that executed the system of market economy and was the most developed country between 19th and 20th century. Though it lost the past glory after the two world wars and the British empire collapsed in the second half of the 20th century, the UK is still a powerful country to influence the world. The UK is rich in petroleum, natural gas, coal and water resources. Its energy industry ranks the first among the West European countries. The UK still enjoys a considerable advantage in the world in finance, insurance, communication, advisory services and certain field of high technology. Dairy livestock is the major industry for the UK agriculture which is highly mechanized. Nowadays, the UK is the sixth largest economy in the world. London, the capital of the country, is the center of finance, shipping and service and is ranked as one of the two world finance centers (the other one is New York). The UK takes a leading position in education, academic field and scientific research. The UK has many world famous universities such as University of Oxford, University of Cambridge and the London School of Economics and Political Science. Besides the United States, the UK is another important education center. Tourism industry is one of the most important sectors in economy. Its annual output value is more than 70 billion pounds. The tourism revenue accounts for about 5% of world tourism income. Different from the countries with the natural scenery, the main attractions for the UK tourism are the royal culture and museums. The economy of the UK is named as economy of Anglo-Saxons.

3. 社会文化

英国人口约6 679万，其中英格兰5 629万，威尔士315万，苏格兰546万，北爱尔兰189万。英国的两种官方语言分别是英语和威尔士语，绝大部分地方都使用英语。苏格兰部分地区使用盖尔语。居民多信奉基督教新教，还有部分人信奉天主教、印度教、犹太教及伊斯兰教等。

The UK has a population of 66.79 million, among which England has 55.29 million, Wales has 3.15 million, Scotland has 5.46 million and Northern Ireland has 1.88 million. The official languages of the UK are English and Welsh. Most people speak English while some from Scotland speak Gaelic. Most of the inhabitants believe in Protestantism, but some believe in Catholicism, Hinduism, Judaism and Islam.

英国是一个具有多元文化和开放思想的国家。英国的艺术、音乐、文化和饮食一直受到来自世界各地不同国家的人民和民族习惯的影响，并与许多国家有着悠久而密切的联系。直到现在，它仍与美国、加拿大、澳大利亚和新西兰等英语国家保持着牢固的关系。

The UK is a country with multi-culture and open mind. Its arts, music, culture and food are affected by different people and customs from all over the world, and have a long and close ties with many countries. Until now, it has had a close contact with some English-speaking countries such as the United States, Canada, Australia and New Zealand.

英国的现代写实主义的文学创作在世界文化史上占有突出的地位。14 世纪的杰弗雷·乔叟（1343—1400）是英国现实主义文学的奠基人，被誉为“英国现代文学之父”，代表作为《坎特伯雷故事集》。而文艺复兴时期英国的代表人物当数威廉·莎士比亚（1564—1616），他一生共写了 37 部戏剧。

The UK's modern realistic literature holds a prominent place in the world cultural history. Geoffrey Chaucer (1343–1400) of the 14th century was the founder of UK realistic literature and was awarded as the Father of the English Modern Literature. *The Canterbury Tales* was his representative work. William Shakespeare (1564–1616) was the greatest master of Renaissance in UK and finished 37 plays in his life.

17 世纪英国的议会制度发展迅速，为了表达不同政见，出现了各种传单和小册子，约翰·弥尔顿（1608—1674）是此时期的代表。18 世纪到 19 世纪，英国的现实主义小说达到巅峰，代表人物有丹尼尔·笛福（1660—1731），代表作为《鲁滨逊漂流记》；乔纳森·斯威夫特（1667—1745），代表作为《格列佛游记》；简·奥斯汀（1775—1817），代表作为《傲慢与偏见》；查尔斯·狄更斯（1812—1870）无疑是最有代表性的人物，主要著作为《雾都孤儿》《双城记》等。其他代表人物还有威廉·梅克皮斯·撒克里（1811—1863），代表作为《名利场》；夏洛蒂·勃朗特（1816—1855），代表作为《简·爱》；艾米莉·勃朗特（1818—1848），代表作为《呼啸山庄》；托马斯·哈代（1840—1928），代表作为《德伯家的苔丝》。诗歌方面的代表人物有乔治·戈登·拜伦（1788—1824），代表作为《唐璜》；珀西·比希·雪莱（1792—1822），代表作为《解放了的普罗米修斯》；约翰·济慈（1795—1821），代表作为《夜莺颂》。20 世纪的代表人物是伟大的戏剧家乔治·伯纳德·萧伯纳（1856—1950），一生创作了超过 60 部作品。

In the 17th century, the British parliament system developed rapidly. In order to express different opinions, there appeared to be a variety of leaflets and brochures. John Milton (1608–1674) was the representative among the political commentators in the 17th century. During the 18th and 19th centuries, the realistic literature of UK reached its climax. The representatives were Daniel Defoe (1660–1731, *The Adventures of Robinson Crusoe*), Jonathan Swift (1667–1745, *Gulliver's Travels*), Jane Austen (1775–1817, *Pride and Prejudice*). Among them, the typical representative should be Charles Dickens (1812–1870), whose major novels were *Oliver Twist, A Tale of Two Cities,* etc. There were some other famous writers like William Makepeace Thackeray (1811–1863, *Vanity Fair*), Charlotte Bronte (1816–1855, *Jane Eyre*), Emily Bronte (1818-1848, *Wuthering Heights*) and Thomas Hardy (1840–1928, *Tess of the D'Urbervilles*). The representatives of poets were George Gordon Byron (1788–1824, *Don Juan*), Percy Bysshe Shelley (1792–1822, *Prometheus Unbound*) and John Keats (1795–1821, *Ode to a Nightingale*). George Bernard Shaw (1856–1950), the greatest dramatist in the 20th century who finished more than 60 works in his life.

作为电影的发祥地之一，英国电影在世界上占有重要的地位。从古典的《傲慢与偏见》到现代的《哈利·波特》，更多人通过电影来了解英国。英国的流行音乐也是其文化的重要组成部分。20 世纪 60 年代初，甲壳虫乐队开创了流行音乐的革命。

As one of the cradles of the film, United Kingdom film occupies an important position in the world. From the classical films like *Pride and Prejudice* to the modern films like *Harry Potter*, more people learn about the UK through the films. United Kingdom pop music is also an important part of its culture. In the early 1960s, The Beatles created a revolution in pop music.

知识拓展

甲壳虫乐队

甲壳虫乐队（The Beatles），又名“披头士”乐队。在英国，甲壳虫乐队影响了20世纪60年代至今几乎每一支乐队的形成和发展。甲壳虫乐队以其反上流社会、反正统艺术的风格，敢于接触社会敏感问题的内容和在舞台上与世俗挑战的举止征服了各国青年。不少歌曲表现了资本主义社会年轻人失望、低落和愤懑的心情。甲壳虫乐队是流行音乐界历史上最伟大、最有影响力、拥有最多歌迷、最为成功的乐队。甲壳虫乐队对于流行音乐的革命性的发展与影响力无人可及，对于世界范围内摇滚的发展做出了非常巨大的贡献。他们不仅拥有世界上最高、令后人难以企及的唱片销售纪录，而且他们的文化影响力也早已超过了艺术本身。甲壳虫乐队在几十年的时间里，已成为流行音乐和流行文化的标志，也成为英国文化和英国历史的象征，他们中有成员被英国女王加封晋爵。

二、民俗风情

（一）礼仪禁忌

长期的王室文化和贵族文化形成了英国人特有的礼仪。保守、矜持、幽默是英国国民的特点。英国人做事有耐心，和蔼，诚实守信。“打扰一下”“对不起”“谢谢”永远都是使用频率最高的词。无论是在售票处、银行、超市，还是在公交车站，都是耐心排队的人。排在队尾的人常被问道：“你在排队吗？”哪怕在公交车站只有两三人也会排队。不管是在拥挤的电梯里还是在排队队伍中，英国人总是缩着身体避免相互碰撞，他们最常说的一句话是“保持距离”。

The UK etiquette adopts the British royal and aristocratic culture. The national characteristics are conservative, courteous and humorous. The people keep patient, good-tempered, honest and trustworthy as a rule. The terms used most often are “excuse me”, “sorry” and “thank you”. People get used to queue no matter where they are: ticket offices, banks, supermarkets or bus stations. The person in the end of the line will be often inquired as “are you in the queue?” Even when there are only two or three persons in the bus station, they will queue to get on the bus. People always avoid touching each other wherever they are in the crowded lifts or in the lines. They always say “keep your distance”.

到英国人家中做客时，不要提前到，最好在约定时间后10分钟到达。客人不要送太贵重的礼物，礼物一般是巧克力、红酒、威士忌或鲜花。当然，民族特色手工艺品也很受欢迎。不要送有公司标志的礼品。不要送菊花，菊花在欧洲只用于万圣节和葬礼。而白色百合在英国象征死亡。

"Ten minutes later than the due time" is the right time when you visit a British family. The gifts you take should not be expensive. Chocolate, wine, whiskey or flowers are more popular. Of course, handicrafts with ethnic characteristics are also acceptable. Don't send the gift with company logos. Don't send chrysanthemums, as they are used only on Halloween or in funeral. White lily is the symbol of death in UK.

在欧洲人看来，英国人最显著的特点是缄默，感情不太外露。英国人爱谈论天气，因为英国的气候常难以预测，故见面时常以谈论天气来代替通常的问候。在与英国人交谈时，切忌谈及个人隐私，如家庭状况、婚姻状况、年龄、职业、收入、宗教等问题。没有邀请不能私自到别人家里。"英国人的家就是他的城堡"，这句话很好地道出了英国人在家里不愿受人打扰的习惯。

In Europeans' opinion, the most notable feature of the British is that they would always strive to be calm and avoid demonstrative words or behaviors. Because of the unpredictable weather, the British love to chat about the weather when they meet with each other. Don't ask the British about their personal affairs like family, marriage, age, occupation, income, religion, etc. The British don't welcome visitors who are not invited to their home. "An Englishman's home is his castle" means that they don't want to be disturbed at home.

英国人讲究穿戴，特别是参加宴会、集会和在特定场合时，都要穿正式的服装，如黑色西装，打不带条纹的领带。"头戴黑皮帽，身穿黑色燕尾服，手拿一把折好的雨伞"这也许是中国人心目中的英国绅士形象。英国的"绅士风度"是对男性行为举止、文明礼貌、尊重女性等一系列行为规范的总称。尊重女性是"绅士风度"的集中体现。"女士优先"贯彻在生活的每一角落。

British people pay attention to wear, especially when they attend the banquets, meetings or some special occasions, they are required to wear formal clothes such as black suits with non-strip tie. In the Chinese mind, an educated British gentleman should wear a black leather hat and a black swallowtail suit with an umbrella in the hand. The British gentleman is a series of codes of conduct of the British male's behavior, courtesy and respect for females. Respect for females is a concentrated expression of the British gentlemen. "Lady first" is carried out in every corner of life.

英国人的饮食简单但注重营养。食物以牛肉、羊肉和土豆为主。炸鱼、薯条和三明治是英国人的发明，也是现代快餐的标志。英国人非常注重餐桌礼仪。进餐时尽量不要出声，不要端着盘子喝汤，喝完汤后汤勺要放在汤盆托上。不能在餐桌上抽烟。茶是英国人的国饮，喝下午茶是英国人的习俗。

British food is simple but nutritious which usually are beef, mutton and potato. Fried fish, chips and sandwich are typical in their cuisine which is the symbol of modern fast food. The British care about the dinner etiquette very much. You should use a spoon to take soup and lay the spoon to the pot with care. Smoking is prohibited during dinners. Tea is the British national drink and drinking afternoon tea is a British custom.

知识拓展

约翰牛

英国人的绰号为“约翰牛”(John Bull)，音译为“约翰·布尔”，其形象为“头戴礼帽，足踏筒靴，身材矮胖的愚笨绅士”。18世纪初，苏格兰一位名叫约翰·阿巴思诺特的医生兼作家出版了一本政治讽刺小说，借以讽刺当时辉格党的战争政策，书名叫《约翰·布尔的历史》。书中的主人公约翰·布尔是一位保守的乡村绅士，他身材矮胖、性情急躁、举止笨拙滑稽，身后总跟着一条斗牛犬。由于这个形象很能代表英国乡绅，因此19世纪以来，英、美等国的漫画家纷纷用约翰·布尔这个形象指代英国人。由于该人物刻画逼真，形象生动，“约翰·布尔”很快传播开来，逐渐成为英国人的代名词。

（二）节庆风情

1. 万圣节（Halloween）

万圣节是在每年的11月1日。10月31日是万圣节前夜。英国是万圣节的起源地。公元前5世纪，当时居住于爱尔兰的凯尔特人将10月31日定为夏末，象征一年的结束。凯尔特人因为怕成为鬼魂的目标，便在夜晚熄灭家中炉火，戴上狰狞可怕的面具，并打扮成鬼怪模样走到街上巡游，以驱赶鬼怪。渐渐地，它成了孩子们的节日，年轻人也会举办化装舞会。万圣节前夜，孩子们会提着南瓜灯，穿着各式各样的稀奇古怪的服装，挨家挨户地去索要糖果，不停地说“trick or treat”，不给糖果就要捣乱，因此这一天孩子们往往收获颇丰。

Halloween is on November 1. October 31 is All Hallow's Eve. The festival originated in UK. In the 5th century BC, the Celtics living in Ireland set the October 31 as the end of the summer day and the symbol of the end of the year. Celtics were afraid of being a ghost goal, so they put on the ghost masks, extinguished the oven and marched in the city to chase away the ghost. Gradually, the festival becomes the kids' favorite. It is also the masquerade festival for young people. On All Hallow's Eve, the children will carry pumpkin lamps, they disguise as little ghosts, knock at the doors of neighbors and ask for candy. "Trick or treat" is the word they continue to say to the host. The kids will receive lots of candies.

2. 复活节（Easter）

据《圣经》记载，耶稣被钉死在十字架上，是为了赎世人的罪，第三天耶稣复活，复活节因此得名。在西方，复活节是仅次于圣诞节的重大节日。通常这个日子是在3月21日或以后的第一个月圆日之后的星期日，一般在3月22日至4月25日之间。复活节是最古老、最有意义的基督教节日之一。它庆祝耶稣的复活，象征着重生和希望。世界各地的基督徒每年都会举行庆祝活动。除了教会的庆典之外，复活节有不少传统习惯。典型的复活节礼物跟春天和再生有关系，最典型的要数复活节彩蛋。

According to the *Bible*, Jesus was crucified on the cross in order to redeem sins of the world. On the third day, Jesus was resurrected from the dead. So the festival got its name. Easter is a major holiday after Christmas in western world. Typically, this day is on March 21 or the Sunday after the first full moon day, generally between March 22 and April 25. Easter is one of the oldest and most meaningful Christian holidays. It celebrates the resurrection of Jesus and also symbolize of rebirth and hope. Christians around the world celebrate it every year. In addition to the celebration of the church, Easter has many traditional rituals. Typical Easter gifts have connections with spring and regeneration, the most typical one is the Easter eggs.

三、主要旅游城市及景点

（一）伦敦（London）

伦敦位于英格兰东南部，跨泰晤士河下游两岸，是英国第一大城市及第一大港，也是欧洲最大的都会区之一、世界金融中心之一及世界十大首都之一，人口 896 万，面积 1 577.3 平方千米。伦敦不仅是英国最重要的政治、金融中心，也是著名的旅游城市。由于历代王朝建都于此，因此伦敦拥有丰富的历史和文化古迹。泰晤士河两岸风光无限，南岸有水族馆、壮观的伦敦眼、别致的泰特现代美术馆、莎士比亚环球剧院，北岸有著名的威斯敏斯特宫（国会大厦）及沿岸的古建筑群，如大英博物馆。

Located on the banks of the River Thames in the southeast of England, London is the largest city and port in the UK. It is also one of the largest capital cities in Europe and one of the largest world financial cities. London is also one of the top ten capital cities in the world, with an area of 1,577.3 square kilometers and population of 8.96 million. London is not only the center of politics and finance but also a well-known tourist city. As the capital for all the British dynasties, London is full of historic and cultural relics. Along the both sides of the River Thames, there are numerous scenic spots. Along the south bank of the River Thames, there appear a large aquarium, the giant London Eye, the elegant Tate Modern and Shakespeare's Global Theatre. On the north bank, there stand the Palace of Westminster (Houses of Parliament) and historic buildings such as the British Museum.

◆ 白金汉宫（Buckingham Palace）

白金汉宫如今是英国女王伊丽莎白二世的王宫，始建于 1703 年，1761 年英王乔治三世购得此屋，改建成国王的寝宫，并沿用至今。目前，白金汉宫是伊丽莎白二世办公、生活的场所以及皇室家庭的行政总部。每天 11:30 开始，持续 45 分钟的卫兵换岗仪式可以说是游客必看的节目。

The Buckingham Palace is currently royal palace of Queen Elizabeth Ⅱ. It was a house built in 1703, but in 1761 King George Ⅲ purchased the house and rebuilt it as a palace. Finally the Buckingham Palace became the official royal palace of the British monarch. Now the palace serves as both the office and

London residence of Queen Elizabeth Ⅱ, as well as the administrative headquarters of the Royal Household. The 45 minutes of daily changing guards, starting from 11:30 am, is the must-see for visitors.

◆ 伦敦塔（Tower of London）

伦敦塔并不是一座塔，而是一座城堡，于1078年由威廉一世下令建造。自12世纪以来，伦敦塔曾被作为王室居所、监狱、军械库、财政部、动物园、皇家造币厂和档案室。目前，伦敦塔是一座王室珍宝展览馆，并被列入世界文化遗产名录。

Actually, Tower of London is not a tower but a castle which was built in 1078 as a fortification under the command of King William Ⅰ. Since the 12th century, it was used as the royal household, a prison, an armory, a treasury, a menagerie, the home of the Royal Mint, a public records office, and now it serves as the home of the Crown Jewels of the United Kingdom. It is listed as a World Cultural Heritage Site by UNESCO.

◆ 大本钟（Big Ben）

大本钟是位于威斯敏斯特宫（又称国会大厦）北面钟楼的昵称，建于1859年，高约96米，是当时英国最高的哥特式建筑。顶部安装了重达13.5吨的当时世界上最大的机械钟，时针和分针的臂长分别为2.75米和4.27米。大本钟的命名来自当时设计和监造此项工程的本杰明·霍尔爵士。2012年6月26日，大本钟所在的钟楼正式改名为伊丽莎白塔，以此纪念女王伊丽莎白二世登基60周年。

Big Ben is the nickname of the clock tower at the north end of the Palace of Westminster which is also known as House of Parliament. The 96 meters height tower was built in 1859 in gothic style and it was the largest in the world at that time. The weight of the clock is 13.5 tons with inside the face, the length of the hour hand is 2.75 meters and the minute hand is 4.27 meters. Big Ben is named after Sir Benjamin Hall who was the designer and construction supervisor of this project. On June 26, 2012, the clock tower was renamed the Elizabeth Tower to mark the Diamond Jubilee of Queen Elizabeth Ⅱ.

◆ 伦敦塔桥（Tower Bridge）

伦敦塔桥是伦敦的标志性建筑，开通于1894年，是维多利亚时代的哥特式建筑，因位于伦敦塔边而得名。伦敦塔桥升起时最为壮观，遇有大船通过或特殊场合时，塔桥桥面会升起，可达40米高、60米宽。伦敦塔桥是体验塔桥、了解塔桥历史和建筑文化及欣赏泰晤士河风光的最佳地点。

The Tower Bridge is the symbol of London. It was open to public in 1894 in gothic style of Victorian Dynasty. It is close to the Tower of London, so it was named as Tower Bridge. The rising of the Tower Bridge is the most spectacular. When big ships go through the bridge or there appears a special occasion, the Tower Bridge deck will rise up to 40-meter-high, 60-meter-wide. Ascending the Tower Bridge is the best venue to experience the bridge, to understand the history and architecture of Tower Bridge, and to appreciate the fantastic scenery of the River Thames.

◆ 大英博物馆（British Museum）

大英博物馆是英国最大的综合性博物馆，亦是世界上著名博物馆之一，与纽约大都会博物馆及巴黎卢浮宫并称为世界三大博物馆。大英博物馆建于1753年，是世界上历史最悠久、最重要的文化和历史博物馆。大英博物馆拥有古埃及馆、古希腊和罗马馆、古中东馆、版画和素描馆、史前历史和欧洲馆、亚洲馆等。大英博物馆以收藏古罗马遗迹、古希腊雕像和埃及木乃伊而闻名于世，是人类文化遗产的宝库。

The British Museum is the UK's largest comprehensive museum and also one of the famous museums in the world. The British Museum, along with the Metropolitan Museum of Art in New York and the Louvre in Paris, is known as one of the world's top three museums. Established in 1753, it is one of the oldest and most important museum of culture and history in the world. The museum owns the departments of Ancient Egypt, Greece and Rome, the Middle East, Prints and Drawings, Prehistory and Europe, Asia and so on. It is famous for the collection of ancient Roman ruins, the ancient Greek statues and ancient Egyptian mummies. It is a treasure trove of cultural heritage of mankind.

◆ 威斯敏斯特教堂（Westminster Abbey）

威斯敏斯特教堂位于伦敦西部，意为“西部大教堂”。威斯敏斯特教堂是11世纪号称“忏悔者”的英王爱德华建立的。教堂的主要特点是大门处有一对塔楼。教堂自建立以来，一直是英国历代国王或女王加冕典礼和王室成员结婚的场所。英国历代国王去世后，大部分葬在这里。英国人把威斯敏斯特教堂称为“荣誉的宝塔尖”。

Westminster Abbey, which means the big church in the west, is located in the west of London. It was built in the 11th century by King Edwards who was named as Confessor. Twin towers in the front feature the Church. It is here that the kings or queens are crowned or the wedding ceremonies of the royal family are held. Kings of many dynasties were buried here. Westminster Abbey is also regarded as the spire of the tower of glory.

◆ 温莎古堡（Windsor Castle）

温莎古堡是世界上最著名、最古老的城堡之一，位于伦敦市郊约40千米处的温莎小镇，始建于1070年，后经历代英王修成行宫，目前仍是英国女王伊丽莎白二世度假小住的行宫。“不爱江山爱美人”的温莎公爵曾在此度过浪漫的蜜月，而世人所知的查尔斯王子和戴安娜王妃的婚姻也由此开始。如今，温莎古堡是重要的王室博物馆，收藏了王室的大部分文物和珍宝。古堡的大部分大厅均对外开放。

Built in 1070 and located at the Windsor Town about 40 kilometers away from London, Windsor Castle is one of the largest and oldest castles in the world. Now it is still a royal palace where Queen Elizabeth Ⅱ usually stays for vacation. For Duke Windsor, who loved his wife more than the kingdom, spent his honeymoon here. The well-known marriage between Prince Charles and Princess Diana also initiated here. Now the Castle is also an important royal museum. Most of the collections are royal artifacts and treasures. And most of the castle halls are open to the public.

（二）爱丁堡（Edinburgh）

爱丁堡自 11 世纪开始一直是苏格兰首府，苏格兰政治、文化和金融中心，位于苏格兰南部低地的中心。爱丁堡得名于 7 世纪诺森伯里亚王国的一位名叫爱德温的国王。爱丁堡于 1392 年建成，1437 年成为苏格兰王国的首都。爱丁堡历史悠久，风景秀丽，是英国最美丽的城市之一，素有“北方雅典”“欧洲最有气势的城市”之称。中世纪以来，爱丁堡在欧洲文化交流中占有重要地位，是苏格兰的文化、艺术中心。1947 年以来，每年 8 月，爱丁堡都会举行为期 3 周的国际艺术节，来自世界各国的艺术团体云集于此，成为世界瞩目的一大盛事，参加艺术节的游客数量相当于爱丁堡的人口数。爱丁堡还是苏格兰民俗和文化的展示中心，尤其是方格薄呢裙与风笛。这里游客到访最多的是爱丁堡城堡，它是苏格兰王国最重要的城堡，屹立于市中心的一座死火山上，在这可以俯瞰整个市区，是英国最古老的城堡之一。据说亚瑟王和他的十二骑士的故事就起源于这个地方。1995 年，联合国教科文组织把爱丁堡老城区列入世界文化遗产名录。

Edinburgh has been the capital of Scotland since the 11th century. It is the political, cultural and financial center of Scotland and located in the center of the southern lowlands of Scotland. Edinburgh was named after King Edwin from the Kingdom of Northumbria in the 7th century. Built in 1392, Edinburgh became the capital of the Kingdom of Scotland in 1437. With long history and charming scenery, Edinburgh is one of the most beautiful cities in the UK, known as the “Athens of the North” and “Europe’s most imposing city”. Since the Middle Ages, Edinburgh has occupied an important position in the European cultural exchanges and has been the Scottish cultural and arts center. Edinburgh has held the annual International Festival which lasts 3 weeks in August 47 since 1974. The art groups from around the world will gather here. The event attracts the world’s attention and the number of visitors attracted to Edinburgh for the festival is roughly equal to the resident population of the city. Edinburgh is also the center of Scottish folklore and culture exhibition, especially thin checkered kilt and bagpipes. The most-visited tourist attraction is the Edinburgh Castle, an important fortress of the Kingdom of Scotland. It dominates the top of the extinct volcano of city of Edinburgh of Scotland, overlooking the whole city, and is one of the oldest castles in the UK. It was said that it was here that the story of King Arthur and his twelve knights happened. The Old City of Edinburgh was listed as a World Cultural Heritage Site by UNESCO in 1995.

（三）利物浦（Liverpool）

利物浦是英国仅次于伦敦的第二大港，位于英格兰西北部，距离伦敦 325 千米。昔日的利物浦是英国著名的制造业中心，今天的利物浦是英国国家旅游局认定的最佳旅游城市，该市最为著名的是音乐（“披头士”乐队的故乡）与足球（有两支参加英超的球队——埃弗顿足球俱乐部和利物浦足球俱乐部）。

Liverpool, located at the northwest of the England, is the second largest port after London in UK and is 325 kilometers away from London. Liverpool was the famous manufacturing center in UK and is the best tourist city certified by National Tourism Bureau of UK. It is the hometown of The Beatles and is most famous for music and football. There are two Premier League teams in the city, Everton Football Club and Liverpool Football Club.

（四）其他著名旅游景点

◆ 巴斯（Bath）

巴斯是英格兰西南部的一座古老小城，距离伦敦约 160 千米，属于英格兰埃文郡东部的科茨沃尔德。巴斯是一个被田园风光包围着的古典而优雅的小城，被誉为英国最漂亮、典雅的城市之一。傅雷曾经形容它是“精致而美丽的城市”。它的典雅来自乔治王时期的房屋建筑风格以及绮丽的乡村风光。每年 5 月末到 6 月初举办的巴斯国际音乐节是世界上最著名的音乐盛典之一。

Bath, a small old city in the southwest of England, is about 160 kilometers away from London. Bath is in Cotswolds which is to the east of Avon. Bath is a small elegant city surrounded by the countryside scenery and is called as one of the most beautiful and elegant cities in UK. Fu Lei, described it as a delicate and pretty city. It is delicate because of its building style of Georgian Era. It is pretty because of its countryside scenery. Bath International Music Festival, held every year from the end of May till the beginning of June, is one of the most famous music festivals in the world.

◆ 剑桥（Cambridge）

剑桥是一座大学城。有人说，一直以来都是牛津和剑桥在“统治”英国。剑桥大学在自然科学领域的成就尤其突出，哺育出牛顿、达尔文这样开创科学新纪元的科学大师。截至 2019 年，共有 120 位诺贝尔奖得主曾在剑桥留下足迹。人们称剑桥为“自然科学的摇篮”。印度前总理尼赫鲁、英国王储查尔斯也曾在剑桥就读。徐志摩的《再别康桥》更是汉语现代诗歌的经典。每年一度的牛津、剑桥赛艇对抗赛是全世界最著名的赛艇对抗赛。

The city Cambridge is a university town. It is said that it is Cambridge and Oxford that have been “governing” the UK. University of Cambridge is the best in the field of natural sciences. Newton and Darwin who opened the new era of science studied here and became the science master. As of 2019, 120 Nobel Prize winners used to study or work here. Cambridge is called the cradle of natural sciences. Nehru, the former prime minister of India and Prince Charles also studied here. *Saying Goodbye to the Cambridge Again* written by Xu Zhimo is the canon of modern Chinese poetry. The annual boat race between Cambridge and Oxford is one of the most famous boat races in the world.

◆ 牛津（Oxford）

牛津大学是英国最古老的大学，位于伦敦西北 87 千米处有“英国雅典”之称的牛津城。牛津大学创办于 1096 年，由 38 所学院组成，以社会科学见长。英国有 28 位首相毕业于该校，牛津大学的校友、教授及研究人员中有 72 位获得诺贝尔奖，因而被誉为“象牙之塔”，以培养政界人士而著名。

University of Oxford, the oldest in UK, is located at Oxford city, 87 kilometers away from the northwest of London and reputed as British Athens. Established in 1096, the university consists of 38 colleges and is famous for its social sciences. 28 prime ministers in British history graduated here. 72 of its graduates, professors and researchers have won the Nobel Prize. Oxford University is acclaimed as the ivory tower and is well-known for training senior politicians.

◆ 巨石阵（Stonehenge）

巨石阵位于英格兰威尔特郡，是世界著名的旅游景点，每年有100万人从世界各地慕名前来参观。巨石阵是欧洲最著名的史前文明的遗址，建于新石器时代末期至青铜器时代。它的建造起因和方法至今在考古界仍是个不解之谜。在人们的心中，这里是一个极为神圣的地方。1986年，巨石阵、埃夫伯里和相关遗址被列入世界文化遗产名录。

Located in the county of Wiltshire, the Stonehenge is one of the world famous sites and attracts 1 million tourists from all over the world every year. As the most famous prehistoric monument in Europe, Stonehenge was built in the late Neolithic Age to the Bronze Age. The cause and method of construction has still been a mystery so far in the archaeological world. In people's minds, here is a very sacred place. Stonehenge, Avebury and Associated Sites were added to the UNESCO's list of World Cultural Heritage Site in 1986.

四、旅游资讯

（一）美食

英国菜选料比较简单，尽管英国是岛国，海域广阔，但受地理、自然条件限制，渔场不太好，所以英国人不像法国人那样崇尚海鲜，而是比较偏爱牛肉、羊肉、禽类等。英国人常自嘲不精于烹调，英国菜相对来说比较简单，口味清淡，忌用味精调味，注意营养成分和餐桌礼仪，对饭菜本身并不在意。但英式早餐比较丰富，炸鱼、薯条是英国的国民小吃。英国人进餐时会喝酒，一般喝啤酒，还喜欢喝威士忌等烈性酒，苏格兰的威士忌在世界上久负盛名。下午茶是英国人生活的一部分，每个英国人年均消费的茶叶量在西方各国中居于首位，茶可谓英国的民族饮料。较为知名的英国菜有牛肉腰子派、炸鱼排等。

The choice of ingredients of British cuisine is relatively simple, although the UK is an island nation with vast sea, it is limited by the geographical and natural conditions and lacks good fishing grounds. So unlike French, the British do not pay attention to seafood, instead they prefer beef, mutton, poultry and so on. The British often joke that they are not good at cooking. British cuisine is relatively simple with light taste and it is a taboo on MSG seasoning. The British pay attention to the nutrients and table etiquette, and do not care of the food itself. However, English breakfast is rich. Fish & chips even becomes the British national food. During meals, British people would have beer, whisky and other spirits. The Scottish whisky is prestigious in the world. The afternoon tea is part of their daily life. The average annual consumption of tea for each British is top one in western countries. The tea can be described as Britain's national beverage. Other famous British dishes include steak and kidney pie, fried fish, etc.

知识拓展

英国下午茶

格调优雅、内涵丰富的"英国下午茶"文化享誉世界。历史上英国人不曾种过一片茶叶，却用从中国进口的茶叶，创造了自己独特的生活方式。据说下午茶发端于维多利亚时代，英国贝德福德公爵夫人安娜难以打发漫长悠闲的下午，百无聊赖中感到有进食的欲望，但此时离晚餐和晚会尚早，就请女仆准备几片烤面包、奶油和茶。后来安娜女士邀请几位知心好友，伴随着茶与精致的点心，同享轻松惬意的午后时光，从此下午茶成了贵族社交圈内的风尚，一直到今天，已形成一种优雅自在的下午茶文化，也成为正统的"英国红茶文化"。其风靡之快、影响之大，恰如一首英国民谣所唱："当时钟敲响四时，世上的一切瞬间为茶而停。"下午茶最初只是在家中用高级、优雅的茶具来享用，后来渐渐地演变成招待友人欢聚的社交茶会，进而衍生出各种礼节，但现在形式已简化不少。虽然下午茶已经简单化，但是冲泡茶的方式要正确、摆设要优雅、茶点要丰盛，这三点被视为下午茶的传统而流传下来。

（二）购物及退税

苏格兰威士忌：闻名于世的苏格兰威士忌历史悠久。苏格兰高地的特殊水质和极为严格的蒸馏工艺，使那里出产的威士忌被誉为"液体黄金"。

Scottish whisky: Scottish whisky is famous in the world for its long history. In Scotland highland the whisky is known as "liquid gold" because of the special quality water and very strict distilling technology.

银器：英国的银器非常华丽，做工精良而复杂，广受各国游客的欢迎，特别是银制的圣诞餐具，除了美观，品种还很多，从蜡烛台到刀叉再到碟子应有尽有，这一类银器展示了英国传统的手工制作技艺。

Silverware: Silverware in UK, especially Christmas tableware with various kinds such as candle sticks, forks and spoons and plates are widely welcomed by tourists all over the world, because they are very beautiful with excellent British traditional handmade technology.

泰迪熊：泰迪熊有着浑圆丰满的身材和四肢，蓬松柔软的安哥拉羊毛，简单的材料和绣线，憨厚的表情，以及百分之百的手工缝制和填塞作业。在白宫的一次宴会上，有几只玩具熊被打扮成猎人、渔夫的模样陈列在桌上当作装饰品，美国罗斯福总统对这些小熊着迷不已。恰巧英国国王爱德华七世小名也叫泰迪，很快泰迪熊便成为英国家喻户晓的宠物。如今的泰迪熊就像芭比娃娃一样，已经不再是一般玩具的概念了，它们成为传承某种文化的载体。尤其是在欧美，一只泰迪熊可以被当作家庭中的一员，甚至陪伴一家三代人成长。

Teddy Bear: Teddy Bear has a round and fleshy body, with arms and legs of bush and tender Angola wool. It appears simple and honest embroidered with simple material. It is completely handmade. Once at a dinner in the White House when President Roosevelt saw the Teddy Bears on the table decorated as hunters and fishermen, he liked them very much. Because the nickname of King Edwards Ⅶ was also Teddy, the Teddy Bear became popular immediately in UK. Nowadays in UK, Teddy Bear is not just a toy, it becomes a kind of media to transport the culture just like Barbie. In Europe and America, a Teddy Bear is likely to accompany the growth of the family from grandfather, father to son.

英国商店一般营业时间是早上 9:00—10:00 开门，下午 5:00—7:00 关门，许多商店周末不营业。商店一般都非常正规，不能讲价，但角落多设有折扣货架。哈罗斯百货商店是有名的折扣商店。英国奢侈品（如博柏利）的价格和国内差价较大。通常，英国的商品标准增值税率是 20%，最低购买金额是 30 英镑，对持中国护照和其他非欧盟国家护照，逗留期在 3 个月内的游客均可实行退税。如果游客在同家商场同日内购物到指定金额，在柜台出示护照领取有商场凭证或印章的退税单及付款凭证，填上名字和护照号码，在出境口岸退税专用柜台海关审核盖章后，可到出境处的指定银行领取现金。如果游客在有些免税店已领退税，在海关审核盖章后要把盖好海关章的退税单寄回商店，否则商店有权从游客担保的信用卡里扣回已退的金额。

Most of the British shops open between 9:00 am to 10:00 am and close between 5:00 pm to 7:00 pm. Many shops close at the weekend. You cannot bargain in the shop but lots of discount shelves can be found at the corner. Harrods is the famous discount shopping mall. There is a big gap for the price of luxury consumer goods (such as Burberry) between China and the UK. Usually the goods sold in the UK contain VAT (20%) and the minimum purchase amount is GBP 30. Tourists from China or other non-EU countries can claim back the VAT if they leave within 3 months. When you buy goods in certain amount in one shop on the same day, you may ask the shop for a refund form signed or stamped from the shop. You need to fill in the refund form with your name, passport number and attach the receipt from the shop and have it stamped by the refund office (the Customs) before leaving. You may have to show the goods to the officer. You can get the refund from the bank after you go through the airport exit. In some duty free shops, the VAT has been deducted directly, but you still need to send back the tax refund form stamped by the Customs. Otherwise, the shop will deduct the tax from your credit cards you have guaranteed.

（三）时差

英国时间又叫格林尼治标准时间，中国比英国早 8 小时。但是由于英国实行夏令时，每年 3 月的最后一个星期天到每年 10 月的最后一个星期天是夏令时，在夏令时期间，英国和中国的时差是 7 小时。

British time is also called Greenwich Mean Time. China is 8 hours ahead of the UK. The UK is a country with a practice of Daylight Saving Time. In British Summer Time (BST) which lasts from last Sunday in March to last Sunday in October, China is 7 hours ahead of the UK.

思考练习

1. 经典旅游线路分析

英国深度 8 日游

第 1 天：上海——伦敦

抵达伦敦后专车前往威斯敏斯特教堂，观看（外观）国会大厦及伦敦的标志性建筑大本钟。走进唐宁街，远眺伦敦塔桥，晚餐后入住酒店休息。

第 2 天：伦敦——剑桥——约克——利兹

早餐后乘车前往剑桥，那里是世界闻名的大学城，参观国王学院（剑桥大学内最有名的学院之一，成立于 1441 年，由当时的英国国王亨利六世创建）和三一学院（剑桥大学中规模最大、财力最雄厚、名声最响亮的学院之一）。可在小镇中自由活动，尽情感受剑桥风情，也可乘坐小船在剑河中畅游，之后乘车前往历史可追溯到古罗马时期的古镇——约克，这里曾被评为“年度欧洲最佳旅游城市”。参观完约克大教堂，之后乘车前往利兹，晚餐后入住酒店休息。

第 3 天：利兹——爱丁堡——格拉斯哥

早餐后前往苏格兰首府爱丁堡，首先参观矗立于嶙峋花岗岩上的爱丁堡城堡，城堡里小巧的玛格丽特皇后礼拜堂是爱丁堡现存最古老的建筑；之后沿着中古石铺大道皇家英里大道（每年 8 月爱丁堡的军乐队游行便在此举行）前行；接着前往绿意盎然的王子街公园，公园里有一座 1903 年建造的世界最古老的花钟，其北侧的王子街名店林立，是购物的好去处。之后乘车前往格拉斯哥，车览当地风光，晚餐后入住酒店休息。

第 4 天：格拉斯哥——湖区——曼彻斯特

早餐后驱车前往英国最美丽的国家公园——湖区国家公园，参观温德米尔湖区。夏季来到这里，满目翠绿，缎面般宁静的湖水，天鹅绒般的草地，翠生生的好像一幅还未干透的水彩画。温德米尔是位于湖区中心的一座保存完好的村镇，堪称“英格兰最美丽的角落”。在湖区小镇悠闲漫步，体验英国本地人的生活，或自费选择湖区游船，观赏湖区景色。之后前往曼彻斯特，车览曼联总部（空气中无处不弥漫着疯狂的足球文化），晚餐后入住酒店休息。

第 5 天：曼彻斯特——斯特拉福德——比斯特——伦敦

早餐后前往斯特拉福德，参观莎士比亚故居外观，莎士比亚被称为“最伟大的戏剧天才”。在小镇中心的埃文河畔，还可以找到众多莎翁剧中的人物雕像。之后前往比斯特购物村购物，这里有大量的折扣商品。之后前往伦敦，晚餐后入住酒店休息。

第 6 天：伦敦

早餐后游览白金汉宫（这里是英国王权的象征，见证了“日不落帝国”的“升起”与“落下”），而后开始世界历史之旅——参观大英博物馆（它是世界上历史最悠久、规模最宏伟的综合性博物馆，收藏了世界各地的许多文物和图书珍品，藏品之丰富、种类之繁多，为全世界博物馆所罕见）。下午在著名的韦斯特菲尔德（Westfield）购物中心尽情购物。

第7天：伦敦——上海

早餐后乘车前往机场办理退税及登机手续，后乘坐国际航班返回上海。

第8天：上海

抵达上海，圆满结束愉快的行程。

分析：这条经典旅游线路的主要旅游景点与行程特色，以及适合旅游的人群。

2. 案例分析

［案例1］游客林平在英国旅游，在伦敦的路上他看到一位英国老人正步履蹒跚地通过车水马龙的马路，出于同情心，他飞步上前搀住老人，要送她过去，但老人拒绝了。出于礼貌，林平说了句："您累了吧？好好休息一下！"然而，普通的问候之语却让英国老人误解为林平是在对她的身体状况表示担忧，脸上露出不悦。林平有点疑惑，尊敬老人是中国人的传统，为什么英国老人不接受呢？

［案例2］张女士对英国的王室文化很感兴趣，在英国旅游期间，她遇到一位英国人，闲聊之余表示了对戴安娜王妃、威廉王子等王室成员的关注，同时发表了自己的不同观点，那位英国人却不理会她。请问张女士哪里做错了？

3. 练一练

（1）试分析英国的王室文化旅游，选择你感兴趣的英国文化写一篇导游词。

（2）《哈利·波特》是英国女作家J.K.罗琳创作的系列小说，共7部。该系列小说被译成近70种语言，在200多个国家累计销量多达4.5亿册。因小说的巨大成功，带动了一系列相关领域的开发，包括电影、玩具、系列景点、相关书籍和相关主题城市等。在电影热映的同时，影片中那些具有魔幻气息的外景拍摄地也成为影迷们追忆《哈利·波特》系列的热门旅游胜地。目前十大最热门的《哈利·波特》外景拍摄地依次为：杜伦大教堂、牛津大学波德林图书馆、国王十字车站、伦敦动物园爬虫馆、艾维克城堡、勒顿豪（Leadenhall）市集、格伦希奥高地、格伦菲南高架桥、格洛斯特大教堂、威尔士的西淡水海滩。你能否结合英国的主要旅游资源和《哈利·波特》的外景拍摄地，设计一条"哈利·波特魔幻之旅"的线路？

第二节 法国

一、国家概况

（一）地理环境

法国位于欧洲大陆西部，西临大西洋，西北隔多佛尔海峡、英吉利海峡与英国相望，南濒地中海，东与瑞士相依，东北毗邻比利时、卢森堡和德国，东南与意大利相连，西南与西班牙、安道尔接壤，是沟通北欧、南欧、西欧、中欧之间的重要纽带。法国版图犹如六边形，三边临水，三边靠陆，距离英国的最短距离仅 33 千米，这 33 千米是连接英国和欧洲大陆的最短海道，因而成为国际重要航道。

France is located in the west of the Continental Europe. To the west is the Atlantic Ocean and the northwest is the Strait of Dover and English Channel which separates UK from France. To its south is the Mediterranean. It connects with Switzerland to the east. It borders Belgium, Luxemburg and Germany to the northeast and Italy to the southeast. It links with Spain and Andorra to the southwest. The location is very important because it is the hub to connect Northern Europe, Southern Europe, Western Europe and Central Europe. The shape of France is like a hexagon. It faces the sea on its three sides and the continent on the other three sides. The narrowest distance of the channel between UK and France is only 33 kilometers so it is the important international channel.

法国地势东南高、西北低。山地集中在东部和南部边境地带，有阿尔卑斯山脉、比利牛斯山脉、汝拉山脉等。南部地中海沿岸平原狭窄，风景秀丽，是世界最重要的游览区。法意边境的勃朗峰是欧洲最高峰。地中海上的科西嘉岛是法国最大的岛屿。法国境内河流众多，主要河流有流入大西洋的卢瓦尔河、塞纳河和加龙河，以及流入地中海的罗讷河。

The terrain of France slopes from the southeast to the northwest. The mountains are concentrated in the eastern and the southern border. The main mountain ranges are Alps, Pyrénées Mountains and Jura Mountains. The plain along the Mediterranean is narrow and long but it is so beautiful that it becomes the most important international attraction. Mont Blanc on the border between France and Italy is the peak of Europe. Corsica in the Mediterranean is the largest island of France. There are many rivers in France among which the major ones are the Loire, Seine and Garonne which flows into the Atlantic, and the Rhône which flows into the Mediterranean.

法国西部濒临大西洋，受西风影响较大，冬暖夏凉，年度温差较小，终年湿润多雨，云雾多；东部和中部距海较远，属大陆性气候，特点为冬季较冷，年度温差较大；南部属亚热带地中海气候，冬季温暖多雨，夏季炎热干燥。

Western France on the Atlantic is influenced by west wind. It is warm in winter and cool in summer. The temperature difference is small with humid, rainy and cloudy days all year round. The climate of the eastern and central France where is far from the sea is continental. It is cold in winter and the temperature throughout the year differs greatly. Southern France belongs to subtropical Mediterranean climate with mild, rainy winters and hot, dry summers.

（二）人文概况

1. 历史

公元前1500年到公元前58年，凯尔特人来到法国的中央高原及周围地区（即高卢地区）定居，并逐渐成为高卢人。公元前58年，恺撒打赢高卢战争。罗马在高卢建省，设立行政中心，将基督教带入高卢，并统治高卢达400年。罗马人在高卢推广拉丁语，在此基础上形成了法语。

During the years from 1500 BC to 58 BC, the Celtics came to the central highland of France, i.e. Gaul, settled down and gradually became Gauls. Caesar won the Gaul war in 58 BC. The Roman Empire set up a province in Gaul and a political center was established. The Romans dominated the Gaul for 400 years and brought Christianity to the Gaul. French was formed on the base of Latin language the Romans brought to Gaul.

公元275年，野蛮人（即日耳曼部落）开始入侵并定居高卢。公元481—751年，其中的一个部落——法兰克人建立了墨洛温王朝，将高卢命名为法兰西，定都巴黎。公元768年，查理曼大帝继位了加洛林王朝，在他统治期间，法国国土从波罗的海地区延伸到地中海地区，包括法国、德国和意大利。他死后，其孙子把帝国分成三部分，即今天的意大利、法国和德国。1066年，征服者威廉一世征服英伦三岛，并建立诺曼底王朝，统治英格兰及法国西北部。1337年，英法两国争夺领土的百年战争爆发了。一开始，法国军队节节败退，直到1431年，一位农村少女贞德带领军队取得奥尔良战役的胜利，法国才开始取得优势。英国人非常害怕贞德，设计抓住贞德并把她烧死，但是法国军队还是在1453年把英国人赶出了法国，并赢得了最后的胜利。17—18世纪路易十四在位时期，法国君主专制制度达到顶峰。然而路易十六在位期间，连年的战争使法国发生了财政危机，人们厌倦了封建专制的统治，呼唤改革。终于在1789年7月14日，法国爆发大革命，人民攻占巴士底狱，废除君主制，并于1792年建立了第一共和国。

In the year of 275, the Barbarian, named as Germanic tribes started to invade Gaul and settled down. One of the tribes, Frank, established the Merovingian Dynasty during 481 and 751, and named Gaul as France and made Paris the capital. Charles the Great became the king of Carolingian Dynasty in 768. The territory he conquered covered most parts of Western Europe from the Baltic Sea region to the Mediterranean including France, Germany and Italy. His grandsons divided the empire into three countries after he died, i.e. Italy, France and Germany. In 1066, William I the Conqueror conquered England, established the Norman Dynasty and ruled England and Northwest France. Since 1337 France and England started the Hundred Years' War for territory. France did not win any wars until Joan of Arc, a rural girl, led an army to defeat the British garrison at Orleans in 1431. The British was so angry that they arrested Joan and burned her death in 1431. However, the British army was chased out of France at last in 1453 and France won the war. During the 17th century to 18th century at the time of Louis XIV, the autocratic monarchy reached its peak. However, a financial crisis arose because of the continuous wars during the time of Louis XVI. People started to complain about the feudal system of autocratic monarchy and continued to call for reform. Finally the revolution occurred on July 14, 1789 and the Bastille was taken over. The French First Republic was established in 1792.

1799 年 11 月 9 日，拿破仑·波拿巴发动政变，成为第一执政者。尽管他统治法国时间不长，却对当时的世界产生了非常大的影响。1848 年爆发“二月革命”，共和党人掌握政权，建立了第二共和国。1852 年，路易·拿破仑建立了第二帝国。1870 年，法国在普法战争中战败后，第二帝国解体，第三共和国建立。1871 年 3 月 18 日，巴黎建立了世界上第一个无产阶级政权——巴黎公社。

On Nov. 9, 1799, Napoléon Bonaparte staged a coup and became the First Consul. Though he ruled the country for a very short time, he influenced the world greatly. The February Revolution occurred in 1848, while the bourgeois republican won the power and established the Second Republic. However, Louis Napoléon took the power and established the Second French Empire in 1852. In 1870 French declared war against Prussia. They were defeated in the war so that the Third Republic replaced the Second French Empire. On March 18, 1871, the world's first proletarian regime — the Paris Commune was established.

第一次世界大战期间，英法领导的协约国战胜德国并签订了《凡尔赛条约》，法国得到大笔赔款，促进了经济的恢复和发展。

During the First World War, the Allies led by France and UK defeated Germany. After the *Treaty of Versailles* was signed, France won a huge amount of compensation and that promoted the economy recovery and development.

第二次世界大战期间，法国遭德国侵略，戴高乐将军在伦敦成立流亡政府领导抵抗运动。1944 年法国解放，1946 年成立第四共和国。1958 年第五共和国成立，戴高乐当选为第五共和国第一任总统。他设计并建立了强大的第五共和国的制度，建立了总统直选制度。法国从此开始了现代化的进程并取得了经济的持续发展。

During the Second World War, when Germany occupied France, Charles de Gaulle set up a government in exile in London and led the people to fight against Germany. France was liberated in 1944 and the Fourth Republic was set up in 1946. In 1958, the Fifth Republic was established and Charles de Gaulle became the first president. After taking the power, he designed and established the strong system of executive power of the Fifth Republic. That is the system allowing people to choose their president by voting. France has begun its modernization since then and has gained continuous development of economy.

知识拓展

高卢雄鸡

高卢是法国的古称。罗马帝国曾把今天法国这块地域叫作高卢，高卢在拉丁语里的另一个意思就是雄鸡。中世纪前期无人作如此联系，大约 14 世纪后，这种联系才普遍起来。法国人也逐渐接受了雄鸡这一代表形象。但直到文艺复兴时期，雄鸡才正式成为法国的象征。法国大革命和七月王朝时期，雄鸡取代了王权的标志——百合花。法兰西第一共和国国旗上有雄鸡形象，是当时法国人民革命意识的象征。在第一次世界大战期间，雄鸡被当作法兰西民族抵抗德国入侵的象征。从 20 世纪 80 年代起，高卢雄鸡（the Gallic Rooster）被当作法国足球队和橄榄球队的标志，由此使得高卢雄鸡举世闻名。

2. 经济

作为第二个完成了第一次工业革命的国家，法国在 19 世纪末就已完成了资本的积累，经济实力一直排在世界前列。目前，法国是世界第七大经济体，经济实力仅次于美国、中国、日本、德国、印度和英国。法国素有“西欧粮仓”之称，是欧盟最大的农业生产国，也是世界主要农副产品出口国，粮食产量占全欧洲粮食产量的 1/3，农产品出口仅次于美国，居世界第二位。法国也是世界贸易大国，出口商品主要有机械、汽车、化工产品、钢铁、农产品、食品、服装、化妆品和军火等。法国葡萄酒享誉全球，酒类出口量占世界出口量的一半。法国时装、法国大餐、法国香水闻名遐迩。法国是个极具魅力的旅游大国，旅游业是法国经济的重要组成部分。风情万种的花都巴黎，美丽迷人的蓝色海岸，阿尔卑斯山的滑雪场等，都吸引着来自世界各地的游客。

France was the second country to finish the first Industrial Revolution so that it had finished the capital accumulation by the end of the 19th century. Its economy strength has always been ranked in the forefront in the world. At present it is the seventh largest economic power after the United States, China, Japan, Germany, India and the UK. France is considered as the granary of Western Europe. France is the largest agricultural country of European Union and the world major exporting country of farm and subsidiary products. Its grain output makes up one third of that of Europe. And the exporting of agricultural products ranks the second of the world only after the United States. France is also a major trading country. The major exporting products are mechanical products, automobiles, chemical products, iron and steel products, agricultural products, foods, garments, perfume and weapons. French wine is well-known in the world. The quantity of wine export is half of the world. France is also famous for its garments, cuisine and perfume. France is one of the largest charismatic tourism countries. Tourism industry is an important part of its economy. Visitors from all over the world are attracted to the exceedingly fascinating and charming city of Paris as well as the beautiful French Riviera and ski resorts in Alps, etc.

3. 社会文化

法国人口为 6 701 万，其中本土人口 6 432 万，海外人口 269 万。通用法语。居民中 64% 的人信奉天主教。

The population of France is 67.01 million, including the 64.32 million at home and 2.69 million overseas. French is the common language. 64% of the inhabitants profess Catholicism.

许多人都是通过法国的文化和艺术（文学、绘画或音乐）了解法国的，可见法国的文化和艺术影响深厚。法国文化历史悠久，法国文学是世界文学的重要组成部分。公元 842 年用古法语写成的《斯特拉斯堡誓言》是法国古文学的起点。18 世纪是法国文学的重要阶段，伏尔泰（《老实人》）、让－雅克·卢梭（《爱弥儿》）等哲学家开始了启蒙文学。19 世纪是法国文学的顶峰，出现了浪漫主义文学，在小说、诗歌和戏剧等方面都取得了很大成就，代表人物是维克多·雨果（《悲惨世界》和《巴黎圣母院》）、亚利山大·大仲马（《基督山伯爵》和《三个火枪手》），这一时期还出现了批评现实主义的新文学流派，代表人物是玛里－亨利·贝尔（《红与黑》）、奥诺雷·德·巴尔扎克（《人间喜剧》）、居斯塔夫·福楼拜（《包法利夫人》）、亚历山大·小仲马（《茶花女》），以及现实主义作家也是现代短篇小说之父居伊·德·莫泊桑（《羊脂球》）等。第二次世界大战后，法国是获得诺贝尔文学奖最多的国家。

People all over the world know France through its arts and culture (literature, painting or music). The influences of French arts and culture are deep. In its long history, the French culture is one of the most important parts of the world literature. Les Serments de Strasbourg written in old French in 842 AD is regarded as the starting point of French ancient literature. The 18th century is the important period for the French literature. The philosopher and writer, Voltaire (1694–1778, *Candide*), and Jean-Jacques Rousseau (1712–1778, *Émile,* or *De l'éducation*) began the Literature of Enlightenment. French literature reached the summit in the 19th century. The Romanticism appeared in novels, poems and plays with representatives like Victor Hugo (1802–1885, *Les Misérables* and *Notre–Dame de Paris*), Alexandre Dumas (1802–1870, *Le Comte de Monte–Gristo* and *Les Trois Mousquetaires*). At the same time, there also appeared the Realism as a new literature genre with the representatives like Marie-Henri Beyle (1783–1842, *Le Rouge et le Noir*), Honoré de Balzac (1799–1850, *La Comédie humaine*), Gustave Flaubert (1821–1880, *Madame Bovary*), Alexandre Dumas, fils (1824–1895, *La Dame aux Camélias*), and the Naturalism Guy de Maupassant (1850–1893, *Boule de Suif*), who is considered as the father of modern short story. Since the Second World War, France has been the top country in terms of the Nobel Prize in Literature.

17 世纪到 19 世纪是法国绘画和雕刻艺术的重要时代，涌现了众多的大师，如巴洛克古典主义代表人物尼古拉斯·普桑，浪漫主义代表人物欧仁·德拉克鲁瓦，自然主义和现实主义代表人物让－弗朗索瓦·米勒和印象主义代表人物保罗·塞尚等。他们的作品多以油画为主。19 世纪到 20 世纪，巴黎成了世界各国画家的圣地，法国成了现代绘画艺术各种流派的源头。巴勃罗·毕加索对现代艺术流派的影响巨大，他一生经历了印象主义、立体主义、新古典主义、现实主义等流派。雕塑艺术也是法国文化的重要组成部分，不少古代建筑如凡尔赛宫、卢浮宫、先圣寺里都有许多完美的作品，如 18 世纪的让－安托万·乌东的历史人物塑像、19 世纪的弗朗索瓦·吕德在凯旋门上的《马赛曲》浮雕、奥古斯特·罗丹的《思想者》等。

The time from the 17th to the 19th century was the most important period for the French painting and sculpture arts. There were lots of masters at that time and oil painting was popular. The representatives are Nicolas Poussin (French baroque and classicism), Eugène Delacroix (romanticism), Jean-François Millet (naturalism and realism) and Paul Cézanne (impressionism). Paris became the holy land for the painters all over the world between the 19th and the 20th century. France was the source for various modern arts of painting. Pablo Picasso's influence on the modern art is great. He experienced various genres of the arts—impressionism, cubism, new classicism, realism and so on. The art of sculpture is also the important part of the French culture. There are lots of perfect works in many ancient buildings such as Palace of Versailles, the Louvre, and the Holy Temple. Those works include historical portraits and figures by Jean-Antoine Houdon in the 18th century, *La Marseillaise* on the Arc de Triomphe in the 19th century by Francois Rude and *Le Penseur* by Auguste Rodin.

二、民俗风情

（一）礼仪禁忌

法国人十分注重礼仪，善于交际。对法国人来说，社交是人生的重要内容，没有社交活动的生活是难以想象的。法国人诙谐幽默，天性浪漫。在人际交往中大都爽朗热情，善于雄辩，高谈阔论，好开玩笑，讨厌不爱讲话的人，对愁眉苦脸者难以接受。在人际交往中，法国人的礼节主要有握手礼、拥抱礼、贴面礼和吻手礼。和不认识的人见面时，一般要说“你好”并加上“女士”“小姐”“先生”或头衔。熟悉的人才称呼名字。初次见面可以握手，但通常是女士先伸手，年长者对年轻者先伸手，上级对下级先伸手。在交谈中不要询问对方的隐私，如收入、年龄、婚姻及宗教等。

The French pay great attention to etiquette and are good at communication. They are characterized with sociability that is very important for their life. It is unbelievable if there is no social life. The French are humorous and romantic. They are warm, kind and talkative. They don't like those who keep silent or always are in low spirits. French people in interpersonal etiquette are mainly taken to shake hands, hug, kiss the check and kiss the hand. When addressing a stranger, you should say “Bonjour” (Hello) and their title or first name if you are friends. The titles are Mademoiselle (Miss), Madame (Ms.) and Monsieur (Mr.). Shaking hands is a popular way to greet somebody, but remember that the lady will give the hand first, and so will the older to the young and the superior to the subordinate. When communicating with someone, it is important not to inquire about their private affairs such as income, age, marriage, religions, etc.

巴黎是时尚的代名词。这里有全世界最负盛名的服饰品牌，因此，法国被称为世界时尚中心。但法国人和其他欧洲人一样，讲究不同场合穿不同的服饰。在选择发型、手袋、帽子、鞋子、手表、眼镜时，都十分强调与着装协调一致。

Paris is synonymous with the fashion. There are the most famous clothing brands in the world. Though France is regarded as the world center of fashion. The French dress themselves differently on different occasions in the same way the other Europeans do. When they choose the style of hair, handbags, hats, shoes, watches and glasses, they will consider if they match their dresses.

法国是欧洲浪漫的中心。受传统文化的影响，法国人不仅爱冒险，而且喜欢浪漫，他们渴望自由，纪律性较差。法国人被视为世界上最著名的“自由主义者”。“自由、平等、博爱”不仅被当作国家箴言写入宪法，而且在国徽上明文写出。法国人把生活中所做的每一件事都当作享受来看待，所以生活节奏很慢。在法国，最先得学会的就是“等待”和“约会”。

France is the center of romance in Europe. Because of their culture, the French not only like risk-taking, but also like experiencing romance. They believe in freedom and discipline is poor. France is believed to be the most renowned liberalist in the world. “Liberty, Equality and Fraternity” is not only stipulated as the national motto in the constitution, but also inscribed on the national emblem. The French regard it as pleasure for everything they do in life. So, the pace of their life is very slow. In France, the first two things you have to know are "wait" and "make an appointment".

在如今的法国，婚恋生活颇为自由。法国的单身者有很多，以35岁以下和50岁以上者居多。传统婚姻的观念受到了极大的冲击。传统上，新郎和新娘在婚礼前会分别举行告别晚会，男方叫"埋葬单身汉生活晚会"，女方称"辞别宴会"。在聚会中，新郎是通过一个象征性的"棺材"举行一次"葬礼"来表示向"单身汉"告别，新娘则是接受姐妹们的花束、花篮，大家同唱辞行歌，共跳送别舞，以示姐妹间眷恋深情。次日婚礼将会在教堂举行。

In present France, people can choose their marriage on their own. Lots of people, most of whom aged under 35 or above 50, keep single. The traditional marital values have suffered great impact. Traditionally, before the wedding ceremony, both the bridegroom and the bride will hold a farewell party respectively. The bridegroom's party is called "to bury the bachelor's life" and the bride's "farewell dinner". In the party, the bridegroom will make a symbol of "coffin" and hold a "funeral" in order to bid farewell to the bachelor's life, while the bride will accept the flowers from her friends, sing the songs of farewell and dance to show their love. The wedding ceremony will be held in a church after the farewell day.

法国女性在家庭和社会中的地位很高。有这样的说法：在法国家庭中，女性排在第一位，狗排在第二位，孩子排在第三位，男性排在最末位。这句话虽带有调侃的成分，但能很好地反映女性在法国的地位。法国的男性非常尊重女性，"骑士风度"是法国人引以为豪的传统。无论是在走路、进屋，还是在入座时，都要让女士优先；介绍两人认识时，一般职务相等时，先将男性介绍给女性；同女性握手时，一定要等其先伸手，女性可戴着手套，而男性一定要脱掉手套。

In France, the status of women is very high both in the family and the society. It is said that in the French family, the woman is the first, the dog is the second, the kid is the third and the man is the last. Though it is kidding, it does show the status of the woman. In France, men always respect women and they are proud of "the conducts of a knight". Ladies are the first when you are walking, entering the house or taking the seat. When you introduce each other, you should introduce gentlemen to ladies first if they are equal. Ladies will give hand first when shaking hands. Ladies can have gloves on when shaking hands but gentlemen should take them off.

法国的国花是鸢尾花。一般不宜随意送给法国人菊花、玫瑰、水仙花、金盏花等。法国人对每一种花都赋予了一定的含义，所以送花时要格外注意。送花的支数不能是双数，菊花是表示对死者的哀悼，红玫瑰象征爱情，水仙花表示冷酷无情，金盏花表示悲伤。

Iris tectorum is the national flower of France. Chrysanthemum, rose, daffodil and calendula should not be chosen as gifts for the French. The French give meanings to every kind of flowers. People must be careful when they send flowers to the French. The number of flowers should not be even. Chrysanthemum is for funeral, red rose for love, daffodil means grim and cold-hearted and calendula means sorrow.

法国人认为鲜艳的色彩即为高贵，认为马是勇敢的象征，认为蓝色是宁静和忠诚的象征色，粉红色是积极向上的象征色。法国人忌讳胡桃色，厌恶墨绿色，忌用黑桃图案，商标上忌用菊花。法国人还视孔雀为恶鸟，并忌讳仙鹤（认为它是蠢汉与淫妇的象征）、乌龟，而且认为杜鹃花、纸花不吉利。

The French regard bright colors as nobility. They regard the horse as the symbol of bravery. They think blue color is the symbol of peace and faithfulness and pink is the symbol of positiveness. They don't like walnuts and hate greenish black and spade pattern. Chrysanthemum should not be used as trade marks. Peacocks are regarded as bad birds. They don't like cranes, which are the symbol of foolishness and intrigant, and turtles. They regard azaleas and paper flowers as unlucky symbols.

在人际交往中，法国人对礼物十分看重，但又有其特别的讲究。客人宜选择具有艺术品位和纪念意义的物品，不宜选择刀、剑、剪刀、餐具或带有明显的广告标志的物品。在接受礼物时，主人若不当着客人的面打开包装，则是一种无礼的表现。如果初次见面就送礼，法国人会认为你不善交际，甚至认为你粗俗。法国人重视情意的表达，例如：在亲友家做客后总要即时写一封措辞美好的感谢信，到远方旅游时不忘给亲朋好友寄张明信片，旅行回来时总要带点小礼物分赠亲友。

During social interaction, the French are always particular about gifts. They pay more attention to the gifts that should be special. Gifts should be artistically tasteful or meaningful which should not be knives, swords, scissors, tableware or articles with commercial marks. It is impolite if the hostess does not open the gift parcels in the face of the guests. Gifts are not appropriate at the first meeting. Otherwise you will be regarded as gauche or even vulgar. The French will always show their affection. For example, they will write a thank-you letter, and they will send a card to their friends or relatives during their journey and bring some souvenirs to them when they are returning home.

（二）节庆风情

1. 国庆节（National Day）

国庆节在7月14日，是法国最隆重的节日。1789年的7月14日，巴黎人民攻占了象征封建统治的巴士底狱，推翻了君主政权。1880年，7月14日被正式确定为法国的国庆日，法国人每年都要隆重纪念这个象征自由和革命的日子。为庆祝国庆节，法国每年都要在香榭丽舍大街上举行大规模的阅兵仪式，总统会发表演讲并颁发奖章。入夜，会燃放五彩缤纷的焰火。

National Day falls on July 14 and is the most important public holiday. On July 14, 1789, people of Paris occupied Bastille, which was the symbol of feudal reign, and ended the monarchy. July 14 was announced officially as National Day in 1880. The French celebrate this important day which means freedom and revolution every year. A series of celebrations will be held in the Avenue des Champs-Élysées. There will be a review of troops and the French president will deliver a speech and award prizes. In the evening, colorful fireworks will be displayed.

2. 诸圣节（All Saints Day）

11 月 1 日是诸圣节，亦称“诸圣瞻礼”，是天主教节日之一。全国放假一天。法国的民间习惯是在这一天到墓地去祭奠，凭吊已故的亲人，相当于中国的清明节。

All Saints Day is on November l. It is also referred to as “Samhain feast”. It is one of the Catholicism festivals. On this day, people usually have the whole day off and visit cemeteries, honor saints and attend the religious service. In a sense, it is like Qingming Festival of China.

三、主要旅游城市及景点

（一）巴黎（Paris）

巴黎是法国的首都，位于法国北部盆地中央，跨塞纳河两岸，故又被称为“塞纳河的女儿”。巴黎的核心是塞纳河上的西提岛，也称西岱岛。巴黎是欧洲最大的城市之一，它是时尚、文明、艺术、文化的代名词，被称为“光明之城”“时装之都”“香水之都”。有人曾这样评价巴黎：“鲜活的建筑史教科书，生动的法国编年史。”作为欧洲一流的旅游名城、浪漫之都，这座有着 2 000 多年历史的文化名城从 12 世纪起就一直是历代王朝的首都，拥有许多世界闻名的历史名胜与艺术建筑。塞纳河把巴黎一分为二，习惯上称为右岸和左岸。对于巴黎人来说，右岸代表贸易和商业、国家级文物古迹和高级时装店，左岸则以知名大学和咖啡馆而闻名。巴黎的主要景点集中在塞纳河的两岸。巴黎的历史中轴线是一条从市中心笔直向西的直线，东端开始于卢浮宫，然后经过杜伊勒里花园、协和广场、香榭丽舍大街，到达戴高乐广场中央的凯旋门。

Paris, the capital of France, is located in the center of the basin in northern France. Straddling the Seine, the city is also known as the “daughter of Seine”. The center of the city is the Île de la Cité, an island on Seine. Paris is Europe’s largest city, it is synonymous with fashion, civilization, art and culture, known as “the city of light”, “fashion capital ”and “perfume capital”. A comment on Paris reads: “Fresh architectural history textbooks and lively France Chronicle”. As the first-class tourist city and the romantic capital in Europe, the cultural city with a long history of more than 2,000 years, it has been the capital of each dynasty since the 12th century. So there are many world-famous historical monuments and art buildings. Paris is divided into right bank and left bank by Seine. The representatives of right bank are trade and commerce, national monuments and fashion. The left bank, for Parisians, is famous for its well-known universities and cafes. The major attractions of the city are along Seine. The historical principle axis is the line from the city center to the west along which there are lots of historical relics. The important attractions from the starting of the line from the east to the west are the Louvre, Tuileries Garden, Place de La Concorde, the Avenue des Champs-Élysées, and Arc de Triomphe at the Place Charles de Gaulle.

◆ 巴黎圣母院（Notre-Dame de Paris）

巴黎圣母院始建于 1163 年，坐落在塞纳河中间的西提岛上，被称为“法国最伟大的艺术杰作”，与卢浮宫、埃菲尔铁塔并称为巴黎三大旅游热点。巴黎圣母院以其哥特式的完美建筑、正门的“玫瑰玻璃窗”和悠久的历史而著称。1804 年 12 月 2 日，拿破仑在此举行盛大的加冕仪式。1996 年，百余国特使在此为前总统弗朗索瓦 · 密特朗举行安魂弥撒。圣母院广场的零起点是法国丈量全国各地里程时所使用的起测点。2019 年 4 月 15 日，巴黎圣母院屋顶尖塔与主体木结构被一场大火烧毁，目前正在修复中。

Notre-Dame de Paris was built in 1163 in the Île de la Cité of Seine. Regarded as "France's greatest masterpieces of art", Notre-Dame de Paris is one of the top three tourist attractions in Paris. The other two are the Louvre and the Eiffel Tower. It is a piece of gothic architectural perfection with the typical rose windows above the portal and represents the history of France. Napoleon crowned himself here on Dec. 2, 1804. Hundreds of special envoys came here to hold Requiem for the late French president François Mitterrand in 1996. The square of Notre-Dame is the zero point from which the nationwide survey on mileage starts. The roof of Notre-Dame de Paris caught fire on April 15, 2019, the construction and the wooden roof were seriously damaged. It is now undergoing renovation and restoration.

◆ 卢浮宫（The Louvre）

卢浮宫是世界上最大的美术博物馆，位于巴黎市中心塞纳河右岸。卢浮宫始建于 1204 年，是法国最大的王宫建筑之一，展示了法国文艺复兴时期建筑的特点和成就。卢浮宫正门入口处的透明金字塔建筑是美籍华裔建筑师贝聿铭的杰作。馆内收藏有大量欧洲文艺复兴期间以及 17 世纪艺术家的作品，共约 40 万件。卢浮宫美术博物馆分为 6 大部分：希腊和罗马艺术馆、东方艺术馆、埃及艺术馆、欧洲中世纪艺术馆、文艺复兴时期和现代雕像馆、历代绘画馆。里程碑式的艺术经典都汇集在这里，名画《蒙娜丽莎》以及雕塑《爱神维纳斯》《萨莫特拉斯的胜利女神》是著名的宫中三宝。

The Louvre is the largest art museum in the world, located on the right bank of Seine of the centre of Paris. It is one of the largest palace architectures in France, which was built in 1204 and shows the features and achievements of French Renaissance architecture. In front of the entrance, there is a glass pyramid designed by I. M. Pei, the Chinese-American architect master. The museum has a large collection of works nearly 400,000 items during the Renaissance and the 17th century. The Louvre art museum is divided into 6 departments including Museum of Greek and Roman Art, Museum of Oriental Art, Museum of Egyptian Art, Museum of the Middle Ages Art, the Renaissance and modern sculpture, and all previous dynasties painting pavilion. Landmark collection of classical art is here. The three masterpieces are *Mona Lisa*, *Venus de Milo* and *The Winged Victory of Samothrace*.

◆ 协和广场（Place de la Concorde）

协和广场是位于塞纳河右岸、香榭丽舍大街东端的一个八角形大广场，是法国最著名的广场和世界上最美丽的广场之一。协和广场始建于 1757 年，它的设计者为著名建筑师雅克 · 昂日 · 卡布里耶。因广场中心曾有路易十五骑像，1763 年曾命名为“路易十五广场”。大革命时期又被改名为“革命广场”。1795 年又将其改称为“协和广场”。协和广场中央矗立着一尊 23 米高、有 3 400 多年历史的埃及方尖碑，这是路易 · 菲利普于 1831 年从埃及卢克索移来的著名文物。

Located on the right bank of the Seine, a large octagonal square at the eastern end of the Avenue des Champs-Élysées, Place de la Concorde is France's most famous square and one of the world's most beautiful squares. The square was built in 1757. Its designer is renowned architect Jacques-Ange Gabriel. There used to be a statue of Louis XV of France in the center of the square, so it was named "Place Louis XV" in 1763. During the French Revolution, the square was called "Place de la Révolution". The square was given the current name, Place de la Concorde in 1795. The famous relic in the center is the giant Egyptian obelisk with a height of 23-meter and a history of more than 3,400 years which was moved from Luxor of Egypt by Louis Philippe in 1831.

◆ 香榭丽舍大街（Avenue of Champs-Élysées）

香榭丽舍大街起始于协和广场，终于凯旋门，全长约 1 800 米，是巴黎最漂亮、最著名的街道。在法文中，"香榭丽舍"是"田园乐土"的意思。香榭丽舍大街齐聚了巴黎最繁华的百货公司、时装店、咖啡馆等。它还是法国许多重大节庆典礼的庆祝中心，如每年 7 月 14 日的国庆阅兵式、新年联欢活动都在这条著名的街道上举行。

Starting from the Place de la Concorde and ending at the Arc de Triomphe with a length of 1,800 meters, the Avenue of Champs-Élysées is the most beautiful and famous among the Paris streets. The meaning of Champs-Élysées is "idyllic paradise" in French. The Avenue of Champs-Élysées is bordered by the most prosperous department stores, boutiques, cafes and so on. It is also France's major festivals ceremony center, for example, the National Day military parade on July 14 of each year and the New Year celebrations.

◆ 凯旋门（Arc de Triomphe）

作为巴黎的三大地标之一，凯旋门坐落在巴黎市中心戴高乐广场的中央，是 1806 年拿破仑为纪念奥斯特利茨战役的胜利而建的，建成于 1836 年，高 50 米，宽 45 米，是世界上最大的凯旋门。凯旋门的每一道外墙上都有巨幅浮雕，其中最著名也是最精美的一幅就是右侧石柱上的《马赛曲》浮雕。门前有建于 1920 年的无名战士墓地，墓前火炬常年不灭。

As one of the three landmarks of Paris, located in the center of Place Charles de Gaulle, Arc de Triomphe was commissioned in 1806 after the victory at Austerlitz by Emperor Napoleon at the peak of his reign and finished in 1836. The Arc is 50 meters high and 45 meters wide. It is the world's largest triumphal arch. Each exterior wall of the Arc de Triomphe has a huge relief, of which the most famous and the most beautiful one is on the right side of the pillars of *La Marseillaise* relief. The ground of the center is tomb of the unknown soldiers built in 1920.

◆ 埃菲尔铁塔（Eiffel Tower）

埃菲尔铁塔位于巴黎市中心塞纳河左岸，是世界上第一座钢铁结构的高塔，也是巴黎的最高建筑物和游览中心，被视为巴黎的象征。1889 年，世界万国博览会在法国巴黎举行，同年也是法国大革命百年纪念日。为纪念这一特殊日子，法国著名建筑师古斯塔夫·埃菲尔设计了铁塔，并由此而得名。塔高 324 米，塔身重达 9 000 吨，分 3 层。埃菲尔铁塔是巴黎最易识别的标志。

Located on the left bank of Seine, Eiffel Tower is the first steel structure of the tower in the world. It is also the highest building in Paris and tourist center. It is regarded as the symbol of Paris. It was built in 1889 in memory of the 100th anniversary of France Revolution and for the Exposition Universelle. The designer was architect Gustave Eiffel and it was named after him. The three-story tower is 324 meters high and 9,000 tons in weight. It is the most recognizable symbol of Paris.

◆ 凡尔赛宫（Palace of Versailles）

凡尔赛宫位于巴黎西南郊的凡尔赛镇，是欧洲最富丽堂皇的皇家宫苑，也是西方古典主义建筑的代表作。它是 17 世纪专制王权的象征，路易十四、路易十五和路易十六三代帝王曾在这里度过一生。许多举世瞩目的大事也在此发生。1979 年，被联合国教科文组织列入世界文化遗产名录。

Located at the Versailles town in the southwest of Paris, Palace of Versailles is the most magnificent palace in Europe. It is the representative work of western classic architecture. It is the symbol of the king of autocracy in the 17th century. King Louis XIV, XV and XVI had spent their lives here. Many remarkable events had happened here. It was listed in the World Cultural Heritage Site by UNESCO in 1979.

（二）马赛（Marseille）

法国南部的尼斯、戛纳、马赛地区被称为“蓝色海岸”。马赛是法国最大的港口和第二大城市，也是仅次于鹿特丹的欧洲第二大港，位于法国南部地中海利翁湾东岸，是普罗旺斯的首府，法国南部的行政、经济、文化和交通中心。著名的《马赛曲》（现为法国国歌）即诞生于此。同时，马赛是几千年来东方货物进入西方世界的重镇，所以马赛城弥漫着混杂的异国气息。马赛法国最古老的城市之一，建于公元前 6 世纪的古希腊时代，已有 2 600 年的历史。马赛拥有众多的文物古迹，距马赛老港 3 000 米处有一座 16 世纪建造的要塞——伊夫堡，传说是大仲马《基督山伯爵》一书中主人公被囚禁的地方，每年吸引着成千上万的旅游者来此参观。

Nice, Cannes and Marseille are regarded as “Côte d'Azur” (Blue Coast) in the southern France. Located along the east bank of the Gulf of Lion of Mediterranean in the south of France, Marseille, the capital of Provence, is the largest port and the second largest city in France, and the second largest port in Europe (after Rotterdam), and the center of politics, economy, culture and transportation in southern France. The well-known song *Le Marseillaise*, now the National Anthem of France, was sung here for the first time. It has been one of the most important cities for the Eastern goods to be imported to the Western countries since several thousand years ago, so the city is mixed with various exotic tastes. Marseille, founded in the 6th century BC by Greek as one of the oldest cities in France, has a history of 2,600 years. Lots of historic relics can be found here. Château d'If, 3 kilometers away from the old port, is an important fortress built in the 16th century which was said to have been the place where the hero in *Le Comte de Monte-Cristo* by Dumas was imprisoned. Thousands of tourists visit here every year.

（三）尼斯（Nice）

尼斯是位于地中海沿岸的法国南部城市，距巴黎 933 千米，是“蓝色海岸”地区的首府，是法国仅次于巴黎的第二大旅游胜地，也是全欧洲最具魅力的黄金海岸。尼斯是欧洲的首选度假地。在地理上，尼斯三面环山，一面临海，有着 7 500 米长的海岸线。群山的阻拦，使尼斯免受寒冷的北风侵凌，冬暖夏凉。尼斯以其全年温和的地中海气候、灿烂的阳光、绵延的海滩，以及晒太阳的美女而闻名。尼斯被人称“世界富豪聚集的中心”。海边的豪华别墅、比比皆是的奢侈品店和艺术气息的交织使尼斯形成富丽堂皇与典雅优美的独特美。尼斯狂欢节是法国最有名的节日之一，也是世界最著名、最盛大的狂欢节之一，创办于 1873 年，最精彩的是花车游行、烛光游行和奇装异服表演。

Located on the bank of Mediterranean in the southern France, Nice, the capital of the Côte d'Azur area, 933 kilometers away from Paris, is the second tourist city after Paris in France and also the most attractive golden beach in Europe. The city is always the first option for holiday in Europe. Geographically, Nice is open to the sea on one side and surrounded on three sides by mountains so that the cold air from the north can not enter, and the weather here is warm in winter and cool in summer. It has a coastline of 7,500 meters. With the mild Mediterranean climate all year round, Nice is noted for bright sunny days, long beaches and lots of beauties in sunbath and it is referred to as “the world center of the riches”. Nice has its unique beauty because the luxury villas along the seashore and the lavish brand shops are mixed with the taste of art. The Nice Carnaval, started in 1873, is one of the most famous festivals in France, and one of the most well-known and biggest carnivals in the world. The most fascinating shows are flower floats parade, candle-lit parade and fancy fashion show.

（四）戛纳（Cannes）

戛纳是欧洲有名的旅游胜地和每年的戛纳名流社交集会场所，因每年的戛纳国际电影节而闻名于世。戛纳位于法国南部地中海沿岸，距尼斯约 26 千米，拥有世界上最洁白、漂亮的海滩。这里气候温和、阳光普照、海水蔚蓝，来自世界各地的游艇汇集于此，主要景点有海滨大道、老城区、建造于 11 世纪的城堡等。戛纳是世界级的影都，著名的戛纳国际电影节被誉为“电影界的奥运会”，每年 5 月举行，该电影节颁发的金棕榈大奖被公认为电影界的最高荣誉之一。

Cannes is a well-known tourist city in Europe and a venue for the world celebrities to have social gatherings. It is famous for its annual Cannes International Film Festival. Located on the coast of Mediterranean in the southern France, Cannes, about 26 kilometers away from Nice, has the clearest and most beautiful beaches in the world. With the mild climate and sunny days, the sea is blue and Cannes is full of yachts from all over the world. The main attractions are seashore avenue, old city, the castle of the 11th century, etc. Cannes is a world-class capital of films. The Cannes International Film Festival held in May every year is honored as the “Film Olympics”. The most prestigious award given out at Cannes is the Golden Palm Award, which is one of the highest honors in the film industry.

四、旅游资讯

（一）美食

作为举世皆知的世界三大烹饪王国之一，法国的饮食文化有着悠久的历史和传统，法国菜不仅做起来复杂，强调色、香、形、味，而且吃起来也很有讲究，从酒与菜的搭配、餐具和酒具的形状乃至服务员上菜、倒酒的方式都有严格的规矩。法国人注重原材料的新鲜和口味的纯正。法国菜选料广泛，法国人主要偏好牛肉、禽类、海鲜、蔬菜等，特别是蜗牛、松露、蘑菇、龙虾、鹅肝、鱼子酱；在配料方面，酒、橄榄油、鲜奶油以及各式香料是他们的最爱。一顿标准法式大餐的上菜顺序为冷盘菜、汤类、主菜和甜品。第一道菜是冷盘菜，一般是沙丁鱼、火腿、奶酪、鹅肝酱和沙拉等，用于开胃。第二道菜是汤类，汤大致为清汤、蔬菜汤、肉汤或者海鲜汤，一般要配面包一起食用。第三道是主菜，鱼类包括淡海水鱼、贝类以及软体动物类，肉类有牛羊肉、家禽等，其中牛排是常见的主菜，常用的烹调方式有烤、煎等。享用完主菜后，便到甜品了。法国人爱好甜食是出了名的，蛋糕、冰激凌、馅饼、酥饼、布丁等，种类口味多样。法国人饭前一般要喝度数不高的甜酒，习惯称之为“开胃酒”；吃饭时要喝不带甜味的葡萄酒或玫瑰酒；吃肉时一般喝红葡萄酒；吃海鲜时喝白葡萄酒或玫瑰酒；饭后要喝一点儿带甜味的“消化酒”；每逢宴请还要喝香槟酒，以增加席间欢乐的气氛。法国的葡萄酒、香槟和白兰地享誉全球。

As one of the three countries with famous cuisine, the cuisine culture of France has a long history and tradition. French cuisine is not only complicated in color, smell, shape and taste, but also has a strict process on table. They will match wine with the dishes, tableware with wine glass, and even the way for the waiters to serve the dishes or fill up the glass. They pay much attention to the freshness of ingredients and the originality of the taste. The material is various but they prefer beef, poultry, seafood and vegetables, especially escargot, truffle, mushrooms, lobster, foie gras and caviar; and the condiments such as wine, olive oil, fresh cream and various spices. The standard order for French dinner will be cold dish, soup, main course and desserts. First course is cold dish, usually sardines, ham, cheese, foie gras and salad for an appetizer. Second course is soup which can be clear soup, vegetable soup, meat soup, or seafood soup, usually with bread. Third one is the main course including fresh or salty water fish, shellfish or mollusks and meat like beef, mutton and poultry. Normally beef is the main course that is usually toasted, grilled or fried. After the main course, it is dessert time. French is known for their love for desserts such as cake, ice cream, pie, pastry, pudding, etc., kinds of flavors for the dinner. Before the dinner, the low degree wine will be served which is usually called aperitif, and during the dinner the wine or rose wine without sweet will be served. Meat is always served with red wine and seafood is with white wine or rose wine. After dinner the digesting wine that is a little bit sweet will be served. In the banquet, champagne will be served to build up the atmosphere. France is well-known to the world for its wine, champagne and brandy.

知识拓展

咖啡文化

法国有句谚语“Un jour sans fromage, c’est un jour sans soleil”。意思是说，对法国人而言，如果哪天少了奶酪，那天就没了阳光。相比阳光和奶酪，如果法国人的生活里少了咖啡，他们会更加无精打采。法国人的日常生活离不开咖啡。咖啡对他们来说不只是一种饮品，它有丰富的文化内涵。遍布城市与乡村的咖啡馆是法国生活方式的一种标志。

“请来一小杯浓咖啡”已经成为融入法国生活的开场白，在咖啡馆的柜台上经常能够听到这句话。不论清晨还是夜晚，人们喜欢坐在露天咖啡馆，谈论着天气、体育赛事、政治时事和时尚等众多话题，欣赏别人或被别人欣赏。法国人曾对外国游客做过一项调查，当被问及巴黎最吸引人的东西是什么时，许多人的回答不是卢浮宫、埃菲尔铁塔等脍炙人口的名胜，而是散落在巴黎大街小巷的咖啡馆。有人曾把咖啡馆比作法国的骨架，如果拆了它们，法国就会散架。徐志摩也曾说过：“如果巴黎少了咖啡馆，恐怕会变得一无可爱。”

咖啡还和法国几个世纪以来的文化息息相关。17世纪法国就出现了许多因为咖啡而形成的文化艺术沙龙。普洛可甫咖啡馆是巴黎第一家咖啡馆，思想家伏尔泰、卢梭、狄德罗等都曾是这家咖啡馆的常客，伏尔泰的几部著作、狄德罗的世界首部《百科全书》都是在这里完成的；文学巨匠如雨果、巴尔扎克、乔治·桑、左拉等还以咖啡馆的名字创立了文学刊物《普洛可甫》。蒙马特的学院咖啡馆是19世纪巴黎大学时代的标志，长期聚居着来自四面八方的艺术家，毕加索、海明威、凡·高、弗洛伊德等曾在这里编织他们的梦想。

（二）购物及退税

时装：法国高级时装是法国服装的精华，每件时装犹如一件艺术作品。在巴黎，每年均举行巴黎春夏时装周和巴黎秋冬时装周。这是世界上最受瞩目的时装盛会，引导着全世界的服装潮流，影响着人们对于流行的观念。著名设计师伊夫·圣罗兰、加布里埃·香奈儿和克里斯汀·迪奥并称法国时装界“三圣”。

Fashion: The superior fashion is the essence of France garment which is just like an art. Every year in Paris, there will be Paris Fashion Week with Spring/Summer and Autumn/Winter events which are well-known all over the world leading the world’s fashion trend and affecting people’s idea of fashion. The well-known three designers, Yves Saint Laurent, Gabrielle Chanel and Christian Dior are considered as “Three Saints” of French fashion.

香水：法国香水以及化妆品举世闻名。香水、时装和葡萄酒并列为法国三大精品产业，是法国人的骄傲。法国香水是全球女性的挚爱，其实巴黎的商店里琳琅满目的香水大都是被誉为“香水之都”的格拉斯生产或提供原料的。在法国，香水业与时装业的结合是一种很有意思的文化现象。20世纪20年代，香奈儿推出了“香奈儿5号”香水，在世界范围内获得了认可，被视为法国香水发展史上的里程碑。至今，各名牌时装公司几乎都保留了自己牌号的香水。

Perfume: Both French perfume and cosmetics are well-known all over the world. Perfume, fashion and wine are listed as the three leading boutique industries, of which the French people feel proud. French perfume is the women’s favorite in the world. Actually most of the perfume or the raw material in Paris is manufactured or supplied in Grasse which is named as “the capital of perfume”. In France, it is a meaningful cultural phenomenon to combine perfume industry with fashion industry. In 1920s, Chanel put out Chanel No.5 perfume and was accepted all over the world. It was regarded as the milestone of the French perfume history. Up to now all the fashion companies have their own brand repertoires of perfume.

葡萄酒：自从古代英勇无畏的水手把葡萄藤从尼罗河的山谷和克里特岛带到希腊、西西里和意大利南部，再由此传入法国之后，葡萄的种植和酿酒技术在法国得到了一代又一代人的改良、提升和发扬光大。葡萄酒文化不仅表现了法兰西民族对精致美好生活的追求，而且是法国文明和文化不可分割的一个重要组成部分。玛格丽红葡萄酒享誉世界，有“法国葡萄酒皇后”的美称。波尔多是公认的世界最大的葡萄酒产地。

Wine: After the brave sailors brought the grapevine branch from Nilotic valleys and Crete to Greece, Sicily and southern Italy and then to France, the technology of vines cultivation and wine brewing has been improved, promoted and carried forward in France by generation after generation. The wine culture shows not only the French pursuit of good life but also the integral part of the French civilization and culture. Margaret Red Wine is known throughout the world and is rated as “the queen of French wine”. Bordeaux is recognized as the largest wine producing area in the world.

芝士：法国出产近 400 种芝士，花样繁多，各具风味，是世界上芝士品种最多的国家。法国芝士有牛奶、绵羊奶、山羊奶或者混合奶制成的不同品种。法国各地都有道地的芝士产品，制法历史悠久，源远流长。

Cheese: France ranks top worldwide in cheese variety, with nearly four hundred in number and taste. French cheese is made from the cow milk, sheep milk, goat milk or mixed milk. Authentic cheese with long history can be found everywhere in France.

在法国退税，持非欧盟国家护照的游客在同一天同一家标有可退税标志的商店购物超过 175.01 欧元，普通商品可享受约 12% 的退税。游客在购物之后的 3 个月内，可凭盖有离境海关签章的退税单办理退税手续。

The visitors from non-EU countries can have about 12% tax refund when they buy goods over 175.01 euros in the same shop in the same day. Within 3 months after the shopping, visitors can get the refund with stamped tax refund form in the customs office.

知识拓展

香水之都——格拉斯

提起法国香水，人们会自然地想到巴黎。其实，真正称得上“法国香水摇篮”的不是巴黎，而是位于法国南部一个不大的城市——格拉斯（Grasse）。17 世纪的欧洲人已经知道，最迷人的香水出自格拉斯。1730 年，法国第一家香精香料生产公司在格拉斯诞生。

从此，香水业逐渐在格拉斯落地生根。如今，这里已成为名副其实的“香水之都”，为法国各大名牌香水销售公司配制香水。法国80%的香水都是在这里制造，格拉斯因此被称为“嗅觉的天堂”。格拉斯至今仍是法国香水的重要产地和原料供应地，它拥有众多的香水博物馆、试验室以及生产厂家，风靡世界的“香奈儿5号”香水就诞生于此。它也为法国赢得了“香水之国”的美誉。格拉斯之所以能成为“法国香水摇篮”，主要是因为它优越的自然环境和传统的手工业。

（三）时差

法国位于GMT+1时区（在3月底到10月底间实行GMT+2时区的夏令时）。在1973年的石油危机后，1975年法国开始实行夏令时制。夏令时制实施的最初目的是节约能源，几乎所有的欧盟国家都实行夏令时制。在10月到次年3月间，法国与中国有7小时的时差；在3月到10月间，与中国有6个小时的时差。

France is in the time zone GMT+1(France practices Daylight Saving Time from end of March to October, GMT+2). Daylight Saving Time started in 1975 after the Oil Crisis of 1973. In order to save the energy, most of the EU countries adopt the Daylight Saving Time. During the October to the next March, there is 7 hours different from China and 6 hours from March to October.

知识拓展

《申根协定》

1985年6月14日签署的《申根协定》(*Schengen Agreement*)，是一项欧洲国家间的条约协定，由德国、法国、荷兰、比利时、卢森堡5个国家在卢森堡小镇申根签署。《申根协定》的签署目的是取消相互之间的边境检查点，并协调对申根区之外的边境控制，即在成员国相互之间取消边境管制，持有任一成员国有效身份证或签证的人可以在所有成员国境内自由流动。根据该协定，旅游者如果持有其中一国的旅游签证即可合法地到所有其他申根国家。

《申根协定》创造了无边界区，即申根区。截至2019年底，申根的成员国增加到26个欧洲国家，包括4个非欧盟国（冰岛、挪威、瑞士和列支敦士登）。26个申根国家是：奥地利、比利时、丹麦、芬兰、法国、德国、冰岛、意大利、希腊、卢森堡、荷兰、挪威、葡萄牙、西班牙、瑞典、匈牙利、捷克、斯洛伐克、斯洛文尼亚、波兰、爱沙尼亚、拉脱维亚、立陶宛、马耳他、瑞士和列支敦士登。

申根国家和欧盟国家是两个不同的概念。虽然有不少国家同属这两个概念的范围，但是也有例外。如属于申根国家的瑞士、挪威、冰岛和列支敦士登不属欧盟，属于欧盟的爱尔兰、罗马尼亚、保加利亚和塞浦路斯等国并不实施《申根协定》。

思考练习

1. 经典旅游线路分析

法国深度8日游

第1天：上海——阿姆斯特丹——尼斯

游客在上海浦东国际机场集合，搭乘国际航班经阿姆斯特丹转机前往尼斯。抵达后入住酒店休息。

第2天：尼斯——戛纳——摩纳哥——尼斯

早餐后，前往戛纳，每年来自世界各地著名的电影人都会云集于这座法国南部城市。“精巧、典雅、迷人”是大多数人对戛纳的评价。后前往只有1.95平方千米的袖珍赌国——摩纳哥，外观蒙特卡洛大赌场、王宫及王宫广场。接着驱车前往尼斯，途经著名的法国香水小镇格拉斯。抵达尼斯后，漫步于有“英国人散步大道”之称的盎格鲁大街，亲身体验蓝色海岸的悠闲气氛。

第3天：尼斯——艾克斯——阿尔勒——阿维尼翁

早餐后，前往印象派画家塞尚的故乡——艾克斯。艾克斯是座拥有林荫大道、喷泉、华宅的中世纪古城，随后前往伫立在罗讷河上的珍宝——阿尔勒。外观阿尔勒最大的纪念馆——圆形竞技场，以及古剧院、市政厅和圣特罗菲姆教堂。后驱车前往阿维尼翁这个1995年被联合国教科文组织列入世界文化遗产名录的美丽城市，罗讷河上的圣贝内泽桥建于公元12世纪初。这座大桥有21座桥墩、22个巨大的拱洞，如今只剩下4孔，长900米，是中世纪建筑的杰作，也是法国民歌的灵感源泉。夜宿阿维尼翁附近宾馆。

第4天：阿维尼翁——酒庄——勾禾德——里昂

早餐后，前往Chareau Neuf du Pape酒庄，参观酒窖，品尝当地美酒。之后到曾被选为法国最美的村庄之一的山城勾禾德，这是一座依山而建的古城，也是普罗旺斯非常著名的观光胜地，在蓝天的映衬下，灰白的建筑煞是好看。随后前往位于法国东南部的里昂。这是一座历史悠久的古老城市，1998年被联合国教科文组织列入世界文化遗产名录。里昂旧城中心布满了中世纪的建筑和教堂，使它获得了“拥有一颗粉红的心脏”的美称。漫步于被称为“皇家广场”的白莱果广场，广场周围都是19世纪初建造的楼房，这里花店、咖啡座、餐馆林立。游览里昂老城，旧街区中保存着许多15世纪到17世纪的旧宅居。

第5天：里昂——舍农索城堡——图尔

早餐后，驱车前往舍农索水上城堡。舍农索城堡是卢瓦尔河谷宫堡群中最富有浪漫情调的“水上城堡”。夜宿图尔附近。

第6天：图尔——巴黎

早餐后，驱车前往法国的时尚之都——巴黎，游览被联合国教科文组织列入世界文化遗产名录的凡尔赛宫。

第 7 天：巴黎

参观世界三大博物馆之一的卢浮宫，将安排专业的中文讲解员讲述这座艺术宫殿的珍贵收藏；午餐后，游览香榭丽舍大街的起点凯旋门、协和广场、埃菲尔铁塔；乘坐塞纳河游船，晚上安排品尝法国特色餐。

第 8 天：巴黎——上海

早餐后，参观蒙帕纳斯大厦（56 层观光厅），矗立在塞纳河左岸的蒙帕纳斯大厦是巴黎古城中除埃菲尔铁塔外最高的建筑。前往老佛爷百货公司或巴黎春天百货公司和 BENLUX 免税店享受一番购物的快乐。在导游的带领下前往机场，办理好退税手续后，搭乘国际航班返回上海。

分析：这条经典旅游线路的主要旅游景点与行程特色，以及适合旅游的人群。

2. 案例分析

[案例 1] 第 64 届戛纳电影节红毯仪式上，某著名影星以一身朱红色仙鹤图案礼服亮相，当晚即有一家法语教学机构通过微博对此影星的礼服做出了点评，称这套礼服不符合法国文化，仙鹤在中国文化中代表长寿、吉祥，同时也寓意着和平、安宁，但是在法国文化中，仙鹤与孔雀均被视为恶鸟。请问在法国着装需要注意什么？

[案例 2] 游客晨晨进行了法国深度 8 日游，她漫步过戛纳、尼斯、摩纳哥，享受过法国的绚丽阳光，并且寻访了印象派画家留下的足迹，感受了普罗旺斯宁静、恬适的生活，至今还沉浸于卢浮宫艺术海洋、浪漫的塞纳河畔和优雅的香榭丽舍大街。她唯一觉得遗憾的是无法与当地人交流，她的英语很好，可是每当她与当地人聊天，当地人总是用法语回答她，而且大多数情况下当地人也听得懂她说的英语。难道法国人天生傲慢、讨厌英语？晨晨想不明白。法国人为什么不愿说英语？

3. 练一练

试分析法国有哪些主题游。选一个你最有兴趣的话题，写一篇导游词。

第三节　德国

一、国家概况

（一）地理环境

德国，全称为德意志联邦共和国，位于欧洲的西部和中部，北接丹麦，东连波兰和捷克，南靠奥地利和瑞士，西南紧临法国和卢森堡，西北连荷兰和比利时。从地图上看，德国位于欧洲的心脏地带，是欧洲邻国最多的国家，水、陆、空条条道路经过德国，故被称为“欧洲走廊”。

The Federal Republic of Germany, briefly Germany, is located in the western and the central of Europe, bordering Denmark to the north, Poland and Czech to the east, Austria and Switzerland to the south, France and Luxemburg to the southwest and Holland and Belgium to the northwest. So Germany is located in the heart of Europe and it is the country with the most of its European neighbors. All roads including water, land and air lead to Germany. That's why it is known as the European corridor.

德国地势北低南高，北部是平均海拔不到100米的平原，中部是由东西走向构成的山地，西南是莱茵河谷区，莱茵河两边的山地为森林和高山牧场，东南是巴伐利亚高原和阿尔卑斯山区，境内最高峰是位于阿尔卑斯山的楚格峰，海拔2 962米。主要河流莱茵河（流经境内865千米）、易北河、美因河均向北流淌，唯有多瑙河自西向东注入黑海。德国湖泊星罗棋布，最大的天然湖康斯坦茨湖位于德国、瑞士和奥地利的交界处。

Its terrain is high in the south and low in the north. The elevation of the northern plain is less than 100 meters and the central is the mountainous area from east to the west. Its southwest is the Rhine Valley, both sides of which are forested mountains and alpine pasture. Its southeast is Bavarian Highland and Alps mountainous region. Its peak is Zugspitze with 2,962 meters high. The main rivers are the Rhine (865 kilometers in the territory), the Elbe and the Main flowing to the north, but the Danube flows from west to east into the Black Sea. Germany is dotted with lakes, among which the largest natural lake is Lake Constance, located at the junction of Germany, Switzerland and Austria.

德国气候：西北为温带海洋性气候，往南部和东部逐渐过渡为温带大陆性气候。德国1月平均气温为0℃，山区为–10℃，夏季平均气温为20℃，适合旅游。

The climate in the northwest is maritime temperate zone. To the south and the east are the transition regions which vary from maritime climate to continental climate. The average temperature is 0℃ in January and –10℃ in mountainous region. The average temperature in summer is 20℃ and it is suitable for traveling.

（二）人文概况

1. *历史*

尽管真正统一的德国历史要从普鲁士王国成立才开始，但是德意志民族却可以追溯到公元前100年，从斯堪的纳维亚半岛至德国北部逐渐形成的日耳曼部落。在奥古斯都统治德意志地区时期，日耳曼部落开始抵抗罗马帝国的统治。公元5世纪末，克洛维一世建立法兰克王国，日耳曼进入法兰克时代。公元800年，查理曼大帝统一了西欧的大部分地区。查理曼死后，其孙子把法兰克王国分成西、中、东三部分。莱茵河以东的东法兰克王国成了后来的德意志王国的基础。公元919年，萨克森公爵亨利一世在东法兰克王国建立萨克森王朝。公元962年，国王奥托一世加冕为神圣罗马帝国皇帝。1806年，拿破仑入侵德意志地区，神圣罗马帝国破裂，建立莱茵邦联。1871年，法国在普法战争中失败，威廉一世加冕为德意志皇帝，德意志帝国成立，定都柏林。1914年，斐迪南大公被杀后，第一次世界大战爆发，1918 年 11 月，德国革命开始，威廉二世政权被推翻。1919 年，建立魏玛共和国。1933 年，希特勒上台，实行独裁统治。德国于 1939 年发动第二次世界大战，给世界人民带来严重灾难。1945 年，苏联红军占领柏林，德国战败投降。1949 年 5 月 23 日，被英、法、美占领的德国西部建立德意志联邦共和国，定都波恩。同年 10 月 7 日，被苏联占领的德国东部成立德意志民主共和国，东柏林为其首都。1990 年 10 月 3 日，德国实现统一，重新定都柏林。

Though the history of the united Germany started from the establishment of the Kingdom of Prussia, the history of the Germanic tribes which were from Scandinavia and northern part of Germany could be traced back to 100 BC. During the period of Emperor Augustus' reign of German area, the Germanic tribes started to fight against the Rome. At the end of the 5th century, the Kingdom of Franks was established by Clovis Ⅰ. In 800 AD, Charles the Great united the most areas of west Europe. After his death, his three grandsons separated the kingdom into three parts—the west, the middle and the east. The Kingdom of Eastern Franks in eastern Rhine was the basic area of the Germany. In 919, Henry Ⅰ, Duke of Saxony established the Saxony Dynasty in the Kingdom of Eastern Franks. In 962, the King Otto Ⅰ was crowned as the emperor of Holy Rome Empire. In 1806, Napoléon invaded the German area and set up the Confederation of the Rhine comprising most of the German states instead of the Holy Rome Empire. In 1871, France was defeated during the Franco-Prussian war, William Ⅰ was crowned as the emperor of the German Empire, hence German Empire was established and Berlin was the capital. In 1914, the First World War started after the Archduke Ferdinand was assassinated. In Nov. 1918, the German Revolution began, William Ⅱ abdicated and Weimar Republic was established in 1919. In 1933, Adolf Hitler came into power and ruled despotically. In 1939, Germany started the Second World War and brought the world disaster. In 1945, the Red Army of the Soviet Union occupied Berlin and Germany surrendered. The Federal Republic of Germany was founded in the area occupied by the Britain, France and United States on 23 May 1949 and Bonn became the capital. On October 7,1949, the German Democratic Republic was established in the area occupied by the Soviet Union and East Berlin was the capital. On October 3, 1990, Germany was reunited and Berlin became the capital again.

知识拓展

勃兰特的下跪

1970 年 12 月 7 日是大雪过后东欧最寒冷的一天。刚刚对捷克、波兰进行国事访问后，当时的联邦德国总理维利·勃兰特冒着凛冽的寒风来到华沙犹太人死难者纪念碑下。他向纪念碑献上花圈后，肃穆垂首，突然双腿下跪，并发出祈祷："上帝饶恕我们吧，愿苦难的灵魂得到安宁。"勃兰特以此举向第二次世界大战中无辜被纳粹党杀害的犹太人表示沉痛哀悼，并虔诚地为纳粹时代的德国认罪、赎罪。当时的联邦德国总统赫利同时向全世界发表了著名的赎罪书。在第二次世界大战中，波兰付出了 600 万人的生命，纳粹德国臭名昭著的奥斯维辛集中营就设在波兰，仅这个集中营就杀害了近 400 万犹太人……勃兰特本人没有责任，恰恰相反，勃兰特在第二次世界大战中是名坚强的反纳粹战士，他被希特勒下令开除国籍，被到处追捕，亡命挪威，直至战后返回祖国……但是，勃兰特现在已是政府首脑，他感到自己有责任代表德国人民向波兰人民表明心迹，保证不再使历史重演。勃兰特在波兰犹太人纪念碑前下跪谢罪，被誉为“欧洲1 000年来最强烈的谢罪表现”。这一跪，淡化了饱受纳粹蹂躏的波兰人民沉积在心底里的愤怒，他们被勃兰特的举动感动得热泪盈眶。这一跪，对德国重返欧洲，赢得自尊，回归正常的发展道路产生了极为深远的影响。1971年，勃兰特因此获得了诺贝尔和平奖。德国还在首都柏林著名的勃兰登堡门附近建立了由2 700余块石碑组成的犹太人大屠杀纪念碑群，以提醒后人德国走过的歧途绝对不能重现。

2. 经济

德国是高度发达的资本主义工业国。德国的经济实力位居欧洲首位，是世界上仅次于美国、中国、日本的第四大经济体。德国的国内生产总值占欧盟的25%，德国经济也因此被称为“欧洲经济的火车头”。其中，汽车工业是德国经济发展的“晴雨表”，德国为第四大汽车生产国，位列中国、美国和日本之后。德国是欧洲货币联盟的创建成员，欧洲中央银行总部设在法兰克福。德国也是西方八国首脑会议的成员国。

Germany is a highly-developed capitalist industrial country. Its economic power is the strongest in Europe and is ranked the fourth after America, China and Japan in the world. The GDP of Germany is accounted for 25% of the total amount of Europe Union. The economy of Germany is called as the locomotive of the train for the European economy. Auto industry is the barometer of German economy. The output is ranked the fourth after China, United States and Japan. Germany is the member of the founders of the European Monetary Union. The headquarters of the European Central Bank is in Frankfurt. Germany is also the member of the G8 summits.

3. 社会文化

德国人口约8 301万，主要是德意志人，还有721.4万外籍人士，占人口总数的9%，其中以土耳其人最多，其次是意大利人和希腊人。德国居民中29.3%的人信奉基督教新教，30.2%信奉罗马天主教。此外，还有少数人信奉伊斯兰教和犹太教。德语为通用语言，也是该国的官方语言。

The population of Germany is 83.01 million, mainly Germans. The expatriates are 7.214 million that is 9% of the population, mainly Turk, then Italian and Greek. 29.3% of the inhabitants profess Protestantism and 30.2% profess Roman Catholicism, while some of others for Islam and Judaism. German is the common and official language.

讲到德国的文化艺术，人们首先想到的是德国的哲学家。德国是许多哲学流派的发源地，如德国唯心论、马克思主义，代表人物有康德、黑格尔、费尔巴哈、马克思、叔本华、尼采等。

When people talk about the culture of Germany, they will think about the philosophers. Germany is the source for lots of schools of philosophy such as German Idealism and Marxism. The representatives are Kant, Hegel, Feuerbach, Karl Marx, Schopenhauer, Nietzsche, etc.

德国文学可以追溯到中世纪时期的瓦尔特·冯·德尔·福格尔魏德。受意大利文艺复兴的影响，18 世纪德国文学走向顶峰，最杰出的作家有歌德（代表作《浮士德》《少年维特的烦恼》）、海涅（代表作《罗蕾莱》）、席勒（代表作《强盗》）和格林兄弟（代表作《格林童话》）等。《格林童话》被译成多国文字，是世界儿童文学的瑰宝。20 世纪德国有许多文学家获得诺贝尔文学奖。

The history of German literature can be traced back to Walther Von der Vogelweide in Medieval Period. In fluenced by Italian Renaissance, German literature reached its summit in the 18th century. The most outstanding authors are Goethe (1749–1832, *Faust, The Sorrows of Young Werther*), Heine (1797–1856, *Lorelei*), Schiller (1759–1805, *The Robbers*) and Brothers Grimm (*Grimms' Fairy Tales*) and so on. *Grimms' Fairy Tales* was translated into many languages and is regarded as the treasure of the children literature all over the world. In the 20th century, lots of writers in Germany have been awarded Nobel Prize in Literature.

音乐是德国人生活中不可缺少的组成部分。德国也是音乐家的摇篮，诞生了许多著名的世界级音乐家，特别是古典音乐家，主要的代表人物是巴赫和贝多芬。其他世界知名的作曲家还有亨德尔、瓦格纳、勃拉姆斯等。柏林爱乐乐团更是享誉世界。可以说，德国是名副其实的音乐之乡。

Music is an integral part of German life. Germany is the cradle of many musicians. Lots of world-class musicians, especially the classic musicians were born here, and the main representatives are Bach and Beethoven. Other world famous composers were Handel, Wagner, Brahms, etc. The Berlin Philharmonic Orchestra is known throughout the world. It can be said that Germany is a truly country of music.

德国有 3 000 多座博物馆，收藏内容十分丰富。每年都会举办各种艺术节、博览会等。德国人喜欢阅读，即使在当今电视通信及网络普及的年代，德国人仍然保持着爱读书的传统。法兰克福和莱比锡是德国图书出版业中心，德国图书出版量在世界上仅次于美国，排第二位。此外，众多的教堂、宫殿和古堡也是德国重要的文化遗产。

Germany has more than 3,000 museums with rich collections. Each year there are lots of festivals and fairs. The Germans like reading. Even today they still keep the tradition though the TV and internet is so popular. Frankfurt and Leipzig are Germany's publishing centers. The quantity of the publishing in Germany is ranked second in the world after the US. In addition, a large number of churches, palaces and castles are important cultural heritages in Germany.

二、民俗风情

（一）礼仪禁忌

在德国文化的不断熏陶下，德国人的性格形成了一些共性：有礼貌、守时、勤奋、节俭、整洁、遵纪守法、做事一板一眼。正如一句谚语所云：“一个德国人可以成为哲学家，三个德国人可以组成一个俱乐部。”共同的特点使德国人几乎都愿意加入各种非营利性质的俱乐部。在公共社交场合，德国人往往显得呆板沉重，拘泥于形式，缺乏幽默感。德国人在工作中一丝不苟，就像一部机器。传统的德国妇女往往可以用三个词来描述：下厨、照看孩子、去教堂做礼拜。然而，正如欧洲其他国家一样，这种传统模式逐渐消失。德国的出生率逐年下降，如今德国相当数量的人信奉独身主义。但是他们仍然喜欢聚会、度假、过节。德国是欧洲公共假日最多的国家。

Germans have developed common features because of their culture background. They are polite, punctual, diligent, frugal, clean, law-abiding and do everything according to the rules. An old saying goes that one German can be a philosopher, and three can organize a club. The common features lead them to join the non-profit clubs. In public, Germans seem to be stiff, formalistic and humorless. They are strict in their work, just like a machine. The traditional role for women can be concluded in three words: kitchen, kid and church. However, just like the people of other European countries, the tradition is gradually disappearing. The rate of birth is declining every year as more people don’t want to get married. But they still love parties, holidays and festivals. Germany is the country which has the most public holidays in Europe.

德意志民族是一个讲究秩序的民族。德国人注重规则和法律。同德国人打交道没有太多的麻烦。多数情况下，他们都比较干脆、直接。他们会直接告诉你什么事能做到，什么事做不到。他们会非常明确地回答。

Germans pay great attention to orders. They do everything according to the rules and law. Without too much trouble to deal with the German, in most cases, they are relatively simple and direct. They will reply immediately what they can do or can’t do. They will answer unambiguously.

德国人非常注重时间，凡事都喜欢提前预约。德语中有一句话：“准时是帝王的礼貌。”德国人非常守时，约定好的时间无特殊情况，绝不轻易变动。应邀到别人家做客或外出拜访朋友时，都会准点，让主人干等或者浪费他人时间，是不礼貌的。如果有特殊原因无法准时赴约，应向朋友表示歉意，并请求原谅。

Germans pay great attention to time. They like to make reservations for everything in advance. The German word goes like that “just-in-time is the courtesy of the emperor”. Germans are very punctual. Appointments could not be easily changed without any special conditions. It should be punctual to pay a visit or to be one’s guest. It is impolite to let the host wait or waste others’ time. If there are special reasons for the lateness for appointments, making an apology and asking for forgiveness is necessary.

德国人讲究礼仪。例如：处处体现女士优先；在日常生活中，“您好”“请问”“谢谢”“再见”等礼貌用语总是不离口；当两人在路上、办公室、宾馆或电梯相遇时，不管认识不认识，都会相互打招呼。在同人交谈时，德国人很注意尊重对方，不过问私事，如不问女性的年龄、不问对方的收入等。

Germans pay attention to the etiquette. Lady first is the rule. In daily life, those terms are often used, such as “hello”, “please”, “thank you”, and “goodbye”. When people meet on the way, in the office, the hotel or the lift, they always say hello to each other no matter whether they are familiar or not. They respect each other. They won’t mention the personal affairs during the social interaction such as lady’s age, salary and so on.

德国人很讲究清洁和整齐，不仅注意保持自己生活的小环境的清洁和整齐，而且十分重视大环境的清洁和整齐。德国人会根据场合搭配服装。工作时会穿工作服，下班回到家里会穿得随便些。但只要外出活动或有客来访，就一定会穿戴得整洁。听歌剧时，女士要穿长裙，男士要穿礼服。参加社会活动或正式宴会时更是如此。

Germans are very particular about cleanliness and tidiness. They not only keep their lives clean and tidy, but also attach great importance to their living environment. Germans will dress themselves according to situation. They will wear work uniforms during the working time and informal clothes at home. They will dress formally when they visit guests or host guests at home. When they go to the opera, a woman will wear a long dress and a man in a suit. And they will be in formal dress to attend a social party or a formal banquet.

德国人大都喜欢清静的生活，除特殊场合外，不喜欢喧闹。例如：晚上8时至第二天早晨8时不可以演奏乐器、大声喧哗。如果晚上要进行聚会活动，事先要向邻居讲明情况，请求他们的谅解，并尽可能安排在周末而且不要大声喧闹。否则，受干扰的邻居会十分恼怒，可能会当面提出抗议，甚至会请警察出面干预。

Germans are quiet. They hate noise except in special situations. They will not play instruments or make any noise from 8：00 pm to the next 8：00 am. If they want to hold a party at night, they will inform the neighbors in advance, and try to choose the weekend and will not make loud noise. Otherwise, the neighbors will complain or even call the police.

送礼物在德国也很受重视。应邀去别人家做客时，一般都会带礼物。大部分人会带束鲜花，也有一些男性客人会带瓶葡萄酒，自己写的书或者画册等。在参加生日宴会、节日聚会或者婚礼时，贺卡更为普遍。德国人不会选择贵重的礼物，而是以实用和有意义为原则。礼物要事先用礼品纸包好，德国人会当着送礼者的面打开包装。

Germans also pay attention to the gifts. When they are invited to visit somebody’s home, normally they will take gifts, most of which are flowers, wine for man, books which were written by themselves, or brochures. When attending the birthday party, festival party or wedding ceremony, greeting cards are more popular. Germans will not choose the most expensive gifts but useful and significant gifts. All the gifts should be in gift wrap which should be opened in front of the guests.

德国人用餐有许多规矩。德国人忌讳张开嘴巴咀嚼或身子凑近盘子吃东西，忌讳含着满口食物说话，忌讳只同右面的女士说话，更忌讳吃饭时谈有关世界观或政治性的话题。德国人忌用“13”这个数字。13 日若和星期五是同一天，被视为最不吉利。德国人最忌讳的是 13 个人坐一桌吃饭。

Germans have lots of rules for dinner. It is a taboo to open mouth chewing or lean the body closely to the dish, speak while eating, talk only to the woman on the right side, or discuss the world view or political affairs. It is a taboo to use the number 13. It will be regarded as unlucky if the date is Friday the 13th. It is a taboo for Germans that 13 persons have dinner in one table.

知识拓展

默克尔的节俭

德国现任总理默克尔以她的低调、朴素、谦和、平易近人的品格给国人留下了深刻的印象。2007 年，默克尔访问南京，坚决不住奢华的总统套房，而是入住价格仅为总统套房 1/20 的普通商务套房。早餐也坚持和一般住店客人一样，在大厅吃自助早餐，而不进 VIP 包间。吃早饭时，她谢绝了工作人员的服务，坚持自己到自助餐台取食物，并自己动手切法式长棍面包。其间发生了一段令工作人员感动的小插曲：默克尔在拿食物时，一不小心把麦片面包掉在地上，她不让赶过来的餐饮经理帮忙，而是自己将面包捡起，放回了自己的盘中。默克尔的早餐很简单，煎鸡蛋卷、奶酪饼、西瓜、面包，也包括掉到地上的那两片麦片面包。对德国人来说，这并不是什么特别的事。这位平民化的女总理平时就经常到超级市场购物，而且跟其他顾客一样排队，绝没有特权。但对中国公众而言，默克尔的行为实在太震撼了。当今最富裕的工业国家之一的德国，总理为何如此节俭？因为默克尔知道她用的是纳税人的钱，不能也不敢铺张浪费。在德国，法律对公务消费奉行“零容忍原则”，即任何铺张浪费都是不可容忍的，都可视为腐败，总理自然也不例外。对德国官员来说，用纳税人的钱大肆铺张是不可想象的事情。正因为如此，德国很多地方的政府大楼都显得破旧、不起眼，官员的公务消费都受到严格限制，公众随时可以查询其消费清单。如果有官员大肆挥霍公款，那不仅会遭到舆论的谴责，还有可能因此丢掉乌纱帽甚至锒铛入狱。

（二）节庆风情

1. 慕尼黑啤酒节（Oktoberfest）

慕尼黑盛产啤酒，饮用量为世界第一，因此人们习惯称慕尼黑为“啤酒之都”。慕尼黑啤酒节于每年 9 月末至 10 月的第 1 个周末举行，一般历时 16 天左右。慕尼黑啤酒节是世界规模的民间节日、慕尼黑一年中最盛大的活动，它完整地保留了巴伐利亚的民间风采和习俗。慕尼黑啤酒节起源于 1810 年 10 月 12 日，为庆贺德国巴伐利亚王储路德维希一世和萨克森－希尔登豪森的特蕾西亚公主共结百年之好而举行的一系列庆祝活动。德国的10月正值大麦和啤酒花丰收的时节，人们在劳动之余，欢聚在一起饮酒、唱歌、跳舞，表达内心的喜悦之情。今天，人们用华丽的马车运送啤酒，在巨大的啤酒帐篷里开怀畅饮，欣赏巴伐利亚的铜管乐队演奏的民歌乐曲和令人陶醉的情歌雅调。人们不仅在啤酒节上品尝美味佳肴，还举行一系列丰富多彩的娱乐活动，如赛马、射击、杂耍、各种游艺活动及戏剧演出、民族音乐会等。

The output of beer in Munich is very large and the consuming is ranked the first in the world, so Munich is named as "the capital of beer". Oktoberfest is a 16-day festival celebrating beer held annually in Munich, running from late September to the first weekend in October. Oktoberfest is a world-class folk festival, and Munich's biggest events of the year, which retains the integrity of the Bavarian folk style and customs. Oktoberfest was first held on October 12, 1810 in honor of the marriage of Crown Prince Ludwig of Bavaria to Princess Therese von Sachsen-Hildburghausen. October is the season for the harvest of barley and hops in Germany. People gather together, drinking, singing, dancing and expressing the inner joy apart from working. Nowadays, people send the beer by beautiful carriages. People appreciate the folk songs and music from the brass band of Bavaria while drinking in the giant tents. Lots of activities will be held such as horse racing, shooting, acrobats, various amusements, opera, folk song concerts, etc.

2. 科隆狂欢节（Cologne Carnival）

科隆狂欢节于11月11日11点11分开始至第二年复活节前40天为止，科隆狂欢节被称为一年中的第五个季节，仅次于巴西狂欢节，是全德国最盛大的节日，有着超过800年的历史。从前，人们为了将冬季恶灵驱逐出城，便头戴面具上街游行，而现在这一惯例被保留了下来。1823年2月10日，科隆狂欢节庆祝委员会在科隆成立，狂欢节就此成为一种独立的形式。除了由狂欢节庆祝委员会举办的众多活动（包含演讲）之外，狂欢节的活动还包括女人狂欢节、“玫瑰星期一”大游行等。

Starting at 11:11 of November 11th and ending 40 days before the next Easter, Cologne Carnival which is called as the fifth season of a year and the second largest after the Brazil Carnival, is the most popular carnival in Germany and has more than 800 years of history. In the past, people with masks marched in the street to chase the bad ghost out of the city in the winter and it then became regular every year. On February 10, 1823, the Cologne Carnival Celebration Committee set up in Cologne, it has thus become a regular festival of the city. Besides the activities including lecture organized by the Cologne Carnival Celebration Committee, there are many other activities such as Women's Carnival, Rose Monday Parade, etc.

三、主要旅游城市及景点

（一）柏林（Berlin）

柏林是德国的首都，全国第一大城市，位于德国东北部。柏林是著名的欧洲古都，始建于1237年。1871年，柏林成为德意志帝国的首都。在第二次世界大战中，柏林受到严重摧毁。战后，柏林被分为东柏林和西柏林。1990年德国统一，柏林重新成为德国的首都。

Located at the northeast of Germany, Berlin, the capital of Germany, is the largest city in Germany. Berlin is also a well-known old capital in Europe built in 1237. It became the capital of the German Empire in 1871. It was destroyed seriously in the Second World War. After the war, the city became divided into East Berlin and West Berlin. Following German reunification in 1990, the city regained its status as the capital of Germany.

◆ 勃兰登堡门（Brandenburg Gate）

勃兰登堡门位于著名的菩提树下大街西端，是柏林的象征。勃兰登堡门是依据雅典城门造型而建的，是德国古典主义建筑的杰作。勃兰登堡门于1791年竣工，门楼上耸立着胜利女神驾驭四马战车的雕塑。在战后东、西德分裂时期，勃兰登堡门内侧筑起柏林墙。1989年柏林墙被拆后，勃兰登堡门与柏林墙一同成为德国统一的象征。

Brandenburg Gate is located at the west of the renowned Unter den Linden as the symbol of Berlin. It was erected according to the design of colonnade of Acropolis of Athens in 1791 and is Germany's masterpiece of classical architecture. On the gate is the sculpture of Goddess of Victory with four-horse carriage. During the post-war partition of Germany, the gate was isolated and inaccessible immediately next to the Berlin Wall. After the Berlin Wall was torn down in 1989, Brandenburg Gate and the Berlin Wall are considered the symbol of united Germany.

◆ 柏林墙遗迹（Ruins of the Berlin Wall）

柏林墙是1961年8月13日东德在柏林城建起的城墙，目的是隔离东德和西德，是第二次世界大战以后德国分裂和冷战的标志性建筑。柏林墙于1989年被拆毁，为了纪念这段历史，保留了其中长约1 300米的一段。墙上绘有来自21个国家的艺术家不同风格的作品，也称东边画廊。

The Berlin Wall was a barrier constructed by the German Democratic Republic starting on August 13, 1961, which completely cut off (by land) West Berlin from East Berlin. It is the symbol of the Cold War and the separation of the Germany. The wall was torn down in 1989 but about 1,300 meters long of the wall was kept for commemorating the history. On the wall, there are different paintings by the artists from 21 countries which also was named East Side Gallery.

（二）慕尼黑（Munich）

慕尼黑位于德国南部，是巴伐利亚州的首府，是仅次于柏林、汉堡的德国第三大城市。慕尼黑位于阿尔卑斯山北麓，多瑙河的支流伊萨尔河流经此地，自古以来就是北欧进入中欧、南欧的交通要冲，故有“通向世界的门户”“欧洲大转盘”之称。慕尼黑建于1158年，1806年成为巴伐利亚王国的都城。此后在路德维希一世时代兴建了大量古典风格的建筑，使慕尼黑成为欧洲著名的城市。慕尼黑素以建筑艺术、博物馆、文化活动以及临近的阿尔卑斯山而闻名，如建于15世纪的慕尼黑的标志性建筑圣母教堂、玛利亚广场的新市政厅、宝马汽车博物馆和奥林匹克中心。作为历史文化名城，慕尼黑与巴黎、维也纳，并列为欧洲三大文化中心。

Located in the south of the Germany, Munich is the capital of Bavaria and the third largest city in Germany after Berlin and Hamburg. It is located on the River Isar—a tributary of the Danube and in the north of the Alps. Since ancient times, it has been the Nordic transportation hub to Central Europe and Southern Europe. So it is known as the "Gateway to the World", "the European Big Wheel". The city was first built in 1158 and became the capital of Kingdom of Bavaria in 1806. During the period of King Ludwig Ⅰ, lots of classic buildings were built and Munich became a famous city in Europe. Munich is known for the architectural art, museums, cultural activities, as well as the nearby Alps, such as the landmark Munich Frauenkirche built in the 15th century, the City Hall in Marienplatz, the BMW Museum and Olympic Center. As a historical and cultural city, Munich, Paris and Vienna are considered as the three major European cultural centers.

◆ 玛利亚广场（Marienplatz）

玛利亚广场是慕尼黑的中心广场，是慕尼黑最繁华的地方。广场的名称来自广场上的"玛利亚"圆柱，设立的目的就是颂扬圣母玛利亚。广场中央是圣母玛利亚的雕像，广场北面是哥特式建筑市政厅，其高达85米的钟楼上有著名的玩偶报时钟。西北面是有两个绿圆顶钟楼的圣母教堂，它是慕尼黑的象征，为哥特式教堂，钟楼高99米，建于1468年。

Marienplatz is in the center of Munich and it's Munich's most prosperous areas. The name of Marienplatz comes from the "Maria" column in the square which was set up just to celebrate the Virgin Mary. In the center stands the sculpture of Mary. To its north is the Rathaus (City Hall). It is a gothic style building with the 85 meters high tower. In the tower, there is a famous doll bell which strikes the hours. To the northwest is the Frauenkirche, the city's cathedral, with two green-domed towers which are the symbol of Munich. They are gothic cathedral built in 1468 with 99 meters high tower.

（三）法兰克福（Frankfurt）

法兰克福位于德国中部的美因河畔，是进入欧洲的交通枢纽，德国商业与制造业的中心，也是德国的金融中心和博览会城市。实行欧元后，欧洲中央银行就设在法兰克福，因此使得法兰克福成为世界著名的金融中心。众多的跨国公司、银行、国际博览会都落户于这座国际大都市，新的"世界金融大厦区"汇集了全世界各大银行和金融机构的摩天大楼。法兰克福是德国摩天大楼最多的城市，被人戏称为"美因哈顿"。法兰克福还是德国文化重镇，大文豪歌德1749年在此地出生。从16世纪起，这里被指定为罗马皇帝选举和加冕的场所。法兰克福还是"德国最大的书柜"德意志图书馆的所在地。

Frankfurt is located on both sides of the Main in Germany. It is the gateway to Europe, the center of Germany's business and manufacturing, and financial center and the trade fair city of Germany. After the introduction of the Euro, the European Central Bank is located in Frankfurt which makes Frankfurt the world's leading financial center. Many transnational corporations, banks, international fairs have settled in this international metropolis. A unique feature of Frankfurt is its significant number of skyscrapers in the city center which form the Frankfurt skyline. Frankfurt is one of the few cities in the European Union that has such a skyline. Because of the city's skyline, Germans sometimes refer to Frankfurt and Main as

"Mainhattan". Frankfurt is also a German cultural center. Great writer Goethe was born here in 1749. From the 16th century, Frankfurt was designated as the election of the Roman emperor and the coronation place. Frankfurt is also the location of the German National Library—Germany's largest bookcase.

◆ 歌德故居（Goethe House）

歌德故居位于法兰克福市中心，大文豪歌德在此出生并度过青年时光。歌德故居虽曾遭受第二次世界大战的战火破坏，但经重建后尽量保持原貌，公开让各界人士参观。歌德在此完成了《浮士德》及《少年维特的烦恼》等著名的作品。

The Goethe House is located in the center of Frankfurt, in which great writer Goethe was born and spent his youth time here. The original home was destroyed near the end of the Second World War, but it was then restored as closely as possible to its original condition. Today, the Goethe House is open to all visitors. It is the place where Goethe completed his *Faust*, *The Sorrows of Young Werther* and other famous works.

（四）科隆（Cologne）

科隆是德国第四大城市，位于德国西部，著名的莱茵河穿城而过。早在公元前 50 年，科隆就已是罗马帝国的重要殖民地，其名字就是由英文“殖民地”演变而来的。至今，科隆仍保留着不少罗马帝国时代的历史遗迹。如今的科隆是莱茵区最大的国际商业中心，经常举办各类国际博览会，有“传媒与通信之城”的美誉。科隆有三宝：香水、狂欢节、教堂，其中最出名的是科隆大教堂。

Located in the west of Germany, Cologne is Germany's fourth largest city with the famous Rhine flowing through the city. As early as 50 BC, Cologne was an important colony of the Roman Empire, whose name is from the word "colonial". Cologne retains many historical monuments of the era of the Roman Empire. Today Cologne is the biggest international business centre of Rhine region. International fairs of various fields are often held here and Cologne wins the "media and communications city" in the world. There are three treasures in Cologne: perfume, carnival and cathedral, of which the most famous is the Cologne Cathedral.

◆ 科隆大教堂（Cologne Cathedral）

科隆大教堂是德国建筑的纪念碑，以轻盈、雅致著称于世，是科隆的象征，也是世界第三高的教堂。作为最完美的哥特式大教堂，科隆大教堂始建于 1248 年，建造期长达 630 多年，堪称世界之最。1996 年，科隆大教堂被列入世界文化遗产名录，与巴黎圣母院、梵蒂冈圣彼得大教堂并称为欧洲三大宗教建筑。

Cologne Cathedral, known for its lightness and elegance in the world, is Germany's architectural monument and a symbol of Cologne, and is also the third tallest churches in the world. As the most perfect gothic Cathedral, Cologne Cathedral was first built in 1248 and the construction lasted for more than 630 years. In 1996, Cologne Cathedral was added to the World Cultural Heritage Site list. Cologne Cathedral, Notre-Dame de Paris and St. Peter's Basilica in Vatican City are regarded as three largest European religious buildings.

（五）海德堡（Heidelberg）

海德堡位于德国的西南部，是德国历史最悠久的古城之一，也是个兼具文艺浪漫气息与热闹活泼气氛的大学城。海德堡过去曾是科学和艺术的中心，在罗马帝国时期，这里成为边陲。1386年，鲁普莱希特选帝侯在这里创办了德国最古老的大学——海德堡大学。今天，海德堡仍是德国乃至欧洲的大学科研基地。这里有哲学家之路，十几座博物馆、艺术馆和剧院，处处散发着文学和艺术的气息。歌德曾赞美道："海德堡是可以忘却一切的地方。"马克·吐温称赞海德堡是其"到过的最美的地方"。

Located in the southwest of Germany, Heidelberg is one of the Germany's oldest cities and is a romantic and lively university town. Heidelberg used to be the center of science and art. In Roman Empire time, it became borderland village. In 1386, Ruprecht established the oldest university—Heidelberg University. Today, Heidelberg is still the university research base in Germany even the Europe. There are Philosophers' Way, a dozen museums, galleries and theaters. The city is full of literary and artistic atmosphere everywhere. Goethe once praised "Heidelberg is the place to forget everything". Mark Twain also said that Heidelberg is "the most beautiful place I have ever been".

（六）其他著名旅游景点

◆ 新天鹅城堡（Neuschwanstein Castle）

新天鹅城堡是德国南部著名的城堡，位于德国浪漫大道的最南端，慕尼黑西南120千米。同欧洲众多的城堡相比，新天鹅城堡算是比较"年轻"的，始建于1869年。它的草图是当时巴伐利亚国王路德维希二世亲自设计的。美国迪士尼乐园的睡美人城堡就是以此为蓝本设计的。

Neuschwanstein Castle is a famous castle in southern Germany. It is located in the south of the Romantic Avenue of Germany and 120 kilometers of southwest of Munich. It is young compared with the other castles of most European countries as it was built in 1869. The first design was made by Ludwig Ⅱ of Bavaria. The Sleeping Beauty Castle in Disneyland was built according to the Neuschwanstein Castle.

四、旅游资讯

（一）美食

德意志不是一个特别讲究吃的民族。德国人喜欢吃猪肉、喝啤酒。德国人注重食材的原味，口味喜清淡、甜酸，不爱吃油腻食品，一般不加太多的作料，不爱吃辣。德国人喜欢吃肉，尤其喜欢香肠。德国的香肠品种多达1 500种。慕尼黑小白肠、纽伦堡指肠非常有名，黑森林火腿销往世界各地。香肠通常与面包和土豆搭配，德国面包的质量和数量位居世界前列。德国人一般不单独食用面包，而是要抹上一层厚厚的奶油，配上干酪和果酱，加上香肠或火腿一起食用。德国人喜食奶酪，其品种多达600多种，奶酪是德国人早餐必备。德国人的早餐较简单，晚餐是一天中最丰盛的一餐，以肉类为主，通常还会有汤。德国比较有特色的菜有巴伐利亚烤猪肘、烤猪肉、醋焖牛肉等。德国猪肘堪称一道享誉世界的名菜，也是德国人的传统美食之一，在巴伐利亚尤其受欢迎，并佐以德国酸菜等进食。德国烤猪肘的特色就在于猪肘皮脆而不干，嚼起来非常有劲，猪肉也饱满入味。在食用德国猪肘的时候，通常还要配上道地的德国啤酒。德国啤酒和葡萄酒以种类繁多而闻名于世。1516 年，巴伐利亚公国的威廉四世大公颁布《纯正啤酒法》，规定德国啤酒只能以大麦芽、啤酒花和水三种原料制作，所以近 500 年来德国啤酒成为纯正啤酒的代名词。今日的德国为世界第二大啤酒生产国，境内共有 1 300 多家啤酒厂，生产的啤酒种类高达 5 000 多种。根据官方统计，每个德国人平均每年喝掉 138 升的啤酒，世界上再也找不到比德国人更热爱啤酒的民族了。

The Germany is not a nation that particularly pays great attention to eating. The native Germans like to eat pork with a big glass of beer. Germans focus on original flavor and they love light, sweet and sour taste. They do not eat greasy and spicy food and generally do not add too much sauce. Germans love meat especially the sausage. There are more than 1,500 kinds of sausage. Both the Weisswurst in Munich and Nuremburg Sausage are quite famous. Black Forest Ham has been sold all over the world. Sausage is always eaten with the bread and potato. The quality and the number of the bread in Germany can rank the top in the world. Germans usually coat the bread with cream, dry cheese or fruit jam, and eat with sausage or ham. Germans love cheese. There are more than 600 kinds of cheese which is the must for German breakfast. Dinner is the most sumptuous meal for a day, and the food is mainly meat and normally with soup. The characteristic German Cuisine are Bavaria roasted pork knuckle, roasted pork and vinegar braised beef. Pork knuckle is Germany's well-known dish in the world and is one of the typical dishes of German cuisine that is popular in Bavaria and always eaten with sour cabbage (sauerkraut). The characteristics of roasted pork knuckle is crispy but not dry, very energetic and also full of taste. In Germany, pork knuckle is always accompanied by authentic Germany beer. Both the beer and wine of Germany are famous in the world. In 1516, William Ⅳ of Bavarian Grand Duchy enacted the rule of *Beer Purity Law* in which only three kinds of raw materials—barley malt, hops and water can be used for producing beer, so German beer has become synonymous with a so-called pure beer for nearly 500 years. Today, Germany is the world's second largest beer producer. There are 1,300 breweries and more than 5,000 species of beer. According to the official statistics, each German drinks 138 liters of beer a year on average. There are no other nations but Germans who could love beer so much in the world.

（二）购物及退税

德国生产的各款名牌产品，因其品质、实用性及耐用性而获得一致的好评，尤其是做工精良的工具，如照相机、光学仪器、钟表、钢笔和刀具。此外，德国的木雕制品、皮革制品、宝石也很精美。每年德国商店都会举行两次降价清仓的活动，特别是圣诞节结束后至 2 月，以及 6 月末至 7 月。

Germany has been unanimously praised for the brand-name products with quality, practicality and durability, especially the good quality tools, mechanical products such as cameras, optical instruments, watches and clocks, pens and knives. Woodcarving, leather and jewelry are also delicate and beautiful. Every year particularly from the end of Christmas to February as well as from the end of June to July, there are two seasons on sale in Germany.

刀具、厨具：德国的钢材全世界有名，以优质钢材制成的刀具耐用持久，刀刃锋利，双立人就是其中之一。德国产的锅具导热性好，油烟少，以菲仕乐和福腾宝最为有名。

Knives and kitchenware: Germany is famous for its steel in the world. The knives made of high quality steel are durable and sharp. Zwilling is one of them. The pot has good thermal conductivity with less smoke. The most famous pot series are Fissler and WMF.

笔和皮具：持久耐用的德国皮具和钢笔有着德国严谨的制造工艺与欧洲先进的设计，深受各界推崇。零钱包、皮夹、手袋、旅行袋等各式产品都有品质保证。知名品牌包括爱格纳、金箭、MCM、BREE 等。此外，户外品牌"狼爪"也是享誉全球，产品包括防水夹克、背包系列等。设计简洁、书写流畅的百利金及万宝龙的钢笔在各大百货店都可以买到。

Pens and leather: Durable German leather products and pen series are deeply respected with stringent manufacturing process and advanced design of Europe. All the products are quality guaranteed such as coin purses, wallets, handbags, travel bags and other various styles of products. Famous brands are Aigner, Gold Pfeil, MCM, BREE and so on. In addition, the brand Jack Wolfskin for the outdoor products is well worldwide known for its outdoor waterproof jackets, backpack series. The easily writing pens of Pelikan and Mont Blanc with simple designs are available in major department stores.

梅森瓷器：德国的梅森市以瓷器著称，以前一直为皇室烧陶瓷。梅森瓷器制作精美，款式多样，风格独特，素有"瓷中白金"之称，可以说是欧洲高级瓷器的代名词。

Meissen porcelain: Meissen, a city of Germany, is known for its porcelain and had supplied ceramic products for the Palace. Meissen porcelain is elegant with diverse unique styles and is known as the porcelain platinum. It is said to be synonymous with the high-class porcelains in Europe.

根据规定，非欧盟国家持短期旅游签证的游客在德国同一天同一家商店购物金额超过 50.01 欧元时，可以享受退税。一般退税率最高为 19%。在购物之后的 3 个月内，游客都可凭盖有离境海关签章的退税单办理退税手续。

According to the regulation, the non-EU tourists with short term visiting visa can get tax refund before they depart the country when they purchase the goods above 50.01 euros in the same shop on the same day. The general tax refund ratio is up to 19%. Within three months after the shopping, visitors can get the refund with stamped tax refund form in the customs office.

（三）时差

德国在 10 月到次年 3 月间与中国有 7 小时的时差。由于德国实行夏令时制，在 3 月的最后一个星期天到 10 月的最后一个星期天，德国与中国有 6 个小时的时差。

China is 7 hours ahead of Germany from October to the next March. Due to the Daylight Saving Time which lasts from last Sunday in March to last Sunday in October, China is 6 hours ahead of Germany.

思考练习

1. 经典旅游线路分析

德国深度10日游

第1天：上海——柏林

游客按照规定的时间在上海浦东国际机场集合，飞往德国首都及德国最大城市柏林。机场接机后前往柏林市中心，参观胜利纪念柱、胜利女神像和柏林墙，然后前往查理检查站。

第2天：柏林——波茨坦——德累斯顿

酒店早餐后，外观德国的“命运之门”——勃兰登堡门。勃兰登堡门建于1791年，全部用乳白色花岗岩筑成，门楼上耸立着用青铜铸造的胜利女神像。东侧是巴黎广场，往南是由2 700余块高低不等的灰色水泥块组成的犹太人大屠杀纪念碑群，用以警示德国纳粹杀害600万犹太人的罪恶。外观著名的德国国会大厦、柏林大教堂和1999年被列入世界文化遗产名录的博物馆岛。后驱车前往普鲁士古都波茨坦，这里素有“宫殿和庭院城市”的美称。1945年盛夏，由于在这里签署了《波茨坦公告》，波茨坦因此而闻名，并于1990年被列入世界文化遗产名录。在此游览仿照凡尔赛宫而建的恢宏建筑无忧宫古堡，这里最主要的景点是1747年建成的中部有圆形屋顶的单层洛可可式宫殿。后前往波茨坦会议旧址——西席林霍夫宫（外观）。后驱车前往文化、自然与建筑“三和弦”的德累斯顿。德累斯顿经常被称为巴洛克城市，精美的皇家建筑和教堂多采用这种风格建造。在德累斯顿市区游览，外观圣母教堂，该教堂是1743年建筑领域中的一个奇迹；外观德累斯顿王宫、茨温格宫、森伯歌剧院。

第3天：德累斯顿——纽伦堡——罗滕堡

酒店早餐后，驱车前往被称为“中世纪明珠城”的纽伦堡，外观纽伦堡法庭，这里是第二次世界大战结束后著名的纽伦堡大审判所在地，作曲家瓦格纳的故乡，也被称为“世界玩具之都”。登上城市制高点——威严的恺撒堡，鸟瞰整个纽伦堡。后驱车前往浪漫之路上最优美的城镇、有“中世纪之珠”美誉的罗滕堡，城内保存着完整的中世纪街道、住宅、城堡、塔楼、石路、喷泉、市集等，然后到罗滕堡市集广场，外观具有传奇色彩的议会会馆。

第4天：罗滕堡——法兰克福——海德堡

酒店早餐后，驱车前往金融之都法兰克福，在法兰克福市区观光，外观市政厅、正义天使像、罗马贝格广场及加冕教堂等。后驱车前往有德国“旅游文化之都”之称的海德堡。海德堡老城在内卡河南岸傍河而建，为长条形。尽管老城也十分现代化，但街道、小巷和主要建筑都保留了原来的古朴风格。

第5天：海德堡——麦琴根——斯图加特

酒店早餐后，前往闻名全欧洲的名牌商品折扣城——麦琴根，这里汇集了近60家德国和世界各地的著名品牌的专卖店，商品以服装、鞋、玩具为主，价格低廉，优惠幅度可达30%～70%。后驱车前往斯图加特，斯图加特是两大世界知名汽车品牌的生产基地：梅赛德斯－奔驰和保时捷。这两家汽车制造商都以建造引人注目的新博物馆来阐述本公司的历史。

第6天：斯图加特——滴滴湖——弗莱堡

酒店早餐后驱车前往著名景区滴滴湖。游览老城门、大教堂，远眺古城堡，著名的黑森林、美丽的滴滴湖，让人可以全身心地放松在这片欧洲的度假胜地，还可以在此挑选购买到闻名于世的咕咕钟。之后驱车前往弗莱堡。

第7天：弗莱堡——新天鹅城堡——富森

早餐后在弗莱堡市区游览，漫步于明斯特广场，周围伫立着几座代表了新哥特式和晚期哥特式的建筑。外观距今已经有700年历史的明斯特大教堂。之后出发前往浪漫之路上最闻名于世的景点——新天鹅城堡。在德国众多的城堡中，最著名的就是这座位于慕尼黑以南富森的阿尔卑斯山麓的新天鹅城堡，也叫白雪公主城堡，它是德国的象征。它的设计者和建造者是巴伐利亚国王路德维希二世。之后驱车前往富森。

第8天：富森——鹰巢城堡——慕尼黑

酒店早餐后，驱车前往希特勒情有独钟的世外桃源，也是他的私人城堡——鹰巢，又称“凯尔施泰因别墅”，它位于阿尔卑斯山脉1 834米高的奥柏萨尔斯堡山顶。从这里向下俯瞰，不仅可以看到希特勒的山间别墅，还可领略湛蓝如镜的国王湖，更可远眺奥地利的萨尔茨堡。之后驱车前往慕尼黑。抵达后参观市中心的玛利亚广场，外观建于1867—1908年的新哥特式的市政厅，有着著名的报时玩偶的85米高的钟楼等。

第9天：慕尼黑——上海

酒店早餐后，前往宝马汽车展厅参观，后游览宁芬堡宫。该宫殿建于1664年至1728年，是一座气势恢宏的巴洛克式宫殿。宁芬堡已有300年左右的历史，是后期巴洛克式宫廷庄园的佼佼者。之后前往机场，办理登机、退税手续，返回上海。

分析：这条经典旅游线路的主要旅游景点与行程特色，以及适合旅游的人群。

2. 案例分析

［案例1］留学生小丁在德国做了3个月的交换生，他住在一个环境优美安静的乡村。离开德国前，他想举办一个小型的聚会，邀请认识的德国朋友来欢聚一堂。结果房东说德

国人多喜欢清静的生活，不大喜欢喧闹，对住宅周围的噪声颇为在意。如果晚上要聚会，事先要向每一位邻居讲明情况，要求他们同意并能谅解，并尽可能不大声喧闹。否则，受干扰的邻居会十分恼怒，可能当面提出抗议，个别人甚至会请警察出面干预。小丁觉得德国人小题大做，就放弃了举办聚会的想法。你如何理解德国人的这种行为？小丁有必要放弃举办聚会吗？

[案例 2] 中学生小青到德国奥古斯堡游学，住在当地一个典型的巴伐利亚家庭里。晚上，主人带小青和她的孩子去当地的一家啤酒花园享用晚餐，小青点了一份巴伐利亚烤猪肘配薯条。由于不习惯当地的口味，她只吃了点肉和几根薯条就说吃饱了。主人有点不悦，请问小青应该如何做？

3. 练一练

德国是一个充满活力的国家，到处都能看到精彩创意；德国也是理想的游学目的地，游学内容包括观光、语言学习、接触德国文化事物，及住宿于德国家庭中。例如：以音乐为游学主题，德国音乐名人辈出，亦有不少与音乐家有关的纪念地，再加上德国拥有众多颇具规模的音乐学院以及知名乐团，适合学习或观摩。又如：以足球为游学主题，内容包括于德国足球学校培训、观看德国足球比赛、参观德国足球俱乐部和球场、旅游观光及住宿于德国家庭中。由此可见，音乐、体育、博物馆和设计已经成为人们开启德国之旅的 4 个关键词。德国国家旅游局也持续推出年度主题进行旅游推广。2018 年，德国国家旅游局全球推广主题为“美食德国”；2019 年为“包豪斯 100 年”；2020 年为“贝多芬诞辰 250 周年”。试分析德国有哪些主题游。选一个你最有兴趣的话题，写一篇导游词。

第四节　意大利

一、国家概况

（一）地理环境

意大利共和国，简称意大利，地处欧洲南部，包括亚平宁半岛、西西里岛和撒丁岛及其他小岛。北方的阿尔卑斯山区和法国、瑞士、奥地利和斯洛文尼亚接壤。国土内包围着两个袖珍国家——梵蒂冈和圣马力诺。意大利的地理位置十分重要，最南端几乎接近非洲大陆海岸，与突尼斯、马耳他和阿尔及利亚隔海相望。意大利是欧洲到达非洲和亚洲的南大门。

The Republic of Italy, briefly Italy, is located in the south of Europe, comprising Apennine Peninsula and a number of islands including Sicily and Sardegna and other small islets. To its north is Alps mountainous area and it borders France, Switzerland, Austria and Slovenia. Inside the territory there are two small countries: Vatican City State and San Marino. Italy's geographical position is very important, its south point is almost close to the coast of the African continent, and Italy can see Tunisia, Malta and Algeria across the sea. Italy is the south gate of Europe to Africa and Asia.

亚平宁半岛的外形像插入地中海的高跟鞋。亚平宁山脉是构成亚平宁半岛的主干，向西北方向延伸 1 000 千米，与阿尔卑斯山相接。亚平宁山脉和阿尔卑斯山脉之间是著名的波河平原。波河平原约占意大利国土面积的 1/6，是著名的农业区和天然粮仓。意法边境的勃朗峰海拔 4 810 米，为境内最高峰。意大利南部多火山，地震频繁。亚平宁半岛西侧有著名的维苏威火山，西西里岛的埃特纳火山海拔 3 323 米，为欧洲最高的活火山。

The shape of Apennine Peninsula is like a boot in the Mediterranean. The Apennine mountains range is the backbone of the peninsula which stretches 1,000 kilometers to the northwest and is connected with the Alps. Between the Apennines and the Alps it is Po River Plain which has an area of the 1/6 of the Italian territory and it is the natural barn. Mont Blanc, on the border with France with 4,810 meters above sea level, is the highest mountain in the territory. There are many volcanoes in the south, and it is on the earthquake zone. There is the famous Mount Vesuvius at the west of Apennine Peninsula. Mount Etna in Sicily is 3,323 meters above the sea level which is the highest active volcano in Europe.

意大利由于地形狭长，境内多山，并且地处地中海腹部，因此南北气温相差较大，气候也相差较大。总的来说，意大利北部为大陆性气候而南部为典型的地中海气候。北部冬季寒冷、湿润和多雪，而南部沿海地区冬季暖和，夏季干燥。

With narrow terrain and mountainous area, Italy is located deep into the Mediterranean. The climate is quite different from the north to the south. Generally speaking, the north belongs to continental climate and the south is typical Mediterranean climate. The north is cold, moist and snowy in winter and the south is warm in winter and dry in summer.

（二）人文概况

1. *历史*

意大利是古罗马帝国的发源地。古希腊文明对古罗马影响巨大，促使古罗马从君主制过渡到共和制（公元前 509 年到公元前 27 年）。罗马共和国通过不断扩张，到恺撒时期已经成为横跨非洲、欧洲和亚洲，称霸地中海的超级大国。恺撒大帝死后，他的养子屋大维获得政权并被元老院赐封为“奥古斯都”，他建立了元首制，罗马帝国进入 100 多年的和平时期。君士坦丁大帝时期，罗马帝国确立基督教为国教。公元 395 年，罗马帝国分为西罗马帝国和东罗马帝国（拜占庭帝国）。公元 476 年，西罗马帝国灭亡。1453 年，东罗马帝国灭亡。直到 1806 年拿破仑推翻神圣罗马帝国，意大利一直陷于分裂状态。1861 年，意大利王国建立。1870 年，法国在普法战争中失败，撤回在罗马的军队，意大利国王乘机吞并教皇国，意大利最终完成统一，迁都罗马。1922年，墨索里尼上台执政，开始实行长达20余年的法西斯统治。1940年，意大利向英、法宣战。1943年，盟军入侵，意大利无条件投降。1946年，意大利共和国正式宣布成立。

Italy was the cradle of Roman Empire. The ancient Rome was affected so deeply by the civilization of ancient Greek that its monarchy was replaced by the Roman Republic (509 BC to 27 BC). Roman Republic became a super country which included some part of Africa, part of Asia and part of Europe in Caesar period after many years of extension and became the No.1 in Mediterranean. After Caesar died, his stepson Octavian controlled the power and was awarded as Augustus by Senatus. He set principate and led to Roman Empire. The empire had been peaceful for more than 100 years. Constantine the Great set the Christianity as the national religion of Roman Empire. In 395, the Empire was separated into two parts—West Roman Empire and East Roman Empire (Byzantine Empire). The West Roman Empire ended in 476 and the East Roman Empire ended in 1453. Italy was in disunion before Napoléon overthrew the Holy Roman Empire in 1806. In 1861, Italy was unified as Kingdom of Italy. In 1870, France was defeated in the Franco-Prussian War and withdrew the army from Italy. The King of Italy took over the papal state, and Italy was unified at last and made Rome as the capital. In 1922, Mussolini took the power and carried out the fascist regime for more than twenty years. In 1940, Italy declared the war on Britain and France. In 1943, the allies invaded Italy and Italy surrendered. The Republic of Italy founded in 1946.

2. 经济

意大利是欧洲的四大经济体之一，也是八国集团和欧盟的成员。第二次世界大战后直到20世纪60年代，意大利经济才开始迅速发展，从农业国家迅速成为高度工业化国家。但意大利世界级的大公司较少，主要依靠中小企业。中小企业在意大利经济中占有重要地位，近70%的国内生产总值由这些企业创造。意大利北部和南部经济发展不平衡。北部人均生产总值高于欧盟，而南部低于欧盟平均水平。意大利拥有高度自由的投资、贸易和商业活动，但是官僚腐败和低效率成为障碍。意大利的汽车工业发达，居欧洲第5位，法拉利、菲亚特畅销海外。家用电器、服装和鞋类在世界上声誉卓著，尤以高级服装著称于世。意大利素有“制鞋王国”之誉，所产皮鞋在很多人眼中是地位和品质的象征。意大利农业发达，是世界三大橄榄油生产国之一。意大利的葡萄和葡萄酒产量位居世界前列，每年都有大量葡萄酒出口到法国、德国和美国，出口量居世界首位。对外贸易是意大利经济的主要支柱，传统产品为其出口创汇的主体。另外，作为古罗马帝国的核心和文艺复兴运动的发源地，意大利旅游业发达，旅游收入是弥补国家财政赤字的重要来源。

Italy is one of the four largest economies in Europe. It is one of the founding members of G8 and European Union. After the Second World War, Italy's economy did not develop quickly until 1960s and became an industrial country instead of the agricultural country. Only a few large group companies exist in Italy. Most of the companies are medium and small in size, but they created the 70% of the GDP. The economy of south and north is uneven in Italy. The average GDP of the north zone is higher than the average of European Union, while the south is lower than that. Italy has a free environment for investment, trade and business, but official corruption and low efficiency are the factors of hindrance. Italy has a large auto industry which is the 5th largest in the Europe, especially the overseas market of Ferrari and Fiat. The electrical household appliances, garments and boots are well-known in the world. The high-class fashion has been ranked first in the world. Italy is known as the kingdom of the boots which is the symbol of status and quality. Italy is also a developed agricultural country. It is one of the three countries that manufacture olive oil. Its output of grape and wine has been ranked first in the world. Italy exports lots of wine to France, Germany and the United States every year, and the quantity has been ranked first in the world. The foreign trade is the mainstay of the economy and the traditional products are the backbone to earn foreign currency. In addition, as the core of the ancient Roman Empire and the birthplace of the Renaissance, Italy has a developed tourism industry whose income is the important resource to compensate for the deficits of the country.

3. 社会文化

意大利人口约 6 087 万，94% 的居民为意大利人，此外还有少量法国人、拉丁人等。大部分地区讲意大利语，个别地区讲法语和德语。大部分居民信奉天主教。

Italy's population is about 60.87 million. 94% residents are Italian and minorities are French, Latin and so on. Italian is the common language while some speak French and German. The majority of the inhabitants profess Catholicism.

意大利是世界文明古国，文艺复兴运动的发祥地。意大利文化别具特色，文学、艺术、建筑设计、雕塑、绘画、军事科学、农业技术、地理、医学等许多方面都达到了很高水平，名人辈出。意大利在艺术、科学和技术上拥有悠久的传统，拥有 48 处世界遗产，位居世界第一。其丰厚的文化艺术遗产是国家的瑰宝，也是发展旅游业取之不尽、用之不竭的源泉。古罗马文明和文艺复兴时期的文化、艺术是其中最重要的。拉丁语是在希腊语的基础上形成的，进而成为现代意大利语。在西方文明发展的历程中，古希腊、古罗马文明达到了高峰 。

Italy is the world's ancient civilized country and the birthplace of the Renaissance. Italian culture has its unique characteristics. Its literature, art, architecture, sculpture, painting, military science, agricultural technology, geography, medicine and many other aspects have reached a very high level with lots of famous persons. Italy has a long tradition on the arts, science and technology, with 48 World Heritage Sites that are ranked the first in the world. Its rich resources of artistic and cultural heritages are the national treasures and inexhaustible sources for the development of tourism. The most important for arts and culture are the ancient Roman civilization, culture and arts of the Renaissance. Modern Italian language has its origin from the Latin language, an ancient Roman language formed on the basis of the Greek language. In general, the ancient civilization of Greece and Roman has reached its peak for the development of the Western civilization.

公元前 2 世纪，诗歌、喜剧、散文等已在意大利产生。安德罗尼柯是第一位诗人，加图是唯一有拉丁散文作品传世的作家。在罗马帝国时期，意大利的建筑及雕刻达到了顶峰。他们利用火山灰加水拌石子发明了原始的混凝土，从而使高大建筑成为现实，并且留下许多传世建筑，罗马斗兽场、君士坦丁凯旋门、古罗马遗址、万神殿等是当时的代表。庞贝古城遗址再现了古罗马时期的城市文明。

In the second century BC, Italy had the works of poem, comedy and prose. Andronicos was the first poet and Cato was the only writer that had helped the Latin prose to be handed down. During the period of Roman Empire, architecture and the art of carving reached its peak. They invented the ancient concrete by mixing volcanic ash and small stones with water. Therefore giant buildings came to the world. The representative buildings are Colosseum, the Arch of Contantine, the ancient Roman remains and Pantheon. The ancient city of Pompeii revealed the city civilization of ancient Roman period.

到了中世纪，基督教成为意大利人的主要宗教，文学作品中也有较浓的宗教色彩。而十字军带来了东方文明，文艺复兴在意大利兴起，意大利成为西方近代文明的发源地。佛罗伦萨作为文艺复兴的中心，产生的大师之多、杰作之盛，是任何城市都不能与其相提并论的。但丁的《神曲》开创了人文主义思想回归，其他的还有薄伽丘的《十日谈》、马基雅维利的《君主论》等。

Christianity became the main religion of Italy during the Middle Ages and all the literature were connected with it. The Crusade brought back the eastern civilization. The Renaissance started from Italy which became the cradle of recent western civilization. No other cities could compare with Florence, the center of Renaissance, where so many masters were born with their great works. Dante's *Divine Comedy* initiated the back of Humanism. The other masters are Boccaccio's *The Decameron* and Machiavelli's *The Prince.*

在绘画、雕塑方面，代表人物有文艺复兴三杰——达·芬奇（1452—1519，代表作《最后的晚餐》《蒙娜丽莎》）、米开朗基罗（1475—1564，代表作《大卫》《创世纪》《最后的审判》）和拉斐尔（1483—1520，代表作《雅典学院》及宗教绘画）。18 世纪下半叶，意大利获得了相对稳定的局面，自然科学、唯物主义哲学和启蒙思想广泛传播，启蒙主义文学出现。19 世纪末，意大利的儿童文学成就非凡，如科洛迪（1826—1890）的《木偶奇遇记》。

The representatives of painting and sculpture are the three outstanding persons of the Renaissance—Leonardo da Vinci (1452–1519, *The Last Super, Mona Lisa*), Michelangelo (1475–1564, *David, Genesis, The Last Judgment*) and Raphael (1483–1520, *The School of Athens* and his religion paintings). Due to the wide spread of nature sciences, philosophy of materialism and enlightenment and the fact that Italy was stable at the end of the 18th century, there appeared enlightenment literature. By the end of the 19th century, the children literature also had made great achievements. The representative writer was Collodi (1826–1890, *The Adventures of Pinocchio*).

17 世纪，歌剧在意大利诞生。佛罗伦萨、罗马、威尼斯和那不勒斯先后成为意大利歌剧艺术的中心。意大利拥有许多历史悠久、世界闻名的歌剧院，如米兰的斯卡拉歌剧院、那不勒斯的圣卡尔洛歌剧院、都灵的皇家歌剧院以及罗马歌剧院。著名的歌剧有焦阿基诺·罗西尼（1792—1868）的《塞维利亚的理发师》和《灰姑娘》、朱塞佩·威尔第（1813—1901）的《茶花女》《阿依达》和《假面舞会》，贾科莫·普契尼（1858—1924）的《蝴蝶夫人》和《图兰朵》等。

In the 17th century, opera was born in Italy. Florence, Rome, Venice and Naples became Italian opera arts centers. Italy has a lot of historic and world-famous opera houses, such as Milan's La Scala, the Theatre of Saint Charles in Naples, the Royal Theatre in Turin, and Rome Opera House. Famous operas include Gioachino Rossini (1792–1868, *Il Barbiere di Siviglia* and *La Cenerentola*), Giuseppe Verdi (1813–1901, *La Traviata*, *Aida* and *Un Ballo in Maschera*), and Giacomo Puccini (1858–1924, *Madama Butterfly* and *Turandot*).

知识拓展

米开朗基罗

米开朗基罗·博那罗蒂（1475—1564），是意大利文艺复兴时期伟大的绘画家、雕塑家、建筑师和诗人，文艺复兴时期雕塑艺术最高峰的代表，与拉斐尔和达·芬奇并称为“文艺复兴三杰”。1475年，米开朗基罗出生于意大利的佛罗伦萨。他25岁时的雕刻作品《哀悼基督》就已表现出很高的艺术造诣，如今被收藏在圣彼得大教堂。《大卫》是米开朗基罗的成名作，米开朗基罗花了大约3年的时间使它几乎达到了完美无缺的境界。《大卫》直到今天还是每一位学画者必须临摹的。如今，《大卫》被收藏在佛罗伦萨美术学院。米开朗基罗最著名的绘画作品是梵蒂冈西斯廷教堂的天顶画《创世纪》和壁画《最后的审判》。米开朗基罗以超人的毅力和勇气，画了4年零5个月，终于给世人留下了无与伦比的杰作——《创世纪》。当整个作品完成时，37岁的米开朗基罗已劳累得像个老人了。由于长期仰视，头和眼长久不能低下，连读信都要举到头顶。而《最后的审判》更是花费了他将近6年的时间，他还曾从脚手架上摔下，跌断了脚，可他仍以刚强的意志完成了这幅气势雄伟的杰作。在生命的最后20年，他以极大的热情设计并主持了圣彼得大教堂的建筑工作。作为文艺复兴的巨匠，米开朗基罗在生前和后世都产生了巨大影响。

二、民俗风情

（一）礼仪禁忌

意大利是崇尚自由的国度，开朗、乐观、热情是意大利人的特点，但他们也懒散、工作效率低。意大利人的作息时间通常会延后，也就是晚睡晚起。午餐一般在1点半左右，晚餐在八九点钟。在意大利人心目中，自由是最重要的，意大利人不喜欢守时，约会时迟到15～20分钟是正常的。在意大利，一年中有很多假期，大都以宗教理由放假。意大利人每日的工作时间不长，大致是上午9点到12点，下午4点到6点，中午休息时间很长。因此不管是在意大利旅游、购物或者办事，都要特别注意各地点的开放或营业时间，以免有所耽误。

Italy is the land of liberty. Italians are cheerful, optimistic and enthusiastic but also lazy and low efficient. The routine time for Italian is later than ours. They go to bed late and get up late. The lunch is generally around 1:30 pm, and dinner at 8:00 pm or around 9:00 pm. Italian are not likely to be punctual so that they are always 15 minutes or 20 minutes late for the appointed time. Italy has lots of holidays all year round, mostly for religious reasons. Their daily work time is not long, usually from around 9:00 am to 12:00 am and 4:00 pm to 6:00 pm. They have a long lunch time, so you must pay more attention to the time to avoid possible delay for visiting, shopping or for business.

意大利人的家庭观念比较重，完全以家庭为中心。祖母非常受人尊重，每年还会举行“最酷奶奶”评选活动。与其他欧美国家相比，1/3 的意大利已婚男女每天都会与他们的母亲见面，50% 的已婚男子与他们的母亲住在一个城市，15% 的人甚至与父母住在同一幢公寓。最离奇的是有 70% 的超过 35 岁的独身男子与他们的父母住在一起，1/4 的离婚男子会搬回与母亲同住。无论何时，意大利的亲情纽带都非常紧密。家人们喜欢周末相聚，也经常一起吃饭，团结和亲情是意大利人力量的源泉。

Italians have a strong family notion and their life center is their family. The grandmother (Nonna) is respected very much so that they will elect a coolest Nonna every year. Unlike people in the other European countries, one third of married Italian meet their mothers every day. 50% of the married men live in the same city with their mothers and 15% even stay in the same building. It is so strange that 70% of the single men at the age up to 35 years old live with their parents. One fourth of the divorced men will come back to live with their mothers. Italy has a tight family bond. They like to stay together at weekends and have dinner together. Solidarity and love for the family is the source of power for Italians.

意大利人善于交际和沟通，也喜欢争论和辩论。在日常生活中，见到长者或不太熟悉的人，要称呼其姓，再加上“先生”“夫人”“小姐”和荣誉职称。“小姐”和“夫人”这两种称谓切忌混用，如果不清楚该如何称呼对方，可以使用意义较为模糊的“女士”一词。意大利人见面时会握手或招手示意，握手时忌四个人同时交叉握手，这样会形成一个十字架形，在意大利人眼中十字架是不吉利的象征。

Italians are good at social interaction and communication. They get used to arguing and debating. In daily life, when you see the elderly, or people who you are not familiar with, you should call his or her surname with “Mr.”, “Mrs.”, “Miss” and the honorary title. The “Miss” and “Mrs.” titles should never be mixed. If you do not know how to greet a female, you can use “Madam”. Italians shake or wave hands when they meet. But it is considered as bad manners if four people shake hands together with their hands crossing, because in Italy the cross is a symbol of bad luck.

意大利人的肢体语言非常丰富，讲话时会配有各种肢体动作。有人开玩笑说：意大利人不做动作就不会讲话了。如果手势表达不正确，很容易造成双方误会。几种常见的手势是：用大拇指和食指围成圆圈，其余三指向上翘起，一般表示“好”“行”或“一切顺利”；在餐桌上表示“好吃极了”或做得“棒极了”，他们会用食指顶住脸颊来回转动；竖起食指来回摆动表示“不”“不行”；耸肩、摊掌加上摇头，表示“不知道”；五指并拢、手心向下、对着胃部来回转动，表示“饥饿”。

Italians have rich body languages. They always use their body languages to express themselves while speaking. It is believed that Italians cannot speak if they don't use their body languages. Wrong hand gestures will cause misunderstandings. When they circle with the thumb and forefinger, and the rest are upturned, it means "good, ok, or everything is going well". When they express satisfaction for dinner, they touch the cheek with their forefinger and move it back and forth. When the forefinger is up and swings back and forth, they mean "no or can't". When they shrug with palms and shake head, it means "I don't know". When they show their hunger, they close fingers with palms down and move back and forth on the stomach.

意大利有“服装之乡”的美称。意大利人穿着讲究，上班着制服，参加宴会或重要活动时穿礼服。意大利人热情好客，但聚餐往往是AA制，除非有人声明请客。他们喜欢和朋友、家人或亲戚一起进餐，边吃边聊，时间非常长。用餐的时候，不要把刀叉弄得叮当作响。在吃面条时，用叉子将面条卷起来往嘴里送，不可用嘴吸，尤其是在喝汤时，不要发出响声。客人一定不可以将盐撒落在地上，这是对主人极大的不尊敬。早在2 000多年前的罗马帝国时期，盐就被看作一种珍贵的商品，还曾用来支付军队士兵的薪饷，主人向客人表示欢迎的方式是敬盐。

Italy is a fashion country. Italians pay particular attention to their dress. They wear uniforms to work, and they dress formally when attending a party or important event. Italians are warm-hearted and hospitable. They always have dinner together but they will go Dutch except when somebody claims to pay. Italians like to have dinner with family, friends or relatives. It will take a long time to have dinner as they talk with each other while eating. During the dinner, it is a taboo to make noise with the forks and knives. When you eat noodles, you must use the fork and don't absorb the noodle directly. When you have soup, never make noise. Never spread the salt on the floor because it is impolite to the host. As early as 2,000 years ago in the Roman Empire, salt was regarded as precious goods and was even used to pay the salary of soldiers. To send the salt to the guests is to welcome the distinguished guests.

受邀到朋友家做客时可以带一些小礼物，包装要精美，但忌讳送十字架形的礼物。意大利人喜欢鲜花，但送花有不少讲究，菊花是丧葬、扫墓之时用以凭吊故人之花，玫瑰花比较普遍，但红玫瑰只送情人或妻子。送花单数为宜。意大利人非常在意礼物的包装。收到礼物后，主人会当着客人的面打开礼物，并说一些感谢的话。意大利人忌讳送手帕，因为手帕是用来擦眼泪的。

It is better to take gifts with fine packings when you visit friends, but it is a taboo to send cross-like items as a gift. Italians like flowers but you must be careful to choose proper ones. Chrysanthemum is for funeral or tombs. Rose is more popular but the red one is for lovers or one's wife. The number of the flowers should be singular. Italians care much about the packing of the gift. They will open the present in front of the guests and express gratitude to them. It is rude to send handkerchief as they think it for wiping tear.

（二）节庆风情

1. 威尼斯狂欢节（Venice Carnival）

威尼斯狂欢节于2月复活节前40天举行。威尼斯狂欢节是当今世界上历史最久、规模最大的狂欢节之一，与巴西狂欢节及法国尼斯狂欢节并列为世界三大狂欢节。威尼斯狂欢节又称威尼斯面具节，这一传统可追溯到1 700年前。那时，权贵和穷人可以通过面具融合在一起，在面具的后面，社会差异暂时被消除，所有的阶级、身份与地位，此时都不再有任何意义。威尼斯狂欢节最大的特点是面具，其次是华丽服饰。在狂欢节期间，人们戴着各种面具，穿着传统的服装，到街上游行、表演。现在每年的狂欢节都会有一个主题。官方的举办中心是圣马可广场。

The Carnival of Venice starts in February 40 days before Easter. It is one of the oldest and biggest carnivals in the world today, and is regarded as one of the three largest carnivals in the world with Brazil Carnival and Nice Carnival in France. The carnival is also known as Venetian Mask Festival. It can be traced back to 1,700 years ago. The rich would mix with the poor with the masks and the class differences would temporarily be eliminated behind the masks. All class, identity and status in this period were no longer meaningful. The biggest feature for the Venice Carnival is the masks and its gorgeous costumes. People in a variety of masks will wear traditional clothes and march into the street for performances. The Venice Carnival is officially held in St. Mark's Square with a theme every year.

2. 圣母升天节（Ferragosto）

圣母升天节在8月15日，是意大利的公共假日。它的历史可以追溯到2 000多年前的古罗马。当年，为了让人们尽情地享受生活，奥古斯都大帝将该节日定在8月1日。从17世纪末，圣母升天节改为8月15日。人们要在圣母升天节前后度假，避免在一年中最热的时候工作，尽情享受生活。

Ferragosto is an Italian public holiday celebrated on the August 15. It can be traced back to the ancient Rome 2,000 years ago. In order to enjoy life, Emperor Augusto stipulated August 1 as the holiday. And since the end of 17th century, the date was changed to August 15. People will have a rest and celebrate the holiday before or after the Ferragosto to avoid working in the hottest weather of the year and to enjoy life.

三、主要旅游城市及景点

（一）罗马（Rome）

罗马位于亚平宁半岛中部的台伯河畔，是意大利的首都和最大城市，全国政治、经济、文化和交通中心。"条条大道通罗马"形象地描述了罗马作为地中海地区交通中心的重要性。罗马于公元前753年4月21日建立，著名的"母狼乳婴"故事记载了有关罗马古城建立的传说。如今，4月21日被定为罗马建城日，"母狼乳婴"成为罗马的城徽图案。作为古罗马帝国的发源地，罗马有着非常丰富的旅游资源，被称为"永恒之都"。罗马还是一座艺术宝库、文化名城，古城酷似一座巨型的露天历史博物馆。在罗马古城遗址上，矗立着帝国元老院、君士坦丁凯旋门、万神殿和罗马斗兽场等世界闻名的古迹。罗马还有文艺复兴时期的许多精美建筑和艺术精品以及市中心的天主教圣地梵蒂冈（梵蒂冈为独立国家）。

Located on the riverside of the Tiber River in the middle of Apennine Peninsula, Rome is the capital of Italy, and the political, economic, cultural and transportation center. The old saying “All roads lead to Rome” can describe how important Rome is as a center of transportation in the Mediterranean. Rome was established on April 21 of the year 753 BC. The myth of she-woof suckling the infant twins recorded the legend of the Roma City. Today April 21 is the date of memorial of establishment of Rome and the city emblem is the she-wolf suckling the infant twins. As a cradle of the ancient Roman Empire, there are lots of tourist resources and it is named as Eternal City. Rome is also an art treasure and cultural city. The old town is a large open museum of history. In the ancient ruins in Rome stand the Imperial Senate, Arch of Contantine, Pantheon, Colosseum and other famous historic remains. There are many beautiful buildings of the Renaissance and art as well as holy land Vatican City in the center of the city.

◆ 罗马斗兽场（Colosseum）

罗马斗兽场，又称弗莱文圆形剧场，是由混凝土和石头建成的圆形剧场，坐落于罗马市中心。作为罗马帝国最大的露天剧场，它被认为是罗马式建筑和工程最伟大的作品之一。罗马斗兽场于公元 72 年罗马皇帝斯佩西安在位时开始建设，由他的继任者提图斯在公元 80 年完成。罗马斗兽场可以容纳 50 000 名观众，主要用于斗兽和角斗士角斗，如模拟海战、狩猎动物、死刑、重演著名战役和古典神话戏剧。中世纪前期，该建筑不再被用于娱乐。进入 21 世纪，罗马斗兽场由于地震和盗石只剩下断墙残壁，但它仍是罗马帝国的一个象征，是罗马最热门的旅游景点之一。

The Colosseum, also known as the Flavian Amphitheatre, is an elliptical amphitheater in the center of the city of Rome. Built of concrete and stone, it was the largest amphitheater of the Roman Empire, and is considered one of the greatest works of Roman architecture and engineering. Construction began under the Emperor Vespasian in 72 AD, and was completed in 80 AD under his successor and heir Titus. The Colosseum seated 50,000 spectators, and was used for gladiatorial contests and public spectacles such as mock sea battles, animal hunts, executions, re-enactments of famous battles, and dramas based on classical mythology. The building ceased to be used for entertainment in the early medieval era. Although in the 21st century, it stays partially ruined because of damage caused by devastating earthquakes and stone-robbers, the Colosseum is still an iconic symbol of Roman Empire. It is one of Rome’s most popular tourist attractions.

◆ 许愿池（Trevi Fountain）

许愿池又名“特莱维喷泉”，位于三条街的交叉口，Trevi 即指此意。罗马有“喷泉之都”的称号，全市有美妙壮观的喷泉 1 300 多个。特莱维喷泉是罗马最大的巴洛克风格喷泉，据说闭着眼睛背对着许愿池投硬币，愿望就会成真。许愿池因电影《罗马假日》而闻名于世。许愿池建于 1629 年，于 1732 年重建，最终于 1762 年完工。它是由 18 世纪建筑师尼科拉·萨尔维设计的。这座巴洛克式的群雕以波里公爵的楼房为依托，呈现了海神得胜的景象。海神的上方有一幅少女浮雕，传说少女曾为干渴的古罗马士兵指明水源所在地，因此该泉也被称为“少女泉”或“童贞之水”。

Trevi Fountain is located at the intersection of three streets which is the name of Trevi from. Rome has got the reputation of Fountain City with more than 1,300 spectacular fountains in the city. Trevi Fountain is the largest baroque fountain in Rome. It is said that when you make a wish with your back to the fountain and throw a coin into the pond, the dream will come true. It became famous after the movie *Roman Holiday*. The fountain was built in 1629, rebuilt in 1732, and finished in 1762. It was designed by Nicola Salvi, an architect of the 18th century. The back of the baroque sculptures is the Palazzo Poli and it is the sign of the victory of Poseidon. There is a girl on top of Poseidon emboss. The legendary girl specified where the water was for thirsty Roman soldiers, so the springs are also known as girl springs or the water of virgin.

◆ 西班牙广场（Piazza di Spagna）

西班牙广场位于罗马市中心，300 多年以来一直是罗马文化和旅游的中心地带，因是 17 世纪西班牙驻梵蒂冈大使馆所在地而得名。自古以来，西班牙广场便是作家、诗人、音乐家、画家聚会的场所。李斯特、拜伦、歌德、考夫曼、巴尔扎克、司汤达、安德逊和另外一些名人曾在广场附近居住过。1821 年，英国诗人济慈在大台阶靠右边的那间屋子里与世长辞。西班牙广场的主要名胜有石阶。具有艺术特色的大台阶是于 1723 年建成的，又名“西班牙之阶”。

Piazza di Spagna is located at the center of Rome which has been the heart of Roman culture and tourism for more than 300 years. It was named because of the location of the Spanish Embassy in Vatican City in the 17th century. Since ancient times, it has been the gathering place of writers, poets, musicians and painters. Many famous people such as Liszt, Byron, Goethe, Kauffman, Balzac, Stendhal, Anderson and others had lived near the square. Keats, a poet of the United Kingdom died in the room on the right near the steps in 1821. The square's main attraction is stone stairs on the hill. The large steps were completed in 1723, with artistic characteristics, and it was named as Spainish Steps.

◆ 威尼斯广场（Piazza Venezia）

威尼斯广场因旁边的威尼斯宫而得名，是罗马最大的广场，也是罗马最热闹的地方。广场上有建于 1911 年的埃玛努埃莱二世的纪念堂、雕塑以及无名烈士墓，许多名人故居也分布在广场附近。意大利人称威尼斯广场为“祖国祭坛”，很多外国元首到意大利正式访问时都要到此敬献花圈，意大利总统接见外国元首等重大活动也都在此地举行。因为威尼斯广场象征团结和自由，所以意大利人引以为豪。

Piazza Venezia is named because of the Venice Palace nearby. It is the largest piazza and the most crowded place in Rome. In the piazza, there is the Vittorio Emmanuele II monument built in 1911, sculptures and nameless revolutionary martyr's tombs. There are also many famous houses for the well-known persons around the piazza. Italians call Piazza Venezia as "the altar of the motherland" and many heads of foreign countries will come here for wreaths. And it is also the place for the president to hold the important welcome ceremony to the heads of foreign countries. Italians are proud of the place as it is the symbol of unity and independence.

◆ 万神殿（Pantheon）

万神殿是唯一保存完整的古罗马帝国时期的古迹。公元前 27 年至公元前 25 年，为纪念奥古斯都皇帝远征埃及的战功而建造了这座神殿。它的历史比罗马斗兽场还要早 100 多年。万神殿的内部为圆形，四面无窗，顶部开有一个直径为 9 米的天窗，是内部唯一的光线来源。殿顶的圆形曲线继续向下延伸，形成一个完整的球体与地面相接。这是建筑史上的奇迹，展现了古罗马建筑师们高深的建筑知识和深奥的计算方法。意大利实现统一后，万神殿成为国王和一些伟大的意大利艺术家的陵墓，其中最重要的人有拉斐尔。万神殿被列为意大利的国家圣地。

Pantheon is the only intact monument of the ancient Roman Empire. It was built during the years from 27 BC to 25 BC that was 100 years earlier than the construction of the Colosseum, to commemorate the Emperor Augustus expedition to Egypt. It is round inside with no windows on the walls but an opening of a diameter of 9 meters on the top, which is the only source for the internal light. The roof curve reaches down, resulting in a complete sphere and phase. This is a miracle in the history of architecture and shows that the ancient Roman architects had deep architectural knowledge and advanced esoteric calculations. After the unification, the Pantheon became tombs of kings and some great Italian artists, of which the most important person is Raphael. The Pantheon is listed as a national holy site.

知识拓展

罗马城徽

在罗马的帝国大道，在台伯河畔桥头，在宽阔广场的旁边，可以看到多处“母狼乳婴”黄铜雕塑。这是一个让罗马人引以为荣的亘古传奇故事。著名的“母狼乳婴”故事记载了有关创建罗马古城的传说。公元前 7、8 世纪，罗马国王努米托雷被其胞弟阿姆利奥篡位驱逐，其子被杀死，女儿西尔维娅与战神马尔斯结合，生下孪生兄弟罗慕洛和雷莫。阿姆利奥把这两个孪生婴儿抛入台伯河。落水婴儿幸遇一只母狼用奶汁哺喂成活，后被一位猎人养育成人。两兄弟长大后杀死了阿姆利奥，并迎回外祖父努米托雷，重登王位。努米托雷把台伯河畔的 7 座山丘赠给他们建新都。后来，罗慕洛私定城界，杀死了雷莫，并以自己名字命名新城为罗马。这一天是公元前 753 年 4 月 21 日，后定为罗马建城日，并将“母狼乳婴”图案定为罗马城徽。

（二）佛罗伦萨（Florence）

佛罗伦萨是意大利中部托斯卡纳大区和佛罗伦萨省的首府。美第奇家族曾经长期控制佛罗伦萨，并把它经营成欧洲中世纪重要的文化、商业和金融中心。在 1865 年至 1871 年间，佛罗伦萨曾是意大利统一后的首都。佛罗伦萨是一座美丽的文化古城。有人称罗马是政治首都，米兰是经济首都，佛罗伦萨则是文艺首都。佛罗伦萨是文艺复兴的发源地，是世界上文艺复兴时期艺术作品保存最丰富的地区之一，是艺术与建筑的摇篮之一，它拥有众多的历史建筑和藏品丰富的博物馆。历史上有许多文化名人在此地诞生、活动，著名的有但丁、达·芬奇、米开朗基罗。整个城市仍保留着文艺复兴时的风貌。佛罗伦萨堪称那个伟大时代留给后人的独一无二的标本，被称为“西方的雅典”。佛罗伦萨旧城区被列入世界文化遗产名录。

Florence is the capital city of the region of Tuscany and of the province of Florence. Medici Family had controlled the area for a long time and it became the medieval center of culture, commerce and finance in Europe. It was the capital of the united Italy (1865–1871). Florence is a beautiful cultural city. It is said that Rome is the political capital, Milan is the commercial capital, but Florence is the cultural and art capital. Florence is the birthplace of the Renaissance. The number of arts of the Renaissance it has collected is ranked the first in the world. It is one of the cradles of arts and architecture. There are numerous historic buildings and museums with rich collections. Many famous men were born or lived here such as Dante, Leonardo da Vinci and Michelangelo. The whole old town still keeps the style of the Renaissance. It is the only specimen left by the great age and is named as the Athens of the West. The old town was listed in the World Cultural Heritage Site by UNESCO.

◆ 圣母百花大教堂（Basilica of Saint Mary of the Flower）

圣母百花大教堂是天主教佛罗伦萨总教区的主教堂，也是佛罗伦萨最著名的建筑物，也称杜奥莫大教堂，是文艺复兴时期第一座伟大建筑。它始建于1296年，为罗马式建筑，外部以白、红、绿三色大理石按几何图案装饰，橘红色巨型圆顶堪称文艺复兴时期的圆顶之最。圣母百花大教堂仅次于梵蒂冈的圣彼得大教堂和伦敦的圣保罗大教堂，是欧洲三大教堂之一。

The Basilica of Saint Mary of the Flower is the mother church of the Roman Catholic Archdiocese of Florence and Florence's most famous building. It was the first great building of the Renaissance known as the Duomo Cathedral. It was set up in 1296, a Roman-style architectural work, with its external wall decorated with white, red and green marble geometric patterns. The orange giant dome is the largest in Renaissance domes. It is the third largest church in Europe after St. Peter Basilica in Vatican City and St. Paul's Cathedral in London.

◆ 维琪奥桥（Ponte Vecchio）

维琪奥桥也称旧桥，重建于1345年，是佛罗伦萨最古老的一座桥，也是世界上最有名的桥梁之一。维琪奥桥的设计者是特达·高迪。14世纪以来，桥上就店铺林立，主要经营金银首饰，故人们称之为“黄金大桥”或“商业大桥”。现在，维琪奥桥已成为佛罗伦萨最大的黄金首饰贸易场所，是许多观光客的必游之地。

Ponte Vecchio also known as Old Bridge, rebuilt in 1345, is the oldest bridge in Florence and one of the famous bridges in the world. The designer of the Ponte Vecchio is Taddeo Gaddi. Since the 14th century, there have been many shops everywhere on the bridge, which were mainly gold and silver jewelry shops. That's why it is known as the “Golden Bridge” or “Commercial Bridge”. Nowadays, the Ponte Vecchio has become the largest gold and jewelry trading place in Florence. It is a must-visit place for many tourists.

（三）威尼斯（Venice）

威尼斯是意大利东北部一座著名的旅游和工业城市。作为亚得里亚海上的一颗明珠，威尼斯城四周环海，由亚得里亚海沿岸和威尼斯咸水泻湖上的118座岛屿、117条水道和400座桥梁组成。它是闻名于世的水上之城，有“水都”“百岛之城”之称。“贡多拉”是威尼斯最具代表性和早期传统的代步小船。威尼斯也是世界著名旅行家马可·波罗的故乡。威尼斯还是一座文化艺术名城。全城有教堂、钟楼、修道院、宫殿、博物馆等艺术及历史名胜450多处。文艺复兴时期，威尼斯是继佛罗伦萨和罗马之后的第三个中心。1932年，威尼斯又创办了世界上第一个电影节——威尼斯国际电影节。作为世界上独一无二的水上城市，威尼斯具有宝贵的历史文化价值，被联合国教科文组织列入世界文化遗产名录。

Located in the northeast Italy, Venice is a famous tourist and industrial city. As a pearl of Adriatic Sea, Venice, surrounded by the sea, consists of 118 islands in the Venice lagoon along the Adriatic coast. 117 canals wind through the 118 islands and 400 bridges were built to connect the Venice islands. Gondola is the traditional small boat for transportation in Venice at the earlier time. Venice is the hometown of Marco Polo, a world famous traveler. Venice is a well-known art and cultural city. There are more than 450 famous historic attractions including cathedrals, towers, monasteries, palaces and museums. Venice is the third center after Florence and Rome during the period of Renaissance. Venice International Film festival established in 1932 is the first film festival in the world. As a unique city on water, thanks to its historic and cultural value, it has been listed as World Cultural Heritage Site by UNESCO.

◆ 圣马可广场（St. Mark’s Square）

圣马可广场（圣马尔谷广场）包括公爵府，圣马可大教堂，圣马可钟楼，新、旧行政官邸大楼，连接两幢楼的拿破仑翼大楼。初建于9世纪的长方形广场长约170米，东侧宽约80米，西侧宽约55米。广场四周的建筑都是文艺复兴时期的精美建筑。马可是《圣经》中《马可福音》的作者，威尼斯人将他奉为守护神。相传828年，两个威尼斯商人从埃及的亚历山大城将耶稣圣徒马可的遗骨偷运到威尼斯，并在同一年为圣马可兴建教堂，教堂内有圣马可的陵墓，大教堂以圣马可的名字命名，大教堂前的广场也因此得名“圣马可广场”。1797年，拿破仑攻占威尼斯后，赞叹圣马可广场是“欧洲最美的客厅”和“世界上最美的广场”。

St. Mark’s Square consists of Duke Palace, St. Mark’s Basilica, the Clock Tower, new and old official buildings and Napoleonic Wing which connects the two official buildings. The long square was built in the 9th century which is 170 meters long, 80 meters wide in the east and 55 meters wide in the west. The surrounding buildings are the elegant buildings of the Renaissance. San Marco was the writer of *Gospel of Mark* and was regarded as the protestant God of Venice. It was said that in 828 the remains of San Marco was moved back to Venice secretly by two Venice businessmen from Alexander of Egypt. The basilica was established in the same year to bury the body of San Marco and thus the piazza was named as well as the basilica. In 1797 when Napoléon invaded Venice and lived here, he praised the piazza as the most beautiful sitting room in Europe and the most beautiful piazza in the world.

◆ 圣马可大教堂（St. Mark's Basilica）

雄伟壮丽的圣马可大教堂始建于 829 年，不久毁于一场大火，重建于 1043 年至 1071 年，它曾是中世纪欧洲最大的教堂，是威尼斯建筑艺术的经典之作。它融合了东、西方的建筑特色：拜占庭式的直线、哥特式的尖拱门、文艺复兴时期的栏杆装饰、伊斯兰式的圆顶。而整座教堂的结构又呈现希腊式的十字形设计，曾有“世界上最美的教堂”之称。圣马可大教堂不仅是一座教堂，而且是一座博物馆，收藏了丰富的艺术品。

Magnificent St. Mark's Basilica was built in 829, but soon destroyed in a fire, and was reconstructed during the years from 1043 to 1071. It was Europe's largest church in the Middle Ages, and it is the classical art of Venice architecture. It combines Eastern and Western architectural features: Byzantine lines, gothic pointed arches, the Renaissance-style railings accessory and the Islamic dome. The entire basilica structure presents a Greece-style cross design and it was once called the most beautiful church in the world. St. Mark's Basilica is not only a church, but also a museum, a collection of a large number of art works.

◆ 里亚托桥（Rialto Bridge）

在威尼斯有 400 多座桥，其中从火车站通往市中心的里亚托桥（又名商业桥）最为有名。里亚托桥全部用白色大理石筑成，是威尼斯的象征。大桥长 48 米，宽 22.9 米，高 7.32 米，建于 1588 年至 1591 年，由安东尼奥·庞特设计。桥顶有一座浮亭，两侧是出售首饰和纪念品的商店，里亚托桥是威尼斯最重要的商业区之一，曾作为欧洲的商业中心达 300 年之久，在世界上的知名度很高。莎士比亚的名剧《威尼斯商人》就是以这里为背景的。

There are more than 400 bridges in Venice, among which Rialto Bridge, also the Commercial Bridge, connected the railway station with downtown is the most famous. The bridge, built of white marble, is a symbol of Venice. Designed by Antonio Ponte and built during the years from 1588 to 1591, it was 48 metres long, 22.9 meters wide, and 7.32 meters high. There is a floating pavilion on the bridge with jewelry and souvenir shops on both sides. It is one of Venice's most important business districts and has served as the commercial center of Europe for more than 300 years. It is quite well-known in the world. William Shakespeare's dramatic work, *The Merchant of Venice,* is set here.

（四）米兰（Milan）

米兰是意大利的第二大城市、伦巴第大区的首府。米兰是意大利最重要的经济中心，有“经济首都”之称，也是艺术家的摇篮和许多天才人物的故乡，更是一种意大利特有的工作方式和生活方式的故乡，因此米兰被认为是意大利最重要的城市。自古以来，米兰就是连接地中海及中欧的主要交通枢纽，是意大利商业及金融中心。米兰工业发达，经济实力雄厚，其工业产值占意大利工业产值的一半以上。米兰是一座现代化的城市，同时蕴藏着大量珍贵的文化艺术遗产及著名古迹。主要名胜古迹有埃玛努埃莱二世长廊、斯卡拉歌剧院等。

Milan is the second-largest city in Italy and the capital of the Lombardy. It is the country's most important economic center, with a name of "economic capital". It is also the cradle of art and hometown of many talented persons. With a special Italian work and life style, Milan is considered to be the most important city in Italy. Since the ancient time, Milan has been a commercial and financial center and an important transportation center as it connects the Mediterranean with Central Europe. Milan has developed industries with strong economic power. Its industrial output value is more than half of the industrial output of Italy. Milan is a modern city, which contains a treasure trove of cultural and artistic heritages and famous monuments. Main attractions are Galleria Vittorio Emanuele Ⅱ, La Scala and so on.

◆ 米兰大教堂（Milan Cathedral）

米兰大教堂是位于米兰市中心的一座哥特式大教堂，是全世界最华丽的教堂之一，规模仅次于梵蒂冈的圣彼得大教堂。米兰大教堂始建于1386年，1965年最后完工，历时5个多世纪，它不仅是米兰的象征，也是米兰的中心。拿破仑曾于1805年在米兰大教堂举行加冕仪式。米兰大教堂的整个外观极尽华美，主教堂用白色大理石砌成，是欧洲最大的大理石建筑之一，有“大理石山”之称，被马克·吐温称赞为“大理石的诗”。米兰大教堂也是世界上雕像最多的哥特式教堂，教堂内外墙等处均点缀着圣人、圣女雕像，共有6 000多座，仅教堂外就有3 159尊之多。教堂顶耸立着135个尖塔，每个尖塔上都有精致的人物雕刻。

Milan Cathedral, one of the world's most magnificent churches, is a gothic cathedral in downtown Milan and second largest after the St. Peter's Basilica in Vatican City. Milan Cathedral was founded in 1386 and completed in 1897 which lasted for more than five centuries. It is not only the symbol of Milan but also the center of Milan. In 1805 Napoléon's coronation ceremony was held in Milan Cathedral. Entire appearance of the cathedral is very gorgeous and decorated with white marbles. It is one of Europe's largest marble buildings and is named as “the mountain of marble”. Mark Twain praised it as “poetry of marble”. Milan Cathedral is a gothic cathedral with the most statues in the world. There are more than 6,000 Saints and Saintess decorated inside and outside the cathedral walls. There are 3,159 statues outside the wall of the cathedral. On the top there stands 135 towers with exquisite engraving.

◆ 圣玛利感恩教堂（Santa Maria delle Grazie）

圣玛利亚感恩教堂是米兰的古迹之一，达·芬奇创作的巨画《最后的晚餐》就画在这座教堂旁的修道院餐厅的墙壁上。达·芬奇于1495年开始动笔，1498年才完成。这幅巨画宽9.1米，高4.2米，画中的人物比真人大一半，画面描绘的是耶稣和12个门徒共进晚餐时的情景。第二次世界大战时，市民们用沙袋将教堂的墙保护起来，使这一杰作得以保存。1980年，圣玛利亚感恩教堂被联合国教科文组织列入世界文化遗产名录。

Santa Maria delle Grazie is one of the monuments in Milan with Leonardo da Vinci's mural of *The Last Super* on the wall of the refectory of the convent. Leonardo da Vinci started painting in 1495 and completed in 1498. This mural painting is 9.1 meters wide and 4.2 meters high. The figures in the painting are 1/2 bigger than real people. The mural depicts the story of Jesus having dinner with his 12 disciples. During World War Ⅱ, the citizens protected the wall with sandbags so that this masterpiece could be preserved. In 1980, the Santa Maria delle Grazie was listed in the World Cultural Heritage Site by UNESCO.

（五）那不勒斯（Naples）

那不勒斯是意大利南部的第一大城市，著名的维苏威火山和庞贝古城就在附近。那不勒斯以其丰富的历史、文化、艺术和美食而著称，这里历史悠久，风光美丽，文物众多，一年四季阳光普照，是地中海最著名的风景区之一。比萨饼起源于那不勒斯。音乐在那不勒斯文化中产生了广泛影响，浪漫的吉他和曼陀林均在此地发明。那不勒斯音乐对歌剧和民谣做出了重大贡献。那不勒斯人生性开朗，充满活力，善于歌唱，那不勒斯的民歌传遍世界。那不勒斯因此被人们称颂为“阳光和快乐之城”，被视作意大利的一颗明珠。那不勒斯历史中心还被联合国教科文组织列入世界文化遗产名录。

Naples is the largest city in southern Italy with the famous Mount Vesuvius and Pompeii nearby. Naples is known for its rich history, culture, art and cuisine. Here is one of the most famous scenic sites in Mediterranean with a long history, beautiful scenery, rich cultural relics and year-round sunshine. Pizza originated in Naples. Music is an important component of culture impact for Naples. Romantic guitar and mandolin were invented here. Naples music also has made great contributions to opera and folk songs. Neapolitans are good at singing with open character and energetic power. Neapolitan folk songs are spread around the world. So it is praised as “city of sunshine and happiness”. Being regarded as a pearl of Italy, it has been listed in World Cultural Heritage Site by UNESCO.

（六）其他著名旅游景点

◆ 梵蒂冈（Vatican City）

梵蒂冈是世界上最小的主权国家，也是世界上人口最少的国家。位于意大利首都罗马城西北角的梵蒂冈高地上，面积为 0.44 平方千米，四面都与意大利接壤，是一个“国中国”，也是全世界天主教的中心——以教皇为首的教廷的所在地。名胜古迹包括圣彼得广场、圣彼得大教堂和梵蒂冈博物馆等。梵蒂冈是伟大的文化瑰宝，城内的建筑如圣彼得大教堂、西斯廷教堂等都是世界重要的建筑作品，蕴藏了波提切利、贝尔尼尼、拉斐尔和米开朗基罗等人的作品。梵蒂冈拥有一个馆藏丰富的图书馆以及一个博物馆，专门收藏具有历史、科学与文化价值的艺术品。圣彼得广场可容纳 50 万人。每逢元旦、复活节、圣诞节，广场上往往都会聚集 20 万人。每逢礼拜日，也总有成千上万的人在此聆听教皇在阳台上播送晨祷词，接受教皇的祝福。1984 年，梵蒂冈被列入世界文化遗产名录。

Vatican City is the world’s smallest sovereign state with the least population in the world. Located in the northwest corner of the highland of the capital city of Rome, Vatican City has an area of 0.44 square kilometers and is bordered by Italy. As a state within a state, Vatican City is also the center of the Catholic world headed by the Pope of the Holy See in Rome. The cultural sites include St. Peter’s Square, St. Peter’s Basilica and Vatican Museum. Vatican City itself is a great master art work. The buildings in the city including St. Peter’s Basilica and Sistine Chapel are very important in the world architecture which include the works of Botticelli, Bernini, Raphael and Michelangelo. Vatican City also has a library with large collections and a museum dedicated to collections of historical, scientific and cultural works of art. St. Peter’s Square can hold more than 500,000 people. There will be more than 200,000 persons gathering in the square every January 1, Easter and Christmas day. Thousands of people will come here every Sunday morning to listen to the Pope’s Matins and receive the Pope’s blessing. In 1984, Vatican City was added by UNESCO to the list of World Cultural Heritage Site.

◆ 比萨斜塔（Leaning Tower of Pisa）

比萨距离佛罗伦萨约 1 小时车程。比萨斜塔实际上是比萨大教堂的钟楼，比萨斜塔修建于 1173 年，由著名建筑师博南诺·皮萨诺主持修建，它位于比萨大教堂右后方，是比萨城的标志。刚开始修建时，塔高设计为 100 米左右，但动工五六年后，塔身从 3 层开始倾斜，直到完工还在持续倾斜，在其完工前，塔顶已南倾（即塔顶偏离垂直线）3.5 米。比萨斜塔还曾因一个著名的科学实验而闻名全世界。1987 年，比萨斜塔和相邻的大教堂、洗礼堂、墓园一起因其对 11 世纪至 14 世纪意大利建筑艺术的巨大影响，而被联合国教科文组织列入世界文化遗产名录。

Pisa is one hour driving from Florence. Leaning Tower in fact is the bell tower of the Cathedral of Pisa. It was built in 1173 by famous architect Bonanno Pisano and is located right behind the Cathedral. It is a landmark of Pisa. At the beginning, the tower height was designed for 100 meters, but five or six years later, the tower started leaning from three-tier and it was still leaning after it was completed. Before it was closed, the tower has been dumping south (namely tower deviation from the vertical line) of 3.5 meters. The Leaning Tower of Pisa is also known for a famous scientific experiment. In 1987, because of the tremendous impact to Italy architectural art from the 11th century to the 14th century, the Leaning Tower of Pisa, the nearby cathedral, baptistery and cemetery were listed in World Cultural Heritage Site by UNESCO.

◆ 维罗纳（Verona）

维罗纳是意大利最古老、最美丽和最荣耀的城市之一，拉丁语意为“极高雅的城市”。维罗纳北靠阿尔卑斯山，西临经济重镇米兰，东接水城威尼斯，南通首都罗马，有“意大利门户”之称。维罗纳也被称作“爱之城”，莎士比亚笔下的罗密欧与朱丽叶的爱情故事就发生在这里。该城市有古代罗马的圆形露天剧场和许多造型精美的教堂。2000 年，维罗纳被联合国教科文组织列入世界文化遗产名录。

Verona is one of the oldest, most beautiful and glorious cities in Italy. Verona in Latin means the most elegant city. To the north of the city is the Alps, to its west is Milan — the important financial city, to its east is Venice and to its south is the capital city Rome. Verona is the gateway to Italy. The city of love is another name of Verona. The love story in Shakespeare's *Romeo and Juliet* occurred here. In the city, there is an ancient Roman arena and many elegant cathedrals. The city was listed in the World Cultural Heritage Site in 2000 by UNESCO.

◆ 庞贝（Pompeii）

庞贝是位于意大利那不勒斯海湾维苏威火山下的一座古罗马城市，始建于公元前 8 世纪，但是公元 79 年维苏威火山爆发，庞贝被埋，1748 年被发现。庞贝是今天世界上唯一的一座构造保留了古罗马时期风貌的城市。庞贝的街道棋盘似的纵横交错，这是传统的古罗马街道。庞贝为研究者了解古罗马社会生活和文化艺术提供了重要资料。

Pompeii is an ancient Roman city located at the foot of the Mount Vesuvius in the Gulf of Naples of Italy. Pompeii was built in the 8th century BC but was buried when Mount Vesuvius erupted in 79 AD, It was discovered in 1748. It is the only one city left in the world that the structure was complete the same as in the ancient time. The streets cross each other like the chessboard and it was the traditional Roman city. From the remains, the researchers can know more about the social life, the culture and the arts of ancient Rome.

四、旅游资讯

（一）美食

意大利是西餐的鼻祖。意大利的美食高贵、典雅、味道独特。精美可口的面食、奶酪、火腿和葡萄酒成为世界各国美食家的向往。意大利菜肴注重原料的本色，成品力求保持原汁原味。在烹调过程中喜欢用橄榄油、黑橄榄、帕玛森干酪、香料、西红柿与马萨拉酒，烹调以炒、煎、炸、烩等方法见长。意大利人喜爱面食，面食往往是第一道菜。面条的做法、吃法甚多，面条的形状、颜色、味道各不相同，每种面还配有不同的调料、酱汁。此外，还有意式馄饨、意式饺子等。面包是意大利非常重要的一种日常食品。意大利面包大致可分为软式（早餐食用）和硬式两种。除面食外，另一种传统的意大利食品是冰激凌。据记载，17 世纪，意大利就出现了冰激凌。意大利从南到北都适宜种植葡萄，所有大区都盛产葡萄酒。

Italy is the ancestor of Western cuisine. Italian cuisine is noble, elegant with unique taste. Beautiful and delicious pasta, cheese, ham and wine are favored by international gourmets. Italian dishes attach most importance to the nature of the raw material, color and original taste of finished food. In the process of cooking, olive oil, black olives, Parmesan cheese, spices, tomatoes and Marsala wine are made best use of. The means of cooking are frying, grilling, deep-frying and stewing. Italians like wheaten food which is usually the first course. They eat noodles in many ways. The shape, color and taste of noodles are various with different seasonings and sauces. And there are Italian ravioli and dumplings. Bread is the important daily food for Italians. The bread can be classified as soft which is for breakfast and hard which is for the main meal. Another traditional food besides wheaten food is ice cream which appeared in the 17th century. Italy is suitable for the grape from south to north and wine is produced in all districts.

（二）购物及退税

威尼斯面具与玻璃：威尼斯的面具文化在欧洲文明中独具一格，在威尼斯的传统文化中占有重要的地位。18 世纪以前，威尼斯居民的生活离不开面具，人们外出时，不论男女，都要戴上面具，披上斗篷。威尼斯面具称为“包塔”。今天，在威尼斯的大街小巷都可以看到各种面具。除此之外，慕拉诺所产的玻璃也是水城的特色。

Venice mask and glass: Venice mask culture is unique in European civilization. It has a very important position in the Venetian tradition. Before the 18th century, Venice residents could not live without masks. People, male or female, had to wear a mask and a cloak to go out. The exclusive mask from Venice is Bauta. A variety of masks can be seen in Venice streets today. Besides, the water capital is also famous for Murano glass.

佛罗伦萨皮制品：在古代，意大利半岛的居民就是闻名遐迩的皮革匠，所以最早的手工制鞋作坊也出现在意大利。几百年来，这种传统的制鞋工艺一直流传至今。如今，意大利有 60% 的制鞋厂仍然在坚持使用手工或者半手工的方式制鞋。佛罗伦萨的皮革品更是声名远扬。

Florence leather products: In ancient times, the residents of Italian Peninsula were famous as leather craftsmen and the earliest handmade shoes workshop also appeared in Italy. For hundreds of years, this traditional shoe-making process has been passed down. Nowadays, 60% of factories still insist on manufacturing shoes by hand or semi-hand. And leather goods in Florence enjoy a widespread reputation.

意大利咖啡：浓咖啡是意式咖啡的精髓，其做法起源于意大利，意大利语意为“特别快”。其特征是利用蒸气压力，瞬间将咖啡液抽出。所有的牛奶咖啡或花式咖啡都是以浓咖啡为基础制作出来的。喝意大利咖啡时，只需尝一小口，就会迅速被其浓郁的口味和香气折服，这正是意大利咖啡与其他咖啡的不同之处。香味和浓度是衡量意大利咖啡是否好喝的两个尺度。

Italian coffee: Espresso, which means “extremely fast” in Italian, is the essence of the Italian coffee whose practice originated in Italy. Its characteristic is that the use of steam pressure makes the liquid of coffee extract momentarily. All milk coffee or fancy coffee is Espresso-based production. With just a sip of Italian coffee, we will quickly be humbled by its rich taste and aroma. And this is how Italian coffee differs from the other coffee. Flavor and concentration is the measure to judge if Italian coffee is good or not.

时装：米兰是世界三大时尚之都之一。意大利设计师的大胆革新和丰富创意使意大利制造的时装能与法国时装分庭抗礼。古驰绝对是意大利的同义词，华伦天奴是高端时尚的代名词，Miu Miu 把尼龙背包化为风尚，菲拉格慕一直在寻找最理想的鞋型，乔治·阿玛尼是低调美学的王者风范，而范思哲则是古典巴洛克的金色风华。

Fashion: Milan is one of the three major fashion capitals of the world. Italian fashion can compete with French fashion because the Italian designers always reform the design and have rich imagination. Gucci is definitely the synonym for Italy while Valentino is the word of high fashion; Miu Miu leads nylon bags to fashion; Salvatore Ferragamo is always looking for the best shoes; Giorgio Armani is the king of low-key aesthetic style and Versace is golden elegance of classical baroque.

游客在意大利购物，必须在同一家店当日满 155.01 欧元才可享受退税。在机场办理登机手续后，把行李拿到海关退税处办理退税检验及盖章再托运。手提物品出境后到海关退税处盖章后再退税。意大利有许多品牌店都可以当场退税，但要把海关盖过章的单子寄回。

Tourists can get tax refund when they buy 155.01 euros or more in the same shop on the same day. After checking in at the airport, you must take the luggage to the Customs with the form of tax refund to be stamped and then send the luggage to the conveyor nearby. The small carry-on goods can have the check stamped by the Customs inside the departure hall and get the refund nearby. Lots of shops in Italy can have the tax refunded in the shop, but you must send back the form of the tax refund stamped by the Customs.

（三）时差

意大利在10月到次年3月间与中国有7小时的时差。由于意大利实行夏令时制，在3月到10月间与中国有6个小时的时差。

In Italy, from October to next March, there is a 7-hour time difference from China. Because of the Daylight Saving Time in Italy, the time difference is 6 hours from March to October.

思考练习

1. 经典旅游线路分析

情定亚平宁10日游

第1天：上海——米兰

游客按照规定的时间在机场集合，搭乘荷兰皇家航空公司的航班，经阿姆斯特丹转机后前往米兰。抵达后入住酒店休息。

第2天：米兰——威尼斯

早餐后，市区游览。外观多姆大教堂，多姆大教堂是世界上最大的哥特式教堂，坐落于米兰市中心的大教堂广场。游览埃玛努埃莱二世长廊，这是一个华丽的购物商场，观光价值高于购物价值。随后前往意大利著名的小城维罗纳，这里是莎士比亚名著《罗密欧与朱丽叶》中朱丽叶的故乡，游览朱丽叶故居，您可以看到朱丽叶和罗密欧幽会的露台。随后驱车前往著名的意大利水城威尼斯，夜宿威尼斯附近。

第3天：威尼斯——意大利小镇

早餐后，游览圣马可广场，圣马可广场竖立着雕刻着威尼斯守护神的白色石柱，外观有“黄金教堂”之称的圣马可大教堂。前往参观传统工艺——FOSCARI水晶玻璃制造工厂和销售商店，在圣马可广场景区自由活动（有兴趣的客人可自费乘坐威尼斯的主要交通工具——贡多拉）。夜宿意大利小镇。

第4天：意大利小镇——比萨——酒庄——佛罗伦萨

早餐后，前往比萨城内，外观著名的比萨斜塔。伽利略的自由落体实验让比萨斜塔闻名于世。随后驱车前往维琦玛乔古堡，参观葡萄酒庄园，品尝意大利美酒。随后前往意大利的皮革之都，也是文艺复兴的发源地——佛罗伦萨，抵达后游览佛罗伦萨的象征，华丽的圣母百花大教堂、乔托钟楼、宏伟气派的市政厅广场。而展现男性身体魅力的米开朗基罗的《大卫》雕像，也体现了这个城市的艺术气息。之后参观代表意大利当地制皮工艺的Peruzzi皮货商店。夜宿佛罗伦萨附近。

第5天：佛罗伦萨——罗马（梵蒂冈）

早餐后，前往意大利首都罗马，参观全世界最小的国家，占地0.44平方千米的梵蒂冈，参观世界第一大教堂圣彼得大教堂和圣彼得广场。之后参观罗马著名的斗兽场、建于公元315年的罗马最大的君士坦丁凯旋门，顺访古罗马废墟。在矗立的断壁残垣、庙墩孤柱前聆听曾经的辉煌。之后享用意大利风味晚餐，体会属于意大利的浓情。夜宿罗马附近。

第6天：罗马——庞贝——那不勒斯

早餐后，前往庞贝古城，参观埋没地下2 000多年的遗迹，并远眺维苏威火山雄壮景观及美丽的地中海景致。随后前往被称为“意大利永恒剧场”的那不勒斯，参观位于那不勒斯市中心的公民投票广场，广场上有壮丽的那不勒斯皇宫、气势非凡的保罗圣方济教堂、闻名的圣卡罗歌剧院，漫步美人鱼大道。夜宿那不勒斯附近。

第7天：那不勒斯——苏莲托——阿玛菲海岸——那不勒斯

早餐后，前往民谣之乡——苏莲托，苏莲托位于苏莲托半岛突出海面的山崖上，依山傍海、风光旖旎，景观奇特壮丽，在古代便已是罗马王公贵族最钟爱的度假胜地及冬季避寒胜地。随后前往《国家地理》杂志所列“人生必游的50个地方”之一的阿玛菲海岸，其与希腊诸岛一起被誉为“人间天堂”。结束后返回那不勒斯，夜宿那不勒斯附近。

第8天：那不勒斯——卡布里岛——罗马

早餐后，乘船前往卡布里岛，卡布里岛又称女妖岛，是意大利享誉国际的观光胜地。这里有迷人的阳光与海滩、优美的海岸、丰富的古迹，有人将之比喻为“人间仙境”。游览结束后返回罗马，夜宿罗马附近。

第9天：罗马——上海

早餐后，在导游的带领下前往机场，办理好退税手续后，搭乘荷兰皇家航空公司的国际航班。

第10天：上海

游客返回上海浦东国际机场，行程结束。

分析：这条经典旅游线路的主要旅游景点与行程特色，以及适合旅游的人群。

2. 案例分析

[案例1] 游客陈先生跟团到意大利旅游。有天在托斯卡纳的一个小镇上看到一幢很漂亮的别墅，别墅门口有几个大人、孩子在刷墙和制作家具，他很好奇地问当地导游：“意大利人怎么还雇用童工？”当地导游解释：“那可不是童工，这是他们的家，很多意大利人都喜欢自己动手，全家一起刷墙、铺地、拉电线、制作家具、装修房间、修整花园，甚至自己制作陶瓷工艺品。这不仅是出于经济考虑，更是把此看作培养个人技能、陶冶个人情操的一种休闲方式。通过自己动手，能使自己的居室更加舒适，更具个性化。家是心灵的港湾，全家一起动手，既能让一家人更和谐，又可以从小锻炼孩子的动手能力。”但是陈先生还是想不明白：既然住得起别墅，为何还要这么辛苦？你如何理解？

[案例2] 张老太太随团到意大利旅游，意大利司机每次上车都会对她堆满笑脸地说：

"Bella"（美女）。一天在那不勒斯，司机用意大利语对张老太太说："如果不是您离不开这位朋友的话（他碰了碰张老太太倚在身边的拐杖），我真想邀请您做我今晚的舞伴。"听了导游的翻译，张老太太咧开戴着假牙的嘴发自内心地笑了，司机还很绅士地弯下腰来亲了她布满皱纹的手。当地导游解释，生活中不带任何功利目的地向女士献殷勤是意大利男人的习惯，他们认为让女人充满自信、心情愉快是男人应有的一种礼仪。你如何理解意大利人的这种行为？

3. 练一练

地中海的蔚蓝天空和碧绿海水令人神往，但这样的美景并非可望而不可即。文艺复兴留下的绘画和雕塑，空气中飘散的淡淡的历史气息，加上美味的地中海式意大利美食，特别是黄昏时落在斗兽场上的那道余晖，让人没有任何理由拒绝意大利。试分析意大利有哪些主题游。选择其中一个主题，写一篇导游词。

第五节　瑞士

一、国家概况

（一）地理环境

瑞士联邦，简称瑞士，是位于欧洲中部的多山内陆国，东与奥地利、列支敦士登接壤，南邻意大利，西接法国，北连德国。全境分为中南部的阿尔卑斯山脉（占总面积的60%）、西北部的汝拉山脉（占总面积的10%）和中部高原（占总面积的30%）三个自然地形区，国境几乎都在阿尔卑斯山脉之中，平均海拔约1 350米，多为高山及湖泊，少女峰是最有名的。瑞士是欧洲大陆三大河流的发源地，有"欧洲水塔"之称。主要河流有莱茵河（在瑞士境内375千米，是瑞士最长的河流）。境内共有湖泊1 484个，其中最大的是日内瓦湖。

The Swiss Confederation, briefly Switzerland, is the mountainous inner land country in the middle of Europe. It borders Austria and Liechtenstein to the east, Italy to the south, France to the west and Germany to the north. Three natural regions are included in the country, including the Alps in the middle and south part (which occupies 60% of the national territory), Jura Mountains in the northwest (which occupies 10% of the national territory) and the middle plateau (which occupies 30% of the national territory). Its major territory is in the Alps area with an average altitude of about 1,350 meters. There are many mountains and lakes, among which the Jungfrau is the most famous. Switzerland has the source of three inner land rivers, thus, enjoying the name of "European Water Tower". The major river is Rhine River (375 kilometers in Switzerland, the longest one in the country). There are 1,484 lakes, including the largest one named Lake Geneva.

瑞士地处北温带，各地气候差异很大。阿尔卑斯山由东向西伸展，形成了瑞士气候的分界线。阿尔卑斯山以北受温和、潮湿的西欧海洋性气候和东欧大陆性气候的交替影响，变化较大，山间谷地气候温和，高山地区较寒冷；阿尔卑斯山以南则属于地中海气候，全年气候宜人。

Switzerland is located in the north temperate zone with various climates in different regions. The Alps stretch from east to west serving as the boundary of Switzerland climate. The north of the Alps is influenced by mild and moist Western Europe maritime climate and east continental climate, so the valleys are warm and the high mountainous areas are cold. The south of the Alps enjoys the comfortable Mediterranean climate with pleasant climate all the year round.

知识拓展

阿尔卑斯山脉

阿尔卑斯山脉是欧洲最高大、最宏伟的山脉。阿尔卑斯山脉从亚热带地中海海岸的法国尼斯附近向北延伸至日内瓦湖，然后向东北延伸至维也纳盆地。阿尔卑斯山脉遍及下列7个国家的部分地区：法国、意大利、瑞士、德国、奥地利、斯洛文尼亚和列支敦士登，仅有瑞士和奥地利可算作是真正的阿尔卑斯型国家。阿尔卑斯山脉长约1 200千米，最宽处201千米以上，是西欧自然地理区域中最明显的景观。瑞士境内有多座数千米的山峰和终年不化的冰河，有欧洲著名山峰——少女峰。1891年，美国作家马克·吐温写道：“少女峰这个名称很好，没有比少女更洁白无瑕和圣洁的了。”发源于少女峰地区的阿莱奇冰川是阿尔卑斯山脉中最美的冰川，也是欧洲第一大冰川。2001年，联合国教科文组织宣布少女峰－阿莱奇冰川地区为世界自然遗产。这是整个阿尔卑斯山脉中唯一获此殊荣的景观。阿尔卑斯山脉的景色十分迷人，是世界著名的风景区和旅游胜地，被世人称为“大自然的宫殿”和“真正的地貌陈列馆”。这里还是冰雪运动的圣地、探险者的乐园。

（二）人文概况

1. 历史

1032年，神圣罗马帝国统治瑞士之前，瑞士相继被罗马帝国、勃艮第和法兰克帝国占领。1291年，为了反抗哈布斯堡王朝的统治，卢塞恩周围的森林三州——乌里、施维茨和尼瓦尔登组成永久同盟。1370年，又和格拉鲁斯、楚格、卢塞恩、苏黎世、伯尔尼签订八州宪章，促使瑞士完成统一。1648年，瑞士宣布独立，并宣布执行中立政策。1798—1803年，拿破仑占领瑞士，改名为海尔维第共和国。1815年，维也纳会议确定瑞士为永久中立国，此后瑞士共有17个州相继加入联邦，定都伯尔尼。联邦政府于1848年成立。第二次世界大战期间，瑞士保持中立。瑞士实行民主制度，公民权利很大，任何重要事务都投票表决。

Switzerland was occupied by Roman Empire, Burgundians and Frankish Empire, and in 1032 the Holy Roman Empire reigned over the country. In 1291, three forest communities of Uri, Schwyz and Nidwalden around Luzern signed the alliance to fight against Habsburg. In 1370, the three cantons joined with the cantons of Glarus, Zug, Luzern, Zurich and Bern and signed the Charter which led to the union of Switzerland. In 1648, Swiss declared independent and the neutrality policy. From the year 1798 to 1803, Napoléon took the control of Switzerland and established the Helvetic Republic. In 1815, the Congress of Vienna formally guaranteed Switzerland's independence and neutrality. The other 17 cantons joined the Confederation one after one, and Bern was established as the capital. The confederate government was established in 1848. Switzerland kept neutral during World War Ⅱ. Switzerland is a democratic country and the citizens enjoy strong civic rights. They vote for important national affairs.

2. 经济

瑞士由于1815年后从未有过大规模的战争，因此是全球最富裕、经济最发达和居民生活水准最高的国家之一。其主要的产业是旅游业、精密机械工业（钟表、光学机械）、化学制药业和金融保险业。钟表业是瑞士的传统工业，有500多年的历史，迄今一直保持世界领先地位，瑞士被称为“钟表王国”。瑞士的金融业非常发达，共有600余家银行，分支机构达5 070家，银行总资本达5 000多亿美元，纳税额占国家税收的20%，在国民经济中居于重要地位。瑞士人均在国外资产和投资居于世界第一位。稳定的政局、较低的通货膨胀率、完善的金融体系及闻名遐迩的“银行保密”制度对国际现金的流动产生了巨大吸引力，从而使瑞士成为继美国、英国和日本之后世界第四大国际金融中心，有“金融帝国”之称。瑞士人的生活很舒适，失业率是欧洲最低。苏黎世和日内瓦分别被列为世界上生活品质最高城市的第一名和第二名。

Switzerland has not been involved in wars since 1815, so it becomes one of the richest and most developed countries with the highest living standard in the world. Its main industries are tourism, precision machinery industry (watches, optical mechanical parts), chemical industry, finance and insurance. The clock and watch industry is the traditional industry in Switzerland with over 500 years of history. Till today, it has kept the leading place in the world and is named the kingdom of clocks and watches. The financial industry in Switzerland is very developed with over 600 banks, 5,070 branches and total capital of 500 billion dollars. Its tax occupies 20% of the national tax income, so the financial industry is very important for the national economy. Switzerland ranks the first in the world in personal foreign assets and investment. The stable political environment, low inflation rate, complete financial system and the famous bank secrecy system have great attraction to international cash. Known as financial kingdom, Switzerland becomes the fourth international financial center after the US, the UK and Japan. Life in Switzerland is comfortable and the country has the lowest unemployment rate in Europe. Zurich and Geneva rank the first and second in terms of its living quality.

3. 社会文化

瑞士人口约857万，其中日耳曼人占74%，法兰西人占20%，意大利人占4%，雷托罗曼人占1%，均属欧罗巴人种。首都伯尔尼。官方语言为德语、法语、意大利语和罗曼什语，前3种为高中学生必修的语言，为大多数瑞士人所通晓。信奉天主教的居民占

36.5%，基督教新教占 24.4%。

The population in Switzerland is about 8.57 million, 74% of which are Teutonic, 20% are French, 4% are Italian and 1% are Rhaeto-Romances. They all belong to European race. Bern is the capital. The official languages are German, French, Italian and Romansh. The first three languages are the compulsory courses in high school. 36.5% of the Swiss are Catholics and 24.4% of the Swiss are Protestants.

地处欧洲一隅的瑞士是一个小国，但却有德语、法语、意大利语和罗曼什语四种官方语言。德意志、法兰西和意大利文化相互融合，各文化区实行独立的文化政策。三个主要邻国对瑞士三大语区产生的直接影响也决定了瑞士多元文化的特点，主要表现在诗歌、音乐、舞蹈、木雕和刺绣等。这里还有历史上著名的朝圣之路，有多处联合国教科文组织指定的世界文化和自然遗产，有历史悠久的古老城堡和众多各具特色的博物馆。历史上，曾有众多著名的艺术家来此游历或定居于此，是音乐家和艺术家云集的地方。

Switzerland is a small country in Europe, but it has four official languages as mentioned above. German, French and Italian cultures mingle together. Those cultural regions have their own cultural policies. The three neighboring countries have direct influence on the three language regions and also the multicultural features of Switzerland are fostered which are reflected mainly on poems, music, dances, wood carvings and embroidery, etc. It also boasts the relics such as the pilgrimage road, the World Cultural and Natural Heritages named by the UNESCO, the historical castles and characteristic museums in Switzerland. Many artists once visited and lived there in the history. It is the place where many musicians and artists gather together.

20 世纪的瑞士艺术非常繁荣，博物馆和艺术画廊遍布各个城市和城镇。全年会举行各种各样的音乐会。20 世纪，这里产生了新的艺术运动：达达主义。著名的画家尚·丁格利和保罗·克莱、伟大的雕塑家阿尔贝托·贾科梅蒂、世界上最有影响的建筑师勒·科尔比西耶等都是瑞士人。20 世纪最著名的两大德语作家——弗里德里希·迪伦马特和马克斯·弗里施也是瑞士人。

The art was developed very prosperously in Switzerland in the 20th century. Museums and art galleries scatter in the cities and towns. Various concerts were held all year around. In the 20th century, new art movements were developed from here: Dadaism. The famous painter Jean Tinguely and Paul Klee, the great sculptor Alberto Giacometti, the most influential architect Le Corbisier are Swiss. The most famous German writers Friedrich Dürrenmatt and Max Frisch are also Swiss.

二、民俗风情

（一）礼仪禁忌

瑞士人举止端庄、感情细腻、注重文明、讲究礼仪、言谈风趣，给人们的第一印象是喜欢安静、习惯轻声细语。在公共场合，瑞士人相互接触时，“谢谢”“请”“你好”一类的礼貌用语使用频繁，这是人们生活中的一种习惯，也反映了国民素养。对于陌生人，他们也总是彬彬有礼，乐于助人，无论你是问路或打听某个人，都会有人热情地为你指点。

Swiss people are very polite, sensitive, civilized, gentle and funny. The first impression that they give to the others is silent and speak softly. In public, "thank you", "please" and "how are you" are the frequently used words. Those living habits reflect the national quality. The Swiss are polite to strangers and happy to offer help. If you ask directions or look for someone, the Swiss people are willing to guide you.

瑞士有一些约定俗成的规矩。在火车站、公交车站、餐厅、咖啡馆等公共场合，不宜大声喧哗，以使对方听清楚为宜。多数火车设有不可以大声说话的车厢，因为人们习惯于在安静的环境中读书、看报或看电脑。即使是在商店中购物或走在大街上，讲话声音也以不影响别人为宜。家里晚上 10 点以后不使用洗衣机，不大声说话，如果你一不小心把收音机或者电视的声音开大了，若是第一次，隔壁的邻居一定会很客气地跑来敲门提醒你注意。晚上 9 点以后，瑞士人不会打电话给他人。如果某家将举办生日聚会或庆祝活动，会提前几天在走廊和电梯里张贴通知，而且一定要写上开始和结束的时间，并注明"希望尊敬的住户们理解和原谅"的字样，否则，邻居一定会投诉甚至报警，由警察出面干涉。

There are some accepted practices in Switzerland. People do not talk loudly in public, such as railway stations, bus stations, restaurants and cafes. Their voices are just enough to be heard. People are not allowed to speak loudly in some carriages of trains because they are used to reading books, papers or watching computers quietly. Even in the shops or on the streets, their voices are not supposed to interrupt anyone else. People do not use washing machine after 10:00 pm in the evening. They talk in a moderate volume. If the volumes of radios or TV are loud, the neighbors will come to remind you to keep quiet with politeness for the first time. People do not call each other after 9:00 pm. If a family is going to throw a birthday party or has something to celebrate, they will put on a notice in the lobby or elevators with starting and ending time of the activity and words like "hope for the forgiveness and understanding". Or the neighbors will come to make complaint and even call the police.

瑞士享有"世界花园"的美称。瑞士人热爱自然、努力不懈地保护环境。在瑞士，家庭垃圾实施严格分类，并按不同的种类在规定的时间扔到指定的地点，乱扔垃圾会被罚款。在每周规定日的晚上 10 点以后，瑞士人把垃圾装进黑色塑料袋，放在指定地点。瑞士人酷爱清洁，他们不仅注意个人住所的干净整齐，而且十分注意保持公共场所的卫生。无论是在城市或乡村，很少有乱扔垃圾的现象。他们不愿看到在公共场所（如公寓、阳台、餐厅等）晾晒衣服。他们认为这样做不雅观，会影响环境的美观。

The Switzerland enjoys the name of "World Garden". The Swiss love the nature and try their best to protect the environment. In Switzerland, family rubbish is classified strictly. People are required to throw rubbish according to the scheduled time and places. If they don't follow the agreement of rubbish disposal, they will be punished. On the day scheduled, the Swiss put the rubbish into black plastic bags and throw them to the appointed place after 10:00 pm. The Swiss love to clean the environment. They not only care about the personal space but also the public places. No matter in cities or towns, the rubbish can not be thrown at people's own will. They do not like their clothes hung in the public space, like apartment, balcony or restaurant. They believe that it is not suitable and would untidy the environment.

瑞士人保守、自信，君子之交淡如水。他们办事井井有条，在允许的范围内会尽其所能，而那些不被允许的事情，他们会礼貌地回绝。瑞士人不仅自己严格遵守规矩，而且会要求别人遵守。瑞士人有互相监督并告发不遵守公德者的习惯，如检举邻居或路人虐待动物或把单独孩子留在车里等。瑞士人严格遵守交通规则。只要遇上红灯，瑞士人就会老老实实等待绿灯。不管有多重要的事情，行人优先、公交车优先是驾驶员永不改变的信条。

The Swiss are conservative, confident and keep friends in a proper distance. They do things neatly. They do their best on the things permitted. They will politely refuse those that are not allowed. The Swiss obey the rules strictly and they require other people to do so. The Swiss supervise each other and will sue those who do not obey the rules, for examples, to report their neighbors or passersby who abuse animals or leave children alone in the car. The Swiss also have high standard for their traffic. If the light turns red, they will wait until the green light turns on. No matter how important things, they believe in the rule of the pedestrians first and the buses first.

守时是瑞士人又一个突出的优点。现代社会生活节奏加快，高效、有序要求人们遵守时间。瑞士人被认为是最遵守时间的民族之一。遵守时间是尊重别人，也是尊重自己的文明礼貌行为。即使是探亲访友，也要预先约定前往，这一点也包括看望父母、子女在内。在通常情况下，所有的公共交通都是准点的。在瑞士，文明、诚信蔚然成风。瑞士大小城市的公交车都不设售票员，司机也从不验票。除了持有月票的乘客，其他乘客都在站台的自动售票机购买公交车票。交通管理部门偶尔才会派出检票员巡查。在瑞士，逃票十分罕见。

Being punctual is another advantage of Swiss people. The pace of life is fast in modern society, people are required to be punctual so as to be efficient. The Swiss are believed to be the nation of being punctual. Being punctual is to respect others as well as respect ourselves. Even if the Swiss visit the relatives and friends, they will make an appointment first, including visiting the parents and children. All the public transportation is punctual. In Switzerland, people respect honesty and civilization. There are no conductors in the buses and the drivers do not check the tickets. Besides those who already have commute tickets, the other passengers buy bus tickets in the auto vending machines. The transportation department will send the conductors occasionally to check the tickets. Stealing a ride is rare there.

保持低调是瑞士人的一大特点，即使是百万富翁也很少张扬。很多瑞士人崇尚简单、自然的生活，他们将大部分金钱用于旅游、健身和参观博物馆。在瑞士，休息是最重要的权利，“会休息的人才会工作”这句话被瑞士人当成座右铭。如何安排每年的休假更是瑞士人的头等大事，许多人通常在前一年就开始计划如何安排日程。相较而言，瑞士人在吃穿上则较随便，即便在联合国和瑞士当地政府部门工作的官员们，除非参加正式活动，日常工作中的衣着并不总是西装革履。无论是在家里还是在餐馆，瑞士人绝不浪费。在朋友家做客时，主人从不劝酒、劝菜。

Keeping a low profile is another character of Swiss. Even the millionaires will not be flamboyant. Many Swiss pursue peaceful and natural life. They spend their money on traveling, body exercising and museums visiting. In Switzerland, rest is the most important right. "Those who know how to rest know how to work" is the motto for most Swiss. How to arrange the vacation every year is the first priority for Swiss. Many people have made a plan a year before. Comparatively, the Swiss pay less attention to their food and clothes. Even the officials who are working in the UN or local governments wear casually unless they participate in some formal activities. The Swiss never waste food. When treating the friends, the host will not overpersuade the friends to eat or drink.

瑞士人就餐时，讲究安静、祥和，忌大声喧哗，宜细嚼慢咽，忌狼吞虎咽。喝汤不能出声音，应用汤勺送入口中。吃意大利面时，要用叉子或筷子把面卷起来送入口中。喝咖啡时，切忌用小勺品尝咖啡，小勺只是用来搅拌奶油和糖的。瑞士有上好的佳酿。在正式场合，主人不劝酒，不豪饮，一般不喝烈性酒，但可以祝酒。不论何种场合，在瑞士人看来，把满杯酒一饮而尽的干杯不够文明。

When the Swiss have dinner, they eat in peace and quietly, swallow food slowly and make no noise when having soup. They use spoons to have soup and forks or chopsticks to eat pasta. When drinking coffee, instead of using the teaspoon to drink, people use the teaspoon to stir the cream and sugar. There are good wines in Switzerland. On the official occasions, the host will not talk the guests into drinking and people do not drink strong alcohol, but people cheer each other while drinking. In Swiss opinion, bottoms-up is not civilized on any occasion.

瑞士人赠花很有讲究，不习惯接受别人赠送 3 支红玫瑰，因为这带有浪漫的含义，但是以 1 支或 20 支作为礼物是可以接受的。他们珍视雪绒花，因为它象征至高无上的荣誉，瑞士人常将它作为最珍贵的礼物献给外宾，以表达友好、诚挚和崇敬。

There are certain rules when giving flowers in Switzerland. People are not used to accepting three red roses because of the romantic meaning, but one or twenty flowers are acceptable. They respect edelweiss for the flower represents the highest honor. The Swiss take the flower as the most precious gift to foreign guests to express friendliness, sincerity and respect.

（二）节庆风情

1. 巴塞尔狂欢节（Basel Carnival）

巴塞尔狂欢节从封斋节开始后的第 1 个星期一至星期三晚上延续 3 天，是瑞士最大的狂欢节，参加者过万。该节源自天主教的习俗。每年 3 月至 4 月的封斋节期间，信徒们本应封斋减食，但人们在此期间尽情欢乐，化装游行。

Basel Carnival, the largest carnival in Switzerland, begins on the first Monday after Fast to Wednesday with participants over 10,000. This festival originates from the Catholic customs. During the Fast from March to April, the disciples are supposed to reduce their food ingestion or stop eating, but now people enjoy themselves during the time, dress up and parade.

2. 伯尔尼洋葱节（Bern Onions Festival）

每年11月的第4个星期天是伯尔尼人如狂欢节一样欢乐的节日，节日的主角是洋葱。该节起源于15世纪伯尔尼每年有半个月的秋季集市。1405年，伯尔尼市发生了一场火灾，城市变为一片废墟，附近农民进城帮助市民重建家园。为答谢农民的帮助，农民被允许在城内出售自己种植的洋葱和蔬菜。到了晚上，人们就会跳舞、举办小丑表演等活动。这个节日传承至今，成为城市生活的一个亮点。

Bern Onions Festival falls on the fourth Sunday of November. It is just like another carnival. The leading role of this festival is onion. The origin of the festival started in the autumn fair lasting for half month in Bern in the 15th century. In 1405, there was a big fire in the Bern city. The whole city was destroyed. The farmers in the suburban areas came into city and helped the citizens rebuild their homes. To thank them, the onions and vegetables grown by the farmers were allowed to sell in the city. In the evening, people dance and clown performances are showed, etc. This festival has been passed down till today and becomes a sparkling spot in the city life.

三、主要旅游城市及景点

（一）伯尔尼（Bern）

伯尔尼是瑞士的首都，位于瑞士的中西部，是联邦政府和议会所在地。它是一座具有中世纪风貌的城市，老城区被联合国教科文组织列入世界文化遗产名录。伯尔尼的气候温和湿润，冬暖夏凉。居民主要讲德语。据传，伯尔尼城名源自800多年前，该地区常有熊出没，当地统治者用他狩猎的第一只动物——熊命名该座城市。德语中“熊”一词的发音是“拜尔”，后渐变为“伯尔尼”。后来，熊便成为伯尔尼的城徽，进而又变为伯尔尼州的标志，熊也就成为伯尔尼的吉祥物和伯尔尼人最喜爱的动物。伯尔尼城始建于12世纪，至18世纪建成现在的规模。伯尔尼市区街道中有许多街心泉，伯尔尼也被称为“泉城”。在瑞士人的眼中，伯尔尼是全国最漂亮的城市，有“花园村庄”的美称。当初为遮风避雨所建的拱形骑楼，长达6 000米，现在已成为知名的精品购物大街。瑞士享有“钟表王国”的美称，首都伯尔尼也以“表都”著称，钟表商店在伯尔尼随处可见。

Bern is the capital of Switzerland, located in the middle and east part, and is home of confederacy government and parliament. It is a city with the Middle Ages style. The old downtown entered the World Cultural Heritage Site of UNESCO. Bern has mild climate and it is warm in winter and cool in summer. The official language of Bern is German. It is said that the name of Bern was called over 800 years ago. At that time, bears appeared often in the area and the local governor named the city with his first hunted animal bear. The German pronunciation of the word “bear” gradually became into “Bern”. Later, the bear becomes the city badge and then the symbol of Bern State. Bear thus is the mascot and favorite animal of Bern people. Established in the 12th century, Bern was built up to the present scale in 18th century. There are many fountains on the streets, thus Bern is also called the “fountain city”. Swiss believe that Bern is the most beautiful city all over the country with the fame of “garden village”. The arched portico originally was built as rain shelter with 6 kilometers long and now it's the famous shopping street. The Switzerland is the "kingdom of clocks and watches", so is its capital. Clocks and watches shops are everywhere in the city.

（二）苏黎世（Zurich）

苏黎世是瑞士最大的城市，苏黎世州的首府和瑞士主要的商业和文化中心，也是全欧洲最富裕的城市。它位于阿尔卑斯山脉北部，苏黎世湖的西北端，利马特河同苏黎世湖的河口。苏黎世在克里特语里的意思是“水乡”。早在2 000年前就已形成村落，1218年成立城邦，1351年加入瑞士联邦。到了18、19世纪，苏黎世成为瑞士德语区的文化、教育和科技中心。苏黎世是瑞士银行业的代表城市和世界金融中心之一。瑞士联合银行、瑞信银行和许多私人银行都将总部设在苏黎世，其中半数以上是外国银行，故享有“欧洲百万富翁都市”的称号。国际足球联合会总部也设在苏黎世。苏黎世还是1916年出现的达达主义的发源地。苏黎世被誉为湖上的花园城，利马特河畔的圣母大教堂和苏黎世大教堂是苏黎世的重要标志。苏黎世连续多年被评为世界“最宜居城市”之一。

Zurich is the biggest city in Switzerland, the capital of canton of Zurich, the business and culture center in Switzerland as well as the richest city in Europe. It is located to the north of the Alps, northwest of Lake Zurich, and the river outlet of Lake Zurich and the Limmat. Zurich means "water town" in Crete language. 2,000 years ago, the villages were set up in this area. The city was built in 1218 and joined into Confederation in 1351. Zurich became the cultural, educational and scientific center of German-speaking nation in the 18th and 19th century. Zurich is the representative city of Swiss bank industry, and it's one of the world financial centers. Many banks set up their headquarters here, such as UBS, Credit Suisse and many other private banks, half of which are foreign banks. The city enjoys the name of "European Millionaire Metropolis". The FIFA sets up its head office here too. Zurich is also the origin place of Dadaism started in 1916. It enjoys the fame of garden city on lake. The Fraumünster and the Grossmünster along the Limmat are the important symbols of this city. Zurich has been selected as one of the best livable cities for several years.

（三）日内瓦（Geneva）

日内瓦是瑞士境内国际化程度最高的城市，是瑞士第二大城市，位于西欧最大的湖泊日内瓦湖畔，阿尔卑斯山脉和汝拉山脉近在眼前。其南、东、西三面都与法国接壤，许多地方的土地都是和法国共有的，自古是兵家必争之地。日内瓦的官方语言是法语和英语。日内瓦尤以国际组织所在地和国际会议城市著称于世，是继纽约之后联合国机构和国际组织最多的城市。亨利·杜南于1859年在日内瓦创立的国际红十字会及1864年由他发起签订的《日内瓦公约》，奠定了日内瓦在外交史上的重要地位。此后，联合国驻欧洲总部、世界卫生组织、世界知识产权组织、关税及贸易总协定、国际劳工组织、国际电信联盟等150多个世界性机构的总部都陆续在日内瓦设立。每年来这里的外国客人达260多万，日内瓦成为一个国际社交活动的大舞台。因此，人们把它称为“国际会议之城”。日内瓦湖光山色，四季皆具吸引力，湖上140米高的大喷泉是日内瓦的象征。日内瓦的名胜还包括花钟、艺术与历史博物馆、国际红十字会和红新月会博物馆和万国宫。

Geneva is a highly internationalized and the second largest city in Switzerland. It is located to the largest lake of west Europe (Lake Geneva) with the Alps and Jura Mountains in sight. It borders by France from south, east to the west. Many of its lands are shared with France, so it is a military important region. The official languages here are French and English. Geneva is famous for being the site of international organizations and conferences. Second only to New York, the city has the most UN and international organizations. Jean Henri Dunant established the International Committee of the Red Cross in 1895, and led and signed the *Geneva Conventions* in 1864, founding the important status of Geneva in foreign policy history. Later, over 150 world organizations set up their headquarters here, such as European Office of the UN, WHO, WIPO, GATT, ILO and ITU. Every year, the diplomatic agents coming here are more than any other cities. The foreign guests are over 2,600,000. Geneva becomes the international social stage with the name of "City of International Conference". The scenery in Geneva is also very attractive. The 140 meters high fountain over the lake is the symbol of Geneva. The famous scenic spots also include the Flower Clock, Art and Historic Museum, the International Red Cross and Red Crescent Museum, and Palace of Nations.

（四）洛桑（Lausanne）

洛桑是瑞士法语区城市，位于日内瓦湖北岸，与法国城市埃维昂莱班隔湖相望，北面是汝拉山脉。洛桑位于日内瓦东北约 50 千米处。它是瑞士联邦沃州和洛桑区首府。洛桑是奥林匹克总部所在地。由于国际奥委会总部和奥林匹克博物馆都设在这里，洛桑又被称为"奥林匹克之都"。国际奥委会是世界上最庞大的国际性组织，在全世界拥有亿万体育爱好者，各国竞相争取奥运会举办权。奥林匹克博物馆位于日内瓦湖畔，建成于 1993 年，是世界上唯一与奥林匹克运动有关的博物馆，这里展览了各种形式的资料和展品，介绍了奥林匹克运动的来源及发展史。洛桑是瑞士的文化和教育中心，这里的酒店学校和洛桑国际芭蕾舞比赛闻名于世。洛桑酒店管理学院有 100 年的历史，教学质量一直处于世界领先地位。许多五星级酒店的经理均出自该校，或在该校接受过培训。老城区的圣母大教堂被称为瑞士最美丽的教堂。

Lausanne is the French-speaking city in Switzerland, located at the north bank of Lake Geneva, opposite to the French city Évian-les-Bains, and north to Jura Mountains. Lausanne is located 50 kilometers away from the northeast of Geneva. It is the capital of the canon of Vaud and Lausanne of Swiss Confederation. Lausanne is home of the International Olympic Committee. Because the headquarters of International Olympic Committee and Olympic Museum are set up here, thus the city is also called "City of Olympic". The International Olympic Committee is the largest international organization with billions of sports fans. Every country competes for holding the Olympic Games. Located to the Lake Geneva, the Olympic Museum was established in 1993 and is the only one related with Olympic Games, exhibiting various materials and exhibits to introduce the origin and developing history of Olympic Games. Lausanne is the cultural and education center of Switzerland. The hospitality schools and Prix de Lausanne are famous in the world. The Lausanne Hotel School has 100 years history and good-quality education. Many managers of five-star hotels graduated from this school or were trained in the school. The Notre-Dame Cathedral in the old downtown is named the most beautiful church in Switzerland.

（五）卢塞恩（Lucerne）

卢塞恩位于瑞士中部，是卢塞恩州的首府，距离苏黎世1小时车程，距离日内瓦2.5小时车程。由于位于欧洲最重要的南北交通要道上，中世纪时这里就形成渔村，并建造了灯塔，为罗依斯河和卢塞恩湖上的船只导航，并得名“卢塞恩”，又称琉森，在拉丁语里的意思是“光明”。历经几个世纪，作为瑞士中部地区的中心，卢塞恩已发展成为金融、经济和文化交流中心，并完好地保存了中世纪的风貌，是瑞士最美丽的城市之一，世界十大旅游城市之一。大仲马曾形容卢塞恩是“世界上最美的蚌壳中的明珠”。俄国大文学家列夫·托尔斯泰曾写短篇小说《卢塞恩》。德国著名诗人歌德曾在此居住。音乐家瓦格纳在这里写出《纽伦堡的名歌手》《众神的黄昏》等著名乐章。卢塞恩的独特之处在于：美丽的湖光山色，古老的中世纪建筑，悠久的文化传统和现代的时尚生活相互映衬的优雅、柔和之美。卡佩尔桥和狮子纪念碑是必到的景点。卡佩尔桥是一座带有古老风貌的、带屋顶的木制廊桥，是这个城市的象征，曾于1993年被烧毁，现已重建。雕在山坡岩石上的狮子纪念碑是为纪念1792年瑞士雇佣兵786名壮士为保卫法国国王路易十六和皇后而全部牺牲的悲惨历史。自那之后，瑞士就废除了雇佣兵制度。美国作家马克·吐温来卢塞恩时，把狮子纪念碑誉为“世界上最悲壮和最感人的雕像”。此外，老城区到处是钟表店，展示了钟表王国的风采。

Lucerne is located in the middle of Switzerland, the capital of canton of Lucerne, one hour drive from Zurich and 2.5 hours from Geneva. Because this city is located on the important crossroad of south and north transportation, its history may be traced back to a fish village set up here in the Middle Ages. The lighthouse was also built at that time to guide the boats on Reuss River and Lucerne Lake. Lucerne means “brightness” in Latin language. As the center of central Switzerland, Lucerne has been developing for centuries and becomes the financial, economic and cultural communication center with complete Middle Ages style. It is one of the most beautiful cities in Switzerland and one of the top ten tourist cities in the world. Alexandre Dumas described Lucerne as “the pearl in the most beautiful shell in the world”. Russian writer Leo Tolstoy wrote the short story *Lucerne*. The famous German poet Goethe once lived here. Musician Wagner used to stay here and wrote the famous *The Mastersingers of Nuremberg* and *The Twilight of the Gods*. The specialty of Lucerne is elegant and gentle, reflecting in the beautiful scenery, ancient Middle Ages architectures, long history, traditional and modern lives. The scenic spots Chapel Bridge and the Lion Monument are not supposed to be missed by. The Chapel Bridge is an ancient style wooden bridge with roof which was burnt in 1993 but rebuilt. It is the symbol of this city. The Lion Monument carved in the mountain slope remembers the tragic history of 786 mercenary soldiers' deaths in 1792 to protect King Louis XVI of French and his queen. The Switzerland has abandoned the mercenary soldier system since then. The American writer Mark Twain once said the dying lions are the most tragic and touching carvings in the world. Besides, the clock and watch shops in the old downtown show the splendors of clock and watch kingdom.

四、旅游资讯

（一）美食

瑞士菜肴深受法国、意大利和德国菜肴的影响，法语区、德语区和意大利语区的饮食各具特色。瑞士各地菜肴中有三种基本食材：洋葱、土豆和胡萝卜。肉类以小牛肉，尤以生长不到一年的小牛肉为昂贵的食材，是国宴、大餐中不可或缺的上等菜肴。其次是猪肉，由于瑞士是内陆国家，因此多数人不吃鱼虾等海鲜产品。在法语区，最受人们喜爱的是干酪火锅和奶酪板烧（奶酪溶化制成的菜肴）；在德语区，最受人们欢迎的是香肠、烤肉和土豆饼；在意大利语区，最受人们欢迎的是风干牛肉片和火腿。瑞士菜肴注重的是精工细作，讲究的是色、香、味、形。就数量而言，他们所举办的宴请简单至极。在瑞士，一道冷盘、一道汤、一道主菜，再加上一道甜品，往往就是宴请客人时所上的全部菜肴。当重要宾客光临时，瑞士人有时还讲究待之以干奶酪、鸡蛋糊，这是传统的待客仪式之一。有人说，中国人不可一日无茶，而瑞士人则不可一日无酒。瑞士人饮酒很讲究，一般与奶酪火锅或烤奶酪搭配。一般吃红肉时饮红葡萄酒，吃鱼时饮白葡萄酒。宴请宾客时，菜单上不仅会列出各道菜、点心、咖啡的名字，而且必定单列出与佳肴匹配的葡萄酒名称、产地和年份，以此显示出宴请的品位和规格。瑞士拥有高品质的葡萄酒，瓦莱州、沃州和日内瓦州是瑞士三大葡萄酒产地，拉沃葡萄园还被联合国教科文组织列入世界文化遗产名录。

The food in Switzerland is influenced by French, Italian and German cuisine. Therefore, food in French, German and Italian speaking areas has its respective specialty. There are three basics in Swiss food: onion, potato and carrot. The expensive meat is the veal, especially that from the cattle younger than one-year old. It is the best and necessary dish in national feast or formal dinner. Then it is the pork. Because the Switzerland is the inner land country, most Swiss do not have seafood. In the French speaking area, people's favorites are cheese pot and Raclette. In the German speaking area, people's favorites are sausage, roasted meat and potato pies. In Italian speaking area, people's favorites are dry beef and ham. The Swiss cuisine pays attention to the cooking methods as well as the color, smell, taste and appearance. When it comes to the quantity, their dinner is quite simple. In Switzerland, a dinner includes just one appetizer, one soup, one main course and one dessert. When the VIP guest comes, the Swiss also serve the dry cheese and egg mixture—one of the traditional treatment. People say that Chinese can not live without tea while Swiss cannot live without wines. The Swiss pay a lot of attention to the drinking. They drink with cheese pot or roasted cheese. When they eat red meat, they drink red wine. When they eat fish, they drink white wine. On a feast, the menu shows not only the names of dishes, desserts, and coffee, but also the wines accompanied, including the names of wines, place of origin and production year so as to show the taste and standard of the feast. Switzerland has high-quality wines. The cantons of Valais, Vaud and Geneva are three major origin places for wines. The Lavaux Vineyard also is in the World Cultural Heritage Site list of UNESCO.

（二）购物及退税

手表：瑞士境内的钟表专卖店内，各式钟表琳琅满目。虽然如今手表已不再是少数人拥有的奢侈品，但那些高档手表依然是社会地位的象征。世界上享有盛誉的瑞士名表有百达翡丽、劳力士、欧米茄、斯沃琪、爱彼、江诗丹顿、萧邦、泰格豪雅、万国和伯爵等。

Watches: Kinds of watches and clocks are in the shops around the country. Nowadays, the watches are no longer the luxuries. Those high-class watches are still the symbol of social status. The famous brands include Patek Philippe, Rolex, Omega, Swatch, Audemars Piguet, Vacheron Constantin, Chopard, TAG Heuer, IWC and Piaget.

瑞士军刀：瑞士军刀是享誉全球的产品，因瑞士军方为士兵配备这类工具刀而得名。第二次世界大战结束后，成为美国军队的大宗采购品。这种军刀因为小巧轻便、制作工艺精良、功能多样、质量上乘，所以深受各国人的喜爱。比较著名的品牌有维氏和威戈。

Swiss army knife: Swiss army knife is another famous product in the country. It is called army knife because the Swiss government sends those knives to the soldiers. After the World War Ⅱ, the Americans purchased a lot of those knives. Because Swiss army knife is compact and super lightweight with sophisticated technology, multifunction and good quality, it is welcomed by clients from all the countries. The famous brands are Victorinox and Wenger.

巧克力：瑞士人均年消费 12 千克的巧克力，被称为“巧克力王国”。瑞士巧克力的种类丰富，价格适中，最适合作为礼物。牛奶巧克力是由丹尼尔·彼得于 1875 年发明的。瑞士的巧克力种类繁多，味道也是各种各样。其中，最有名的是瑞士莲巧克力，配料达 170 多种，这种采用上乘可可豆、可可脂制成的巧克力可谓巧克力中的极品。

Chocolate: The annual chocolate consumption in Switzerland is 12 kilograms each person, thus this country is known as the kingdom of chocolate. Various chocolates are with proper prices which is most suitable as a gift. Milk chocolate is invented in Switzerland by Daniel Peter in 1875. There are kinds of chocolates in Switzerland with different tastes. The most famous one is Lindt. It has over 170 ingredients for chocolates and adopts the best cocoa and cocoa butter to make the best chocolate.

瑞士的手表和军刀是中国游客必购商品。由于瑞士不是欧盟成员，因此游客在商店购物退税后拿到的退税单必须在出瑞士边境时到海关盖章寄回。在有免税标志或者免税商店购物一次性购物满 300 瑞士法郎以上的中国游客可以享受大约 7.5% 的退税。手续需要在离开瑞士前，在瑞士海关办理。以机场为例，在办完登机手续，持护照经过海关后，找有“Zoll”“Customs”或“Export Documents”标志的小亭子或柜台，工作人员审完单后会在单据上盖章。在有些大的钟表店，会为外国享受退税的游客提供特别的当场扣税服务，在这样的商店里，应退的税款已从购物款中扣除，但仍须在离开瑞士前履行上述程序，但只需将盖完章后的单据放到海关便可。没有享受当场退税的客人，在履行完上述盖章程序后，可以持单据到附近的现金退税柜台拿到退税款。

Swiss-made watches and army knife are Chinese favorites. Because Swiss is not the member of European Union, you must have the tax refund form stamped and mail back to the company at the customs office before you depart from Switzerland. Chinese tourists who buy more than 300 swiss francs in the shops with signs of “Tax Free” or in its membership shops may enjoy about 7.5% tax refund. The procedure must be dealt with before departing from the Switzerland at the customs. Take the airport for example:

after check in, people pass the Customs and see counters of "Zoll", "Customs" or "Export Documents". They may deal with the tax refund there. The tax form will be stamped after checked by the staff. Some large clocks and watches shops will deduct the tax right after the guests' shopping. People enjoy the tax refund directly in such kind of shops, but they still need to deal with the refund process. The process is very simple, just hand in the form with stamps to the customs. Guests who are not paid back the tax right away may receive the refund at the counters "Cash Refund" nearby after getting the form stamped.

（三）时差

瑞士属于东一时区，比中国慢7个小时，但从3月的最后一个星期天到10月的最后一个星期天采用夏令时制，因此与中国的时差为6个小时。

Switzerland belongs to the first east time zone, seven hours later than Chinese time. But it adopts the Daylight Saving Time from the last Sunday of March to the last Sunday of October. The Daylight Saving Time is six hours later than Chinese time.

思考练习

1. 经典旅游线路分析

瑞士深度10日游

第1天：北京——慕尼黑——苏黎世

乘坐德国汉莎航空公司客机，经慕尼黑转机前往被誉为瑞士"湖上的花园城"、瑞士最大城市的苏黎世。抵达后，入住酒店，倒时差。

第2天：苏黎世——圣加伦——达沃斯

早餐后，参观具有历史意义的林登霍夫公园、圣母大教堂，并在古朴的老城区鹅卵石铺成的街道漫步，欣赏苏黎世湖宁静的美。随后游览著名的班霍夫大街，这条1.4千米长的大街，两旁商店林立，装潢考究，陈列着名贵皮草、高级时装，以及手表、珠宝、古董、首饰、法国香水等，是追求顶级名牌者的圣地。随后乘车前往欧洲学术中心——圣加伦，欣赏16—18世纪的带有非常漂亮的彩绘凸窗的中产阶级住宅，游览当地标志性建筑大教堂及其修道院图书馆。随后乘车前往世界经济论坛举办地——达沃斯。

第3天：达沃斯——圣莫里茨

早餐后，前往旅游胜地、冰雪运动的天堂——圣莫里茨。之后在小镇游览，欣赏小镇特有的苏格拉费蒂花纹装饰的房屋，了解古老的恩嘎丁人独特的山居文化。这里有全瑞士第一盏路灯、第一家宾馆和建于12世纪的圣莫里茨斜塔。此外，街道上林立的高级酒店、名牌汇集的商店及世界贵族的聚集游览胜地，也显示了它的优雅和高贵。

第4天：圣莫里茨——蒂拉诺——卢加诺

早餐后，搭乘伯尔尼快车前往瑞士和意大利交接的小镇——蒂拉诺。窗外呈现给游客的是变化万千的景色。那截然不同的城镇和乡村景色也很吸引人。随后乘车穿越意大利前往“阳光之都”——卢加诺。欣赏从典型的阿尔卑斯风貌到充满了地中海风貌的沿途风光。在瑞士境内，卢加诺的阳光最多，在“退休后最想居住城市”的评选中，卢加诺位列榜首。它紧邻意大利，从城市气候、建筑风格到风俗民情，都是一副典型“意大利”的模样，在巍峨高山的怀抱和奇花异草的簇拥之中，这是一个在卢加诺湖畔散发着光明和活力的城市。

第5天：卢加诺——卢塞恩

早餐后，游览卢加诺老城区，参观圣玛丽·德里·安杰奥利教堂，它是15世纪时的修道院，可以看到16世纪绘画巨匠伯纳迪诺·卢伊尼亲手绘制的壁画。卢加诺还有著名的步行街Via Nassa，这里将瑞士的品质和名牌以及意大利的周到服务集于一身，琳琅满目的珠宝衬托出瑞士手表和军刀等商品的华贵。随后乘车前往瑞士中部第一度假胜地——卢塞恩。

第6天：卢塞恩——因特拉肯

早餐后，游览卢塞恩城区，这里拥有许多15世纪彩绘壁画的建筑与搭有高塔的城墙，具有中世纪所特有的优美、和谐及生命力。8世纪建城的卢塞恩在中世纪曾是瑞士的首都，是到瑞士不可错过的地方。参观著名的狮子纪念碑，整座纪念碑是雕刻在整块崖壁上的石像，意在祈求世界和平。之后领略建于14世纪、风格独特的卡佩尔桥及群山环抱、风景如画的卢塞恩湖。随后乘车前往坐落在少女峰间的美丽小镇——因特拉肯。

第7天：因特拉肯

早餐后，游览这座美丽的湖边小镇——因特拉肯。因特拉肯是伯尔尼高地的中心，其位于图恩湖及布里恩茨湖之间．拉丁文原意是“两湖之间”。因特拉肯是著名的维多利亚式度假胜地。在维多利亚时代，这里已经是向往湖光山色的人士所倾心的一座城镇了。如今它作为少女峰地区的门户而闻名，站在镇中心的何维克街的一片宽广绿地上，就可以清楚地远望美丽的少女峰。

第8天：因特拉肯——采尔马特

早餐后，乘车前往位于“阿尔卑斯山的象征”——马特宏峰脚下的采尔马特，这里因为禁止机动车进入，所以成为世界上空气最清新的城市之一，田园诗般的山间小镇定会给您一种前所未有的恬静安详的感受。乘坐欧洲最高的露天齿轨火车升至海拔3 012米的戈尔内格拉特观景台，眺望海拔4 478米、“浪费欧洲人胶卷最多的地方”——马特宏峰。这里未曾受过人为破坏的冰川拥有独特的自然景致，在皑皑群峰之间，享受极致的阿尔卑斯风情。

第9天：采尔马特——蒙特勒——日内瓦

早餐后，乘车前往日内瓦湖区的观光城市蒙特勒，参观代表瑞士的水上古城堡——西庸城堡，它是瑞士最古老的城堡之一。随后前往联合国总部所在地——日内瓦，游览日内瓦市区，这里汇集了包括联合国驻欧洲总部、国际红十字会总部、世界贸易组织总部在内的众多国际机构。以大教堂为中心的日内瓦老城，其古朴的建筑向世人展示着过去岁月中的繁华。

第10天：日内瓦——慕尼黑——北京

乘坐德国汉莎航空公司客机，经慕尼黑转机返回北京，结束愉快的旅程。

分析： 这条经典旅游线路的主要旅游景点与行程特色，以及适合旅游的人群。

2. 案例分析

[案例1] 留学生小乐到瑞士洛桑酒店管理学院学习酒店管理，租住在老城区的一套公寓房内。一个周末，小乐同学聚会回来已是半夜12点，他习惯于睡前洗澡，由于兴奋，他一边洗澡一边大声哼着家乡的小调，结果还没等澡洗完，邻居就来敲门投诉了。原来不少瑞士人喜欢早上上班前冲澡让自己精力充沛地投入到一天的工作中，而晚上10点以后洗澡，水声会影响邻居休息。小乐觉得挺委屈的，难道在自家洗澡也会妨碍别人？你觉得呢？

[案例2] 留学生小维到瑞士苏黎世学习，租住在老城区的一套公寓房内。小维习惯每天洗衣服并将衣服晒在室外，晚上闻着阳光的味道入睡是她从小养成的习惯。由于房间里没有阳台，小维就把衣服还有被子晒在楼下院子的树杈上，结果没多久，就有邻居来投诉了。他们认为这样做不雅观，会影响环境的美观。他们一般使用烘干机来烘干衣服。小维觉得不可理解，你如何看待？

3. 练一练

说到瑞士，大家会想到阿尔卑斯山的马特洪峰、艾格峰、少女峰。瑞士不仅拥有雄伟壮丽的高山，而且拥有约1 484个湖泊、120多条冰河，无数瀑布、峡谷、山洞、绵延数千米的河流，还是四大著名航道的发源地。因此，瑞士被称为“欧洲的水库”，2019年瑞士的旅游主题是“徒步瑞士，回归自然”。试分析瑞士的旅游资源，并以此为主题写一篇导游词。

第六节　西班牙

一、国家概况

（一）地理环境

西班牙王国，简称西班牙，位于欧洲西南部的伊比利亚半岛。东临地中海，北濒比斯开湾，东北有比利牛斯山和法国、安道尔交界，西邻葡萄牙和大西洋，南部的直布罗陀海峡扼地中海和大西洋航路的咽喉要道，与非洲大陆的摩洛哥隔海相望（最窄处只有14千米）。西班牙的国土还包括在大西洋中的加那利群岛，地中海的巴利阿里群岛以及位于北非的休达和梅利利亚两块景色别致的领地。西班牙是南欧一颗璀璨的明珠。

The Kingdom of Spain, briefly Spain, is located in the Iberian Peninsula of Southwestern Europe. It is bordered by the Mediterranean Sea in the east and the Bay of Biscay in the north. It borders with Portugal and the Atlantic Ocean in the west, France and Andorra in the northeast, characterized by Pyrenees Mountains. In the south, it borders with the Strait of Gibraltar, which is the thoroughfare of the Mediterranean Sea and the Atlantic Ocean. It lies opposite to Morocco of African continent (with the narrowest distance of 14 kilometers). Its territory also includes the Canary Islands in the Atlantic Ocean, Balearic Islands in the Mediterranean Sea and the beautiful Ceuta and Melilla in the North Africa. Spain is known as the pearl in Southern Europe.

西班牙占伊比利亚半岛的 85%，88% 的边界均临海。西班牙境内多山，是欧洲海拔仅次于瑞士的高山国家，全国 35% 的地区海拔 1 000 米以上，平原仅占 11%。西班牙中部的梅塞塔高原是一个被山脉环绕的闭塞高原，约占全国面积的 60%。北部有东西走向的连绵不断的比利牛斯山。

Spain occupies 85% of Iberian Peninsula with 88% boundaries on the sea. It has many mountains and ranks right after the mountainous country Switzerland with 35% of its territory above elevation of 1,000 meters and 11% plain. The Meseta Central in the central Spain is around by mountains, occupying 60% of the national territory. In the north is the Pyrénées Mountains heading east.

伊比利亚半岛受大西洋气候、欧洲大陆气候和地中海气候的影响，分为三大气候带。西班牙气候宜人，终年阳光充足，有“太阳王国”之称，已成为各国游客特别是缺少阳光的西欧、北欧人旅游甚至定居的首选地之一。

The Iberian Peninsula is affected by three climates: Atlantic climate, European continental climate and Mediterranean climate. Spain has enjoyable climate with sunshine all the year round, known as sunny kingdom. It has been the first choice of traveling even settling down for tourists from different countries, especially those from Western and Northern Europe where sunshine is something very scarce.

（二）人文概况

1. 历史

公元前 7 世纪开始，迦太基和罗马一直争夺对西班牙的控制。公元前 19 年，奥古斯都控制了西班牙，罗马人的占领给西班牙带来巨大的影响，整个半岛的政治、经济、语言都发生了变化。公元前 5 年，哥特人入侵西班牙。公元 711 年，穆斯林统治西班牙，阿拉伯文化得到传播。公元 8 世纪，基督教开始收复家园的“收复失地运动”。1492 年，阿拉伯统治者被赶出半岛。1512 年，西班牙完成统一。15 世纪末，西班牙已成为殖民大国，在美洲的殖民统治使西班牙获利不少，西班牙帝国成为当时欧洲最强大的国家。18 世纪，君主王位战争使西班牙失去了比利时、卢森堡和米兰。19 世纪拿破仑入侵，西班牙全国都在进行反抗斗争，最终失去美洲殖民地。1936 年，西班牙内战爆发。1939 年 3 月，佛朗哥将军的民族主义阵线占领马德里。1939 年 4 月，佛朗哥任国家元首和政府首脑，实行独裁统治达 36 年之久。1947 年，西班牙宣布为君主国，佛朗哥自任国家元首和政府总理。1975 年 11 月，佛朗哥病逝，胡安·卡洛斯一世登基。

Since the 7th century BC, the Roman had continued to fight against Carthaginians to control Spain. Augustus ruled Spain at last in 19 BC. Great changes were brought to Spain in the political system, the economy and the language under the rule of Roman Emperor. The gothic tribe occupied Spain in 5 BC. In 711, the Muslim conquered most of Spain and thus Arabic culture was brought into the civil life. In the 8th century, the Christian started the Reconquista and in 1492 the Arabic conqueror was driven away from the Peninsula. In 1512, the Spain completed the unity. At the end of the 15th century, Spain became the colonist empire who benefited from the colony of America and became the strongest country in Europe. In the 18th century, because of the War of the Spanish Succession, Spain lost the control of Belgium, Luxembourg and Milan. In the 19th century, Napoléon invaded Spain, the country struggled against the invaders in the whole century and led to the loss of America colony. In 1936, the civil war occurred. In March of 1939, the nationalist forces occupied Madrid under the leader of General Franco who became the chief of the government and the country in April 1939 and started his 36 years of the dictatorial regime. Spain declared a monarchy in 1947 and Franco appointed himself as head of state and the prime minister. After his death in November 1975, Juan Carlos Ⅰ became the king of Spain and head of the country.

2. 经济

西班牙虽然在世界上属中等发达国家，市场经济发达，但在欧盟人均国民生产总值中处于平均线以下。西班牙的制造业、旅游业发达，是世界上最大的造船国之一，也是最大的汽车生产国之一，却仅拥有少量的民族品牌。西班牙是欧盟水果、蔬菜的主要生产国和出口国之一，橄榄油产量和出口量居世界首位，柑橘年产量居世界第四位、年出口量居世界第一位，葡萄酒产量居世界第三位。畜牧业是西班牙的传统产业，肉制品产量居欧盟第二位。西班牙是渔业大国，在欧盟中居首位。水产品消费量仅次于日本，居世界第二位。制鞋业是西班牙传统的手工业，十分发达，西班牙是欧洲第二大制鞋国。旅游业是西班牙三大支柱产业之一。在希腊神话中，西班牙是大力神的金苹果园。今天的西班牙以其绮丽风光、多元文化和异域风情的无穷魅力每年吸引了约 8 000 多万国际游客，成为世界第二大旅游国。西班牙每年的旅游收入及入境旅游人数均列世界前茅。世界旅游组织总部设在马德里。

Though Spain is ranked as the middle developed country in the world, and has a developed system of market economy, its GDP is below the average of European Union. Spain has a developed industry of manufacturing and tourism. Spain is one of the biggest countries manufacturing automobile and vessels but with fewer national brands. Spain is also the main producer and exporter of fruits and vegetables. Its output and export of olive oil ranks the first, orange production ranks the fourth and annual export ranks the first, and the wine production ranks the third in the world. The animal husbandry is its traditional industry with meat production the second place in the European Union. Spain is also a country of fishing, ranking the first, in the European Union. The consumption of aquatic products is just behind Japan, winning the second place in the world. Shoe making is the traditional handicraft industry in Spain, which gets the second place in Europe. The tourism is one of the three pillar industries in Spain. Spain is the gold apple garden of Hercules in the Greek legends. The beautiful scenery, multiple cultures and exotic style of Spain attract about over 80 million international visitors every year, which makes Spain the second tourism country in the world. The income from the tourism industry and inbound tourists go among the top of the world. The headquarter of UNWTO is in Madrid.

3. 社会文化

西班牙人口约 4 695 万，民族比较单一，由一个主体民族和若干少数民族构成。其中主体民族是卡斯蒂利亚人（即西班牙人），约占人口的 73%。少数民族主要有加泰罗尼亚人，约占人口的 15%，主要居住在巴塞罗那及周边地区；加里西亚人约占人口的 7%，主要居住在西大西洋沿岸；巴斯克人约占 5%，主要居住在北边靠近法国的边境地区。在西班牙境内，还生活着约 1 万名吉卜赛人。西班牙政府以前不愿承认他们为境内合法的少数民族，但近年来，政府专门拨出款项为他们建造房屋，使其安居乐业。西班牙的官方语言为西班牙语。96% 的居民信奉天主教。首都为马德里。

The population of Spain is 46.95 million. The nationality in Spain is quite simple. The country consists of one major ethnic and several ethnic groups. The major ethnic is Castilians with 73% population and the ethnic groups include Catalan people with 15% population, living in Barcelona and around, Galician with 7% population, living along the west Atlantic Ocean, Basque with 5% population, living near France in the north. There are about 10,000 Gypsies in Spain. Previously, the Spanish government was not willing to admit them the legal residents, but recently the government specially allocated fund to build up houses for them. The official language of Spain is Spanish. 96% residents believe in Catholicism. Its capital is Madrid.

西班牙的 40 多处历史古迹被联合国教科文组织列入世界文化遗产名录，居世界第三。从 1.5 万年前阿尔塔米拉洞窟形象逼真的动物壁画到毕加索震撼世界的名画《格尔尼卡》，从仍在使用的、古老的洞穴式住房到圣家族大教堂、米拉之家等如梦如幻的超现实主义建筑，西班牙拥有灿烂的文化。

More than 40 historic places in Spain are named the World Cultural Heritage Site by UNESCO, ranking the third in the world. Spain owns splendid culture, such as the vivid animal cave paintings in the Cave of Altamira 15,000 years ago, *Guernica* by Picasso, the old cave house and surrealistic constructions like Sagrada Familia or Casa Milà.

古西班牙文化深受古罗马和阿拉伯文化的影响。西班牙各个城市矗立着许多古罗马时期的建筑。10 世纪时就建有收藏 30 万册图书的图书馆，众多学者把阿拉伯文、希伯来文和拉丁文的著作翻译成西班牙文。西班牙文学在世界上占有重要的地位。约写于 1140 年的《熙德之歌》是流传至今比较完整的史诗。14 世纪中叶就出现了骑士小说。15 世纪受意大利人文主义思想的影响，世俗小说开始流行。《塞莱斯蒂娜》是世俗小说的代表作，在西班牙文学史上的地位仅次于《堂・吉诃德》。西班牙文学的黄金时期是 16 世纪，巅峰之作是塞万提斯・萨维德拉的《堂・吉诃德》，剧作家洛佩・德・维加一生写了《羊泉村》等 1 800 部作品。

The culture of ancient Spain was influenced deeply by the Ancient Rome and Arabian culture. The ancient buildings passed down from Roman period stand along the streets in the cities. The library was established in the 10th century and contained more than 300,000 books. Lots of articles in Arabian, Hebrew and Latin were translated into Spanish. Spanish literary also has an important role in the world. *El Cantar de Mio Cid* written around 1140 AD is an almost complete epic. The tales of the knight appeared in the middle of the 14th century. Influenced by the humanism of Italy, the secular fiction became popular in the 15th century. *La Celestina* was the greatest work in Spanish literature and was just ranked after *Don Quixote* in Spanish Literature. The golden era of Spanish literature appeared in the 16th century. The peak work is *Don Quixote* written by Miguel de Cervantes Saavedra. Lope de Vega, the dramatist, finished 1,800 works including *Fuente Ovejuna*.

知识拓展

堂·吉诃德

一提起西班牙，人们就会想到塞万提斯。他开创了现代小说的先河，他的不朽名著《堂·吉诃德》自1605年问世以来，已被译成70多种文字，仅中文版本就有几十个，是继《圣经》后译本最多的书籍。塞万提斯是文艺复兴时期的西班牙小说家、剧作家、诗人，1547年出生，1616年在马德里逝世。他被誉为西班牙文学史上最伟大的作家。评论家们称《堂·吉诃德》是文学史上的第一部现代小说，也是世界文学的瑰宝之一。《堂·吉诃德》的背景是那个早没有骑士的年代，主角堂·吉诃德幻想自己是个骑士，因而做出种种匪夷所思的行为，最终从梦幻中苏醒过来。这部小说原是反讽当时流行的骑士传奇小说，嘲讽那些不自量力、脱离现实、自以为是的人，其象征意义不知不觉渐渐转化，如今已多被用来指那些勇敢坚持自己的理想、敢于挑战社会不合理现象、不顾众人嘲笑仍坚持一己信念的人。堂·吉诃德的形象在今天仍有它的意义。通过《堂·吉诃德》，塞万提斯描写了西班牙人性格的精髓，无论是斗牛士、传教士，还是诗人、画家，每一个人都有堂·吉诃德的影子。

西班牙的绘画艺术在世界上也成就非凡，从16世纪以来就涌现了许多天才画家。在世界先锋派绘画中，多位西班牙画家占有举足轻重的地位，如毕加索。他于1909年创立了立体派，翻开了20世纪现代绘画的第一页，是20世纪世界上最伟大的画家之一。他最珍贵的作品《格尔尼卡》现珍藏于马德里的索菲亚王后国家艺术中心博物馆。此外，西班牙著名的画家还有萨尔瓦多·达利、胡安·米罗等，对世界现代艺术的发展都有重要贡献。而在世界建筑史上，西班牙也占有重要地位。建筑家安东尼奥·高迪无疑是建筑史上极其重要的人物。他的许多作品如今都已成为重要景点。

The Spanish painting arts are also very important in the world. There have been lots of talented artists since the 16th century. In the Avant-garde paintings field, many Spanish painters are listed, such as

Pablo Picasso who is the greatest among all. He created cubism in 1909, opening the first page of the 20th century's modern painting. His precious painting *Guernica* now is in the Museum of the Queen Reina Sofia National Center in Madrid. Besides, the famous Spanish painters also include Salvador Dali and Joan Miró. In the history of world architecture, Spain plays an important role too. Antonio Gaudi is undoubtedly one of the most important masters. Many of his works become important scenic spots nowadays.

知识拓展

高迪和毕加索

巴塞罗那以独特的建筑艺术著称于世，城市几乎所有最负盛名的建筑物都出自一人之手。这位被称为巴塞罗那建筑史上最前卫、最疯狂的建筑艺术家，名叫安东尼奥·高迪。他是塑性建筑流派的代表人物，属于新艺术建筑风格。许多人正是因为高迪的建筑而认识了巴塞罗那。安东尼奥·高迪为世界留下了古埃尔公园、米拉之家、巴特罗之家、圣家族大教堂等18处不朽的建筑杰作，其中有17处被西班牙列为国家级文物，7处被联合国教科文组织列入世界文化遗产名录。这位被誉为“上帝的建筑师”的天才大师的建筑被认为是20世纪世界上最具原创精神、最重要的建筑，是现代建筑艺术的代表。东方伊斯兰风格、新哥特主义以及现代主义、自然主义等诸多元素被“高迪化”后，都在他的建筑中得到完美呈现。在高迪的作品中，大量使用彩色瓷砖和锻铁栏杆等来诠释神话和大自然的主题，同时衍生出“非直线”的建筑风格。这些建筑呈现的是万物的生机、自然的生命和对神的虔诚。巴塞罗那是安东尼奥·高迪作品的露天博物馆，被誉为“高迪之城”。

毕加索是西班牙伟大的现代派画家，也是世界上最具影响力的现代艺术大师之一。他是现代艺术的开创者，立体派的创始人。他擅长以各种线条勾勒人物和动物，以鲜艳的色彩来触动人们的心灵，在抽象的构图中展现自己的思想和理念。他在绘画艺术上无可比拟的成就为西班牙带来了巨大的世界声誉。毕加索从19世纪末就开始从事艺术活动，一直持续到20世纪70年代。他一生的绘画风格有过数次改变。早期绘画近似表现派的主题，较为抽象，而后开始吸收原始艺术手法。1915以后画风一度转入写实。1930年后又明显地倾向于超现实主义。第二次世界大战前后，他的画风开始趋向于立体主义、现实主义和超现实主义风格的结合，着重表现痛苦、受难和兽性等与战争有关的主题。在艺术生涯的晚期，毕加索制作了大量的雕塑和陶器等，亦有杰出的成就。他的作品对现代西方艺术流派有很大的影响，代表作品有《格尔尼卡》《和平鸽》等。毕加索是位多产画家。据统计，他的作品总计近37 000件。跟一生穷困潦倒的凡·高不同，毕加索的一生辉煌之至，他是有史以来第一位亲眼看到自己的作品被收藏进卢浮宫的画家。1999年12月，法国一家报纸进行了一项民意调查，毕加索以40%的高票当选为20世纪最伟大的十位画家之首。对于作品，毕加索说：“我的每一幅画中都装有我的血，这就是我的画的含义。”

二、民俗风情

（一）礼仪禁忌

悠久的历史和多元文化的交汇使西班牙人具有鲜明的个性：腓尼基人的务实、希腊人的理性、犹太人的精神至上、罗马人的直率、西哥特人的一丝不苟、阿拉伯人的激情、法兰西人的时尚以及拉丁人的浪漫和热情，这些造就了西班牙人热情奔放、乐观向上、无拘无束、助人为乐、诙谐、健谈的性格特点。无论走到哪里，只要遇上熟人或朋友，甚至有时是素不相识的过路人，他们总会打招呼、问好。西班牙人的见面礼节一般采取握手、亲吻和拥抱三种方式。两人初次见面时会握手。一般而言，长幼之间，由长辈先伸手；上下级之间，由上级先伸手；宾主之间，由主人先伸手；男女之间，由女士先伸手。男士握手时不能握得太紧，如对方无握手之意，可点头说“你好”致意。熟人之间，朋友之间，同事之间，亲属之间，大多以亲吻、拥抱为主。最常见的是男女相互施亲吻礼。拥抱也是在西班牙人相见时常见的礼节。西班牙人的姓名常有三四节，前一二节为本人姓名，倒数第二节为父姓，最后一节为母姓。通常口头称呼父姓。

The long history and multi-cultures create Spanish people's distinguished characteristics: the Phoenician pragmatism, Greek rationality, Hebrew spirit-oriented, Roman frankness, Visigoth squareness, Arabian passion, French fashion and Latin romance and enthusiasm. Those characteristics make Spanish people open and enthusiastic, optimistic, unconstraint, willing to help others, humorous and talkative. Wherever you go, the Spanish people greet you with “Hola” no matter who you are: acquaintance, friends or even just passers-by. There are three types of greeting—handshaking, kissing and hugging. When two people meet each other for the first time, they shake hands. Generally speaking, the elder generation, the superior in companies, the host and the lady initiates the handshaking. Gentleman may not hold the hand very tightly. If the other one has no intention for handshaking, you may just nod and say “Hola”. People kiss and hug among acquaintances, friends, colleagues and relatives. The commonest etiquette is the kissing between males and females. Hugging is another usual way to greet each other. The Spanish name usually has three to four parts. The first one or two parts are the name. The third part is father's family name and the last part is mother's family name. People usually call each other by the father's family name.

传统的西班牙人非常看重自己的空闲时间，家庭对西班牙人来说是最重要的，他们通常要与自己的家人共度休闲时光。这种对待生活的态度贯彻始终，而不单指假期。在他们的生活中，家庭聚餐是一种美德而不是奢侈。对西班牙人来说，每天的生活琐事，如在市场闲谈、与家人共进晚餐或是看望朋友等，都是很重要的。西班牙人很会享受生活，终年节日不断，并想方设法使假期延长。每年 8 月，多数西班牙人会外出旅游、度假，找人办事很不容易。西班牙人一般晚睡晚起，早上 9 点上班，中午 2 点午餐后一直午休至下午近 5 点才开始工作。不少商店中午会打烊休息。晚餐通常在晚上 9 点以后。大部分餐馆晚上 9 点半才开门营业，晚上 11 点才是最热闹的。

The traditional Spanish people think highly of their spare time. The family is the most important to them. They like to spend time with families. This attitude is carried out all over their lives, not only in the vacations. In their lives, the family dinner is not a luxury but a virtue. Daily routines such as chatting in the market, dining with family, visiting friends are very important to Spanish people. They enjoy their lives with continuous festivals all around the year. Meanwhile, they try their best to prolong the vacations. Spanish people are out for traveling or vacations in August every year. It is hard to get things done in this month. Spanish people sleep late and get up late. In the morning, they go to work at 9:00 am. They have lunch at 2:00 pm then take a rest until 5:00 pm. Many shops are closed at noon. The dinners often start after 9:00 pm in the evening. Most restaurants open at 9:30 pm. 11:00 pm is the rush hour for Spanish people.

西班牙是一个受天主教影响很深的国家，上帝是西班牙人的精神支柱。西班牙也是一个极为重视礼仪的古老欧洲国家。在西班牙人家中做客，哪怕是熟人、朋友、亲属之间，都需事先约定。如果不事先打招呼，就贸然到主人家里或办公室，是一种失礼行为。西班牙人赴约时一般会迟到一会儿，尤其是应邀赴宴时。西班牙人只有在参加斗牛比赛时才严守时间，但客人应当守时，即便对方晚到，主人也不应责怪。参加宴会的服装宜正式、保守。西班牙人喜欢谈论政治，但不要把西班牙政治和他国政治进行比较。西班牙人也喜欢谈论体育和旅行，但避免谈论宗教、家庭和工作。不要说有关斗牛的坏话，西班牙人具有强烈的民族自豪感。中国游客拜访当地人时，可以赠送给对方具有中国民族特色的小礼物，也可携带一瓶葡萄酒、巧克力或鲜花。如果送花最好是石榴花，因为石榴花是西班牙国花。不要送大丽花和菊花，因为这两种花和死亡有关。收到礼物后，西班牙人习惯当面打开包装并表示感谢。在任何场合，女士优先是惯例。在宴会桌旁，男士要为身旁的女士挪椅，离开时为女士披上外套。

The Catholicism has rooted deeply in Spain. God is Spanish people's spiritual pillar. Spain is also an old European country that pays a lot attention to etiquette. To be a guest in Spain, one should make an appointment first no matter what is among acquaintances, friends or relatives. It will be considered rude if people fail to make an appointment and go to others' home or office. It is common for Spanish people being a little late for a date, especially for a banquet. Spanish people are on time only when it is a bullfight. The guests are required to be punctual, but the host will not blame the lateness as well. The clothes should be formal and conservative. Spanish people love to talk about politics, but do remember not to compare the politics of other countries with Spain. They often talk about sports and traveling, while avoid religion, families and work. Do not speak evil about bullfight. Spanish people have strong patriotic feelings for their country. It is appropriate to bring some Chinese style gifts or wine, chocolates, flowers when visiting the locals. It is better to bring pomegranate for it is the national flower. Giving dahlia or chrysanthemum is a bad idea because these two types of flowers are related to death in Spain. Spanish people have the habit to open the gift and give appreciation when receiving it. Lady-first is always the routine. For example, the gentleman is supposed to move the chair for the lady as well as help lady put on the coat when leaving.

西班牙人的穿着相对比较随意，特别是在休闲场所以舒适为主，但在正式社交场合，男士通常穿样式保守的西装，内穿白衬衫，打领带。他们喜欢黑色，因此一般穿黑色的皮鞋。职场女性喜欢穿职业装（或套装），尽量避免穿裤装（她们更钟情于裙装）。西班牙人去剧院看演出或去赌场时，也会穿正装，而在外出旅游观光时，会穿休闲服装。参观教堂等相关场所时，要着装整齐。西班牙女性外出时，大多会戴耳环。

Spanish people like casual clothes especially in casual occasion, but they dress formally on the formal social occasions with conservative suits, as white shirts and ties. They like black, thus they usually wear black shoes. Ladies like to wear professional suits (or two piece set) and avoid the trousers (they prefer skirts). Spanish people wear formal clothes when they go to the theatre or casino, while wear informal clothes when traveling. You should pay attention to your clothes when you visit the church or the similarities. The Spanish women wear earrings when they are out.

西班牙的传统服饰就像西班牙人的性格一样，热情开朗，有着丰富且强烈的色彩对比。较为人所熟知的是南部安达卢西亚地区的弗拉明戈舞者身着色彩艳丽、大波浪裙摆及袖口的传统服饰。这些地区独特的地方服饰以及有着浓厚民族色彩的音乐，形成了非常吸引人的西班牙传统舞蹈。

The traditional Spanish clothes are just like their characteristics — enthusiasm with strong color contrasts. It is well-known that the Flamenco dancers in south Andalusia wear the bright colorful traditional clothes with expansion skirts and sleeves. The special local clothes and the fork music form the attractive Spanish traditional dance.

知识拓展

弗拉明戈

人们总是把吉卜赛人与看手相占卜算命、乘大篷车浪迹天涯联系在一起。然而，500多年前从印度北部迁徙到西班牙的吉卜赛人却与当地的安达卢西亚人一起创造了西班牙国粹——弗拉明戈。15世纪，吉卜赛人背井离乡，大批移居至安达卢西亚，那里是阿拉伯、希腊、罗马、犹太、拜占庭、拉丁音乐的大熔炉，他们带去的印度歌舞的特有风格融入了安达卢西亚异彩纷呈的音乐世界，弗拉明戈由此诞生。弗拉明戈是指西班牙安达卢西亚地区吉卜赛人的音乐和舞蹈。它来源于吉卜赛、安达卢西亚、阿拉伯以及西班牙犹太人的民间歌曲和印度的宗教圣歌，融合了浓厚的吉卜赛文化元素，并带有非洲、拉美特点，是集歌唱、舞蹈、器乐于一体的综合表演艺术。从19世纪起，吉卜赛人开始在小酒馆里跳舞，并以此为业。构成弗拉明戈三大灵魂的是吉他、舞蹈和歌唱，歌手唱着传统的乐曲，吉他手伴着歌手的演唱弹奏，而舞者可以和着节奏即兴舞上一段，用脚踏出扣人心弦的旋律。作为西班牙国内最具代表性的艺术流派和当今世界最富感染力的流行舞种，弗拉明戈是吉卜赛文化和西班牙安达卢西亚民间文化的结合，与斗牛并称为西班牙两大国粹。吉卜赛人总爱说："弗拉明戈就在我们的血液里。"今天，弗拉明戈早已走出西班牙国门，蜚声世界，并在拉美、美国、日本等地迅速推广。弗拉明戈有60多种不同风格，演员少则几人，多则数十人。无论是唱、跳还是弹，弗拉明戈舞者都是在用心灵深处最真挚、最强烈的感情在演绎，宣泄对历史沧桑、贫困逆境的忧郁悲愤，抒发对爱的狂热激情。

（二）节庆风情

1. 圣费尔明节（San Fermin）

每年7月6日至14日是西班牙东北部纳瓦拉自治区首府潘普洛纳市的圣费尔明节，以惊心动魄的奔牛闻名世界。圣费尔明节又称为奔牛节。节日期间，潘普洛纳市人口从平时的19万猛增至280万。圣费尔明节的奔牛活动的起源与西班牙斗牛传统有直接关联。惊险的奔牛活动始于1591年，从中世纪节庆期间的集市斗牛逐渐演变而来。牧民在将公牛从养牛场赶往城里斗牛场的过程中发现牛有追人的习性，于是一种娱乐游戏应运而生。1923年，美国著名作家欧内斯特·海明威首次来到潘普洛纳观看奔牛活动并创造了著名小说《太阳照样升起》，他在作品中详细描述了奔牛节，奔牛节因而声名远播。1954年，海明威获得诺贝尔文学奖后，西班牙奔牛节更是名声大噪。

Every year, from July 6th to 14th is the Festival of Pamplona City in Navarre in northeast Spain—San Fermin. It is famous for the running of the bulls in the world, thus this festival is also called Bull Running Festival. During the festival, the population of Pamplona increase to 2.8 million from 0.19 million in common days. The origin of bull running is closely related to Spanish bullfight. The race between men and bulls started in 1591, and was evolved from the street bullfight in the Middle Ages. When the cowman drove the bulls to the bullfight area from the cattle breeding area, they found the bull's habit—chasing people, thus a game came into the world. In 1923, American author Emest Miller Hemingway came to Pamplona and watched the bull running. Later, he wrote the famous novel *The Sun Also Rises*. In this novel, he described the festival in detail and made it known by the world. In 1954, Hemingway won the Noble Prize in Literature. Consequently, the Bull Running Festival becomes more famous.

知识拓展

斗牛

斗牛（Bullfight）被认为是西班牙的“国粹”和“国技”，西班牙素有“斗牛王国”之称。一直以来，西班牙的斗牛受到了世界公众的注目和赞赏，如今更是西班牙旅游业的重要项目。西班牙斗牛历史由来已久。在阿尔达米拉岩洞中发现的新石器时代的岩壁画中，就有人与牛搏斗的描绘。西班牙斗牛起源于西班牙的古代宗教活动（杀牛供神祭品）。13世纪西班牙国王阿方索十世将这种祭神活动演变为赛牛表演（真正的斗牛表演则始于18世纪中叶）。现今，在伊比利亚半岛上，斗牛被视为一种高贵的艺术，每年3月至11月是西班牙斗牛季，通常以星期天和星期四为斗牛日（使用体重400～500千克的非洲纯种公牛）。现在西班牙拥有300多处斗牛场（最大的是马德里的文塔斯斗牛场，可容纳2.5万人）。斗牛场面壮观，格斗惊心动魄。当斗牛士在场上挑逗、戏弄公牛时，他也将生命祭奠给这项疯狂的运动。在西班牙乃至整个西班牙语世界里，斗牛士以其高雅、勇敢的灵魂和技术以及柔美和勇猛完美的结合，被视为英勇无畏的男子汉，备受西班牙民众的敬仰与崇拜，其地位高出一般的社会名流和演艺界人士。无论是毕加索，还是海明威，这些艺术大师都沉醉于斗牛的魅力。后者在其经典著作《死在午后》中这样描绘斗牛："它使人陶醉，能让人有不朽之感，使人入迷。"如今，西班牙国内对斗牛活动的辩论一直很激烈。许多动物权利保护者抵制斗牛。西班牙的加泰罗尼亚地区自 2012 年 1 月 1 日起禁止在当地举行斗牛活动。

2. 番茄节（La Tomatina）

每年 8 月的最后一个星期三，在西班牙巴伦西亚地区的布尼奥尔小镇都要举行一年一度的民间传统节日番茄节——"番茄大战"。当地居民和来自世界各地的游客以番茄为武器，在街头展开混战，把整个市中心变成了一片"番茄的海洋"。布尼奥尔的"番茄大战"始于 1945 年。由于人们通过扔番茄的活动可以尽情放松压抑的心情，并重新找到童年的感觉，因此这个奇特的节日在西班牙变得越来越盛行。2002 年，西班牙政府将布尼奥尔镇"番茄节"列入西班牙国家文化遗产。

Bunyol town in Valencian community holds a folk festival—La Tomatina, tomato fight on the last Wednesday of August every year. The locals and the tourists from all over the world use the tomatoes as weapons to fight each other in the streets. The whole city becomes sea of tomatoes. The tomato fight started in 1945. People get relaxed after they throw tomatoes and find back their feelings in childhood. This amazing festival becomes more and more popular in Spain. In 2002, this festival was listed into the Spanish Cultural Heritage.

三、主要旅游城市及景点

（一）马德里（Madrid）

马德里是西班牙的首都、欧洲著名历史古城，它位于伊比利亚半岛梅塞塔高原中部，海拔 670 米，是欧洲地势最高的首都之一。历史上马德里曾历经罗马人、西哥特人、阿拉伯人等异族统治，遭遇过拿破仑军队的侵略和内战的破坏，从 2 000 多年前曼萨纳雷斯河畔的一个小镇变成如今的国家首都，政治、经济、文化中心，世界旅游组织总部所在地，素有"欧洲之门"之称。同时，马德里是欧洲数一数二的艺术中心，每年都吸引来大批的观光客。这里自然风光绚丽，阳光灿烂。每年晴天时间在欧洲各大城市中排居首位，空气十分清新。马德里也被称为"梦幻之城"，游客在此可以品味最纯正的西班牙。

Madrid is the capital of Spain, the famous historical ancient city in Europe. It is located in the Meseta Central of Iberian Peninsula, with altitude of 670 meters, making it one of the highest capital in Europe. It has been ruled by Roman, Visigoth, Arabian, invaded by Napoléon's troop and destroyed by the civil war. Madrid was developed from a small town along the bank of Manzanares River 2,000 years ago, and now it is the capital, the center of politics, economy and art, the headquarters of the UNWTO and gets the fame of "Gate of Europe". Meanwhile, Madrid is also the art center in Europe, attracting many tourists every year. It has beautiful scenery and sunshine. Madrid enjoys the sunny days with fresh air more than any other cities in Europe. Madrid is also called the fantasy city. People can enjoy the most classic Spain here.

◆ 马德里皇宫（Royal Palace of Madrid）

马德里皇宫是欧洲第三大皇宫，仅次于巴黎凡尔赛宫及维也纳霍夫堡皇宫，其豪华壮丽程度，在欧洲各国皇宫中数一数二。马德里皇宫是世界上保存最完整，而且最精美的宫殿之一，它融合了西班牙传统王室建筑风格和巴洛克式建筑风格。它既是一直使用的王宫，也是一座艺术宝库，珍藏着大量油画、挂毯、古家具等文物、艺术品。卡洛斯国王登基后，马德里皇宫对市民开放，但一些重要的典礼活动仍在此举行，如国王宴请来访的外国国家元首、举行国内最高规格的官方活动以及接受外国大使的国书等。

Royal Palace of Madrid is the third largest palace in Europe, after Palace of Versailles in Paris and Hofburg Palace in Vienna. The palace is so magnificent that it has been ranked among the top in European palaces. The Royal Palace of Madrid is one of the palaces which have preserved the most complete and finest in the world. It combines the traditional Spanish royal architecture style and baroque style. It is a royal palace and it is also an art treasure house with lots of paintings, tapestries, ancient furniture and so on. After the enthronization of King Carlos, it opens to the citizens. Some important ceremonies are still held here, such as the King inviting the foreign leaders to have dinners, holding the highest level official activities and accepting foreign ambassadors' credentials, etc.

◆ 普拉多博物馆（Prado Museum）

马德里共有 30 多座博物馆，其中世界闻名的绘画展览馆——普拉多博物馆，有着“欧洲古典美术宝库”的美誉。普拉多博物馆建于 18 世纪，被认为是世界上最伟大的博物馆之一，亦是收藏西班牙绘画作品最全面、最权威的美术馆。普拉多博物馆内设有 30 个展厅，收集了 15—19 世纪西班牙和意大利艺术家的 3 000 多幅作品。另外，还有许多史前时代的资料及罗马人、摩尔人和中世纪的遗物。

More than 30 museums are located in Madrid, including the famous painting museum — Prado Museum which has the name of “Classic European Art Treasury”. Established in the 18th century, Prado Museum is considered as one of the greatest museums as well as the most complete and authorized art gallery of Spanish works. There are 30 exhibition halls, collecting over 3,000 fine works from Spanish and Italian artists of the 15th century to 19th century. Besides, there are lots of documents from prehistory and relics of Roman, Maure and Middle Ages.

（二）巴塞罗那（Barcelona）

巴塞罗那是西班牙的第二大城市，是一个工商业、文化艺术非常发达的城市，也是西班牙的文化古城和最大海港，有“地中海曼哈顿”之称。巴塞罗那的历史可追溯到公元前 2 世纪，曾被罗马人和西哥特人统治过。巴塞罗那对外来文化高度接受与包容，加上西班牙的友好与法国的浪漫情调，又有“欧洲之花”的美誉。作为伊比利亚半岛最富欧洲气质的大都会，巴塞罗那又被称为“伊比利亚半岛的明珠”。西班牙大作家塞万提斯称赞巴塞罗那是西班牙的骄傲和世界上最美丽的城市。西班牙的现代艺术巨匠如毕加索、米罗、达利等人都诞生于此，天才建筑师高迪的作品是这座城市的骄傲，圣家族大教堂是这座城市的标志性建筑。作为艺术之城，巴塞罗那是古代文明和现代文明结合得最完美的城市。整座城市依山傍海，气候舒适宜人，市区的哥特式、文艺复兴式、巴洛克式的建筑和现代化楼群交相辉映。以圣家族大教堂为中心，有无数值得参观的建筑物，地中海的黄金海岸则是著名的海滨度假胜地。1992 年奥运会的举办更使这座城市在国际上享有了极高的知名度。

Barcelona is the second largest city in Spain. It is also a city with developed industry, art and culture. It is an ancient and cultural city and the largest harbor with the name of Mediterranean Manhattan. The history of Barcelona can be traced back to the 2nd century BC. It was ruled by Roman and Visigoth. Barcelona has great compatibility to other cultures, together with Spanish friendliness and French romance, the city wins the fame of the "Flower of Europe". As the European style metropolis in Iberian Peninsula, Barcelona is also called the "Pearl of Iberian Peninsula". The great Spanish author Cervantes praised it the pride of Spain and the most beautiful city in the world. Many great artists were born here, such as Picasso, Joan Miró, Salvador Dali. The works of the talented architect Gaudi are the pride of the city. The landmark of the city is Sagrada Familia. As the art city, Barcelona combines ancient and modern cultures. The whole city faces the sea and backs upon the mountain with comfortable climate. The architecture of gothic style, Renaissance style and baroque style reflect with the modern constructions in the city. Centered around the Sagrade Familia and the surrounding buildings worth visiting as well as the famous golden seaside resort in the Mediterranean Sea, Barcelona gains more popularity after the 1992 Olympic Games.

◆ 圣家族大教堂（Sagrade Familia）

圣家族大教堂堪称上帝的建筑，它是建筑大师安东尼奥·高迪的毕生代表作，位于巴塞罗那市中心，始建于 1882 年，目前仍在修建中。尽管是一座未完工的建筑物，但丝毫无损于它成为世界上最著名的景点之一，2005 年联合国教科文组织将高迪建成的那一部分列入世界文化遗产名录，是世界上唯一一座还未完工就被列入世界遗产名录的建筑物，它还被提名为新的世界七大奇迹之一。这是一座象征主义建筑，根据高迪的设计，圣家族大教堂拥有耶稣降生、耶稣受难和天国三座外立面。每面上方都建有 100 米左右高低不等的 4 座尖塔，象征耶稣的十二门徒。有人说，圣家族大教堂是超越了一般意义的建筑，是巴塞罗那的象征。

Sagrade Familia is known as the God's architecture. Built in 1882, it is the representative work of great master Antonio Gaudi, located at the center of downtown Barcelona. This building is still under construction now. Though unfinished, it is the one of the most famous scenic spots in the world. In 2005, the UNESCO made the finished Gaudi part enter into the World Cultural Heritage Site. Thus it becomes the only unfinished architecture in the World Cultural Heritage Site list. It is also nominated as one of the new Seven Wonders of the World. It is a symbolized building. According to Gaudi's design, the Sagrade Familia has three outer faces with pictures of the birth of Jesus, suffering of Jesus and Heaven. Four towers about 100 meters high stand upon every face, representing the 12 disciples of Jesus. People say that the Sagrade Familia is beyond the common sense of architecture, it is the symbol of Barcelona.

◆ 毕加索博物馆（Picasso Museum）

世界上有两座毕加索博物馆，一座在巴黎，另一座就在巴塞罗那。巴塞罗那毕加索博物馆是一间建于15世纪的优美宅邸。1963年由贵族宅邸改建而成的毕加索博物馆，有着幽静的庭院、华丽的墙壁和窗棂。馆中藏有毕加索的3 500多幅作品，从油画到素描、版画、陶塑等，种类繁多。其中很多是由画家本人于1970年捐献的作品，还有一些是作者早期甚至其幼年时期的画作。

There are two Picasso museums in the world. One is in Paris and the other is in Barcelona. Picasso Museum in Barcelona is a beautiful house established in the 15th century. It was reconstructed from a noble's house to the museum in 1963. With quiet yard, splendid wallpaper and adjacent of windows, the museum has over 3,500 Picasso's works, from oil paintings to sketches, prints, potteries and so on. Most of the works were donated by the painter himself in 1970, and some were the painter's early works even including the paintings from his childhood.

（三）其他著名旅游景点

◆ 塞维利亚（Sevilla）

塞维利亚坐落在瓜达尔基维尔河右岸，是塞维利亚省省会和安达卢西亚自治区首府，西班牙第四大城市，南部地区第一大城市，是一座有着2 000多年历史的著名文化古城，以优美的吉卜赛音乐、弗拉明戈舞和斗牛著称。格兰德河是西班牙境内唯一能通航的内陆河，当年哥伦布就是从这里扬帆入海的。哥特式的塞维利亚大教堂（建于15世纪），是西班牙最漂亮的教堂之一。

Sevilla is located at the right bank of Guadalquivir. It is the capital of the province of Sevilla and the autonomous community of Andalusia. Sevilla is the fourth largest city in Spain, the largest city in southern area, a famous ancient city with over 2,000 years and known for the beautiful Gypsy music, Flamenco and bullfight. The Grand River is the only inner land river for ship passage in Spain. Columbus started his journey on this river. The gothic style Cathedral of Sevilla (established in the 15th century) is one of the most beautiful churchs in Spain.

◆ 巴利阿里群岛（Balearic Islands）

西班牙拥有4 964千米长的海岸线，3 000多个洁净沙细的海滩点缀在漫长的海岸线上，湛蓝的海水在灿烂的阳光辉映下耀金泛银，这就是阳光（Sun）、海滩（Sand）、大海（Sea）构成的一幅西班牙“3S画卷”。巴利阿里群岛因首创裸体浴场而以“地中海浴池”驰名世界，年日照超过300天。因有国际知名海滩，也有一个个被断崖隔开静谧的小海湾，巴利阿里群岛已成为国际明星、名模、富豪的第二故乡。

Spain owns 4,964 kilometers long coastline which is dotted with over 3,000 beaches. The blue seawater reflects golden and silver under the sunshine. Sun, sand and sea consist of the 3S Spanish scroll. Balearic Islands are famous for its first naked bath spot with annual sunshine over 300 days. Because of the famous beaches, the quiet bays separated by the cliffs, the islands become the second hometown of many international stars, models and rich people.

四、旅游资讯

（一）美食

西班牙人非常讲究饮食。西班牙菜肴具有独特的风味。由于长期受到外族的入侵与统治，加上大航海时代对于新大陆的探索、发掘，西班牙对于其他民族文化的包容性也展现在食物上，它融合了地中海和东方烹饪的精华。西班牙菜肴多用橄榄油和大蒜，做法考究。西班牙盛产各种蔬菜、水果、海产品及牛羊肉，而且质量上乘。西班牙人最爱吃海鲜饭，是用鲜虾、鱿鱼、鸡肉、西班牙香肠，配上洋葱、大蒜、番茄汁等焖制而成。此外，西班牙中部地区的烤羊肉非常著名。生火腿、鸡蛋土豆煎饼和香肠是西班牙的三大特色小吃。其中，生火腿最著名。西班牙的生火腿几乎全部只用粗盐调味，自然风干，少见熏火腿，外形上很像我国浙江的金华火腿。享用西班牙大餐时，当然少不了西班牙产的葡萄酒，如干红葡萄酒、干白葡萄酒、雪利酒及用水果酿制的餐后酒。

Spanish people pay a lot of attention to their food. The Spanish cuisine has unique flavor. Spain was invaded and ruled by outer powers for a long time and explored the new continent in the Age of Sail, so it has great compatibility for different cultures. Such feature is also presented in the food. The Spanish food combines the essence of Mediterranean and oriental cuisine. The typical Spain cuisine delicately uses olive oil and garlic. Spain produces different kinds of vegetables, fruits, seafood, beef and mutton with good quality. The favorite food of Spanish people is Paella which is cooked with shrimp, squid, chicken, Spanish sausage, onion, garlic and tomato juice. Besides, the roasted mutton in central Spain is very famous. Green ham, egg and potato cake, and sausage are three typical foods in Spain. The green ham is the most famous. It only uses raw salt as its flavoring and is naturally dried. The shape is like Jinhua ham in Zhejiang Province. When people enjoy Spanish dinner, the wine is a necessity, such as red wine, white wine, sherry and fruit wine.

（二）购物及退税

手工艺品：南部的格拉纳达是摩洛哥手工艺品的最大集散地，你可以找到价廉物美的摩洛哥皮件、铜器、坐垫、地毯、吊灯、拖鞋、木雕等。此外，格拉纳达出产的青蓝绘陶品、安达卢西亚式吊灯、瓷砖、家具以及西班牙风格的大花裙、蕾丝披肩，也是十分具有特色的旅游纪念品。

Handicrafts: Granada in Southern Spain is the largest distributing center of Morocco handicrafts, providing fine and cheap Morocco leather piece, bronzes, cushions, carpets, droplight, slippers, wooden carvings. Besides, the blue painted pottery products, Andalusia droplight, tiles, furniture, Spanish skirts, lace shawl are all typical tourist souvenirs.

皮具：西班牙皮具在质量和设计方面并不比意大利差，价格相对便宜，皮具名牌有罗意威等。西班牙的皮鞋业发达，皮鞋的质量上乘、设计出彩。西班牙的皮鞋厂遍布全国各地，以沿海城市阿利坎特一带最多，也最有名。

Leather: Spanish leather is as good as Italian's in quality and design but with lower price. It has brands such as Loewe and so on. The leather shoe industry in Spain is very prosperous. The shoes have good quality and designs. The shoe factories are all over the country, especially in the coastal city Alicante.

陶瓷：素有"瓷器之城"之称的瓦伦西亚是西班牙瓷器艺术爱好者的天堂。安达卢西亚南部的彩绘陶瓷包括餐具、灯具和家具，风格十分传统，很受欢迎。中部古城托莱多的金银镶嵌饰品，是西班牙最著名的工艺。这种古老技艺是西班牙王公贵族的最爱。在许多西班牙博物馆里保存下来的文物中，都可看到这种技艺。

Pottery: Valencia is known as "the city of pottery". It is the heaven of Spanish pottery lovers. The colorful pottery in southern Andalusia include plates, lights and furniture with traditional style. They are very popular. The gold and silver accessories in the central ancient city Toledo is the most famous crafts in Spain. This ancient skill is the favorite of Spanish nobles. You will find this skill in the antiques in Spanish museums.

西班牙的消费水平不高，物价较低，皮鞋及服装品质优良，实用性也很高。西班牙法律规定，要获得免税卡，游客同一天在同一家店的购物额不能低于90.15欧元。一般可获退税金额大约是消费金额的12%，若消费金额超过一定范围，则退税金额比例将高于12%。游客出境前应把所购物品和退税单一起提交给海关查验。如果游客要随身携带所购物品，最好将之放置在行李的最上方，便于检查。对于要托运的货物，要在办理登机手续时声明行李中有要办理退税的货物并拴上托运牌。之后，将行李送至海关办理验货手续，海关在退税单上加盖验货章。持海关验货后的退税单到机场或边境的现金返还处领取现金。

The price of goods in Spain is not very high. High-quality shoes and fashion garments are popular here. The Spain law stipulates that you can get tax refund when your consumption is up to 90.15 euros in the same shop one day. Generally, the rate of refund is 12% of the total consumption amount or higher if the consumption exceeds certain amount. Before you depart from the country, you need to hand in the refund forms and goods to the customs for checking. If you want to take goods with you, you should put them on the top of the luggage so as to have goods checked easily. You should claim that the goods which you want tax refund is in the luggage before you check in and have them tagged. Send the tagged luggage to the customs office to be checked and have the form stamped before you go to the refund office at the airport or border to cash the tax money.

（三）时差

西班牙的夏季比中国慢6个小时，冬季比中国慢7个小时。从3月份的最后一个星期天，到10月份的最后一个星期天，西班牙实行夏令时制。

In summer, Spain time is six hours later than Chinese time. In winter, Spain time is seven hours later than Chinese time. Spain adopts the Daylight Saving Time from the last Sunday in March to the last Sunday in October.

思考练习

1. 经典旅游线路分析

西班牙深度10日游

第1天：北京——巴黎——巴塞罗那

游客于指定时间在北京首都国际机场集合，搭乘法航国际航班经巴黎转机前往巴塞罗那，游客抵达后，导游接机入住酒店休息。

第2天：巴塞罗那

与瑞士的宁静与巴黎的浪漫相比，西班牙第二大城市巴塞罗那，有的是地中海式热情的阳光与自由奔放的气息。动工100多年至今仍未完成、天才建筑家高迪的代表作圣家族大教堂以完美而协调的手法呈现，线条简洁而利落，令人叹为观止。散步在古埃尔公园中，如蛋糕一般的梦幻小屋、希腊式的白柱，让人不由自主地再一次为高迪的才能所折服。参观和平广场上的哥伦布纪念碑、大都会里的旧城哥德区、13世纪阿拉贡的旧王宫、孟特惠克山丘、1992年奥运会会址。

第3天：巴塞罗那——塞维利亚

早餐后乘车前往西班牙安达卢西亚自治区的首府——塞维利亚。塞维利亚曾是摩尔王朝的首都、西班牙文艺复兴的焦点、安达卢西亚文化的"守护天使"。如同热情的弗拉明戈婀娜多姿、风情万种、令人不可抗拒，塞维利亚的独特之处就是散发着多彩多姿、兼容并蓄的美感。参观塞维利亚大教堂，伟大的航海家哥伦布曾葬于此地。之后游览美丽的西班牙广场、黄金塔，领略传统与现代建筑艺术的完美融合。

第4天：塞维利亚——隆达——马拉加

塞维利亚是西班牙弗拉明戈的发源地，观看一场地道的弗拉明戈舞蹈表演是游览西班牙的精华，千万不要错过。乘车前往被深谷断崖绝壁环绕、风景如画的隆达，这里也是近代西班牙斗牛的发源地。游览位于西班牙著名阳光海岸的度假胜地——马拉加，这里的阳光海岸是欧洲人度假的首选地点之一，这个气质高贵的海滨城镇常常聚集了许多巨贾富商，港口停满了大大小小的游艇。在夏季，更不乏有人在沙滩上来个全裸日光浴。

第5天：马拉加——格拉纳达

早餐后乘车前往格拉纳达。格拉纳达是与之同名的格拉纳达省的首府，位于安达卢西亚自治区的东部。地理和自然景观的多样性是这里的主要特点：沿海地区气候温暖，山区气候寒冷，伊比利亚半岛上的最高峰——海拔3 481千米的穆拉森峰便坐落其中。特殊的历史背景赋予了这座城市丰富的艺术财富，既有摩尔人修建的宫殿，也有基督教文艺复兴时期的建筑瑰宝。由于这里曾是阿拉伯人在伊比利亚半岛上的最后一个王国的首都，格拉纳达因此而成为具有伟大象征意义的城市。入内参观阿尔汗布拉宫。

第 6 天：格拉纳达——科尔多瓦

乘车前往科尔多瓦的标志性建筑——清真寺。许多游客来到科尔多瓦，就是为了能亲眼看见这座举世闻名的清真寺。这座清真寺是伊斯兰教王朝在安达卢西亚所遗留下来的最佳文化遗迹。这座具有双重功能的建筑，不仅是现今西方世界中的最大清真寺（占地 24 000 平方米），也是表现伊斯兰教艺术最佳典范的重要宫殿。

第 7 天：科尔多瓦——托雷多——马德里

上午乘车前往托雷多，这里曾作为西班牙帝国的首都达千年之久，可以说是西班牙历史文化的缩影，在犹太教、伊斯兰教、基督教和摩尔人文化的交汇、冲击之下，保留着相对完整的中世纪风貌。时间仿佛在托雷多停留下来，整座城都是依旧维持着数百年前风貌的古迹，托雷多可以说是一部活的历史教科书，并已被联合国教科文组织列入世界文化遗产名录。游客参观比萨格拉门、大寺院、圣托马斯教堂、诺曼底哥德教堂。夜宿马德里。

第 8 天：马德里

全天在马德里市区观光。“零公里”标志是一块正方形的瓷砖，建在太阳门广场的人行道上。哥伦布广场是西班牙的骄傲，是为纪念哥伦布发现新大陆而修建的。随后怀着朝圣般的心情参观普拉多博物馆，西班牙早期三大艺术家委拉斯开兹、哥雅、葛雷科的佳作尽收眼底，毕加索、拉斐尔、阿尔布雷特·丢勒等的巨作更能震撼每一个人的心灵，让你心生共鸣且深深感到艺术的力量竟是如此神奇。市政广场是西班牙最宽广、最古老的广场，可容纳 5 万人。结合巴洛克式与新古典主义建筑风格的皇宫是西班牙王室鼎盛时的建筑，金碧辉煌且美轮美奂，呈现出昔日强大帝国神圣的余晖。西班牙广场则象征西班牙文学在世界上的重要地位，广场上伫立着塞万提斯塑造的梦幻骑士堂·吉诃德及其仆人的塑像。

第 9 天：马德里——巴黎——北京

早餐后收拾行李，搭乘法航国际航班前往巴黎转机返回北京。

第 10 天：北京

游客于上午抵达北京，结束此次温馨的西班牙之旅。

分析：这条经典旅游线路的主要旅游景点与行程特色，以及适合旅游的人群。

2. 案例分析

［案例 1］ 游客小卢随团到西班牙旅游。在自由活动期间，他想去巴塞罗那的海滨酒吧感受当地文化，他看到门口有一排小吧台，但没有椅子，而里面的桌子都配有椅子，就选择坐在里面。结果买单的时候，小卢被要求付小费，他心里纳闷了：坐外面和坐里面有区别吗？当地导游解释，在西方国家，给服务行业的工作人员付小费已成为习惯，小费已成为服务员的重要收入来源。给小费不仅是对其服务的一种酬劳，也是对别人劳动的尊

重，特别是对饭店招待、门房、服务员、房间清洁工、旅馆中的行李搬运员等。如果选择站在外面自助式，就不需要付小费了，但在酒吧里面有人服务就需要付小费。难怪在欧洲很多城市可以看到许多人在咖啡馆门口站着喝咖啡。你的选择呢？

[案例2] 在马德里，小江意外遇到了以前认识的一位西班牙朋友。这位朋友提议与小江共进晚餐。他选好餐厅，并帮助不熟悉当地菜肴的小江点了菜。结账时，侍者把账单放在了两个人中间，这时西班牙朋友说："我们AA制，各付一半吧。"小江虽然付了50%的餐费，心里却认为西班牙朋友先提出一起吃饭的建议，他没有尽地主之谊也未免太小气了。你觉得小江的想法正确吗？

3. 练一练

（1）2018年，约59.7万位中国游客前往西班牙旅游。任何季节都适宜去西班牙旅行，因为这个欧洲国家具备所有的"元素"可以让游客度过难忘的假日：被联合国教科文组织列入世界文化遗产名录的继承了多元文化的城市、名胜古迹和自然景观，世界一流的博物馆，适合各类人群的海岸，全年宜人的气候，健康的地中海饮食（如道地的海鲜饭、烤肉），弗拉明戈和斗牛等西班牙传统表演，西班牙全年不断的体育赛事（尤其是足球）等。试分析西班牙的旅游资源，选一个你感兴趣的主题写一篇导游词。

（2）西班牙开发了可以满足游客个人品位的多种文化旅游路线，其中，朝圣旅游线路——圣地亚哥之路是西班牙开发得非常成功的、引导来自世界各地的朝圣者穿越西班牙西北部七个大区前往圣地亚哥朝圣的著名旅游路线，堪称"欧洲第一文化旅行路线"。除宗教信仰的因素外，由于朝圣之旅途经不同的地区，各地不同的文化传统、当地居民的热情好客以及沿途动人的美景、奇闻轶事也成为朝圣者的又一精神支柱，并赋予圣地亚哥之路以极强的文化色彩。请谈谈这条线路的特点。

第七节 俄罗斯

一、国家概况

（一）地理环境

俄罗斯联邦，简称俄罗斯，位于欧洲东部和亚洲大陆的北部，其欧洲领土的大部分是东欧平原。俄罗斯与挪威、芬兰、爱沙尼亚、拉脱维亚、立陶宛、波兰、白俄罗斯、乌克兰、格鲁吉亚、阿塞拜疆、哈萨克斯坦、中国、蒙古、朝鲜接壤，与日本、美国、加拿大、格陵兰岛、冰岛、瑞典隔海相望。俄罗斯绵延的海岸线从北冰洋一直伸展到北太平洋，还包括内陆海黑海和里海。俄罗斯是世界上面积最大的国家，亦是世界第二大军事强国。

Russia, officially known as the Russian Federation, is a country in Eastern Europe and Northern Asia. Most of Russian territories are in East European Plain. Russia shares borders with Norway, Finland, Estonia, Latvia, Lithuania, Poland, Belarus, Ukraine, Georgia, Azerbaijan, Kazakhstan, China, Mongolia and DPRK. It also has maritime borders with Japan, the United States, Canada, Greenland, Iceland and Sweden. Its extensive coast stretches from the Arctic Ocean to North Pacific Ocean, including the Black Sea and Caspian Sea. Russia is the largest country and the second military power in the world.

俄罗斯的大部分地区为平原，山脉集中在俄罗斯南部和太平洋沿岸，乌拉尔山脉是欧洲和亚洲的分界线。俄罗斯境内的主要河流包括欧洲第一长河——伏尔加河（全长 3 692 千米、是俄罗斯的母亲河）、鄂毕河、叶尼塞河、勒拿河以及阿穆尔河（即黑龙江）。主要湖泊有贝加尔湖（世界上最深的淡水湖）等。

Most area in Russia is plain. In the south and along the Pacific Ocean are some mountain ranges and among which Ural Mountains divide Europe from Asia. The major rivers in Russia include the longest river in Europe — Volga River (3,692 kilometers, the mother river of Russia), Ob River, Yenisei River, Lena River and Amur River (Heilong Jiang in Chinese). The major lakes include Lake Baikal (the world's deepest fresh water lake) and so on.

俄罗斯幅员辽阔，纬度较高，国土跨寒带、亚寒带和温带三个气候带。俄罗斯大部分地区处于北温带和北寒带。气候以大陆性气候为主，冬季严寒漫长。

The enormous territory size of Russia and the high latitude result in the country in three climate zones — Frigid Zone, Subfrigid Zone and Temperate Zone. Most of its territory is in the North Temperate Zone and North Frigid Zone. Its main climate is dominant by continental climate with a long term of winter.

（二）人文概况

1. *历史*

公元 9 世纪，维京人建立了第一个东斯拉夫人的国家——基辅罗斯。1547 年，伊凡四世建立莫斯科大公国，开始吞并周边地区，逐渐成为多民族的国家。后经历代沙皇的扩张，发展成为横跨亚欧大陆的帝国。18 世纪到 20 世纪初是俄罗斯帝国的全盛时期，第一次世界大战末期陷入内战。1917 年，列宁领导“十月革命”的胜利使共产党取得政权，建立了世界上第一个社会主义国家。1922 年 12 月 30 日，根据列宁的提议，俄罗斯联邦、外高加索联邦、乌克兰、白俄罗斯成立苏维埃社会主义共和国联盟，简称苏联。在斯大林领导期间，苏联从农业国家转变成了工业化国家。第二次世界大战后，苏联成了唯一能和美国为首的西方国家对抗的超级大国。1991 年 12 月 21 日，苏联 11 个加盟共和国领导人在哈萨克斯坦的阿拉木图决定，苏联在联合国安理会的席位由俄罗斯继承。同年 12 月 25 日，俄罗斯苏维埃联邦社会主义共和国最高苏维埃决定，将国家正式名称改为“俄罗斯联邦”（简称俄罗斯）。1992 年 4 月 16 日，第 6 次人民代表大会决定将国名改为“俄罗斯”，从而恢复了历史上的名称；4 月 17 日，最后决定使用两个同等地位的正式国名“俄罗斯联邦”和“俄罗斯”。

In the 9th century, Vikings established the first East Slavic State of Kievan Rus. In 1547, Ivan Ⅳ established Grand Duchy of Moscow and started to overcome the neighboring lands. At last, the country was transformed into a multi-ethnic country. Extending the borders by the Tsars, Russia became a transcontinental empire. During the period from the 18th century to the beginning of the 20th century, Russian Empire had been in its heyday. At the end of the First World War, it was involved in the civil war. In 1917 led by Lenin, the communist gained the reign of the country and established the first socialist country after the victory of the October Revolution. On December 30, 1922, proposed by Lenin, Russian Federation, South Caucasus, Ukraine and Belarus unified into the Union of Soviet Socialist Republics, Soviet Union for short. In the period under Stalin's reign, the Soviet Union turned into an industrial country from an agriculture one. After the Second World War, the Soviet Union was the only superpower capable of struggling against the Western countries led by the United States. On December 21, 1991, eleven leaders from the Union decided the seat in the UN would be inherited by Russia in Alma-Ata of Kazakhstan. On December 25, the Highest Soviet of Russian Soviet Federative Socialist Republic decided to change the name of the country into Russia Federation (Russia for short). On April 16, 1992, the sixth congress decided to change the name into Russia. Later on April 17, Russia Federation and Russia were considered the two official names for the country.

2. 经济

俄罗斯是世界经济大国。苏联时期，它是世界第二经济强国。苏联解体后，俄罗斯从中央计划经济体制向市场经济体制过渡。由于石油价格的上升和卢布的疲软，俄罗斯经济走向好转。2000年之后，俄罗斯经济在大量出售资源的情况下得以迅速发展。俄罗斯拥有丰富的自然资源，如世界上最大的矿产储量、能源储量和森林资源，其淡水储量占世界储量的1/4。目前，俄罗斯经济主要依靠自然资源的出口，其中石油、天然气、金属以及木材的出口占到80%。俄罗斯是世界上最大的天然气输出国和OPEC（石油输出国组织）以外的最大石油输出国。近年来，俄罗斯的计算机工业、航空业、高科技产业迅速崛起。特别是俄罗斯的国防工业在世界上占有重要的地位，其武器产品出口到全球各地。俄罗斯的核工业和航空业也占重要地位。

Russia is a large economy entity in the world. It ranked the second in the world in Soviet period. After the disintegration of the Soviet Union, the economic policy of Russia turned into the market economic system instead of central planned system. Because of the rising of the oil price and the weakening of the Ruble, Russian economy became better. After 2000, the economy of Russia has increased rapidly based on the selling of large amount of its resources, because the country has enormous natural resources, such as the largest mineral reserves, energy and forest reserves as well as it has 1/4 fresh water on the earth. Currently, Russian economy depends on the export of natural resources, 80% of which are oil, natural gas, metals and timber. Russia is the largest oil producer and exporter except the OPEC. In recent years, computer industry, aviation and high-tech industry have developed fast. The national defense industry of Russia occupies special status in the world. Its weapons are exported to many countries and regions in the world. Russian nuclear, industry and aviation industry also enjoy important status in the world.

3. 社会文化

俄罗斯人口为1.46亿，首都为莫斯科，官方语言为俄语。俄罗斯有194个民族，其中俄罗斯族占 77.7%。主要少数民族为鞑靼、巴什基尔、车臣、楚瓦什、亚美尼亚、乌克兰、达吉斯坦、哈萨克、阿塞拜疆和白俄罗斯等。主要宗教为东正教，其次为伊斯兰教。

Russia has a population of 146 million.The capital is Moscow. The official language is Russian. It has 194 nationalities. 77.7% of the population is Russian and the main ethnic groups are Tatars, Bashkirs, Chechens, Chuvash, Armenians, Ukrainians, Daghestan, Kazakhs, Azerbaijanis and Belarus. The major religion in Russia is Orthodox Church followed by Islam.

俄罗斯领土跨越欧、亚两大洲，俄罗斯文化融合了东西方两种文化，有近千年的历史。俄罗斯文化与俄罗斯的历史密切相关，是世界文化遗产中不可分割的一部分。俄罗斯文学是世界文坛上最伟大的文学遗产之一，其每一个阶段都反映了俄罗斯悲壮的、喜剧的和光荣的历史。俄罗斯文学源远流长，包括沙俄和苏联时期的文学，在世界文学史上占有重要的地位。列夫·托尔斯泰的《战争与和平》《复活》《安娜·卡列尼娜》，奥斯特洛夫斯基的《钢铁是怎样炼成的》，高尔基的《母亲》《海燕》，肖洛霍夫的《静静的顿河》，都是世界文学宝库中的杰作。俄罗斯艺术也有着悠久的历史，著名的艺术大师有艾萨克·列维坦、苏里科夫、克拉姆斯科伊等。俄罗斯交响乐团有着悠久的历史和优秀传统，在世界上占有一定的地位。俄罗斯的戏剧艺术体裁和形式多样，最早出现在宫廷里，19 世纪进入繁荣时期。果戈理的《钦差大臣》等戏剧充满强烈的时代气息，具有鲜明的民族特色。同时，俄罗斯涌现了许多杰出的艺术大师。奥斯特洛夫斯基是 19 世纪 50 年代以后俄罗斯文坛众多的戏剧作家中最杰出的代表，被称为“俄罗斯戏剧之父”。俄罗斯的芭蕾舞艺术具有独特的风格，在世界上享有很高的声誉。著名的芭蕾舞剧有《天鹅湖》《罗密欧与朱丽叶》《灰姑娘》等。俄罗斯马戏团也很受人们的欢迎，马戏团团员训练有素，技艺精湛。俄罗斯人有着卓越的民间艺术，最有名的工艺品有木制套娃、木刻勺、木盒、木盘等木制品。

The territory of Russia is across Asian and European continents. The Russian culture combines the eastern and western cultures with almost a thousand year of history. The Russian culture is closely related to the Russian history and an integrated part of world culture heritage. The Russian literature is one of the greatest world literature heritages. Every stage of the literature reflects Russian tragic, comedic or glorious history. The Russian has long literature history. The Russian literature mainly refers to the literatures both in Tsardom of Russia and Soviet period, which occupies important status in world's literature history. Those masterpieces include Lev Tolstoy's *War and Peace*, *Resurrection*, *Anna Karenina*; Nikolai Ostrovsky's *How the Steel Was Tempered*; Gorky's *The Mother*, *The Song of the Stormy Petrel*; Sholokhov's *Quiet Flows the Don*. The Russian art also has long history and the famous artists include Isaac Levitan, Vasily Surikov, Ivan Kramskoi, etc. The Russian Symphony Orchestra has long history and excellent tradition, enjoying high status in the world. The Russian drama has various styles and genres. Its first appearance was in the palace and went into prosperous period in the 19th century. Gogol's *The Government Inspector* was full of the time spirit and vivid ethnic feature. At that time, a lot of artists came into stage, such as the father of Russian drama Ostrovsky, who was the great representative in the Russian literature after 1850s. The Russian ballet has special style and enjoys great honor in the world. The famous ballets are *Swan Lake*,

Romeo and Juliet, Cinderella and so on. The Russian circus is also very popular. The circus members are well-trained and skillful. The Russian people have excellent folk art as well as the famous crafts, such as Matryoshka doll, wooden spoons, wooden boxes and wooden plates, etc.

二、民俗风情

（一）礼仪禁忌

俄罗斯人素来以热情、勇敢、耿直而著称于世。俄罗斯人比较注重礼貌。“您好”“早安”“万事如意”“请原谅”等礼貌语经常挂在嘴上，即使是在亲人间也常用。俄罗斯人最常用的问候语是“你怎么样”“你好”。俄罗斯人认为，两人相遇时，一定要先问好；在咖啡馆或饭店里用餐时，应先向邻桌的人问好，再入座；问路时，也要先问好。在俄罗斯的农村，人们至今还保持着向陌生人问好的习惯。问好的时候，男士要先向女士问好，戴帽子的应把帽子抬一抬，戴有色眼镜的也应把眼镜摘下来。拥抱、亲吻和握手是俄罗斯人的重要礼节。在正式的场合，如国家领导人见面时，为了表示尊敬和友好，俄方领导人会与对方拥抱并握手。俄罗斯人对女性颇为尊敬，在比较正式的场合，男士会弯腰并亲吻女士的右手背，以表示尊重。好友相见时，女士一般会拥抱或亲吻，男人则只是拥抱。兄弟姐妹重逢或分别时，要拥抱、亲吻。人们见面握手时，既不能过于用力，也不能过于无力。如果是男女间握手，男士不能先伸手，男士如戴手套应在握手前脱下，女士则不用脱。年轻人与年长者握手时，也需等年长者先伸手。

The Russian people are famous for their enthusiasm, braveness and frankness. They pay much attention to their politeness. They greet each other with “hello”, “good morning”, “wish you all good”, “excuse me”, even among the relatives. The most frequent-used greetings are “how are you” and “how do you do”. Russian people believe that when two people meet with each other, they should greet first. In a café or a restaurant, people should give their greetings firstly and then take their seats. People say “hello” before asking for directions. In the Russian villages, people still keep the customs of greeting strangers. When people give their greetings, men make greetings to women first. If people wear hats, they should lift the hat a little higher. If people wear color glasses, they should take off them for a while too. Hugging, kissing and hand shaking are important etiquette in Russia. On a formal occasion, when two national leaders meet, Russian leader hugs and shakes hands with the other leader to show friendliness and respect. Russian people give much respect to women. On the formal occasion, men bend forward to kiss the right hand of women. When friends meet each other, women hug or kiss while men hug. When brothers and sisters reunite or leave for another place, they hug and kiss. When people do the hand shaking, they do it in a moderate way. If men shake hands with women, men should not hand out first. If men wear gloves, they should take off the gloves first and then shake hands while women do not have to take off the gloves. When young people shake hands with the old, they should also wait until the old hands out first.

俄罗斯人的姓名很长，一个人的姓名由名、父名和姓组成。如何称呼这么长的姓名呢？在庄重、严肃的场合用全称，有时会稍简化一点，略去父名，只用名和姓。在日常场合，同龄人间可直呼名字。对长辈或上级，为了表示尊敬，就称呼名字加父名。学生对教师也称呼其名和父名，并不叫老师。教师对学生则直呼其姓，有时也可直呼其名以示亲切。

Russian people have long names. Their names consist of first name, father's name and family name. How to call their names? People use the full name on the formal occasion, sometimes the father's name can be omitted. First name can be used on daily occasions among people of same age. First name plus father's name may be used to call the old or the supervisors to show the respect. The students may address their teachers with first names and father's names together. The teachers may call the students their first names or family names.

俄罗斯人有尊重女性的美德，“女士优先”很盛行。凡在公共场所，无论是行走让路，还是乘车让位，男士会特别优待女士。在剧院中，男士要协助女士脱掉大衣，入场时为女士开路并找座位，而且要等女士落座后男士才能入座。男女同行时，男士空手，而让女士拎重物是不允许的；男士要走在女士的左侧，保护女士；男士要陪伴女士过马路。在社交场合，交谈中不要讨论女士的长相、年龄；临别时，男士要帮助女士穿上大衣、拉开门，要让女士先行，不能自己开门拂袖而去。

Russian people respect the ladies. “Lady first” is applied everywhere. In the public places, on the streets or on buses, men treat women specially. At the theater, men are supposed to help ladies take off their coats, show the way to the seat and wait until the lady to sit down first. When men and women are walking together, it is not allowed to see a man carry nothing while a woman carries the heavy stuff. While walking, men are supposed to walk at the left side of the women to protect them. When women are crossing the roads, men have to accompany with them. During the conversation, people don't discuss about the appearance of the women and their ages. At the moment of goodbye, men should help women put on coats, open doors and let the women leave first. Men are not allowed to leave first.

俄罗斯人喜欢文学，酷爱读书。在汽车上、地铁里，随处可见看报、读书的人。很多俄罗斯人的家里都有丰富的藏书，有人甚至有自己的家庭图书馆。俄罗斯人忌讳谈论政治争端、经济问题、宗教等问题，如苏联解体、阿富汗战争以及大国地位。

Russian people love literature and reading. People read on the buses, trains and so on. Many Russian people have volumes of books in their home, some of which even have their own family libraries. Russian people are not willing to talk about political disputes, economic problems or religions, such as disintegration of Soviet Union, War in Afghanistan or super power status.

俄罗斯人性格豪爽，一般在饭桌上离不开酒。俄罗斯人善饮酒，大部分男士和一部分女士喜欢饮用烈性酒，伏特加特别受欢迎。在饮酒时，俄罗斯人习惯上每次举杯都要说祝酒词，如为身体健康、为了友谊等。此时，客人也要避免无祝酒词的干杯，应找到一些理由来祝酒，如祝主人身体健康、为在座的女士干杯等。

Russian people are generous and they like to drink wines during the meal time. They are also good at drinking. Most men and some women like to drink liquor, thus vodka is very popular. When Russian people are drinking, they like to propose toasts. The toasts may include wishes for health, friendship and so on. At this time, the guests should avoid the cheers without toasts, and try to find out some reasons to drink wines, such as wishes for the host's health, for the ladies and so on.

俄罗斯人捧出“面包和盐”来迎接客人，是向客人表示最热烈的欢迎。俄罗斯人对盐十分崇拜，并将盐视为珍宝和祭祀用的供品。他们认为盐具有驱邪除灾的力量。如果有人不慎打翻了盐罐或是将盐撒在地上，便认为是家庭不和的预兆。为了摆脱凶兆，他们总习惯将打翻在地的盐拾起来撒在自己头上。因为在古代俄罗斯，盐要从很远的地方运来，价格昂贵，而用盐腌制的食物可以长时间保存，不易腐烂，由此产生了盐的象征意义：可靠性、持久性、友谊和尊重。

"Bread and salt" is the most warming welcome to the guests. Russian people admire the salt and consider salt as the sacrifice and treasure. They believe salt has the power of driving away the devil. If someone breaks the salt jar accidentally or spreads the salt on the ground, it is believed a bad sign for family peace. To avoid the bad luck, they usually pick up the salt on the ground and scatter it on the head. Because in the ancient Russia, the salt was transported from far away with high price and the food salted can be kept long time, the symbols of salt are reliability, durability, friendship and respect.

在俄罗斯，被视为“光明”象征的向日葵最受人们的喜爱，是俄罗斯的国花。拜访俄罗斯人时，送给女士的鲜花数量宜为单数。在数字方面，俄罗斯人和其他西方人一样，忌讳 13 这个数字，因为在基督教的传说中，背叛耶稣的犹大正好排 13 位。他们也厌恶 666 这个数字，因为在《圣经》中这是魔鬼的代号。他们常用 7 这个数字，认为“7”象征幸福和成功。有些新婚夫妇在婚礼后乘坐彩车要经过 7 座桥才心满意足。

In Russia, the sunflowers are popular for the symbol of "brightness". It is the national flower of Russia. When visiting Russian people, the number of flowers sent to the ladies is better to be singular. When talking about numbers, the Russian people are just like the westerners, they don't like the number 13. Because according to the Christian legend, the betrayer Judah ranked 13. They dislike 666 either, because in the *Bible* this number is the code for devil. They like to use 7, because they believe this number represents happiness and success. Some newly-married couple would like to go through 7 bridges by car.

（二）节庆风情

1. 洗礼节（Epiphany）

洗礼节在 1 月 19 日，这是东正教节日。洗礼原本是一种入教仪式。圣水祭是洗礼节的一项重要活动。在洗礼节前一天，将水放入教堂，之后进行隆重的祷告仪式。在祈祷后，信徒们用圣水洗去自己的罪恶。此外，有的人还会跳入河中的冰窟窿里洗一洗。洗礼节通常是冬季最冷的时候，因此有“洗礼节严寒”之说。按风俗习惯，1 月 18 日晚是占卜日，女孩子们要预卜自己的终身大事。

Epiphany which traditionally falls on January 19 is the Orthodox Church believers' festival. Ablution is originally admittance rites. The Holy Water is an important activity in the Epiphany. Before the holiday, water is put into the church, followed by formal praying. After the praying, the disciples use holy water to wash away the evil on their bodies. Besides, some people will jump into the holes in icy river to wash themselves. The Epiphany is usually in the depth of winter. Thus it comes the saying "the holiday is very cold". In the evening of January 18, people practice divination. Especially, the girls will predict their marriages at that night.

2. 谢肉节（Maslenista）

每年2月底3月初会举行谢肉节，又称送冬节。它的前身为春耕节。信奉多神教的古斯拉夫人认为，冬去春来是太阳神战胜了严寒和黑夜，令其所喜爱的春天回归的结果。东正教传入俄罗斯后，教徒在无力取消这一个已经深深扎根于民间的异教节日的情况下，只得将春耕节改称“谢肉节”，并将节期安排在大斋节前1周、复活节前的第8周进行，称之为“干酪周”。此周一过即进入长达40天的东正教大斋节，期间禁止人们娱乐、吃肉，故名“谢肉节”。如今，人们在谢肉节期间会举行宴会、跳假面舞、做游戏等。

From the end of February to the beginning of March is the Maslenista, also called Winter Farewell Festival. Originally, it was the Spring Ploughing Festival. Ancient Slavs who were polytheist believed that the winter went away and the spring came because the Sun God conquered the coldness and darkness and brought back his favorite spring. When Orthodox came to Russia, they can not change the rooted idea and pagan festival. They changed the name into Maslenista and arranged it a week before Lent, the 8th week before Easter, and the festival was also named "cheese week". After this week, it is the Lent when people are forbidden to have entertainment or have meat. The Lent usually lasts 40 days. Nowadays, people celebrate Maslenista with feasts, dances and games.

三、主要旅游城市及景点

（一）莫斯科（Moscow）

莫斯科是俄罗斯首都，政治、经济、文化、科技和交通中心。人口为1 230万，是世界上特大都市之一和欧洲人口最多的城市。莫斯科地处俄罗斯欧洲部分中部，跨莫斯科河及其支流亚乌扎河两岸。莫斯科和伏尔加流域的上游入口和江河口处相通。莫斯科建城于1147年，迄今已有800余年的历史。从1147年的莫斯科大公国时代开始，到沙皇俄国至苏联及俄罗斯联邦政权，莫斯科都一直担任着国家首都的角色。俄罗斯有数个被列入世界文化遗产名录的建筑群，其城市布局以克里姆林宫和红场为中心，呈环形放射形展开，其中阿尔巴特大街、列宁大街和特维尔大街最为著名。莫斯科的剧院现在还在上演高尔基的名著《海燕》，音乐大厅里一直传出柴可夫斯基的音乐，“每个俄罗斯人都把莫斯科当作自己的母亲”，列夫·托尔斯泰在《战争与和平》里如此描述莫斯科。

Moscow is the capital of Russia and the center of the politics, economy, culture, technology and transportation with a population of 12.3 million. It is one of the metropolises in the world and the most populous city in Europe. Moscow is in the center of the European territories of Russia, situated across the Moscow River and its branch Yauza. Moscow connects with the upper river of Volga. Established in 1147, Moscow has over 800 years history. In the course of its history, the city has served as the capital of many states, from the medieval Grand Duchy of Moscow and the subsequent Tsardom of Russia to the Soviet Union and Russian Federation. Architecture in the city is listed into the World Cultural Heritage Site. With Kremlin and Red Square as the center, the city spreads out in the form of circle. The Arbat Street, Lenin Street and Tverskaya Street are very famous. Gorky's *The Song of the Stormy Petrel* is still on show in the theatres now. Tchaikovsky's music is played in the concert halls. Lev Tolstoy described Moscow in *War and Peace*: "Every Russian takes Moscow as their mother."

◆ 红场（Red Square）

红场是俄罗斯首都莫斯科市中心的著名广场，与克里姆林宫一样是俄罗斯的标志，是俄罗斯历史的见证，也是俄罗斯举行各种大型庆典及阅兵活动的中心地点。红场原名“托尔格”，意为“集市”。1662年改为“红场”，意为“美丽的广场”。红场的地面很独特，全部由条石铺成。红场上的建筑群是在数百年的时间里逐渐建成的。红场的历史与俄罗斯的历史有着密不可分的联系。红场上的每一座建筑物都与某个重大历史事件有关。著名的建筑物包括：西侧是列宁墓和克里姆林宫的红墙及三座高塔；在列宁墓与克里姆林宫之间有12块墓碑，是包括斯大林等在内的苏联政治家的墓碑；南侧是莫斯科的象征——圣瓦西里升天大教堂，这座大教堂是伊凡四世下令建造的，约建于1555年至1561年间，由9间礼堂组成，采用了当时流行的穹顶教堂风格；北侧是国家历史博物馆，建于1873年，也是莫斯科的标志性建筑；附近还有为纪念第二次世界大战胜利50周年而建造的英雄朱可夫元帅的雕像，以及无名烈士墓；东侧是世界知名的十家百货商店之一的古姆商场。红场是俄罗斯举行各种活动的主要场所，也是俄罗斯人举行婚礼必到之地。

The Red Square is a famous square in Moscow. Just like the Kremlin, the Square is another symbol of Russia and the witness of Russian history. It is also the central site for various public ceremonies and parades. The original name of this square is Torg meaning the marketplace. In 1662, the name was changed into Red Square, meaning beautiful square. The ground of the Red Square is very special and made of lath stone. The architecture groups on the square have been built up for hundreds of years. The history of this square is closely connected with Russian history. Every architecture on the square is linked with certain important historical event as well. The famous buildings include Lenin's Mausoleum, Red Walls of Kremlin and three towers in the west, 12 tombstones between Lenin's Mausoleum and the Kremlin, including the Soviet politicians' such as Stalin, and the classic symbol Saint Basil's Cathedral in the south. Saint Basil's Cathedral was built from 1555 to 1561 ordered by Ivan Ⅳ, consisted of nine auditoriums, and adopted the popular arch roof church style at that time. In the north, it is the State Historical Museum, which was established in 1873, also a symbol of Moscow. Nearby, there is a hero sculpture of the General Zhukov for celebrating the 50th anniversary of the victory of the Second World War and anonymous graves. In the east, it is the Gum Department Store, one of the ten famous department stores in the world. The Red Square is the major site for kinds of activities held by Russian, the wedding included.

◆ 克里姆林宫（Kremlin）

克里姆林宫是莫斯科最有名的观光地，既是政治中心，又是俄罗斯东正教的中心。作为俄罗斯国家的象征，克里姆林宫位于俄罗斯首都的中心，是世界上最大的建筑群之一，也是历史瑰宝、文化和艺术古迹的宝库。它已经被联合国教科文组织列入世界文化遗产名录。克里姆林宫始建于1156年，曾为18世纪以前的沙皇皇宫，“十月革命”胜利后，成为苏联党政领导机关所在地。现为俄罗斯联邦总统府等政府机关所在地。克里姆林宫初为木墙，后屡经扩建，至20世纪40年代成为现在的样子，为一古老建筑群。克里姆林宫城堡内有精美的教堂、宫殿、钟塔等。在克里姆林宫的中心教堂广场，有圣母升天大教堂、报喜大教堂以及天使大教堂。克里姆林宫东侧是国家庆典中心——红场。

Kremlin is the most famous tourist attraction in Moscow, the center of politics and the Orthodox Catholic. As the national representative, the Kremlin is located in the center of Russian capital. It is one of the largest architecture groups in the world. It is also the historic, cultural and art treasure, listed by UNESCO as the World Cultural Heritage Site. Established in 1156, the Kremlin was Tsar's palace before the 18th century. After the victory of October Revolution, it became the Soviet's headquarters. Now it is the site for government offices including the President House. The Kremlin started with wooden walls, and later it was rebuilt several times. Till 1940s, it became the large Kremlin. Inside the Kremlin, there are churches, palaces, clock towers and so on. On the center of the Cathedral Square, there are the Assumption Cathedral, the Cathedral of the Annunciation, and the Cathedral of the Archangel Michael. The east side of the Kremlin is the national ceremonial center—Red Square.

（二）圣彼得堡（Saint Petersburg）

圣彼得堡位于俄罗斯西北部，波罗的海沿岸，是列宁格勒州的首府，也是仅次于莫斯科的俄罗斯第二大城市，俄罗斯最大的港口，是世界文化名城之一，也是重要的旅游城市。整座城市由40多个岛屿组成，市内水道纵横，700多座桥梁把各个岛屿连接起来。风光旖旎的圣彼得堡因而有“北方威尼斯”的美誉。因其地处北纬60°，每年初夏都有“白夜”现象，是世界上少数具有白夜的城市。圣彼得堡始建于1703年，至今已有300多年的历史，市名源自耶稣的弟子圣徒彼得。1712年，圣彼得堡成为俄罗斯帝国首都。其后200余年，它始终是俄罗斯帝国的中心。1914年改称彼得格勒，1924年列宁逝世后又命名为列宁格勒，1991年经市民投票恢复原名。圣彼得堡市中心的建筑多为18、19世纪的巴洛克和新古典主义风格。著名的建筑物有彼得保罗要塞、彼得大帝夏宫、斯莫尔尼宫、冬宫、喀山大教堂、伊萨基辅大教堂。俄罗斯的许多著名作家诞生于此，如普希金、莱蒙托夫、高尔基等人。著名的音乐大师柴可夫斯基也诞生于此地。圣彼得堡还是花样滑冰的发源地。

Saint Petersburg is the second largest city of Russia which is located in the northwest of Russia along the coast of Baltic Sea. It is the capital of Leningrad, one of the world's cultural and tourist cities. The whole city consists of over 40 islands. In the city, channels are everywhere and over 700 bridges connect those islands. The beautiful Saint Petersburg thus enjoys the name of "Venice of the North". Because the city is located at 60°N latitude, it has sleepless nights every summer. It is one of the cities that have sleepless night. The city was built in 1703 and named after the Saint Peter. It has 300 years history. In 1712, the city was the capital of Russian Empire. Later, it remained being the heart of Russian Empire for 200 years. It was renamed Petrograd in 1914 and Leningrad in 1924 after the death of Lenin and then back to the name of Saint Petersburg in 1991 based on the votes by the public. The buildings in the central district of the city were constructed in baroque and neoclassicism style of the 18th and 19th century, including Peter and Paul Fortress, Summer Palace of Peter the Great, Smolny Palace, Winter Palace, Kazan Cathedral and Siant Isaac's Cathedral. The city is also the birthplace of many famous authors such as Pushkin, Lermontov and Gorky, etc. The great musician Tchaikovsky was born here too. Saint Petersburg is also the original place of figure skating.

◆ 冬宫（Winter Palace）

冬宫坐落在圣彼得堡宫殿广场上，初建于 1754 年至 1762 年，是 18 世纪俄罗斯巴洛克式建筑艺术最伟大的纪念物。1837 年一场大火将其焚毁，1838 年至 1839 年间重建。冬宫原为俄国沙皇的皇宫，现为艾尔米塔什博物馆，与巴黎卢浮宫、纽约大都会博物馆、伦敦大英博物馆齐名，是世界四大博物馆之一。

The Winter Palace is located at the Palace Square. Established in 1754 to 1762, it is the greatest memorial of Russian baroque architecture art in the 18th century. It was destroyed by a fire in 1837 and rebuilt in 1838 to 1839. The Winter Palace was originally the Tsars' palace. Now it is the Hermitage Museum, enjoying the fame as the Louvre in Paris, the Metropolitan Museum of Art in New York and British Museum in London. It is one of the largest museums in the world.

◆ 彼得大帝夏宫（Summer Palace of Peter the Great）

彼得大帝夏宫位于芬兰湾南岸的森林中，距圣彼得堡市约 30 千米，占地近千公顷，是历代俄国沙皇的郊外离宫。18 世纪初，俄国沙皇彼得大帝下令兴建夏宫，其外貌简朴、庄重，内部装饰华贵。如今，夏宫已成为包括 18 世纪和 19 世纪宫殿花园的建筑群，该宫殿以其直通芬兰湾的喷泉阶梯和园林内众多设计巧妙的喷泉而闻名，被誉为“俄罗斯的凡尔赛宫”。

The Summer Palace of Peter the Great is located in the forests near Gulf of Finland, 30 kilometers away from Saint Petersburg. It occupies nearly a thousand hectares. It was the Tsars' suburban palace. In the early 18th century, Peter the Great ordered to build up the Summer Palace. Its appearance is simple and solemn but the inside decorations are luxurious. Now, the Summer Palace becomes the architecture complex including palaces built during the 18th and 19th century. The palace is famous for its fountain stairs going directly to the Gulf of Finland and many delicate designed fountains, enjoying the name of "Russian Versailles".

四、旅游资讯

（一）美食

俄罗斯人的饮食习惯有着鲜明的民族特色。他们讲究烹调，因此俄罗斯菜肴闻名于世。俄罗斯人讲究量大实惠，喜欢酸、辣、咸味，尤其爱吃冷菜和油炸食品。面包，尤其是黑面包，是俄罗斯人的主食。土豆被称为俄罗斯人的“第二面包”，俄罗斯人十分爱吃土豆。据统计，俄罗斯每年人均消费土豆为100多千克，与粮食的消费量差不多。俄罗斯由于夏短冬长，日照不足，因此一年四季以土豆、圆白菜、胡萝卜、洋葱为主，新鲜的时令蔬菜和水果很少，也很难储存。俄罗斯人特别爱喝红菜汤，也称罗宋汤。在宴席上，一般还有鱼子酱，它是菜肴中的上品，也是俄罗斯有名的美食。俄罗斯人不太讲究菜肴，有酒喝就行，尤其喜欢喝烈性酒，而且一般酒量都大，女士们一般喝香槟和果酒，男士们则偏爱伏特加。俄罗斯人喜欢喝红茶，喝红茶时加糖、蜂蜜或果酱。俄罗斯的饮茶文化源远流长。茶炊是俄罗斯传统饮茶文化的象征。

Russian people have distinguished features in their cuisine. They love to cook and Russian cuisine is famous all over the world. Russian people do not care too much about the food but the quantity and price. Their taste is a little bit sour, spicy and salty. They like cold and fried dishes. Bread, especially the black bread, is the major food for the Russian. Potato is considered the second bread for Russian people. They love potatoes. According to the statistics, Russian people consume over 100 kilograms potatoes per person in a year, almost equal to the consumption of grains. Because the summer is short and the winter is long in Russia, the major plants are potatoes, cabbages, carrots and onions. Russia does not have much fresh vegetable or fruit, let alone storing them. Russian people love to drink red vegetable soup, also called borsch. In a feast, the caviar is the regular course. The caviar is a very famous food in Russia. Russian people care little about the dishes, they love drinking, especially the liquor. They are good at drinking a lot of wines. The ladies love to drink champagne and fruit wine while the gentlemen love vodka. Russian people like to drink black tea with sugar, honey or jam. The tea culture in Russia has long history. The tea-urn is the symbol of the traditional Russian tea culture.

（二）购物及退税

套娃：套娃是俄罗斯的一种民间木制玩具。它一般由七八个木娃，由大到小依次套合在最大的一个的体内。套娃的由来不算久远，据说在19世纪末，一位侨居日本多年的俄罗斯基督教传教士，看到日本的套瓷玩具受到启发，就用木料削制了世上第一套套娃。他把这一套套娃绘成了俄罗斯农家姑娘形象，以寄托他的思乡之情。后来，套娃流传到莫斯科，被一位玩具制作高手仿制成现在的套娃。1900年，俄罗斯套娃参加了巴黎万国博览会，受到大家的欢迎并获得了奖章。一时间莫斯科郊区的很多手工艺作坊，都开始生产套娃。不久，这些地区就成了“套娃之乡”。如今，俄罗斯套娃已名扬四海，它也就成为俄罗斯的独特标志及文化使者。

Matryoshka dolls: A matryoshka doll refers to a set of seven to eight wooden dolls of decreasing size placed one inside the other. The first set of Russian matryoshka doll was carved in late 19th century by Russian Christian missionary who was living in Japan for a long time and inspired by the Japanese ceramic dolls. He made the dolls look like the girls in his hometown to comfort his homesickness. Later, the matryoshka doll came back to Moscow, and was copied by a doll craftsman into matryoshka dolls. In 1900, the matryoshka doll participated in the Exposition Universelle in paris, got the popularity and won the medal. Suddenly, many factories in the Moscow suburban began to make the dolls. Then the area became the hometown of Russian matryoshka dolls. Now, the doll is famous all over the world. It is a kind of Russian special symbol as well as the cultural ambassador.

伏特加：伏特加是俄罗斯的国酒。伏特加的做法是先将酒精经过活性炭处理，除去不纯正气味，然后加上水，到酒精含量达到 36% ～ 60% 时便算制成。市场上出售的伏特加多为 42 度。用粮食制成的伏特加口感清冽，余味悠长。

Vodka: Vodka is Russian national wine. The production of vodka starts with the alcohol being dealt with in active carbon to get rid of the impure smell and then the water is added till the alcohol content reaches 36%—60%. Most vodka in the market is 42 degree. The vodka made from grain has clear taste and long flavor.

裘皮大衣：在俄罗斯人眼中，裘皮大衣不仅可以彰显富贵，而且是生活的第一必需品。由于俄罗斯大部分地区冬季长达 6 个月，为了抵御寒冷的冬天，俄罗斯人历来就有穿着裘皮大衣的习惯。购买裘皮大衣是俄罗斯人继住宅、汽车之后的第三大需求。俄罗斯至今仍是世界上最大的裘皮消费国。俄罗斯是紫貂皮的发源地，也是紫貂皮的生产国之一。

Fur clothes: Russians believe that the fur clothes can not only show the status but also be the first necessity in life. Because the winter in Russia lasts for six months, Russians have the tradition to wear fur clothes to defend the cold winter. Fur clothes are the third demand of Russian people after houses and cars. Russia is the biggest fur consumption country. Russia is the place of origin of zibeline and one of the countries that has zibeline.

琥珀：琥珀是数千万年前的树脂被埋藏于地下，经过一定的化学变化后形成的一种树脂化石，是一种有机的似矿物。俄罗斯最西端的加里宁格勒州集中了世界琥珀藏量的 90% 以上，是俄罗斯的一块“飞地”，以“琥珀之都”闻名遐迩。位于加里宁格勒的琥珀大厅是世界上唯一的琥珀建筑，其使用了 6 吨琥珀，多数来自加里宁格勒的琥珀矿区，最大的一整块琥珀原料重约 1 000 克。

Amber: Amber is the colophony buried tens of million years ago. Through several chemical changes, the colophony becomes some kind of colophony fossil, organic mineral-like matter. The Kaliningrad in western Russia has over 90% amber in the world. It is famous for “enclave” and “capital of amber” in Russia. The Amber Room in this area is the only building made of amber in the world. It uses over 6 tons amber, and the largest one weights about 1 kilogram.

在俄罗斯，免税的最低购物金额为 1 万卢布。一般退税比例为 15% 左右。在购物之后的 3 个月内，游客可以凭盖有离境海关签章的退税单办理退税手续。

In Russia. the minimum tax-free purchase amount is 10,000 rubles. The general tax refund ratio is about 15%. Within 3 months after shopping, visitors can get the refund with stamped tax refund form in the Customs office.

（三）时差

北京位于东八区，莫斯科位于东三区，所以北京和莫斯科相差5个小时。2014年起，俄罗斯永久使用冬令时制，取消夏令时制。

Beijing is located in the eastern eighth time zone while Moscow is in the eastern third time zone, thus there is 5 hours difference between the two cities. In 2014, Russia decided to cancel Daylight Saving Time forever and use the standard time.

思考练习

1. 经典旅游线路分析

俄罗斯深度8日游

第1天：北京——莫斯科

在北京首都国际机场集合，乘航班前往莫斯科，开始愉快旅程。

第2天：莫斯科

早餐后游览革命圣地——红场（这里是莫斯科的心脏，南北长697米，东西宽130米，原为一个集市，17世纪改为现在的名字，意为“美丽的广场”）。参观列宁墓（周一和周五不开放）、圣瓦西里升天大教堂（外观）、克里姆林宫、无名烈士墓、亚历山大花园、俄罗斯最大的百货商店——古姆商场。晚餐后入住酒店休息。

第3天：莫斯科——谢尔盖耶夫镇——圣彼得堡

早餐后，乘车前往位于莫斯科东北71千米处的谢尔盖耶夫镇。游览著名的谢尔盖圣三一修道院——圣三一大教堂、圣母升天大教堂和特拉别茨纳亚大教堂（谢尔盖圣三一修道院是俄罗斯驰名世界的宗教圣地，也是俄罗斯最古老的大修道院之一）。午餐后，乘车返回莫斯科。晚餐后乘火车赴圣彼得堡。

第4天：圣彼得堡

早抵圣彼得堡，早餐后在市区观光，游览狮身人面像、瓦西里岛古港口灯塔、打响十月革命第一枪的阿芙乐尔号巡洋舰，参观世界四大博物馆之一的艾尔米塔什博物馆——冬宫，圣彼得堡的中心广场——冬宫广场。圣彼得堡不仅以其雄伟的建筑而闻名，也是俄罗斯历史上众多历史事件的见证。晚餐后入住酒店休息。

第5天：圣彼得堡

早餐后游览夏宫花园，午餐后游览圣彼得堡的发源地——彼得保罗要塞。1703年彼得大帝下令修建，彼得保罗要塞曾作为沙皇俄国的巴士底狱关押政治犯。其中的彼得保罗教堂是罗曼诺夫王朝的沙皇陵寝所在地，参观青铜骑士像。晚餐后入住酒店休息。

第6天：圣彼得堡——莫斯科

早餐后参观滴血大教堂（1881年3月1日沙皇亚历山大二世在此遇刺身亡，该教堂由此得名），喀山大教堂，十二月党人广场，十月革命胜地——斯莫尔尼宫（原为叶卡捷琳娜二世时期的贵族女子学院，十月革命期间布尔什维克军事革命委员会设于此地，现在为圣彼得堡市政府办公所在地）。漫步涅瓦大街，选购纪念品，晚餐后乘火车返回莫斯科。

第7天：莫斯科

早餐后参观莫斯科地铁站、俄罗斯的最高学府莫斯科大学（位于莫斯科西南部的列宁山上，中央主楼32层，顶部是穗形环绕的五角星，两翼为18层高楼，顶部装有大钟，培养出了多位诺贝尔奖获得者）。游览列宁山、观景台，参观二战胜利公园、凯旋门、阿尔巴特大街（一条古老的文化商业大街，是外国游客经常光顾的地方，主要出售手工艺品等各种纪念品）。晚餐后入住酒店休息。

第8天：莫斯科——北京

乘飞机返回北京，结束愉快的旅程。

分析：这条经典旅游线路的主要旅游景点与行程特色，以及适合旅游的人群。

2. 案例分析

[案例1] 领队小王带领游客前往俄罗斯旅游，在与当地人的一个交流项目中，一位美丽的俄罗斯女孩捧着托盘迎接客人，铺着绣花的白色面巾的托盘上放着大圆面包，面包上面放着一小纸包盐，请客人品尝。其中一位游客品尝了面包后把那小包盐扔到了地上。俄罗斯女孩脸上露出不悦的神情。请问这位游客哪里做错了？

[案例2] 某商务旅游团赴俄罗斯旅游。为迎接这些游客，接待方在莫斯科当地一家有名的餐厅请他们享用风味餐。用餐期间，一名游客不小心把盘子摔碎了，她当时显得很尴尬，在这么隆重喜庆的场合做了一件不吉利的事。结果主办方俄罗斯人却兴高采烈，还为她敬酒。为什么？

3. 练一练

近年来，赴俄罗斯旅游的绝大多数游客都是40岁以上的人。2018年，俄罗斯公民访华241.4万人次，同比增长3%。中国公民访俄203.7万人次，同比增长21.3%，中俄旅游互访人数约444万人，中国和俄罗斯互为重要的客源国和目的地国。试分析这些中国游客的俄罗斯情结，选择一个你感兴趣的主题写一篇导游词。

第四章
北美地区

本章导航

联合国按照政治地理学标准，将北美地区（Northern America）定义为拉丁美洲国家以北的美洲地区，位于西半球北部，东滨大西洋，西临太平洋，北濒北冰洋，南为墨西哥。与北美洲有明显的不同，北美地区不包括同属于北美大陆的中美（即墨西哥、中美洲和加勒比地区），主要由加拿大、美国、格陵兰（丹麦的自治领地和岛屿）、圣皮埃尔和密克隆群岛（法国的海外领地）和百慕大（英国的海外领地）组成。本区通用英语，为发达国家。北美地区最早的居民为印第安人和因纽特人（爱斯基摩人），其余大部分居民是欧洲移民的后裔，以盎格鲁-撒克逊人最多。北美地区人口约为33 500万，约占世界总人口的5%。美国和加拿大都是旅游业非常发达的国家。自2008年美国、2010年加拿大正式成为中国出境旅游目的地国家以来，中国赴美国和加拿大的游客数量大幅增长。本章主要从国家概况、民俗风情、旅游景点和旅游资讯等方面增加学习者对美国和加拿大的认识和了解。

第一节　美国

一、国家概况

（一）地理环境

美利坚合众国，简称美国，地处北美洲中部，东临大西洋，西濒太平洋，南靠墨西哥和墨西哥湾，北邻加拿大。美国由 50 个州和华盛顿哥伦比亚特区组成，其中 48 个州位于本土，2 个州在本土以外，即北美西北部的阿拉斯加州和太平洋的夏威夷州。此外，还有关岛、美属维尔京群岛、塞班岛等海外属地和托管地。美国的面积达 937 万平方千米，仅次于俄罗斯、加拿大和中国，居世界第四位。

The United States of America, briefly America or the United States, is located in the central North America, bordering the Atlantic Ocean to the east, the Pacific Ocean to the west, Mexico and the Gulf of Mexico to the south, and Canada to its north. The country consists of 50 states and Washington, D.C. (District of Columbia), 48 of which are on the mainland of the United States and the remaining two: the state of Alaska in the northwestern part of North America and the state of Hawaii in the Pacific Ocean. Its territory also includes other overseas trust territories such as Guam, American Virgin Islands and Saipan. With an area of 9,370,000 square kilometers, it is the forth largest country in the world by area, next to Russia, Canada and China.

美国地势东西高，中央低，可以分为三个地形区。东部是阿巴拉契亚山脉构成的古老山地及大西洋沿岸平原；西部是科迪勒拉山系构成的高原和山地，包括落基山脉、海岸山脉、内华达山脉以及一系列山间高原、盆地和谷地；中部为大平原，约占美国面积的一半，是美国的主要农业区。美国的河流、湖泊众多，水系复杂，其中密西西比河全长 6 020 千米，是世界第四长河。北美洲中东部的苏必利尔湖、休伦湖、密歇根湖、伊利湖和安大略湖五大湖为世界最大的淡水湖群，总面积为 24.5 万平方千米，素有“北美地中海”之称。

The land of America is high in both east and west and low in the midland, divided into three terrains: Appalachian Mountains and coastal plain in the east, American Cordillera range in the west including the Rocky Mountains, Coast Mountains, Sierra Nevada, as well as other plateaus, basins and valleys, and the central plain in the middle, which is the major agricultural area, covering the half area of the country. America has rich water resources from rivers and lakes, and its waterways are complicated. Mississippi River running 6,020 kilometers is the fourth largest river in the world. Located in the mid-east of North America, the Great Lakes, consisting of Lake Superior, Lake Huron, Lake Michigan, Lake Erie and Lake Ontario, is the largest freshwater lakes group in the world with an area of 245,000 square kilometers and is known as “Northern American Mediterranean Sea”.

美国幅员辽阔，地形复杂，各地气候差异较大，大体可分为 5 个气候区：东北部为沿海的温带气候区、东南部为亚热带气候区、中央平原为大陆性气候区、西部高原为干燥气候区、太平洋沿岸为海洋性气候区。其中，佛罗里达半岛南端属热带；阿拉斯加位于北纬60° 至 70° 之间，属北极圈内的寒冷气候；夏威夷位于北回归线以南，属热带气候。

The vast land and complex terrains give rise to varied regional climates of the country. Generally, there are five climatic regions in America — the coastal temperate zone in the northeast part, the subtropical zone in the southeast part, the continental zone in the central great plain, the arid climate zone in the western highlands and marine climate along the Pacific coast. The southern tip of Florida Peninsula is in the tropical zone. Alaska located between 60°N and 70°N latitude has an Arctic frigid climate; and Hawaii which is in the south of the Tropic of Cancer has a tropical climate.

（二）人文概况

1. 历史

在哥伦布发现美洲大陆以前，北美洲生活着印第安人和因纽特人。15 世纪末期，新大陆的发现引起了欧洲殖民国家的关注，大批殖民者蜂拥而至。西班牙、荷兰、法国和英国相继在此建立殖民地。到 1773 年，英国已拥有 13 个殖民地。1775 年，美国爆发了反对殖民统治的独立战争。1776 年 7 月 4 日，13 个州的代表在费城召开了第二次大陆会议，组成大陆军团，华盛顿任总司令，并发表《独立宣言》，成立美利坚合众国。1788 年，华盛顿任美国第一任总统。1861 年，林肯当选为美国总统后，反对取消奴隶制的南方 7 个州宣布退出联邦并另外成立邦联，导致南北战争的爆发。1862 年，林肯宣布废除奴隶制。1865 年，南北战争结束。联邦政府权力得到加强。政府通过了许多刺激经济发展的法案，大大加快了美国的工业化进程。1898 年，美西战争爆发，美国最终取胜，标志着美国正式步入帝国主义强国行列并开始对外扩张。第一次世界大战的胜利使美国获利不少，而第二次世界大战的胜利奠定了美国世界第一强国的地位。20 世纪末随着苏联解体及冷战结束，美国国力更是空前强大。自 1870 年以来，美国国民经济就高居全球第一。如今的美国是联合国安理会 5 个常任理事国之一，其在全球的政治、经济、军事、娱乐等众多领域的庞大影响力更是其他国家无法匹敌的。

Before discovered by Columbus, the North American continent was inhabited by American Indians and Inuits. At the end of the 15th century, the discovery of the new continent drew the attentions from the European colonial countries and a large number of colonists flocked here. Spain, Holland, France and United Kingdom established colonies here one after another, and United Kingdom took the lead with 13 colonies in 1773. In 1775, American Revolutionary War was launched against the colonial rule. On July 4, 1776, the representatives of 13 states held the Second Continental Congress in Philadelphia and organized the Continental Army with George Washington as the commander. The *Declaration of Independence* was issued and thereafter, the United States of America was established. In 1788, Washington was elected as the first president of the United Stated. In 1861, with the election of Abraham Lincoln as the president, southern slave states declared their secession and formed Confederate States of America (the "Confederacy" or the "South"). The American Civil War thus broke out. In 1862, President Abraham Lincoln issued the *Emancipation Proclamation*. The American Civil War ended in 1865. The slavery was abolished and the power of the federal government was strengthened. Different bills were passed to stimulate the economy, accelerating the pace of industrialization of America. In 1898, America won the war against Spain, growing into one of the powerful imperialist countries, and embarked on foreign expansion. America benefited a lot from the victory of the First World War, and the victory in the Second World War secured its status as the most powerful country in the world. At the end of the 20th century with the ending of Cold War and disintegration of the Soviet Union, the national power of America rose to an unprecedented level. Since 1870, the national economy of America has topped the world. Nowadays, America is one of the five permanent members of the United Nations Security Council and its powerful influences in such areas as politics, economy, military and entertainment are unparalleled by any other countries.

2. 经济

美国于 19 世纪末期就已超越英国成为世界第一大经济体。发达的经济使美国成为全球最富裕和民众生活水平最高的国家。美国是典型的从殖民经济到最强的工业化经济的典范。美国经济高度发达，其劳动生产率、国内生产总值和对外贸易额均居世界首位，而且有较为完善的宏观经济调控体制。美国的工业以技术先进、门类齐全、生产实力雄厚而著称于世。其中，汽车工业和建筑业是美国经济的两大支柱产业。美国的科技先进，航空和宇航工业居世界第一位，新兴的硅谷成为世界资讯产业的龙头重镇。美国的服务业特别发达，金融、保险、航运和商业服务行业在国民经济中所占比重较大，全国 3/4 的劳动力从事服务业。纽约是美国最大的城市及金融中心，也是世界最大的金融、航运服务中心。美国农业高度发达，是世界最大的农产品出口国。自 2008 年底至 2012 年，美国经济陷入次贷危机，经济增长缓慢。

By the end of the 19th century, America had already surpassed the United Kingdom in economy and it has become the No.1 economy of the world ever since. The strong economy makes America the richest country and Americans enjoys the highest living standard in the world. The country is the typical of the industrial economy which developed from the colonial economy. The economy of the country is highly-developed. The labor productivity, GDP and value of the foreign trade are leading the world. It has a complete system of regulation and control of the macro economy. The industry is known for its developed technology, a complete range of products and powerful production strength. Auto industry and building industry are two mainstay industries of American economy. America's science and technology are advanced, and its aviation and aerospace industry top the world. The newly booming Silicon Valley has become the world center of IT industry. America has vigorous service industry. The services like finance, insurance, shipping and business take up large percentage in the national economy. Almost three fourths of labor force engage in the service industry. New York is the largest city and the largest financial center in America, and it is also the largest center of the shipping and commercial service in the world. The agriculture industry of America is highly-developed. It has the biggest volume of agricultural products for export. From the end of 2008 to 2012, American economy has been sluggish as a result of the subprime mortgage crisis.

3. 社会文化

美国人基本上都是移民或是移民的后裔。印第安人、因纽特人和夏威夷人是最早安居在美国土地上的土著人。美国人口为 3.3 亿，白人占 62.1%，拉美裔占 17.4%，非洲裔占 13.2%，亚裔占 5.4%。其中，华裔是亚裔中人口最多的一个族裔。美国没有法定的官方语言，但英语是事实上的国家语言。由于地理的阻隔、时间的流逝，美、英两国语言已产生了很大的差异，演变出了具有美国特色的美式英语。除了英语外，使用人口超过 100 万人的语言包括西班牙语、法语和汉语。54.6% 的居民信奉基督教新教，23.9% 信奉天主教，1.7% 信奉犹太教，此外还有东正教、佛教、伊斯兰教和印度教等。

Americans are mostly immigrants or the descendants of immigrants. American Indians, Inuits and Hawaiians are the earliest inhabitants of America. The population of America is 330 million, mainly composed of four ethnic groups, the whites (62.1%), the Hispanic and Latino American (17.4%), African American (13.2%) and the Asian American (5.4%). Ethnic Chinese is top in number of the population of Asian American. America does not have an official language by law, but English is actually the national language. As a result of geographical barriers and the passage of time, the languages of America and United Kingdom have differed greatly, and American-featured English has evolved from the original one. Besides English, the languages with more than 1 million speakers also include Spanish, French and Chinese. 54.6% of the American are Protestant, 23.9% are Catholic, 1.7% are Jew, and the rest are Orthodox Christians, Buddhists, Muslim and Hindu, etc.

美国是个移民国家，移民文化的融入是美国文化的最大特色。由于不断涌入的人口带来了文化与传统的完美融合，因此美国通常被称为“大熔炉”。多元文化遍及美国社会，而欧洲文化对美国文化的影响最为深刻。早期的移民把欧洲文化带到美国。这些文化很快遍及美国各地，形成美国独有的特色，并成为世界文学的主流之一。早在建立初期，美国就产生了许多杰出的作家。多位美国人曾经获得诺贝尔文学奖，如剧作家尤金·奥尼尔与小说家索尔·贝娄、赛珍珠、威廉·福克纳、欧内斯特·海明威、辛克莱·刘易斯以及约翰·斯坦贝克。如今，美国的文学作品被翻译为世界各种语言。

The United States is a nation of immigrants, and the cultural feature of which is the fusion of immigrant cultures. The inpouring population created a perfect blend of cultures and traditions, which is normally referred to as the “melting pot”. American society is diverse culturally, while the European culture influenced the American culture most significantly. The early immigrants brought European culture to the United States. And the culture spread and grew into one of the mainstreams of world literature which also has unique American features. As early as the beginning of the nation, many outstanding writers sprung up. Several Americans have been awarded Nobel Prize in Literature, such as the playwright Eugene O’Neill, and writers including Saul Bellow, Pearl S. Buck, William Faulkner, Ernest Hemingway, Sinclair Lewis, and John Steinbeck. Nowadays, American literature works have been translated into many other languages in the world.

虽然法国是世界电影的发源地，但是在当今全球化背景下，美国好莱坞电影的影响力首屈一指，处处体现了美国文化的软实力。电影、电视艺术的发展使英语迅速成了世界通用语言。

France is the birthplace of movie, but in the current globalization context, American Hollywood movies have the greatest influence, representing the soft power of American culture. The fast development of film and TV arts in the world contributed to the spread of English as the universal language.

美国的音乐起源于基督教传统音乐。随着非洲移民的加入，形成了爵士乐、摇滚乐、布鲁斯和乡村音乐等多种形式。爵士乐是19世纪末20世纪初在新奥尔良发展起来的一种流行音乐，是美国本土产生的最有分量的艺术。它最早来源于非洲音乐。17—18世纪，非洲黑人被贩运到北美做奴隶，他们用音乐来表达心中的痛苦。爵士乐保持了非洲音乐的传统——音乐与舞蹈相结合。布鲁斯是爵士乐中最主要的一种音乐形式，形成于1900年左右，源自黑奴的劳动歌曲。摇滚乐始于1952年的一次布鲁斯音乐会上青年人欢呼跳跃的“摇滚”，这一年也被称为“摇滚乐之年”。摇滚乐由爵士乐派生而来，摇滚总被认为浪荡不羁，反叛精神是其标签。如今，摇滚乐已成为一种最受美国人喜欢的流行音乐。

American music derived from the traditional Christian music. With the coming of the African immigrants, it evolved into various styles such as jazz, rock, blues and country music. Jazz, the most valuable art form native to America, is a type of new pop music which originated in New Orleans at the end of the 19th century and the beginning of the 20th century. Jazz has its root in African music. From the 17th to 18th century when Africans were transported from Africa to North America in slave trade, they expressed their bitterness with music. Jazz music retains the tradition of African music which is the combination of music and dance. Blues, which appeared around 1900, is the most important form of Jazz. It originated from the songs the slaves sang when they were in labor. Rock and roll music emerged in 1952 when a group of young men shouted and danced in a blues concert, and that year was referred to as the Year of Rock and Roll. Derived from Jazz music, Rock and Roll has always been considered wild and unrestrained, and the rebellious spirit is its label. Nowadays, Rock and Roll has become one of the most popular styles of pop music in America.

知识拓展

美国梦

许多生活在美国的人，无论是土生土长的美国人，还是漂洋过海来到美国的外国移民，都有一个梦，即通过自己的努力，改变自己的社会地位，实现自己的人生梦想，这就是人们常津津乐道的“美国梦”（American Dream）。400年前，当英格兰移民乘坐着“五月花”号横穿大西洋来到马里兰，寻找一块清教徒能居住的“净土”时，“美国梦”已开始悄然萌芽。自1776年以来，世世代代的美国人都深信不疑，只要经过努力不懈的奋斗便能获得更好的生活，而非依赖于特定的社会阶级和他人的援助。今天，每年有超过100万的人成为美国公民，来到这片土地创造自己的价值，美国成为世界上最受欢迎的移民目的地。一般而言，“美国梦”包含几个要素：美国提供了人人都能成功的机会；成功取决于自己的才能和努力，而不是家世和背景；人人都拥有平等的权利；人人都有信仰的自由。“美国梦”是美国文化精神的缩影，是个人至高无上的各种价值的实现和实际利益的满足。但是近年来，随着美国经济的持续疲软和社会问题的集中显现，很多人心中的“美国梦”正在破碎。

二、民俗风情

（一）礼仪禁忌

美国一直被视为一个大熔炉。美国公民原本来自世界各地，美国文化是由许多不同的文化、种族和宗教经过长时期的共存、结合而形成的，因此，美国人以身为美国人而自豪。美国人待人热情、开朗大方、易于接近，在人际交往上比较随意。朋友之间通常是不拘礼节地招呼一声“你好”。不论职位、年龄，美国人总是尽量喊对方的名字，以拉近相互间的距离，并把它视为亲切、友好的表示。美国人很少用正式的头衔来称呼别人。正式的头衔一般只用于法官、高级政府官员、军官、医生、教授和高级宗教人士等。大多数美国人都乐于帮助外来游客。

The United States has always been considered as a melting pot. Its citizens were originally from different parts of the world and its culture was shaped on the basis of different cultures, races and religions. Thus, the citizens are all proud of being an American. Americans are generally warm-hearted, outgoing, easygoing and casual on social occasions. A simple “hello” or “hi” is appropriate when friends greet each other. Regardless of their positions and ages, they usually address the other with the first name to show their friendliness and kill the distance between people. Formal titles are seldom used in daily life, except for the professionals such as the judges, senior government officials, military officers, doctors, professors and senior religious people, etc. Most of Americans are willing to help foreign visitors.

美国人会经常使用肢体语言。耸肩而面带不高兴的表情表示惊讶；耸肩而面带笑容表示肯定；食指和中指构成“V”字形，表示“胜利、加油”；把手搭在他人的肩膀上，表示肯定与鼓励；手掌朝上并来回运动，表示招呼人过来；单用食指，表示挑衅或不礼貌的行为，因这一行为是用来招呼动物的。小孩子犯了错，可以吐吐舌头，显得天真、可爱，但美国人认为成年人如在别人面前伸出舌头是一件既不文雅又不礼貌的行为，给人以庸俗、下流的感觉，甚至可以解释为瞧不起人。

Americans use body language frequently. When they feel surprised, they will shrug their shoulders with a sad look. And they shrug their shoulders with a smile to express approval. They use middle finger and index finger to make a “V” shape to show victory or encouragement. They pat on your shoulders to show affirmation or encouragement. When they turn their hands upward and move back and forth, it is a sign to ask someone to come over. If it is a single index finger instead of hand, it is defiant and impolite as it is used for animals. Sticking out your tongue is acceptable for kids when they make mistakes, while it represents contempt, impoliteness and vulgarness for adults before the others.

“残疾人优先、老人优先、儿童优先、女士优先”是美国人的习惯。因为他们是弱势群体，理应得到健康人士的照顾。从历史角度分析，美国人尊重女士的传统习俗受到了欧洲中世纪骑士作风的影响。若从宗教的角度分析，它是出于对圣母玛利亚的尊敬。按照美国人的习惯，在社交场合，男士处处都要谦让女士，爱护女士。

"The disabled first, the elderly first, kid first and lady first" is the common practice for Americans, because they are the vulnerable groups and deserve concerns. Historically speaking, the respect of women in America can be traced back to the knight-erranty in Medieval Europe. Religiously speaking, it is rooted in the respect for Virgin Mary. It is customary for men to give precedence to women and take care of them on social occasions.

美国人格外看重成功的价值。美国人认为只有打败所有的对手，才是成功者。在美国人眼里，重要的不是一个人的家庭背景，而是他本人的才华和能力。个人价值比什么都重要。个人价值能否实现被看作成功与否的重要标志。美国总统林肯曾经十分幽默地说过："我不知道我的祖父是何许人。我更为关心的是他的孙子将成为一个怎样的人。"因此，美国人非常独立、进取，从小便养成独立奋斗、自强自立、不依赖父母的习惯。当他们还是学生时，会打工赚取学费；成年后，离开父母自立门户，自己抚育孩子，完全靠自己的本事谋生。美国人视工作为生命的一部分。无论多么富裕，他们都要有自己的一份工作。他们对工作很敬业，工作效率很高，但工作与休息时间很分明。美国人喜欢当面或者在谈判桌上拍板，而不喜欢在事后或私下找关系解决问题。

Americans greatly value success. They believe only when you beat all the rivals are you the winner. They also have the view that it is not your family background that counts, but your own talent and capability. Nothing is more important than personal value. To realize your personal value is an important symbol for success. President Abraham Lincoln once said with his sense of humor:" I have no idea who my grandpa was. I am more concerned about what his grandson will be like." Therefore, Americans are usually very independent and aggressive as they were told to be independent and rely on themselves rather than their parents since childhood. When they are students, they work to pay for their own tuitions. When they grow up, they start their own families, raise kids and earn a living by themselves. Work is part of their life. No matter how rich they are, they all want jobs of their own. They are dedicated and efficient workers, but there is clear boundary between work and rest. They tend to make decisions face to face or put things on the table, rather than solve problems by networking afterwards.

美国人喜欢争论，不喜欢沉默不语。他们会通过争论达成共识，若达不成共识，会通过举手或投票表决，少数服从多数，这也就是美国式的民主。在美国社会中，一切行为都是以个人为中心，个人利益是神圣不可侵犯的。这种准则渗透于社会生活的各个方面。在人们的日常交谈中，忌谈有关年龄、婚姻状况、收入、宗教信仰、竞选中投谁的票等非常冒昧和失礼的问题。美国人十分讲究"个人空间"。和美国人谈话时，不可站得太近，一般保持在50厘米为宜。在餐厅或图书馆等公共场合，也要尽量同他人保持一定距离。不得已与别人同坐一桌或紧挨着别人坐时，最好打个招呼，问一声："我可以坐在这里吗？"得到允许后再坐下。

Americans like to argue rather than keep silence. They argue to reach agreement, if cannot they vote, and the majority wins. This is the American democracy. In American society, everything is oriented to the individuals, and personal interests are sacred and inviolable. This principle is reflected in any aspect of social life. The daily conversation shall not touch upon the rude and impolite questions such as age, marital status, income, religious belief, the votes in the election, etc. Americans are particular about personal space. When talking to an American, it is proper to keep the distance of 50 cm. On public occasions like restaurants or libraries, you should also keep certain distance with others. You'd better ask:" May I sit here?" if you really have no choice but to share a table with others. Never sit before being permitted.

美国人讲求实际。他们喜欢一切都自己动手，多数美国人懂得怎样使用机器、修理电气设备、油漆家具和粉刷墙壁。美国人在金钱方面也非常务实，付出劳动便要取得报酬，求助他人便应以惠相报。

Americans are very pragmatic. They love doing things all by themselves. Most of Americans know how to use machine, fix electrical equipments, paint furniture and walls. Americans are very practical about money. Any work should be paid for and they will do something in return for any favor from others.

美国人喜欢冒险。他们总是追求新奇的事物，不断地改变环境，在冒险中寻求刺激。他们从来不满足于稳定的生活和安宁的环境，喜欢运动、旅行等。美国人不喜欢串门，而喜欢在周末邀上一些亲近的朋友一同外出观光、钓鱼、聚会等。

Americans like adventures. They always pursue novel items, change living environment constantly and seek thrills in adventures. They are not satisfied with stable life and peaceful environment. They love sports and travel. They do not visit their neighbours very often, but like going out for sightseeing, fishing or party with a couple of close friends during the weekends.

美国人很珍惜时间，浪费他们的时间等同于侵犯他们的个人权利。因此，拜访美国朋友时需预先约好。美国人一般乐于在家中宴请客人，因此如被邀请到美国人家中做客，应带小礼物。美国人待客的家宴讲究经济实惠、不摆阔气、不拘泥形式。通常的家宴包括一大盘沙拉、一大盘烤鸡或烤肉、各种凉菜、一盘炒饭、面包片以及甜食、水果、冷饮、酒水等。在餐桌上，女主人动手开始就餐后，客人才能用餐。客人只有得到主人的同意后才能参观房间。受款待后，客人应给主人打电话或寄一张卡片以表示谢意。

Americans cherish time. Waste of their time is violating their personal rights. Before you visit an American friend, it would be better to make an appointment in advance. Americans would like to entertain their guests at home, so when you are invited to their homes, you'd better bring some gifts. The dinner at home is usually economical and practical rather than lavish. A home dinner usually includes a large plate of salad, a large plate of roast chicken or pork, different cold dishes, a plate of fried rice, slices of bread, dessert, fruits, cold drinks, wines, etc. At the table, you are not supposed to eat until the hostess begins. Guests should not visit the rooms without the permission of the host. After the dinner, guests should give a call or send a card to express gratitude for hospitality.

美国人把过度谦虚视为虚伪的代名词。如果一个能讲流利英语的人自谦说英语讲得不好，美国人便会认为他撒了谎，是个口是心非、装腔作势的人。因此，与美国人交往时，应该大胆展示自己的能力，不必谦虚，否则会事与愿违。

Modesty is a virtue for Chinese but a synonym for hypocrisy for Americans. If you speak fluent English and apologize for poor English, they will think you lie and behave affectedly. Therefore, when you are socializing with Americans, you should show your capability and not humble yourself. Otherwise, things will go contrary to your own wishes.

美国人对平时的穿着打扮不太讲究，他们偏爱宽松和休闲的服饰，讲究着装要彰显个性。但在一些正式场合，穿衣要得体，如周末人们去教堂时，每个人都穿得比较正式。

Generally speaking, Americans are not particular about what to wear. They prefer casual and loose clothes, but the clothes should reflect your own individuality. Appropriate dress is required on some occasions, for instance, when going to church at the weekends, people need to observe formal dress code.

（二）节庆风情

1. 独立日（Independence Day）

独立日是美国的主要法定节日之一，在每年的7月4日，以纪念1776年7月4日第二次大陆会议在费城正式通过《独立宣言》。《独立宣言》是具有历史意义的伟大文献。这一天也是美国的国庆日。在这一天，美国会举办各种活动，其中最重要的就是敲响位于费城的自由钟。其他的庆祝活动包括花车游行、节日游行等。

Independence Day, one of the major federal holidays in the United States, falls on July 4 each year to commemorate July 4, 1776 when the Second Continental Congress officially passed *the Declaration of Independence* in Philadelphia. *The Declaration of Independence* is a great document which has historic significance. On this national day of the United States, variety of activities will be held nationwide, the most important of which is striking the Liberty Bell in Philadelphia. Other celebrations include floats parades, festive parades, etc.

2. 感恩节（Thanksgiving Day）

感恩节在每年11月的最后一个星期四。感恩节是美国人独创的一个古老节日，也是美国人全家欢聚的节日。感恩节的由来可以一直追溯到美国历史的发端。1620年，著名的"五月花"号轮船满载不堪忍受英国国内宗教迫害的清教徒到达北美洲。一些心地善良的印第安人帮助了这些饥寒交迫的清教徒。按照宗教传统习俗，这些移民确定了特别的一天以感谢上帝，他们邀请印第安人共同庆祝，以感谢印第安人的帮助。美国独立后，感恩节成为全国性的节日。在这一天，家庭成员团聚在一起，吃着传统风味的火鸡，沉浸在亲情之中。而城乡市镇到处都会举行化装游行、戏剧表演和体育比赛等。

Thanksgiving Day falls on the last Thursday of November every year. It is an old festival only celebrated in America and a time for family reunion. The origin of the festival can be traced back to the beginning of American history. In 1620, the well-known Mayflower arrived in North America carrying puritans who suffered from religious prosecutions. Some kind-hearted Indians helped them when they were in hunger and cold. According to religious traditions, those immigrants designated a special day to express their gratitude to God, and invited the Indians over to celebrate together to thank for their help. After the independence of America, Thanksgiving Day became a national holiday. During the festival, family members get together, enjoying the turkey prepared in the traditional way and the company of family. In the towns and cities, other activities are held such as costume parade, theatre performances and sports games, etc.

三、主要旅游城市及景点

（一）华盛顿（Washington, D.C.）

华盛顿是美国的首都，正式称法为华盛顿哥伦比亚特区，通常称为华盛顿。华盛顿位于美国的东北部，靠近弗吉尼亚州和马里兰州。华盛顿是为了纪念开国元勋乔治·华盛顿和美洲新大陆的发现者哥伦布而命名的。作为“国家的心脏”，华盛顿受到世界各国的瞩目，它是名副其实的世界政治中心。而法国著名建筑师皮埃尔·朗法的设计，则使它成为全世界少有的美丽都市之一。华盛顿是世界各国少有的仅以政府行政职能为主的现代化大城市，白宫、国会、美国最高法院等政府机构均设在此地。华盛顿被认为是美国标志性的旅游胜地，市内数百处纪念建筑物、纪念碑、雕像等大都与历届总统有关，如华盛顿纪念碑、林肯纪念堂、杰弗逊纪念堂等。

Washington, D.C., formally the District of Columbia and commonly referred to as Washington, is the capital of the United States. It is located in the northeast of America, neighboring Virginia and Maryland. It was so named to commemorate the farther of the nation George Washington and Columbus who discovered America. As the heart of the nation, Washington draws the attention of the world. It is truly the political center of the world. Designed by French architect Pierre Charles L'Enfant, it was made one of the few beautiful cities. Washington is one of the modern cities which has solely the administrative functions, where you can find the government agencies like the White House, Congress, the Supreme Court, etc. Washington has been considered as the symbolic tourist resort, where you can see hundreds of memorial buildings, monuments and statues, which are all related to the former presidents, for instance, Washington Monument, Lincoln Memorial, Jefferson Memorial, etc.

◆ 国会大厦（The Capitol）

国会大厦是美国国会的办公大楼，因坐落在一处高约 30 米的高地上，故名“国会山”。1793 年，华盛顿曾亲自为大厦奠基。圆顶建筑呈半球形，为华盛顿的制高点，也是华盛顿的象征。国会大厦的圆顶已经成为电视中美国政治新闻报道的最佳背景，四年一度的总统就职典礼在主楼的平台上举行。美国参、众两院构成的国会就在这里举行会议。国会大厦内天花板与墙壁上绘满了以建国史为题材的壁画。游客可自行前往参观国会大厦，也可参加配有向导的观光团。国会大厦东侧的国会图书馆是世界上最大的图书馆之一。

The Capitol is the office building for the US congress. It is also called the Capitol Hill as it sits atop a 30-meter high small hill. In 1793, president Washington laid the foundation stone himself. The Rotunda, built in hemispherical shape, is the highest peak and symbol of Washington. The dome of Rotunda has been the best backdrop for political news broadcasting on TV. The inauguration ceremony is held on the platform of the main building every four years. Composed of the Senate and House of Representatives, the US Congress holds meetings here. On the ceiling and walls of the Rotunda are painted with the murals featuring the founding of the nation. The Capitol is open to the public for free. You can also join the guided tour to visit. The Library of Congress is one of the largest libraries in the world.

◆ 林肯纪念堂（Lincoln Memorial）

林肯纪念堂，被视为美国永恒的建筑及华盛顿的标志。它位于华盛顿的国家广场西端，与国会大厦、华盛顿纪念碑在同一轴线上。林肯纪念堂是为纪念美国南北战争时期的林肯总统而兴建的。林肯是美国历史上最受尊敬的总统之一，他维护美国的统一以及解放南方黑奴的伟大历史功绩为今日美国的繁荣昌盛奠定了坚固的基础。林肯纪念堂是仿古希腊帕特农神庙而建的，正中是林肯坐像。

Lincoln Memorial is viewed as the eternal architecture and symbol of Washington. Located in the west of the National Mall, it sits on the axis of the Capitol and Washington Monument. It was built in memory of President Abraham Lincoln during the Civil War. President Abraham Lincoln is one of the most respected presidents in history, for his great efforts in unifying the nation and emancipating the black slaves in the south laid solid foundation for the the United States today. The memorial was modeled on the Parthenon in Greece, enshrining Abraham Lincoln at the central position.

◆ 白宫（White House）

白宫是美国总统府所在地。白宫的基址是美国开国元勋、第一任总统乔治·华盛顿选定的，始建于 1792 年，因外墙为白色砂砾石，故名“白宫”。最先使用此官邸的是美国第二任总统约翰·亚当斯。从此，美国历届总统均以白宫为官邸，白宫成为美国政府的代名词。白宫的设计者是著名的美籍爱尔兰建筑师詹姆斯·霍本。白宫分主楼和东、西两翼，总统办公室呈椭圆形，南草坪是欢迎国宾的场所。根据白宫支出由全体纳税人负担的原则，白宫的一部分在规定时间内向全世界开放，因此成为游人观光的热点。毕竟它是世界上唯一定期向公众开放的国家元首官邸。

The White House is the official residence and principal workplace of the president of the United States. Its location was chosen by George Washington, the founder of the nation and first president of the United States. It was first built in 1792 out of white-painted sandstone, hence its name the White House. The first one to actually reside here was John Adams, the second president of the United States. Since then, it has been the residence of every president, making it a synonym for American government. The designer of the White House was the famous American Scottish architect named James Hoban. The White House Complex mainly includes the Executive Residence, East and West Wings. The Executive Office of the president takes the shape of an oval and the South Lawn is where the welcome ceremonies of visiting heads of state are held. As the expenses of the White House are borne by all the taxpayers, part of the White House is open to the public as a popular sightseeing attraction for a certain period of time. It is the only presidential residence in the world which is open to the public at regular intervals.

（二）纽约（New York）

纽约，别称大苹果、哥谭镇、不夜城、帝国之城等，于1624年建城，是美国最大的城市及最大的商港，也是世界经济中心之一。纽约地处纽约州东南部，在华盛顿和波士顿的中间，紧邻的哈德逊河让纽约市享有航运之便。纽约由布朗克斯区、布鲁克林区、曼哈顿、皇后区（昆斯区）、斯塔滕岛五大区组成。其中，曼哈顿是纽约的核心和象征、美国的金融中心，有"纽约市的心脏"之称。位于曼哈顿的华尔街是美国财富和经济实力的象征，也是美国垄断资本的大本营和金融寡头的代名词，美国最大的500家企业中，有1/3以上把总部设在这里。纽约是国际级的经济、金融、交通、艺术及传媒中心，更被视为都市文明的代表地，由于联合国总部设在此，因此被世人誉为"世界之都"。纽约与伦敦、巴黎、莫斯科并称为世界四大国际大都会。纽约的旅游景点主要有自由女神像、帝国大厦、时代广场、中央公园、联合国总部大楼、百老汇、华尔街、大都会博物馆等。

Built in 1624, New York is the biggest city and port in the United States, as well as one of the economic centers in the world. New York is also nicknamed the Big Apple, Gotham, the City that Never Sleeps and the Empire City, etc. New York is located in the southeast of the State of New York and that is about in the middle of Washington, D.C. and Boston. Close to the Hudson River, New York enjoys the great shipping convenience. New York consists of 5 boroughs, namely Bronx, Brooklyn, Manhattan, Queens and Staten Island, among which Manhattan is the core and symbol of New York. It is the financial center of the United States and known as the heart of New York. Wall Street in Manhattan is the symbol of wealth and economic power of United States and it is also synonymous with the monopoly capital base and financial tycoons. More than one third of Top 500 enterprises are headquartered in the Wall Street. New York is the center of international economy, finance, transportation, art and media, and it is regarded as the typical representative of urban civilization of the world. New York, together with London, Paris, Moscow are called the world's four major international metropolises. The main tourist attractions of New York are the Statue of Liberty, the Empire State Building, Times Square, Central Park, United Nations Headquarters, Broadway, Wall Street, the Metropolitan Museum of Art, etc.

◆ 帝国大厦（Empire State Building）

帝国大厦和自由女神像一起被称为纽约的标志。帝国大厦于1931年建成，当时正是美国经济大萧条时期，因此被认为是美国经济复苏的象征。帝国大厦高443米，是纽约摩天大楼的象征。至今，这幢装饰艺术派的杰作仍然是曼哈顿最特别的一道风景。在第86层和102层上有观景台，天气晴朗时，可以眺望周围80千米以内的景色。

The Empire State Building, together with the Statue of Liberty are known as the landmarks of New York. It was finished in 1931 when the US was in the Great Depression, thus it served as the sign of economic revival. With a height of 443 meters, it is a representative of New York skyscrapers. This art deco masterpiece is the most characteristic view of Manhattan. On the observation decks of the 86th and 102nd floor, you can have a panoramic view of the scenery within 80 kilometers.

◆ 自由女神像（Statue of Liberty）

自由女神像正式的名称是"照耀世界的自由女神"，它高高地耸立在纽约港口的自由岛上，是美国的象征，象征着美国人民争取自由的崇高理想。自由女神像是法国在 1876 年送给美国独立 100 周年的礼物。整座铜像以 120 吨的钢铁为骨架，80 吨的铜片为外皮，30 万只铆钉装配固定在支架上，总重量达 225 吨。自由女神像由法国雕塑家巴托尔迪创作，内部钢架由巴黎埃菲尔铁塔的设计师古斯塔夫·埃菲尔设计。自由女神像高 46 米，右手高举火炬，左手捧着《独立宣言》，内有 22 层，可以前往自由女神像顶端的皇冠处，游客可透过皇冠上的小窗饱览纽约美景。1984 年，自由女神像被联合国教科文组织列入世界文化遗产名录。

The official name of the Statue of Liberty is Liberty Enlightening the World. Towering on the Liberty Island of New York harbour, it is an icon of the US, representing the lofty ideal to obtain liberty. The statue was a gift from France for the 100th anniversary of the founding of the US in 1876. The interior of the statue is composed of 120 tons steel and its surface is covered by 80 tons copper sheet nailed by 300,000 rivets. Its weight amounts to 225 tons. The Statue of Liberty was created by French sculptor Bartholdi. The interior framework was designed by Gustave Eiffel who designed the Eiffel Tower. The whole statue is 46 meters high, holding a torch in her right hand and *the Declaration of Independence* in the left. It has 22 floors inside, with an interior staircase leading to the crown of her head, where you will be able to have a panorama of the scenery of the city. In 1984, the Statue of Liberty was inscribed in the list of World Cultural Heritage Site.

◆ 联合国总部大楼（United Nations Headquarters）

现代世界史与联合国密切相关。联合国总部大楼是世界各国的“大家庭”，每年世界上许多大事情都在这里展开讨论并最终得以解决。联合国成立于 1945 年。1946 年，美国纽约富商约翰·洛克菲勒出资买下曼哈顿的大片街区赠予联合国，希望能把联合国总部留在纽约以巩固纽约的世界地位。联合国的 6 个主要机构，除了国际法院外，均设在这里。因此，联合国总部大楼被视为联合国的象征。目前，联合国总部大楼已成为纽约重要的观光点之一。

The modern world history is correlated with the United Nations. The United Nations Headquarters is the home for nations worldwide, where many issues are discussed and solved. After the establishment of the UN in 1945, John Rockefeller, a business tycoon, purchased large area of blocks which were later bestowed to the UN in 1946, hoping that the headquarters of UN would be kept in New York so as to enhance its world central status. There are 6 major organs which are all in this building except International Court of Justice. Thus, the United Nations Headquarters is considered the symbol of UN, and is also one of the important sightseeing attractions in New York.

（三）圣弗朗西斯科（San Francisco）

圣弗朗西斯科又称“旧金山”、粤语叫“三藩市”。19 世纪，这里是美国“淘金热”的中心地区，早期华人劳工移居美国后多居住于此，称之为“金山”，但在澳大利亚的墨尔本发现金矿后，为了与被称作“新金山”的墨尔本相区别，而改称“旧金山”。旧金山位于加利福尼亚州西北部，美国西海岸中点，是太平洋沿岸仅次于洛杉矶的第二大港口，也是美国西部的金融中心，人们常把旧金山称为美国西部的大门，素有“西海岸门户”之称。旧金山原为西班牙的一个殖民据点，1848 年，附近地区发现金矿，大批淘金者涌入，城市迅速发展。作为加利福尼亚州的门户，今天的旧金山是一座国际大都市，与众不同的城市魅力让其多年蝉联“全球最受欢迎的美国城市”，拥有众多世界知名的标志性景点，如金门大桥、旧金山-奥克兰海湾大桥、伦巴底街、联合广场、渔人码头等。

The Chinese equivalent of San Francisco is Jiu Jin Shan (old gold mountain) or Sheng Fu Lang Xi Si Ke in Mandarin or San Fan Shi in Cantonese. It used to be the center of gold rush in the United States in the 19th century when the early Chinese labors migrated and settled down here, calling it Jinshan which means gold mountain. But after the discovery of gold mines in Melbourne of Australia, its name was changed to Jiu Jin Shan (old gold mountain) to distinguish it from the new one. San Francisco is located in the northwest of California, the middle point of American west coast. San Francisco is the second biggest commercial port just next to Los Angeles, and the financial center of the western US, thus, gaining itself a title of “west coast gateway”. San Francisco was first set up as a Spanish colonial settlement and saw the quick development with a large number of gold hunters flooding in as a result of the discovery of gold mine here in 1848. As the gateway of California, present San Francisco is a cosmopolis, honored as the most popular city of the US for consecutive years for its distinctive glamour. Well-known iconic attractions of San Francisco are Golden Gate Bridge, San Francisco-Oakland Bay Bridge, Lombard Street, Union Square, Fisherman’s Wharf, etc.

◆ 金门大桥（Golden Gate Bridge）

横跨金门海峡的金门大桥建于 1937 年，是世界上最大的单孔吊桥之一，也是旧金山的象征。金门大桥全长 2 780 米，以气势雄伟被誉为“美国最美丽的大桥”。金门大桥在桥梁建筑学上也是一个创举，它不是利用桥墩支撑桥身，而是利用桥两侧的弧形吊带产生的巨大拉力，把沉重的桥身高高吊起。金门大桥的设计者——工程师约瑟夫·施特劳斯的铜像被安放在桥畔，以纪念他的杰出贡献。如今，金门大桥是世界上无数桥梁中最繁忙的桥梁之一，每天约有 10 万辆汽车从桥上驶过。

Built in 1937, Golden Gate Bridge, the largest single arch suspension bridge spanning Golden Gate, is recognized the symbol of San Francisco. With a length of 2,780 meters, it is heralded the most beautiful bridge of the US for the grandeur. The bridge is hailed as great achievement in bridge construction history. Its weight does not rely on the piers, but the pulling strength produced by two arc-shaped suspension cables on both sides. The statue of Joseph Strauss, the designer of the bridge, stands by the bridge, remembered by people for his outstanding contribution. Nowadays, Golden Gate bridge is one of the busiest bridges with more than 100,000 vehicles across the bridge each day.

（四）洛杉矶（Los Angeles）

洛杉矶位于充满阳光的西海岸，是仅次于纽约的美国第二大城市。洛杉矶意指“天使之城”，坐落在一个三面环山、一面临海的开阔盆地中，一年四季阳光明媚，干燥少雨，气候温和宜人。当地人常用昵称“L.A.”或用“南方”称呼洛杉矶。洛杉矶是美国的科技中心之一，科学家和工程技术人员的数量位居全美第一，享有“科技之城”的称号。近年来，洛杉矶的金融业和商业也迅速发展，是仅次于纽约的金融中心。洛杉矶还是美国的文化娱乐中心。闻名遐迩的“电影王国”好莱坞、引人入胜的迪士尼乐园和峰秀地灵的比弗利山使洛杉矶成为一座举世闻名的“电影城”和“旅游城”。

Los Angeles, the second largest city in the United States after New York, is located on the sunny west coast. Los Angeles means “City of Angels”. Situated in an open basin with one side facing the sea and the other three nestled by mountains, it is sunny all year round with a dry and mild climate. Nicknamed as “L.A.” or “Southern”, Los Angeles is one of the technology centers in the United States. Known as “City of Technology” , Los Angeles boasts more scientists, engineers and technicians than any other states. It has experienced rapid developments in the financial and commercial sectors in recent years. Los Angeles is the financial center just next to New York. As the cultural and entertaining center of the United States, Los Angeles has become a world famous “film city” and “tourist city”, thanks to the Kingdom of Movie—Hollywood, fascinating Disneyland and spectacular Beverly Hills.

◆ 好莱坞（Hollywood）

加利福尼亚州是古典艺术的中心、世界娱乐产业的首都、时尚潮流的标杆、大明星们出入的大本营，更是全球影迷魂牵梦萦的圣地。20 世纪福克斯、哥伦比亚电影公司、环球影片公司、华纳兄弟娱乐公司等电影巨头都汇集在好莱坞。主要旅游景点有好莱坞日落大道、星光大道、中国剧院、举办奥斯卡颁奖典礼的柯达剧场和好莱坞环球影城等。

California, the center for classic arts and the capital of the world entertainment industry, plays the leading role in fashion. It is the place where super stars gather and the holy land the movie fans worldwide dream of. Movie giants like 20th Century Fox, Columbia Pictures, Universal Studios, Warner Bros. Entertainment all settled down in Hollywood. The main attractions are Hollywood Sunset Boulevard, Walk of Fame, TCL Chinese Theatre, Kodak Theater where Academy Awards ceremony is held, and the Hollywood Universal Studios, etc.

◆ 迪士尼乐园（Disneyland）

迪士尼乐园是由美国动画片大师华特·迪士尼于 1955 年推出的世界上第一个迪士尼主题乐园，也是世界上第一个现代意义的主题公园。它以丰富的想象力设计出的人间幻境招徕游客，号称“全世界最快乐的地方”。

Disneyland, the first Disney theme park launched in 1955 by the American animation master Walt Disney, is the world’s first modern theme park. Known as “the happiest place in the world”, it appeals to millions of tourists by creating a supernatural imaginative realm.

（五）其他著名旅游景点

◆ 拉斯维加斯（Las Vegas）

拉斯维加斯，别名“世界娱乐之都”“罪恶之城”“赌城”，是美国内华达州的最大城市，是一个涵盖赌博、购物和度假产业的大型旅游中心，是世界知名的度假胜地之一。拉斯维加斯是一座从沙漠里建起来的神奇城市。经过 100 多年的发展，凭借温和的冬季气候和紧邻洛杉矶和盐湖城之间繁忙的15号州际公路的有利位置，每年吸引了近4 000万的游客到访。有时，游客们甚至把婚礼都搬到了拉斯维加斯。拉斯维加斯现已跻身于美国头等旅游和会议目的地。

Las Vegas, the largest city in Nevada and alias of "the entertainment capital of the world", "sin city," "gambling city", is the huge tourist center for the gambling industry, shopping and vacation. It is one of the world-famous resorts. Las Vegas is a magical city rising from the desert. After over 100 years of development, Las Vegas attracts nearly 40 million visitors a year, thanks to its mild winter climate and favorable position close to the No.15 Interstate Highway linking Los Angeles and Salt Lake City. Some tourists even move their weddings to Las Vegas. Las Vegas is now among the first-class tourism and convention destinations in the United States.

◆ 夏威夷（Hawaii）

夏威夷群岛，位于北太平洋，距离美国本土5 000多千米。夏威夷州的城镇包括欧胡岛上的火奴鲁鲁、大岛（夏威夷岛）上的希洛与科纳，考艾岛上的利胡埃以及毛伊岛上的卡胡鲁伊。夏威夷州的首府火奴鲁鲁，以洁白海滩闻名世界的威基基海滩以及钻石山，都位于欧胡岛。欧胡岛上的火奴鲁鲁国际机场（丹尼尔·伊努耶国际机场）是国际人士出入夏威夷州的大门。夏威夷拥有全世界最活跃的火山，是现代冲浪、草裙舞和夏威夷地方美食的发源地。夏威夷也是前国王的王室所在地，是美国领土唯一的皇家官邸所在地。夏威夷是全世界地质构造最年轻的地区之一，也是美国最年轻的州。夏威夷最与众不同之处就是它的阿罗哈精神：夏威夷人的热情好客与岛屿四季宜人的完美风光相得益彰。夏威夷的每座岛屿都有着鲜明的个性，马克·吐温称赞夏威夷是大洋中最美的岛屿，是停泊在海洋中最可爱的岛屿舰队。

Hawaiian Islands are located in the North Pacific Ocean, over 5,000 kilometers from the United States. Hawaiian towns consist of Honolulu on Oahu, Hilo and Kona on Big Island (Hawaii Island), Lihue on Kauai and Kahului on Maui. The capital Honolulu, Waikiki Beach known for its world-famous white beach, and Diamond Hill are all on the island of Oahu. Honolulu International Airport (Daniel K. Inouye International Airport) on Oahu is the gateway for the international guests to travel to and out of Hawaii. Hawaii is home to the most active volcanoes in the world, and is the birthplace of modern surfing, hula dancing and Hawaiian regional cuisine. It is also the royal seat of the former king, and the only royal residence location. Hawaii is the youngest region in terms of the geological structure in the world, and also one of the youngest states in the United States. Of Hawaii's most distinctive is its Spirit of Aloha, the Hawaiian style hospitality. The spirit and the charming scenery all years around complement each other perfectly. Hawaiian Islands have a distinct personality as Mark Twain described it as the most beautiful island in the North Pacific Ocean, and the cutest fleet of islands in the sea.

◆ 波士顿（Boston）

波士顿是美国马萨诸塞州的首府和最大城市，也是新英格兰地区的最大和最有活力的城市，位于美国东北部的大西洋沿岸。波士顿创建于1630年，是美国最古老、最有文化价值的城市之一。波士顿的发展与许多历史事件都有联系，如1770年发生的英军枪杀四位平民的“波士顿惨案”，1773年出现的反英抗税的“倾茶事件”。1775年4月在这里打响了美国独立战争的第一枪。这些政治事件已经影响了整个国家的历史，波士顿在其中扮演了重要角色。作为一座文化城市，波士顿常被誉为“美国雅典”，这是因为在波士顿大都会区拥有超过100所大学，超过25万名学生在此接受教育。1636年成立的美国第一所大学——哈佛大学，现在是全美最杰出的教育机构之一。此外，还有著名的麻省理工学院、东北大学和波士顿大学等高等学府，每年吸引了众多来自世界各地的学子。此外，波士顿交响乐团享有很高的国际声誉。

Boston is the capital and the largest city of Massachusetts, as well as the largest and most vigorous city of New England. Boston is situated on the Atlantic coast of northeastern America. Established in 1630, Boston is one of the oldest and most culturally-valued cities in the United States. The development of the city has been correlated with many historical events, such as Boston Massacre in 1770 when British soldiers shot four civilians, and the Boston Tea Party of 1773 when American colonists dumped tea into Boston harbor to protest taxes imposed by ruling Britain. It was in Boston that the first shot of American Independence War was fired in April 1775. Those political issues have transformed the history of the entire nation and Boston played an essential role. As a cultural city, Boston is often reputed as the Athens of the US, for Boston metropolitan area boasts over 100 universities with a total enrollment of more than 250,000 students. Created in 1636, Harvard University is the first university of the United States, as well as one of the most outstanding educational institutions. There are other well-known higher education institutions such as Massachusetts Institute of Technology, Northeastern University and Boston University, etc., which attract a large number of students from different parts of the world. Besides, Boston Symphony Orchestra also enjoys high international reputation.

◆ 费城（Philadelphia）

费城是美国历史的摇篮。“Philadelphia”是希腊语，意为“兄弟之爱”。费城是宾夕法尼亚州的最大城市，是美国最具历史意义的城市，也是美国和美国民主的诞生地。1774年至1775年，两次大陆会议在此召开，通过了《独立宣言》；1787年，在此举行了制宪会议，诞生了第一部联邦宪法。1790年至1800年，这里曾是美国首都。19世纪以来，铁路和港口发展很快，制造业兴起，1860年制造业产值曾占全国的30%。现在仍为美国主要的经济、交通、文化中心之一。费城的著名旅游景点有费城艺术博物馆、自由钟、独立宫、宾夕法尼亚大学等。

Philadelphia is the cradle of American history. It means “brotherly love” in Greek. Philadelphia is the largest city of Pennsylvania, and the most historic city of the United States. Philadelphia is also the birthplace of the nation and American democracy. Two Continental Congresses were held here in 1774 and 1775 respectively, and *the Declaration of Independence* was signed here; The first Constitution of the United States was drafted in the Constitutional Convention in Philadelphia in 1787. The city once served as the capital of the nation from 1790 to 1800. Since the 19th century the fast development of railway and harbour contributed to the rise of manufacturing industry. In 1860, manufacturing output of Philadelphia accounted for 30% of the entire country. Till now it is still one of the major centers of economy, transportation and culture. The famous tourist attractions are Philadelphia Museum of Art, the Liberty Bell, Independence Hall and University of Pennsylvania, etc.

◆ 迈阿密（Miami）

迈阿密位于美国佛罗里达州东南角的比斯坎湾、佛罗里达大沼泽地和大西洋之间。迈阿密被认为是文化的大熔炉，受庞大的拉丁美洲族群和加勒比海岛国居民的影响很大（当地居民多使用西班牙语和海地克里奥尔语），与北美洲、南美洲、中美洲以及加勒比海地区在文化和语言上关系密切，因此有时还被称为“美洲的首都”。因为此地气候温暖，所以是美国退休人士最爱居住的城市之一。现在的迈阿密是老年人与时装设计师、比基尼泳装模特和古巴移民的天堂。迈阿密是美国最受欢迎的旅游胜地之一，温暖的阳光、新鲜的橙子、高尔夫、水上运动等每年吸引着来自世界各地的游客。迈阿密港是世界上最大的邮轮港，每年有超过 350 万人次游客在此乘坐邮轮，占全球总数的 1/3，迈阿密也因此被称为“世界邮轮中心”。

Miami lies among Biscayne Bay, the southeast corner of Florida, the Everglades and the Atlantic Ocean. Greatly affected by the huge ethnic group of Latin America and the Caribbean island residents (most local residents speak Spanish and Haitian Creole), Miami—a melting pot—has a close relationship with North America, South America, Central America and Caribbean regions in culture and language, thus it is entitled as “the capital of the Americas”. It is one of the American retirees’ favorite cities to live for the warm climate, known as the heaven for the old, fashion designers, bikini models and Cuban immigrants. Miami is one of the most popular attractions in the United States, where the warm sunshine, fresh oranges, golf, water sports appeal tourists from around the world annually. The Port of Miami is the largest cruise port in the world. Over 3.5 million passengers start their cruise here every year, accounting for one third of the global amount, therefore Miami is also known as the World Cruise Center.

◆ 大峡谷（Grand Canyon）

世界闻名的大峡谷位于亚利桑那州的西北部，它是美国的象征。大峡谷是从太空中可以用肉眼看得见的地球自然景观之一。它是科罗拉多河旧时河谷的一部分。大峡谷由科罗拉多河侵蚀切割而成，峡谷两岸随处显露着形成于不同地质年代的地层断面，自谷底到北壁峰顶分成四个各不相同的气温层与植物带，是一部生动的“地质教科书”。1919 年，威尔逊总统批准将它辟为国家公园。1979 年，联合国教科文组织将大峡谷国家公园列入世界自然遗产名录。

Located in northwestern Arizona, the world-famous Grand Canyon is the symbol of the United States. The Grand Canyon is one of the visible natural landscapes seen from the space. It is part of the primitive valley of the Colorado River. Grand Canyon was carved as a result of the erosion of the Colorado River. Sections which formed in different geological ages expose here and there on both sides of Canyon. From the bottom of valley to the top of its north wall lies four distinct layers of climate and plants, virtually a living geological textbook. In 1919, President Wilson approved it as a National Park. In 1979, UNESCO included the Grand Canyon National Park on the World Natural Heritage Site.

◆ 尼亚加拉瀑布（Niagara Falls）

尼亚加拉瀑布源自印第安语，意为“雷神之水”，位于加拿大安大略省和美国纽约州的交界处，距离纽约州第二大城市布法罗仅 32 千米，是世界著名奇观。它与南美洲的伊瓜苏瀑布及非洲的维多利亚瀑布合称“世界三大瀑布”。在这里，尼亚加拉河跌下一个 52 米高的悬崖，创造出全世界最宏伟的自然奇观之一——尼亚加拉瀑布。尼亚加拉瀑布由两个主流汇合而成：一是美国境内的“美国瀑布”和“新娘面纱瀑布”，二是加拿大境内的“马蹄瀑布”。两个瀑布奔腾交织在一起，从高达 35 ～ 58 米的峭壁上倾注而下。尼亚加拉瀑布以美丽的景色、巨大的水力发电能力和极具挑战性的环境保护工程而闻名于世，是非常受游客欢迎的旅游景点。

The name of Niagara Falls was derived from the American Indian language, meaning “the water falling from the thunder god”. It is located at the border of Ontario of Canada and the state of New York in the US, 32 kilometers away from Buffalo, the second largest city in the state of New York. The Niagara Falls, together with Iguazu Falls in South America and Victoria Falls in Africa, are known as the three largest falls of the world. Niagara River falls off the 52 meters cliff, creating the most splendid natural scene—Niagara Falls. American Falls and Veil of Bride Falls in the US converge with Horseshoe Falls in Canada into Niagara Falls, pouring down from the cliff of 35 to 58 meters high. Niagara Falls is well-known for its charming view, huge hydropower generation capacity and the challenging environment protection.

◆ 黄石公园（Yellowstone National Park）

美国目前一共有 62 座国家公园，14 座被列入世界遗产名录。黄石公园是美国的第一座国家公园，也是世界第一座国家公园，由尤利塞斯·S. 格兰特于 1872 年签署法令成立。公园位于美国西北部的爱达荷、蒙大拿、怀俄明三州交界处的落基山区，以多间歇泉著称，被称为“水与火构成的自然界奇异景色”。1978 年，被联合国教科文组织列入世界自然遗产名录。

There are altogether 62 national parks in the US, among which 14 have been listed as the World Heritage Site. Approved by Uylissis S. Grant in 1872, Yellowstone National Park is the first national park of the country, as well as the world. It is situated at Rocky Mountains bordering the states of Idaho, Montana and Wyoming. It is well-known for its geysers and is praised for the “unique natural scenery created by water and fire”. In 1978, it was included on the list of World Natural Heritage Site.

四、旅游资讯

（一）美食

美国是快餐文化的代名词。由于美国人生活节奏较快，人们更注重效率和快捷，讲究吃得是否科学、营养、方便，一般不会在食物的精美、细致上下功夫。很多美国人习惯吃快餐，速食成为美国餐饮界的发展方向。蔬菜大都生吃，菜肴味道较清淡。早在 20 世纪 50 年代，快餐就开始在美国风行，经过几十年的发展，各式各样的快餐遍布美国。人们最常吃的快餐是热狗、汉堡包、三明治以及速溶咖啡。当然，美国饮食吸收了土著人的烹饪法和食材，如火鸡、马铃薯、玉米、南瓜，这些都成了美国文化不可或缺的一部分。美国人的饮食主要取决于其所居住的地区和文化背景。移民国家的性质使得人们在美国可以品尝到全世界各国的地道美食。美国西部有丰富的太平洋海鲜及各种河鲜，全美品质最新鲜、品种最多的蔬菜水果，有著名的加州菜及具有亚洲元素的菜肴；美国南部有墨西哥特色的得克萨斯州菜，具有法国、西班牙、非洲特色的路易斯安那州菜，具有古巴、巴西特色的佛罗里达州菜；中西部有德国、荷兰及北欧特色的芝加哥菜；东部有英国、法国、爱尔兰特色的新英格兰菜系及纽约菜；此外，还有日本特色的夏威夷菜。

The United States is synonymous with fast-food culture. Due to its fast life pace, people focus more on efficiency and speed. They pay attention to whether their diet is scientific, nutritious or convenient rather than the appearances. Many Americans prefer fast food. Quickness is what American food is oriented to. Vegetables are mostly eaten uncooked. Dishes are light in taste. Fast food became popular in America as early as in the 1950s. Now after decades of development, various fast foods are all over the country. The most popular fast food are hot dog, hamburger, sandwich and instant coffee. Of course, American food also takes in the cuisine and ingredients from the Native Americans. Turkey, potato, maize and pumpkin are indispensable parts of American culture. American diet mainly depends on the cultural environment they live in. As a nation of migrants, one can taste authentic food here from all over the world. In western America, there are rich Pacific seafood and all kinds of river food. The vegetables and fruits there are the freshest and most varied. The Californian cuisine and the Asian featured dishes are well-known. The south boasts of Mexican-style Texas food, the French, Spanish and African featured Louisiana food, and the Florida food which has tropical taste like in Cuba and Brazil. In the mid-west, there are German, Dutch and Northern European flavored Chicago food. The food in New England and New York in the east falls into English, French and Irish styles. Hawaiian food has the Japanese characteristics.

（二）购物及退税

在美国购物必须另外付消费税。消费税在各级政府的收入来源中占相当大的比重。购物退税在绝大多数州都行不通。只有一些大的旅游城市及国际机场才有免税商店。但是美国有许多的折扣商店，如奥特莱斯等。

In America, a consumption tax is added to people's purchases. The consumption tax is a large proportion of sources of income in all levels of government in the country. Tax refund does not work in the vast majority of America. Duty-free shops are only available in some large tourist cities and international airports. However, there are many stores like outlets offering discounts.

花旗参：提起美国，很多人会想到花旗参，威斯康星州被誉为“花旗参之乡”，全美90% 以上的花旗参都产自这里。美国花旗参的品质好，药用价值高，出口世界各地。

American ginseng: When mentioning America, many people would think of American ginseng. With 90% of ginseng production in America, Wisconsin is reputed as the home of American ginseng which boasts high quality, high medicinal value and is exported to all over the world.

电脑产品：硅谷聚集了全美甚至全世界最顶尖的科技人才，因此这里也有全世界最多、最新的数码设备。

Computer products: Silicon Valley holds the top-notch talents of science and technology of America and even the whole world. Therefore, it has the world's largest number of the latest digital products.

篮球用品：美国是世界公认的篮球王国，篮球水平居世界领导地位。因此，篮球装备的数量和质量也是世界上独一无二的，在这里你可以买到最新款的篮球鞋和球衣，如阿迪达斯、耐克等品牌。

Basketball products: With the leading position in the world, the United States is a world recognized nation of basketball. As a result, the quantity and quality of basketball products is unique in the world. The latest fashion of basketball shoes and shirts such as Adidas and Nike are sold here.

印第安人传统工艺品：在遭受到种族残酷灭绝之后，印第安人留下的东西已经很少了，但现在仍有一部分印第安人在美国生活着。他们传承着祖先留下来的文化，而这些文化恰以手工艺品作为载体，具有代表性的有巴拿马草帽、披肩饰品、印有印第安图腾的各种器具。

The traditional American Indian handicrafts: After suffering the cruel racial elimination, few American Indian relics remain. Nevertheless, there are still a few American Indians living in the United States. They inherit from their ancestors the culture which is embodied in the traditional handicraft. The representatives include Panama straw hat, ornamental wraps, and various articles with prints of Indian totem.

（三）时差

美国自东海岸至西海岸横跨西 5 区至西 10 区，共 6 个时区。

From the east coast to the west coast, the United States covers six time zones from the east 5th to the west 10th.

东部时间：代表城市纽约、华盛顿，比北京晚 13 小时。
中部时间：代表城市芝加哥，比北京晚 14 小时。
山地时间：代表城市盐湖城，比北京晚 15 小时。
太平洋时间：代表城市洛杉矶，比北京晚 16 小时。
阿拉斯加时间：代表城市费尔班克斯，比北京晚 17 小时。
夏威夷时间：代表城市火奴鲁鲁，比北京晚 18 小时。

East Time: represented by New York, Washington, D.C., 13 hours later than Beijing.
Middle Time: represented by Chicago, 14 hours later than Beijing.
Mountainous Time: represented by Salt Lake City, 15 hours later than Beijing.

Pacific Time: represented by Los Angeles, 16 hours later than Beijing.
Alaska Time: represented by Fairbanks, 17 hours later than Beijing.
Hawaii Time: represented by Honolulu, 18 hours later than Beijing.

美国实行夏令时制。美国夏令时始于每年 3 月的第 2 个星期天，止于每年 11 月的第 1 个星期天。夏令时比标准时早 1 小时，夏威夷州不实行夏令时制。

Daylight Saving Time which starts from the second Sunday of March and ends on the first Sunday of November and is one hour earlier than the standard time, and it is practiced throughout the United States except Hawaii.

知识拓展

美国的文化象征

举世闻名的自由女神像、富有美洲气息的《美国哥特式》画像、风靡全球的芭比娃娃、野牛镍币及亲切可爱的“山姆大叔”组成了美国的五大文化象征，它们从不同方面和角度代表了美国的文化，充实了美国文化的内涵。自由女神像于 1886 年起就屹立于纽约湾，它一直代表新移民向往自由的美国梦。在《美国哥特式》画像中，老屋上的哥特式窗户和农夫庄重的表情以及长脖子的妻子使画家于 1930 年一夜成名，该幅画表现了美国农民庄重的自豪感。芭比娃娃几乎是所有女孩，甚至成年女性心仪的玩偶。芭比的创作灵感来源于美国一家玩具公司创始人汉德勒夫妇的女儿芭芭拉，他们在一个德国的成人用性感洋娃娃的基础上，于 1959 年推出了一个美国娃娃芭比。野牛镍币是由美国著名艺术家詹姆斯·厄尔·弗雷泽于 1911 年开始设计的，1913—1938 年间生产的一种硬币，也是艺术家对美国西部开发的牺牲品野牛和印第安人的纪念。在 1812 年美国第二次独立战争期间，美国纽约特罗伊城商人山姆·威尔逊在供应军队牛肉的桶上写上“U.S.”，表示这是美国的财产。这恰与他的昵称“山姆大叔”（“Uncle Sam”）的缩写（“U.S.”）相同，于是人们便戏称这些带有“U.S.”标记的物资都是“山姆大叔”的。“山姆大叔”就逐渐成了美国的绰号。1961 年美国国会通过决议，正式承认“山姆大叔”为美国的象征。

思考练习

1. 经典旅游线路分析

美国经典 14 日游

第 1 天：上海——东京——夏威夷

游客于上海浦东机场集合后出发，乘坐豪华客机，经东京转机，前往美国的夏威夷。之后展开环岛精致游。前往游览库克船长登岸地“钻石山”，随后前往白沙湾海滩、恐龙湾、喷泉喷口，远观兔子岛、乌龟岛。之后来到夏威夷族保护区景区“巴里大风口”，这里也是第二次世界大战时日军空袭珍珠港时进入夏威夷的入口。之后前往酒店入住。

第2天：夏威夷

乘车前往第二次世界大战著名的战场——珍珠港，远观港中央被日军炸沉的“亚利桑那号”战舰的遗骸以及1 000多名阵亡将士的纪念碑。返回途中，外观美国最早的中国城、唐人街、夏威夷州议会大厦以及小白宫州长官邸，以及夏威夷第一任国王塑像和依兰尼皇宫。下午自由活动。游客可逛一逛夏威夷著名的商业街卡拉卡瓦大街，那里有名牌专卖店、免税店、独具夏威夷风情的跳蚤市场。

第3天：夏威夷——旧金山

上午自由活动。下午搭乘美国夏威夷航空豪华客机前往旧金山，抵达后享用晚餐，前往酒店办理入住手续。

第4天：旧金山——洛杉矶

清晨开始游览著名的金门大桥，它是旧金山的象征，也是世界上最伟大的桥梁之一。参观艺术宫、联合广场。午餐后游览“世界上最弯曲的街道”——伦巴底街，路面坡度达40度以上。之后前往渔人码头中的39号码头，它是从意大利渔民聚集的港口发展起来的。下午乘车前往国际机场，乘坐美国达美航空公司豪华客机前往洛杉矶。抵达洛杉矶后入住酒店。

第5天：洛杉矶

前往游览全世界最大的电影制片厂——好莱坞环球影城。置身神奇的电影银幕世界中，目睹电影中灾难、惊险镜头等的拍摄及特效制作过程。亲身体会侏罗纪公园、未来水世界、木乃伊墓穴，乘坐环影城游览车进行摄影棚巡礼等。游览活动约晚餐前结束，之后返回酒店。

第6天：洛杉矶——拉斯维加斯

早餐后乘车前往著名赌城拉斯维加斯，这里有米高梅、威尼斯、恺撒宫、纽约纽约、蒙特卡罗等知名豪华酒店，以及设计精美的喷泉与雕塑。抵达后自由活动，感受不夜城的迷人景色，体验美国的奢华和疯狂。

第7天：拉斯维加斯

游览大峡谷，约需1天时间。上午出发，单程行车约2.5个小时后抵达大峡谷，途中经过著名的胡佛水坝。抵达后在大峡谷内游览，之后可以得到一张峡谷游览证书，约晚餐时分返回拉斯维加斯。

第 8 天：拉斯维加斯——布法罗

乘坐美国达美航空公司豪华客机经明尼阿波利斯飞往美国东部城市布法罗（水牛城）。布法罗是美国与加拿大的交界城市，是美国最具特色的城市之一。世界七大自然奇景之一的尼亚加拉瀑布流经于此。当天抵达后，前往酒店休息。

第 9 天：布法罗——尼亚加拉瀑布——布法罗

早餐后乘车前往参观尼亚加拉瀑布，当汽车驶近瀑布时，可以听到瀑布的轰鸣声，好像来自远方的呼唤。站在瀑布观景台欣赏加拿大及美国境内的瀑布景观，水花四溅，汹涌澎湃，经历千亿年演变而成的奇景异石。乘坐“雾中少女号”游船近观大瀑布。下午乘车返回布法罗。晚餐后入住酒店休息。

第 10 天：布法罗——纽约

早餐后乘车前往纽约。预计于傍晚抵达纽约，纽约是世界金融、商业、贸易大都会、美国最大的城市。

第 11 天：纽约

早餐后前往曼哈顿，乘坐双层游船游览代表美国国魂的自由女神像。之后前往华尔街游览，这里有纽约证券交易所、华尔街铜牛。下午游览誉满全球的联合国总部大楼（外观）。乘车游览光彩夺目的百老汇大街、撩人眼球的时代广场、名牌商店遍布的第五大道和气度非凡的洛克菲勒中心广场。

第 12 天：纽约——华盛顿

早餐后从纽约出发，驱车前往美国的首都——华盛顿。抵达后，游览巍然屹立的华盛顿纪念碑、举世闻名的总统官邸——白宫、宏伟壮观的国会山、神圣的林肯纪念堂、设计独特的越战纪念碑、朝鲜战争老兵纪念碑和杰弗逊纪念堂。后入住酒店。

第 13 天：华盛顿——东京

早餐后乘车前往国际机场，乘坐豪华客机返回上海，并在东京转机。

第 14 天：东京——上海

从东京出发抵达上海，结束愉快的旅行。

分析：这条经典旅游线路的主要旅游景点与行程特色，以及适合旅游的人群。

2. 案例分析

［案例 1］某商务旅游团在美国参加当地商人的宴会，席间一位游客看见同桌有一位年长的美国老妇人，为了表示礼节，他起身端起酒杯，微笑着向她敬酒：“祝您老身体健康，福寿延年！”可是，老妇人并没有接受他的敬酒，反而脸色骤变，一句简短的“对不起”后，就离开了座位。游客不知所措。请问：这位游客表达错了吗？正确的表达应该是怎样的？

[案例 2] 某游客在纽约中央公园的长凳上休息。看见一位美国人牵着一只可爱的雪纳瑞犬走过来，心生欢喜，便不由自主地迎了过去。他一边向主人打招呼，一边蹲下抱起狗狗，拿出包内的烤肉和面包，毫不吝惜地拿在手里喂给狗吃。狗主人惊愕地看了几秒后，飞快地拉着狗快步跑开，游客愣住了。请问：那位美国人为什么飞快地拉着狗快步跑开？游客哪里做错了吗？

[案例 3] 美国所有公共停车场必须按照规定设立一定数量的残疾人停车位，位置往往设在最便利的地方，车位宽敞且设有醒目的"蓝色轮椅"标志，只有持残疾人车牌的人才可在此泊车。杜先生参加美国自驾游，有天逛超市直接把车停到了残疾人专用车位，结果几分钟后就有当地人报警，警察给他开了 500 美元的高额罚单。杜先生很懊恼，觉得美国人小题大做。请问：美国人的罚单开得合理吗？

3. 练一练

请分析美国各州有哪些主题游。选择一个你最感兴趣的州，写一篇导游词。

第二节　加拿大

一、国家概况

（一）地理环境

加拿大位于北美洲北部，除阿拉斯加半岛和格陵兰岛外，整个北半部均为加拿大领土。地理上，加拿大东临大西洋，西濒太平洋，南接美国本土，北临北冰洋。美、加两国边界长达 8 892 千米，为全世界最长的不设防疆界。海岸线约长 24.4 万多千米，是世界上海岸线最长的国家，加拿大人习惯称自己的国家是"从海洋到海洋的国家"。加拿大面积为 998 万平方千米，仅次于俄罗斯，是世界第二大国。

Located in the north of North America, the territory of Canada covers nearly the entire north, except the Alaska Peninsula and the Greenland Island. Geographically, the country is surrounded by the Atlantic Ocean to the east, the Pacific Ocean to the west, the United States to the south, and the Arctic Ocean to the north. Canada shares a boarder of 8,892 kilometers with the United States, the longest unguarded boarder in the world. With the longest coast line, over 244,000 kilometers, Canadians are accustomed to nickname Canada "the country stretching from ocean to ocean". Second only to Russia, Canada ranks No.2 in the world in terms of national territory with 9.98 million square kilometers.

加拿大是世界上地形最复杂的国家之一，地势东西高，中间低。东南部多为低山和丘陵，与美国接壤的五大湖和圣劳伦斯河地区地势平坦；中部为大平原区，约占全国面积的一半；西部为科迪勒拉山系，是加拿大地势最高的地区，有许多海拔 4 000 米以上的高峰，包括落基山脉、海岸山脉，最高峰洛根峰海拔 5 951 米。

With one of most varied terrains of the kind, the country features east-west highlands and mid lowlands. Scattered in southeast are mountains of low altitudes and hills. The smooth areas are close to Great Lakes and St. Lawrence River neighboring the US. The great plains in mid Canada account for approximately half the total national territory. The highest lands are found in west Canada where the overwhelming Cordillera Mountains ranges give rise to mountains at high altitudes over 4,000 meters, among which are the Rocky Mountains, Coast Mountains with Mount Logan boasting the highest altitude at 5,951 meters.

加拿大位于北半球的高纬度地带，约有 1/5 的领土位于北极圈内，近一半的国土面积为冻土。加拿大国土辽阔，各地气温差异较大。加拿大的冬季比较漫长，1 月份 2/3 地区的平均气温在零下 18℃左右，北部地区一年仅两三个月温度在 0℃以上。南部气候温和，四季分明。西海岸由于受太平洋暖湿气流的影响，夏季凉爽干燥，冬季温和潮湿。秋季是加拿大最漂亮的季节，漫山遍野的枫叶使加拿大有了"枫叶之国"的美誉。

Canada belongs to high latitude belts in the northern hemisphere with one fifth of its territory falling within the Arctic Circle, and therefore half of its territory is frozen soil. The vast expanse of territory of the country gives rise to reasonably a spectrum of temperature. Relatively long in winter, two thirds of the country features an average temperature of around minus 18℃ in January, with only 2 or 3 months a year rising above zero in temperature in the north. South Canada presents a mild climate with clear-cut four seasons. As a result of warm and wet currents coming from the Pacific Ocean to its west coasts, summer here is normally cool and dry while winter is mild and humid. Canada is best in autumn as vast stretches of maple trees with blazing leaves justifying its name as "the country of the maple leaf".

（二）人文概况

1. 历史

加拿大的名字来源于印第安语"棚屋"。加拿大的历史是一部移民史。最早的居民是很早以前从亚洲东北部越过白令海峡来到美洲的印第安人和因纽特人。加拿大在 16 世纪以前是印第安人和因纽特人的居住地。法国最先在加拿大建立殖民地。1608 年，法国人萨缪尔·德·尚普兰建立了第一个永久性殖民点——魁北克，他也被誉为"新法兰西之父"。从 16 世纪起，加拿大沦为法、英殖民地。1756 年至 1763 年，英、法两国在加拿大爆发战争，法国战败，将殖民地割让给英国。1867 年 7 月 1 日，英国通过《英属北美法》，成立加拿大自治领。1926 年，英国承认加拿大在外交上的独立。1931 年，加拿大成为独立国家，属英联邦成员国。1982 年，英国通过《加拿大宪法法案》，加拿大从此获得了立法和修宪的全部权力，但仍为英联邦成员国。

Today's geographical name Canada finds its origin in Indian "kanata". The development of Canada is virtually the history of immigration, the earliest inhabitants being the Indians and the Inuit people crossing the Bering Straits from northeast Asia to America far back in the ancient times. Therefore, prior to the 16th century, Canada remained a land of Indians and Inuit. French were the first settlers to colonize today's Canada. In 1608, Samuel de Champlain created the first truly permanent French settlement in the area where the Quebec City stands today which earned Champlain the name of "Father of New France". Since the 16th century, Canada was reduced to French and British colonies. 1763 witnessed France ceding its Canadian colonies to the United Kingdom after the former lost to the latter in the war that broke out in 1756 in Canada. *British North America Act of 1867* was passed on July 1, 1867 which gave rise to the establishment of the Dominion of Canada. In 1926, the United Kingdom acknowledged Canadian autonomy in its diplomacy and further on its national independence in 1931, an independent country thereof founded. In 1982, with the passage of *Constitution Act of Canada* recognized by the United Kingdom, Canada was empowered complete rights to legislation and amending its Constitution, although still a member of the British Commonwealth.

2. 经济

加拿大是世界上最富有的国家之一，是世界第八大经济体。它是典型的服务型经济为主的国家，经济增长率居世界七大工业国的第二位，仅次于日本。劳动生产率排名世界第二，仅次于美国，是世界上经济最发达，也是经济最稳定的国家之一，其福利制度非常完善。加拿大资源丰富，森林业、采矿业、能源业、农业及渔业是加拿大传统的重要经济支柱。加拿大以贸易立国，其最大的贸易伙伴是美国，经济上受美国影响较深，对外资、外贸依赖程度很高。加拿大的旅游业也十分发达，在世界旅游收入最高的国家中排在第九位。此外，加拿大是全球最重要的教育枢纽之一，教育也是加拿大最重要的经济产业之一，每年吸引了不少来自世界各地的留学生，这不仅为国家带来了丰厚的外汇，而且为这个属于知识型经济体系的国家吸纳了不少人才。

Canada is among the world's most wealthy nations with its economy ranking 8th in the world. Second only to Japan, Canada ranks No.2 among G7 in terms of economic growth which is grounded firmly in the pillar industries of service; second only to the US in terms of labor productivity, Canada is one of the most advanced and stable economies with sophisticated welfare provisions; rich in natural resources, the country relies heavily on resource industries with forestry, mining, energy, farming and fishery as its traditional pillars. Rooted in trading, the country is greatly influenced by the US, its largest trading partner, and relies enormously on foreign investment and international trade. It also has a well-developed tourist industry and ranks No.9 in terms of tourist revenues. Besides, education also plays an important role in its economy as Canada is one of the educational hubs where international students flood in for quality educational services and bring with them large sums of foreign currencies, at the same tine attracting good talents for Canada where knowledge economy prevails.

3. 社会文化

加拿大人口约 3 707 万，人口密度为 4.1 人 / 平方千米，是世界上人口密度较低的国家之一。加拿大人口分布极不平衡，绝大部分居民集中居住在南部沿加拿大、美国边界的狭长地带，而占国土总面积 89% 的地区均无常住居民。受投资、技术移民和家庭团聚移民两大政策的驱使，加拿大成为世界上最热门的移民国家之一。在全部人口中，英裔占 42%，法裔占 26.7%，其他欧洲人后裔占 13%，土著居民（印第安人、米提人和因纽特人）约占 3%，其余为亚洲、拉美、非洲裔等。其中，华裔人口占加拿大总人口的 4.5%，现已成为加拿大最大的少数族裔，大部分集中在多伦多、温哥华及蒙特利尔等大都市。英语和法语同为官方语言，加拿大多数居民讲英语。全国英语使用者约占总人口的 70%，法语使用者占 17%，英、法语兼用者占 15%。加拿大是个宗教信仰自由的国家，居民多信奉天主教和基督教新教。居民中信奉天主教的约占 45%，信奉基督教新教的约占 36%。

Canada is scarcely populated (37.07 million in total and 4.1 person/km^2) and extremely uneven with the majority of its citizens living in the narrow strip along the Canada-US boarder in the south while 89% of its territory is home to few permanent inhabitants. Driven by two types of immigration policies, namely investment and skill immigration and family reunion immigration, Canada has emerged as one of the world's most favored destinations for immigrants. Among the population, 42% are Canadian British, 26.7% are Canadian French, 13% are other Canadian European, approximately 3% are aboriginal, including American Indian, Métis and Inuit, and the rest are Asian, Latin, African origins. Today, Chinese is the largest ethnic minority group in Canada, accounting for 4.5% of its population, who are mainly concentrated in mega cities like Toronto, Vancouver and Montreal. Both English and French are official languages, and English is used by the majority of its citizens. Among all the citizens, approximately 70% speak English and 17% speak French, English / French bilinguals are at around 15%. Canada upholds freedom in religion, and most citizens believe in either Catholicism or Protestantism. Approximately 45% of the citizens are Catholics and 36% are Protestants.

土著人文化是唯一真正属于加拿大自己的本土文化。随着 19 世纪移民浪潮的出现以及各种各样移民计划的实施，世界各地的移民者开始涌向加拿大。加拿大是个名副其实的移民国家，移民来自世界 200 多个国家和地区，因此，加拿大其他的文化都是由来自世界各地的移民引进的。加拿大的城市融合了欧洲、亚洲、拉丁美洲和非洲的各种文化，与美国的“熔炉文化”相比，加拿大文化往往被称为“马赛克文化”。例如：温哥华是众多的亚裔人聚居之地；多伦多融合了欧、亚及其他文化；魁北克则为北美洲添上一份英、法双语的欧洲韵味。“马赛克”式的民族人口结构和文化的多元性是加拿大的基本国情。1988年，加拿大通过了《多元文化法案》，从而使加拿大的多元文化得到了正式承认，加拿大政府尽力为一切愿意发展自己文化传统并为加拿大做出贡献的群体提供财政资助。2003 年，加拿大政府确定每年的 6 月 27 日为加拿大多元文化节，以促进加拿大多民族文化的共同发展。

Aboriginal culture is exclusively the truly native culture born in Canada. Immigrants across the globe began to flood in following immigrant flows in the 19th century combined with implementation of various immigrant policies. Canada truly lives to its name of an immigrant country with immigrants coming from over 200 countries and areas. Thus, cultures, except the aboriginal, in Canada are imported with the influx of immigrants. In contrast to the American culture labeled as "melting pot", Canada is better known for its "mosaic culture" where European, Asian, Latin American and African cultures coexist in the cities across the country. Vancouver is home to concentration of Canadian Asian; Toronto features a close fusion of European, Asian and other cultures; Quebec adds to the North America cultural menu a European course of British and French bilingual hybrid. Given its national context of the mosaic-like population structure and cultural diversity, Canada passed *Canadian Multiculturalism Act* in 1988, officially recognizing its multicultural identity. The Canadian government does its utmost to boost cultural traditions and finance communities that make contribution to the country. In 2003, the Canadian government designated June 27 as annual celebration of Multicultural Festival to facilitate the development of its multinational culture.

二、民俗风情

（一）礼仪禁忌

广阔而美丽的风景是加拿大的一个鲜明特征，徒步旅行、滑雪和水上泛舟都是加拿大人十分喜爱的户外运动形式。加拿大人酷爱体育运动，尤其是冬季冰雪运动。冰球、棒球、篮球以及加拿大足球都吸引了大批的观众。加拿大是世界上驰名的“枫叶之国”。加拿大人民对枫叶有极其深厚的感情，视枫叶为国宝、友谊的象征和国家的骄傲。他们还偏爱白雪，视白雪为吉祥的象征，常用筑雪墙、堆雪人等方式来助兴，认为这样可以防止邪魔的入侵。

Canada features a vast and beautiful landscape. Popular outdoor activities in Canada range from hiking, skiing to paddling. The Canadian are sports lovers, especially winter sports. Ice hockey, baseball, basketball and Canadian football hold millions of audience in fascination. Known as "the country of the maple leaf", the Canadian are deeply attached to the maple leaf which is in effect regarded as national gem, symbol of friendship and national pride. The Canadian favor snow as a token of luck, and therefore entertainments like snow walls and snowmen are Canadian ways to guard against intrusion of the devil.

作为一个多民族的移民国家，加拿大各民族宽容待人、和睦相处。加拿大人热情好客、待人诚恳、平易近人、风趣幽默。加拿大人生活习性包含英、法、美三国人的综合特点。他们既有英国人的含蓄，又有法国人的明朗，还有美国人的无拘无束。“CCATR”这五个字母可以很好地概括和描绘加拿大人的价值观，即谦让、合作、接纳、宽容和尊重。加拿大人往往温和又耐心，处处体现出轻松和随意，工作和生活节奏较慢，常是“一天只做一件事”。加拿大人充分肯定自我价值，认为每个人只有自己会对自己的成功和失败负责，不用在乎别人怎么看自己，只要在乎自己的感受。“I don't care”是加拿大人常说的一句话。加拿大人特别喜欢别人赞扬他们美好的国家和勤劳智慧的人民。加拿大的因纽特人慷慨大方、友善和气、喜欢说笑、异常好客，被喻为世界上“永不发怒的人”。

Citizens of different national backgrounds live in harmony and openness in this multinational country. They are hospitable, candid, easy-going and witty. The Canadian lifestyles are hybrids of British, French and American. They are subtle as the British, open and forthright as the French, and out-going as the American. CCATR captures well the Canadian values: compromise, cooperation, acceptance, tolerance and respect. They are mild and patient, easy-going, not hasty in life or work following the Canadian rule of "one thing a day". The Canadian highly recognize individuality, believing that one shall follow his own heart and hold responsibility for the consequences of his personal conduct irrespective of the other's finger-pointing. "I don't care" is a Canadian slogan. The Canadian are obsessed with compliments on their motherland and civic ingenuity and diligence. The Inuit people are nicknamed "people know no rage" as they are generous, friendly, witty and extremely hospitable.

加拿大人大多为欧洲后裔，故习俗多与欧洲接近，文化的多元性使得加拿大人更具有包容性。他们不太讲究礼仪，但有礼貌。相识的人见面要问好。一般请客吃饭都会在家里，应邀之人通常会带一些小礼物或一束花给女主人，宴会后会写信感谢女主人。在加拿大，白色的百合花主要用于悼念死者，因其与死亡相关，所以绝对不可以作为礼物送给加拿大人。

Canadian customs are close to Europe as most Canadians are European descendants, and yet cultural diversity drives them toward a more tolerant end. They are less rigid in etiquette yet equally polite. For example, acquaintances greet each other; dinners are usually held at home; no formal gifts are customary for the invited, although a small gift or a bunch of flower never fail to surprise the hostess. A thank-you letter to the hostess after the event is, however, customary. It is a Canadian convention that white lily is ceremonially for the dead; so no white lily is given as gifts to the Canadian due to its close cultural connection to death.

与加拿大人交谈时，不要插嘴打断对方，或是与对方争辩。与美国人相比，加拿大较为保守。交谈要选择众人共同关心的话题，如加拿大的经济、文化、天气、体育、旅游、风俗等话题。不能询问年龄、收入、家庭状况、婚姻状况、女士体重等私人生活问题。避免将加拿大与美国相比，不谈政治、血统、宗教、语言、魁北克法语区等社会敏感问题。

Do not cut short or argue to win when talking with a Canadian. The Canadian are more reserved compared with their US neighbors. Safe topics are those of shared interest, such as economy, culture, weather, sports, travel and customs. Age, salary, family, marriage, women's weight are too private and therefore are taboo. Comparison and contrast between Canada and US should be avoided, and social irritations like politics, lineage, religion, language and French Quebec should also be screened out.

（二）节庆风情

1. 枫糖节（Maple Syrup Festival）

每年 3 月的枫糖节是加拿大的传统节日。加拿大人热爱枫树并把枫叶作为国家的象征。在加拿大的枫树品种中，最著名的一种叫糖枫，它的树叶含糖量达 3.5%，可熬制香甜的枫糖浆，制作太妃糖。据说，在300多年前，是印第安人发现了枫树的秘密，并向人类提供了这种清香可口、甜度适宜、润肺健胃的甜食。每年枫糖节期间，生产枫糖的农场会向国内外游客开放，届时不仅有游行和歌舞晚会，还会放焰火庆祝。

Maple Syrup Festival is a traditional Canadian holiday held in annual March. The Canadian people love maple tree and crown maple leaf as the symbol of the country. Among the many maples in Canada, the most famous is named sugar maple, 3.5% of whose leaves is sugar for making maple syrup, which is a raw material for toffee. Legend has it that it was the Indians that discovered the mystery of maple trees about 300 years ago, and therefore presented to the world a refreshing, tasty and mild desert that nourishes the lung and enhances the spleen. During the festival, syrup farms are open to the tourists from home and abroad combined with parades, parties and firework shows.

2. 魁北克冬季狂欢节（Quebec Winter Carnival）

一年一度的冬季狂欢节是魁北克省居民最盛大的节日，具有浓郁的法兰西色彩。狂欢节一般是在2月份举行，为期10天。魁北克冬季狂欢节的吉祥物是“博纳”，他像圣诞老人一样。狂欢节期间会举行冰雕比赛、划船比赛、越野滑雪比赛、轮胎滑雪比赛、大型滑车比赛、狗拉雪橇比赛、冰上赛马等各种体育活动。冰雕比赛是狂欢节的主要活动项目之一。魁北克冬季狂欢节已成为魁北克市第三大产业，被公认为全世界最大的冬季狂欢节之一。

The Quebec Winter Carnival, a ten-day February tradition featuring French style, is the most magnificent annual event celebrated by citizens in the Quebec Province. Bonhomme, someone like Santa Claus, is the mascot of the carnival. Games like ice sculptures, canoe races, cross-country skiing, snow-tubing, snow-boarding, dog-sled races and horse races on ice. Among them, ice sculptures are the highlight. The Winter Carnival is now the 3rd largest industry of the Quebec City and is listed among the world's top three winter carnivals.

3. 加拿大郁金香节（Canadian Tulip Festival）

加拿大郁金香节诞生于和平。第二次世界大战期间，荷兰皇室来到加拿大避难，受到加拿大人的热心帮助。战争结束后，荷兰赠予加拿大10万株郁金香，以表达感激之情。此后，荷兰皇室每年都会向加拿大赠送1万株郁金香。1953年5月，首届加拿大郁金香节在渥太华举办。如今，加拿大郁金香节已成为世界上最大的郁金香节，并为渥太华赢得了“北美郁金香之都”的称号。

The Canadian Tulip Festival is a product of peace during the Second World War when the Royal Dutch Family received enthusiastic aid in Canada for refuge. After the war, Holland sent 100,000 tulips to Canada in gratitude and from then on the Royal Dutch Family sends 10,000 tulips to Ottawa each year. The first Canadian Tulip Festival was held in Ottawa in May, 1953. Today, the Canadian Tulip Festival is the largest of the kind and has won Ottawa the crown of "North America Capital of Tulips".

三、主要旅游城市及景点

（一）渥太华（Ottawa）

渥太华是加拿大的首都，位于安大略省东部与魁北克省交界处。渥太华在印第安语中是“贸易”的意思，早期的欧洲殖民者使这里变成了一个经营木材和皮毛生意的伐木小镇。1867年，渥太华被英国维多利亚女王钦定为加拿大的首都，故又被称为“锯与法之城”。渥太华是世界上最寒冷的首都之一，每年约有8个月夜晚温度在0℃以下，最低气温可以达到零下39℃，有“严寒之都”之称。正因为其气候寒冷、冬季漫长，渥太华的冰上运动非常发达，特别是冰球运动，加拿大素有“冰球王国”之称，渥太华则是“冰球之城”。每年2月初，渥太华里多运河成为世界上最大的天然滑冰场，为期10天的冰上狂欢节吸引了世界各地的滑冰爱好者。渥太华河畔的联邦国会大厦不仅是渥太华的标志，而且是加拿大的象征。其居民一半讲法语，一半讲英语。渥太华风景优美，每年吸引着来自世界各地的200万名游客。当年荷兰皇室为感谢加拿大政府而赠送的10万株郁金香每到春天就开满全城，因此渥太华又被称为“郁金香城”。

Capital of Canada, Ottawa is sandwiched between Ontario and Quebec. In American Indian language, Ottawa means “trading”, for early European settlers turned where today’s Ottawa stands into a lumbering town for timber and fur trades. In 1867, with Queen Victory’s regius decision, Ottawa was made capital of Canada, giving rise to its nickname of “City of Saw and Law”. As one of the coldest national capitals in the world, Ottawa is known as “Capital of Cold”, with average night temperature below zero in 8 months around the year, lowest falling to minus 39℃. A cold climate and a long winter, however, attribute to advanced ice sports, especially ice hockey. Whilst Canada is nicknamed “Kingdom of Ice Hockey”, Ottawa is “City of Ice Hockey”. Early February finds Rideau Canal in Ottawa the world’s largest natural ice stadium when the ten-day ice carnival attracts ice fans from across the world. The waterfront Parliament Buildings in Ottawa is not only a landmark of the city, but also a symbol of the nation. Half the citizens here speak French and the others speak English. The landscape of Ottawa is a magnet for over 2 million international visitors each year. Ottawa is also known as “City of Tulips”, for 100,000 tulip plants were once bestowed by the Royal Dutch Family in gratitude to the Canadian government, and tulips spread all over the capital in full blossom when spring comes.

（二）多伦多（Toronto）

多伦多是安大略省省会，加拿大第一大城市和金融中心，也是加拿大英语区的经济、文化中心，位于世界最大的淡水湖群五大湖的中心安大略湖的西北岸，与美国隔湖相望。多伦多的城市名来源于休伦湖边的印第安人，在印第安语中意为“汇集之地”。1996年，联合国正式确认多伦多是世界上最有多元文化特色的城市之一，全市人口的50%都是在加拿大以外的地方出生的，市内的“小意大利”“小波兰”和“希腊城”等社区的不同韵味是多伦多并存的各种文化的代表。多伦多也是华裔在加拿大居住最集中的地区之一。多伦多的标志性建筑有市政厅和加拿大国家电视发射塔，高达553米的国家电视发射塔是多伦多的标志性建筑，占据世界第一高塔的位置长达34年，也是多伦多的标志、加拿大的象征。在塔上可俯瞰多伦多市和安大略湖。从多伦多开车 1 小时，便可到达位于美、加边境的尼亚加拉瀑布，位于加拿大境内的“马蹄瀑布”气势最大、最为惊险，是世界著名的奇观。得天独厚的优越地理位置使得只有加拿大境内才能观赏到美、加两大瀑布的全貌，因此加拿大尼亚加拉瀑布城的旅游业格外发达，是世界著名的“蜜月之都”。

Sitting at the northwest shore of Ontario Lake which is the center of the largest fresh water lake, Toronto, looking across Ontario to the US, is the capital of Ontario Province, Canada's largest city and its financial center, as well as the economic and cultural hub of Canadian English district. Toronto, "land of gathering" in Indian language, is a city with its name deriving from Indians living around Huron Lake. In 1996, the United Nations officially recognized Toronto one of the most multicultural cities in the world, where 50% of the citizens are born outside Canada. Urban communities such as Little Italy, Little Poland, and Greek Town are cultural representatives of distinctive styles living in harmony. Toronto is one of the Canadian regions with densest Chinese concentrations. Landmarks in Toronto are City Hall and the Canadian National Tower (CN Tower) of 553 meters high, and CN Tower is Toronto's landmark and Canada's symbol, where one commands a bird's eye view to the city and the Ontario Lake, CN Tower stood highest of the world's high-rise for 34 years. Within one-hour drive from Toronto is the Niagara Falls bordering Canada and the US. The Horseshoe Falls in Canada, the most massive and thrilling of its kind, is a world wonder. By virtue of geography, it is only in Canada that one commands paramount views to both falls, which endows Niagara city, a well-known honeymoon capital of the world, and an exceptionally developed tourist industry.

（三）蒙特利尔（Montreal）

蒙特利尔位于渥太华河和圣劳伦斯河交汇处，是魁北克省最大的城市和加拿大第二大城市。蒙特利尔是加拿大历史最悠久的城市之一，约在 350 年前由法国人建立。蒙特利尔居民中 75% 是法裔，深受法国文化的影响，城市处处体现出独特的法国文化底蕴，是加拿大最具欧洲韵味的城市。法语是该市的官方语言，蒙特利尔也是世界上最大的双语系城市。蒙特利尔在法语世界里地位仅次于巴黎，是全球第二大法语城市，有“北美巴黎”“小巴黎”之称。作为北美的浪漫之都，蒙特利尔以法式建筑为主，有“尖塔之城”的美誉。蒙特利尔老城是一座魅力无穷的 18 世纪城市，到处可见马车及咖啡馆。蒙特利尔圣母大教堂和美术馆以及闻名加拿大的地下城是必游景点，而著名的国际爵士音乐节、国际焰火大赛等更是吸引了世界各地的游客。蒙特利尔被联合国评定为最适合人类居住的城市之一。

Sitting where Ottawa River converges with St. Lawrence River, Montreal is the largest city in Quebec Province and the second largest in Canada. Built by the French around 350 years ago, Montreal has the longest history among Canadian cities. With 75% of its citizens being Canadian French, the city features rich French culture and is the most European city in Canada. Montreal is the largest bilingual city in the world, and French is an official language here. Known as "Paris in North America" and "Little Paris", Montreal is the second largest French-speaking city in the world following Paris. As the romantic city of North America, Montreal features dominant French architecture and is acclaimed as "City of Towers". The old town of Montreal is an 18th-century city with great charm where wagons and coffee houses compete.

Notre-Dame Basilica in Montreal, Montreal Museum of Fine Arts and the Montreal Underground City are must-sees. Besides, events like the International Jazz Festival and Montreal Fireworks Competition attract visitors from the world over in fascination. Montreal is recognized by the United Nations as one of the most livable cities for human habitation.

（四）魁北克市（Quebec City）

魁北克市是魁北克省省会，是北美洲独一无二拥有城墙的城市，也是加拿大最古老的历史文化名城。该城最早是由法国人所建的第一个永久性殖民据点，绝大多数居民为法国人后裔，通用法语。魁北克市有着狭窄的鹅卵石铺就的街道和 18 世纪的古建筑，颇具欧洲风韵，是法裔加拿大人的真正代表城市，加拿大境内法国文化的发祥地，被所有法裔居民视为精神首都。魁北克的老城区是北美堡垒式殖民城市的完美典范。1985 年，魁北克老城区被联合国教科文组织列入世界文化遗产名录，这在北美大陆是少有的荣誉。

As capital of Quebec Province, Quebec City is the exclusively walled city in North America and Canada's famous cultural city with the longest history. The city has morphed from the first permanent colony established by the French, and therefore most of the citizens are French off-springs who speak French. Laced with narrow, cobblestone-paved streets and scattered with 18th-century architectural structures, Quebec City is very European. It is truly an urban representation of Canadian French descendants who take the city as their spiritual capital where Canadian-French culture takes its origin. The old town of the city, a monument to Château-style colony cities in North America, was inscribed on the UNESCO World Cultural Heritage Site list in 1985, a rarity in North America.

（五）温哥华（Vancouver）

温哥华是不列颠哥伦比亚省第一大城市和加拿大第三大城市，也是加拿大西海岸最大的港口、文化中心和国际贸易中心，被誉为加拿大的“西部天堂”“加拿大通向东方的门户”。温哥华的名称源自到此探险的英国航海家乔治·温哥华，起初为渔业和锯木业小镇。如今的温哥华三面环山，西面傍海，是一个把现代都市与自然美景汇聚一身的花园城市。温哥华的气候与加拿大其他地区不同，由于靠近太平洋而十分温和，夏季温度在 20℃左右，而冬季也很少低于 0℃，气候四季宜人，连续多年被选为世界上最适合人类居住的城市之一。温哥华的旅游景点众多，包括北美最大的城市公园——史丹利公园，北美第二大“中国城”，北美洲最大的滑雪场——威斯勒滑雪场。温哥华也是华人聚集地之一，汉语是第二大语言。

Vancouver, the largest city in British Columbia, the 3rd largest city in Canada and the largest port and center of culture and international trade in its west coast, is crowned “West Heaven of the Country” and “Gateway to the Orient”. A town of fishery and saw-milling in its early days, Vancouver as a city, traces its name back to George Vancouver, the British navigator. Today's Vancouver city, surrounded with mountains in three sides and facing the Pacific Ocean in the west, is a garden city of dynamic modernity and picturesque landscape. In the proximity of the Pacific Ocean, Vancouver features a mild climate deviant from its cousins elsewhere. Agreeable year round, summer here averages 20 ℃ and winter rarely goes below zero, truly living up to its name of the most livable city consecutively. Vancouver is home to a range of tourist attractions from Stanley Park, which is the largest of the kind in North America, the 2nd largest China Town in North America and Whistler Skiing Resort, which is again the largest of the kind in North America. Chinese is the second mostly used language in Vancouver where there are highly concentrated Chinese communities.

（六）维多利亚（Victoria）

维多利亚是不列颠哥伦比亚省省会，位于温哥华岛的最南端。充满田园景致的维多利亚素有“海与花园的城市”之称，而浪漫的海景及温和的气候，更让它成为退休者的天堂。维多利亚秀美、宁静、精致，是以英国女王维多利亚的名字命名的，因受到传统英式生活的影响，在维多利亚，游客仿佛置身于欧洲。维多利亚享有“世界最美花园”之誉，5月中旬至9月下旬时百花齐放的布查花园是维多利亚最著名的观光景点。

Capital of the province of British Columbia, Victoria is located at the southern end of the Vancouver Island. Idyllic in landscape, Victoria is known as the city of sea and parks. Its romantic seascape and mild climate make it a paradise for the retired. Named after Queen Victoria, the city preserves well traditional British lifestyles in an idyllic and tranquil aura that gives you a real European experience. Butchart Gardens, hailed as the world's most beautiful park, stand out brilliantly amidst all the attractions in Victoria when flowers compete and contend in spring.

（七）其他著名旅游景点

◆ 班夫国家公园（Banff National Park）

加拿大落基山区的国家公园不少于6座，其中4座被联合国教科文组织列入世界自然遗产名录。班夫国家公园是加拿大设立的第一个国家公园。到加拿大西岸旅游，班夫国家公园几乎是不可缺少的景点安排。班夫位于艾伯塔省卡尔加里西面，被称为“落基山脉的灵魂”，有“人间仙境”的美誉。在这个国家公园里，分布着数不尽的瀑布、溪流、山峰和温泉，是游览观光的最佳去处。露易斯湖是班夫的精华，也被称为“一年四季的魔鬼”。班夫国家公园也是加拿大最大的自然动物保护区。

There are at least six national parks surrounding the Rocky Mountains of which four have been inscribed on the List of UNESCO World Natural Heritage Site. Banff National Park is the first national park of Canada. It is a must-see for visitors to the west coast of the country. Crouching west of Calgary in Alberta Province, Banff, a wonderland on earth, is enshrined the soul of the Rocky Mountains, where waterfalls, brooks and creeks, peaks and thermal springs create a magnet for sightseers. Lake Louise is the gem of the park and is nicknamed “devil of four seasons”. The Banff National Park is the largest nature reserve in Canada.

四、旅游资讯

（一）美食

在加拿大，东西被海包围的广阔国土上有着无数的湖泊和河流以及适合于农产牧畜的土壤，物产富饶，如卡尔加里的野味驯鹿肉、艾伯塔的特色牛肉，两大洋岸的鳕鱼、鲑鱼，淡水湖和河流中盛产的鳟鱼、鲈鱼等，大西洋沿岸的纽芬兰岛和爱德华王子岛所产的龙虾、大西洋鲑鱼、贻贝、海扇等海鲜，以及加拿大的特产枫糖浆。

In the vast expanse of Canada sandwiched between oceans lie fertile land studded with countless lakes and rivers productive in farming and stockbreeding. You will find on the menu a complete range of Canadian specialties from wild reindeer meat in Calgary, Alberta beef, sea codfish and salmon along the two oceanic coasts, freshwater tuna and bass abundant in lakes and rivers, seafood like lobster, Atlantic salmon, mussel and scallop found in the waters surrounding the Newfoundland Island and Prince Edward Island by the Atlantic coast, to the Canadian delicacy of maple syrup.

总体而言，加拿大人的饮食习惯与英、法两国较为接近，不同地区可以品尝到英国风味和法国风味的佳肴。主要食物是牛肉和新鲜的鱼类、贝类，蔬菜以生吃为主。在口味方面，加拿大人比较喜清淡，爱吃酸、甜的食物，不喜辣味，以食肉为主，黄油、奶酪必不可少。加拿大人在饮食上的一大独特之处是特别爱吃烤制的食品，如烤牛排、烤鸡、烤土豆。加拿大人习惯餐后喝咖啡或吃水果。与欧洲人相比，加拿大人喝酒不多。加拿大人喜欢喝凉水，无论档次多高的宴席，加冰块的凉水总占一席之地。由于加拿大华人较多，因此有许多的中餐馆，多数以粤菜为主。

In general, the Canadian adopt a food style close to the British and French food that varies from region to region. Staples are beef, fresh fish and clams, and vegetables are typically consumed raw. The Canadian have a bland diet of sweet and sour, distant from spicy or hot taste; they feed on meat, and butter and cheese are must. Roasts are distinctively Canadian cuisine personality, grilled steak, roasted chicken, baked potato, and the like. The main course is usually followed by coffee or fruit. They do not drink that much like their European cousins; instead, cold water is popular among sumptuous banquets or home dinners where ice-cubed water has its role to play. Given the large body of Chinese, it is easy to find Chinese restaurants in Canada where Cantonese style is the mainstream.

（二）购物及退税

印第安人和因纽特人的工艺品：印第安人和因纽特人制作的木偶、手工艺品、金银加工的装饰品、木雕的摆饰品、铜制品、玻璃制品、毛皮和皮革等种类繁多，颇值得收藏。毛皮为加拿大代表商品，价钱便宜、种类繁多。

Indian and Inuit handicrafts: Ideal collections are puppet, handmade art-ware, gold and silver accessory, wooden carvings, copper, glass decorations, fur and leather. Fur is a Canadian commodity representative, available at reasonable price and rich in choice.

枫糖浆：美丽迷人的枫树，除了观赏之外，还是加拿大重要的经济来源之一。早在1600年前后，已有“印第安糖浆”的记载。加拿大的糖枫树，树汁含糖量极高，可熬制成枫糖浆。目前，全世界70%的枫糖制品集中在魁北克。这种从树龄40年以上的糖枫中所采集的汁液非常珍贵，平均40升的枫树浆只能提炼出1升的枫糖浆。枫糖浆能补充营养不均衡的虚弱体质。枫糖产品还有很多，如枫糖黄油、枫糖果酱、棉花糖等，是加拿大最有名的特产之一。

Maple syrup: Beautiful and attractive, the maple tree is more than a landscape decoration, but more importantly a major source of revenue. As long as 1,600 years, there were records of Indian syrup. With high content of sugar, the sugar maple is extracted of juice to process syrup. Of today's maple syrup products, nearly 70% comes from Quebec. The maple juice contained in maple trees that are 40 years old is a rarity, because on average out of 40 liters of maple juice only 1 liter of maple syrup could be extracted. Syrup is ideal for rebalancing poor physique resulted from malnutrition. And there are more Canadian specialties — syrup butter, syrup flavor jams, marshmallow — you name it.

冰酒：冰酒是加拿大独特且稀有的特产，举世闻名，乃葡萄酒中之极品，享有“加拿大国酒”的美誉。真正的冰酒不仅要用优质的葡萄品种和非常严格的酿造工艺，更取决于天气的因素和时机，且其出汁率极低。冰酒最初于 1794 年诞生在德国的弗兰克尼。由于加拿大尼亚加拉半岛的气候特别适合冰酒的生产，且经过 200 多年的发展，冰酒已经成为酒中极品，因此加拿大冰酒在国际上一直享有很高的声誉。加拿大安大略省的尼亚加拉地区是目前世界上最著名的冰酒产区。

Ice wine: Ice wine, a gem in the family of wine, is a Canadian rarity known around the world. It is crowned the national wine of Canada. Good ice wine is a product of not only fine vine that contains extremely low juice content and prudent brewing processes, but more importantly climate and timing. Ice wine was born in Franconia in Germany in 1794. By virtue of climate in the Niagara Peninsula, ice wine brewed in Canada has emerged as best of the kind after 200-some years of refinement, claiming high repute at the international scale. The Niagara region in Ontario Province is the best-known ice wine origin in the world today.

游客在加拿大购物单张收据满 50 加元，总额满 200 加元，可以申请退税（GST 和 HST 退税）。2010 年 7 月 1 日实施的 HST 税率如下：安大略省为 13%，新斯科舍、新不伦瑞克省、纽芬兰省、拉布拉多半岛和爱德华王子岛为 15%，不列颠哥伦比亚为 12%。除一些特定免税店可当场退税，且退税金额不超过 500 加元，其他都必须回国后办理。游客所购物品及收据或住宿收据（连续住宿不超过 1 个月）正本必须在出境时由海关验明并盖章，然后在机场领取表格填好，附上机票或登机证正本就可以退税了。

Visitors to Canada can obtain a refund for GST paid for some purchases. The total value (excluding taxes) of the purchases for which you are claiming a GST/HST refund must be at least CAD 200. The value (excluding taxes) of each individual item must be at least CAD 50. As of July 1, 2010, HST rate is as follows: 13% / Ontario; 15% / Nova Scotia, New Brunswick, Newfoundland, Labrador Peninsula, Prince Edward Island; and 12% / British Columbia. All tax refunds shall be processed outside Canada, except on-the-spot refund service at special duty free stores providing total refund does not exceed CAD 500. The original copy of goods receipts or accommodation receipts (provided that the consecutive accommodation does not exceed one natural month) must be checked and sealed by customs officers before leaving Canada, and pertaining forms must be filled at the airport affiliated with your air ticket or boarding card.

（三）时差

加拿大共分 6 个时区。

There are six time zones in Canada.

纽芬兰时间：代表城市圣约翰斯，比北京时间晚 11.5 小时。
大西洋时间：代表城市哈利法克斯，比北京时间晚 12 小时。
东部时间：代表城市渥太华，比北京时间晚 13 小时。
中部时间：代表城市温尼伯，比北京时间晚 14 小时。
山地时间：代表城市埃德蒙顿，比北京时间晚 15 小时。
太平洋时间：代表城市温哥华，比北京时间晚 16 小时。

Newfoundland Time: represented by Saint John's, 11.5 hours later than Beijing time.
Atlantic Time: represented by Halifax, 12 hours later than Beijing time.
Eastern Time: represented by Ottawa, 13 hours later than Beijing time.
Central Time: represented by Winnipeg, 14 hours later than Beijing time.
Mountain Time: represented by Edmonton, 15 hours later than Beijing time.
Pacific Time: represented by Vancouver, 16 hours later than Beijing time.

由于加拿大纬度偏高，因此每年夏季加拿大都会实施夏令时制。夏令时始于每年 3 月的第 2 个星期天，止于每年 11 月的第 1 个星期天。夏令时比标准时早 1 个小时。

Due to its high latitudes, Daylight Saving Time is observed in Canada, which begins from the second Sunday of March and ends on the first Sunday of November. Daylight Saving Time is one hour earlier than the standard time.

思考练习

1. 经典旅游线路分析

加拿大东西岸精华 10 日游

第 1 天：北京——多伦多

由北京首都国际机场集合出发，搭乘加拿大航空公司豪华客机前往加拿大西岸第一大城市多伦多。因时差原因，当日抵达，之后晚餐，入住酒店休息。

第 2 天：多伦多

早餐后前往尼亚加拉瀑布区，参观世界七大奇景之一的尼亚加拉瀑布。尼亚加拉瀑布位于北美洲五大湖区尼亚加拉河上，平均流量 5 720 立方米/秒，与伊瓜苏瀑布、维多利亚瀑布并称为世界三大瀑布。到达瀑布后乘坐“雾中少女号”游船，体验瀑布扑面的刺激与紧张，亦可自费乘坐直升机，全方位体验瀑布的磅礴气势。随后，返回多伦多，途经号称“世界七大童话小镇”之一的尼亚加拉湖滨小镇。在这里，我们既能看到19世纪维多利亚时代留下的小洋房，又能了解和品尝道地的加拿大特产冰酒，冰酒是游客不可错过的加拿大著名特产。之后参观多伦多市内新旧市政厅、多伦多大学。晚餐后返回酒店休息。

第3天：多伦多——渥太华

早餐之后前往渥太华，途经加拿大东部最佳旅游地之一的千岛群岛和加拿大建国时的首都金斯顿参观。金斯顿既有水城风韵，又有古都风貌。抵达后参观皇后大学、市政厅、皇家军事学院。千岛群岛是加拿大十大自然景观之一。千岛之名来源于圣劳伦斯河上镶嵌的1 864个岛屿，岛上树木郁郁葱葱，各种风格的建筑遍布其中，夏季这里是有名的避暑胜地。乘坐千岛群岛游船，一览千岛群岛美景。继而前往渥太华，晚餐后入住酒店。

第4天：渥太华——蒙特利尔

早餐后，前往渥太华拥有瑰丽雕刻艺术的国会大厦，外观自1967年7月1日引燃后至今仍在水面上熊熊燃烧的“不熄之火”、和平塔；之后于加拿大总督官邸的庭院中漫步，手抚克林顿、曼德拉、叶利钦等昔日政要亲手种植的树木，之后游览丽都运河。约下午抵达蒙特利尔市区观光，前往宏伟的圣约瑟大教堂并入内参观；游览极具历史价值的旧城部分：外观蒙特利尔圣母大教堂、肃穆雄峙的市政大厦、浪漫的市政厅广场。

第5天：蒙特利尔——卡尔加里——班夫

早上前往机场转机飞往艾伯塔省第一大城卡尔加里，此城兼具牛仔韵味与现代都市风情，由于石油天然气的开发，让卡尔加里成为大草原上商业繁盛的“水泥森林”，是北美地区的石油重镇。抵达加拿大第一座国家公园——班夫国家公园。在班夫国家公园，搭缆车登上硫黄山顶，眺望落基山脉的磅礴气势。下午，前往玛丽莲·梦露拍摄电影《大江东去》的著名场景——弓河瀑布，来到惊奇角远眺弓河谷地及以群峦叠翠为背景的百年班夫温泉城堡。晚上住宿班夫镇上特色酒店。

第6天：班夫

早餐后，沿着有世界景观最美公路之一的冰原大道而上。抵达冰原后，搭乘特制的巨轮冰河雪车，直上2 210米的阿塔巴斯卡冰河，体验踩在万年冰河之上的神奇感觉。随后沿着冰河景观公路，即冰原大道（它被《国家地理杂志》评为世界上景色最美的高山公路），沿途不仅可以欣赏高山、湖泊、冰河奇景，而且可以见到生生不息的野生动物，此条公路也被称为“荒野之窗”。顺着冰原大道，欣赏悬吊在断崖绝壁的乌鸦脚冰河，游览呈现令人惊异颜色湖水的沛托湖。之后参观落基山中最特别的、风景绝美的一座国家公园——优鹤国家公园，欣赏大自然的雕塑品——天然石桥和宛如落基山的翠玉——翡翠湖。

第7天：班夫——卡尔加里——维多利亚

早餐后，前往卡尔加里国际机场直接飞往维多利亚岛，它位于温哥华最南端，别具英伦风情。这里是加拿大西岸最大的岛屿，面积与中国台湾相等，而人口却只有中国台湾的

1/10。游览布查花园。午后前往滨海风景区，参观议会大厦、帝后饭店、贯穿加拿大的一号公路起点“Mile 0”。夜宿维多利亚。

第 8 天：维多利亚——温哥华

早餐后乘渡轮前往温哥华。畅游加拿大第一座植物展示园——伊丽莎白女王公园。之后游览北美第二大唐人街及温哥华的诞生地煤气镇，它也是温哥华历史最悠久的街区。之后前往史丹利公园，它是北美最大的城市公园，园中有美丽的洛斯特湖、图腾柱、九时古炮等，还有温哥华的地标性景点——展望角，它是整个公园的制高点，可以一览狮门大桥、温哥华内港以及北温哥华绵延的山脉。前往加拿大广场，这里集邮轮基地、国际会议中心、酒店三位一体，是 1986 年世博会地标。

第 9 天：温哥华——北京

午餐后乘车前往温哥华国际机场办理登机手续，乘坐加拿大航空公司豪华客机，经国际日期变更线返回，于次日抵运北京。

第 10 天：北京

结束丰富多彩的加拿大东西岸 10 日精华之旅。

分析：这条经典旅游线路的主要旅游景点与行程特色，以及适合旅游的人群。

2. 案例分析

[案例 1] 李先生初次随团前往加拿大旅游，途中在加油站休息时与一位加拿大人用英语聊天。闲聊中，那位加拿大人问李先生对加拿大的印象，李先生把加拿大与美国做了比较，认为两国有许多相似之处，加拿大的自然景观比美国更胜一筹，但美国更繁荣一些。那位加拿大人没有说什么，耸耸肩，满脸不悦地走了。请问：李先生说错了什么？作为游客，应该如何与当地人交流才能避免文化冲突？

[案例 2] 陈先生带孩子去加拿大旅游，孩子在路上耍脾气，陈先生非常生气地当众教训了他，结果路人叫来了警察。警察问清情况后，对陈先生进行了教育并警告他不能打骂自己的孩子，否则将被请进警察局。由于在异国他乡，陈先生没有与警察辩解，却对爱管闲事的加拿大人愤愤不平，认为他多管闲事，扰了自己的游兴。你如何理解？

3. 练一练

请以“枫叶之国”为主题写一篇关于加拿大的导游词。

第五章
非洲

本章导航

非洲（Africa）的全称是阿非利加洲，意思是阳光灼热的地方。非洲位于亚洲的西南面，东濒印度洋，西临大西洋，北隔地中海与欧洲相望，东北角以苏伊士运河为非洲和亚洲的分界。非洲为高原大陆，地势比较平坦。东南部高，西北部低。大陆海岸线平直，缺少海湾和岛屿。非洲沙漠面积约占全洲面积的1/3，为沙漠面积最大的洲。其中，撒哈拉沙漠是世界上最大的沙漠。非洲东部有世界大陆上最大的断裂带——东非大裂谷。除了沙漠，非洲大陆还是一片人与自然、人与动物和谐相处的乐土。在地理上习惯分为北非、东非、西非、中非和南非五个地区，共54个独立国家。埃及、南非、肯尼亚、毛里求斯、塞舌尔、坦桑尼亚、突尼斯等旅游业相对成熟的国家和地区都成为中国公民自费出境旅游的目的地，其旅游产品呈现“神秘”和“高端”的特点。本章主要介绍埃及、南非两个非洲国家的国家概况、民俗风情、主要旅游城市及景点、旅游资讯等。

第一节　埃及

一、国家概况

（一）地理环境

埃及，全称为阿拉伯埃及共和国，英语中“埃及”一词是从古希腊语演变而来的。阿拉伯人称之为“米斯尔”，在阿拉伯语中意为“辽阔的国家”。埃及又被誉为“金字塔之国”“棉花之国”。埃及横跨亚、非两大洲，大部分位于非洲东北部，只有苏伊士运河以东的西奈半岛位于亚洲西南角。埃及北濒地中海，西面连接利比亚，南面为苏丹，东临红海和以色列及巴勒斯坦接壤。埃及是欧、亚、非三大洲的交通枢纽和战略要地，它在阿拉伯世界扮演了“橱窗”的角色，也为整个中东地区开启了一扇大门。

The full name of Egypt is the Arab Republic of Egypt, of which the word “Egypt” comes from the ancient Greek. The word “Egypt” means “vast country” in its Arabian equivalent. It is also called the country of the Pyramids and cotton. Egypt spans the two continents of Africa and Asia, mostly in the northeast of Africa, with only the Sinai Peninsula to the east of Suez Canal lying at the southwest corner of Asia. With the Mediterranean Sea in the north, Libya in the west, Sudan in the south, the Red Sea, Israel and Palestine in the east, Egypt is the traffic hub that is of strategic significance. It has played the role of a show window for the Arabian world and opened a door to the Middle East.

从地理上，埃及分为 4 个地区——尼罗河流域及尼罗河三角洲地区、西部沙漠地区、东部沙漠地区和西奈半岛地区。开罗以南是宽 3 000 米～16 000 米的尼罗河绿色长廊，一般称为上埃及；开罗以北称为下埃及。埃及 96% 的地区为沙漠，尼罗河横贯全境，并在开罗以北形成三角洲。尼罗河是世界第一长河，在埃及境内有 1 530 千米，两岸的狭长河谷及三角洲地带生活着全国 96% 的人口，但面积只占全国面积的 4%。

Geographically, Egypt can be divided into four parts: the Nile Valley and the Nile Delta, the western desert, the eastern desert plus the Sinai Peninsula. The oasis stretches southwards from Cairo for about 3—16 kilometers like a long green corridor along the Nile which is usually called Upper Egypt. The other part northwards from Cairo is called Lower Egypt. 96% of this country is covered by desert. The Nile, the longest river in the world with 1,530 kilometers in Egypt, runs across it to form the long and narrow valley and delta where 96% percent of the population inhabit on 4% of the land.

埃及气候干旱少雨。尼罗河三角洲及北部的沿海地区属地中海气候，气候相对温和，其他大部分地区属热带沙漠气候，夏季气温较高，昼夜温差较大。游览埃及的最佳时间是 11 月至次年的 3 月，这段时间气候较为凉爽。一般情况下，埃及不会下雨。

It is a dry place with little rain. The Nile Delta and the northern coastland enjoy the mild Mediterranean climate, while the other parts are under the tropical desert climate where it is hot in summer and the temperature varies greatly between day and night. The best time to visit Egypt is from November to next March when it is cool. Normally, it doesn’t rain.

（二）人文概况

1. 历史

埃及是个具有悠久历史和文化的古国，人类文明的发源地之一。古埃及和古巴比伦、古印度、中国并称“四大文明古国”。埃及在公元前3100年就出现了统一的奴隶制国家，当时的国王被称为法老。公元前525年，波斯帝国占领埃及并在此设省。公元前332年，马其顿亚历山大大帝打败波斯帝国，将埃及纳入其国土。公元前30年，罗马帝国出兵埃及，统治埃及达600多年，基督教传入埃及。公元640年左右，阿拉伯人进入埃及，并把埃及建成阿拉伯国家。1517年，土耳其侵入并将埃及纳入奥斯曼帝国，成为一个省。1798年，拿破仑率兵攻占埃及，但1882年英军打败法军占领埃及，并在1914年将埃及纳入其保护国。1922年，英国承认埃及为独立国家。1953年，埃及废弃君主制，建立共和国。1956年，埃及宣布收回苏伊士运河，英军全部撤出埃及。1958年，埃及联合叙利亚成立阿拉伯联合共和国。1961年，叙利亚独立。1971年，埃及改名阿拉伯埃及共和国。2011年伊始，阿拉伯世界多国发生社会动荡。埃及成为这台“大戏”中的重要一幕，运动导致执政30年的穆巴拉克总统下台。

Egypt is one of “the Four Cradles of Civilization”, together with ancient Babylon, India and China, known for their long history and rich culture. In 3100 BC there was already centralized slavery country in Egypt where Pharaoh ruled. In 525 BC, Persians invaded it and made it a province of theirs. In 332 BC, Alexander the Great of Macedonia beat the Persians to become the new ruler. In 30 BC, the Romans conquered it and began their control of Egypt for over 600 years when Christianity was introduced into it. In 640 AD or so, Arabians came and changed it into an Arabian country. In 1517, Turks took it over and made it a province of the Ottoman Empire. In 1798, Napoléon captured it, while in 1882, the British beat the French to take it and make it a protectorate in 1914. In 1922, the British were made to admit the independence of Egypt. In 1953, Egypt witnessed the abolition of monarchy and the establishment of the republic. In 1956, Egyptian government declared the resumption of the Suez Canal and the British army had to withdraw from Egypt. In 1958, the United Arab Republic was founded to consist of Egypt and Syria while in 1961, Syria declared its independence. In 1971, the country was renamed the Arab Republic of Egypt. Since the beginning of 2011, social turbulence swept the Arabdom. Egypt played an important role in this campaign and President Mubarak who had been in power for 30 years was forced to resign.

2. 经济

埃及的经济主要是农业、石油、旅游、劳务出口和苏伊士运河的船运税收。1/3的人口从事农业。埃及的长绒棉占世界长绒棉总产量的1/3以上，是世界上长绒棉产量最大的国家。1970年建成的阿斯旺大坝改变了尼罗河的生态，并影响了埃及的农业。埃及的石油、天然气储量丰富，石油及制品占出口总值的一半以上。埃及的旅游资源丰富，在于其拥有悠久的历史和古老的文化，在2009年和2010年，埃及超越沙特阿拉伯成为中东地区（不含以色列）游客到访最多的国家，旅游业为国家带来巨额收入，成为国家经济支柱之一。另外，有300万埃及人在沙特阿拉伯、海湾国家和欧洲等地工作。埃及的贫富差距比较大，近年来失业率居高不下，也是2011年埃及革命的导火线之一。

The main revenue of Egypt comes from agriculture, oil, tourism, labor export, and the Suez Canal transportation. One third of its population are engaged in agriculture. Its output of long-staple cotton is the highest among all countries so as to occupy at least one third of the world market. The Aswan Dam set up in 1970 changed the ecology of the Nile River and influenced the agriculture of Egypt. With abundant reserve of oil and gas, over one half of the exportation comes from crude oil and oil products. Egypt is rich in tourism resources as it enjoys long history and brilliant culture. From 2009 to 2010, Egypt exceeded Saudi Arabia to become the most frequently visited country in the Middle East (not including Israel) and tourism has brought huge revenue to the country to become one of the its mainstays. Besides, 3 million of Egyptians are working overseas in Saudi Arabia, the Gulf States and Europe. But the big gap between the rich and poor, the high unemployment rate in recent years also helps to bring about the revolution in Egypt in 2011.

3. 社会文化

埃及是阿拉伯世界中人口最多的国家，人口达1亿，主要是阿拉伯人，其中绝大多数生活在尼罗河河谷和尼罗河三角洲。伊斯兰教为国教，其信徒主要是逊尼派。官方语言为阿拉伯语，通用英语和法语。

Having a population of 100 million, Egypt is the most populous country in the Arab World, mostly Arabs who live in the Nile Valley and the Nile Delta. The national religion is Islam, especially Sunnite sect, and the official language is Arabic, with English and French widely-used.

公元前5世纪，古希腊著名的历史学家希罗多德曾说过，埃及是“尼罗河的赠礼”，意为尼罗河每年泛滥所带来的沃土使古埃及的农业得以发展，从而造就了这一古代文明。作为古文明的发源地之一，埃及的文化艺术非常丰富。埃及经历了法老时期、古希腊罗马时期、科普特时期及伊斯兰时期，每个时期都留下了永恒的遗迹。所以，埃及文化是具有非洲特点的阿拉伯文化，夹杂着法国、希腊、土耳其和叙利亚文化的特点。随着7世纪阿拉伯人的入侵，新的统治者和自身文化的保护者将阿拉伯语和伊斯兰教传播开来，其中禁止偶像崇拜，对大部分埃及人从过去法老和古希腊罗马时代的宗教中解脱出来产生了重大影响。而游客到埃及旅游，主要是针对古埃及的文化而来的。概括而言，古埃及时期的主要贡献是：（1）创造了象形文字，对腓尼基字母影响很大，而希腊字母是在后者基础上创造出来的；（2）法老时期的金字塔体现了古埃及在建筑和绘画艺术及数学上的高超成就，是古埃及文明的集中表现；（3）木乃伊体现了古埃及人在化学及医学上的成就；（4）古埃及人在2 600年前就制成纸莎草纸，它对传播埃及文明做出了非常大的贡献；（5）古埃及人在天文学领域成就非凡，发明了第一部太阳历法。目前，埃及共有六处世界文化遗产和一处世界自然遗产。

In the 5th century BC, Herodotus, the famous Greek historian said, Egypt is “the gift of the Nile”. That is to say, it was the fertile soil brought by the annual flood of the Nile that made it possible for Egypt to develop its agriculture, and thus its ancient civilization. As one of the cradles of human civilization, Egypt is rich in art and literary legacy. The eras of the Pharaohs, ancient Greece and Rome, the Copts, and the Islam have all left their perpetual brands on it, so Egypt's culture is what is called African Arabian and also a mixture of French, Greek, Turkish, and Syrian features. With the invasion of the Arabs in the 7th century, Arabian and Islam were spread, including prohibition of idolatry, which result in the casting off the old religion of the Pharaohs as well as the Greeks and Romans. Whereas, most visitors come for the ancient Egyptian culture, which can be summarized briefly as follows: a. the creation of hieroglyphics which greatly influenced Phoenician alphabet, the origin of Greek letters; b. the pyramids of the Pharaohs which is the epitome of ancient Egyptian civilization, especially their achievements in architecture, art and mathematics; c. mummies that reveal the medical accomplishments of the ancient Egyptians; d. papyruses that Egyptians used 2,600 years ago, which helped in spreading Egyptian civilization; e. astronomy achievement, e.g. the first solar calendar. So far, there are six World Cultural Heritage Sites and one World Natural Heritage Site in Egypt.

二、民俗风情

（一）礼仪禁忌

埃及的伊斯兰教信徒虔诚信仰“五行”（自白、礼拜、绝食、布施、参拜麦加圣地），并力所能及地完成信徒分内的事。“五行”已经跟日常生活融合，成为伊斯兰教信徒的生活习惯。伊斯兰教信徒每天祈祷 5 次，每次祈祷时间大约 15 分钟，第一次祈祷是在破晓前，第二次是在中午 1 点，第三次是在午后 3 点或 4 点，第四次是在日落时分，第五次是在晚上 8 点或 9 点，即晨礼、晌礼、晡礼、昏礼、宵礼。每逢周五是埃及人传统的“主麻日聚礼”，当清真寺内传出悠扬的唤礼声，伊斯兰教信徒便纷纷涌向附近的清真寺，做集体礼拜。每逢宗教节日，电视中还会播放总统及政府首脑去清真寺礼拜的镜头。如果游客参观清真寺正好赶上祈祷时间，就会被要求在主厅外等候片刻，等祈祷完毕方可进入。游客进清真寺时，务必脱鞋。

Muslims in Egypt believe in "Five Pillars" (five basic religious practices, including Profession of Faith, Prayer, Fasting, Alms, Pilgrimage to Mecca), and try their best to fulfill what a believer should do. The "five pillars" have been mixed with everyday life to be a daily routine. The Muslims should pray five times a day, about 15 minutes every time. The first prayer should be given before daybreak, the second at 1:00 pm, the third at 3:00 or 4:00 pm, the fourth at sunset, the fifth at 8:00 or 9:00 pm, that is, early morning prayer, noon prayer, mid-afternoon prayer, sunset prayer and evening prayer. Friday is the traditional "Jumu'ah" (Friday prayer) when the bells ring in the mosques, Muslims will flow into the nearby mosque to attend the congregation prayer. In every holyday, the scene of the president and other heads of the government praying in the mosque will be on TV. If the tourists come at the time of praying, they will be asked to wait a while outside the main hall and won't be allowed to come in until the end of the prayer. Before entering the mosque, please do remember to take off your shoes.

如今，埃及人不仅遵循着传统的礼仪习俗，而且有西方的做法。埃及人很热情，一般见面互致问候语：“祝你平安”“真主保佑你”“早上好”等。如果是老朋友，特别是久别重逢时，则拥抱行贴面礼，即用右手扶住对方的左肩，左手搂抱对方腰部，先左后右，各贴一次或多次，还会连珠炮似的发出一串问候语。贴面礼问候分为三种：一是吻面礼，一般用于亲友之间，尤其是女性之间；二是吻手礼，是向尊长表示敬意或是向恩人致谢时用的；三是飞吻礼，多见于情侣之间。

Nowadays, the Egyptians practice both their traditional etiquette and the western one. The friendly Egyptians will greet each other "May you be safe and sound", "May Allah bless you", "Good morning", etc. Old friends, especially those who meet again after a long separation, will hug each other to have the "cheek kiss", that is, to hold the other's left shoulder with one's right hand and put the left arm around his or her waist with cheek to cheek, first left cheek, and then the right one, to offer one "cheek kiss" or more as well as greetings in quick succession. There are three kinds of "cheek kiss", e.g. kissing the cheek, which is widely-used in the relatives and friends, especially among the women; kissing the back of the hand, which is used to show respect to the elders or to offer thanks; blowing a kiss, which is common in the lovers.

埃及人认为"右比左好"，右是吉祥的，埃及人做事都是从右手、右脚开始的，握手、递东西、用餐必用右手。不论送给别人礼物，或是接受别人礼物时，要用双手或者右手，千万别单独用左手。穿衣先穿右袖、穿鞋先穿右脚。进家门或寺庙时先迈右脚。伊斯兰教信徒上厕所或做脏活时都是使用左手的，他们认为左手是不干净的，因此用左手同人握手及递东西带有侮辱含义。

The Egyptians think that "right is better than left". Believing that right means lucky, they start doing everything with the right hand or foot and are obliged to shake hands or pass something with the right hand. Use the right hand or both hands to offer or receive the present, but never the left hand alone. Put on the right sleeve or right shoe first, and step with the right foot first when coming back home or entering the mosque. The Muslims use left hand when going to the washroom or doing dirty work and they believe that left hand is impure, so shaking hands or pass someone something with the left hand is deemed insult.

埃及人认为女人"最迷人的地方"只能给丈夫看，哪怕是同性之间也不可以互相窥探，所以女性不可穿着短、薄、透、露的服装。严禁穿短袖、短裤、背心到清真寺。交谈时不要夸女性身材苗条，埃及人认为瘦的人像针，而针在埃及人眼里是非常神秘的，特别是农村地区。传说每天下午 3 点到 5 点，天神会下凡赐给人们财富，而穷人一天到晚都在缝缝补补，穿针引线，所以他们得到的财富就很少，久而久之，针就成了不祥的象征，甚至成了骂人的话。在埃及，一到了下午 3 至 5 点之后，人们大都忌讳针。商人决不卖针，人们也不买针，即使有人愿出 10 倍的价钱买针，店主也会婉言谢绝，绝不出售。在埃及，也不可向人借针。

As the Egyptians believe that "the most charming part" of a woman's body should only be exposed to her husband instead of other people, including those of the same sex, women could never wear short, thin, transparent, bare clothes. It is forbidden to enter the mosque with short-sleeved shirt, shorts, camisole. Don't flatter a woman that she is slender as the Egyptians think a thin person is like a needle which is very mysterious in the eyes of the Egyptians, especially those in the rural areas. The legend goes that the God will come down every afternoon, at about 3:00 to 5:00 pm, with gifts for people, while the poor are so busy sewing with needles and threads all day long that they get the little wealth from the God. In the long run, needle becomes the ominous symbol, or even a bad word. In Egypt, people avoid needle all the way. Merchants will not sell needles then, nor will the people buy them. Even if there is someone who offers to to buy it at ten times the original price, the shopkeeper will decline it with thanks, politely but firmly. In Egypt, it is also not allowed to ask other people to lend you a needle.

（二）节庆风情

1. 闻风节（Sham el-Nessim）

每年的4月中下旬到5月初的某一天是埃及的“闻风节”。“闻风节”又称春节、踏青节，意味着可以闻到春天的气息。其历史可追溯到公元前2700年甚至更早。传说这天，慈善神战胜了凶恶神。经过约5 000年的历史演变，人们就在“闻风节”里祈求人间祥和、太平、春光永驻，这个习俗经久不衰。该节也是埃及最古老的传统节日之一。每年春天，古埃及人会在“闻风节”这天举家外出踏青，品尝彩蛋、咸鱼等各种象征吉祥的食品。

Sham el-Nessim (the Day of Beneficial Wind, or literally, smelling the breeze) happens between mid-late April and early May in Egypt. It is also called Spring Festival when people can go for a walk in the country to “smell” its coming. The tradition can be dated back to 2700 BC or earlier and it is said that Ormazd (the God of All Goodness) defeated Ahriman (the God of Evil). Lasting for about 5,000 years, it now becomes a day for people to pray for happiness as well as everlasting spring in the world. As the most ancient festival in Egypt, the tradition is still observed and in every spring, the family members will go out for a walk on Sham el-Nessim when the grass has just turned green, and they will not forget to bring the lucky food with them, that is, colored eggs and salted fish.

2. 斋月（Ramadan）

斋月是伊斯兰历第9个月，该月名字意为“禁月”，《古兰经》里明言规定此月符合条件的伊斯兰教信徒必须守斋戒，从日出到日落停止一切饮食、性事等活动，日落后即可进食恢复正常作息，直到晨礼（也就是日出）前都能吃喝，晨礼后便又进入斋戒状态。为期一个月的斋月期间，肃静的气氛只出现在白天，斋月期间的夜晚是一年中最热闹的，各大城市都会举行音乐会及各种演出。

Ramadan is the ninth month according to Islamic calendar, which means “the Month of Fast”. It is required in *the Quran* that the qualified Muslims must fast from sunrise to sunset with no food and no sex, etc. The fast is broken at sunset and people can drink and have meal until next morning (before the sunrise) when the fast starts again. The fast month is solemn in the daytime while the nights during the fast month are the most lively and dynamic in the year when concerts and other performances are held in the big cities.

三、主要旅游城市及景点

（一）开罗（Cairo）

开罗位于埃及北部，尼罗河三角洲的顶端，是埃及首都。开罗人口为2 280万，是整个中东地区阿拉伯世界和非洲最大的城市，中东地区的政治、经济、文化中心，世界上最古老的城市之一。开罗西南约 30 千米的孟菲斯是埃及的古都，其历史可以追溯到公元前 3100 年的前王朝时期的首位法老美尼斯，古埃及许多王朝都在此定都，并在附近修建金字塔和陵墓。现代的开罗建于公元 973 年，被喻为“胜利之城”。如今，开罗城的西部以现代化的高楼建筑为主，东部则是以古老的阿拉伯建筑为主，250 多座清真寺集中于此。开罗城内清真寺随处可见，有“千塔之城”的称呼。开罗的主要景点有吉萨金字塔群、狮身人面像、埃及博物馆等。

Cairo, capital of Egypt, is situated in its north part, at the top of the Nile Delta. With a population of 22.8 million, Cairo, one of the most ancient cities in the world, is now the biggest city in Africa and Arabdom of the Middle East, the center of politics, economy and culture in the Middle East. Memphis, the ancient capital of Egypt, lies about 30 kilometers to the southwest Cairo. It can be dated back to the first Pharaoh Menes in 3100 BC, and afterwards, many dynasties had chosen it for the capital and founded the pyramids and royal tombs nearby. Modern Cairo, literally “the Vanquisher”or “the Conqueror”, was built in 973. Now the west of the city is occupied by modern high-rise buildings, while the east is still the world of ancient Arab buildings, including over 250 mosques. There are mosques everywhere in Cairo to win it the name “City of a Thousand Minarets”. The attractions include the Giza Pyramids, Sphinx, the Egyptian Museum, etc.

◆ 金字塔（Pyramids）

金字塔是古埃及法老为自己修建的陵墓。埃及共发现金字塔 96 座，最大、最有名的是位于开罗西南面的吉萨高地上的金字塔。它们是祖孙三代法老（包括胡夫、哈夫拉、孟卡拉）的金字塔。大金字塔是法老胡夫的陵墓，建于公元前 2580 至公元前 2560 年，据说，10 万人用了 20 年时间才建成了这座埃及现存规模最大的金字塔，被喻为“世界古代七大奇迹之一”。第二座金字塔是胡夫的儿子法老哈夫拉的陵墓，建于公元前 2650 年左右，建筑形式更加完美壮观，塔前建有庙宇等附属建筑和著名的狮身人面像。第三座金字塔是胡夫的孙子法老孟卡拉的陵墓，建于公元前 2600 年左右。而著名的阶梯金字塔位于开罗南郊 30 千米的塞加拉，为古埃及第三王朝法老左塞尔的陵墓，建于公元前 2700 年左右。该金字塔是埃及现有金字塔中年代最早的，也是世界上最早用石块修建的陵墓。

Pyramids are the tombs built by the pharaohs of ancient Egypt for themselves. There are altogether 96 pyramids discovered in Egypt, of which the biggest and most famous lies in Giza, a highland in the southwest of Cairo. They are the pyramids for three generations of pharaohs, that is, Khufu, Khafre, and Menkaure. The Great Pyramid of Khufu was set up in about 2580–2560 BC and it is said to cost 100,000 people 20 years building it. It is the biggest pyramid existent in Egypt, one of “the Seven Wonders of the Ancient World”. The second pyramid is for Khafre, son of Khufu. Built in about 2650 BC, the architecture form is more perfect and magnificent, with the auxiliary buildings like temple, as well as the famous Sphinx before it. The third one is built in about 2600 BC for Menkaure, Khufu’s grandson. The famous Step Pyramid (Pyramid of Djoser), or Stepped Pyramid, is located in Saqqara, 30 kilometers of southern suburb of Cairo, which was built in about 2700 BC for Zoser, pharaoh of the Third Dynasty. It is the oldest pyramid now in Egypt and the earliest stone-made tomb in the world.

◆ 埃及博物馆（Egyptian Museum）

埃及博物馆是世界上最著名的博物馆之一，由被埃及人称为“埃及博物馆之父”的法国著名考古学家马里埃特设计，建于1858年，收藏了12万件历史超过3 000年的代表古埃及文明的历史文物，主要以法老时期的文物为主，埃及人又习惯地称之为“法老博物馆”，是世界上收藏古埃及文物最多的博物馆。参观埃及博物馆是直观了解古埃及文化的最好选择。

As one of the world-famous museums, Egyptian Museum, designed by Mariette, French archaeologist who was titled “Father of Egyptian Museum” by the Egyptians, was built in 1858. With 120,000 historical relics of ancient Egyptian culture over 3,000 years ago, mainly those from the era of the Pharaohs, it is the museum with the most ancient Egyptian antiques in the world and is usually called “Museum of Pharaohs” by the Egyptians. Visiting Egyptian Museum is the best choice of getting into the ancient Egyptian civilization visually.

◆ 尼罗河（Nile River）

尼罗河发源于埃塞俄比亚高原，流经布隆迪、卢旺达、坦桑尼亚、乌干达、肯尼亚、刚果民主共和国、苏丹和埃及9国，全长6 671千米，是非洲第一大河，也是世界上第一长河。尼罗河在埃及境内长度为1 530千米，两岸形成3 000米～16 000米宽的河谷，到开罗后分成两条支流，注入地中海。世界四大文明古国之一的古埃及，就是在尼罗河的哺育下发展了其光辉灿烂的古文化。尼罗河河谷和尼罗河三角洲是埃及文化的摇篮，是世界文化的发祥地之一，也是世界上人口最密集的地区之一，埃及96%的人口集中于此。因此，尼罗河是埃及的生命线，是“埃及的母亲”。如今，开罗的尼罗河上有许多游船，其中仿法老时期修造的船只又名“法老船”。夜晚泛舟河上，既可游览两岸旖旎风光，又可观赏船上著名的东方舞表演。尼罗河上约有200艘游船，多数在卢克索和阿斯旺之间航行。

The Nile River springs from the Ethiopian Highlands and runs through the nine countries of Burundi, Rwanda, Tanzania, Uganda, Kenya, Democratic Republic of the Congo, Sudan and Egypt. It is 6,671 kilometers long, the longest river in the world, and 1,530 kilometers is within Egypt to form the valley 3–16 kilometers in width. In Cairo, it splits into two branches that empty into the Mediterranean Sea. As one of “the Four Cradles of Civilization”, Egyptian civilization has its own cradle in the Nile Valley and Delta where 96% of Egyptian population concentrates to be one of the biggest population centers in the world. So the Nile is the lifeblood and Mother River of Egypt. Nowadays, there are many cruise ships along the Nile in Cairo, including some Pharaoh-styled ones that are named Pharaoh Cruises. Sailing in the river at night, you can feast on the beautiful landscape on both sides as well as enjoy the world-famous performance of oriental dance (Belly Dance) on the cruise. There are about 200 cruises along the Nile, and most of them shuttle between Luxor and Aswan.

（二）亚历山大（Alexandria）

亚历山大是埃及的最大海港和全国第二大城市，是历史名城、地中海沿岸的避暑胜地、埃及最具有欧洲风格的城市，是埃及开放度最高的城市。亚历山大的名字来源于马其顿亚历山大大帝，约建于公元前 331 年，曾经是古希腊的文化中心。亚历山大大帝死后被他的将军引渡葬在亚历山大。亚历山大见证了古罗马帝国的安东尼和埃及王后克里奥佩特拉之间的爱情。之后阿拉伯人、土耳其人先后在此登陆。拿破仑到来时，亚历山大已成为只有 8 000 人的小镇。英国统治埃及后，亚历山大成为重要的军港。今天的亚历山大被称为“地中海的新娘”，干净整洁，有浓厚的地中海气息。

Alexandria, the largest harbor and the second largest city of the country, is a famous historical city as well as the summer resort in the Mediterranean Sea. It is the most westernized and liberal city in Egypt. The name “Alexandria” derives from Alexander the Great, emperor of Macedonia. Built in about 331 BC, it used to be the cultural center of ancient Egypt. After his death, Alexander was buried by his general in the town across the Mediterranean Sea which witnessed the love story between Antony of ancient Rome and Cleopatra, queen of Egypt. Since then, Arabs and Turks landed on it one after another. When Napoléon came, it was already a town of 8,000 people. During the rule of Britain, Alexandria became an important military harbor. Now it is called “the Bride of the Mediterranean”, which is clean and tidy with the strong Mediterranean flavor.

亚历山大灯塔位于法洛斯岛上，建于公元前 283 年，被誉为“世界古代七大奇迹之一”，但由于地震，灯塔毁于 1435 年。1480 年，在原址上利用其石头修建了卡特巴城堡。庞贝柱是亚历山大灯塔遗留下来的仅有的古迹，附近有阿匹斯神庙遗址。

The Lighthouse of Alexandria used to be on an island named Pharos. It was built in 283 BC and was known as one of “the Seven Wonders of the Ancient World”. While due to the earthquake, it collapsed in 1435. In 1480, Citadel of Qaitbay (or the Fort of Qaitbay) was built on the ruin of the lighthouse, using the remaining stones. Pompey’s Pillar is the only relic of the Alexandria Lighthouse, and there is also the relic of the Temple of Apis nearby.

（三）卢克索（Luxor）

代表古埃及文明最繁盛时期的卢克索位于开罗以南 675 千米（属于上埃及）。古称底比斯，因埃及古都底比斯遗址在此而著称，距今已有 4 000 年的历史，是底比斯文物集中地。底比斯处于鼎盛时期，跨尼罗河两岸，《荷马史诗》把这里称为“百门之都”，有“100 个城门的底比斯”的描述，它毁于公元前 88 年。沿尼罗河南下，这里是游客必游之地，埃及文化古迹集中的旅游胜地。卢克索古迹中最引人注目的是尼罗河东岸的卡纳克神庙和卢克索神庙。如今的卢克索是世界上最大的露天博物馆，有着“宫殿之城”的美誉。每年都有几十万游客从世界各地慕名而来。埃及人常说：“没有到过卢克索，就不算到过埃及。”

Luxor, 675 kilometers south of Cairo (in Upper Egypt), represents the most prosperous period of Ancient Egypt. Originally called Thebes, it is known for the site of the ancient capital Thebes, which started 4,000 years ago to leave numerous cultural and historical relics there. In its heyday, Thebes strode across the Nile to be “the Capital of a Hundred Gates” that was described in *Homer’s Epic* as “Thebes of a Hundred Gates”. It was destroyed in 88 BC. Going down the Nile to the south, it is the must-see for the tourists where the relics of ancient Egypt can be found everywhere. Among them, the Karnak Temple Complex and Luxor Temple are the most attractive. Nowadays, Luxor has become the biggest open-air museum in the world to win the reputation of "City of Palace" that has attracted hundreds of thousands visitors from all around the world to admire it every year. The Egyptians always say: "He who has not been to Luxor has not been to Egypt."

（四）阿斯旺（Aswan）

阿斯旺是埃及文化古城，阿斯旺省的首府，是埃及南部的一个重要城市。阿斯旺位于首都开罗以南 900 千米的尼罗河东岸，是埃及的南大门，也是非洲的门户和唯一一条由海上进入非洲腹地的通道。阿斯旺是埃及阳光最充足的南部城市，具有非洲的气候特征，是埃及最热、最干燥的城市之一。阿斯旺的气候冬季温和，是世界闻名的冬季休养地，夏季炎热，全年几乎没有任何降水。阿斯旺是埃及自然风光最优美的地方，南部观光的起点站。阿斯旺的氛围比卢克索或开罗更为轻松惬意，是尼罗河帆船观光以及纳赛尔湖巡航游的中心。在这里，既有古代的遗迹，又有现代文明的成果，世界第七大水坝——阿斯旺大坝就建在附近的尼罗河上。滨河大道上 1899 年开业的老瀑布饭店激发了阿加莎·克里斯蒂创作《尼罗河上的惨案》的灵感。

The ancient city Aswan, capital of Aswan Governorate, is an important city of Southern Egypt, which lies 900 kilometers to Cairo at the eastern bank of the Nile. It is the southern gate of Egypt, door to Africa and the only passage to the interior of Africa from the sea. Aswan is the sunniest city in Southern Egypt, and one of the hottest and driest cities with typical African climate. In winter, it is sunny and warm to be world-famous, while in summer, it is too hot and dry with scarcely any rain. With the most beautiful landscape in Egypt, Aswan is the first stop of the sightseeing tour around Southern Egypt. More relaxing than Luxor or Cairo, it attracts flocks of sailing boats along the Nile and the cruises on the Lake Nasser. There are both ancient relics and modern civilization, including Aswan Dam, one of the top 7 dams in the world, nearby across the Nile. On Abtal El Tahrir Street, there is Old Cataract Hotel that was opened in 1899 at the riverside and inspired Agatha Christie to write her famous novel *Death on the Nile* then.

四、旅游资讯

（一）美食

埃及的饮食是比较典型的阿拉伯传统饮食。埃及菜肴简单而美味，埃及人通常以“耶素”为主食，进餐时与“富尔”（煮豆）、“克布奈”（传统白乳酪）、“摩酪赫亚”（汤类）一并食用。耶素是一种不用酵母的平圆形埃及面包。埃及人喜食羊肉、鸡、鸭、鸡蛋以及豌豆、洋葱、南瓜、茄子、胡萝卜、土豆等，很少吃鱼、虾、海鲜。肉类以牛、羊、骆驼和家禽类为主，肉类通常以烧烤为主。烤羊肉串和切片烤肉十分流行，串烤全羊是他们的待客佳肴。蚕豆是埃及的“国菜”，是必不可少的一种食品。其制造方法多种多样，制成的食品也花样百出，例如：蚕豆酱、油炸蚕豆饼、炖蚕豆、干炒蚕豆和生吃青蚕豆等。埃及人喜吃甜食，正式宴会或富有家庭正餐的最后一道菜都是甜食。著名的甜食有“库纳法”和“盖塔伊夫”。

Egyptian food is typical of traditional Arab style which is simple and delicious. The Egyptians usually live on Aish (Arabic name for bread), together with Ful (pronounced “fool”, creamy bean paste made from fava beans), Kareish (traditional white cheese) and Molokhia (soup). Aish is a kind of flat round bread without yeast. They prefer mutton, chicken, duck and eggs as well as beans, onions, pumpkins, eggplants, carrots, potatoes, etc. with little fish, shrimp, or seafood. They have much meat, including beef, mutton, camel and poultry. Most meat is roasted or grilled. Mutton shashlik and roast sliced meat is very popular and one of the delicacies to feast their guest is the grilled whole lamb. Fava bean (broad bean) is the “national dish” of Egypt, an essential part of every meal, with different recipes to make a variety of dishes, e.g. bean paste, deep fried bean cake, boiled beans, fried beans, or green beans to be eaten raw. The Egyptians love desserts and the last course of a family dinner or a dinner party is necessarily a dessert, e.g. the famous Egyptian dessert Kunāfah (cooked batter stuffed with nuts) or Qatayef (sweet crepe filled with cheese or nuts).

（二）购物及退税

一般而言，外国游客到埃及都会买些当地特色的商品作为纪念。埃及比较有特色的商品包括纸莎草制品、香精、香水、铜盘、银器等。除国营商店和超市明码标价外，埃及许多市场的商品没有固定的标价，讨价还价是日常生活的一部分。作为游客，在埃及购物时，首先要学会讨价还价。讨价还价并不是打仗，而是能让买卖双方达成各自理想价位的手段。讨价还价时应该保持礼貌和幽默。

Usually, the overseas visitors would like to buy some local specialties as souvenirs, for example, papyrus products, essence, perfume, copper dish, silverware, etc. In Egypt, bargaining is a part of life as in most markets, they have no fixed price tags for the goods they sell, except in the state-owned stores or supermarkets. Bargaining is not a battle, but a way for both parties to reach an ideal price that can make them satisfied, so politeness and sense of humor is important.

香水：埃及是法国许多著名香水的原产地，也是香料的生产大国。1 000 多年以前，开罗就已经是世界上最大的香料贸易中心了。埃及香料的品种繁多，功能各异，像麝香、玫瑰、荷花香精等是专门制作香水用的，而枯茗、红番花、樟脑可用于治疗疾病。

Perfume: Egypt is a country of spice as well as the place of origin of many famous brands of French perfume. Over a thousand years ago, Cairo had already become the biggest trade center of spice in the world. There are a large variety of perfume and spice produced in Egypt for various purposes, e.g. musk, rose, lotus essence that are used for fragrance, cuminum, crocus, camphor that are used for treatment of diseases.

纸莎草制品：纸莎草是尼罗河三角洲生长的一种类似芦苇的水生植物，可以用来造纸。纸莎草是古埃及文明的一个重要组成部分，纸莎草纸画是埃及文化瑰宝、世界上最早的纸画。纵使过去了几千年，在埃及，制作纸莎草纸画的每一个步骤都不曾变过，目前有许多以纸莎草创作的彩绘作品，题材多取自于古埃及神庙和宫殿的壁画。

Papyrus Products: Papyrus is a weed-like water plant that grows in the Nile Delta, which can be used as raw material for papermaking. It's an important part of ancient Egyptian civilization to contribute papyrus painting, the earliest paper painting in the world. Although thousands of years have passed, the process of making papyrus painting is still there with every step unchanged. You can see many papyrus color paintings whose subject matters are mainly drawn from the wall paintings of ancient temples and palaces in Egypt.

地毯：埃及的地毯在大街上随处可见，是埃及的著名特产，西奈半岛的达哈布有许多商店出售贝都因人制作的既便宜又色彩缤纷的棉制地毯 。

Carpet: As a famous local specialty, carpet can be seen everywhere in Egypt. There are many stores in Dahab, Sinai Peninsula to sell inexpensive, colorful cotton carpets made by the Bedouins.

水烟袋：水烟袋在阿拉伯语中称为"nargileh"，是埃及人抽烟用的器具。制作得较精致的水烟袋是一种很有意思的纪念品，以玻璃的为贵，黄铜的次之。

Hubble-bubble: Called "nargileh" in Arabic, it is the tool for people to smoke with. Now the delicately made nargilehs have become interesting souvenirs for the visitors, of which the glass ones are more expensive than the brass ones.

在埃及购物超过 1 000 埃及磅，就可以到机场退税柜台办理退税。游客购物时，需要求购物点开具退税的证明发票（不是购物收据）。到机场后要先办理登机牌，出境时声明要办理退税，并出具退税发票，再回到出境大厅。游客需在退税柜台出示登机牌、护照、退税发票、购物清单及发票办理退税手续。

If you buy things over EGP 1,000, you can apply for tax refund at the refund desk of the airport. While shopping, please ask for the certified invoice for tax refund (not the receipt). Having arrived at the airport and got the boarding pass, please make the tax refund declaration and show the invoice, and then come back to the departure lobby. You are required to show the boarding pass, passport, tax refund invoice, shopping list and invoice to apply for the tax refund.

（三）时差

埃及与中国时差是 6 小时。埃及是非洲国家里少数实行夏令时制的国家之一。通常，埃及的夏令时开始于 4 月的最后 1 个星期四，结束于 9 月的最后 1 个星期四。在夏令时期间，开罗与北京的时差从 6 小时变为 5 小时，与格林尼治时间相差 3 小时。

The time difference between Egypt and China is 6 hours. Egypt is one of the few countries in Africa that have the official Daylight Saving Time, which usually starts from the last Thursday in April and ends on the last Thursday in September. During the Daylight Saving Time, the time difference between Cairo and Beijing is shortened to be 5 hours, and that between Cairo and Greenwich is 3 hours.

思考练习

1. 经典旅游线路分析

埃及经典8日游

第1天：广州——开罗

游客在广州白云国际机场出境大厅集合，由专业领队带领办理登机手续后乘坐埃及航空公司航班飞往埃及首都开罗（全程飞行时间约13小时）。

第2天：开罗

抵达开罗后前往世界古代七大奇迹之首的吉萨金字塔群和金字塔守护神——狮身人面像。前往埃及博物馆，这是典藏最丰富的博物馆之一，内藏有古埃及历代法老的陪葬品、纯金宫廷御用珍品、木乃伊、纯黄金面罩及金棺材等。

第3天：开罗——亚历山大——卢克索

从开罗出发前往亚历山大（约3小时）。亚历山大是埃及第二大城市，距开罗约225千米，由亚历山大大帝于约公元前331年创建，参观25米高的红色圆柱形建筑——庞贝柱，外观古代七大奇迹之一的亚历山大灯塔遗址、亚历山大图书馆、古罗马剧场、蒙塔扎皇宫花园（又名夏宫），眺望美丽的地中海。晚乘夜火车前往卢克索。

第4天：卢克索

卡纳克神庙是有史以来规模最大的神庙群，它是经过历代法老的不懈努力，在漫长的1 500年间逐步完成的。卢克索神庙位于尼罗河畔，在现代城区的环绕之中，埃及法老时代的建筑数不胜数，但这是其中最引人入胜的一座。帝王谷是内容最丰富的考古遗址，在古埃及最辉煌的时期，几乎每一位法老都埋葬在这里。参观著名的女王神殿、孟农巨像，其中，孟农巨像是新王国时期法老阿蒙霍特普三世的雕像，用整块石料雕琢而成。

第5天：卢克索——洪加达

乘车前往洪加达（车程4小时）。洪加达位于埃及东部红海沿岸，是埃及的著名旅游景点。洪加达在20世纪80年代开始成为一个度假城市，市内兴建了多间酒店。洪加达有多个海滩，阳光充沛，游客可游泳及进行如滑浪、钓鱼等水上活动，也可乘潜艇或玻璃底船欣赏红海海底的珊瑚景色。

第6天：洪加达——开罗

早上自由活动，午餐后返回开罗（车程6小时）。晚上乘坐尼罗河游船。

第7天：开罗——广州

前往古埃及首都孟菲斯古城，参观孟菲斯博物馆及塞加拉梯形金字塔。前往圣母玛利亚教堂（又名悬空教堂），因为该教堂建在罗马塔上，也可以说是高悬在罗马塔的上空，是开罗科普特区6座古教堂中最漂亮的一座。有600多年历史的著名的汗哈利利大市集，是地中海和阿拉伯世界的著名交易中心。晚餐后去机场，飞回广州。

第8天：广州

抵达广州，结束愉快旅行。

分析：这条经典旅游线路的主要旅游景点与行程特色，以及适合旅游的人群。

2. 案例分析

[案例1] 某旅游团到埃及旅游，埃及人非常热情。大街上，好客的人们不时地主动打招呼，游客们很兴奋。但前往卢克索的途中，在中午1点左右，司机和导游突然让游客中途休息一下，他们却跪趴在地上念念有词，足有15分钟，游客们疑惑不解。请问：司机和导游的行为是否反常？他们会做多久的祷告？领队应该如何和客人解释？

[案例2] 埃及是非洲少数实行夏令时制的国家之一。通常，埃及的夏令时开始于4月的最后1个星期四，结束于9月的最后1个星期四。2010年，埃及政府宣布，于8月10日，也就是埃及斋月的前一天，停止使用夏令时，斋月结束时，也就是9月10日恢复夏令时，然后就到9月末夏令时结束。请问：埃及政府为何要宣布在斋月期间停止实行夏令时的规定？

3. 练一练

请以埃及的文化和古迹为主题写一篇关于埃及的导游词。

第二节 南非

一、国家概况

（一）地理环境

南非，全称南非共和国，有“彩虹之国”之誉，位于非洲大陆最南端，北邻纳米比亚、博茨瓦纳、津巴布韦、莫桑比克和斯威士兰，另有“国中之国”莱索托。南非是世界上独一无二的拥有三个首都的国家：行政首都（中央政府所在地）为茨瓦内，司法首都（最高法院所在地）为布隆方丹，立法首都（议会所在地）为开普敦。南非东、南、西三面被印度洋和大西洋环抱，地处两大洋间的航运要冲，地理位置十分重要。其西南端的好望角航线，历来是世界上最繁忙的海上通道之一，有“西方海上生命线”之称。

South Africa, officially the Republic of South Africa, is reputed as “the Rainbow Nation”. It is located at the southern end of African continent, with Namibia, Botswana, Zimbabwe, Mozambique and Swaziland to the north, and Lesotho, a “A State within a State” in it. South Africa is the only country in the world that has three capitals: Tshwane, the administrative capital with the seat of President and Cabinet; Bloemfontein, the judicial capital with the seat of Super Court of Appeal; Cape Town, legislative capital with the seat of Parliament. Embraced by the Indian Ocean and the Atlantic Ocean from eastern, southern, and western sides, South Africa is the communications hub of the two oceans that is very important geographically. The shipping route of the Cape of Good Hope has long been one of the busiest sea passages known as "Sea Lifeline of the West".

南非气候多样，西部干燥无雨，东部属亚热带湿润气候，而西南部属地中海气候。全境气候分为春、夏、秋、冬四季。12 月至 1 月为夏季，最高气温可达 32℃～38℃；6 月至 8 月是冬季，最低气温为 -12℃～ -10℃。南非全年平均日照时数为 7.5 ～ 9.5 小时，尤以 4、5 月间日照最长，故以“太阳之国”著称。由于风光秀美，气候宜人，南非被称为“人间天堂”。欧洲人尤其喜爱来南非休闲度假，因此，南非又被冠以“欧洲后花园”的美誉。

The climate varies in South Africa, dry and rainless in the west, subtropical moist weather in the east, Mediterranean climate in the southwest. There are four seasons of spring, summer, autumn and winter in the whole country. Summer lasts from December to January when the highest temperature reaches 32℃—38℃, and winter is from June to August when the lowest temperature is minus 12℃—minus 10℃. The average sunshine of the year is 7.5—9.5 hours per day, especially in April and May when the sun sets very late to win it the name "Sunshine State". Owing to the beautiful landscape and pleasant climate, South Africa is reputed as "Paradise on Earth", and as the Europeans are fond of taking vacation there, it is nicknamed "the Backyard Garden of Europe".

知识拓展

野生动物天堂

南非以其丰富、珍稀的野生动植物和美丽的自然风光著称。到南非 90％的外国游客是来看野生动物的。没有游览过南非的公园，就不能算来过南非。南非的硬币上印的是野生动物头像，而不像一般国家印的是领导人的头像，这个细节印证了南非这个“野生动物天堂”的美称。南非的动物也许是世界上幸福指数最高的动物，它们的生命价值和生存环境得到了最大限度的保护和尊重，人类与自然十分友好、和谐。南非人建立了多个保护区，以保持国有资源的存续。南非被认为是地球上展示野生动物最多的地方，哺乳类动物占全球的 6%，鸟的种类约占全球的 7%。南非公私拥有的动物保护区约 580 座，克鲁格国家公园是世界上最大的野生动物园之一。南非的五大动物有“百兽之王”狮子、最凶猛的食草动物水牛、惊人的巨兽犀牛、“偷袭王子”花豹和“力量之王”大象。

（二）人文概况

1. 历史

（科）桑人、科伊人和班图人为南非最早的土著居民。15 世纪欧洲人前往亚洲时，将好望角作为补给停靠点。1652 年，荷兰开始远征开普半岛。1657 年，荷兰人在开普半岛建立荷属殖民地并从欧洲招来大批雇员，欧洲各国移民在此逐渐融合，形成阿非利卡人（旧称布尔人）。1795 年，英国占领开普殖民地，并将殖民地英国化。随着黄金和钻石的发现，大批欧洲移民蜂拥而至，他们占领了大部分土地并迫使大部分黑人沦为奴隶和劳工。1910 年，英国把开普、纳塔尔、德兰士瓦、奥兰治 4 个自治州合并组成南非联邦，成为英国的自治领。由于南非政府推行白人至上的种族政策，1912 年为反对种族主义，南非土著人国民大会（现为南非非洲人国民大会）成立。20 世纪 40 年代后期，南非的种族歧视日益严重，种族隔离成为南非的政策，黑人不能和白人交往，他们的生活受到歧视。20 世纪 60 年代，南非内部出现反对种族隔离政策的骚乱和斗争，这一时期，纳尔逊·曼德拉当选南非非洲人国民大会领导人。1961 年，南非退出英联邦，成立南非共和国。1962 年 8 月，曼德拉被捕并被判终身监禁。20 世纪 80 年代，南非国内民主运动达到高潮，曼德拉利用自己的威望和地位，在狱中和当局谈判，1990 年获得自由。曼德拉坚持和解政策推动多党谈判，加上国际社会对南非种族隔离政策的制裁，1993 年多党制制宪会议通过了《临时宪法》。在 1994 年 4 月的不分种族大选中，曼德拉当选为南非首任黑人总统。

The earliest natives were Khoisan, Khoikhoi and Bantu. During the 15th century, the European stopped at Cape of Good Hope for supplies during the sailing to Asia. In 1652, the Dutch began to overcome Cape Peninsula. In 1657, the Dutch established the colony at the peninsula and hired lots of employees from European countries. Those European settled here and joined together to become a race called Afrikaners. In 1795, the British took Cape colony and made it anglicized. With the discovery of diamond and gold, flocks of European came and occupied most of the land, enslaved the black and forced them to do hard work. In 1910, British united the four free states, Cape, Natal, Transvaal and Orange as Union of South Africa which became a British dominion. Because the South African government carried out the ethnic policy of White Supremacy, the African National Congress was established against the racism. In the late 1940s, racial discrimination reached its top when the black are forbidden to be in contact with the white and the discrimination can be seen everywhere in their life. In 1960s, riots broke out to resist the policy of racial segregation in South Africa, and Nelson Mandela was elected as the president of the African National Congress. In 1961, South Africa quit the Commonwealth and became the Republic of South Africa. In August 1962, Mandela was arrested and sentenced to life imprisonment. In 1980s, the democratic movement in South Africa reached its top and Mandela, the prestigious domestic leader, commenced negotiating with the government in prison. He was released in 1990. Mandela insists on the policy of conciliation to promote multi-party negotiations and owing to the joint effort of international sanctions again, *the Interim Constitution* was adopted by the multiparty constitutional convention in 1993. In April 1994, Mandela was elected as the first black president.

2. 经济

根据联合国的分类，南非是非洲唯一的发达国家。丰富的资源、廉价的劳动力，加上先进的管理，使南非成为当今非洲经济最发达的国家，有“小欧洲”“非洲经济巨人”之称。但南非贫富悬殊，2/3 的国民收入集中在占总人口 20% 的富人手中。南非发展程度最高的区域包括开普敦、约翰内斯堡、德班以及伊丽莎白港，但这些区域外的其他地区发展程度非常有限。此外，南非国内不同人种收入悬殊造成黑人对外国移民的抵制、罪案率与贪污问题严重。更为严峻的是，附近国家难民的持续涌入，以及艾滋病发病率的高升，使南非经济发展受到限制。

Classified by the United Nations, South Africa is the only developed country in Africa. With abundant resources, cheap labor as well as advanced management, South Africa has become the richest country in Africa to have the name of "Mini Europe" or "Economic Giant of Africa". However, there is a huge gap between the rich and the poor when two thirds of the national income comes to 20% rich people. The most developed areas of South Africa include Cape Town, Johannesburg, Durban, and Port Elizabeth, while the other parts of the country are still very poor. Besides, the different income among different races results in the black people's opposition to foreign talents and immigration, crime and corruption. To make matters worse, the continuous influx of the refugees from the surrounding countries, and the climbing rate of AIDS add to the drag on its development.

南非是世界上矿产最丰富的国家之一，目前其矿产额约占整个非洲的一半，主要矿产为金、铬、钻石、白金。南非是世界上最大的黄金生产国和出口国之一，黄金出口额占全部对外出口额的 1/3，因此又被誉为“黄金之国”。南非还是世界主要的钻石生产国，产量约占世界的 8.7%。南非戴比尔斯公司是世界上最大的钻石生产和销售公司，其营业额一度占世界钻石供应市场 90% 的份额，目前仍控制着世界毛坯钻石贸易 60% 的份额。

South Africa is one of the countries which has the richest mineral resources. Its mineral output is half the sum of the whole Africa's, mainly in gold, chromium, diamond and platinum. Being one of the largest gold producers and exporters, the value of gold export is one third of the total exports, so South Africa is reputed as "The Gold Kingdom". It is also the main producer of diamond in the world whose output is 8.7% of the world market. De Beers is the largest diamond production and sales company in the world whose sales turnover was once 90% of the diamond supply of the world market and now still occupies 60% of the world trade of rough diamonds.

旅游业是当前南非发展最快的行业之一，南非旅游资源丰富，设施完善，生态旅游与民俗旅游是南非旅游业两大最主要的增长点。旅游业是南非第三大外汇收入和就业部门。2010 年南非世界杯吸引大量游客前往，但南非的治安问题一直备受关注。

Tourism is one of the fastest-growing industries in South Africa. With rich tourism resources and perfect amenities, ecotourism and folklore tourism are the major two growth points. Tourism is the third important source of foreign exchange and the employment. The 2010 South Africa FIFA World Cup has attracted a large number of visitors to come, but the problem of public security has also become the major concern.

3. 社会文化

南非人口为 5 652 万，有黑人、有色人、白人和亚裔四大种族，分别占总人口的

80.7%、8.8%、8% 和 2.5%。黑人主要有祖鲁、科萨、斯威士等 9 个部族，白人主要是荷兰血统的阿非利卡人（约占 57%）和英裔白人（约占 39%）。有色人是殖民时期白人与当地黑人所生的混血人种，亚裔主要是印度人（超过 90%）和华人。南非有 11 种官方语言，英语和阿非利卡语为通用语言。白人、大多数有色人和 60% 的黑人信奉基督教新教或天主教；亚裔约 60% 信奉印度教，20% 信奉伊斯兰教；部分黑人信奉原始宗教。

With a population of 56.52 million, South Africa is composed of four races, that is, the black, colored, white and Asian, who occupies 80.7%, 8.8%, 8% and 2.5% respectively of the population. The black people mainly come from 9 tribes, e.g. Zulu, Xhosa, Swazi, etc., and the white people are mainly Afrikaners who are of Dutch descent (about 57%) and those of British descent (about 39%). The colored people are mixed-blood of the white and the black, and the Asians are mainly the Indian (over 90%) and the Chinese. There are 11 official languages in South Africa, with English and Afrikaans as the common languages. The white people, most colored people and 60% of the black people believe in Protestantism or Catholicism, while among the Asians, 60% of them believe in Hinduism, 20% in Islam, and some black people believe in primitive religion.

南非有着丰富多彩的文化历史传统，各种族都对南非的文化做出了巨大的贡献。1996 年，南非颁发了《艺术、文化和遗产白皮书》，这是南非历史上第一次根据公正、民主、不分种族和性别的原则制定文化政策。手工艺、电影、出版和音乐是南非四大支柱性文化产业。

South Africa is of splendid culture and all races have contributed to it. In 1996, the government issued *White Paper on Arts, Culture and Heritage*. It is the first time in South African history to make a cultural policy on the principle of fairness, democracy, regardless of the race and sex. Handicraft art, movie, publishing and music are the four pillars of South African cultural industry.

土著文化表现在有着悠久历史的绘画和雕刻艺术上。布希曼人的洞穴壁画及雕刻留下了远古狩猎时代和现代原始部落非洲黑人生活的记录，这是人类艺术的宝贵财富，也是南非艺术的组成部分。

The native culture is well presented in the traditional painting and carving art. In the Bushman's caves, the murals (cave paintings) and carvings are vivid records of either the life of the black people in the ancient hunting times or that of the primitive tribes in modern times. They are treasure of the world as well as elements of South African art and culture.

南非的白人都是从欧洲移民过来的，其绘画艺术和欧洲一脉相承，又结合了南非土著艺术特点。从 20 世纪 30 年代的自然写意、现实写意到现代的许多创作流派，最初表现的多是移民历史和南非的风土人情，现在多以城市建筑雕塑或环境雕塑为主，并诞生了许多杰出的作品。

The white people of South Africa are immigrants from Europe who have combined the tradition of European art of painting and the features of the native art of South Africa. From the natural style, realistic style in the 1930s to many schools of modern art, they have created numerous masterpieces, first the representation of the immigration history and the description of South African manners and customs, now the achievements in city architectural or environmental sculptures.

除了绘画和雕塑，南非人也同样擅长音乐和舞蹈。南非的音乐文化集非洲、欧洲和东方印度音乐之大成，将黑人的鼓声、欧洲古典音乐的韵律和印度人的宗教音乐融为一体，其自由、奔放的节奏又为黑人传统舞蹈伴奏出丰富多彩的音乐旋律。二者默契，融为一体。其中的音乐剧《非洲脚印》被誉为南非的“舞之魂”。

Besides the painting and sculpture, South African people are also good at music and dance. South African music is a comprehensive expression of African, European and Oriental, especially Indian music to combine the drum of the black, rhythm of European classic music, and Indian sacred music. It is well-known for the free and hot rhythm accompanied by the black people's folk dance to present a charming melody where music and dance fuses in harmony. The musical *African Footprint* is reputed as “Soul of Dance” of South Africa.

南非是荣获诺贝尔奖人数最多的非洲国家。在文学上，女作家纳丁·戈迪默荣获1991年度诺贝尔文学奖，她的作品以关注黑人的平等与自由为焦点。约翰·马克斯维尔·库切荣获2003年度诺贝尔文学奖，库切的数部小说“精准地刻画了众多假面具下的人性本质”，是“后种族主义时代”文学的代表作。

South Africa is the African country whose people have won the most Nobel Prizes. To narrow it down to literature, there are Nadine Gordimer, the 1991 Nobel Prize winner, who has focused her works on the freedom and equality of the black people, and John Maxwell Coetzee, the winner of the 2003 Nobel Prize in Literature, who “in innumerable guises portrays the surprising involvement of the outsider” to present the world the masterpieces “after the collapse of white supremacy”.

二、民俗风情

（一）礼仪禁忌

南非人深受英国的文化和礼仪的影响。信仰基督教的南非人忌讳数字13和星期五。一般见面礼节是握手礼。对交往对象的称呼是“小姐、夫人、先生”。在黑人部族中，流行的打招呼方式是举起右手，手掌向着对方，目的是表示“我手里没有石头”，它是友好与和平的象征。在广大农村，南非黑人还会将鸵鸟毛或孔雀毛赠予贵宾，客人则把这些珍贵的羽毛插在自己的帽子或头发上。

Deeply influenced by British culture and etiquette, number 13 and Friday are taboos for the South African who believe in Christianity. Usually they shake hands and address people they meet “Madam, Miss, Sir”. In some tribes of black people, a popular way of greeting is to lift you right hand with the palm toward each other to show that “I have no stone in my hand”, which is a sign of friendliness and peace. In the vast countryside, South African black people will give their honored guests the plume of ostrich or peacock as gifts and the guests will wear it on their hat or hair.

南非黑人受到西方文化的影响，经常身着西式服装，偏爱色彩鲜艳的服装，尤其爱穿花衬衣。南非黑人通常还有穿着本民族服装的习惯，特别是女性保持着传统的服饰风格。不同部落的黑人，在着装上往往会有自己不同的特色。例如：有的部落黑人喜欢用兽皮做成斗篷，有的部落黑人则喜欢上身赤裸，仅在腰间围上一块腰布。

Influenced by the western culture, South African black people often wear the western style suit and prefer the colorful clothes, especially the colorful shirt. And they are also in the habit of dressing themselves in the national costume, especial the women who still keep the traditional dress style. People from different tribes can be distinguished from each other by their unique habits. For example, some people are fond of making cloak with the hide (animal skin), while others like to be bare to the waist where there is a loincloth as the only ornament.

在南非黑人家做客时，主人一般会送上刚挤出的牛奶或羊奶，有时是自制的啤酒，出于礼貌客人要喝一点，最好一饮而尽。若是百般推辞、一口不喝，主人多会不悦。在非洲很多地方，吃饭不使用刀叉，更不用筷子，而是用手。吃饭时，大家围坐一圈，用右手手指抓自己面前的饭和菜。客人吃饭时，应注意切勿将饭菜撒在地上，这是主人所忌讳的。

To be a guest at a South African person's home, it is most usual to be treated with the milk or goat's milk that is fresh, or the home-made beer. You'd better have a try out of politeness and it's best to toss it off. Refusing to have even a sip will make the hostess unhappy. In many places in Africa, people use hands to have meals instead of knife and fork, let alone chopsticks. During the meal, they sit around, reaching the food before oneself with the fingers of one's right hand. Please avoid spilling any food on the ground because it is something of a taboo.

在非洲，最大的禁忌是强调肤色不同。称呼非洲人时，最好按他们的国籍来称呼。非洲人的国家意识相当强烈，喜欢直呼其国名。南非黑人非常敬仰自己的祖先，特别忌讳外人对自己的祖先言行失敬。跟南非人交谈时，有四个话题不宜涉及：为白人评功摆好；评论不同黑人部落或派别之间的关系及矛盾；非议黑人的古老习惯；为对方生了男孩表示祝贺。非洲人普遍认为相机对准某物时，某物的"精气"就会被吸收殆尽。人、房屋、家畜一律不准拍摄，也不要拍体现他们发展落后的镜头。游客如果想拍摄，最好先向对方打个招呼，以免被投石、被吊或被打。

The biggest taboo in Africa is to emphasize the difference in the color of skin. The best way to address African people is to address them according to their nationality because they have very strong sense of nationality and appreciate being called so. African black people revere their ancestors very much so it is a taboo for the guests to show any disrespect for their ancestors. It is suggested to avoid the following four topics when talking with the South African: singing high praise for the white people, making comments on the relationship and disputes between different tribes or groups of black people, criticizing the ancient tradition of the black people, congratulating someone on his or her birth of a son. There is a popular belief in South Africa that he who is aimed at by a camera will have his "essence" sucked up by it. It is prohibited to take photos of men, women, houses, their livestock, and the scene to show their backwardness. The tourists had better ask their consent before taking photos lest they be thrown a stone at, hung up, or beaten by them.

（二）节庆风情

1. 自由日（Freedom Day）

4月27日的自由日是新南非首次不分种族的大选日，为南非国庆节。1994年废除种族隔离制度之后，南非进行了历史上第一次不分种族的全民大选。这次大选，凡是年满18岁的南非国民，不分种族，都有投票权。而在此之前，在种族隔离制度下，南非有色人种在大选中投票只有有限的权利。

Freedom Day, the National Day, falls on April 27, which was the first Election Day of all races in South African history. In 1994 when social segregation was abolished, the first national election in South African history was held among people of all races. All citizens aged above 18, irrespective of the race, have the right to vote. Whereas during the period of racial segregation, the colored people in South Africa had only limited right to vote in the election.

2. 和解日（Day of Reconciliation）

每年的12月16日是南非政府法定的“种族和解日”，原称“誓言日”，教育国人吸取黑人、白人“血河之战”的历史教训。1994年新南非政府成立后，这一天被改名为“和解日”，寓意是希望南非黑、白两大种族面向未来，和平共处。

December 16 is the day of racial reconciliation determined by the government of South Africa. Formerly called as “Day of the Vow”, it was for both the black and white people to learn from the “Battle of Blood River” in history. In 1994, the new government of South Africa changed its name into “Day of Reconciliation” in hope of the peaceful coexistence of the biggest two races in South Africa, that is, the black and the white, to win a better future for them and for the country.

三、主要旅游城市及景点

（一）开普敦（Cape Town）

开普敦位于非洲大陆西南端、好望角北端的狭长地带，是南非议会的所在地，故称立法首都。开普敦是开普省的省府，人口374多万，是南非的第二大城市，也是重要港口。开普敦是欧裔白人在南非建立的第一座城市、南非的发祥地，故有“南非诸城之母”之称，也被称为“母亲城”。经过300多年的演变，开普敦从原来的不毛之地变成了南非最古老且最富特色的城市。历经荷、英、德、法等欧洲诸国的统治及殖民，开普敦充满欧洲殖民地的多元文化色彩，为南非的文化古都，集欧洲和非洲人文、自然景观特色于一身，被誉为“非洲明珠”“南半球花园”，是世界上最美丽的都市之一，也是南非最受欢迎的观光都市。开普敦气候温暖、景色宜人，每年10月至次年的3月是最佳旅游季节。城区内多种风格的欧洲古老建筑，围绕着桌山而建。桌山因山顶平整如桌而得名，是开普敦的地标，在此可以观赏大西洋和印度洋的不同风光。

Cape Town lies in the southwest tip of African continent to form a narrow belt north of Cape of Good Hope. It is the legislative capital with the seat of Parliament of South Africa. It is also the capital of Cape Province, the second largest city in South Africa with a population of 3.74 million as well as an important harbour. Cape Town is the first city that was built by European immigrants, so it is also known as “South Africa’s Mother City” to be the cradle of South Africa. Over 300 years later, it has been turned from a barren land to the richest and the most special city in South Africa. As a European colony that has been ruled by the Dutch, British, German and French in succession, Cape Town is well-known for its multi-culturally colonial style. As an ancient capital, it combines the natural scenery and cultural heritage to be one of the most beautiful metropolises in the world and the most popular tourist city in South Africa, which is called “Pearl of Africa”, “Garden of the Southern Hemisphere”. It is warm and beautiful here. The best tourism time is from October to the next March. There are various old style of European buildings surrounding the Table Mountain which is the landmark of the city and is famous for its top as flat as a table. From the top of the mountain you can enjoy the beautiful but different scenery of the Atlantic Ocean and the Indian Ocean.

（二）约翰内斯堡（Johannesburg）

约翰内斯堡是南非最大城市，人口 388.81 多万，是南非采矿业、工业、商业、金融和经济中心，南非交通中心和国际航运站，被称为南非的经济首都。约翰内斯堡是世界最大的产金中心，素有“黄金之城”之称。1880 年，这里只是一座以两头牛的价值换来的农场，随着金矿的发现和开采，历经发展，1928 年建为市。今天的约翰内斯堡已发展成为繁华的现代化大都市，融合了东方、西方、非洲三种文化色彩。主要旅游景点有黄金城、人类摇篮遗址等。黄金城是建立在旧金矿遗址上的主题公园，园内逼真地重现了 18 世纪后期到 19 世纪初期淘金热潮时黄金城的建筑。人类摇篮遗址有占全世界一半的人类祖先化石，1999 年被列入世界文化遗产名录。

Johannesburg is the biggest city of South Africa, with a population of over 3.8881 million. It is also the center of mining, industry, trade, finance, economy as well as the hub of land transportation and airline traffic so that it is called the economic capital of South Africa. It is the biggest gold production center in the world to be known as “City of Gold”. In 1880, it was still a farm acquired at the cost of two cows, and with the discovery of gold mines and its development, the city of Johannesburg was established in 1928. Now it has become a prosperous modern metropolis to fuse the cultural elements of the East, West and Africa. The main tourist attractions include Gold Reef City, Cradle of Humankind, etc. Gold Reef City is a theme park which offers a vivid depiction of the gold rush at the turn of the 19th century with the old buildings there. Cradle of Humankind is included in the list of UNESCO World Cultural Heritage Site in 1999, and it is the richest hominid site where half the fossils of human ancestors in the world are discovered and kept there.

（三）茨瓦内（Tshwane）

茨瓦内是南非的行政首都，南距约翰内斯堡约 60 千米，城中居民白人多于黑人。原名比勒陀利亚，于 1855 年创建，为纪念布尔共和国第一任总统马蒂纳斯·比勒陀利乌斯而命名，2005 年 3 月 7 日改名。因为每年 10 月间，市内有 7 万多株紫薇树花朵盛开，所以又名“紫葳之城”，1999 年被评为世界上最美的花园城市。各国驻南非使馆皆设立于此。

Tshwane is the administrative capital of South Africa, about 60 kilometers south of Johannesburg, with more white people than black people in its population composition. It was founded in 1855 in honor of the first president of Boer Republics, Marthinus Wessel Pretorius, hence the original name was Pretoria. On March 7, 2005, the name was changed. Every October, over 70 thousand of jacaranda in the city will be in bloom to bring it a beautiful name, "Jacaranda City". In 1999, it is appraised as the most beautiful garden city in the world where the embassies of all countries are located.

（四）其他著名旅游景点

◆ 太阳城（Sun City）

太阳城是南非的著名旅游胜地，约翰内斯堡向西北方向驱车约 140 千米即可到达。太阳城集娱乐、体育、休闲、博彩和观光为一体，是南半球最大的娱乐中心，是仅次于美国拉斯维加斯的全球第二大赌城，有“世外桃源”、非洲的“拉斯维加斯”的美誉，也是世界小姐大赛的举办地。太阳城并非是一座城市，而是一个青山绿水的超豪华度假村。太阳城之所以能够名噪非洲南部，除了其在贫瘠地区创造奇迹外，1993 年落成的“失落之城”也是其备受世人瞩目的一大原因。太阳城和“失落之城”已成为国际知名度很高的顶级娱乐中心，这里常年举办大型国际文艺演出和国际体育赛事。游览太阳城已成为南非之旅的一大亮点，每年约有 300 多万游客前来观光和消闲。

The famous tourist attraction, Sun City, is located 140 kilometers northwest of Johannesburg. It is the largest recreation center in the Southern Hemisphere to integrate recreation and entertainment, sports, leisure tourism, lottery and sightseeing into one. It is the second largest entertainment casino in the world, next to Las Vegas of the US, to be called "an Arcadia", or "Las Vegas of Africa". It is also a famous host city of the Miss World Pageant. But indeed, it is not a city. It's just the most luxurious holiday village with beautiful landscape. It is well-known not only because it has created "miracle" in poorer areas, but because of the Lost City that was built in 1993. Both the Sun City and Lost City have become world-famous top recreational centers to hold many international theatrical performances and sports games. Visiting Sun City has become a highlight of South African tour and has attracted about 3 million tourists yearly to come for sightseeing or entertainment.

◆ 克鲁格国家公园（Kruger National Park）

克鲁格国家公园位于姆普马兰加省、林波波省和莫桑比克交界的地带，从约翰内斯堡驱车东北方向约 6 小时可达，是南非最大的野生动物保护区。克鲁格国家公园南北纵贯约 400 千米，东西横跨约 70 千米，面积相当于英国的威尔士，总面积达 2 万平方千米。克鲁格国家公园创建于 1898 年，由当时布尔共和国最后一任总统保尔·克鲁格所创立。保尔·克鲁格为了阻止当时日趋严重的偷猎现象，保护萨贝尔河沿岸的野生动物，宣布将该地区划为动物保护区。随着保护区范围的不断扩大，这一地区的自然环境和生态平衡得以完美保持。克鲁格国家公园是世界上自然环境保持最好的、动物品种最多的野生动物保护区，也是南非旅游的精华之一。

Kruger National Park is located in the border region of Mpumalanga, Limpopo and Mozambique. About 6 hours' drive northeast of Johannesburg, it is the biggest wildlife reserve in South Africa. About 400 kilometers from south to north, and about 70 kilometers from west to east, Kruger National Park covers an area of 20,000 square kilometers, amounting to that of Wales of the United Kingdom. It was built in 1898 by the last president of Boer Republic, Paul Kruger, who declared it as wildlife refugee to prevent the increasingly serious problem of poaching and protect the wildlife along the Sable River. The reserve has been expanding to retain the natural environment and ecological balance of this region perfectly. Now it is the best wildlife reserve in the world with the most original natural environment and the richest wildlife species to be the soul of South African tour in a sense.

四、旅游资讯

（一）美食

南非美食受到东、西方和非洲传统饮食的影响，形成“彩虹之国”多元文化特色的饮食文化。南非的美食主要分为两大流派：一种是豪放的土著美食，南非黑人喜欢吃牛肉、羊肉，主食是玉米、薯类、豆类，不喜生食，爱吃熟食；另一种是来自英国等地的西餐，当地白人经常吃牛肉、鸡肉、鸡蛋和面包，爱喝咖啡与红茶，特别是当地著名的饮料，如路依保斯茶。因为地理环境的特殊性，南非被印度洋和大西洋所环绕，海产品十分丰富，尤以龙虾、对虾、牡蛎、鲍鱼、鳕鱼等出名。这些海味通常是用香浓的奶油煎烤而成，佐以南非出品的白葡萄酒，味道十分鲜美。常见的南非菜的烹制手法有烧烤、炖和烩，讲究调汁，善用南非特有的香料、咖喱。比较有代表性的菜肴是龙虾餐、鸵鸟餐和烤肉。烤肉是南非生活方式中不可缺少的组成部分。

With the influence of both the Eastern and Western style and African traditional food, a multi-cultural food style of “Rainbow Nation” has come into being. South African food and cooking can be divided into two groups, one is the crude style of the native people, the other is the Western style from Britain, etc. South African black people favor beef, mutton, and live on corns, potatoes, beans, and prefer cooked food to uncooked one. The local white people usually have beef, chicken, eggs and bread, together with coffee and black tea, especially Rooibos tea, the popular local drink. As South Africa is surrounded by the Indian Ocean and the Atlantic Ocean, seafood abounds here including the most famous lobsters, prawns, oysters, abalone and codfish. Seafood is usually roasted with thick cream, which tastes very good when served with the local white wine. The common ways of cooking include roasting, stewing and braising. South Africans are particular about the sauce they use and know how to make delicious food with the spice peculiar to South Africa. Typical South African dishes are lobster, ostrich and roasted meat. Barbecue is an inseparable part of South African style of life.

（二）购物及退税

由于外国游客购物可以退税，因此南非是国外游客购物的天堂。钻石、黄金、珠宝、皮货、非洲手工艺品及时装是游客的最爱。各大城市均有现代化的购物中心，还有街头的集市和旧货市场，国外游客可买到物美价廉的物品。南非的治安状况不好。最好不要携带大量现金，在南非可以用银联卡、维萨卡和万事达卡。

As the foreign tourists can get tax refund, South Africa is the international shoppers' paradise. Diamond, gold, jewelry, leather, fur, African handicraft, and fashionable dress are among the favorites of the overseas shoppers. There are modern shopping centers in every big city, besides the fairs and flea markets here and there where the tourists can buy some goods cheap and fine. It is not safe to carry much cash in South Africa, you can use UnionPay Card, VISA Card and MasterCard.

黄金：南非是黄金生产大国，从 1898 年起，南非黄金产量一直高居世界第一。南非的黄金主要出口国际市场。

Gold: South Africa is the major producer of gold whose output has ranked first in the world since 1898. The gold in South Africa is mainly for exportation to the international market.

钻石：钻石号称"宝石之王"，南非是世界重要的钻石生产国，而且以生产名钻闻名于世。南非生产的钻石大多属于珍品级，在国际市场上有很高的声誉。

Diamond: Diamond is known as "the King of Precious Stones". South Africa is the most important producer of diamond and is known to the world for the famous diamonds it has produced. They are for the most part rarities and enjoy very high reputation in the international market.

非洲木雕：在非洲黑土地上，最有民族特色的东西莫过于木雕艺术品。非洲木雕大都具有宗教神圣性，一般认为放在家里能镇宅驱邪。种种因素使得从民间收藏家，到普通的老百姓，越来越多的人爱好收藏非洲木雕艺术品。

African wood carvings: Wood carvings may be the most ethnic keepsake in Africa. African wood carvings are mostly religiously sacred and believed to have the power of driving away the evil spirits. A variety of reasons have made it become a favorite of both the private collectors and the ordinary people.

南非葡萄酒：南非是目前世界上六大知名的葡萄酒产区之一，产量约占世界的 3%，是非洲的葡萄酒王国。南非的葡萄酒价廉物美。

South African wine: South Africa is one of the top six wine producing areas in the world to produce about 3% that of the world. It is Africa's kingdom of wine where you can pay a small price for very good wine.

路依保斯茶：路依保斯茶富含矿物质，非常有益健康。它不含色素、防腐剂和咖啡因，丹宁酸的含量也非常低，还不含草酸，因而对易患肾结石的人来说，是非常好的一种饮料。

Rooibos tea: It is rich in minerals and is very good for health with no artificial coloring, no preservatives, and no caffeine. With very little content of tannic acid and no oxalic acid, it is a pretty good drink for those who are liable to suffer from kidney stones.

游客一定要保留购物后开具的小票，这点非常重要，因为在南非购物退税很方便。游客购物超过 250 兰特以上，即可在离境时，在机场退税柜台办理 14% 的退税。退税时，需要出示付款单和对应的物品，该物品必须是未使用的。核对无误后，退税柜台会填写一张退税支票。办理完出境手续后，凭支票到海关退税处领取退回的税款。在退税柜台和海关都要支付手续费，扣除手续费后退回的金额约为总价格的 10% ～ 12%。

It's very important to keep the receipt after shopping as it is convenient to apply for tax refund in South Africa. If you buy things over ZAR 250 , you can apply for 14% drawback at the tax refund desk of the departure airport. You are required to show the bills of payment and the corresponding articles which are supposed to be unused. Having being checked, you will be given a tax refund check with which you can claim your tax refund at the customs drawback. Commissions should be paid at both the tax refund desk and the customs drawback, and the net drawback you can get after deducting the commission is about 10%—12% of the total amount.

（三）时差

南非在东二区，和中国相差 6 小时。

South Africa is in GMT+2 Time Zone, and the time difference between South Africa and China is 6 hours.

思考练习

1. 经典旅游线路分析

南非经典 8 日游

第 1 天：北京——约翰内斯堡

游客在北京首都国际机场集合，办理登机手续，搭乘南非航空公司客机，飞往非洲大陆最南端的国家——南非。

第 2 天：约翰内斯堡——茨瓦内——太阳城

乘车前往南非行政首都茨瓦内，参观庄严的开拓者纪念堂、教堂广场、希腊式建筑风格的总统府。总统府大楼正面的花园花团锦簇，争奇斗艳，美不胜收，在此可眺望市街美丽的景致。之后前往“世界小姐”选美大赛的场地——有“南非拉斯维加斯”之称的太阳城，太阳城以豪华而完整的设备及浑然天成的自然美景吸引了世人的目光，几乎是所有到南非旅游的观光客不会错过的好地方。抵达后，游客于太阳城内可享受其内部的各项游乐设施，如游泳、骑马、打高尔夫球，或前往赌场小试身手，晚餐后入住太阳城的五星级酒店休息。

第 3 天：太阳城——约翰内斯堡

早餐后，乘车前往南非第四大野生动物园——匹林斯堡野生动物园。乘旅游车进入园内，这里拥有各种野生动物和超过 350 种鸟类，在这里欣赏那些在苍茫的大草原、起伏的山坡、草丛中、大树下生活的各种野生动物，是一项不可错过的体验。之后乘车返回约翰内斯堡，前往南非钻石切割中心参观，游客可以亲眼看见神奇的钻石加工过程。晚餐后入住酒店休息。

第4天：约翰内斯堡——开普敦

早餐后，前往狮子园，在这里有机会欣赏狮子在草地上漫步的英姿，并可与小狮子合影留念。午餐后乘车前往机场办理登机手续，乘机飞往非洲南端、世界最美丽的城市之一的开普敦。开普敦是南非文化的发源地，许多南非人称它为“母亲城”，是南非召开共和国会议的立法首都。抵达后享用晚餐，入住酒店休息。

第5天：开普敦——好望角——开普敦

早餐后，乘车前往豪特湾，在天气许可的情况下乘船前往著名的海豹保护区，观赏上百只海豹聚集在一起嬉戏的自然生态景象。途经企鹅保护区，参观著名的南非斑嘴环企鹅。之后经开普半岛的海滨公路，游览好望角自然保护区，乘缆车登上好望角山顶，俯瞰印度洋及大西洋交会的壮阔景色，晚餐后入住酒店休息。

第6天：开普敦

早餐后，在天气许可的情况下，搭乘360度旋转缆车登上桌山游览，在山上可以俯瞰整个港湾，远近海景尽收眼底。之后前往鸵鸟园，在此可了解鸵鸟的生态及习性。前往马来区，这里是1652—1806年荷兰东印度公司从东南亚带来大量的马来奴工所建的住宅。平顶、色彩亮丽是马来后裔独特的风格，区内大多数房屋都已被列为古迹保存。之后前往宝石中心参观，晚餐后入住酒店休息。

第7天：开普敦——约翰内斯堡——北京

早餐后，前往世界闻名的葡萄酒原产地康斯坦夏，展开浪漫的酒乡之旅，这里属于地中海气候，温暖湿润，土地肥沃，因此成为重要的葡萄酒产地，沿途果园风光引人入胜。有专人带领，实地参观酒窖并详细了解各种葡萄酒的生产过程。在此游客不仅可以了解到关于葡萄酒的各种知识，还可以品尝数种红、白葡萄美酒。午餐后前往康斯坦博西植物园，它是世界上最早的植物园，园内只栽种南非原产植物，尤其是南非的国花——帝王花。之后乘车前往机场办理登机手续，乘坐南非航空公司飞机经约翰内斯堡转机返回北京。

第8天：北京

抵达北京，旅行中的美好回忆将成为游客铭记今生的挚爱珍藏。

分析：这条经典旅游线路的主要旅游景点与行程特色，以及适合旅游的人群。

2. 案例分析

[案例1] 2002年，某旅游团在开普敦市附近的企鹅滩参观时，其中一人出于好奇心捡了一只企鹅蛋。当地人发现后向执法部门举报，结果整个旅游团被扣留，护照被收缴，还差点儿被送上法庭。后经多方努力，双方达成庭外和解协议，最终旅游团赔了3 000兰

特，但此事造成的恶劣影响延续至今。如何理解一只企鹅蛋引起的风波？作为领队和游客，该如何避免类似冲突？

[案例2] 在南非，保护大自然、保护动植物已成为一种可贵的社会风气。南非人喜欢说，保护大自然既是给自己，也是给子孙后代造福，是件功德无量的事。但某旅游团在参观某野生动物园时，由于害怕，一名游客当着当地地陪的面踢一只靠过来的不知名的小动物，地陪和旁边的一些当地人非常气愤，纷纷指责这名游客。作为领队，应如何提高游客的环保意识，真正做到入乡随俗？

3. 练一练

（1）自从1994年以来，南非习惯上被称为“新南非”，因为创新的精神鼓舞了整个民族，数以百万的南非人能够接受教育，拥有住房、医疗和选举权等，而在以前他们完全是被排除在外的。如何理解南非的变化？

（2）请以“发现新南非”为主题写一篇导游词。

第六章
中国港澳台地区

本章导航

中国港澳台地区（Hong Kong，Macau and Taiwan，China）是对我国的香港特别行政区、澳门特别行政区和台湾地区的统称，三地在经济和文化体制上有诸多类似之处。自2003年开放内地居民赴港澳个人游和2008年7月启动大陆居民赴台个人游以来，中国内地/大陆出境旅游者绝大多数集中于中国香港、澳门、台湾地区，以及韩国、日本、东南亚等周边国家与地区，其中赴港澳台地区的游客最多，2018年占出境总人数的52.7%。2019年8月1日起，鉴于当前两岸关系，47个城市大陆居民赴台个人游试点暂停。

第一节　香港特别行政区

一、地区概况

（一）地理环境

香港，全称为中华人民共和国香港特别行政区，位于中国东南部，北隔深圳河和深圳相连，西望澳门特别行政区，由香港岛、九龙、新界和周围262个岛屿组成，面积为1 106.66平方千米。九龙及香港岛之间的维多利亚港，港阔水深有利于船只航行，是世界三大天然良港之一。香港最初就是从维多利亚港两岸的平地开始发展的，至今该区仍然是香港都市命脉所在。深圳河是香港和内地的边界线。

Hong Kong, whose full name is Hong Kong Special Administrative Region of the People's Republic of China, is located in southeastern China, facing Shenzhen across the Shenzhen River in the north, and Macau Special Administrative Region in the west. It is made up of Hong Kong Island, Kowloon and New Territories, with other 262 islands, covering an area of 1,106.66 square kilometers. Victoria Harbor, located between Kowloon and Hong Kong Island, is one of three largest natural harbors in the world, and ideal for the navigation of vessels as the harbor is wide and deep. Hong Kong originally developed from both sides of Victoria Harbor, and the area has been the urban lifeline for Hong Kong till today. The Shenzhen River is the natural boundary line between Hong Kong and the mainland of China.

香港属亚热带气候，全年的气温较高，年平均温度为22.8℃。夏天炎热且潮湿，温度约在26℃～30℃；冬天凉爽而干燥，但很少会降至5℃以下。

Hong Kong enjoys a subtropical climate. The temperature is a bit high all year round. The average annual temperature is 22.8℃. Summer is hot and humid, with a temperature around 26℃ to 30℃ ; winter is cool and dry, but rarely drops below 5℃.

（二）人文概况

1. *历史*

公元前214年，秦朝设置南海郡，香港列入管辖之地。唐朝设立屯门军镇以保护海上贸易。1840年，鸦片战争爆发，清政府战败，被迫割让香港岛给英国，由此英国开始了长达156年的殖民统治。随后在第二次鸦片战争和甲午战争中，英国又强迫清政府出租九龙和新界。第二次世界大战期间，日本发动太平洋战争同时侵占香港，统治香港3年零8个月。1945年，日本投降，英国继续对香港实行殖民统治。20世纪80年代，中国政府在邓小平提出的"一国两制"原则下，开始和英国谈判，两国在1984年9月18日达成协议。同年12月19日，两国于北京签署了《中华人民共和国政府和大不列颠及北爱尔兰联合王国政府关于香港问题的联合声明》（简称《中英联合声明》）。1997年7月1日，中国政府恢复对香港行使主权，成立中华人民共和国香港特别行政区。

In 214 BC, Qin Dynasty set up the Nanhai County and Hong Kong was in its jurisdiction. In Tang Dynasty, Tunmen military town was set up to protect the maritime trade. In 1840, the First Opium War broke out and Qing government was defeated and Hong Kong Island was ceded to the United Kingdom. Since then, the United Kingdom started its 156 years of colonizing Hong Kong. And Qing government was forced the cession of the Kowloon to the United Kingdom after the Second Opium War II and the lease of New Territories after Sino-Japanese War of 1894–1895. During the Second World War, Japanese launched the Pacific War and at the same time invaded Hong Kong and had occupied for 3 years and 8 months. In 1945, Japan surrendered and the United Kingdom continued to implement the colonial rule over Hong Kong. In 1980s, Chinese government started to negotiate with the United Kingdom under the principle of "One Country, Two Systems", an idea put forward by Deng Xiaoping, and reached the agreement on September 18, 1984. On December 19, 1984, both governments signed *The Joint Declaration of the Government of the United Kingdom of Great Britain and Northern Ireland and the Government of the People's Republic of China on the Question of Hong Kong* (briefly *Sino-British Joint Declaration*). On July 1, 1997, China resumed sovereignty over Hong Kong and the Hong Kong Special Administrative Region of the People's Republic of the China was established.

2. 经济

香港是一个自由港，对大多数进口物品不征收关税。香港是亚太地区乃至全球的金融中心、国际航运中心、国际贸易中心以及旅游和信息中心，在全球金融中心指数中，有超过 160 家银行机构和相同数量保险公司的香港名列第三，仅次于纽约和伦敦。尽管 2020 年香港金融地位受创，但其“全球金融中心第一梯队”的地位依然稳固。香港以社会廉洁、治安优良、自由的经济体系以及法制完备而闻名于世，为全球最安全、富裕、繁荣和生活水平高的城市之一，有“东方之珠”“美食天堂”“购物天堂”及“亚洲国际都会”等美誉。香港在回归后保持自己原有的社会制度和经济运作模式，发行和流通自己的货币——港币，独立发行邮票（邮戳是“中国香港”）。在国际体育比赛中，以“中国香港”的名义参与国际体坛的盛事，并加入世界贸易组织等国际组织。

Hong Kong is a free port. Most of the imported goods are exempted from tariff. Hong Kong is a financial center of the Asia-Pacific region and even the world, an international shipping center, an international trade center, a tourism and information center. Hong Kong, with more than 160 banks and the same number of insurance companies, ranked the third next to New York and London in the global financial centre index. Although Hong Kong's financial position was damaged in 2020, it is still stable in the position of "first echelon of global financial center". Hong Kong, often referred to as "the Pearl of the Orient", "gourmet paradise", "shopping paradise" and "Asia's world city", is known in the world for its clean society, good public order, free economic system and a complete legal system, thus, gained itself the reputation as the world's safest, most prosperous city with the highest standard of living. After the reunification, it still keeps its existing social system and operational mode of economy. Hong Kong issues and circulates its own currency. It independently issues postage stamps (stamps marking is "Hong Kong China"). Under the name of "Hong Kong China", Hong Kong participates in international sports events and the international organizations such as WTO.

3. 社会文化

香港总人口约750万，以华人为主，占总人口的91.4%，华人以外的种族，以印度尼西亚人及菲律宾人人数最多，其次为白人及印度人。香港华人普遍讲粤语，当地习惯称为广东话。由于香港曾经受英国管治，英语和中文同样享有官方语言地位，英语也是香港常用语言，广泛用于商业及教学中。香港回归之后，普通话变得越来越重要，政府的语言政策是"两文三语"，即书面上使用中文和英文，口语上使用粤语、普通话和英语，香港学校亦增设普通话为一门学科。世界各大宗教在香港几乎都有人信奉。华人主要信奉佛教、道教。

Hong Kong has a total population of about 7.5 million, predominantly Chinese, taking up 91.4% of the total population, with Indonesians and Filipinos coming the next, followed by Whites and Indians. Chinese residents in Hong Kong mostly speak Cantonese, a local dialect. Since Hong Kong was under British rule, both English and Chinese are used as the official languages. English is also the common language in Hong Kong, widely used in business and education. After the return of Hong Kong, Mandarin is becoming increasingly important. The government's language policy is "two written languages and three spoken languages", namely Chinese and English as the written languages, and Cantonese, Mandarin and English as the spoken languages. Schools also offer Mandarin course. The major world religions are worshiped in Hong Kong. Chinese mainly believe in Buddhism and Taoism.

香港被称为"流行文化之都"，并将流行文化带入华人世界。哪里有华人哪里就有香港文化，香港文化将"东方之珠"的魅力向全球输出，被称为"华人娱乐码头"，无论是在电影、电视、广播，还是乐坛，一直是潮流的领导者。

Hong Kong has been called the "the Capital of Pop Culture", and the popular culture is deep into the Chinese world. Where there are Chinese, there is the culture of Hong Kong. Hong Kong, known as "Chinese Entertainment Pier", spreads oriental charm to the world, leading the trend in film, television, radio and music in Chinese community.

粤语歌是香港早年普及的大众娱乐，自20世纪70年代起，由"歌神"许冠杰带动的中文歌潮流，掀起了后来蓬勃发展的"粤语流行曲"，并影响了中国内地的流行文化。

Singing Cantonese songs was the popular entertainment in the early time. Since the 1970s, the trend of singing Chinese songs led by the "God of Singing" Samuel Hui, opened a new chapter for "Cantonese pop music" and affected Chinese popular culture.

有华人的地方就有港产片，香港被誉为"东方好莱坞""华语梦工场"。香港的电影业起步较早，第二次世界大战后内地大批电影人南下，成立了许多著名的制片公司，粤语片开始流行，同时，中西合璧、自由创作的氛围使香港成为除美国以外的第二大电影出口基地，是全球华人社会中最为瞩目的电影天堂。香港电影金像奖创立于1982年，与台湾电影金马奖和大陆电影金鸡奖并称为华语电影最高成就的三大奖，在华语电影圈中具有举足轻重的地位。

Where there are Chinese, there will be Hong Kong movies, and Hong Kong is known as the "Hollywood of the East" and "Chinese Dreamworks". Hong Kong film industry started early. After the Second World War, a large number of film makers from Chinese mainland settled down here and established many famous studios, thus, Cantonese speaking movies became popular. Due to the combination of Chinese culture with Western culture and the free atmosphere for creation, Hong Kong became the second largest film exporting base just next to the US, and became the film heaven in the global Chinese community. Hong Kong Film Awards was founded in 1982 and is called as one of three top Chinese film awards together with Golden Horse Film Awards of Taiwan region and Golden Rooster Awards of Chinese mainland. They play a decisive role in the Chinese movie circles.

在文化方面，香港报人兼作家金庸（查良镛）以其风靡全球华人读者的武侠小说系列，脍炙人口数十年，是新派武侠小说最杰出的代表作家，被誉为武侠小说作家的“泰山北斗”。香港作家亦舒、梁凤仪、梁羽生等都是当代在香港、亚洲乃至华人世界知名的文化名人。

In culture, Hong Kong journalist and writer Louis Cha (Zha Liangyong) has won universal praise for decades for its martial arts novel series popular with Chinese readers at home and abroad. He is the most outstanding writer in the field of martial arts novels, known as "the master of martial arts novels". Other Hong Kong writers such as Yi Shu, Liang Fengyi, Liang Yusheng are also contemporary famous cultural celebrities in Hong Kong, Asia and even the world.

二、民俗风情

（一）礼仪禁忌

香港华人祖籍多为广东，故仍保留着许多中国的传统礼仪，同时中西文化的融合又使其呈现自己的特点。华人多信奉佛教、道教，信“神”最多，多供奉祖先神位、门神。商人多供奉关帝，船员和渔民还供奉天后。农历初一、十五或其他节日时，香港人喜欢到庙宇求神，烧香拜佛。

Hong Kong Chinese are mostly of Cantonese descent, so they still retain lots of traditional Chinese etiquette, while cultural blend of the east and west has formed their own characteristics. Chinese people believe in Buddhism and Taoism, and most of them believe in "deity". They enshrine ancestor's memorial tablet and Door God. Most of businessmen believe in a deity named Guangdi. And the seaman and fisherman also worship a goddess named Tin Hau. On the first day and fifteenth day of the Chinese lunar months and other holidays, they like to go to the temple to burn incense and pray to the gods.

香港人比较随和，注重礼貌及秩序。如果游客寻求帮助，香港人都乐意提供帮助。一般而言，无论在公车或在大街上，香港人的说话声音不会太大，避免对他人造成干扰。香港人乘坐巴士、地铁或购物时都会排队，很有公共意识。搭乘扶梯时，会靠右站。让赶时间的人从左边走。所有公共交通工具（巴士、地铁、火车）上一律禁止吃东西。

Hong Kong people are easy-going, courteous and obey the public order. If the tourists ask for help, Hong Kong people are willing to give their hands. In general, Hong Kong people speak in a low voice on the bus or in the street to avoid disturbing others. With strong public consciousness, they queue for bus, subway or shopping orderly. When taking the escalator, they will stand to the right, waiting for people on the run to pass from the left. Eating is prohibited in all the transportation (bus, subway, train).

香港人忌讳别人打听自己的家庭地址，因为他们不欢迎他人到家里做客，一般都乐于到茶楼或公共场所。交流时忌讳询问个人的工资收入、年龄等情况，认为个人的私事不需要他人过问。忌称丈夫或妻子为“爱人”，在香港，“爱人”有“第三者”的意思，一般称“我的先生”或“我的太太”，称别人的丈夫或妻子则是“您的先生”或“您的太太”。忌称中老年人为“伯父”“伯母”，应该称“伯伯”“伯娘”，因为“伯父”“伯母”与“百无”谐音，即“一无所有”的意思。与人见面前应该先电话预约。拜访亲朋时，忌伸“香蕉手”，香港民间称空手上门的客人为“香蕉手”，意为“两手空空”，让人看不起。探望病人或亲友时，忌送剑兰、茉莉、梅花，因为剑兰与“见难”（意为日后难见）谐音，茉莉和“没利”“末利”谐音，“梅”与“霉”谐音。送礼也不能送钟、书籍和毯子，因“书”与“输”同音，因此当地人把“历书”更名为“历本”或“通胜”。香港人过年过节从不说“新年快乐”“节日快乐”，写信也不用“祝您快乐”，因为“快乐”与“快落”（失败、破产的意思）谐音，而说“恭喜发财”“新年发财”“万事如意”。赌马、打麻将时，忌人来借钱和取钱。

It is not advisable to inquire about home addresses of Hong Kong people, because they usually don’t welcome people to their home. Generally, they tend to meet at the teahouse or public places. When talking, personal income and age are taboos as they think these are personal affairs. “Lover” can not be used for the husband or wife as “lover” in Hong Kong refers to mistress. Generally they will call their husband or wife as “my sir” or “my lady”, and call other’s husband or wife as “your sir” or “your lady”. Never call old person “Bofu” or “Bomu” as they should be called “BoBo” or “Boniang”, because “Bofu” and “Bomu” pronounce the same as “Baiwu” (which means “nothing”). And people should call first before they meet. When visiting the relatives, you should avoid “banana hands”. Hong Kong folk call those guests without gift “banana hands”, meaning “nothing” and will be looked down upon. To visit patients or relatives, you should not bring gladiolus, jasmine or plum, because gladiolus and “hard” (meaning difficult to meet in future), jasmine and “no interest”, “the end benefit”, “mei” and “bad” are homophonic. Neither should gifts be clocks, books or blankets, because “book” and “lose” are a pair of homophonic words. The local people call “lishu” (almanac) as “liben” or “tongsheng”. When Hong Kong people spend the Spring Festival holiday, they never say “Happy New Year”, “Happy holidays”, also do not write “wish you happy”, because the “happy” in Cantonese sounds like “going down” (failure, bankruptcy), instead they usually say “wish you every success”, “wish you a prosperous new year”, “good luck in everything”, etc. When they bet on the horse or play mahjong, it is considered a taboo to borrow or take money.

香港人早上喜欢到餐馆喝早茶，晚餐较为丰盛。香港人喜欢吉利，对菜名特别讲究，不吉祥的字都会改为吉祥字，如称“猪肝”为“猪润”、“丝瓜”为“胜瓜”、“苦瓜”为“凉瓜”等。以冷盆菜“猪舌”为例，因地方方言，“舌”与“独”同音，独就是亏本、倒霉的意思，香港人因此喜称“猪舌”为“猪利”或“赚头”。去饭店用餐时，遇上刚开市不能说“炒蛋”“炒饭”之类的话。“炒”字在香港是解雇的意思，俗称“炒鱿鱼”。上鱼时，鱼头对客人以表尊敬，吃鱼时不要翻转鱼身（寓意翻船）。香港人逢年过节最喜欢吃发菜和年糕，因为“发菜”被当地读成“发财”，是合人心的彩头，“年糕”则被称为“年高”或“年年高”，也是好兆头。

Hong Kong people love to go to the restaurant for breakfast, and dinner is usually very abundant. Hong Kong people have a special bond with auspiciousness, especially for the name of dishes, lucky words will be used to take the place of ominous words, such as “zhu run” for “pig liver”, “sheng gua” for “towel gourd”, “liang gua” for “bitter gourd”. Take cold dish “pig’s tongue” as an example, “tongue” in Cantonese sounds like “du” which means losing money in business or bad luck, thus Hong Kong people pronounce “pig’s tongue” as “zhu li” or “zhuan tou” which means profit. You cannot say “scrambled eggs”, “fried rice” or something like that, when going to a restaurant, as “fry” in Hong Kong means to sack, commonly known as “fried squid fish (be fired)”. When eating fish, the fish head pointing to the guest shows respect to him or her. You should not flip the fish body as it implies shipwreck. Seaweeds and New Year cakes are the favorite foods during festivals, because “seaweed” in Cantonese is pronounced “fortune”, while “New Year cake” is called “nian gao”in Chinese which means rising higher each year, which is considered a good sign.

香港人喜欢吉祥号码，特别喜欢数字“3、6、8、9”，“3”粤语发音为“生”，“6”为“禄”，“8 ”为“发”，“9”为“久”，“6、8、9”即“禄、发、久”，是大吉大利的意思，很受香港人欢迎。家庭汽车牌号也争配吉祥号码，以“2、3、8”最受欢迎，因为它们在粤语中谐音为“易、生、发”。香港人最忌讳的数字是“4”，因为“4”与“死”谐音，认为是不吉利的象征，送礼等也避开“4”这一数字，非说不可的情况下，常用“两双”或“两个二”来代替。

People in Hong Kong love auspicious numbers, especially “3, 6, 8, 9”. “3” in Cantonese sounds similar to “life”, “6” to “high position”, “8” to “fortune”, “9” to “longevity”. “6, 8, 9” together represent good fortune and good luck. People also want lucky numbers such as “2, 3, 8” for their automobile license plate, because “2, 3, 8” are homophonic with “easy, life, fortune” in Cantonese. Nevertheless, “4” is a taboo in Hong Kong, because “4” and “death” are homophonic, so “4” is an ominous sign. You should try to avoid “4” in daily life. When you really need to say it, you’d better say “two pairs” or “double two” instead.

（二）节庆风情

香港享有“亚洲盛事之都”的美誉，精彩节日及盛事包罗万象，从热闹缤纷的本土节庆活动，到世界级的艺术文化节日、国际体育盛事，精彩纷呈。此外，还有国际知名艺术家和本地流行歌手演出的音乐会，世界级的戏剧及舞蹈表演。

Hong Kong, the events capital of Asia, offers a smorgasbord of fascinating and exciting events ranging from colorful local festivals to world-class arts and sports events. Concerts, theatre and dance performances by famous international artists and local Canton-pop singers create dynamic experiences.

1. 春节（Spring Festival）

香港人非常注重春节。红包分为压岁钱和“利市”，压岁钱是除夕时长辈给晚辈的，给小孩的压岁钱一般会给两个，代表好事成双，红包里还会放进一个硬币，象征小孩以后“有出头”。“利市”是香港人最为看重的习俗，意为万事大吉。“利市”里面一般装有10港元，可以从年初一派发到正月十五。“利市”传统上是由已婚的发给未婚的，现在则是雇主发给员工、上级发给下属、主人发给客人、业主发给物业、店家发给顾客等。香港政府自1982年开始每年春节在维多利亚港举行烟花会演，以增加节日气氛。

Hong Kong attaches great importance to Spring Festival. There are two types of red envelopes of Spring Festival, gift money for children and lucky money for good business. The elders give gift money to younger people at Spring Festival's Eve. Usually they give a child two red envelops which represent that good things come in pairs. They usually put a coin in red envelops, meaning future success. Giving lucky money is Hong Kong's most valued custom, representing everything goes well. An envelope usually contains 10 Hong Kong dollars, distributed from the first day till the fifteenth day of the first lunar month. Lucky money is traditionally given by the married to the unmarried but now by employers to employees, superiors to subordinates, hosts to guests, property owners to property personnel, shop owners to customers and so on. The government of Hong Kong has launched firework show every Spring Festival in Victoria Harbor since 1982 in order to promote the atmosphere of festivity.

2. 鬼节（Ghost Festival）

每年的农历七月是中国传统的盂兰节，又称鬼节，香港人在这个月有“烧衣”的习俗。在这个节日的前后几天，不少人家在自家门口或者人行道上摆放米饭、肉食等祭品，并且燃烧香烛冥镪，各处火光闪闪，烟雾弥漫，气氛很是诡秘。人们相信无论是自己的祖先或游魂野鬼都能“享受”这些祭品。

The traditional Chinese Ghost Festival or Yu Lan falls on the seventh Chinese lunar month. In order to appease the ancestors' souls and all the forgotten spirits, people make small paper models of various objects, and burn it all with incense. Some place rice and meat on the pavements of the streets or at the entrance door of their houses. They worship the gods to protect those beloved ones and for that purpose prepare dishes of meat and fruits. They believe the spirits of their ancestors and wandering ghosts will come to enjoy the sacrifice.

三、主要旅游城市及景点

（一）太平山顶（The Victoria Peak）

太平山顶是香港最高点，海拔554米，位于香港岛西北部，一直是香港的标志。太平山顶是港岛最负盛名的豪华、高级住宅区所在地，也是香港最著名的旅游胜地之一，是俯瞰港岛两岸摩天高楼、享誉全球的维多利亚港和欣赏香港夜景的最佳之地。前往太平山顶的最佳交通工具是乘坐山顶缆车，太平山顶缆车自1888年就开始营运，已有100多年历史。

554 meters above sea level, Victoria Peak is the highest point, located in the northwest of Hong Kong Island, and has been a symbol of Hong Kong. It is the very location for the most prestigious luxury upscale residential area. It is one of the most famous tourist attractions in Hong Kong. Overlooking the skyscrapers of Hong Kong Island, the world-renowned Victoria Harbor, it is the best place where you can enjoy the night view of Hong Kong. The best transport to Victoria Peak is Peak Tram which has been in operation since 1888, and has a history of more than a hundred years.

（二）维多利亚港（Victoria Harbor）

维多利亚港是世界三大深水港之一，香港最珍贵的财富之一。登上太平山顶，沿尖沙咀海滨花园中的星光大道或湾仔金紫荆广场海滨长廊漫步，可饱览海港的壮丽风光，更可观赏已列入《吉尼斯世界纪录》的“幻彩咏香江”。在这项全球最大型的灯光音乐会演中，维多利亚港两岸超过40幢建筑物逐一亮起璀璨夺目的灯光，景致格外迷人。

Victoria Harbor, one of the world's top three deepwater ports, is one of the Hong Kong's greatest assets. Climbing up to the Victoria Peak and visiting the Avenue of Stars along the Tsim Sha Tsui Promenade or Wan Chai's Golden Bauhinia Square can enjoy the spectacular harbor views. Moreover, you can watch the magnificent "A Symphony of Lights", an event listed in the *Guiness World Records*. This music extravaganza, considered the world's largest of its kind, features the bewitching seaside scenary with dazzling one-by-one lights from more than 40 skyscrapers along the both banks of the Victoria Harbor.

（三）海洋公园（The Ocean Park）

香港海洋公园是一个世界级的海洋动物主题乐园，集娱乐、教育及保育于一体，位于香港岛南面，占地面积超过87万平方米，拥有全东南亚最大的海洋水族馆及主题游乐园，包括高峰乐园与海滨乐园两个景区，由架空缆车及海洋列车连接。

The Ocean Park is a world-class marine theme park that offers guests an experience that blends entertainment with education and conservation. It is located on the southern side of Hong Kong Island, covering more than 870,000 square meters and boasting the largest aquarium and amusement park in the Southeast Asia. Two scenic areas, the Summit and the Waterfront area are connected by cable car and Ocean Express.

（四）浅水湾（Repulse Bay）

位于香港岛南区的浅水湾，英文名源自一艘昔日的英国皇家军舰，是香港著名的旅游景点，也是高级住宅区。这一新月形状的沙滩是香港最美丽的海滩之一。沙滩上具有中国古典色彩的镇海楼公园里有天后娘娘、大慈大悲观音神像，她们都是渔民的保护神，伫立在风景如画的花园中直至海滩。

Located in the southern area of Hong Kong Island, Repulse Bay, named after a British Royal Navy warship, is a famous tourist attraction and an expensive housing development. This crescent-shaped stretch of sand is one of the most beautiful beaches in Hong Kong. The beach features a lifeguard clubhouse built in classical Chinese style. Towering twin statues of Tin Hau and Guanyin, both protectors of fishermen, dominate the picturesque gardens that lead down to the beach.

（五）兰桂坊（Lan Kwai Fong）

兰桂坊是香港最时尚的餐饮、休闲胜地，位于中环一条短小、狭窄，呈L形并用鹅卵石铺成的街巷，街巷布满西式餐馆和酒吧。兰桂坊酒吧街缘起于20世纪70年代初期，当时一位意大利籍商人在这里开设了一间意大利餐厅，部分在中环上班的“优皮士”，下班后想找一个地方谈天，这家餐厅便成为他们欢乐时光的聚集点。香港华洋共处，居港的外籍人士、时尚男女和年轻的专业人士在兰桂坊内流连忘返，通宵达旦地酌酒消遣。如今，兰桂坊已由一条小巷发展成一个富有西方文化的地区，被誉为“香港特有的文化特区”。

Lan Kwai Fong is Hong Kong's most fashionable diet leisure paradise of eatery and leisure. Located in Central, it is a short, narrow, L-shaped cobbled street. The street is full of western-style restaurants and bars. Lan Kwai Fong bar street originated in the early 1970s when an Italian businessman opened an Italian restaurant here. Some Yuppies who worked in Central needed a place to chat after work, so the restaurant became the first gathering place for their happy hour. No matter Chinese or expatriates, male or female, and young professionals, they love Lan Kwai Fong so much that they indulge in happy hour here overnight. Today, Lan Kwai Fong has developed from an alley into a unique region featured with western culture, known as the characteristic cultural district of Hong Kong.

（六）黄大仙祠（Wong Tai Sin Temple）

黄大仙祠是香港最出名的道教庙宇。相传祠内所供奉的黄大仙是有求必应的，所以香火十分鼎盛。在每年农历年底及正月初一至十五，有大量善信前往黄大仙祠，为过去一年酬谢神恩及为未来一年求神庇佑。

Wong Tai Sin Temple is the most well-known Taoism temple in Hong Kong. According to the legend, Wong Tai Sin is responsive to every prayer. That is the reason why lots of worshipers gather here. From the first day to the 15th day of the first Chinese lunar month during the Spring Festival, a large number of worshipers will gather in the temple to thank for his mercy and also pray for his blessing in the coming year.

（七）香港迪士尼乐园（Hong Kong Disneyland）

香港迪士尼乐园位于香港大屿山岛，2003年正式开始建设，2005年投入营运。虽然香港迪士尼乐园是世界六座迪士尼乐园中最小的，但它拥有巨大的吸引力。香港迪士尼乐园包括七大主题园：美国小镇大街、探险世界、幻想世界、明日世界、反斗奇兵大本营、灰熊山谷、迷离庄园，每个主题园都能给游客带来无尽的奇妙体验。

Hong Kong Disneyland is located on Lantau Island. It was constructed in 2003 and opened in 2005. Though significantly smaller in size than other Disneylands elsewhere, it does offer some great attractions. Everyone visiting Hong Kong Disneyland will embark on a magical journey through seven themed areas—Main Street U.S.A., Fantasyland, Adventure Land, Tomorrow Land, Toy Story Land, Grizzly Gulch and Mystic Point.

四、旅游资讯

（一）美食

香港人对饮食极为重视，享有“亚洲美食之都”“美食天堂”的称号。香港不仅有一流的粤菜馆和其他中国菜，更有亚洲各国的知名菜肴和西方美食。

Hong Kong people are food lovers. Hong Kong enjoys the reputation of the "Culinary Capital of Asia" and the title of "gourmet paradise". Hong Kong has not only high-class Cantonese restaurants and Chinese cuisine, but also well-known Asian countries' dishes and western food.

传统本地菜以粤菜、客家菜及潮州菜为主。盆菜则是新界原居民在节日时的传统菜。由于香港临近海洋，因此海鲜也是常见的菜肴。香港人口味较为清淡，爱喝汤滋身。

Traditional local cuisine is based on Guangdong cuisine, Hakka cuisine and Chiu Chow cuisine. Poon Choi is a traditional dish in the holiday of indigenous residents in New Territories. Hong Kong is near the ocean, so seafood is also a common dish with lighter taste. Hong Kong people love soup for health reasons.

由于受英国的影响，香港人同样喜欢喝下午茶。在华洋共处的环境下，最富当地特色的是港式茶餐厅，它是感受道地的香港市民文化的绝佳地。茶餐厅是适应香港人快节奏生活的餐厅，不同于一般的快餐店，它可以提供早餐、午餐、晚餐和夜宵等，同时提供咖啡、茶和冷饮。主菜通常是罐头类或加工好的食品（如叉烧、香肠、午餐肉、回锅肉、猪扒等，搭配米饭、意粉、公仔面等），汤是早就煲好的。“快、靓、正、平”是此类餐厅的写照。

Under the British influence, Hong Kong people also like to have afternoon tea. In a multi-national environment, the typical of local specialties is Hong Kong style tea restaurant where you can enjoy the authentic Hong Kong-style civic culture. Tea restaurant is a restaurant to adapt to the fast-paced life of people in Hong Kong. Unlike the ordinary fast-food restaurants, it can provide breakfast, lunch, and supper as well as midnight snack, also coffee, tea and cold drinks at the same time. The main course is usually canned or processed food (such as roasted pork, sausage, luncheon meat, twice cooked pork, pork chop, etc., along with rice, pasta, noodles, etc.), the soup is ready made for you. "Fast, pretty, delicious, reasonably priced" is the portrayal of such a restaurant.

香港人习惯上茶楼，“饮茶”是港人不可或缺的习惯。早上冲一壶茶、叫两份点心，中午茶则是三五知己或亲戚共聚，也有谈生意的。如有必要，他们也会点其他菜。这便是西方人眼中香港饮食文化的典型。

Hong Kong people get used to the restaurant for morning tea. "Drinking tea habit" is an integral part of the people of Hong Kong. Make a fresh pot of tea and order two snacks in the morning, for afternoon tea with rich variety of dim sum when a couple of friends or family relatives stay together, or for business. If necessary, they will order other dishes. In Westerners' view, this is typical of Hong Kong's cuisine culture.

（二）购物及退税

由于香港是自由港，加之特区政府实施低税率，而且对大部分商品都不征税，因此在香港，可以以相对较低的价格买到全世界各种品牌的商品，而且香港的服务人员都受过培训，服务非常好。香港每年都会吸引大量来自全世界的游客，因此也就拥有了“购物天堂”的美称。香港的购物点充满各个角落，购物区主要集中于香港岛的中环、金钟及铜锣湾，以及九龙的尖沙咀、油麻地及旺角等地。香港较著名的大型购物商场包括中环置地广场、金钟太古广场、铜锣湾时代广场、尖沙咀海港城等，游客可以购买化妆品、手表、数码产品和首饰等。此外，香港还有多条主题购物街，如以女性商品为主的旺角女人街、男性商品为主的油麻地庙街和电器店林立的旺角西洋菜南街等。

Hong Kong is a free port, the SAR government collects low tax, and most commodities are not taxed, so you can buy a variety of brand goods from all over the world at relatively low prices. And the well-trained personnel provide excellent service. That's why a large number of foreign tourists from all over the world flood to Hong Kong every year. Hong Kong also has a reputation of "shopping paradise". Shopping outlets can be found at every corner of the city. The shopping areas are mainly concentrated in Central, Admiralty and Causeway Bay in Hong Kong Island, and Tsim Sha Tsui, Yau Ma Tei and Mong Kok in Kowloon. Hong Kong's famous shopping malls are the Landmark in Central, Pacific Place in Admiralty, Times Square in Causeway Bay, Harbor City in Tsim Sha Tsui where you can choose cosmetics, watches, digital products and jewelry, etc. In addition, Hong Kong has a number of themed shopping streets, for example, the women goods in Mong Kok Ladies Market, men goods in Yau Ma Tei Temple Street, and the electrical appliances shops along Mong Kok Sai Yeung Choi Street South and so on.

思考练习

1. 经典旅游线路分析

香港4日游

第1天：上海——香港

游客由上海乘国际航班至购物天堂香港。赴大屿山乘坐360度昂平缆车，参观大屿山宝莲禅寺及昂平市集等；游览海洋公园，欣赏精彩的海豚表演，还可参观熊猫馆、蝴蝶馆、水母馆等；更可体验多种机动游戏的惊险刺激；最后乘坐东南亚最长的户外电梯下山。晚上登太平山顶，欣赏香港的璀璨夜景。

第2天：香港

早餐后前往香火鼎盛、有求必应的黄大仙祠；漫步星光大道，这里游客不仅能欣赏到诸多著名电影明星的手印，而且能饱览壮丽的维多利亚港风光以及香港岛的繁华都会景致；游览香港的风水宝地——浅水湾，这里是香港最有名的海滩；前往香港标志性建筑之一的香港国际会展中心，在此可与香港回归祖国纪念碑——金色紫荆花铜像合影；最后参加特色节目——维多利亚港夜游。

第 3 天：香港

香港是享誉世界的购物天堂，各种商品价格相对较低，种类繁多，服务水平较高。安排自由活动，尽享购物乐趣。

第 4 天：香港——上海

乘国际航班返回上海，结束愉快旅程。

分析：这条经典旅游线路的主要旅游景点与行程特色，以及适合旅游的人群。

2. 案例分析

［案例 1］春节期间，内地游客陈先生前往香港旅游并顺道探望香港朋友，他提出要去香港朋友家看看，香港朋友婉拒了，而是请他去茶楼喝早茶。陈先生送给香港朋友四盒家乡特产茉莉花茶，出于礼貌，陈先生问："你的爱人可好？伯父伯母也安康吧？"最后告别时，他又按照习惯对朋友说："新年快乐！"香港朋友却满脸不悦。请问：陈先生哪些地方做得不对？香港朋友为何不悦？

［案例 2］在中国香港，拜访亲朋时，忌伸"香蕉手"，送礼也不能送钟、书籍和毯子，探望病人或亲友时，忌送剑兰、茉莉、梅花，为什么？

3. 练一练

了解中国香港的热门景点、购物、美食等最新信息，试分析为何中国香港被称为"亚洲国际都会"。

第二节　澳门特别行政区

一、地区概况

（一）地理环境

澳门，全称为中华人民共和国澳门特别行政区，总面积为 32.8 平方千米。澳门位于中国南海，北面与珠海相连，东北与香港隔海相望，由澳门半岛、路环岛及氹仔岛两个离岛组成。氹仔和路环本是两个分离的离岛，但后期填海工程把两个离岛完全连接，两个离岛之间填海形成的地段称为路氹城。

Macau Special Administrative Region of People's Republic of China, briefly Macau, covers an area of 32.8 square kilometers. Situated at the coast of the South China Sea, it connects with Zhuhai to the north and is separated from Hong Kong by the sea to the northeast, including Macau Peninsula, Coloane Island and Taipa Island. Taipa and Coloane are two separate outlying islands, but later reclamation fully connected two outlying islands and is called Cotai reclamation drawn between two outlying islands.

澳门气候为亚热带季风气候，年平均气温为22.6℃左右，最低温度约为10℃。

Macau is in subtropical monsoon climate zone with average temperature 22.6℃ all year around and 10℃ in the coldest month.

（二）人文概况

1. 历史

澳门本名濠镜或镜海，秦朝时澳门就已列入中国版图，属南海郡番禺县。南宋时属香山县。明朝时，葡萄牙人于1535年通过贿赂当地官员把此地作为与中国贸易的落脚点，并在1557年取得当地的正式居住权。1623年，葡萄牙政府正式委任马士加路也为第一任总督。第一次鸦片战争爆发清政府战败后，1844年，葡萄牙女王宣布澳门为自由港。1849年，葡萄牙停止向清政府交付澳门地租。1887年，葡萄牙迫使清政府签订《中葡和好通商条约》，取得"永久管理澳门"的权力。1961年，葡萄牙海外部确立澳门为旅游区，特准设赌博。1986年，中国和葡萄牙开始对澳门问题展开谈判，并于1987年在北京签订《中华人民共和国政府和葡萄牙共和国政府关于澳门问题的联合声明》及两个附件。1999年12月20日，中国对澳门恢复行使主权，设立澳门特别行政区。

The original name of Macau was Haojing or Jinghai. Macau was under jurisdiction of Panyu of Nanhai County since Qin Dynasty. It belonged to Xiangshan County in Song Dynasty. In Ming Dynasty, Portuguese settled here temporally in order to trade with China in 1535 and obtained the right of permanent residence in 1557. In 1623, Portuguese government assigned D.Francisco Mas Carenha as the first governor. After the First Opium War when the Qing government was defeated, Portuguese Queen declared Macau as the free port in 1844. In 1849, Portugal stopped paying rent fee to Qing government. In 1887, Portuguese government forced Qing government to sign *The Sino-Portuguese Treaty of Peking* and obtained the permanent right to administrate Macau. In 1961, Portugal overseas department established Macau as tourist area and authorized to set up gambling. In 1986, China started the negotiation on Macau with Portugal and signed *The Joint Declaration of the Government of People's Republic of China and the Government of the Republic of Portugal on the Question of Macau* and the other two attachments in the following year. On December 20, 1999, China resumed the right of sovereignty over Macau, then Macau Special Administrative Region was established.

2. 经济

澳门是微型海岛经济，开埠400余年，由于受到海浅港窄的自然条件以及市场、资源和结构等方面的局限，经济发展一直比较缓慢。但澳门确定了"以博彩旅游业为龙头，以服务业为主体，其他行业协调发展"的目标，加上澳门是开放的自由港，有优越的地理位置和日趋完善的城市基础设施，在赌权开放、自由行政策的支持下，澳门仍然是亚太地区极具经济活力的一员。博彩业和旅游业是澳门经济的主要来源，并带动了酒店、餐饮和零售业的发展。澳门成为“一国两制”的成功典范，是亚洲最发达、最富裕的地区之一。

Macau is a mini-island economy area with a history of over 400 years. Economic development has been relatively slow, due to the limitations on the natural conditions such as shallow bay and narrow harbor and resources and structure of the market. Macau is still one of the great economic dynamisms in the Asia-Pacific region, because the SAR government has adopted the policy of “gambling and tourism leading the service industry which is in co-ordination with the development of other industries”, and Macau is an open free port with excellent geographical location and gradually improving urban infrastructure and with the opening of gambling right and the policy of individual visit from Chinese mainland. The gambling industry and tourism industry are the main source of the Macau economy and has led to the development of hotels, catering and retail industry. Macau becomes the successful example of the principle of “One Country, Two Systems” and it is one of Asia’s most developed and affluent areas.

知识拓展

澳门的博彩业

以博彩业著称的澳门，与美国的拉斯维加斯、大西洋城，摩纳哥的蒙特卡洛，南非的太阳城均为世界著名赌城。博彩业在澳门历史悠久，已有170多年的历史。早在1847年，澳门便颁布法令宣布赌博合法化。1961年，葡萄牙批准在澳门正式开设博彩旅游业。1962年，由香港的何鸿燊、叶汉合组的何氏澳门旅游娱乐公司竞标成功，获得赌业管理权。2002年，澳门特别行政区政府向三家公司发出博彩经营权牌照，分别是澳门博彩股份有限公司、永利度假村（澳门）股份有限公司和银河娱乐场股份有限公司。2003年在内地“自由行”政策的拉动下，澳门博彩业更获得了历史性的大丰收。自澳门赌权开放以来，澳门政府已把博彩业的税收收入作为财政收入的主要来源。根据资料显示，从2000年以后，博彩税一直占据财政收入的50%以上，特别是在2008年博彩税所占比例高达82.03%。由于澳门财政对博彩业的高度依赖，澳门旅游娱乐公司也因此被称为“镶嵌在澳门这顶皇冠上的最大的一颗明珠”。来澳门的游客中80%以上是慕博彩之名而来。澳门的博彩业大概可以分成五大类：娱乐场赌博、赛马、赛狗、彩票和足球博彩。澳门的赌场与美国的拉斯维加斯、大西洋城相比，虽然其建筑、设施和繁华程度都较为逊色，但这里的一些赌客所下的赌注却大得惊人。娱乐场可自由进出，不用入场费，18岁以下的游客及21岁以下的本地人不准进入。在澳门，各娱乐场的规则一致。娱乐场只接受澳门币或港币的投注，如游客所持的为外币，可在邻近的兑换店或银行兑换。

3. 社会文化

澳门人口约67.96万，以华人为主，占总人口的97%，葡萄牙人（包括在澳门的土生葡萄牙人）及其他外国人占3%，汉语和葡萄牙语是现行官方语言。居民日常沟通普遍使用粤语，但许多居民也能听懂普通话。英语在澳门也很通行，可应用于很多场合。由于澳门是华洋共处和实行信仰自由的地区，其居民的宗教亦呈多元化。由于多数居民为华人，因此信仰以儒、佛、道及民间神祇为主，如妈祖文化在澳门得到广泛传播，澳门仅供奉妈祖的庙宇就有10多间，作为民间信仰的妈祖信仰融入佛教、道教，成为多元信仰。

Macau's population is about 679,600, the predominant Chinese accounting for 97% of the total population, compared to 3% of the Portuguese in Macau (including those native-born) and other expats. Chinese and Portuguese are the two official languages. The residents commonly use Cantonese in daily communication, but many residents also can understand Mandarin. English is very common in Macau and can be applied on many occasions. In Macau, people of Chinese and Western origins inhabit together and have rights to choose religions themselves, so the religion of its inhabitants is diversified. The majority of the residents are Chinese, most of them believe in Confucianism, Buddhism, Taoism and folk deities, for example, Matsu culture is widely disseminated in Macau. In Macau, there are more than 10 Matsu temples. The Matsu, as the folk belief, has been mixed with Buddhism and Taoism and has become a multi-faith.

由于澳门独特的地理位置和历史背景，澳门文化是一种以中华文化为主、兼容葡萄牙文化的具有多元文化色彩的共融文化。澳门文学可追溯到1590年，明代以写《牡丹亭》著称的戏剧家汤显祖来到澳门游览后，把他对澳门的新奇印象写进五首诗和《牡丹亭》中。这是关于“香山澳”最早的文学记录。而比汤显祖早来约30年的葡萄牙大诗人卡蒙斯也在澳门南湾的岩石洞内写下了8 800多行的长诗《葡国魂》，由此被文学史家称作“葡萄牙文学之父”。随着移民的涌入，澳门文学也开始蓬勃发展。《七子之歌》是中国著名学者闻一多于1925年在美国留学期间创作的组诗，共七首，象征被外国列强侵占的七处中国国土，即澳门、香港、台湾、威海卫、广州湾（广东湛江）、九龙、旅顺－大连。我们常听的《七子之歌·澳门》，就是七首之中的一首。

As Macau has unique geographical location and historical background, it has an inclusive culture based on Chinese culture and integrated with Portuguese culture. Macau literature can be traced back to 1590, in the Ming Dynasty. Tang Xianzu who was famous for *The Peony Pavilion* put his impression of Macau into his five poems and masterpiece *The Peony Pavilion* after he had visited Macau. This is the earliest literary records about Macau. Luis de Camões, the great poet of Portugal who came to Macau about 30 years earlier than Tang Xianzu wrote his poem *The Lusiads* of more than 8,800 lines engraved in the rock cave in Nam Van of Macau. Thus he is regarded as the "Father of Portuguese Literature" by historian scholars. With the influx of immigrants in recent years, Macau literature begins to flourish. *Song of Seven Sons* is a group poem, which contains 7 poems written by the famous Chinese scholar Wen Yiduo while studying in the United States in 1925. The seven poems are the symbol of the seven Chinese territories occupied by foreign powers, Macau, Hong Kong Island, Taiwan, Weihaiwei, Guangzhou Bay (Zhanjiang, Guangdong), Kowloon Island and Lvshun-Dalian. *The Song of Seven Sons · Macau*, which we often hear, is one of them.

作为近代中西文化交流一个最重要的桥头堡，几百年来，各种文化在澳门这块土地上互相碰撞、交流，形成了今天澳门独特的文化氛围。2005年7月15日，澳门历史城区的

22座建筑及8个广场被列入世界文化遗产名录，成为中国第31处世界文化遗产，是世界对中华文化、对澳门400多年中西文化交汇、结晶的肯定。

As one of the most important bridgeheads for the exchange of the modern Chinese culture with Western culture, different cultures have impacted and communicated here for hundreds of years, and the unique culture environment has formed. On July 15, 2005, 22 buildings and 8 squares in Macau were listed in the World Cultural Heritage Site, and became the thirty-first of its kind in China. This is the affirmation of Chinese culture and the result of the exchange of Chinese culture with Western culture over a history of more than 400 years.

二、民俗风情

（一）礼仪禁忌

虽被葡萄牙统治了400多年，澳门人还是保留了较传统的文化理念。虽与香港仅一海之隔，香港拥挤、繁闹，而澳门却始终保持安静、悠闲。澳门人好客有礼，“谢谢”“你好”是常用的词语。澳门的礼仪禁忌和香港差不多，如澳门人不喜欢在家里招待客人，忌讳数字“13”和“星期五”，也不喜欢别人询问个人年龄、婚姻和收入等。

Though Portugal has ruled Macau for more than 400 years, Macau people still keep traditional idea of Chinese culture. Compared with Hong Kong's crowded and noisy life, Macau is quiet and easy, though Hong Kong is just located across the sea. Macau people are hospitable and courteous. Both “thank you” and “how are you” are daily expressions. The etiquette is almost the same as Hong Kong, for example, Macau people don't like to treat guests at home. They don't like the number “13” and “Friday”. And they don't like to ask the privacy about age, marriage, income and so on.

澳门融合了中西文化，仍保留了许多中国的传统礼仪。早期澳门人多靠海为生，故大多数人信奉妈祖。妈祖崇拜是澳门重要的民间信仰之一。妈祖是中国渔民和船民奉祀的海神。妈阁庙是澳门最早的庙宇，除夕时多数居民都会去祭拜。

With the blend of both Chinese and Portugal culture, Macau still keeps the traditional Chinese etiquette. The early inhabitants made a living by sea, so most of them believe in Matsu. Matsu worship is one of the major folk beliefs in Macau. Matsu is the deity Chinese fishermen honor. A-Ma Temple is the oldest temple in Macau. Most of the residents will go for praying on the last day of the Chinese calendar.

（二）节庆风情

1. 浴佛节、谭公诞、醉龙节（Feast of Buddha，Tam Kung Festival, Feast of Drunken Dragon）

每年的农历四月初八是佛教的浴佛节，道教的谭公诞，也是醉龙节，都要举行庆祝活动。浴佛节原是佛教的“释迦佛祖诞”。根据习俗，这一天澳门的佛教寺庙内要举行“浴佛”活动：僧人用五香水浴佛，作龙华会，象征佛陀降生。这是佛教的一个重要庆典。谭公诞是庆祝谭公诞辰的节日。据说谭公幼为牧童，所以显灵时化身为小孩，或为渔民预测天气，或治疗疾病。他是继妈祖后，深受渔民崇拜的另一位海上之神。每到诞期，路环村的谭公庙前会举行声势浩大的庆祝活动，包括上演粤剧、巡游、舞醉龙等。醉龙节是渔业行会的传统节日，渔业人士每年都举行独有的醉龙醒狮大会庆祝。他们以舞醉龙的方式到澳门各区巡游。舞醉龙与中国其他地方盛行的方式很不同，醉龙只有头和尾，用坚实木料制成，没有龙身，由两名艺人各执头、尾舞动。他们一边舞龙，一边喝酒，舞步似醉非醉。

Every April 8th of the Chinese lunar calendar is the Feast of Buddha, Tam Kung Festival in Taoism and the Feast of Drunken Dragon.The Feast of Buddha is the birthday of Sakyamuni. According to the custom, all the temples in Macau will hold a ceremony for bathing the Buddha: the monk will bathe Buddha with five scents water to clean and purify the Buddha. This is an important day for Buddhism to celebrate the birthday of Buddha. Tam Kung Festival is to celebrate the birthday of the God Tam Kung. This child god is said to control the weather and help the sick. Among the fishing community, he is second only to Matsu in popularity. There will be a Chinese opera, a procession through the streets and lively lion dances, while traditional offerings are made and firecrackers are set off near Coloane Village's Tam Kung Temple. The Feast of Drunken Dragon is the traditional festival of fisherman organization. The fishermen will hold the ceremony every year. They usually play dragon in drunken feet throughout every district of Macau. Drunken Dagon play is different from the other areas in China. There are only the drunken dragon head and tail made of hard wood and there is no dragon body. Two men will hold the head and the tail to play. While they are playing, they are drinking all the way and they seem to be drunken while playing the dragon.

2. 端午节 / 龙舟竞渡（Dragon Boat Festival）

农历五月初五是纪念爱国诗人屈原投江自尽的日子。这天全澳门粽子飘香。如今，龙舟竞渡是端午节的一项重要活动，每年在南湾湖内举办。许多本地队伍和国外队伍都会参加这项精彩赛事。

Every May 5th of the Chinese lunar calendar is the day when Qu Yuan, a patriotic poet drowned himself. Today all celebrations are concentrated on the famous Dragon Boat Races, which takes place on the Nam Van Lake in Macau. Many local teams and foreign teams take part in this colorful event.

三、主要旅游城市及景点

（一）大三巴牌坊（Ruins of St. Paul's Cathedral）

大三巴牌坊，其正式名称为圣保罗大教堂遗址，是澳门最具代表性的名胜古迹，澳门的象征。400 多年前，葡萄牙人侵占了澳门，也把天主教带到了澳门。该教堂建于 1602 年，由一名意大利籍耶稣会神父设计，历经 35 年，于 1637 年完工，是当时东方最大的天主教堂，号称“东方梵蒂冈”，为意大利文艺复兴时期巴洛克式建筑。然而 1835 年的一场大火把教堂烧毁，只剩下教堂门前的 68 级石阶和以花岗岩材质构筑的大教堂前壁，因教堂前壁形似中国传统牌坊，故称“大三巴牌坊”。2005年，大三巴牌坊与澳门历史城区的其他文物被联合国教科文组织列入世界文化遗产名录。

Dasanba Archway, whose official name is the Ruins of St. Paul's Cathedral, is the symbol of Macau and the most representative monument. Over 400 years ago, the Portugal occupied Macau and Catholicism was introduced here. The cathedral was designed by an Italian Jesuit priest and constructed in 1602 and completed in 1637. It was the largest Catholic church and an Italian Renaissance-Baroque style building in East Asia known as the "Oriental Vatican". However, in 1835, the cathedral caught fire and the 68 stone stairs and the granite front facade were the only remains of the grand cathedral. Because the front facade looks like traditional Chinese archway, so it is known as the Dasanba Archway. In 2005, Ruins of St. Paul's and other relics of the Historic Centre of Macau were listed into the World Cultural Heritage Site by UNESCO.

（二）大炮台（Macau Fort）

位于大三巴牌坊东边的大炮台（又名圣保罗炮台、中央炮台或大三巴炮台）是澳门最古老的大炮台，为中国现存最古老的西式炮台建筑群之一。300多年前为防海盗、保护传教士及居民安全而建，曾是军事防御的重心。现在，大炮台的中央为1998年建成的澳门博物馆。

Macau Fort (also known as Fort St. Paul, Central Fort or Ruins Fort), is one of China's oldest Western-style fort buildings. Of all the forts in Macau, the Fort is the oldest, lying to the east of the Ruins of St. Paul's Cathedral. It was constructed to defend the cathedral from the pirates and protect missionaries and local residents over 300 years ago. It later became solely a military fort. Now the Fort is the Macau Museum built in 1998.

（三）妈阁庙（A-Ma Temple）

妈阁庙是澳门最古老的庙宇，始建于明朝（1488年）。妈祖是中国的海神，又称娘妈、天妃、天后。早年澳门人除经营海上贸易外，多为水上居民，特别是来此经商的福建人，为了祈求海上安全，把源于福建的妈祖崇拜带入澳门。每年农历三月的妈祖诞辰日，澳门居民多会赴妈阁庙上香。

A-Ma Temple is the oldest of its kind in Macau which was first built in 1488 in Ming Dynasty. Matsu is the sea goddess whose other names are Niangma, Tianfei and Tin Hau. In the early days, majority of Macau people were boat dwellers and undertook the marine trade. Those people from Fujian brought Matsu to Macau in order to protect their safety on board. The birthday of the Matsu falls in the third lunar month of Chinese calendar. On this day, Macau people will come to A-Ma Temple to offer incenses to the goddess.

（四）赌场（Casino）

澳门是世界四大赌城之一。建于1970年的葡京大酒店是一座完善的旅游娱乐和赌博的综合体，是澳门赌场的标志。2007年开业的威尼斯人酒店，再现威尼斯水城风采，风格完全和拉斯维加斯的威尼斯人酒店一样，集大规模的博彩、会展、购物、体育、综艺及休闲设施为一体。

Macau is one of the four largest casino cities in the world. Hotel Lisboa built in 1970 is a complex building for tourism and entertainment. Its gambling hall was once the symbol of Macau gambling industry. The Venetian Macau, opened in 2007, is completely the same style as the one with the same name in Las Vegas, a more comprehensive complex of gambling, expo, shopping, sports, variety shows and leisure facilities.

四、旅游资讯

（一）美食

澳门不仅有博彩，而且有丰富的文化内涵。澳门的饮食文化展现出中西方交融多彩的地域特色和浓厚的文化内涵。澳门荟萃了东西南北的美食，在这里可以品尝到澳门菜、粤菜、上海菜、日本菜、韩国菜和泰国菜等，澳门美食主要由粤菜与葡国菜组成。

Macau has not only gambling, but also rich cultural connotations. Macau's culinary culture shows the perfect blend of Eastern and Western colorful geographical features and rich cultural connotations. Macau provides all sorts of cuisines, from both home and abroad, north and south, such as the Macanese, Cantonese, Shanghainese, Japanese, Korean and Thai cuisine, etc. Macanese cuisine is mainly composed of Cantonese and Portuguese dishes.

中餐构成了澳门美食的主题，中餐以粤菜为主，澳门地处南海，海鲜十分丰富，烹调风格上偏重“粤式海味”。澳门豆捞是来自澳门的时尚休闲火锅，主要由海鲜构成。

The theme of Macau Food is Chinese food, especially Cantonese cuisine. Macau is located offshore to the South China Sea, so it is very rich in seafood and the cooking style emphasizes on Cantonese seafood. Macau Doulao comes from Macau's popular casual hot pot which is mainly composed of seafood.

澳门最有特色的菜肴就是澳门式葡国菜，它融合了中国菜和葡萄牙菜的特点。自16世纪葡萄牙人抵澳后，他们从非洲、印度、马来西亚带来的辣椒、咖喱、香料、虾酱，配上新鲜的蔬果、肉类、海鲜、家禽，用古老的葡萄牙和东方特有的方式，烹调出世上独一无二的澳门式葡国菜，更适合东方人特别是中国人的口味。其中最著名的菜有马介休（即腌鳕鱼）、葡国鸡、咖喱蟹等。

Macau's most distinctive dishes is Macau-Portuguese style dish which combines the characteristics of Chinese cuisine and Portuguese cuisine. Since the 16th century when the Portuguese arrived in Macau, they brought from Africa, India and Malaysia pepper, curry, spices, shrimp paste and matched them with fresh fruits and vegetables, meat, seafood and poultry to prepare the dish by combining the unique ancient Portuguese and oriental methods. So it becomes the unique Macau-Portuguese cuisine in the world which is more suitable for the tastes of the East, especially Chinese people. The most famous dishes are Bacalhau (i. e., pickled cod), Portuguese chicken and curry crab.

（二）购物及退税

澳门的低税率、地理条件和低消费水平，造就了澳门物美价廉的购物环境。出口制造业是澳门的重要行业之一，因此有大量便宜货品出售，首饰（特别是金饰）、名牌服饰、古董、瓷器、葡萄酒、电子产品及手机、手表、羊毛衫及丝织品，应有尽有。

Macau's low tax rate, geographical conditions and the low level of consumption create its inexpensive shopping environment. Manufacturing for export is one of the important industries in Macau with a large number of cheap goods to sell including jewelry (especially gold), famous brand clothes, antiques, porcelain, wine, electronic products and mobile phones, watches, cashmere sweaters and silk clothing, etc.

澳门素有"小吃王国"之称，很多著名的小吃享誉海内外。"手信"也是澳门的一张"王牌"，澳门人把特产统称为"手信"。在澳门，"手信"是指像葡式蛋挞、杏仁饼、老婆饼、蛋卷、肉干、花生糖等具有澳门特色的小食的总称。当地许多饼店都出售各种美味的糖果和糕饼，游客非常喜欢将这些"正宗澳门风味"作为手信带回家。最有名和最特别的糕点是葡式蛋挞。

Macau is known as the kingdom of snacks. Many snacks are well-known over the world. "Shouxin" (Souvenirs) is the "golden name card" of Macau. In Macau, "shouxin" means specialty including Portuguese egg tart, almond cake, sweet flaky pastry ("Laopo Bing" in Chinese), egg roll, charqui, peanut candy and other snacks. Many local bakeries sell variety of delicious candy and pastry. Visitors always buy some authentic Macanese souvenirs as gifts. The most famous and most special pastries is Portuguese egg tart.

思考练习

1. 经典旅游线路分析

澳门3日游

第1天：珠海——澳门

从珠海拱北口岸出关，抵达澳门后游览赛马会及闻名中外的西环双层跨海大桥，前往澳门最具代表性的古迹大三巴牌坊、大炮台，随后参观最古老的庙宇妈阁庙、澳门金莲花广场，途中观望海观音像、澳门新景点旅游观光塔，晚餐后入住酒店。

第2天：澳门

威尼斯人酒店自由活动，在仿真的蓝天白云下，踏过意式拱桥，乘着贡多拉在水道中悠闲穿梭，听船夫哼唱迷人歌谣，恍如真的来到了意大利威尼斯，感受前所未有的新体验。

第3天：澳门——珠海

经拱北口岸返回珠海。

分析：这条经典旅游线路的主要旅游景点与行程特色，以及适合旅游的人群。

2. 案例分析

［**案例**］许多外地人对澳门人有句评价："澳门人不怕请客。"意思是说澳门人请客人吃饭，绝不会为请吃什么饭而发愁。如何理解这句话？澳门美食有何特色？

3. 练一练

寻找以下线路，并手绘一张澳门主题旅游线路地图。

葡式风情建筑线路：议事亭前地→市政署大楼→仁慈堂大楼→旧城墙遗址→大炮台→东方基金会会址→基督教坟场→岗顶前地→岗顶剧院→何东图书馆大楼→亚婆井前地→港务局大楼。

南粤文化探幽线路：三街会馆→哪吒庙→卢家大屋→郑家大屋→妈阁庙。

寻访宗教文化线路：大三巴牌坊→玫瑰堂及板樟堂前地→主教座堂及大堂前地→圣奥斯丁教堂→圣老楞佐教堂→圣若瑟修道院及圣堂→圣安多尼教堂（花王堂）→东望洋炮台（包括圣母雪地殿圣堂及灯塔）。

经典博物馆游览线路：海事博物馆→澳门博物馆→林则徐纪念馆→澳门艺术博物馆→葡萄酒博物馆→大赛车博物馆→龙环葡韵住宅式博物馆。

第三节　台湾地区

一、地区概况

（一）地理环境

台湾岛是中国的第一大岛，位于中国东南沿海的大陆架上。西与西北临台湾海峡，距福建省海岸平均距离约 200 千米；北边隔东海与朝鲜半岛相望；东北隔海与琉球群岛相望；西南边为南海，距广东省海岸距离约 300 千米；东边为太平洋；南边则隔巴士海峡与菲律宾群岛相邻。台湾扼西太平洋航道的中心，是中国与太平洋地区各国海上联系的重要交通枢纽。

Located on the continental shelf of the southeast coast of China, the island of Taiwan is China's largest island. To the west and northwest is the Taiwan Strait. The average distance to the coast of Fujian province is about 200 kilometers. To the north across the East China Sea is the Korean Peninsula. To the northeast across the sea is Ryukyu Islands. To the southwest is the South China Sea, 300 kilometers away from the coast of Guangdong province. To the east is Pacific Ocean, and to the south across the Bashi Strait is the Philippine Islands. Taiwan is in the center of Western Pacific channel which is an important transportation hub of China to communicate with the countries in the Pacific Ocean.

台湾由台湾本岛、金门群岛、马祖列岛、澎湖列岛及其他岛屿组成，面积 3.6 万平方千米，岛屿整体形状似长条番薯状。台湾岛内多山，高山和丘陵面积占全部面积的 2/3 以上。东部多高山，中部以丘陵为主，西部多为平原。

Taiwan consists of Taiwan Island, Kinmen Islands, Matsu Islands, Penghu Islands and other islands, covering an area of 36,000 square kilometers. The overall form of Taiwan island looks like a long sweet potato. The island of Taiwan is mountainous. The mountains and hills cover two-thirds of the total area with high mountains in the east, hills in the center and plains in the west.

台湾气候冬季温暖，夏季炎热，雨量充沛。台湾也是我国台风过境最频繁的地区之一，其中7月至9月这3个月台风最多，时常引发洪水和泥石流等灾害，对旅游业具有很大的负面影响。

Taiwan's climate is warm in winter, hot in summer, and has abundant rainfall. Taiwan is one of the most frequently typhoon-stricken areas in China. From July to September, typhoon occurs frequently leading to disasters such as floods and landslides and affects the tourism greatly.

（二）人文概况

1. 历史

隋朝时期，汉人开始迁居台湾。南宋时期，澎湖正式划入晋江县，并有驻兵。17世纪，荷兰和西班牙相继入侵台湾，后荷兰打败西班牙，强占台湾。南明末期的1661年，郑成功渡海东征。1662年，荷兰人投降，结束了对台湾的统治。1683年，清政府收复台湾，设台湾府。甲午战争失败后，1895年，清政府被迫割让台湾给日本。1945年，日本投降，台湾光复，结束了日本人50年的侵占。1949年，中华人民共和国成立，国民党的一部分军政人员退到台湾。

During Sui Dynasty, Chinese began to migrate to Taiwan. Penghu was under jurisdiction by Jinjiang County during Song Dynasty and troops were stationed here. During the 17th century, Holland and Spain invaded Taiwan one after another. Spain was defeated by Holland and Taiwan was occupied by Holland. At the end of Ming Dynasty, i.e., in 1661 General Zheng Chenggong led an expedition to Taiwan and ended the rule of Dutch in 1662. In 1683, Qing government recovered Taiwan and established Taiwan Prefecture. After the failure of Sino-Japanese War of 1894–1895, Qing government was forced to concede Taiwan to Japan in 1895. In 1945, Japan surrendered and Taiwan was recovered, and ended the occupation of Japan of 50 years. In 1949, the People's Republic of China was established, some Kuomintang military and administrative personnel retreated to Taiwan.

1987年，台湾当局宣布开放台湾同胞回大陆探亲。由于台胞大规模到大陆探亲、旅游、经商，为方便两岸事务，1990年，台湾成立了海峡交流基金会（简称海基会），而大陆相应成立了海峡两岸关系协会（简称海协会）。1992年，两岸达成“海峡两岸都坚持一个中国的原则，谋求国家的统一”的共识，简称“九二共识”。2008年6月，台湾正式启动大陆居民赴台旅游。

In 1987, the government announced the Taiwan compatriots could go back to visit their relatives in the Chinese mainland. Because large number of Taiwan compatriots came to visit their relatives, travel and do business in Chinese mainland, in order to control the cross-strait affairs, in 1990 Taiwan set up the Straits Exchange Foundation (SEF). And in the mainland of China the Association for Relations Across the Taiwan Straits (ARATS) was set up accordingly. In 1992, the two organizations reached a consensus across the Taiwan Strait to "adhere to the one-China principle, to seek the reunification of the country", which simply briefed as the "1992 Consensus". In June 2008, Taiwan began to open for people from the mainland to visit Taiwan.

2. 经济

1960年以前，台湾经济以农业为主，20世纪70年代开始，台湾形成了众多以出口业务为主的中小企业，并吸引了大量的外资和先进技术。快速的工业化和经济增长速度创造了台湾奇迹，被称为"亚洲四小龙"之一。台湾的电子业特别发达，目前，台湾以高科技电子产业为主，世界上大多数的计算机电子零件都是台湾生产。国际贸易是台湾经济命脉，大陆是台湾最大的贸易伙伴。

Before 1960 its economy mainly relied on the agriculture. After 1970s, lots of small and medium sized enterprises were established mainly to manufacture for exporting and absorbed a large sum of foreign investment and high technology. The quick industrialization and rapid growth of economy created the Taiwan miracle and thus was proclaimed as one of the Four Asian Dragons. At present, the mainstay of economy is high-tech electronic industries. Because of the highly-developed electronic industries, most of the computer components are manufactured in Taiwan. International trade is the lifeline of Taiwan's economy. Chinese Mainland is the largest trade partner of Taiwan.

3. 社会文化

目前台湾人口约2 360万，可分为四大族群：台湾原住民、闽南人、客家人、外省人。在台湾活动已有约8 000年之久的少数民族约占总人口的2%，其余绝大多数为汉族。汉族人又分为"本省人"（85%）和"外省人"（13%）。本省人主要为闽南人（70%）和客家人（15%），已经在台湾生活许多代。外省人是指1949年跟随国民党来台的人员及其后代。由于混居及通婚，两者已不易分辨。台湾的主要语言有普通话、闽南话、客家话及少数民族诸语。台湾民间普遍祭拜释迦牟尼佛、观音、玉帝、妈祖、孔子、关公、城隍等神祇。如今，佛教、道教、儒教等宗教在台湾相互影响、融合，在寺庙中各种不同宗教的神灵被共同祭祀也是常见的事。

Taiwan has a population of about 23.6 million, and can be divided into four major ethnic groups: Taiwanese aborigines, Minnanese, Hakka and Chinese mainlanders. Taiwanese aborigines have lived in this island for about 8,000 years and accounted for about 2% of the population. The vast majority is Han, which is divided into the "natives" (85%) as well as "Chinese mainlanders" (13%). The natives are mainly composed of Minnanese people (70%) and Hakka (15%). They have been living in Taiwan for many generations. The Chinese mainlanders are the new immigrants following the Kuomintang to Taiwan in 1949 and their descendants. All inhabitants mixed together and intermarried, so they are not easy to distinguish. Mandarin language, Taiwanese (Minnan with Taiwan accent), Taiwan Hakka and aboriginal languages are the main languages. The local Taiwanese generally worship Sakyamuni Buddha, Goddess of Mercy, the Jade Emperor, Matsu, Confucius, Guan Gong and Cheng Huang. Today, Buddhism, Taoism, Confucianism and other religions influence and integrate each other in Taiwan. It is normal that the gods of different religions are worshiped in the same temples.

台湾文化最明显的特点是多元化。少数民族的音乐和工艺、客家人独特的建筑特色、台湾和大陆一脉相承的儒家文化等形成了现代台湾文化的多元性。以闽南人为代表的闽南文化、客家人为代表的客家文化与外省人带来的新文化以及少数民族所代表的南岛文化在台湾共处、融合。除此之外，由于台湾日据时期长达50年（1895—1945年），加上当代的欧美与东亚流行文化对台湾的深刻影响，台湾文化也融合了日本、欧美等地的文化特色。日本文化对台湾的影响很大，如日本的温泉、酒、和室、日式料理、卡拉OK、电视剧、漫画、游戏等。美国文化和欧洲文化也对台湾文化影响深远，早期因殖民和传教，逐渐对台湾文化产生了影响。而今欧美教育在台湾教育界更是被视为典范。

The typical characteristics of Taiwan culture is pluralism, shaped by the music and arts of aborigines, the featured buildings of the Hakka and the Confucian culture sharing the same source as in Chinese mainland. The culture of Minnan, the culture of Hakka, the new culture brought by the Chinese mainlanders and the south island aborigines coexist and integrate with each other in Taiwan. In addition, Japan has governed Taiwan for 50 years (1895–1945), Japanese culture has deeply influenced Taiwan's culture, for example, Japanese hot spring, liquor, tatami room, the cuisine, Karaoke, TV series, cartoon, video games and so on. Taiwan has also been deeply influenced by current American culture and European culture. In the early times, they colonized and missionized in Taiwan and gradually influenced the culture of Taiwan. At present, the system of American and European education has been adopted as the model in Taiwan.

二、民俗风情

（一）礼仪禁忌

台湾居民多数为汉人后裔。1949年前，前往台湾的多为福建人及广东人，因此，这些人的后裔仍保持着福建、广东的习俗。而1949年后到台湾的各省人都有，因此台湾的风俗习惯和大陆非常接近。一般而言，台湾人讲究礼仪，孝顺父母，供奉祖先，爱面子，尊重他人，讨厌虚伪、狡诈。

The majority of Taiwan residents are the Han Chinese descendants. Before 1949, most of them were Fujian Minnanese and Cantonese and their descendants still maintain the customs of Fujian and Guangdong. Because people from different provinces came to Taiwan after 1949, therefore the custom of Taiwan is very close to the mainland of China. In general, Taiwanese pay attention to etiquette, they are filial to their parents, they worship their ancestors, they are sensitive to their reputation and respect others, and they hate hypocrisy and deceit.

台湾主要受福建、广东的影响。例如：到别人家中做客，不能随便进卧室和厨房，不能站或坐在门槛上，进屋也不能踩踏门槛；不能穿草鞋去别人家，因为台湾民间送葬时才穿草鞋；门板不能当床板，厅堂忌讳搭铺睡人；灶头上不能放鞋、袜、裤等东西；吃饭时不能说“吃白饭”，也不能把筷子插在饭上（为了对刚死不久的亲人表示敬意，才把筷子插在饭上）；吃鸡、鸭、鹅时，不能吃头、尾、翅膀；在渔民家中吃饭时，不能翻碗，吃鱼时也不要翻转鱼身。

Taiwan is mainly affected by Fujian and Guangdong. When they visit other families, they can't enter the bedroom or kitchen. They can't stand or sit on the threshold step or stamp on threshold when entering the house. They can not wear straw sandals to visit someone's home, because Taiwanese wear straw sandals only for funeral. The door panel can not be used for bed panel. It is a taboo to make a bed in the hall. Shoes, socks and trousers can't be put on the stove. You can't say "eat rice" when you are eating and can't insert the chopsticks vertically into the rice (it is used only to honor the newly dead relatives). Don't eat head, tail, wings of chicken, duck and goose. And don't turn over the bowl or fish when having dinner in fisherman's house.

台湾的送礼禁忌较多：不送粽子，因为居丧之家习惯包粽子；不送手帕，因为手帕是葬礼后送吊丧人的礼物，送手帕有永别之意；不送扇子，送扇子意味着要抛弃对方；不送刀剪，因为意味着一刀（剪）两断；不送钟，因为与“送终”谐音；不送雨伞，闽南话音同“给散”（使人分离之意）；不送鸭子给坐月子的女性，鸭子属凉性，产妇不宜吃。

There are many taboos on gift giving in Taiwan. Glutinous rice dumplings, handkerchiefs, fans, scissors, clocks and umbrellas are forbidden to send each other. Glutinous rice dumplings are used for mourning. Handkerchiefs are used in funeral which mean separating from the dead. Fan means separation. Scissor means "I will break relationship with you". Clock sounds "end or dead". Umbrella means lovers will be separated. Don't send duck to the woman who has just given birth to a baby because the duck is usually regarded as cool in nature and is not suitable for a puerperal woman.

台湾少数民族人口最多的高山族有着自己独特的习俗：他们的服饰有精美刺绣的几何图案，色彩鲜艳，衣料大多用手织麻布、兽皮，并用贝壳、兽牙、鹿角装饰。高山族以阔额为美，有黥面习俗，能歌善舞。婚姻上遵守一夫一妻制，但是妻权很大，留有母系氏族的痕迹。

Gaoshan, the most populous ethnic minority group, has its own unique custom. They dress colorfully with exquisite embroidery geometric patterns. The materials of clothes are mostly handmade woven linen, animal skins, and decorated with shells, animal teeth, and antlers. Gaoshan regards wide forehead as beauty. They have custom of tattooing on face and are good at singing and dancing. They adhere to monogamy marriage, but wives have more power which has the remains of matriclan.

（二）节庆风情

1. 妈祖祭典（Matsu Memorial Ceremony）

“大甲妈祖回娘家”是台湾最为盛大的宗教仪式。妈祖生日那天（农历三月二十三日），全台妈祖信徒云集大甲镇，抬着妈祖神像步行到北港再回到大甲，往返需八天七夜，沿途经过大小 30 多个乡镇，参拜 80 余座庙宇，游行队伍长达 5 000 米，非常壮观。1920 年以前，台湾妈祖信徒云集北港镇，推出千人“进香团”奉妈祖“金身”，乘船渡海回到福建湄洲岛“割香”。后来由于日本人断绝两岸交通，以及 1949 年台湾当局中断两岸交流，才改在北港遥祭。台湾有“拜妈祖，怀故国”之民谚。

"The Matsu returning home" is Taiwan's most grand religious ceremonies. On Matsu's birthday (lunar March 23), Taiwan Matsu believers gather in Tachia town, carrying the Matsu statue to Beigang and then back to Tachia. The round-trip takes eight days and seven nights, passing by more than 80 temples in over 30 villages. The spectacular procession is more than 5 kilometers long. In fact, prior to 1920, Taiwan's Matsu believers gathered in Beigang town and organized a thousand pilgrim group and took boat across the sea with Matsu golden sculpture back to Meizhou Island in Fujian for sharing blessing. But when Japanese stopped the cross-strait transportation, and later the government stopped cross-strait exchanges in 1949, the sacrifice could be held only in Beigang. In Taiwan, there is a folk saying "Worship Matsu, miss hometown".

2. 孔子诞辰祭典（Birthday Ceremony of Confucius）

至圣先师孔子在台湾民俗信仰中，地位相当特殊。早期祭孔大典分春、秋两季举行，后改在每年农历九月二十八日孔子诞辰纪念日举行，并将这一天确定为教师节。台湾全岛共建有 12 座孔庙。祭孔大典这天，要举行隆重而庄严的仪式，不仅学校的师生都要参加，而且各部门官员也要全部出席，以示尊师重教。

The greatest sage and teacher Confucius has a special position in the local people in Taiwan. In the early times, memorial ceremony is held in spring and autumn, and then it is changed to every September 28 of the lunar calendar which is also assigned as Teacher's Day. There are 12 Confucius temples in the whole island. During the memorial ceremony day, in order to show their respect to teachers and education, all teachers, students and government officials at all levels should attend the ceremony.

三、主要旅游城市及景点

（一）台北（Taipei）

台北位于台湾北部，地处台北盆地中央，是台湾的政治、经济和文化中心。1875 年，清政府在此建府，管辖台湾。日本占据时期，这里也是总督府所在地。1949 年，台北成为台湾的行政中心。台北地处亚热带季风区，四季不明显，是台湾北部的旅游中心，名胜古迹许多，有台北城门、孔庙、101 大楼、台北“故宫博物院”等。夜市也是游客必去的地方，如士林夜市，西门町则是另类次文化的代表。

Located in the center of the Taipei Basin in the northern part of the island of Taiwan, Taipei is Taiwan's political, economic and cultural center. In 1875, the Qing government built a prefecture here to govern Taiwan. During the period of Japanese occupation, it was also the location of the Governor's House. And it became the administrative center in 1949. Taipei is in subtropical monsoon region and the four seasons are not obvious. It is the tourist center of the northern Taiwan with many historical sites such as Taipei City Gate, Confucius Temple, Taipei 101 Tower, and Taipei "National Palace Museum". And also the night markets such as Shilin Night Market are the visitors' must-see places. Ximending is representative of the bizarre subculture.

◆ 台北“故宫博物院”（Taipei “National Palace Museum”）

台北“故宫博物院”建于1965年，位于台北市东北的群山中，是一座仿北京故宫式样的建筑。拥有“中华文化宝库”之名的台北“故宫博物院”藏有全世界最多的无价中华艺术珍宝，收藏品主要承袭自宋、元、明、清四代，几乎涵盖5 000年的中国历史，收藏文物总数高达69.6万余件。台北“故宫博物院”馆藏以多样镇馆稀世珍宝为其一大特色，翠玉白菜、肉形石、毛公鼎为三大镇馆之宝。

"National Palace Museum" in Taipei was built in 1965. Located in the mountains in the northeast of Taipei city, the building resembles the Forbidden City. The museum has been awarded the "Chinese culture treasure house" and has the valueless collections of Chinese arts treasures which rank the first in the world. Most of the collections are inherited from the dynasties of Song, Yuan, Ming and Qing, covering almost the whole Chinese history of 5,000 years. The museum features up to over 696,000 works of art. One characteristic of the "National Palace Museum" is that it collects the various unique treasures in the world. Jadeite Cabbage with Insects, Meat Shaped Stone and Mao Gong Ding are the three most precious in the museum.

◆ 台北101大楼（Taipei 101 Tower）

台北101大楼坐落于台北市精华地段的信义商圈，楼高508米，由于地面楼层多达101层而得名，是台湾建筑界有史以来最大的工程项目。每逢跨年的倒数晚会，101大楼壮观的烟花秀都会汇集来自世界各国的游客一同迎接新的一年。登上101大楼观景台可以鸟瞰台北市全貌。

Located in bustling Xinyi business center of Taipei, Taipei 101 Tower is 508 meters high. It is so named because it has 101 floors from the ground, making it the biggest project in Taiwan architecture history. Every year it holds a ceremony of counting number over the year. It attracts thousands of visitors all over the world for fireworks show to countdown for the new year. You can have bird's eye view of the whole city on the platform of Taipei 101 Tower Observatory.

（二）台湾中部（Central Taiwan）

台湾中部包括台中市、南投县和嘉义县。台湾五大山系中的中央山脉、玉山山脉和阿里山山脉都位于台湾中部。

Central area of Taiwan includes Taichung, Nantou and Chiayi. Three of five mountain ranges including Central Range, Yu Shan and Mount Ali ranges are located here.

◆ 阿里山风景区（Mount Ali Scenic Area）

俗话说："不到阿里山，就不知道台湾的美丽。"阿里山位于嘉义县东北，纵贯台湾岛西部，是台湾著名的风景游览区。由于山区气候温和，盛夏时依然清爽宜人，加上林木葱翠，是全台湾最理想的避暑胜地。若想了解真实的阿里山，应深入阿里山邹族文化村。攀天神木、云海奇观、日出奇景、艳红樱花是该景区最著名的四大奇观。它还是台湾著名的天然森林区，素有"神秘的森林王国"之称，拥有长达 72 千米的森林铁道，被称为世界铁路建筑史上的"奇迹"，其"螺旋形铁道"和"伞形齿轮直立汽缸式火车头"，被认为是"疯狂的设计"，它使登山旅游更为便捷。

The old saying goes that "without visiting Mount Ali you will never truly know the beauty of Taiwan." Mount Ali, located in the northeast of Chiayi and across the west part of Taiwan island, is a well-known scenic area. Because the weather here is mild, it is cool even in summer. Full of lush trees it is the best summer resort in Taiwan. If you want to know real Mount Ali, you must go to Tsou cultural tribe. The four spectacles in the area are towering ancient trees, grand cloud sea, sunrise views and colorful cherry blossoms. It is also the natural forest region as the mysterious forest kingdom. The 72 kilometers long forest railway is the miracle of the world railway. The spiral railway and vertical-cylinder-gear-driven locomotive is regarded as the crazy design but it is convenient for visitors to climb the mountains.

◆ 日月潭（Sun Moon Lake）

台湾的天然湖泊很少，最大和最有名的就是日月潭。日月潭位于南投县，是台湾最重要的天然湖泊。日月潭中有一个小岛，远望好像浮在水面上的一颗珠子，名为拉鲁岛，以此岛为界，北半湖形状如圆日，南半湖形状如弯月，日月潭因此而得名。日月潭之美在于环湖重峦叠嶂，湖面辽阔，潭水澄澈；一年四季，晨昏景色各有不同，是台湾的风景绝胜，素有"双潭秋月"之称，也被称为台湾"天池"。

Taiwan only has a few natural lakes, among which the largest and most well-known is Sun Moon Lake. Sun Moon Lake is located in Nantou and is the most important natural lake. There is a small island on the lake like a bead floating in the water when looked from far away thus it is named La Lu Island. The island serves as the middle point to separate the lake into two parts, with the southern part shaped like a new moon, and the northern part shaped like a sun, hence the name Sun Moon Lake. The beauty of Sun Moon lake is that the lake is surrounded by mountains with wide and deep clean water. The views are different in the morning and evening in four seasons. For the famous scenery, it is known as "Autumn Moon in Twin Pools", or "Heavenly Pool" in Taiwan.

（三）台湾南部（Southern Taiwan）

◆ 高雄（Kaohsiung）

高雄市位于台湾南部，西面濒临台湾海峡，是台湾第二大城市，台湾最大的国际港口。高雄港内水不扬波，巨轮进出频繁，是世界十大港口之一，有"港都"之名。有"台湾西湖”美誉的西子湾风景区，拥有多处独具特色的旅游景点，为台湾南部最负盛名的观光地区，如打狗英国领事馆等历史久远的文物古迹。除了观光外，高雄的夜市和小吃也久负盛名，尤其是六合夜市。

Located in southern Taiwan, Kaohsiung is the second largest city in Taiwan. To its west is Taiwan Strait. It is the largest international port in Taiwan. Kaohsiung Harbor owns calm water and the giant vessels sail in and out frequently. As one of the world's top ten ports, it is known as Harbor Capital. Often referred to as West Lake of Taiwan, the West Bay National Scenic Area has many unique tourist attractions, and is the most famous tourist area in southern Taiwan, including former residence of the British Consulate at Takao and other historic heritage. Besides sightseeing, Kaohsiung's night markets and snacks also enjoy a long-standing reputation, especially Liuhe Night Market.

◆ 台南（Tainan）

台南市是台湾最古老的古都，旧名赤崁，位于台湾西南海岸，嘉南平原南端，以古建筑和美食闻名。建于明朝1665年的台南孔庙是台湾历史最悠久的建筑群；赤崁楼是荷兰人建于17世纪的普罗民遮城，1862年地震时被毁，1942年重修，现为台南历史博物馆；台南妈祖庙是1684年清康熙在位时所建，也是第一座“官建”的妈祖庙。

Formerly named Chikan, Tainan is the oldest ancient capital of Taiwan. Located at southwest coast of Taiwan and south of Jianan Plain, Tainan is famous for its ancient building and cuisine. The Confucius Temple in Tainan was built in 1665 of Ming Dynasty and is the largest building complex with the longest history. Chikanlou, originally called Provintia, was built in 17th century by Dutch. It was ruined in 1862 and was rebuilt in 1942. It is Tainan History Museum now. Tainan Matsu Temple was built in 1684 during the rule of Kangxi by Qing government and it is the first officially-built Matsu temple .

◆ 垦丁“国家公园”（Kenting “National Park”）

垦丁位于台湾最南端的恒春半岛，它是最能代表台湾阳光气候的地方。垦丁“国家公园”建成于1984年，它是第二次世界大战后最早建成的“国家公园”，东邻太平洋、西邻台湾海峡、南濒巴士海峡，三面环海，是台湾唯一拥有海域与陆域的公园，也是台湾本岛唯一的热带地区。垦丁的魅力在于其独一无二的自然景观。其中，位于台湾岛最南端突出的两大峡角“鹅銮鼻”和“猫鼻头”是来垦丁必游的两大热门景点。现在的垦丁四处散发着电影《海角七号》的浪漫。

Located in the southern Hengchun Peninsula, Kenting has unique landscape and rich resources of animal and plants. The park was established in 1984 and is the first "national park" after the Second World War. To its east is the Pacific Ocean, to its west is Taiwan Strait and to its south is Bashi Strait. It is surrounded by sea in three sides and is the only park in Taiwan with both sea and land and only tropical park in Taiwan Island. The unique beauty of the park lies in natural views, among which Eluanbi and Miaobitou on the southern tip of Taiwan are the must-see hot spots. Kenting now is full of the romance of the film *Cape No.7*.

（四）台湾东部（Eastern Taiwan）

◆ 太鲁阁“国家公园”（Taroko “National Park”）

太鲁阁“国家公园”位于台湾岛东部山区花莲县，是台湾著名的“国家公园”旅游胜地之一，以峡谷和断崖为特色。从太鲁阁到立雾溪，河谷两岸皆由大理石岩层构成，所以有“大理石峡谷”的美称。东段主要风景区有清水断崖、长春祠、布洛湾、九曲洞、太鲁阁等。由于强烈的造山运动，地壳持续上升，河流相应地强烈持续下切，形成了这座自然公园的V形峡谷——太鲁阁大峡谷。东段的清水断崖号称“世界第二大断崖”，前后绵延达20千米，是苏花公路最惊险、壮丽的代表景观，也是台湾八大奇景之一。

Located in the eastern mountains of the island of Taiwan, Hualian County, it is one of Taiwan's famous tourist sites in national parks. The typical is canyons and cliffs. From Taroko to the Liwu River, the cliffs on both banks of Liwu Valley are made of marble valley, hence the name of Marble Valley. The main attractions in eastern region include Ching-shui Cliff, Changchun Temple, Buluo Bay, Tunnel of Nine Turns, Taroko, etc. Due to the intense orogeny, the rising crust and the river going down straightly and thus the natural park with V type canyon is formed—Taroko Grand Canyon. Ching-shui Cliff is known as "the world's second largest cliff" stretching for 20 kilometers, and is the most thrilling and spectacular representative landscape of Suhua Highway, which is also one of the eight wonders of Taiwan.

四、旅游资讯

（一）美食

台湾为“美食岛”，有“食在台湾”的说法。由于五谷、瓜果、蔬菜、海鲜品种众多，台湾民间对饮食十分讲究。台湾美食大致与闽菜、粤菜相同，其特色主要有三：第一，类似闽、粤，但加以变化而有台湾特色，作料常用沙茶酱、咖喱、花生酱等，多用清汤炖、煮，味道清淡；第二，台湾风味小吃特别多，拥有许多特色夜市，如六合夜市、士林夜市；第三，台湾食品中以米制品居多，以甜为特色。在台湾，游客不仅能品尝到传统的中华美食，而且可以品尝到结合福建、广东菜肴和本地饮食文化发展而来的、有自己特色的台湾菜，蚵仔煎、虱目鱼肚粥、炒米粉、台南担仔面、棺材板、生炒花枝、卤肉饭，都是独具台湾风味的知名小吃。

Taiwan is a "Gourmet Island" as in a saying that goes "Gourmet Food in Taiwan". Taiwan is rich in food materials such as grains, fruits, vegetables and seafood. People care much about the diet. Taiwan cuisine is roughly similar to Min (Fujian) cuisine and Yue (Guangdong) cuisine with three features. Firstly, it is similar to Fujian and Guangdong cuisine but it has characteristic of its own, it uses barbecue sauce, curry and peanut butter as condiments, natural original flavors are preserved and the main focus is on light-seasoned, fresh, and simply flavored dishes. Secondly, Taiwan has various snacks and special night markets such as Liuhe Night Market, and Shilin Night Market. Thirdly, there are more rice products and the characteristic of Taiwan food is sweet. In Taiwan, you can taste not only the traditional Chinese cuisine, but also Taiwan gourmet food which combines Fujian and Guangdong cuisine with local food and snacks which has its own characteristics; oyster omelette, milkfish maw porridge, fried rice noodle, Tainan peddler noodle, Guancaiban (fried bread with chichen liver), fried squid, minced pork rice, are unique Taiwanese snacks.

（二）购物及退税

台湾是个美丽的宝岛，也是个富饶的宝岛。水稻、甘蔗、茶叶被誉为“台湾三宝”，其中，冻顶乌龙茶驰名中外。台湾盛产香蕉、菠萝、木瓜、柚子、龙眼、槟榔、荔枝等 80 多种热带、亚热带水果，有“东方甜岛”“水果之乡”之美誉。此外，台湾还有“兰花王国”“蝴蝶王国”“珊瑚王国”“鱼仓”等称号。台湾物产丰富，有许多的特产。

Taiwan is a beautiful island and also a fertile island. Rice, sugar cane, and tea are known as “three treasures of Taiwan”, among which Dongding Oolong tea is well-known all over the world. Taiwan produces banana, pineapple, papaya, pomelo, longan, betel nut, litchi etc., over 80 kinds of tropical and subtropical fruits in total, so it owns the reputation of “Oriental Sweet Island” and “Kingdom of Fruits”. In addition, Taiwan also has the reputation of “Orchid Kingdom”, “Butterfly Kingdom”, “Coral Kingdom”, and “Fish Warehouse”. Taiwan is rich in natural resources. There are many specialties.

乌龙茶：冻顶乌龙茶是台湾人眼中的宝贝。该茶在台湾极具盛名，广受欢迎，被品茗人士推崇为上品。在台湾可以买到的茶叶品种众多，其中以文山包种茶、冻顶乌龙茶、白毫乌龙茶和铁观音为四大主流。

Oolong tea: Dongding Oolong tea is precious in the eyes of the Taiwanese. The tea is famous in Taiwan and it is very popular and is regarded as the best by tea lovers. Many kinds of tea can be supplied in Taiwan, of which Wenshan Pouchong, Dongding Oolong tea, Pekoe Oolong tea and Tieguanyin tea are the most popular.

凤梨酥：凤梨酥是台湾最著名的点心之一。台湾盛产菠萝，在民间，菠萝含有“旺来”（闽南话菠萝的发音）的吉利之意。菠萝在台湾被称作“凤梨”，凤梨酥即是一种以菠萝为馅料的糕饼。

Pineapple cake: It is one of the most famous snacks in Taiwan. Taiwan is rich in pineapple. Pineapple also means rich for the local people (it sounds like “Wanglai”, fortune is coming). Pineapple has another name of “ananas” in Taiwan. Pineapple cake is a confectionery with pineapple pastry.

在台湾，购物场所集中在台北，台北各大商场有世界各地的名牌包、服饰等，同时化妆品种类齐全。目前，在台北大多数大商场都能刷银联卡，对于大陆游客非常方便。在同一家商店当天购物（食品除外）满 3 000 新台币，并在 30 天内将所购物品带出境的话，出示证件即可办理退税手续，享受 5% 的退税。退税的办理时间是游客在出境时，海关审核过并在退税单上盖章后可到退税处领取现金。

In Taiwan, Taipei will be the major shopping city. Visitors can find world famous goods such as branded bags, clothes and full range of authentic cosmetics. UnionPay card is acceptable now in most of the shopping malls which is very convenient for the tourists from Chinese mainland. Visitors can have 5% tax refund if they leave Taiwan in 30 days after they buy goods (except food) over TWD 3,000 in one shop in a day and have tax refund documents with their credentials. Before going to collect cash in the Refund Office, the refund form should be checked and stamped by the customs before departure.

思考练习

1. 经典旅游线路分析

"宝岛台湾"环线经典8日游

第1天：杭州——台北

游客搭乘豪华客机经香港抵达台北桃园国际机场。专车进入市区，之后可逛台北地区最具规模的士林夜市，领略台湾闻名全球、种类多样、精彩绝伦的夜市文化。

第2天：台北——新竹

酒店享用丰盛的早餐后，乘车前往台湾北部最负盛名的地质公园——野柳风景区。由于波浪侵蚀、岩石风化等地壳运动形成罕见地形，海滩上奇岩、怪石密布，有脍炙人口的女王头、仙女鞋……午后参观藏品数量巨大的台北"故宫博物院"。翠玉白菜和肉形石形态逼真，乃镇馆之宝，不可不看。之后参观珊瑚博物馆，台湾四面环海，珊瑚资源丰富，有"珊瑚王国"之称，游客可自行挑选珊瑚纪念品。

第3天：新竹——日月潭

前往有"台湾天池"之称的日月潭，乘船遨游于如诗般的湖光山色美景之中，四周群山环抱，以湖中光华岛为界，北潭状似日，南潭形如月，故称"日月潭"。沿途可见文武庙、慈恩塔、玄奘寺、德化社等名胜。然后前往邵族文化村用餐，邵族文化村集餐饮、娱乐、购物为一体，用餐时有少数民族丰富多彩的歌舞表演助兴。参观台湾宗教重地——中台禅寺，它是众多佛教信众的信仰中心，也是融合了中西特色的佛教寺院。

第4天：日月潭——高雄

酒店享用早餐后，前往阿里山森林游乐区，阿里山海拔2 216米，四周高山环绕，气候凉爽，以日出、云海、晚霞、森林、高山茶闻名中外。著名的森林游乐区内还拥有非常珍贵的桧木原始林，千年树龄的红桧神木群、三代木等自然奇景。品尝台湾高山茶顶级的茶品，并可选购阿里山高山乌龙茶。之后前往高雄夜游灯光璀璨、享有"东方威尼斯"美誉的爱河及夜市。

第5天：高雄——垦丁——台东

酒店享用早餐后，游览西子湾风景区。打狗英国领事馆是清朝时外国人正式在台湾兴建的第一座领事馆。驱车前往台湾第一座大型森林公园——垦丁"国家公园"风景区。游览裙礁、长方石等生态地质景观丰富的“猫鼻头”，在此可观赏巴士海峡与台湾海峡交会之处的壮丽海景。

第6天：台东——花莲

酒店内享用早餐后，沿途游览绵延曲折的峭壁、花东海岸公路，参观北回归线牌楼、水往上流奇景，途经石梯坪等风景区，由花莲进入太鲁阁“国家公园”，沿线主要景点有：长春祠、燕子口、九曲洞。之后参观大理石工厂，游客可以选购大理石雕刻品。

第7天：花莲——台北

酒店内享用早餐后，沿苏花公路前往宜兰，途经台湾八景之一的清水断崖，高1 000多米，以极近90°的角度紧临太平洋，令人叹为观止。抵达宜兰后经由雪山隧道返回台北，大自然的神奇与奥妙，在此可一览无遗。之后参观台北中山纪念馆，远眺高度508米的台北101大楼。

第8天：台北——杭州

酒店享用早餐后，由领队协助办理离境手续，搭乘豪华客机经香港返回杭州，结束此次愉快而又难忘的台湾环线之旅。

分析：这条经典旅游线路的主要旅游景点与行程特色，以及适合旅游的人群。

2. 案例分析

有一次，一位大陆女游客在台北叫了一辆出租车：“师傅，请载我到101大楼。”没想到年轻的司机却回答道：“我不是出家人，小姐你怎么叫我‘师傅’呢？”原来，在台湾，“师傅”是弟子对授艺人的尊称，与“师傅”同音的“师父”是对出家人的尊称。对出租车司机的通称则是“运将”，闽南话叫“稳炯”。女游客反应很快：“那你也不能叫我‘小姐’哦，在我们那里，‘小姐’指的是‘特殊行业’。”这下，台湾司机不知该如何回答了。这种由于生活环境不同演化出来的常用语还有很多，例如：“地铁”，台湾人称“捷运”；“盒饭”，台湾人称“便当”；“鼠标”和“网络”，台湾人则称“滑鼠”和“网路”等。请找出大陆与台湾在食物、地名、交通、学术、称谓和问候等习惯用语方面的差异。

3. 练一练

自2001年起，长达10年的时间中，中国台湾以“Taiwan, Touch Your Heart”品牌向国际推广台湾，成功展现了台湾人民友善、热情的形象，也获得了大陆游客的喜爱，将台湾旅游推升到一个新阶段。 2011年，中国台湾又推出新品牌“Taiwan—The Heart of Asia”，是台湾观光“从心出发”不变的坚持。如何理解台湾旅游新、旧两个品牌？请写一篇相关主题的台湾旅游导游词。

参考文献

[1] 王昆欣，鞠海虹．中国旅游客源地和目的地概况 [M]. 2 版．北京：高等教育出版社，2012.

[2] 中国旅游研究院．中国出境旅游发展年度报告 2019 [M]. 北京：旅游教育出版社，2019.

[3] 邬宏．真正欧洲 [M]. 长沙：湖南地图出版社，2003.

[4] 刘列励．欧洲大陆 [M]. 北京：中国水利水电出版社，2001.

[5] 许颖之，王庆忠．湖光山色：瑞士 [M]. 上海：上海锦绣文章出版社，2010.

[6] 汤永贵．热舞弗拉门戈：西班牙 [M]. 上海：上海锦绣文章出版社，2010.

[7] [澳] 彼得·特纳．新西兰 [M]. 北京：旅游教育出版社，2010.

[8] 赵春珍．中外礼仪故事与案例赏析 [M]. 北京：首都经济贸易大学出版社，2011.

[9] 英国 DK 公司．加拿大 [M]. 李伟涛，张寿峰，李剑锋，译．北京：中国旅游出版社，2009.

[10] Fodor's 编写组．埃及 [M]. 刘艳霞，孙慧敏，栗丽娟，译．北京：电子工业出版社，2010.

[11] 陆苗耕．彩虹之国——南非 [M]. 上海：上海锦绣文章出版社，2010.

[12] 徐博东，张明华．台湾传统文化溯源 [M]. 北京：中国国际广播出版社，2011.

[13] 徐辉．国际旅游业对客服务艺术案例 [M]. 杭州：浙江科学技术出版社，2008.

[14] 夏林根．旅游目的地概述 [M]. 北京：旅游教育出版社，2005.

[15] 王佩良．中国主要旅游客源国与目的地国概况 [M]. 北京：中国旅游出版社，2006.

[16] 王兴斌．中国旅游客源国概况 [M]. 北京：旅游教育出版社，2003.

[17] 黄荣鹏．领队实务 [M]. 5 版．新北：扬智文化事业股份有限公司，2012.

图书在版编目（CIP）数据

中国出境旅游目的地概况：双语 / 饶华清主编．--2 版．--北京：中国人民大学出版社，2020.9

21 世纪高职高专规划教材．旅游管理系列

ISBN 978-7-300-15104-5

Ⅰ．①中…　Ⅱ．①饶…　Ⅲ．①国际旅游—旅游地—概况—高等职业教育—双语教学—教材　Ⅳ．① K917

中国版本图书馆 CIP 数据核字（2020）第 157281 号

21世纪高职高专规划教材·旅游管理系列

中国出境旅游目的地概况（双语）（第2版）

主　编　饶华清

副主编　李德煜

主　审　袁　青

Zhongguo Chujing Lüyou Mudidi Gaikuang (Shuangyu)

出版发行	中国人民大学出版社		
社　址	北京中关村大街31号	**邮政编码**	100080
电　话	010-62511242（总编室）		010-62511770（质管部）
	010-82501766（邮购部）		010-62514148（门市部）
	010-62515195（发行公司）		010-62515275（盗版举报）
网　址	http://www.crup.com.cn		
经　销	新华书店		
印　刷	天津鑫丰华印务有限公司	**版　次**	2014年5月第1版
开　本	787mm×1092mm　1/16		2020年9月第2版
印　张	22.5插页1	**印　次**	2024年12月第4次印刷
字　数	498 000	**定　价**	48.00元